CORAL

Part One
Workbook Answer Guide

Mosdos Press
CLEVELAND, OHIO

MOSDOS PRESS
Literature

EDITOR-IN-CHIEF
Judith Factor

EXECUTIVE EDITOR
Libby Spero

CREATIVE/ART DIRECTOR
Carla Martin

CURRICULUM
Jill Brotman

SENIOR EDITOR
Abigail Rozen

COPY EDITOR
Laya Dewick

LESSONS IN LITERATURE
Tim Tibbits

TEXT AND CURRICULUM ADVISOR
Rabbi Ahron Dovid Goldberg

MOSDOS PRESS

Literature

ANTHOLOGY SERIES

RUBY

CORAL

PEARL

JADE

GOLD

acknowledgments

ILLUSTRATORS

Tsippora Degani: *The Black Stallion, The Whimbrel*

Aviva Gross: *Afternoon on a Hill, The Birds' Peace, The Eagle, Figures in the Field Against the Sky, My House, Waking*

George Kocar: *The Greatest Snowball Fight in History, A Niche in the Kitchen, The Quangle Wangle's Hat, The Speckled Hen's Egg, The Street Boy, The Streets are Free*

Eva Martin: *Kate Shelley*

Lydia Martin: *The Day of the Turtle*

Sue McDonald: *74th Street, Hattie's Birthday Box, Kate Shelley, The Memory Box, Truth, The Whippoorwill Calls*

Leah Neustadter: *The Butterfly and the Caterpillar*

UNIT ONE

Samuel's Choice
SAMUEL'S CHOICE by Richard Berleth. Text copyright © 1990 by Richard J. Berleth. Reprinted by permission of Albert Whitman & Company. All rights reserved.

Slower Than the Rest
Reprinted with the permission of Simon & Schuster Books for Young Readers, an imprint of Simon & Schuster Children's Publishing Division from EVERY LIVING THING by Cynthia Rylant. Copyright © 1985 Cynthia Rylant.

Kate Shelley
KATE SHELLY written by Robert San Souci and illustrated by Max Ginsburg. Text copyright © 1995. Published by arrangement with Dial Books for Young Readers, a member of Penguin Group (USA) Inc.

New Providence
NEW PROVIDENCE: A CHANGING CITYSCAPE copyright © 1987 by Renata von Tscharner and Ronald Lee Fleming and The Townscape Institute, Inc., illustrations copyright © 1987 by The Townscape Institute, Inc. and Denis Orloff, reprinted by permission of Harcourt, Inc.

The Silent Lobby
"The Silent Lobby" by Mildred Pitts Walter; reprinted by permission of the author.

To a Daughter Leaving Home
"To a Daughter Leaving Home", from THE IMPERFECT PARADISE by Linda Pastan. Copyright © 1988 by Linda Pastan. Used by permission of W. W. Norton & Company, Inc.

Whatif
From A LIGHT IN THE ATTIC by SHEL SILVERSTEIN. COPYRIGHT © 1981 BY EVIL EYE MUSIC, INC. Used by permission of HarperCollins Publishers.

The Whippoorwill Calls
"The Whippoorwill Calls" first appeared in *Cobblestone*, February, 1981. Reprinted by permission of the author.

UNIT TWO

Gold-Mounted Guns
Copyright © 1922 by F. R. Buckley. Reprinted by permission of Curtis Brown, Ltd.

The Disappearing Man
"The Disappearing Man" by Isaac Asimov, from Boys' Life, June 1978; copyright © 1978, Boy Scouts of America, published by permission of The Estate of Isaac Asimov c/o Ralph M. Vicinanza, Ltd.

The Speckled Hen's Egg
From THE TALKING CAT AND OTHER STORIES OF FRENCH CANADA by NATALIE SAVAGE CARLSON. COPYRIGHT © 1952 BY NATALIE SAVAGE CARLSON. Used by permission of HarperCollins Publishers.

The Black Stallion
From THE BLACK STALLION by Walter Farley, copyright 1941 by Walter Farley. Copyright renewed 1969 by Walter Farley. Used by permission of Random House Children's Books, a division of Random House, Inc.

By the Shores of Silver Lake
BY THE SHORES OF SILVER LAKE by LAURA INGALLS WILDER. TEXT COPYRIGHT 1939, 1967 Little House Heritage Trust. Used by permission of HarperCollins Publishers.

UNIT THREE

One Throw
Copyright © 1950, renewed 1978 by W. C. Heinz Reprinted by permission of William Morris Agency, Inc. on behalf of the Author.

The Birds' Peace
"The Birds' Peace" from *The Big Book for Peace* © 1990, reprinted by permission of Mr. Ted Rand.

Hattie's Birthday Box
From BIRTHDAY SURPRISES: TEN GREAT STORIES EDITED by JOHANNA HURWITZ. BIRTHDAY SURPRISES COPYRIGHT © 1995 BY JOHANNA HURWITZ. Used by permission of HarperCollins Publishers.

I Am Winding Through a Maze
From IT'S RAINING PIGS AND NOODLES. TEXT COPYRIGHT © 2000 BY JACK PRELUTSKY. Used by permission of HarperCollins Publishers.

74th Street
From THE MALIBU AND OTHER POEMS by Myra Cohn Livingston. Copyright © 1972 by Myra Cohn Livingston. Used by permission of Marian Reiner.

UNIT FOUR
The Day of the Turtle
From THE WRECK OF THE ZANZIBAR by Michael Morpurgo, illustrated by Francois Place, copyright © 1995 by Michael Morpurgo, text. Used by permission of Viking Penguin, A Division of Penguin Young Readers Group, A Member of Penguin Group (USA) Inc., 345 Hudson Street, New York, NY 10014. All rights reserved.

Prairie Fire
TEXT COPYRIGHT 1935, 1963 Little House Heritage Trust. Used by permission of HarperCollins Publishers.

The Streets are Free
© First printed in Spanish by Ediciones EkarÈ, Caracas, Venezuela, Original Title: La calle es libre

One Day in the Desert
ONE DAY IN THE DESERT by JEAN CRAIGHEAD GEORGE. TEXT COPYRIGHT © 1983 BY JEAN CRAIGHEAD GEORGE. Used by permission of HarperCollins Publishers.

Choose a Color
© 1993, 1994 by Jacqueline Sweeney. All rights reserved. Reprinted by permission of Marian Reiner for the author.

For Crows and Jays
"For Crows and Jays" first appeared in *Cricket*, November, 2000. Reprinted by permission of the author.

One Day
"One Day" first appeared in *Cricket*, November, 2002. Reprinted by permission of the author.

A City Ditty
From A POEM FOR A PICKLE by Eve Merriam. Copyright © 1989 Eve Merriam. Used by permission of Marian Reiner.

UNIT FIVE
The Memory Box
THE MEMORY BOX by Mary Bahr. Text copyright ©1992 by Mary Bahr. Reprinted by permission of Albert Whitman & Company. All rights reserved.

Founders of the Children's Rain Forest
"The Founders of the Children's Rain Forest" from IT'S OUR WORLD, TOO! by Phillip Hoose. Copyright © 2002 by Phillip Hoose. Reprinted by permission of Farrar, Straus and Giroux, LLC.

Jessica Govea
"Jessica Govea: Education of a Union Organizer" from WE WERE THERE, TOO! by Phillip Hoose. Copyright © 2001 by Phillip Hoose. Reprinted by permission of Farrar, Straus, and Giroux, LLC.

The Street Boy
From MIRROR, MIRROR: TWISTED TALES by Norman Silver. Published by The Chicken House/Scholastic Inc. Copyright © by Silverman. Reprinted by permission of Scholastic Inc.

Waking
From I FEEL THE SAME WAY by Lilian Moore. Copyright © 1967 Lilian Moore. Copyright renewed and reserved. Reprinted by permission of Marian Reiner for the author.

UNIT SIX
Small Steps
SMALL STEPS: THE YEAR I GOT POLIO by Peg Kehret. Text copyright © 1996 by Peg Kehret. Excerpt reprinted by permission of Albert Whitman & Company. All rights reserved.

What a Wild Idea
With permission of Louis Sabin (text) and Christine Mortensen (illustrations) and *Boys' Life*, September 1990, published by the Boy Scouts of America.

Flight Into Danger
"Flight Into Danger" by Arthur Hailey; reprinted by permission of the author.

Passage to Freedom
Passage to Freedom: The Sugihara Story Text copyright © 1997 by Ken Mochizuki. Permission arranged with LEE & LOW BOOKS Inc., New York, NY 10016.

unit 1

COURAGE

unit 2

GROWING

CONTENTS

unit 3

AIMING HIGH

unit 4

THE WORLD AROUND US

CONTENTS

unit 5

FINDING OUT WHAT'S INSIDE

unit 6

THE GRAND FINALÉ

CONTENTS

MOSDOS PRESS Literature

CORAL TEACHER'S EDITION

- Scope and Sequence

- Getting Started Activities

- Annotated Teacher's Edition

- Workbook Answer Guide

UNIT ONE: *Courage • Exploring Elements of a Story*

Elements of a Story—plot, character, setting, and theme—are introduced in this unit. The first selection introduces students to the basic structure of a story. In each of the four prose works that follow, the elements of plot, character, setting, and theme are explored.

SELECTION	FOCUS			WORKBOOK
	Genre • Unit Theme	Literary Element	Eyes On...	
Samuel's Choice Richard Berleth p. 16 *Lesson in Literature* **What is a Story?** p. 14	• Historical Fiction • *Unit Theme— Courage:* This work of Revolutionary War fiction explores the courageous choices Samuel, a black slave, makes. Readers realize that choice is equated with freedom.	• Asking the question "What is a story?" • For students to understand the literary elements of a piece of literature, they must first be introduced to the basic concept of what makes a story a story.	• Eyes On...Historical Fiction and the Elements of a Story: Explanation of exposition, setting, rising action, turning point, climax, falling action, resolution	Pp. 1-6 • Vocabulary, I: p. 1 • Vocabulary, II: p. 2 • Comp. Questions: pp. 3-4 • Graphic Organizer: pp. 5-6
Slower Than the Rest Cynthia Rylant p. 34 *Lesson in Literature* **What is Plot?** p. 32	• Contemporary Fiction • *Unit Theme—Courage:* The need to respect the unique abilities of each and every individual is explored in this story. The courage of a young boy shines as his best is recognized.	• Exploring plot • In this simple but realistic story, students will easily identify the literary elements of plot. • *Language Alert:* Discussion of "then" and "than"	• Eyes On...Plot • Exposition • Characters: internal/ external conflict • Setting • Rising action • Climax • Falling action • Resolution	Pp. 7-12 • Vocabulary, I: p. 7 • Vocabulary, II: p. 8 • Comp. Questions: pp. 9-10 • Graphic Organizer: pp. 11-12
Kate Shelley Robert D. San Souci p. 44 *Lesson in Literature* **What is Character?** p. 42	• Historical Nonfiction • *Unit Theme—Courage:* In this work of historical nonfiction, Kate Shelley shows us the courage it takes to be responsible for the welfare of many.	• Exploring character • In this character-driven piece, students will identify the literary elements an author uses to develop a story's character. • *Language Alert:* Word etymology	• Eyes On...the Character	Pp. 13-18 • Vocabulary, I: p. 13 • Vocabulary, II: p. 14 • Comp. Questions: pp. 15-16 • Graphic Organizer: pp. 17-18
New Providence The Townscape Institute p. 64 *Lesson in Literature* **Setting** p. 62	• A Graphic Story • *Unit Theme—Courage:* This graphic story demonstrates the courage and resiliency a town has to recognize its past and build on it for its future survival.	• Exploring setting (place, time, mood) • The literary elements of setting are essential to understanding the theme of a piece. Students will understand how critical setting is, as they read this unique graphic story.	• Eyes On...Setting • Recognizing the recorded details of the physical features of setting	Pp. 19-24 • Vocabulary, I: p. 19 • Vocabulary, II: p. 20 • Comp. Questions: pp. 21-22 • Graphic Organizer: pp. 23-24
The Silent Lobby Mildred Pitts Walter p. 82 *Lesson in Literature* **Theme** p. 80	• Realistic Fiction • *Unit Theme—Courage:* This work of realistic fiction embraces the determination and courage of the human spirit, as a group of black citizens lobby for their civil right to vote.	• Exploring theme • How one feels after reading a strong work of realistic fiction is how we get to theme. This piece will help students begin to define the literary elements of theme.	• Eyes On...Theme (Review elements of theme: TE, page 15)	Pp. 25-30 • Vocabulary, I: p. 25 • Vocabulary, II: p. 26 • Comp. Questions: pp. 27-28 • Graphic Organizer: pp. 29-30
To a Daughter Leaving Home Linda Pastan, p. 96 **Whatif** Shel Silverstein, p. 97 **The Whippoorwill Calls** Beverly McLoughland, p. 98 **Figures in the Field Against the Sky** Antonio Machado, p. 99	• Poetry Style: Free Verse • Poetry Style: Rhyming Verse • Biographical Poem Style: Free Verse • Poetry Style: Free Verse	• Extended metaphor • Personification • Onomatopoeia; stanza; repetition of rhythm • Repetition of consonant and vowel sounds	• Eyes On...First-Person Voice • Eyes On...Rhyming Verse with a Semi-Regular Rhythm • Eyes On...Biographical Poem, Third-Person Voice, and Stanzas • Eyes On...Repetition in Free Verse	

UNIT TWO: *Growing* • *Exploring Elements of Plot*

Elements of Plot—conflict, sequence, cause and effect, and predicting outcome—are taught in this unit. As students explore a variety of genre, they will be guided toward understanding how the attributes of plot are the foundation to understanding literature.

SELECTION	FOCUS			WORKBOOK
	Genre • Unit Theme	Literary Element	Eyes On...	
Gold-Mounted Guns F. R. Buckley p. 110 *Lesson in Literature* **Conflict** p. 108	• Wild West Fiction • *Unit Theme—Growing:* An encounter with a stranger changes the course of a young man's life. He grows to understand the results of his actions, and the pain he can cause others.	• Exploring conflict in plot • Conflict is the essence of theme. Students are introduced to the most basic literary elements of plot—conflict. Identifying and understanding conflict will ultimately help students recognize theme.	• Eyes On...External Conflict • Internal conflict as it leads to revelatory ending	Pp. 31-36 • Vocabulary, I: p. 31 • Vocabulary, II: p. 32 • Comp. Questions: pp. 33-34 • Graphic Organizer: pp. 35-36
The Disappearing Man Isaac Asimov p. 128 *Lesson in Literature* **Sequence** p. 126	• Contemporary Mystery • *Unit Theme—Growing:* In this contemporary mystery, growth is attained through deductive reasoning and careful thought.	• Understanding plot • Students will be taught how to sequence the events in a plot. Plotting sequence will lead to recognizing the literary elements of exposition, rising action, climax, falling action, and resolution.	• Eyes On...Sequence • Understanding the most important points to include when trying to outline the sequence of events in a story	Pp. 37-42 • Vocabulary, I: p. 37 • Vocabulary, II: p. 38 • Comp. Questions: pp. 39-40 • Graphic Organizer: pp. 41-42
The Speckled Hen's Egg Natalie Savage Carlson p. 140 *Lesson in Literature* **Cause and Effect** p. 138	• Fable • *Unit Theme—Growing:* In this fable, a silly woman's self-centered vanity leads her on an adventure that ultimately reveals her weaknesses, and helps her grow and improve.	• Understanding cause and effect as it aids analyzing plot • Understanding the characteristic components of folktales • Defining types of folktales • What is a legend?	• Eyes On...Cause and Effect • Learning to recognize cause and effect in literature	Pp. 43-48 • Vocabulary, I: p. 43 • Vocabulary, II: p. 44 • Comp. Questions: pp. 45-46 • Graphic Organizer: pp. 47-48
The Black Stallion Walter Farley p. 156 *Lesson in Literature* **Predicting** p. 154	• Adventure Fiction • *Unit Theme—Growing:* A boy's kindness and his selfless actions in saving a black stallion reveals the theme of growth.	• Understanding and recognizing foreshadowing • Students are taught to recognize the clues that lead to an author's intention.	• Eyes On...Predicting • Teaching students the best way to predict outcome by searching for clues in a work of fiction	Pp. 49-54 • Vocabulary, I: p. 49 • Vocabulary, II: p. 50 • Comp. Questions: pp. 51-52 • Graphic Organizer: pp. 53-54
By the Shores of Silver Lake Laura Ingalls Wilder p. 180 *Lesson in Literature* **Unit Review** p. 178	• Memoir • *Unit Theme—Growing:* In this childhood memoir, Laura overcomes her fears. We see a family grow through honest communication, and they ultimately find their homestead.	• Reviewing literary components in Unit 2 • This important review lays the groundwork for the next unit's exploration of the literary element of character. Students will understand that a story's character develops within the framework of plot.	• Eyes On...Pulling It All Together • Helping students see how the literary elements of conflict, sequence, cause and effect, and predicting work together to understand plot	Pp. 55-60 • Vocabulary, I: p. 55 • Vocabulary, II: p. 56 • Comp. Questions: pp. 57-58 • Graphic Organizer: pp. 59-60
A Niche in the Kitchen Ouida Sebestyen p. 194	• Narrative Poetry Style: Free Verse	• The components of plot, character, setting, and theme are introduced in the first seven lines of this free verse poem.	• Eyes On...Free Verse, First Person, Narrative Poetry	

UNIT THREE: *Aiming High • Exploring Elements of Character*

Elements of Character—conflict, a character's dialogue, and point of view—are taught in this unit. As students explore how we get to know a character in a work of literature, they will understand how an author uses a character's actions and reactions to tell the story.

SELECTION	FOCUS			WORKBOOK
	Genre • Unit Theme	Literary Element	Eyes On...	
Gramp Joan Tate p. 208 *Lesson in Literature* **Character** p. 206	• Contemporary Fiction • *Unit Theme—Aiming High:* In spite of obstacles, a young boy keeps trying to help his beloved grandfather. Simon does not accept defeat as he aims high towards a solution.	• How do we get to know a character? • This selection will help students understand how an author uses the interaction between characters, characters' moods, and dialogue to tell the story.	• Eyes On...Character • Helping students understand how they get to know a character through adjectives used in the narrative, dialogue, character's thoughts (internal dialogue), and character's actions	Pp. 61-66 • Vocabulary, I: p. 61 • Vocabulary, II: p. 62 • Comp. Questions: pp. 63-64 • Graphic Organizer: pp. 65-66
After School V. Zheleznikov p. 236 *Lesson in Literature* **Conflict** p. 234	• Russian Fiction • *Unit Theme—Aiming High:* As a young boy helps a little girl in this story, the reader will see that compassion and understanding can be attributes of aiming high.	• Categorizing conflict in fiction • Students will identify the conflict in a work of literature, and in doing so, will be able to discuss the theme the writer is revealing.	• Eyes On...Internal and External Conflict • Categorizing external/internal conflict to help isolate single qualities, ideas, and events • Understanding a character's conflict helps the reader understand the author's intent	Pp. 67-72 • Vocabulary, I: p. 67 • Vocabulary, II: p. 68 • Comp. Questions: pp. 69-70 • Graphic Organizer: pp. 71-72
One Throw W. C. Heinz p. 248 *Lesson in Literature* **Dialogue** p. 246	• Sports Fiction • *Unit Theme—Aiming High:* Refusing to compromise his personal ethics, the main character in this story shows us to aim high for professional success, one must have integrity.	• Recognizing revelatory ending • Students will learn to use varied verbs associated with vocal expression—for example, *gasped, uttered,* and *declared*—in their own writing.	• Eyes On...Dialogue • Students will recognize how dialogue introduces the reader to characters and their basic conflicts.	Pp. 73-78 • Vocabulary, I: p. 73 • Vocabulary, II: p. 74 • Comp. Questions: pp. 75-76 • Graphic Organizer: pp. 77-78
The Birds' Peace Jean Craighead George p. 262 *Lesson in Literature* **A Character's Inner Thoughts** p. 260	• Contemporary Fiction • *Unit Theme—Aiming High:* Aiming to accept her situation, a young girl matures as she calls upon her personal strength and finds peace.	• Understanding the device of "the one-person dialogue" • Students will recognize that a conversation with a non-verbal listener is a technique an author uses to tell the story.	• Eyes On...When a Character Speaks to Someone Who Can't Answer • Helping students understand that verbalizing emotions and anxiety can lead to a problem's solution	Pp. 79-84 • Vocabulary, I: p. 79 • Vocabulary, II: p. 80 • Comp. Questions: pp. 81-82 • Graphic Organizer: pp. 83-84
Hattie's Birthday Box Pam Conrad p. 270 *Lesson in Literature* **Point of View and Narration** p. 268	• Fiction as Memoir • *Unit Theme—Aiming High:* In this uplifting story of the strength of the human spirit and enduring love of two siblings, aiming high for a productive life takes on several meanings.	• Students learn the concept of a story within a story, a technique authors use to bring greater detail and background to a work of fiction.	• Eyes On...Changing Point of View • Understanding the use of past tense and the changing voice of the narrator in a story	Pp. 85-90 • Vocabulary, I: p. 85 • Vocabulary, II: p. 86 • Comp. Questions: pp. 87-88 • Graphic Organizer: pp. 89-90
The Whimbrel Colin Thiele p. 284 *Lesson in Literature* **Pulling It All Together** p. 282	• Fiction • *Unit Theme—Aiming High:* Aiming to care for the creatures of the world, two people take practical steps to assist an injured animal.	• This review of the literary components primary to character development is an important stepping stone to identifying conflict and defining theme.	• Eyes On...Pulling It All Together • Recognizing the techniques an author uses to help the reader get to know a character	Pp. 91-96 • Vocabulary, I: p. 91 • Vocabulary, II: p. 92 • Comp. Questions: pp. 93-94 • Graphic Organizer: pp. 95-96

SELECTION	Genre • Unit Theme	Literary Element	Eyes On...	WORKBOOK

I Am Winding Through a Maze
Jack Prelutsky, p. 302
A Tooter Tutor
Carolyn Wells, p. 302
A Bear in Reverse
Anonymous, p. 303
74th Street
Myra Cohn Livingston, p. 304
This Is the Day
June Crebbin, p. 305
	• Concrete Poem
	  Style: Form Poem
	• Limerick
	• Limerick
	• Poem
	  Style: Free Verse
	• Poetry
			• Eyes On...Concrete or Form Poems. Concrete poetry looks like what it is.
			• Eyes On...Limerick
			
			• Eyes On...Metaphor, Rhythm	

UNIT FOUR: The World Around Us • Exploring Elements of Setting

Elements of Setting—mood, imagery, language, conflict, dialogue, and reading drama—are taught in this unit. As students explore the many elements of setting, they will understand how an author uses setting and how characters interact to tell the story.

SELECTION	FOCUS			WORKBOOK
	Genre • Unit Theme	Literary Element	Eyes On...	

The Day of the Turtle
Michael Morpurgo
p. 316
 	
Lesson in Literature
Mood
p. 314
	• Fiction as Told Through a Diary
	
	• *Unit Theme—The World Around Us:* The mood of this story takes all the forms of human emotion as a girl and her elderly friend help a beached turtle back to sea.
		• Students are taught how setting and a character's external conflict creates tension and suspense in fiction.
		
		• *Language Alert:* Exploring the use of lie, lay, and lain
			• Eyes On...Mood
			• Teaching that mood is established by setting, characterization, conflict, dialogue, events, and plot
			• The mood of a story takes all the forms of human emotion
				Pp. 97-102
				• Vocabulary, I: p. 97
				• Vocabulary, II: p. 98
				• Comp. Questions:
				          pp. 99-100
				• Graphic Organizer:
				          pp. 101-102

Prairie Fire
Laura Ingalls Wilder
p. 332
 	
Lesson in Literature
Imagery
p. 330
	• Memoir
	
	• *Unit Theme—The World Around Us:* In this story of strong family values at work, we see a family whose lives are filled with hard labor and basic pleasures as they strive to settle their land.
		• Understanding how vividly drawn images enable us to see the setting and the characters, as well as enable us to visualize external conflict.
		• Students recognize that vivid images can convey strong emotions.
			• Eyes On...Vivid Images
			• Teaching how nouns, verbs, adjectives, and adverbs work together to create the language of vivid images
			• Understanding repetition of ideas and onomatopoeia
				Pp. 103-108
				• Vocabulary, I: p. 103
				• Vocabulary, II: p. 104
				• Comp. Questions:
				          pp. 105-106
				• Graphic Organizer:
				          pp. 107-108

How to Bring Up a Lion
Rudyard Kipling
p. 346
 	
Lesson in Literature
Paraphrasing
p. 344
	• Fiction
	• *Genre Alert:* Review of folktales, fables, parables, and legends
	• *Unit Theme—The World Around Us:* Can a wild animal be a pet? The children in this story learn to understand their world as they raise a baby lion.
		• Students practice restating and rewriting in their own words by using this simple fable-like tale.	• Eyes On...Paraphrasing
			• Teaching students the essential tool of paraphrasing to enable them to use the writings of others without direct quotes
				Pp. 109-114
				• Vocabulary, I: p. 109
				• Vocabulary, II: p. 110
				• Comp. Questions:
				          pp. 111-112
				• Graphic Organizer:
				          pp. 113-114

The Streets are Free
Kurusa
p. 364
 	
Lesson in Literature
Establishing Setting
p. 362
	• Play Based on Real Events
	
	• *Unit Theme—The World Around Us:* With the help of a respected librarian, children bring about change in their world, as they campaign for a new park.
		• Reviewing drama format
		
		• *Language Alert:* Learning the Spanish words, their pronunciation, and English translation present in the play's dialogue
			• Eyes On...Drama	Pp. 115-120
				• Vocabulary, I: p. 115
				• Vocabulary, II: p. 116
				• Comp. Questions:
				          pp. 117-118
				• Graphic Organizer:
				          pp. 119-120

One Day in the Desert
Jean Craighead George
p. 384
 	
Lesson in Literature
Pulling It All Together
p. 384
	• Nonfiction Science/ Environmental
	
	• *Unit Theme—The World Around Us:* This piece about the natural world shows us a working ecosystem. We learn to understand the inter-dependence of all species.
		• Helping students understand the balance between a story and scientific information
		• Students learn how all the elements of setting work together in this environmental narrative.
			• Eyes On...Pulling It All Together
			• Recognizing all of the elements of storytelling that have been previously discussed, particularly the elements of setting
				Pp. 121-126
				• Vocabulary, I: p. 121
				• Vocabulary, II: p. 122
				• Comp. Questions:
				          pp. 123-124
				• Graphic Organizer:
				          pp. 125-126

Choose a Color Jacqueline Sweeney, p. 408	• Ode Style: Free Verse	• Personification; metaphor; repetition	• Eyes On...Consonant and Vowel Repetition	
For Crows and Jays/ One Day Beverly McLoughland, p. 409	• Poetry	• Rhyme; alliteration; ono-matopoeia	• Eyes On...Switching Course at Midstream	
A City Ditty Eve Merriam, p. 410	• Poetry	• Rhyme	• Eyes On...Regular Alternate Line Rhyme	
Afternoon on a Hill Edna St. Vincent Millay, p. 411	• Poetry	• Repetition; punctuation; mood	• Eyes On...Traditional Poetry	

UNIT FIVE: Finding Out What's Inside • Exploring Elements of Theme

Elements of Theme—the joys and sorrows of the human conditions—are explored in this unit. As children learn to discuss how a work of literature makes us feel after we read it, they will begin to understand how one comprehends theme.

SELECTION	FOCUS			WORKBOOK
	Genre • Unit Theme	Literary Element	Eyes On...	
The Memory Box Mary Bahr p. 422 *Lesson in Literature* **Symbol** p. 420	• Contemporary Fiction • Coming of Age Story • *Unit Theme—What's Inside:* In this coming of age story, a young boy learns ways to honor his beloved grandfather.	• Understanding how theme is revealed in a *poignant* story • Literature grapples with both the joys and sorrows of the human condition. Students are helped to understand that theme is how a piece of literature makes us feel.	• Eyes On...Rite of Passage • Understanding that a rite of passage is a series of actions that we perform with life-changing events	Pp. 127-132 • Vocabulary, I: p. 127 • Vocabulary, II: p. 128 • Comp. Questions: pp. 129-130 • Graphic Organizer: pp. 131-132
The Greatest Snowball Fight in History William Graves p. 436 *Lesson in Literature* **Author's Viewpoint** p. 434	• Historical Fiction • *Unit Theme—What's Inside:* This humorous piece subtly condemns war. We watch soldiers reach inside and demonstrate a humanity that is heartwarming.	• Understanding how history is written • In identifying the historical setting in this work of fiction, students will be helped to comprehend its theme.	• Eyes On...Historical Fiction • Helping students understand the historical accuracy of a work of historical fiction, by examining different sources • Learning to identify where historical records diverge	Pp. 133-138 • Vocabulary, I: p. 133 • Vocabulary, II: p. 134 • Comp. Questions: pp. 135-136 • Graphic Organizer: pp. 137-138
Founders of the Children's Rain Forest Phillip Hoose p. 446 *Lesson in Literature* **Theme in Nonfiction** p. 444	• Nonfiction Narrative • *Unit Theme—What's Inside:* In this nonfiction piece, we see that a group of highly motivated children can make a difference.	• Nonfiction as journalism • Nonfiction literature can include any sort of account that is supposed to be factual. In understanding the message of this story, students will be helped to recognize theme.	• Eyes On...Nonfiction and Theme	Pp. 139-144 • Vocabulary, I: p. 139 • Vocabulary, II: p. 140 • Comp. Questions: pp. 141-142 • Graphic Organizer: pp. 143-144
Jessica Govea Phillip Hoose p. 464 *Lesson in Literature* **Biography** p. 462	• Biographical Nonfiction • *Unit Theme—What's Inside:* This short biography about personal courage and dedication to a cause demonstrates the power of one person who works for the good of many.	• A short biography about personal courage and dedication to a cause becomes an excellent vehicle for understanding theme.	• Eyes On...Biography Created from Interview • Students learn the author's technique of using the language of the interviewee to best represent her	Pp. 145-150 • Vocabulary, I: p. 145 • Vocabulary, II: p. 146 • Comp. Questions: pp. 147-148 • Graphic Organizer: pp. 149-150
The Street Boy Silverman p. 478 *Lesson in Literature* **Pulling It All Together** p. 476	• Fantasy • *Unit Theme—What's Inside:* Do we feel greater compassion for others when we actually experience their lives? This story of switched identities explores this intriguing question.	• Students recognize what makes a story a fantasy. • Students learn how realism can make a story of fantasy work, telling a legitimate tale with characters that are believable.	• Eyes On...Fantasy and Pulling It All Together • All the elements of theme work together in this selection as students identify a realistic theme.	Pp. 151-156 • Vocabulary, I: p. 151 • Vocabulary, II: p. 152 • Comp. Questions: pp. 153-154 • Graphic Organizer: pp. 155-156

Waking
Lilian Moore, p. 500
 	
First Day Back
Yuka Igarashi, p. 501
 	
Truth
Barrie Wade, p. 502
 	
My House
Annette M'Baye D'Erneville, p. 503
	• Poetry
	  Style: Free Verse
	
	• Poetry
	  Style: Free Verse
	
	• Poetry
	
	• Poetry
	  Style: Free Verse
		• Rhyme; alliteration; metaphor
		
		• Metaphor
		
		• Alliteration; metaphor
		
		• Metaphor; repetition
			• Eyes On...Repetition
			• Eyes On...Rhythm and Syllabification to Convey Feeling
			• Eyes On...Slant Rhyme
			• Eyes On...Chant and Repetition	

UNIT SIX: The Grand Finalé

Students will read a poignant memoir, a humorous narrative, a suspenseful play, a nonsense poem, and a powerful true story in this unit. They will recognize how all the literary elements of plot, character, setting, and theme work together in excellent literature.

SELECTION	FOCUS			WORKBOOK
	Genre • Unit Theme	Literary Element	Eyes On...	

Small Steps—Part I
Peg Kehret
p. 514
 	
Lesson in Literature
Autobiography
p. 512
	• Autobiographical Memoir
	
	• *Unit Theme—The Grand Finalé:* We experience the resilience of the human spirit in this well-written autobiography. All the elements of a well-told story work together in this suspenseful piece.
		• Students will understand how an autobiography can have all the elements of a good story—suspenseful plot, dynamic characters, interesting setting, and a powerful theme.	• Eyes On...Autobiography/Author's Purpose
			• Students recognize the choices an author has when including incidents from the past in a memoir.
			• Identifying the author's purpose will aid students in their own writing.
				Pp. 157-162
				• Vocabulary, I: p. 157
				• Vocabulary, II: p. 158
				• Comp. Questions:
				      pp. 159-160
				• Graphic Organizer:
				      pp. 161-162

Small Steps—Part II
Peg Kehret
p. 538
	• Autobiographical Memoir	• Students are helped to recognize all of the elements of plot and character development.	• Eyes On...Autobiography/Author's Purpose	Pp. 163-168
				• Vocabulary, I: p. 163
				• Vocabulary, II: p. 164
				• Comp. Questions:
				      pp. 165-166
				• Graphic Organizer:
				      pp. 167-168

Small Steps—Part III Peg Kehret p. 552	• Autobiographical Memoir	• Students will recognize the turning point in a suspenseful story, and will learn how an author uses the tools of reconstructing past events to explain important scenes that they remember.	• Eyes On...Autobiography/Author's Purpose	Pp. 169-172 • Vocabulary, I: p. 169 • Vocabulary, II: p. 170 • Comp. Questions: pp. 171-172

What a Wild Idea
Louis Sabin
p. 566
 	
Lesson in Literature
Nonfiction
p. 564
	• Humorous Narrative
	
	• *Unit Theme—The Grand Finalé:* In this funny, factual piece, we see that human beings constantly strive to beat the odds against making things easier.
		• Students will explore theme in this funny, factual piece.	• Eyes On...Humorous Fiction	Pp. 173-178
				• Vocabulary, I: p. 173
				• Vocabulary, II: p. 174
				• Comp. Questions:
				      pp. 175-176
				• Graphic Organizer:
				      pp. 177-178

Flight Into Danger
Arthur Hailey
p. 580
 	
Lesson in Literature
Drama
p. 578
	• Drama
	
	• *Unit Theme—The Grand Finalé:* This is a classic drama of suspense. Its exciting plot and easy to understand characters, will make this a fun play to read and perform.
		• Students will learn to recognize the power of dialogue and plot in suspenseful drama.	• Eyes On...Theater
			• This is a good play in which to compare the relative importance of scenery, lighting, sound effects, costumes, and props to plot.
				Pp. 179-184
				• Vocabulary, I: p. 179
				• Vocabulary, II: p. 180
				• Comp. Questions:
				      pp. 181-182
				• Graphic Organizer:
				      pp. 183-184

The Quangle Wangle's Hat Edward Lear p. 638 *Lesson in Literature* **A Nonsense Poem** p. 636	• Nonsense Poetry • *Unit Theme—The Grand Finalé:* When we explore the language of nonsense, we learn more about the language of literature and the tools of writing.	• Do nonsense rhymes have a hidden meaning? Students will explore this in Edward Lear's wonderful poem.	• Eyes On...Nonsense • Students learn to recognize the elements of nonsense. Is it silly words, silly ideas and situations, or talking animals?	Pp. 185-186 • Comp. Questions: pp. 185-186
Passage to Freedom Ken Mochizuki p. 646 *Lesson in Literature* **Author's Viewpoint** p. 644	• Fictionalized Nonfiction • *Unit Theme—The Grand Finalé:* In this powerful finale, we read about true altruism. This is a story about a fearlessness engendered by a strong moral conscience.	• Recognizing the powerful theme—pure altruism, the unselfish regard for the welfare of others—is discussed in this piece. Using the skills previously learned to recognize theme, students will gain a great deal from this story.	• Eyes On...Fictionalized Nonfiction • Students learn the unique first-person narration device the author uses in this piece. Though the author is not actually the main character's son, he assumes the narrator's voice as if he is.	Pp. 187-192 • Vocabulary, I: p. 187 • Vocabulary, II: p. 188 • Comp. Questions: pp. 189-190 • Graphic Organizer: pp. 191-192
The Butterfly and the Caterpillar Joseph Lauren p. 658 **The Eagle** Alfred Lord Tennyson p. 660 **Traveling in a Comfortable Car** Bertolt Brecht p. 661	• Poetry • Poetry • Narrative Poetry Style: Free Verse	• Rhyming couplets • Rhyme scheme; alliteration; consonance; assonance • Repetition; alliteration	• Eyes On...Fable and Traditional Poetic Form • Eyes On...Greatness in Verse • Eyes On...Narrative Poem	

SAMUEL'S CHOICE (P. 16)

A good way to start this unit—and the semester in literature—is to have a class discussion about stories.

Ask your students the questions below, and any others that you feel will be helpful to get them talking and thinking. Remember that storytelling is common to all human cultures, whatever their level of "sophistication."

- What *is* a story? (After all, if a series of events is described, it is not necessarily a story!) What does a narrative have to have in order to *be* a story?
- What makes a story a *good* story?
- Does anyone read them stories now?
- Did anyone read to them, when they were younger?
- Has anyone ever told them a story, without reading it from a book?
- Do they, themselves, ever read stories to younger children?
- What is their favorite story? Why do they especially like it?

You can finish this **Getting Started** discussion by talking, just briefly, about the elements of a story. The definitions in quotation marks below are included to be helpful to the teacher, and are not intended for most students at the fifth grade level.

A story starts with a **beginning,** or **exposition,** "a setting forth of the meaning or purpose in a piece of writing," when we are introduced to

- the **characters** (the people in the story)
- the **setting** (the time and the place)
- the **situation** ("a combination of circumstances at a particular moment; a critical, trying, or unusual state of affairs; the problem in the action of a narrative or drama").

(You can talk with your students about any story using these terms or more familiar synonyms. It may be useful and funny for you to apply them—or ask your students to apply them—to the popular children's stories with which they are familiar.)

Then there is **rising action**, as events unfold, and we see what sort of **conflict** or problem the main character has. Is the main character having a problem with another person? With a set of circumstances? Within himself or herself, as in a personal struggle over what is the right thing to do?

At some point, the **main character** has to make a decision, or take action, in order to deal with the conflict. When the main character does this—or decides to do it—is the **turning point** in the story.

The turning point may or may not be the **climax** or highest moment of the story. In the story that follows, the turning point is *not* the climax. This is because the emotional climax for the main character is not the situational climax of the story.

(Specifically, on page 24, the **turning point** comes when Samuel says, "I looked at my hands, grown strong from pulling ropes and oars and sacks. Then I knew my choice. Those hands now were going to pull people, pull them to freedom."

A **not-quite-the-climax** comes on page 26, when Major Mordecai Gist (who actually commanded the Maryland 400 at the Battle of Long Island) says to Samuel, "out in that creek you did more than many a free man for your country. I'd take it as a privilege if you'd consent to be my orderly and march beside me." The **situation climax** occurs on page 29, when Samuel tells us, "We stumbled ashore on Manhattan Island, where kind people wrapped us in blankets. They were smiling—the rope was across!")

After the climax of a story—and you may want to tell your students that people will not always agree regarding the moment at which the climax comes—there is **falling action,** as the story unwinds, and events come to a **resolution**, or **conclusion**. It is this cycle of opening, rising, peaking, falling, and resolving that makes stories so satisfying.

In the **Literary Components** that are given page for page, the elements of the story are indicated in the appropriate places.

SLOWER THAN THE REST (P. 3

You can begin this selection by asking students, what is a turtle Then have students write down three facts about turtles. At the en of the discussion below, they can see if they got the facts right.

Here are some words you may want to write on the board with their definitions.

chelonian: resembling, having the characteristics of, or being a tortoise or turtle

cold-blooded: having a body temperature that is not regulated by the body, but by the temperature of the environment (captive turtles need to live in glass boxes, so that sunlight reaches then

herpetology: a branch of zoology that deals with reptiles and amphibians

reptile: air-breathing vertebrates that are cold-blooded and hav scales. Most have short legs (or no legs), and lay eggs.

vertebrate: a class of animals that includes fishes, amphibians, reptiles, birds, and mammals. Vertebrates have an internal skel eton formed of cartilage, bone, or both. The skeleton consists o a backbone, which partly encloses a spinal cord; a skull, which encloses the brain; and usually two pairs of limbs.

Turtles are four-legged reptiles. The special feature of the turtle its shell, which has a different shape and different markings depen ing on the species. The shell consists of an arched upper shell gro fast to the backbone and a flat lower shell grown fast to the breast bone. The upper and lower shells are connected by a bony bridge either side. Box turtles have a hinged lower shell. This allows then to close the two shells together and completely hide head, tail, and limbs.

Turtles live in water all or some of the time, but all breathe air, which means they can drown. All turtles lay their eggs on land in nests that vary with each species. Although the eggs are covered, they hatch from the heat of the sun. Many animals like to eat turtle eggs, and the young are very vulnerable before their shells harder Freshwater and marine turtles always return to the same shoreline lay their eggs, which enables humans to kill large numbers of then

Turtles live on every continent except Antarctica in ponds, rivers oceans, forests, grasslands, and deserts. Turtles really like tropica and subtropical climates, because they are cold-blooded.

Turtles come in many sizes. The great leatherback sea turtle has a shell length up to eight feet, and can weigh as much as 200 lbs. The Galapagos Islands near South America and the Island of Aldabra off the coast of East Africa are known for their giant tortois es. These reach up to four feet in length. The Galapagos tortoises were captured and killed by whalers. They were an easy kill, beca they move so slowly. In 1900, only a few remained. Strenuous effo by conservationists to breed them in protected places saved them from extinction.

Turtles have no housing problem. Their greatest enemy is man. Their next greatest enemy is fire.

Turtles are fascinating and there is a great deal of interesting material to teach you about them.

KATE SHELLEY (P. 44)

It is important for children to develop the ability to listen to liter ture, and to be able to understand what they are hearing. This is a skill that we can start to develop in the early grades.

These aural comprehension exercises will make up 25% of the **Getting Started** activities. These are not graded, nor are student answers passed in. This is a chance for students to see how well they do, and to make progress with this skill over the school year. Please read the first three paragraphs of *Kate Shelley: Bound for Legend* aloud to your class. Read them aloud a second time, and ask students to pick the best multiple-choice answer to each of ter questions. If any student has difficulty with this at first, go over the st three paragraphs and point out the correct answers—which are dicated below in **bold.**

Honey Creek was located not far from Kate Shelley's home, and was
a. used as a swimming hole in the summer by all the farm children.
b. the beginning of a water route that led to the Mississippi River.
c. crossed by a railroad bridge.
d. named for the honey bees and special honey for which Iowa was famous in those days.

Every day,
a. boats sailed back and forth under the Des Moines River Bridge.
b. trains sped back and forth over the trestle, east to Chicago or west toward Salt Lake City.
c. people bicycled past, as Kate was plowing the field.
d. planes could be heard in the sky, flying east to Chicago or west to Salt Lake City.

Before Kate's father had died, he had been
a. a farmer.
b. an airplane mechanic.
c. a telegraph operator.
d. a section foreman on the railway.

At the beginning of the story, the year is
a. 1881.
b. 1981.
c. 1771.
d. 2071.

The trains that roared past the farm
a. irritated the Shelley family, because of their noisy choo-choo.
b. carried coal and steel, as they traveled west.
c. were always on schedule—you could set your clock by them.
d. brought excitement to Kate Shelley's life.

In this early part of the story, the author describes Kate as
a. good-natured and sturdy.
b. sensitive and shy.
c. very thin and pale.
d. hard working, but unfriendly.

After her father died, Kate took charge of the family because
a. her mother was no longer alive.
b. she was a terribly bossy girl.
c. her mother was in poor health.
d. her mother had to go to work.

The Shelley farm was pasture and timber set amid rugged hills of
a. Ohio.
b. Iowa.
c. Nebraska.
d. Kansas.

Kate's chores included
a. digging ditches to irrigate the farmland.
b. painting the farmhouse and hanging wallpaper.
c. helping with plowing and planting and gathering firewood.
d. setting fence posts, building rock walls, and nailing No Trespassing signs to the posts.

). Kate Shelley taught herself to shoot
a. so she could go hunting for extra food.
b. because she wanted to be a good marksman.
c. in order to enter a contest at the county fair.
d. to keep hawks away from the chickens.

IEW PROVIDENCE (P. 64)

Activity I

Here is a second set of learning and listening exercises to follow on students' first exposure to this type of activity in *Kate Shelley.* ew Providence: A Changing Cityscape has a lot more detail, so tell udents they may need to focus more intently as you read. Again, s is not a graded exercise.

You will read the year followed by the first (or first and second) ntence(s) for that section. These should be read to your students

twice through, followed by two multiple-choice questions about the passage. The questions should also be read twice, to make sure students have understood the choices.

1910: *New Providence is thriving. Cobblestone streets bustle with activity—Model T Fords, streetcars, and horse-drawn carts carrying meat, milk and ice.*

1. It is clear that New Providence is
    a. a farm community.
    b. a city on the Mississippi River.
    c. a busy, growing city.
    d. a small Asian town on the outskirts of Hong Kong.

2. It can also be figured out from the description that in 1910,
    a. most people in the city used the subways.
    b. there were no supermarkets or refrigerators.
    c. a lot of children did not go to school.
    d. people only ate meat, milk, and ice.

1935: *As a mist rolls into New Providence, effects of the Great Depression are visible; the city has fallen on hard times. Gone is the bandstand from the courthouse square, where homeless men now huddle over trash can fires for warmth.*

3. What has happened to New Providence?
    a. The city has had to make way for an airport.
    b. The city has been replaced by a hundred acres of corn.
    c. Summer has come and it is hot and humid.
    d. The city is much poorer because it is the time of the Great Depression.

4. There is no longer a bandstand in the square. In its place,
    a. men with no place to go are warming themselves at fires that have been started in garbage cans.
    b. a statue has been erected of General Leroy Brown riding his favorite horse, Chester.
    c. a large and ornate fountain is spraying water at passersby.
    d. is an ice skating rink. Everyone is doing fancy figure eights.

1955: *A postwar prosperity settles over New Providence, although there are signs that downtown is deteriorating. The night sky glows with neon, holiday lights, and lighted billboards advertising bread and used cars.*

5. New Providence is
    a. becoming one of the largest cities in the United States.
    b. now the coal capital of Pennsylvania.
    c. celebrating the World Series victory of the Provident Players.
    d. thriving because of the end of the war, but is also becoming rundown.

6. The night sky is lit up by
    a. neon lights, holiday lights, and lighted billboards.
    b. the full, silver moon and white cumulus clouds.
    c. softly falling snow.
    d. 4th of July fireworks.

1970: *By 1970, downtown New Providence is an uninspired jumble of old and new. To attract people from thriving suburbia, part of Main Street has been converted into a pedestrian mall, dominated by a harsh concrete fountain.*

7. In 1970, downtown New Providence has become
    a. terribly congested with traffic.
    b. crime-ridden and dangerous.
    c. an unplanned and confused mixture of old and new buildings.
    d. one of the most beautiful cities of the nation.

8. In order to attract people from the suburbs to the city,
    a. town officials have built an airport next to town hall.
    b. part of Main Street has been turned into a mall.
    c. five new pizzerias have been opened.
    d. a lake has been dug in the middle of town.

1980: *Ten tears later, there are signs that downtown New Providence is sadly in need of recovery—and also signs that help is on the way. Chief Tenebo's statue has been vandalized; debris blows around its dry base and across the square.*

9. In 1980, there are signs that
   a. a highway is going to replace Main Street.
   b. New Providence is going to host the next World Olympics.
   c. the downtown area needs serious work.
   d. New Providence is going to build a new high school.

10. However, there is room for hope, because
    a. the highway will bring new customers.
    b. the city is kind of attractive for a slum.
    c. there are signs that help is on the way.
    d. a better education will make better citizens.

1992: *In the sunny afternoon sky a flock of birds heads back to its winter home. Below, people have returned to the city—living, shopping, working, playing. New Providence has never looked better.*

11. The year 1992 is
    a. the one hundredth anniversary of New Providence.
    b. a very good year for New Providence.
    c. a tough year for the steel workers in the city.
    d. the year Chief Tenebo finally gets elected mayor.

12. The city is now
    a. bustling with active people.
    b. dying, because most people and businesses have moved to the suburbs.
    c. predicting lots of sunshine and good weather.
    d. hoping to host the 1994 Olympics.

Activity II
What Is a City?

Ask your students that question. What is it, after all, that makes a city a city?

The following questions and activities will make a nice lead into *New Providence: A Changing Cityscape.* (This discussion, and material from **Background Bytes,** will help students complete one of the **Wrap-Up** Exercises.)

The Merriam-Webster Unabridged Dictionary offers these definitions of the word *city:*

(1) A city is a municipal corporation in the United States that occupies a definite geographic area and is subject to the State in which it is located; it exists as an area of local government governed under a legal charter by a mayor and council, by a commission, or by a city manager and council; it is usually more populous than a town, borough, or village.

The word *municipal* means "of or relating to a *municipality.*" A *municipality* is an urban political unit with corporate status and powers of self-government.

(2) A city is "a populous place, a place larger than a village or town; a large, prominent, or important center of population; a relatively permanent and highly organized center having a population with varied skills," that does not produce its own food and depends on manufacture and commerce to support the needs of the people who live there.

What do we learn from these definitions? A city is large. A city has a lot of people living in it. A city is a legal entity, with a government. What else?

In the United States, a city has a relationship to the State in which it is located. In Canada, a city has a relationship to the Province in which it is situated. In other countries, which governmental or regional category is the city a part of?

Here are questions for discussion with students.

1. Do you live in a city? If not, which city is closest to where you live? What is its name? What is its population?

2. How is your life linked to the city in which you live? What services does the city supply to you and your family? If you live *near* a city, what does living near the city mean to you?

3. Make a list of five things you associate with a city—things that perhaps can't be found anyplace but in a city. (This may turn out to be a mini-definition of a city.)

4. What are some of the positive things about the city you live in or near? What are some of the negative things?

5. As cities grow, what may be some of the problems they face?

THE SILENT LOBBY (P. 82)

The following activity gives students a chance to see how it feels to be arbitrarily denied fair and equal treatment. It is a powerful experience, and some teachers may not find it appropriate for their classes. You may wish to use a milder exercise or tell a story to convey the same message.

A more complex version of this activity has been used in social studies classrooms across the U.S.A. But even this simpler exercise may take more than one class period. The activity may also be upsetting to some of your students. Time needs to be set aside at conclusion of the exercise for airing feelings.

Use a random distribution of cards, to divide your class into two groups.

From a shuffled deck comprised only of aces, 2's, 3's, 4's, 5's, and 6's (24 cards) pass out one card to each student. (If you have more than 24 students, some students just won't receive a card.)

After the cards are distributed, direct those students who received 2's, 4's, and 6's to sit in the rows at the front of the classroom—horizontal rows 1 through 3, for example. Students with aces, 3's, and 5's, must move to seats in the back rows. Students who received no cards will also sit in the back rows of the classroom.

The two groups cannot share a row, even if this means leaving seats empty in the last row occupied by 2's, 4's, and 6's. Also, a row of seats—or the equivalent floor space—must remain empty between the two groups of students.

If necessary, students with aces, 3's, 6's, and no cards will have to double up in their seats, or take turns sitting. Given the cards they are holding, they are lucky to have any seats.

After students are settled in their new seats, you make an announcement:

1. All students sitting in the back rows will automatically have their grades lowered one grade for each assignment.

2. Students in the front rows may not try to communicate, either by voice or gesture, with students sitting in the back rows during class.

3. An election will be held for class president. Candidates cannot be from those students sitting in the back rows, and only students in the front rows get to pick the candidates. Have students vote on paper ballots. The ballots should be collected so that those from the back rows remain separate from those in the front rows. After all the ballots are collected, tell the students in the back rows that their votes do not count. Dump those ballots in the trash.

Call for a few minutes of silence. Then pass out paper to each student. Ask them to write down how he or she is feeling at that moment in one or two sentences. After papers are passed forward, have students move back to their own seats. Tell your class that this exercise is related to the story they will be reading. The story is about people fighting for equal treatment.

Students may need to talk about how they were treated during this class exercise and how it made them feel. This is a difficult activity, but it has been shown to be a powerful teaching and learning tool. The better you can act your part during the exercise, the more students will learn from the experience.

Three important issues should be talked about in subsequent discussion:

1. Why is the right to vote important?

2. How does one group of people make another group of people feel bad?

3. How does one group of people take away rights from another group of people, even when the law says they *have* those rights?

GOLD-MOUNTED GUNS (P. 110)

This **Getting Started** activity can be used as a forum for the discussion of three topics with your class:

) What do your students think of when you mention cowboys, gunslingers, the old West, and, for example, Dodge City? What do your students imagine life was like for cowboys? What was life like in a town like Dodge City?

) What does the word *conflict* mean? What are examples of conflict? Do students have any idea what the difference is between an external conflict and an internal conflict? You will have to be prepared to talk a little about external (outer) conflicts and internal (inner) conflicts. Tell them that external conflicts can be with other people, with nature (earthquakes, tornadoes, and so forth), and with society (as, for example, in the case of segregation. The conflict described in *The Silent Lobby* is a good example of a group at conflict with society.).

) What type of person do you think would leave a secure home to "go out West"? What character traits—good and bad—might have been found in the people who lived in towns like Dodge City?

THE DISAPPEARING MAN (P. 128)

We are indebted to John P. Gunnison of Adventure House ublishers for much of the historical material below.

Pulp magazines are magazines or books printed on cheap aper (such as newsprint) that deal with "sensational" material. *ensational,* here, means that readers have a quick, intense, but not ery deep experience.) These magazines became popular just before orld War I. The magazines began as "dime novels," cheap publica- ns that were directed towards an audience of young boys and girls ho had little money to spend on books. The pulp magazines that ew out of the dime novels had more pages, boasted color covers, d were directed towards an adult audience.

When publishers Street & Smith created their first pulp maga- ne, it was called *Detective Story Magazine.* Subsequently, Street & mith also sponsored *The Shadow,* a radio show that aired stories m *Detective Story Magazine.* The stories were adapted for public oadcast. The program's host was someone known only as "The hadow." People who listened to *The Shadow* thought there was so a magazine called *The Shadow.* This led to the creation of a cond magazine from Street & Smith.

Pulp magazines were extremely popular between the first and cond World Wars. They became a "cultural force," in the way that levision and, to a lesser degree, radio are today. Magazines came d went, as did their writers. Some of the writers were very good riters and are still well known. These include Edgar Rice Burroughs ho wrote *Tarzan*), Dashiell Hammett, Raymond Chandler, Louis Amour, Ray Bradbury, Isaac Asimov, Arthur C. Clark, Cornell oolrich, and H. P. Lovecraft.

The magazines were not restricted to mystery or detective sto- s. Some were devoted to westerns, others, to science fiction, and t others to just plain "fright." They had interesting names: *Black ask, Weird Tales, Amazing Stories, The Shadow, The Phantom etective, Argosy, Doc Savage, The Spider, G-8 and His Battle ces, Dime Detective Magazine,* and *Weird Menace.*

Now it is time for a class activity. Ask each student to make up a me for his or her detective magazine. Tell students that the names n be serious, scary, humorous, or witty. They will be using this title hen they create a cover for their own detective magazines in the al exercise of this selection.

THE SPECKLED HEN'S EGG (P. 140)

Folktales and fables have developed in every culture across the globe. They have been with us for centuries, and were told and retold for generations before they were written down. Although we may think of them as entertainment, especially as entertainment for children, in fact every society throughout history has used them to communicate values.

For this reason, the **Getting Started** activity is about communication. This exercise can be a lot of fun, and shows that there are many different ways to talk. In addition to words, we use gestures, mime, body movements, charades, sounds, tone, and pitch.

For the activity that follows, you will want to remind your students that an important part of oral communication is repetition of sound: rhyme and alliteration, for example. Even nonsense sounds can be rhymed. Another kind of repetition is rhythm. Studies have shown that repetition of all types—including repeating single words and phrases—helps human beings store and draw on such information in the brain.

This exercise also offers students the opportunity to learn how to speak up and to be verbally and emotionally expressive in front of an audience. This is training for any form of recitation—as removed as it may seem from memorizing and reciting fine poetry!

The Game of GIBBERISH

Gibberish is unintelligible or meaningless language. This is a "theater game" that emphasizes communication, using gibberish. Students work in pairs for the game. If your class is large, you may want to use trios. We discourage using more than three students in a group.

The idea is to have a two- or three-way conversation in which the participants use nonsense syllables instead of their standard language. (Students may need some rehearsal time—in or out of school.) As your students proceed with the exercise, they are likely to realize that gestures, body language, tone, inflection, and rapidity of speech are part of communicating—in any language. In addition to speaking in gibberish, students will also be called upon to switch to intelligible English, when you shout, "Change!" or to switch back to gibberish when you repeat the order.

Each pair or trio should tell the class, in advance of their non- sense discussion, what it is they are talking about.

THE BLACK STALLION (P. 156)

The Horse Lovers Quiz is fun for students and introduces the sub- ject of horses. Even a basically silly quiz such as this reinforces the importance of paying attention and *listening.*

1. Does your family own a horse?
   a. Yes.
   b. No, but I'd like to.
   c. I would not want to have a horse.
   d. Horses. Yuck!
2. I have always wanted to
   a. pet and ride a horse.
   b. see horses, but not close up.
   c. move away quickly when I got close to a horse.
   d. I've never been near a horse and I never want to be.
3. I would like to
   a. have friends who own horses.
   b. have friends who like horses.
   c. leave horses out of my life.
   d. never hear the word, *horses.*
4. In my life, I have read
   a. lots of books about horses.
   b. one or two books about horses.
   c. no books about horses.
   d. Horses?! Who would want to read about horses?
5. I think I should learn
   a. a lot about horses.

b. at least something about horses.

c. nothing about horses.

d. to close my ears when I hear the word, *horses.*

6. To be honest,

   a. I have spent time with horses throughout my life.

   b. I have only seen horses at petting zoos and maybe have gone riding on a horse once or twice.

   c. I have never seen a horse in real life.

   d. I'd move, if someone with a horse moved in next door.

7. If a horse were suffering or starving or being mistreated,

   a. I would definitely tell someone and call the SPCA or another animal protection organization.

   b. I would care, but I wouldn't try to do anything about it.

   c. I probably wouldn't notice.

   d. If I noticed, I wouldn't care.

8. As far as art and horses goes,

   a. I draw horses all the time.

   b. I would like to draw horses, but I'm not very good at it.

   c. I can't draw horses and it's no big deal.

   d. I wouldn't draw horses if I could.

9. If I had a horse, I would

   a. know how to take care of it and put it through its paces.

   b. learn how to care for it.

   c. not want to spend the time taking care of it.

   d. get rid of it.

10. When an animal is suffering,

    a. I can't stand it. I have to do something about it.

    b. I can't stand it. But I feel helpless.

    c. It is not my concern.

    d. I don't care.

Score each a. answer 3.
Score each b. answer 2.
Score each c. answer 1.
Score each d. answer 0.

26 to 30 points: You are a real horse lover!

19 to 25: You have the makings of a real horse lover!

15 to 18: You should find out more about horses. You might really like them!

 0 to 14: Well, hopefully you are really interested in something else.

Students who are interested in horses but who have no contact with them will be inspired by the story of author Walter Farley. When Mr. Farley was a child, his greatest desire was to have a horse. Like Alexander Ramsay, however, he lived in New York City, certainly no place for raising and riding a horse. Through his yearning, he began writing the story of a boy and a horse. Like Alexander Ramsay, too, young Walter Farley had an uncle whose life revolved around horses: this real-life uncle was a horse trainer. *The Black Stallion* was first published in 1941 and is today regarded as a contemporary classic. The money he earned from his horse books enabled him to have the experiences with horses that he had dreamed of as a child.

BY THE SHORES OF SILVER LAKE (P. 180)

This is the third set of learning and listening exercises. The first two sets of aural comprehension exercises were the **Getting Started** activities in Unit I's *Kate Shelley: Bound for Legend* and *New Providence: A Changing Cityscape.* Once again, these exercises are not to be graded, and the students should know this. This is a chance for students to see how well they do, and to make progress with this skill over the school year.

Please read aloud to your class the first two paragraphs and the five short paragraphs of conversation that follow. (Read up through "So Ma told them, 'You may go for a quick run. Don't stay until you get too cold.'") Read the passage aloud to your class twice, and ask students to pick the best multiple-choice answer to each of ten

questions. Try to read the passage with sufficient expression in you voice, so that students will pick up on the dialogue and know who speaking. If any student has difficulty with this, go over the first thr paragraphs and point out the correct answers—which are indicate below in **bold.**

1. There came a night when

   a. **the moonlight shone silver clear.**

   b. the moon was a big silver disk and snow was falling.

   c. Laura wished her cousins would visit from the East.

   d. the lake was silver and there was no sound.

2. Beyond every window,

   a. there was snow and Laura knew she could have fun outside.

   b. **the white world stretched far away in frosty glitter.**

   c. the sky was a curve of light, and there was a half moon.

   d. planes could be heard in the sky, flying east to Chicago or west to Salt Lake City.

3. Laura could not settle down to anything. She didn't even want

   a. bake oatmeal cookies with her mother.

   b. sing songs with Carrie and Mary, while Pa played the fiddle.

   c. help Carrie make doll clothes.

   d. **play games.**

4. She felt she must be going somewhere. Suddenly she exclaim

   a. "Pa, please take us sledding!"

   b. "Carrie! Let's go exploring in the woods!"

   c. **"Carrie! Let's go slide on the ice!"**

   d. "Ma! The bread's burning!"

5. Ma was astonished, because

   a. Laura hated to go sledding.

   b. Laura was usually scared to go outside at night.

   c. **it was nighttime.**

   d. never before had she let the bread burn.

6. In this early part of the story, the author describes Laura as

   a. **restless and wanting to move swiftly.**

   b. sensitive and shy.

   c. very generous.

   d. unable to tell the difference between day and night.

7. What reason does Laura give her mother that it's okay outside that night?

   a. All the streetlamps are lit.

   b. All her friends are doing it.

   c. **It's almost as light as day.**

   d. All the wolves are at a convention in Georgia.

8. Pa says to Ma that it's okay, there's nothing to hurt them unles

   a. they are attacked by a grizzly bear.

   b. they walk by the water hole and fall in.

   c. they behave foolishly.

   d. **they stay out too long and freeze.**

9. So Ma tells them that they can

   a. **go for a quick run.**

   b. run back and forth across the lake.

   c. help with plowing and planting and gathering firewood.

   d. make snow angels if they hurry back inside.

10. Three people are talking in the conversation:

    a. Ma, Pa, and Caroline.

    b. Laura, Caroline, and Ma.

    c. Carrie, Ma, and Pa.

    d. **Pa, Caroline, and Laura.**

GRAMP (P. 208)

This **Getting Started** activity can be used to discuss one of two topics with your class:

How does each of your students imagine the day-to-day life of a grandparent or a person who is in their late sixties or older? What makes an older person happy? What makes an older person worry? Do your students think that older people are lonelier? What do students think their grandmothers and grandfathers think about?

What is the difference between living in a house or a flat (an apartment on one floor of a two- or three-family house) and living in an apartment building? Does each situation have advantages and disadvantages?

AFTER SCHOOL (P. 236)

Do young people act with a conscience towards people their own age?

Discuss the following situations. Use the first situation in italics for girls, and the second situation in italics for boys. The final question is for all students.

Your parents invite a family over for a special meal. It turns out that you don't know their daughter very well. In fact, your own friends have talked about her (and maybe you have, too), because they think that she is uncomfortable with people, definitely not "cool." You find that it is difficult to be friendly to her. How would you like to behave? How do you behave?

Your parents have invited over a new family on the block. Their son is younger than you are. You just ignore him. He's just a little kid and you don't like to talk to guests, anyway. How should you treat him? How do you treat him?

Why is it so difficult for us to act as we know we should in social situations?

ONE THROW (P. 248)

An idiom is a phrase of two or more words that means something other than the literal meaning of its individual words. For example, when we say that someone has *hit the nail on the head,* we mean that they have said precisely the right thing or have gotten to the crux of the matter, not that they are skillful with a hammer. English has thousands of idioms. Studying them is fascinating. Understanding them is important. But overusing them is a transgression of good speaking and good writing. It is irritating to hear everyone talking about *the bottom line, pushing the envelope, the whole nine yards, and having too many things on one's plate.* We have a language with millions of words. Each of us is capable of doing the not-so-hard work of expressing our own thoughts in our own words. We hope you will encourage your students to do so.

Interestingly, many sports expressions have been incorporated into American speech as idioms. U.S. President Bill Clinton once told reporters that he felt his "environmental program was in the **home stretch**" and that he had **"hit a home run** with his appointment of Mr. X as ambassador." The President talked this way, because a *lot* of people talk this way in the United States.

Some teachers of English-as-a-Second Language maintain that American English cannot be understood if one does not understand sports idioms. Certainly as part of our language, these idioms have broader application and wider meaning than they do in sports. Here are some idioms from sports other than baseball:

football	*fumble the ball, game plan, Monday morning quarterback, the whole nine yards, run with the ball*
basketball	*a slam dunk, out of bounds, working against the clock, that's the way the ball bounces*
horse racing	*isn't up to scratch, a long shot, jockey for position, not*

by a long shot, dark horse

boxing	*ring-side seats, a heavyweight, hitting below the belt, saved by the bell, throw in the towel, take it on the chin*
wrestling	*no holds barred*
card-playing	*lay your cards on the table, dealt a bad hand in life, have the cards stacked against you, under the table, a bad deal, a good deal, call a spade a spade*
gambling	*you can count on it, you bet I will*

Understanding Baseball Idioms

This activity is fun. Do your students know the English translation of the idioms in our **Baseball Idioms List** below? Read them the idiom. Then have students volunteer the meaning. (For much of the list of baseball idioms below, we are indebted to *U.S. Society & Values* (December 2003), Kaye Mastin Mallory's *English Zone.*)

Baseball Idioms List

It's a whole new ball game: a new chance, a fresh slate; a situation in which you can start *from scratch.* A situation that now has different rules.

Play hard ball: play with no rules, with *no holds barred*; tough negotiations with no pretense of politeness or civility.

Throw a curve ball: mislead a person

Two strikes against it: close to not succeeding

Two strikes against him: he's down to his last option, there won't be a second chance

No-win situation: impossible to succeed

Out of our league: better than we are

Not in our league: Inferior to us

Major, big leagues: highest level of professionalism; have most money and power

Bush league: cheap, lower-than-acceptable professionalism or ethics

Batting 1000: doing perfectly, really successful at every stage, in every way

Play ball: cooperate with someone

Ballpark figure: general financial number; estimate

Bench (verb): withdraw someone; stop someone from participating

On the ball: knowledgeable; competent; attentive

Step up to the plate: act; take or accept responsibility

Strike out: fail completely

Off base: unrealistic; way wrong

Out of left field: irrelevant; unexpected

7th-inning stretch: pause near end of an activity to refresh or to reflect on an encounter

Throw a curve: deceive; trick; tactically confuse

Squeeze play: sneaking something through with a minor action, where a major action might normally have been expected

To field questions: Handle questions with dexterity

Doubleheader: an event that has two main parts or features

Double play: two successes brought about by one action

THE BIRDS' PEACE (P. 262)

A Philosophy of War for the Fifth Grade

In *The Birds' Peace,* Kristy's father "went off to war." Do students know what that means? For the story, the notion of war needs to be placed in some context.

Discussing war with fifth graders involves a narrow focus and a bit of care. This is not a political discussion. This is an opportunity to give children practice thinking analytically, and to apply ethical ideals to real-life situations. In such a discussion, the participants must support their conclusions—although no one should be put on the spot for being unable to articulate reasons for strong feelings. This is a thinking person's discussion, and we certainly want our children to have practice thinking about things. Have students keep their dictionaries out. They may need their dictionaries to look up *war, fair, just…*

Begin by asking students **what is war?** If they have difficulty with specifics, have them look the word up in the dictionary. War is usually an **open or declared conflict between states or nations** in which **weapons are used.** Several elements are important here:

(1) it's a conflict
(2) it's a conflict between nations
(3) the hostilities have been declared verbally
(4) arms are used

Now broaden the discussion.

What is the point of a war? What is a war for?

Wars have been fought for a huge variety of reasons, some of which your students will be able to provide. Before enumerating reasons for war, it would make your job simpler if you immediately distinguished between offensive wars and defensive wars. [As adults, we know that offensive wars have sometimes been termed defensive by the aggressors, we know that people on the defensive have been labeled aggressors by their enemies and attackers, we know that in our mixed-up world, politicians, dictators, terrorists, and a host of others will turn truth on its head. But none of this will we discuss with a fifth grade! We will keep things simple and basic.]

To return to the question: why are wars fought?

The first and most obvious answer is: to protect a nation from its enemies. Either the enemy has attacked or the enemy is believed to be on the verge of attacking.

Some of your students will have learned about wars that were fought to acquire land, power, wealth, navigational routes, or for other reasons that could not be called defense of the homeland. It is in relation to these wars that the question could be posed: Is it morally right to go to war for any reason other than that you have been attacked?

Guide students in their discussion. You may want to discuss some of the following traditional positions on war:

(1) **War is sometimes, but not always, morally right.** A war that is morally right is fought for a just cause. **(What is a just cause?)** A war that is morally right is fought for its stated reason, not for some ulterior, profit-driven motive. A war is only morally right if all peaceful means (such as diplomatic negotiation) have already been tried first. In a moral war, soldiers do not hurt anyone unnecessarily. In a just war, prisoners of war are not treated badly.

(2) **A war must be essential/necessary/helpful to a nation's security to be just.** Wars are necessary and make sense because states or nations need to protect themselves from other nations. Nations need to protect their people, their land, and their resources. Related, but less often stated openly, are some of the following stances: Nations may make war in order to acquire more land and/ or more resources. The more valuable things a nation has, the more power it will have. The more power a nation has, the more likely it is to survive. Every detail and degree of these statements have been argued pro and con by thinking people.

(3) **War cannot ever be morally right.** This view, held by many in theory but few in practice, is the pacifist view. It leaves completely unanswered what recourse victims of aggression have, but we bring it here because it is held by some. In brief, this view is: in war, people kill people. Killing is wrong; it goes on and on and just creates more violence in the world. The only way for violence and killing to stop is for each person to say, "I will not be violent, no matter what." Mahatma Ghandi of India was the world-famous person who held this viewpoint.

Remind your students that this is a very complex subject with which humanity has struggled for generations. Sadly, no simple solution (Fluter's singing notwithstanding) has presented itself.

HATTIE'S BIRTHDAY BOX (P. 27

This is the fourth set of aural exercises. (*Kate Shelley: Bound for Legend, New Providence: A Changing Cityscape,* and *By the Shores of Silver Lake* were the first three.) Please read the first fou paragraphs aloud to your class. (Read up through "And she keeps reciting the list of everyone who's coming, and he ticks them off on his fingers, but before she's even through, he asks impatiently, 'Bu Hattie coming? My baby sister? Are you sure she's coming?'")

Read the passage aloud to your class twice, and ask students pick the best multiple-choice answer to each of ten questions. Try read the passage with expression in your voice, so that students w pick up on the dialogue and know who is speaking. If any student has difficulty with this, go over the first three paragraphs and point out the correct answers—which are indicated below in **bold**.

1. A party is being held to celebrate
   a. Spencer McClintic's 100th birthday.
   b. the arrival of officials from Washington.
   c. the first landing of men on the Moon.
   d. the McClintic family reunion.

2. The person who is telling the story is
   a. the great-great granddaughter of Civil War General Jeb McClintic.
   b. Spencer McClintic's 90-year-old sister, Hattie.
   c. a very hardworking nurse.
   d. the great-great granddaughter of 100-year-old Spencer McClintic.

3. Momma says that the war is over, most everyone is back, and
   a. nations are a thing of the past.
   b. rations are a thing of the past.
   c. racism is a thing of the past.
   d. she has lost her patience.

4. They are having the birthday party
   a. outside on the lawn and hanging balloons from the trees.
   b. at Spencer McClintic's old homestead.
   c. in the recreation room of the nursing home.
   d. at the high school gymnasium.

5. Momma wants the narrator to come, because
   a. he is the only one who hasn't heard the story.
   b. she doesn't like to drive alone at night.
   c. she has been afraid to be alone since the war.
   d. she wants her daughter to help her blow up balloons and put up decorations.

6. Grandaddy is nervous. He is
   a. sitting in a chair near the window rubbing his hands together.
   b. blowing up balloons and hanging crepe paper.
   c. very sad that great-great grandma isn't there to share the fun.
   d. doing meditation exercises to relax himself.

7. He keeps asking Momma over and over again,
   a. what the weather is supposed to be today.
   b. if she knows where he put his pocket watch.
   c. who is coming to the party.
   d. if he should change his tie.

8. Grandaddy is most concerned about whether
   a. there will be enough birthday cake.
   b. people will have fun at the party.
   c. he's going to be able to blow out 100 candles.
   d. Hattie is coming.

9. Hattie is Grandaddy's baby sister, so
   a. she is probably an infant.
   b. they probably see each other often.
   c. she must also be old, if he is 100.
   d. of course she wouldn't miss the party.

From just these few paragraphs, we can tell that Grandaddy

a. is very much loved by his family.

b. was once a world-class ice skater.

c. has always liked animals.

d. would really like to have the party outside.

THE WHIMBREL (P. 284)

This is the fifth set of aural exercises. (*Kate Shelley: Bound for Legend, New Providence: A Changing Cityscape, By the Shores of Silver Lake,* and *Hattie's Birthday Box* are the other four.) Please read the first four paragraphs aloud to your class. (Read up through "he thought he was one of the Wise People of the World.")

Read the passage aloud to your class twice, and ask students to pick the best multiple-choice answer to each of ten questions. If any student has difficulty with this, review the passage and the questions. Point out and explain the reason for the correct answers. Don't forget to read the title of the piece!

How many people live in the town of Snapper Bay?

a. about a hundred

b. exactly one hundred, no more, no less

c. It depends upon the season.

d. six hundred

Axel Jorgensen is

a. pretty old, and he looks like a banana.

b. deaf—he says it feels like his ears are stuffed with cotton wool.

c. 72, and usually carries a white mop to wash the deck of his boat.

d. 72. He has white hair, a beard, and his legs bow outward.

Tessa Noble

a. also has a mop, but hers is brown.

b. is 12, has freckles and her legs bow inward.

c. has bent sticks instead of legs, like the whimbrel.

d. *loves* to eat tapioca.

There is only one street in Snapper Bay,

a. but it's not the main street.

b. and it's called Hammerhead Handle Street.

c. and so it has to be the main street.

d. Snapper Avenue.

The house that Tessa lives in

a. is made of bent sticks.

b. looks like a Hammerhead.

c. used to be an inn for fisherman.

d. is painted white.

Axel has taught Tessa many things. He has taught her about

a. seashells, albatrosses, summer sedges, snails, and spoonbills.

b. boats, beaches, and foraging.

c. what it feels like to have an albatross around your neck.

d. rusty oarlocks, rudder pins, grappling hooks, and old craypots.

Axel lives by himself in

a. a wooden shack that looks like it's collapsing.

b. a two-family house far around the curve of the bay.

c. a hut away from the town.

d. a high-rise apartment building.

Tessa has walked with Axel

a. on the streets of Perth, the capital of western Australia.

b. down Fifth Avenue, when they visited New York City.

c. up and down main street a thousand times.

d. along the coast and by the lakes and marshes.

Tessa thinks that Axel is

a. her best friend.

b. like a whimbrel.

c. one of the Wise People of the World.

d. a really good teacher.

10. From just these few paragraphs, it is likely that this story is about

a. an older man, a young girl, and a whimbrel, in a small town by the sea in Australia.

b. a boy, his mother, and their cat in the moors of South Wales.

c. a girl, an older man, and the experiences they have when they hike up the coast together.

d. Tessa and Jody's wife, Bridget, when they study French together.

WHAT IS A STORY?

- A story has four elements: plot, character, setting, and theme.
- The **plot** is the action of the story. It is what happens to the characters from the beginning to the end of the story.
- The **characters** are the people, animals, or even objects (for example, robots) that the story is about. The action happens to, or is caused by, the characters in the story.
- The **setting** is the time and place in which the story's events occur. The setting may be described in great detail or hardly at all. When you remember a story, you almost always remember its setting.
- The **theme** is the main idea presented in the story. It is the idea that the author wishes to present through the plot, characters, and setting.

THINK ABOUT IT!

1. Can you summarize the story's plot in one sentence? Try it!

2. The story is really about three characters. Who are they?

3. Where does the main character live? What time of day is it? What is the weather like? Does the action take place indoors or outside? Together, these details make up the setting of the story.

4. In your opinion, who is the most important person in this story? What is his connection to the main idea, or theme, of the story?

To Know Freedom

Robert stood on what looked like a narrow stone path, only the path didn't go anywhere. Instead, it made a hexagon on the ground.

Robert reread the directions Grandpa had scrawled from memory.

Follow picket fence out back to white gazebo with wrought iron trim.

"Gazebo." That was a word he'd had to look up. "A free-standing, roofed, usually open-sided structure providing a shady resting place."*

Where was that gazebo? Except for the abandoned farmhouse and the rickety picket fence, Robert didn't see any structure of any sort.

Not being certain where he was made Robert uneasy. How much more frightening his great-great grandfather's journey must have been to this same spot, heading north from Virginia to this Pennsylvania town.

Frustrated and hot from the late afternoon sun, Robert plopped down on the grass in the center of the hexagon. No shade here.

Shade! That was it!

Suddenly Robert realized that he was in the exact right spot. He had found the gazebo—or where it used to be. Someone must've torn down the gazebo's structure. The stone hexagon was the foundation.

He leaped to his feet.

From the center of the gazebo, head due north 150 paces.

Grandpa had told him countless times the way his own grandfather had used the moss on the trees, the wind, and the North Star to keep his course his journey to freedom.

Robert looked up at the sun. At 4 p.m. the sun would be to the west. Robert turned north and started counting steps.

At 120 Robert noticed a small cluster of simple stone grave markers peeking out amid tall weeds up ahead. He broke into a trot.

Pushing aside the weeds, Robert found the headstone he was looking for Tearing a sheet of paper from his notebook, he held the paper up to the stone began rubbing with the edge of his pencil. Slowly, the inscription came into view:

"Here lies Nathan R. Smith,
Who by the Grace of the Almighty
Lived to Know Freedom."

Grandpa was going to be very proud!

---

* Definition from *The American Heritage Dictionary*. Second College Edition. Boston: Houghton Mifflin, 1982.

LESSON IN LITERATURE

1. A young boy searches for, and finds, the grave of his great-great grandfather, who was an escaped slave.

2. Robert, his grandfather, and his great-great grandfather.

3. Robert lives in a Pennsylvania town. It is late afternoon. It is hot. The action takes place out of doors.

4. The great-great grandfather is the main character. The theme of the story is freedom and how some must struggle to achieve it.

SELECTION VOCABULARY

barges: flat-bottomed vessels, usually pushed or towed through the water, for carrying freight or passengers

bayonet: a long-pointed steel weapon attached to the open end of a gun

buoys: a floating object, fastened or anchored so that it remains in one place

gale: a strong wind

glimpsed: saw for a brief moment

musket: an old-fashioned gun used by foot soldiers

recruits: new members of the army

retreat: move back, away from the enemy

wharf: a pier; a wooden walkway built next to or jutting ino the water so that boats can come alongside it to load or unload

wounded: injured

| barges | buoys | glimpse | recruits | wharf |
| bayonet | gale | muskets | retreat | wounded |

1. The war raged. Everywhere, men in uniform could be seen marching, their rifles and _____ (*old-fashioned guns*) slung over their shoulders.

2. Some of the men carried guns with long, polished barrels and gleaming _____ (*pointed steel weapon on barrel of guns*).

3. These were the new _____ (*new members of the arm*). They had an eager, youthful look.

4. Some of the older soldiers had weary, careworn expressions. These men had seen their fellow soldiers lying _____ (*injured*) or dying on the battlefield, with no one to help them.

5. Today, all the soldiers, young and old, were headed to the _____ (*pier*) at the beach, to meet the ship that would bring them weapons and ammunition.

6. Papers and dust swirled in the wind as a fierce _____ (*wind*) from the ocean made its way inland.

7. The red and white _____ (*floating markers*) in the water bobbed up and down furiously as the waves grew choppier.

8. Little boys ran to the edge of the water, hoping to get a _____ (*look*) of the big ship from across the ocean.

9. Although the soldiers kept shooing them away, they refused to _____ (*go back*).

10. Finally, a loud ship's horn was heard. The tugboats slowly pulled the _____ (*flat-bottomed boats*) out to sea to meet the ship.

The sailors would load them with the precious cargo they had brought, and the war would be won.

Workbook p. 1   Answer Guide p. 1

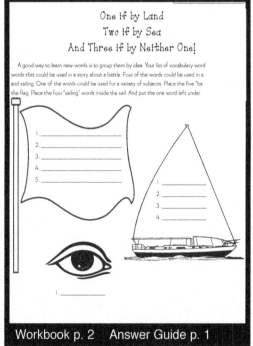

One if by Land
Two if by Sea
And Three if by Neither One!

A good way to learn new words is to group them by idea. Your list of vocabulary word words that could be used in a story about a battle. Four of the words could be used in a and sailing. One of the words could be used for a variety of subjects. Place the five "ba the flag. Place the four "sailing" words inside the sail. And put the one word left under

1. _____
2. _____
3. _____
4. _____
5. _____

1. _____
2. _____
3. _____
4. _____

1. _____

Workbook p. 2   Answer Guide p. 1

Samuel's Choice affords rich possibilities for discussion. Literature offers us broad possibilities for educating our children. Moreover, it is important that students learn that we do not just pass over clues and data that we do not understand. In order for students to be steeped in what they read, and in order for them to learn how to create their own literature, they must understand the need to familiarize themselves with the "current events" of historical fiction. Moreover, they need to see that writers of any kind of fiction ought to be sticklers for the truth—historical fact, contemporary culture, and emotional truth.

Among other things, the events of *Samuel's Choice* commemorate the Battle of the Maryland 400, the first major battle of the American Revolution. In fact, there is today a monument in Prospect Park, Brooklyn, that commemorates the Maryland 400, their contribution and sacrifice.

As *Samuel's Choice* repeatedly attests, Washington's Continental Army was "outnumbered, outgunned, and outsupplied." On August 27, 1776, four hundred Maryland troops "led a rear-guard action to check the British advance and allow the retreat of Washington's greatly outnumbered army." The American Army was surrounded by the British, when Mordechai Gist lead "a desperate movement to cover the retreating American troops." The men from Maryland launched six counter attacks to meet the British in and around the two-story Cortelyou House, which commanded the only escape route for the Americans.

History tells us that the lands surrounding the stone house were soaked with blood. The sixth attack of Gist and his Marylanders was shattered by British reinforcements. With the British in control of the Cortelyou House, the surviving Marylanders were unable to cross the creek at Dam Road. They stumbled across the marsh into the swamp. When the fight was over, only ten of the 250 heroic Marylanders had returned. Major Mordecai Gist was one of the ten survivors.

Another subject for discussion—given the thematic importance of freedom and liberty in the piece—is the circumstances of slaves during the Revolutionary War period.

In *Samuel's Choice*, the character Sana identifies wholeheartedly with the war effort. She believes that freedom for America will mean freedom for her, personally. As the story unfolds, the author portrays an environment in which the norms and restraints of the old order are shattered, where liberty and freedom are the bywords. In this environment, Sana believes, even a former slave will find freedom.

At the outset of the story, Samuel attributes his slavery to "the laws of the Crown Colony." The implication seems to be that, once free of those laws, the Americans will choose freedom for all. Historically, this may or may not be an accurate picture of the environment in which an escaped slave found himself when he joined Washington's army. As the Revolutionary War progressed and moved into every region of the colonies, slaves, in fact, sided with whichever army promised them their personal freedom. Since the British actively attempted to recruit slaves, more African

the same time, other African Americans fought side by side with white soldiers during the battles of Lexington, Concord, and Bunker Hill, and the first man to die in the war was Crispus Attucks, a black man. At one point, George Washington barred recruitment of black soldiers. However, towards the end of the war, a black regiment was established.

Although the hero and heroine of the story are slaves under *British* law, the author makes no reference to the complex issue of racial prejudice in colonial America. Nor is the status of escaped or freed slaves under the Revolution made clear. It is obvious that the author does not wish to enter these murky waters. He limits himself to inspiring his young reader with a tale of courage and patriotism.

Language Alert

What explains the repeated mention of **buttermilk** in the story? Have any of your students ever drunk buttermilk? In times gone by (and this is probably still true in countries where people have less money and fewer refrigerators) nothing was wasted in the kitchen—even the liquid that remained after butter was churned. A *churn* was a vessel for making butter in which milk or cream was agitated in order to separate the oily globules from the watery medium. The liquid was set aside and allowed to combine with airborne bacteria. It became thicker and developed a delicious, tangy flavor. Buttermilk is not only good to drink, but also is a useful ingredient in waffles, pancakes, cakes, and biscuits.

is (a) a difficult concept to grasp in the abstract, and (b) difficult to articulate in words for specific works. Tell your students that the theme is usually what we react to most powerfully when we read a story. It is the source of the feelings we are left with when we are done reading. But feelings can be very hard to put in words. Looking for the theme, trying to find the words to express it, is a delicate undertaking. Students should know that you, yourself, may have difficulty with theme at times—and that not only is there often more than one theme, people sometimes do not even agree about the theme.

So, what is theme, after all?

The theme is the meaning of a story.

The theme is the message of a story.

The theme stands above the facts and setting of the story. It is what the author wants to tell us about what it is like to be human, or what it is like to be a creature with feelings. The theme is what gives us the feelings we are left with when the story ends. The theme of the story is what the author believes to be true not just for *that* story or poem, but for human beings in every time and in every land. Themes speak to such issues of the human condition as struggle for freedom, bravery, courage, personal responsibility, fairness, the individual versus government, the occasional need to put principles over laws, and a host of other truths and conflicts.

What does it mean to be free?

How does a person change his or her life, and thereby gain greater freedom?

How can one group of people be kept slaves, when they live among another group fighting for self-government and liberty?

How does a person make a decision, when they have no experience making decisions or choices?

Can a person be sympathetic, when no one has ever sympathized with him or her?

Why may it be important to be alone at times?

EYES ON...HISTORICAL FICTION

Historical fiction is based on, or set within, actual historical events. Historical fiction is peopled by important historical figures, whose behavior within the story should make sense given what evidence exists in the historical record. Most writers of historical fiction do meticulous research. An error would make their story absurd.

The great pleasure and puzzle of historical fiction always comes from the clever mixing of fact with fiction—that *could have been fact.* After reading historical fiction, it is fun to do research to determine what the historical records show and what is the author's invention. History does not occur without people: people being good, people being bad, and people trying to figure out how to gain the advantage or avoid suffering. Remind your students that dialogue in historical fiction is virtually always invented—unless the author has quoted from actual letters, diary entries, newspaper articles, and speeches written at the time.

The **Elements of a Story** are discussed above in **Getting Started**. As this is just the beginning of the

Blueprint for Reading

INTO . . . *Samuel's Choice*

Samuel is 14 years old. He is a slave in Brooklyn, New York, at the time of the American Revolution. He sees American soldiers losing in a battle with the British. Samuel has his master's boat; he could help rescue wounded soldiers. But Americans have made his people slaves. Freedom from the British will not mean freedom for slaves. Samuel must decide whether to risk his life to save George Washington's soldiers, or simply stand and watch the fight.

When you have finished the story, think about whether Samuel has made the right choice. What would have become of him had he remained loyal to Isaac van Ditmas? What would he have thought of himself if he had remained "neutral," refusing or afraid to help either side?

EYES ON . . . *Historical Fiction*

This is a story that *might* have occurred in Brooklyn, New York in 1776. The background and some of the details are true. The Revolutionary War, fought between the American colonies and England did, of course, take place. It is a fact, too, that in 1776, one-third of the people in Brooklyn were slaves. However, the characters and the plot of *Samuel's Choice* are **fictional**, that is to say, made up by the author. Stories whose backgrounds are true but whose plot and characters are made up, are called **historical fiction**. *Samuel's Choice* is a good story with interesting characters. The time and place are clearly described. Samuel makes a difficult choice. This is a story of hope.

16 ~ Unit I

book, work with your students to understand and find the **exposition,** and to express it in words.

Have your students name the **characters**, and help them determine which of the characters are most important and which are secondary. Samuel is both the main character and the narrator. The story is told through his eyes. Calling all of the rest of the characters **secondary characters** hardly seems fair or accurate, since they are of varying importance. In historical fiction, it is often the secondary characters that were famous in history. They may or may

not directly participate in the action of the story. Here, George Washington is only mentioned, but Major Mordecai Gist talks with Samuel and engages him.

In historical fiction, **setting** must be very specific, and true to the time.

As you move with your students through the story, point out the **rising action**, the **turning point** for Samuel, and the **situational climax.** As the story winds down, point to the **falling action,** and **the resolution** or **conclusion**.

SUMMING UP THE PLOT

- A young slave writes that when he was 14, Isaac van Ditmas, a rich farmer, bought him.
- The slave was taken from his parents to work in the Ditmas flour mill in Brooklyn.
- Van Ditmas bought other slaves at the same time, including Sana and Toby, to care for the kitchen and gardens of his big house on New York Harbor.
- The Heights of Brooklyn overlook the East River and Manhattan Island; in those days the town of Brooklyn was small.
- The flour mill stands on Gowanus Creek, and winds out of the harbor into green fields, ponds, and marshes.

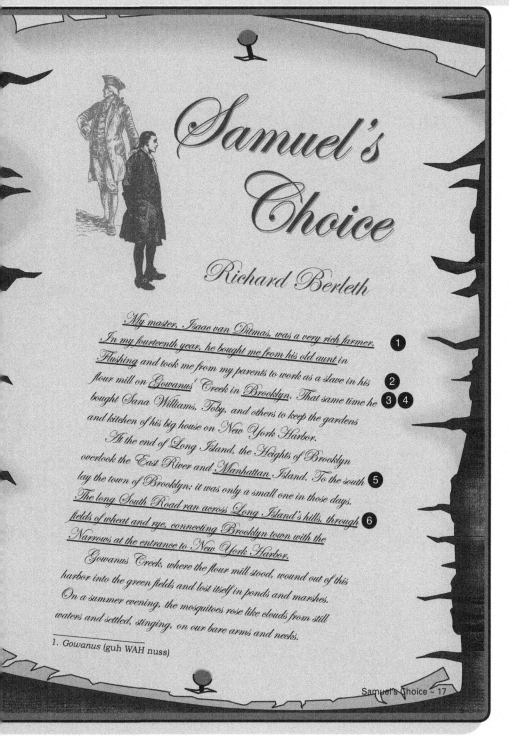

Samuel's Choice
Richard Berleth

My master, Isaac van Ditmas, was a very rich farmer. In my fourteenth year, he bought me from his old aunt in Flushing and took me from my parents to work as a slave in his flour mill on Gowanus' Creek in Brooklyn. That same time he bought Sana Williams, Toby, and others to keep the gardens and kitchen of his big house on New York Harbor.

At the end of Long Island, the Heights of Brooklyn overlook the East River and Manhattan Island. To the south lay the town of Brooklyn; it was only a small one in those days. The long South Road ran across Long Island's hills, through fields of wheat and rye, connecting Brooklyn town with the Narrows at the entrance to New York Harbor.

Gowanus Creek, where the flour mill stood, wound out of this harbor into the green fields and lost itself in ponds and marshes. On a summer evening, the mosquitoes rose like clouds from still waters and settled, stinging, on our bare arms and necks.

1. Gowanus (guh WAH nuss)

LITERARY COMPONENTS

▶ **1. Exposition; Characters; Source of Modern Name:** The first two sentences establish the master/slave relationship between Isaac van Ditmas and the unnamed narrator. We see the Dutch name *van Ditmas* today in Brooklyn's *Ditmas Avenue*.

▶ **2. Geographical Reference:** Flushing, New York is an actual city. The English called the town Flushing, because they were anglicizing the Dutch city name *Vlissingen*. In Vlissingen, the Dutch had harbored English refugees before they embarked for the New World.

▶ **3. Geographical Reference:** The Gowanus Creek is likely today's polluted Gowanus Canal. The name is also used in the Gowanus Expressway, a 6.1 mile elevated highway built in 1941 that connects Brooklyn, Manhattan, Queens, and Long Island. The highway is one of the most congested in the nation.

▶ **4. Origin of City Name; History in Historical Fiction:** The name *Brooklyn* is an adaptation of the Dutch name *Breukelen,* which means broken land. The Dutch established the village with the help of the Dutch West India Company in 1646, and named it after a town in the Netherlands. During the 1770s, one-third of the population of Brooklyn was slave.

▶ **5. Origin of City Name:** Manhattan Island was originally named *Man-a-hat-a* by the Algonquin Indians.

▶ **6. Setting; Geographical Reference:** Setting is gently and clearly established in paragraphs 2 and 3. *The Narrows* refers to a strait (a narrow passage of water connecting to larger bodies of water) between Staten Island and Long Island in New York Bay.

GUIDING THE READING

LITERAL

Q: Who is telling the story?
A: The young slave.

Q: How old is the slave, when Isaac van Ditmas purchases him?
A: He is fourteen years old.

Q: Where does the slave work?
A: The slave works in a flour mill on Gowanus Creek in Brooklyn.

Q: Where does the slave live?
A: The slave lives in Brooklyn.

Q: What connects Brooklyn town with the Narrows?
A: The long South Road that runs across Long Island's hills, through fields of wheat and rye.

ANALYTICAL

Q: Why doesn't the slave who narrates the story live with his parents?
A: When Isaac van Ditmas buys the slave from Ditmas's aunt, he does not buy his parents. So the slave can no longer live with his mother and father.

Q: What kind of land does Gowanus Creek wind out into?
A: Green fields, ponds, and marshes.

SUMMING UP THE PLOT

- Farmer Isaac is strict: The slaves work from sunrise to sunset.

- The stone wheel of the mill is driven by the water flowing in and out of the creek. They grind wheat to make bread.

- Van Ditmas is stingy, and the slave goes to sleep hungry.

- When van Ditmas sees that the slave has grown strong, he teaches him about the currents between Brooklyn and Manhattan, so that he can row Mrs. van Ditmas and her daughters over to Manhattan and Staten Island.

- After teaching him to use the boat, Isaac shakes Samuel and warns him never to row anywhere except where his master sends him.

- Samuel says that he is Isaac's property, to do with as he pleased.

- Work you do not choose to do is always tiring, he says.

- Whenever Samuel feels the breeze on his face, he looks up at the gulls and imagines what it would be like to be free.

LITERARY COMPONENTS

▶ **7. Characterization:** We learn about Farmer Isaac when the slave writes, "Our day began at sunrise and ended when the light faded."

▶ **8. Characterization of Farmer Isaac and of the Narrator; Onomatopoeia:** The farmer does not feed his slaves. The boy is so hungry that when he goes to bed, his stomach is *growling*.

▶ **9. Idioms:** *Setting a sail* means putting the sail in position to catch the wind; *holding a course* means not veering from the right path or direction the boat or ship is traveling.

▶ **10. Understanding the Character and the Nature of the Conflict; Theme:** *I was his property . . . and he could do what he wanted with me.* What the slave says here goes to the heart of his difficulty making a decision further along in the story. Here is a person who experiences himself as having no rights and no autonomy. He is not a person. He is owned, like a thing.

▶ **11. Historical Reference:** *According to the laws of the Crown Colony.* Crown colonies were part of the British system of colonial administration. Crown colonies were governed internally by a British-appointed governor and a locally elected assembly. A modern example of a crown colony was Hong Kong until 1997. The motto of the British Commonwealth of Nations was, "May the sun never set on the British Empire."

▶ **12. Powerful Characterization:** *Work you do not choose to do is always tiring.*

GUIDING THE READING

LITERAL

Q: Which two words does the narrator use to describe Farmer Isaac?

A: The narrator uses the words strict and stingy.

Q: Is the bread made at the mill?

A: No. The flour is brought to bakers in Manhattan.

Q: What does Farmer Isaac do when he sees that his young slave has grown strong and can row a boat?

A: He teaches him about the currents that flow between Brooklyn and Manhattan, about how to set a sail, and how to hold a course. In other words, he teaches him how to sail the boat.

Q: Why does Farmer Isaac want the slave to know how to use the boat?

A: He wants the slave to row Mrs. van Ditmas and her daughters over to Manhattan or down the Brooklyn shore to Staten Island.

Q: After Isaac van Ditmas teaches the slave how to use the boat, what does he do to him?

A: Van Ditmas shakes him by the collar and warns him never to use the boat unless he is told to do so.

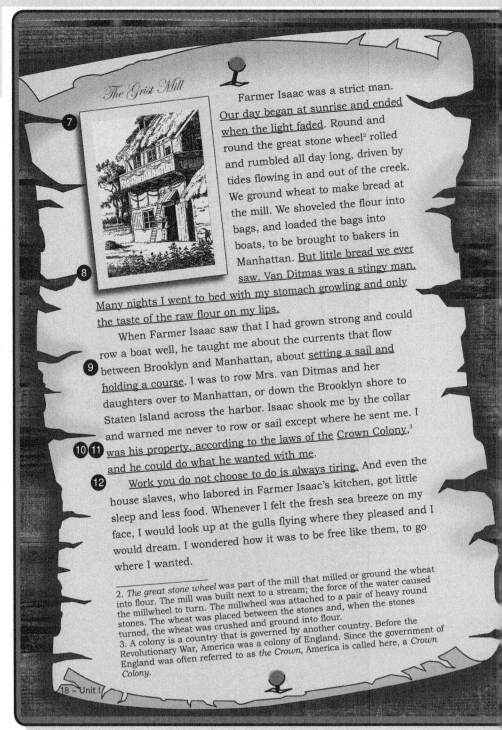

The Grist Mill

Farmer Isaac was a strict man. Our day began at sunrise and ended when the light faded. Round and round the great stone wheel[2] rolled and rumbled all day long, driven by tides flowing in and out of the creek. We ground wheat to make bread at the mill. We shoveled the flour into bags, and loaded the bags into boats, to be brought to bakers in Manhattan. But little bread we ever saw. Van Ditmas was a stingy man. Many nights I went to bed with my stomach growling and only the taste of the raw flour on my lips.

When Farmer Isaac saw that I had grown strong and could row a boat well, he taught me about the currents that flow between Brooklyn and Manhattan, about setting a sail and holding a course. I was to row Mrs. van Ditmas and her daughters over to Manhattan, or down the Brooklyn shore to Staten Island across the harbor. Isaac shook me by the collar and warned me never to row or sail except where he sent me. I was his property, according to the laws of the Crown Colony,[3] and he could do what he wanted with me.

Work you do not choose to do is always tiring. And even the house slaves, who labored in Farmer Isaac's kitchen, got little sleep and less food. Whenever I felt the fresh sea breeze on my face, I would look up at the gulls flying where they pleased and I would dream. I wondered how it was to be free like them, to go where I wanted.

---

2. *The great stone wheel* was part of the mill that milled or ground the wheat into flour. The mill was built next to a stream; the force of the water caused the millwheel to turn. The millwheel was attached to a pair of heavy round stones. The wheat was placed between the stones and, when the stones turned, the wheat was crushed and ground into flour.
3. A colony is a country that is governed by another country. Before the Revolutionary War, America was a colony of England. Since the government of England was often referred to as *the Crown*, America is called here, a *Crown Colony*.

Q: Which kind of grain is ground at the mill to make flour for bread?

A: Wheat is ground into flour to be made into bread.

Q: According to which laws does Isaac say the slave is his property?

A: According to the laws of the Crown Colony.

Q: What does Samuel do, whenever he feels a fresh sea breeze on his face?

A: He looks up at the gulls flying and dreams, wondering what it would be like to be as free as they are.

ANALYTICAL

Q: The slave describes Farmer Isaac as strict. Strict usually means that a person insists that others follow the rules exactly. How is Farmer Isaac worse than strict?

A: Farmer Isaac makes his slaves work from morning to night. He does not feed them. This has nothing to do with rules. Rather, Isaac is inhumane, irresponsible, and cruel.

Q: When Samuel looks at the gulls, what does freedom mean to him?

A: When he looks at the gulls, being free means to go wherever he would want.

SUMMING UP THE PLOT

- America is ruled by the King of England, and these are troubled times.
- A night comes when Manhattan Island is lit up with a hundred bonfires.
- The slaves gather and hear cheers and shouts from Manhattan Island.
- There is the sound of drums and fifes, songs, and cannon firing.
- Old Toby says that that is the sound of people going free.
- The narrator wonders, What is it, that makes people think they can change their lives?
- When the Sons of Liberty come by, van Ditmas locks the slaves in the house.
- The slaves argue. Liberty has nothing to do with Africans.
- Sana maintains that none of them will be free unless they take the risk.

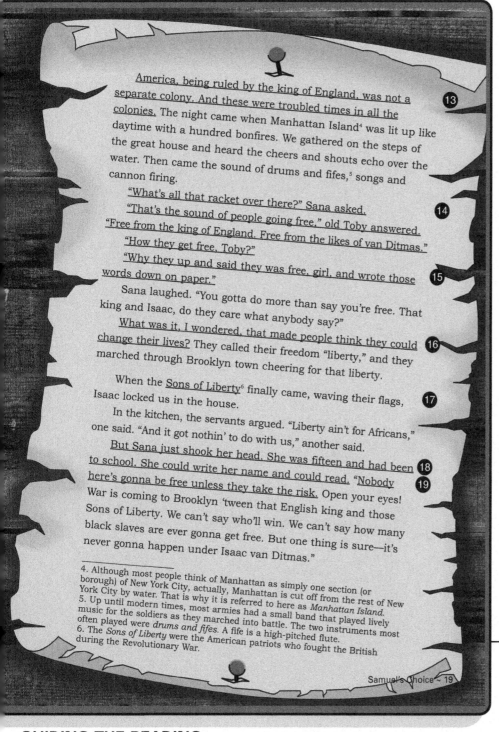

America, being ruled by the king of England, was not a separate colony. And these were troubled times in all the colonies. The night came when Manhattan Island[4] was lit up like daytime with a hundred bonfires. We gathered on the steps of the great house and heard the cheers and shouts echo over the water. Then came the sound of drums and fifes,[5] songs and cannon firing.

"What's all that racket over there?" Sana asked.

"That's the sound of people going free." old Toby answered. "Free from the king of England. Free from the likes of van Ditmas."

"How they get free, Toby?"

"Why they up and said they was free, girl, and wrote those words down on paper."

Sana laughed. "You gotta do more than say you're free. That king and Isaac, do they care what anybody say?"

What was it, I wondered, that made people think they could change their lives? They called their freedom "liberty," and they marched through Brooklyn town cheering for that liberty.

When the Sons of Liberty[6] finally came, waving their flags, Isaac locked us in the house.

In the kitchen, the servants argued. "Liberty ain't for Africans," one said. "And it got nothin' to do with us," another said.

But Sana just shook her head. She was fifteen and had been to school. She could write her name and could read. "Nobody here's gonna be free unless they take the risk. Open your eyes! War is coming to Brooklyn 'tween that English king and those Sons of Liberty. We can't say who'll win. We can't say how many black slaves are ever gonna get free. But one thing is sure—it's never gonna happen under Isaac van Ditmas."

---

4. Although most people think of Manhattan as simply one section (or borough) of New York City, actually, Manhattan is cut off from the rest of New York City by water. That is why it is referred to here as *Manhattan Island*.
5. Up until modern times, most armies had a small band that played lively music for the soldiers as they marched into battle. The two instruments most often played were *drums and fifes*. A fife is a high-pitched flute.
6. The *Sons of Liberty* were the American patriots who fought the British during the Revolutionary War.

Samuel's Choice ~ 19

LITERARY COMPONENTS

▶ **13. Setting Expanded; Rising Action:** *America, being ruled by the king of England, was not a separate country. And these were troubled times in all the colonies.*

▶ **14. Characters; Characterization; Rising Action; Theme:** The reader is introduced to Sana and old Toby through their dialogue. Toby compares King George III with van Ditmas. Sana asks Toby how people become free. We see from their discussion that Toby is aware of events occurring in the colonies, and that the slaves think seriously about their lives. What is not discussed is the possibility of the slaves joining up with the British. In fact, many more slaves joined the British than fought on the side of the colonists.

▶ **15. Historical Reference:** When Toby says that the people became free by writing the words down on paper, he is referring to the writing and signing of the Declaration of Independence.

▶ **16. Theme; Characterization; Inner Dialogue:** It is clear the events and the discussion lead the yet-unnamed narrator to think about personal freedom—and the notion that some people feel they can change their lives. Stated as the question, *What was it...that made people think they could change their lives?*, underscores the novelty of such an idea and its poignancy.

▶ **17. Historical Reference:** The first Sons of Liberty organizations were in New York City and Boston. They corresponded and communicated with other Sons of Liberty groups that grew up in New England, the Carolinas, Virginia, and Georgia. Sons of Liberty were members of the upper and middle classes.

▶ **18. Characterization:** We learn more about Sana and that she can write her name and she can read.

▶ **19. Foreshadowing; Theme; Samuel's Fundamental Conflict:** Sana says that, "Nobody here's gonna be free unless they take the risk."

ANALYTICAL

Q: Why does Samuel say that "these . . . [are] troubled times"?

A: Answers will depend on students' knowledge of American history. But this is the time when the colonies are trying to break from British rule.

Q: Do you know what the paper is called, on which the colonists wrote down the words saying they were free?

A: The very famous paper is called the Declaration of Independence.

Q: Why does the narrator wonder what makes people think they can change their lives?

A: He wonders, because he is a slave and he would like to know what it is to be free.

Q: Isaac, however, does not want his slaves to see the Sons of Liberty or the Proclamation. Why?

A: Perhaps Isaac realizes that words about freedom will fire the imaginations of his slaves.

GUIDING THE READING

LITERAL

Q: Who rules America at the time of this story?

A: The King of England rules America (which is why it is a Crown Colony).

Q: What do the slaves hear from across the water?

A: They hear the echo of cheers and shouts, and the sound of drums and fifes, songs, and cannon firing.

Q: According to old Toby, what is making all that racket?

A: He says that it is the sound of people going free.

Q: What does Toby answer, when Sana asks how the people could become free?

A: Toby says that they just said they were free, and wrote the words down on paper.

Q: What is Sana's response to this?

A: She laughs and says that to be free you've got to do more than say so—such people as the King of England and Isaac van Ditmas don't care what people say.

Q: What does Isaac van Ditmas do when the Sons of Liberty come waving flags?

A: He locks the slaves in the house.

Q: What does Sana claim it takes to be free?

A: She says that none of them will be free unless they take a risk.

SUMMING UP THE PLOT

- The talk among the slaves makes the narrator's head spin.
- When the Declaration of Independence is nailed to a tree, Isaac van Ditmas tears it down and stamps on it.
- Sana promises she will teach Samuel, the narrator, to read.
- Sana brings Samuel jars of buttermilk for him to drink and then fill with flour.
- She says the flour will be bread for their freedom day.
- One morning they awake in the slave quarters to the thunder of great guns in the harbor.
- Sana grins and says Washington's come to New York. The Americans are practicing with their guns on Governors Island, to scare off the British.
- Isaac van Ditmas sends his wife and daughters to live with an old uncle in Staten Island.
- Samuel sees the British army in Staten Island, where they have pitched their tents by the thousands.

LITERARY COMPONENTS

▶ **20. Characterization; Idiom:** The narrator is not used to standing firm on one side of an issue or the other. He just doesn't know what to make of things. The talk among the slaves just *makes his head spin.*

▶ **21. Characterization:** The narrator is finally identified by name, as *Samuel*. He is no longer just a generic slave.

▶ **22. Setting; History in Historical Fiction; Rising Action:** *So the summer of 1776 ...passed on.* This will be an important summer. The final draft of the Declaration of Independence will be ratified on July 9, 1776. On August 22, the British will land 20,000 troops on Long Island. On August 27, the Continental Army will fight its first battle of the Revolutionary War. Defending Gowanus road will be a major element—and a major disaster—for the Americans.

▶ **23. Sensory Image, Appeal to Sense of Taste:** *...a cool jar of buttermilk...*

▶ **24. Symbolism; Theme:** A loaf of bread and the flour used to make it are going to be a symbol of freedom. This harkens back to earlier in the story, when Samuel goes to bed hungry with just the taste of raw flour on his lips. As a slave, he is not given bread to eat.

▶ **25. Rising Action:** The war is moving towards Brooklyn. The slaves awaken one morning in the slave quarters to the sound of thunder from great guns.

▶ **26. Historical (and Contemporary) Reference:** Governors Island is a 172-acre island located a half-mile from the southern tip of Manhattan in New York harbor. Its name comes from the time when New York was a British colony and the colonial assembly reserved the island for the exclusive use of New York's royal governors.

▶ **27. Rising Action:** Samuel hoists sail and carries Mrs. van Ditmas and their daughters to Staten Island. On Staten Island, Samuel sees the king's army.

GUIDING THE READING

LITERAL
Q: Samuel sends back the buttermilk jar filled with flour. What is the flour for?
A: Sana is going to use the flour to make bread for their freedom day.

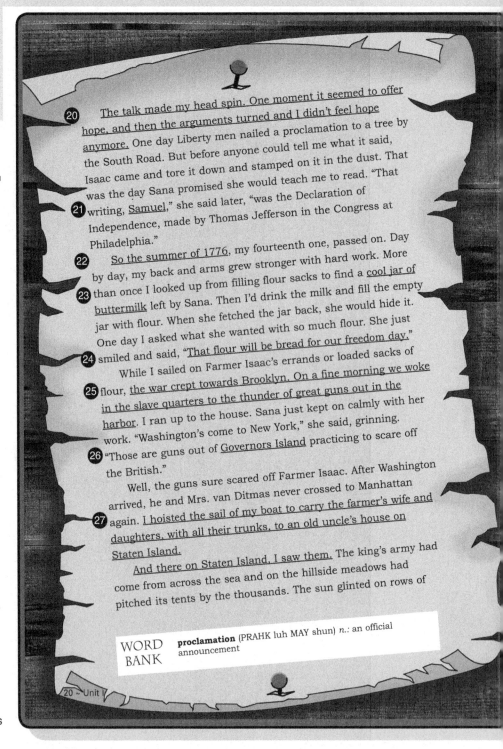

20　The talk made my head spin. One moment it seemed to offer hope, and then the arguments turned and I didn't feel hope anymore. One day Liberty men nailed a proclamation to a tree by the South Road. But before anyone could tell me what it said, Isaac came and tore it down and stamped on it in the dust. That was the day Sana promised she would teach me to read. "That 21 writing, Samuel," she said later, "was the Declaration of Independence, made by Thomas Jefferson in the Congress at Philadelphia."

22　So the summer of 1776, my fourteenth one, passed on. Day by day, my back and arms grew stronger with hard work. More 23 than once I looked up from filling flour sacks to find a cool jar of buttermilk left by Sana. Then I'd drink the milk and fill the empty jar with flour. When she fetched the jar back, she would hide it. One day I asked what she wanted with so much flour. She just 24 smiled and said, "That flour will be bread for our freedom day."

While I sailed on Farmer Isaac's errands or loaded sacks of 25 flour, the war crept towards Brooklyn. On a fine morning we woke in the slave quarters to the thunder of great guns out in the harbor. I ran up to the house. Sana just kept on calmly with her work. "Washington's come to New York," she said, grinning. 26 "Those are guns out of Governors Island practicing to scare off the British."

Well, the guns sure scared off Farmer Isaac. After Washington arrived, he and Mrs. van Ditmas never crossed to Manhattan 27 again. I hoisted the sail of my boat to carry the farmer's wife and daughters, with all their trunks, to an old uncle's house on Staten Island.

And there on Staten Island, I saw them. The king's army had come from across the sea and on the hillside meadows had pitched its tents by the thousands. The sun glinted on rows of

| WORD BANK | **proclamation** (PRAHK luh MAY shun) *n.:* an official announcement |

20 ~ Unit 1

Q: What does Isaac van Ditmas do when he is frightened by the gunfire on Governors Island?
A: He sends his wife and daughters off to Staten Island, with all of their trunks, to live with an old uncle.

Q: How do we know from Samuel's account that the king's army has many soldiers?
A: He says that they had pitched their tents on the hillside meadows by the thousands.

ANALYTICAL
Q: Why does the talk among the slaves make Samuel's head spin?
A: At one moment the talk makes him hope to be free, and then the talk turns and he feels discouraged. He doesn't know how to think about this by himself—he is just a boy and has never been allowed to think for himself—and so his hopes and fears ride on the words of the others.

SUMMING UP THE PLOT

- Back at the big house, Samuel tells what he's seen. The slaves predict that the thousands of Redcoats will whip the Liberty Boys but good.

- Sana insists that General Washington will find a way.
- Joseph Martin comments that it is no business for them, black slaves.

- Samuel thinks the slaves are right. How can American farmers and merchants defeat an army of real soldiers?

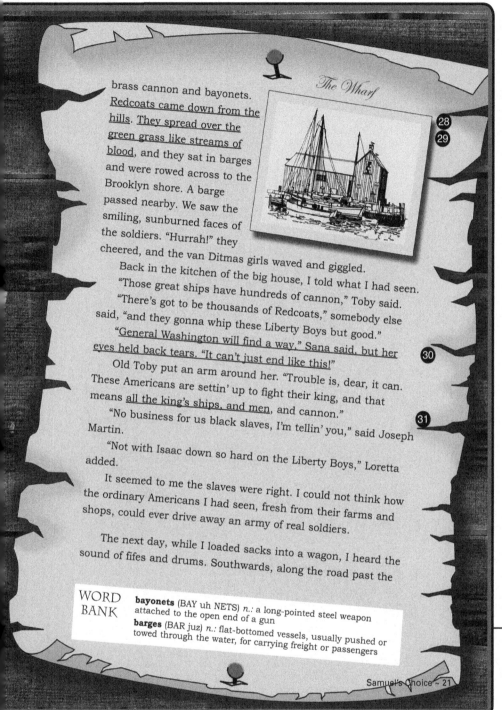

brass cannon and bayonets. <u>Redcoats came down from the hills. They spread over the green grass like streams of blood</u>, and they sat in barges and were rowed across to the Brooklyn shore. A barge passed nearby. We saw the smiling, sunburned faces of the soldiers. "Hurrah!" they cheered, and the van Ditmas girls waved and giggled.

Back in the kitchen of the big house, I told what I had seen. "Those great ships have hundreds of cannon," Toby said.

"There's got to be thousands of Redcoats," somebody else said, "and they gonna whip these Liberty Boys but good."

"<u>General Washington will find a way</u>," Sana said, but her eyes held back tears. "<u>It can't just end like this!</u>"

Old Toby put an arm around her. "Trouble is, dear, it can. These Americans are settin' up to fight their king, and that means <u>all the king's ships, and men</u>, and cannon."

"No business for us black slaves, I'm tellin' you," said Joseph Martin.

"Not with Isaac down so hard on the Liberty Boys," Loretta added.

It seemed to me the slaves were right. I could not think how the ordinary Americans I had seen, fresh from their farms and shops, could ever drive away an army of real soldiers.

The next day, while I loaded sacks into a wagon, I heard the sound of fifes and drums. Southwards, along the road past the

The Wharf

WORD BANK

bayonets (BAY uh NETS) *n.*: a long-pointed steel weapon attached to the open end of a gun
barges (BAR juz) *n.*: flat-bottomed vessels, usually pushed or towed through the water, for carrying freight or passengers

Samuel's Choice ~ 21

LITERARY COMPONENTS

▶ **28. Historical Referent:** The term *Redcoat* comes from their uniform, and denotes a member of the British armed forces in America during the Revolutionary War.

▶ **29. Simile; Foreshadowing:** They spread over the green grass *like streams of blood*. Samuel's vision is appropriate for the fate of the Continental Army, which suffered a devastating loss at the Battle of Brooklyn.

▶ **30. Characterization; Question Historical Accuracy:** Sana clearly identifies with the colonial cause. Did slaves always support the colonists? Would they have been better off siding with the British? Or would it make no difference to them, personally, either way?

▶ **31. Echoic of Nursery Rhyme:** When Toby says "that means all the king's ships, and men...," it echoes the line from Humpty Dumpty: "All the king's horses and all the king's men..."

Q: Why do you think Sana becomes so upset by the thought that Washington might be defeated?
A: There is no single answer to this question—nor is any answer clear from the text. This is a chance for students to try to empathize with Sana and what she may be feeling. One answer is that Sana identifies her own freedom with the freedom of the colonists from British rule. She may feel friendship towards the colonists' cause, because van Ditmas is clearly a royalist and sympathizes neither with the "Americans" nor with his own slaves.

Q: How does Samuel compare the Continental Army and the Redcoats?
A: If students are confused by the question, point them to the [last] paragraph. Samuel describes the Americans as having just come from their farms and their shops—as farmers and merchants. But the British are "an army of real soldiers."

GUIDING THE READING

LITERAL

Q: With what does Samuel compare the Redcoats coming down the hills?
A: He says that they spread over the green grass "like streams of blood."

Q: Why do the slaves think the British will defeat the "Liberty Boys"?
A: The British have thousands of men and hundreds of cannon.

Q: Samuel says that he agrees with the other slaves—that they are right. What does he think they are right about?

A: He also does not see how ordinary Americans, fresh from their farms and shops, can drive away an army of real soldiers.

ANALYTICAL

Q: Why is Samuel's saying that the Redcoats were spread over the green grass "like streams of blood" appropriate for this story?
A: This is a story that occurs at the beginning of the Revolutionary War, and during wars there is bloodshed.

SUMMING UP THE PLOT

- The next day, Samuel sees a hundred of Washington's "soldiers" shuffling past him in the dust.
- Sana cries out to their captain that thousands of British are landing on the shore.
- He tells her that George Washington himself is coming to Brooklyn.
- The men walking past Sana and Samuel look frightened, sick, and hungry. Some are barefoot.

LITERARY COMPONENTS

▶ **32. Metaphor:** British soldiers wore red uniforms in those days. In addition to calling them the literal "Redcoats," Americans also labeled them "lobster backs," because lobsters (especially when they are dead) are red.

▶ **33. Characterization; Theme:** Samuel's observation of Sana shows us that he is growing up, relating more to the people around him. Also, his understanding of her reasons, and saying that "freedom had to start somewhere," shows that he has become more astute and wiser.

▶ **34. Characterization; Theme:** Samuel gives freely of his buttermilk, when he himself has so little food.

GUIDING THE READING

LITERAL

Q: What does Samuel see as he is loading sacks onto a wagon?
A: He sees a hundred of Washington's recruits, with their feet shuffling in the dust.

Q: What does Sana shout to their Captain?
A: She tells him that thousands of British soldiers are landing on the shore.

Q: How do the Americans look?
A: Samuel says many seem frightened, some look sick and hungry, some are barefoot, and their flags droop.

ANALYTICAL

Q: Why do the Americans call the British soldiers lobster backs?

- Farmer Isaac tells Sana to be quiet; if fools want to break the king's law, they can do it without the help of his slaves.
- Samuel knows Sana feels sorry for the men and boys marching past. They aren't fighting

for her freedom—but freedom has to start somewhere.

- Samuel offers his jug of buttermilk to a colonial soldier who has stopped and is staring at him.

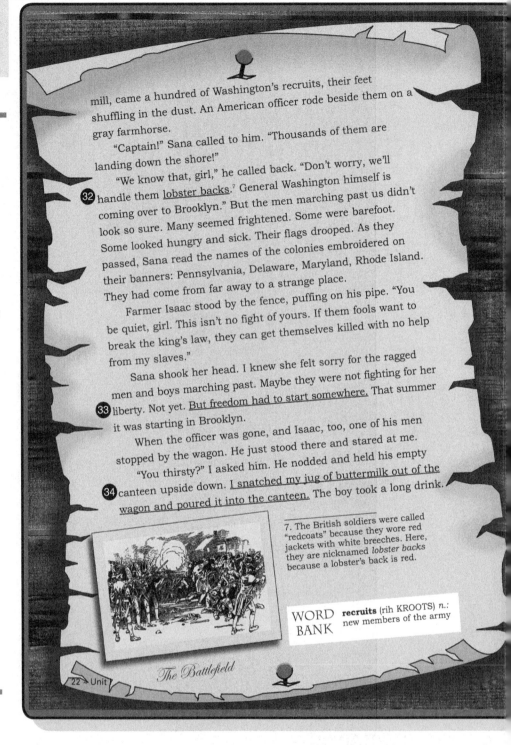

mill, came a hundred of Washington's recruits, their feet shuffling in the dust. An American officer rode beside them on a gray farmhorse.

"Captain!" Sana called to him. "Thousands of them are landing down the shore!"

"We know that, girl," he called back. "Don't worry, we'll handle them lobster backs.[7] General Washington himself is coming over to Brooklyn." But the men marching past us didn't look so sure. Many seemed frightened. Some were barefoot. Some looked hungry and sick. Their flags drooped. As they passed, Sana read the names of the colonies embroidered on their banners: Pennsylvania, Delaware, Maryland, Rhode Island. They had come from far away to a strange place.

Farmer Isaac stood by the fence, puffing on his pipe. "You be quiet, girl. This isn't no fight of yours. If them fools want to break the king's law, they can get themselves killed with no help from my slaves."

Sana shook her head. I knew she felt sorry for the ragged men and boys marching past. Maybe they were not fighting for her liberty. Not yet. But freedom had to start somewhere. That summer it was starting in Brooklyn.

When the officer was gone, and Isaac, too, one of his men stopped by the wagon. He just stood there and stared at me.

"You thirsty?" I asked him. He nodded and held his empty canteen upside down. I snatched my jug of buttermilk out of the wagon and poured it into the canteen. The boy took a long drink.

7. The British soldiers were called "redcoats" because they wore red jackets with white breeches. Here, they are nicknamed *lobster backs* because a lobster's back is red.

WORD BANK — **recruits** (rih KROOTS) *n.:* new members of the army

The Battlefield

22 ~ Unit

A: The British soldiers wear red uniforms (as in Redcoat). When lobsters die they are red.

Q: Why do you think the American soldiers are in such poor condition?
A: Answers will vary. But it is clear that the American forces do not have money to feed or dress their soldiers. They do not have money for shoes, or adequate weapons. Remind students that armies are paid for with taxes levied on the population. But the Americans did not yet even have a government that could legislate taxes. Also, farmers and merchants aren't soldiers. They have not been trained

to fight and kill. The British force based on Staten Island had 27,000 men, including 7,000 Hessian mercenaries, and 400 ships of war manned by 10,000 seamen.

Q: What do you think Samuel means when he says that freedom has to start somewhere?
A: Answers will vary.

Q: Why does Samuel offer the recruit his own buttermilk?
A: Answers will vary.

SUMMING UP THE PLOT

- Samuel asks the young soldier, Nathaniel, if he's scared, and adds that he ought to be.
- All day long Samuel hears the crash and boom of guns in the Long Island hills.

- American soldiers rush down the South Road and suddenly one cries, "The British are coming!"
- Cannonballs whiz through the air and one crashes through the roof of the mill.
- Farmer Isaac has disappeared.

- Sana bandages the wounded soldier, Nathaniel, and orders Samuel to wrap him in empty sacks.
- Nathaniel has swum across Gowanus Creek to escape the British.
- The Continental Army is trapped without boats in the swamps around the creek.
- Washington's men need help badly.

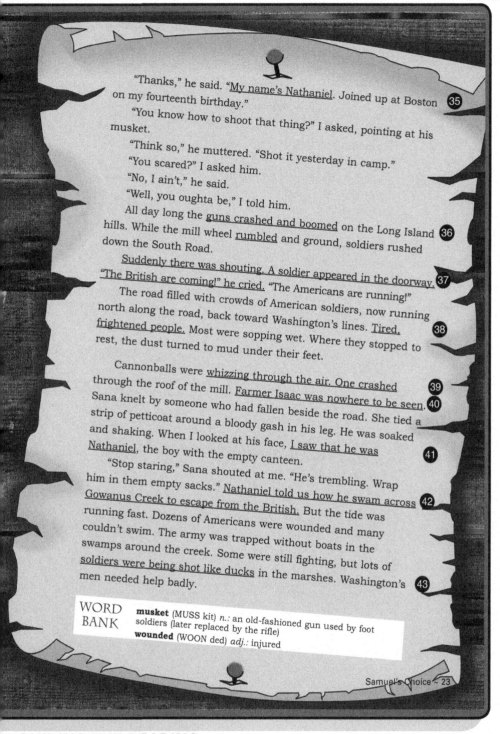

"Thanks," he said. "My name's Nathaniel. Joined up at Boston on my fourteenth birthday." **35**

"You know how to shoot that thing?" I asked, pointing at his musket.

"Think so," he muttered. "Shot it yesterday in camp."

"You scared?" I asked him.

"No, I ain't," he said.

"Well, you oughta be," I told him.

All day long the guns crashed and boomed on the Long Island **36** hills. While the mill wheel rumbled and ground, soldiers rushed down the South Road.

Suddenly there was shouting. A soldier appeared in the doorway. **37** "The British are coming!" he cried. "The Americans are running!"

The road filled with crowds of American soldiers, now running north along the road, back toward Washington's lines. Tired, **38** frightened people. Most were sopping wet. Where they stopped to rest, the dust turned to mud under their feet.

Cannonballs were whizzing through the air. One crashed **39** through the roof of the mill. Farmer Isaac was nowhere to be seen. **40** Sana knelt by someone who had fallen beside the road. She tied a strip of petticoat around a bloody gash in his leg. He was soaked and shaking. When I looked at his face, I saw that he was **41** Nathaniel, the boy with the empty canteen.

"Stop staring," Sana shouted at me. "He's trembling. Wrap him in them empty sacks." Nathaniel told us how he swam across **42** Gowanus Creek to escape from the British. But the tide was running fast. Dozens of Americans were wounded and many couldn't swim. The army was trapped without boats in the swamps around the creek. Some were still fighting, but lots of soldiers were being shot like ducks in the marshes. Washington's **43** men needed help badly.

> WORD BANK
> **musket** (MUSS kit) *n.:* an old-fashioned gun used by foot soldiers (later replaced by the rifle)
> **wounded** (WOON ded) *adj.:* injured

LITERARY COMPONENTS

▶ **35. Introduction of Secondary Character:** Nathaniel is the first American recruit we meet.

▶ **36. Onomatopoeia:** *crashed, boomed,* and *tumbled* are all onomatopoeic words.

▶ **37. Rising Action; Suspense:** A soldiers shouts, "The British are coming!"

▶ **38. Simple Language Is Powerful:** Samuel sees the soldiers for what they are: *Tired, frightened people.*

▶ **39. Onomatopoeia:** *Whizzing* and *crashed* are examples of onomatopoeia.

▶ **40. Plot; Character; Symbol:** Van Ditmas has disappeared. He will not appear in the story again. This makes it possible for these slaves—Sana, Samuel, old Toby, *et alia*—to consider themselves free. This makes the story an easier one to write, since most slaves were re-enslaved at the war's conclusion no matter how important their service had been to the winning of the war.

▶ **41. Rising Action; Characters:** Nathaniel is injured; Sana is bandaging his wound.

▶ **42. Historical Authenticity:** Indeed, this is the only way soldiers were able to escape.

▶ **43. Simile:** The "soldiers were being *shot like ducks* in the marsh."

GUIDING THE READING

LITERAL

Q: How old was Nathaniel when he joined the Continental Army?
A: Nathaniel was fourteen years old.

Q: In this scene, who disappears from the story?
A: Isaac van Ditmas is gone.

Q: Give two reasons why it is that the American soldiers cannot get across the creek.
A: The tide is rising, many of them cannot swim, many are wounded—and as we know from the discussion in Background Bytes, the British have taken Cortelyou House, which commands Dam Road, the only escape route.

ANALYTICAL

Q: Samuel is now the age that Nathaniel was when he joined the Continental Army. They are both young for the burdens they bear. Who is in the worse position?
A: Answers will vary. Nathaniel may be killed. But Samuel is a slave for life. Ask students if they know anyone who is fourteen. Can they imagine that person a slave? Can they imagine that person fighting in a war?

Q: When Nathaniel says that he isn't scared, do you think he is telling the truth?
A: Answers will vary. Ask students to explain their answers.

Q: What do you think has happened to Farmer Isaac?
A: Again, answers will vary. See how imaginative your students are!

Q: Sana shouts at Samuel, "Stop staring!" What does this tell us about Samuel's frame of mind?
A: It sounds like Samuel is immobilized, shocked, stunned—and who wouldn't be?

SUMMING UP THE PLOT

- Sana knows that Samuel always ties up "his" boat in the reeds along the creek. She tells him, "It's up to you, Samuel."

- Toby repeat Sana's words. "You got the boat, Samuel. It's your choice."

- Sana and Toby leave the scene carrying the wounded Nathaniel up the road.

- Sana is carrying her freedom flour in a sack hanging from her shoulder.

- Samuel realizes that everyone is gone and that he is alone. He asks, Is this freedom?

- He looks at his hands that have grown strong from work, and he knows his choice.

- Samuel runs to the creek and pushes the boat out into the rushing tide.

- On the opposite bank, Americans are wading in the muddy water and shouting for help.

- Gun smoke rolls over those brave soldiers and when it clears, Samuel sees fewer of them.

- Samuel pulls wet and weary men into the boat.

LITERARY COMPONENTS

▶ **44. Pivotal Moment:** Sana tells Samuel that it is up to him.

▶ **45. Source of Title:** Toby says to Samuel, "You got the boat, Samuel. It's your choice."

▶ **46. Symbol; Theme:** Sana is taking her *freedom flour* to a place where she can bake her *freedom loaf*.

▶ **47. Moment Preceding Turning Point:** *I was alone.* This may be the first time in his life Samuel is truly alone. His aloneness comes primarily from the disappearance of his master, his "owner," and from an abrupt and complete change of circumstances.

▶ **48. Theme; Internal Monologue:** Samuel asks, *Was this freedom*? Is fighting and dying freedom? Is freedom being in a position to save other people?

▶ **49. Characterization:** Indeed, many slaves decided to help the enemies of their masters.

▶ **50. Turning Point/Emotional Climax:** Samuel says, "Then I knew my choice. These hands now were going to pull people to freedom."

▶ **51. Powerful Visual Image:** It is like a magician's act, when Samuel says, "Great clouds of gunsmoke rolled over these brave soldiers. When the air cleared, I could see fewer and fewer of them."

GUIDING THE READING

LITERAL

Q: Why does Sana tell Samuel that it is up to him?
A: Samuel has been trained to use the boat. In some sense it is "his." Presumably no one else knows how to row a boat.

Q: Why do Toby and Sana carry Nathaniel?
A: Nathaniel is wounded and cannot walk.

Q: What is in the bag on Sana's shoulder?
A: The flour that she has accumulated over time from Samuel.

Q: What can Samuel hear in the distance as he stands alone on the road?
A: He hears the roar of muskets.

Q: What does Samuel think about as he stands alone in the road?
A: He thinks about the boy Nathaniel from far away, about how a lot more people just like him are trapped in the marshes, and how Isaac sneered.

Q: How have Samuel's hands grown strong?
A: His hands have grown strong from pulling ropes and oars and sacks.

Q: Where are the Americans and what are they doing?
A: The Americans are on the opposite shore wading in muddy water up to their waists.

ANALYTICAL

Q: Why is the boat, which belongs to Isaac van Ditmas, considered Samuel's?
A: Answers will vary. Presumably he is identified with the boat because he uses it. If no one else knows how to row a boat, that would surely contribute to the impression that Samuel owns the boat.

Q: What do you think it means that Samuel is finally alone? Why is it such a powerful moment?

A: Samuel cannot fall back on anyone. He cannot get advice from anyone. He has no parents. He has no teachers. He has no siblings. Now Samuel has to grow up fast, without any assistance.

Q: Why is the American artillery in the distance trying to hold the British back from the water?
A: If the British get near or in the water, they will kill the Americans.

Q: When the gunsmoke clears, why are there fewer and fewer Americans?
A: The Americans are drowning or being shot and killed.

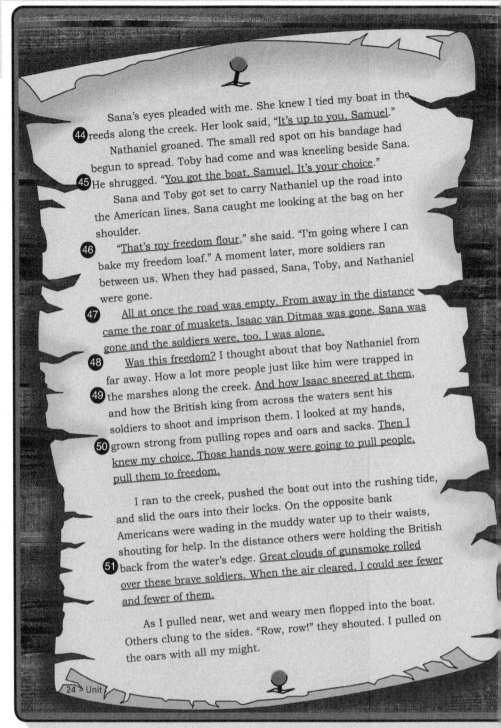

Sana's eyes pleaded with me. She knew I tied my boat in the reeds along the creek. Her look said, "It's up to you, Samuel." Nathaniel groaned. The small red spot on his bandage had begun to spread. Toby had come and was kneeling beside Sana.

He shrugged. "You got the boat, Samuel. It's your choice."
Sana and Toby got set to carry Nathaniel up the road into the American lines. Sana caught me looking at the bag on her shoulder.

"That's my freedom flour," she said. "I'm going where I can bake my freedom loaf." A moment later, more soldiers ran between us. When they had passed, Sana, Toby, and Nathaniel were gone.

All at once the road was empty. From away in the distance came the roar of muskets. Isaac van Ditmas was gone. Sana was gone and the soldiers were, too. I was alone.

Was this freedom? I thought about that boy Nathaniel from far away. How a lot more people just like him were trapped in the marshes along the creek. And how Isaac sneered at them, and how the British king from across the waters sent his soldiers to shoot and imprison them. I looked at my hands, grown strong from pulling ropes and oars and sacks. Then I knew my choice. Those hands now were going to pull people, pull them to freedom.

I ran to the creek, pushed the boat out into the rushing tide, and slid the oars into their locks. On the opposite bank Americans were wading in the muddy water up to their waists, shouting for help. In the distance others were holding the British back from the water's edge. Great clouds of gunsmoke rolled over these brave soldiers. When the air cleared, I could see fewer and fewer of them.

As I pulled near, wet and weary men flopped into the boat. Others clung to the sides. "Row, row!" they shouted. I pulled on the oars with all my might.

SUMMING UP THE PLOT

- As Samuel rows into the current, bullets splash the water.
- He crosses the creek six times.
- A big man in a blue coat and a three-cornered hat throws himself into the boat and orders Samuel to sail for Washington's camp.
- His passenger is Major Mordecai Gist, the commander of the Maryland soldiers who held the British back while the other Americans escaped.

LITERARY COMPONENTS

▶ **52. New Character:** A military man of obvious authority emerges from the bullreeds and gets into the boat. His name is withheld for two paragraphs.

▶ **53. Historical Reference:** General Charles Cornwallis (1738-1805). History shows that he was politically opposed to Britain's policies toward the American colonies, but when the war began he volunteered to fight. He started as a major general under Generals Howe and Clinton. After the 1780 American surrender of Charles Town, South Carolina, Cornwallis was put in charge of the British soldiers in the South. Cornwallis was unable to adapt his strategies to the guerilla techniques Continental Army troops *had learned from Native Americans*. He eventually surrendered at Yorktown.

▶ **54. Internal Monologue:** Here, Samuel is thinking in terms of a reality that appears to no longer exist. It is an interesting juxtaposition of Samuel's slave self and his heroic actions in the boat.

▶ **55. Historical Reference:** Major Mordecai Gist (1742-1792) was a merchant who joined the Maryland Line. During the Battle of Long Island, he led the Maryland regiment that became known as the Maryland 400. Gist was one of only ten men to survive the battle. Gist's force was the final stand of the devastated American line, allowing Washington and much of the remaining Continental Army to escape capture. Gist stayed the course during the war and was promoted to Brigadier General. He retired to his plantation near Charleston, South Carolina. The Mordecai Gist Papers at the Maryland Historical Society make Gist's personal life easily accessible and are a fascinating look at the man and the period. His family tree reveals that his first two wives died in childbirth and that two of his four children died in infancy.

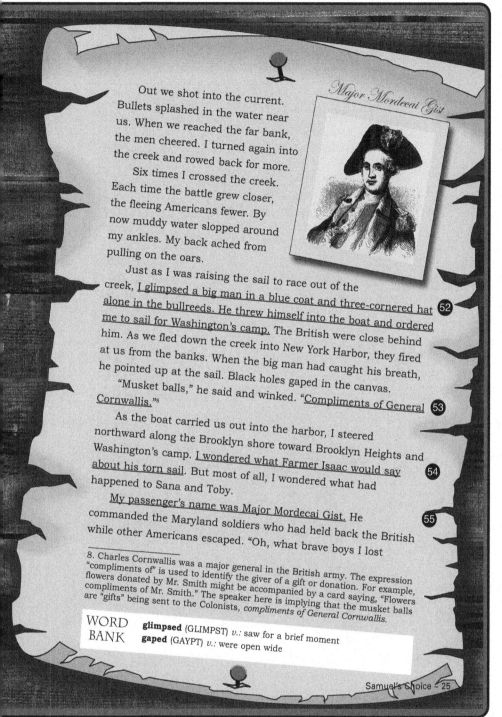

Major Mordecai Gist

Out we shot into the current. Bullets splashed in the water near us. When we reached the far bank, the men cheered. I turned again into the creek and rowed back for more.

Six times I crossed the creek. Each time the battle grew closer, the fleeing Americans fewer. By now muddy water slopped around my ankles. My back ached from pulling on the oars.

Just as I was raising the sail to race out of the creek, I glimpsed a big man in a blue coat and three-cornered hat alone in the bullreeds. He threw himself into the boat and ordered me to sail for Washington's camp. The British were close behind him. As we fled down the creek into New York Harbor, they fired at us from the banks. When the big man had caught his breath, he pointed up at the sail. Black holes gaped in the canvas.

"Musket balls," he said and winked. "Compliments of General Cornwallis."[8]

As the boat carried us out into the harbor, I steered northward along the Brooklyn shore toward Brooklyn Heights and Washington's camp. I wondered what Farmer Isaac would say about his torn sail. But most of all, I wondered what had happened to Sana and Toby.

My passenger's name was Major Mordecai Gist. He commanded the Maryland soldiers who had held back the British while other Americans escaped. "Oh, what brave boys I lost

---

8. Charles Cornwallis was a major general in the British army. The expression "compliments of" is used to identify the giver of a gift or donation. For example, flowers donated by Mr. Smith might be accompanied by a card saying, "Flowers compliments of Mr. Smith." The speaker here is implying that the musket balls are "gifts" being sent to the Colonists, *compliments of General Cornwallis*.

WORD BANK
glimpsed (GLIMPST) *v.:* saw for a brief moment
gaped (GAYPT) *v.:* were open wide

GUIDING THE READING

LITERAL

Q: How many trips does Samuel make back and forth to rescue the American soldiers?
A: He crosses the creek six times.

Q: Why is it so dangerous for him to be going back and forth?
A: The British are shooting at him and bullets are splashing in the water around him.

Q: What happens just as Samuel is raising the sail to race out of the creek?
A: A big man in a blue coat and a three-cornered hat steps out of the bullreeds and throws himself into the boat.

Q: What does the man order Samuel to do?
A: He orders Samuel to sail for Washington's camp.

Q: Who is this man?
A: His name is Mordecai Gist and he is a Major who has led those Maryland soldiers that held back the British while the other Americans escaped.

ANALYTICAL

Q: How is Samuel able to bring out so many men?
A: The soldiers ride both in the boat and hanging from the sides.

Q: What suggests that the man in the bullreeds is a person of authority?
A: The author describes him as a "big man." He seems to be wearing a Patriot uniform with his "blue coat" and "three-cornered hat." This certainly is in contrast to the barefoot recruits. He orders Samuel to sail for Washington's camp—which makes it sound as though he has the rank to talk with Washington.

Q: When the stranger says that the musket balls are "compliments of General Cornwallis," what does he mean?
A: He means that the musket balls have been shot by the British, who are led by General Cornwallis.

SUMMING UP THE PLOT

- Major Gist tells Samuel that out in the creek Samuel did more than many a free man has done for his country.
- Major Mordecai Gist asks Samuel to be his orderly and march beside him.
- Samuel says that the next day he looks everywhere for Sana.
- He is alone and frightened in Washington's camp, which is crowded with soldiers.
- Major Gist and an officer in a fine blue uniform ask Samuel how deep the water is between Brooklyn and Manhattan. Can British ships sail between the two points?
- Only the fog is keeping the British men-of-war from trapping Washington's army on Long Island.
- The next day the rains continue.

LITERARY COMPONENTS

▶ **56. Theme; Characterization:** We learn about both Samuel and Gist, when Gist says he has done more for his country than many free men.

▶ **57. Setting:** *The next day it rained and rained. A thick sea fog covered the land.* This is a good example of setting establishing mood.

▶ **58. Characterization:** Samuel's setting and role have changed radically. This is frightening for him. Where are his friends?

▶ **59. New Character:** Another character is introduced without a name. But he is wearing "a fine blue uniform." Students may guess that this is none other than George Washington.

▶ **60. Rising Action; Suspense:** If only the fog is keeping the British from attacking, what will happen when the fog lifts?

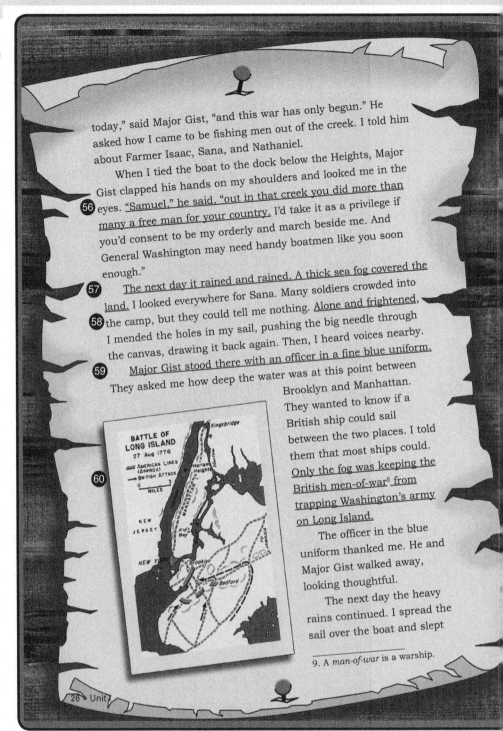

today," said Major Gist, "and this war has only begun." He asked how I came to be fishing men out of the creek. I told him about Farmer Isaac, Sana, and Nathaniel.

When I tied the boat to the dock below the Heights, Major Gist clapped his hands on my shoulders and looked me in the eyes. **56** "Samuel," he said, "out in that creek you did more than many a free man for your country. I'd take it as a privilege if you'd consent to be my orderly and march beside me. And General Washington may need handy boatmen like you soon enough."

57 The next day it rained and rained. A thick sea fog covered the land. I looked everywhere for Sana. Many soldiers crowded into **58** the camp, but they could tell me nothing. Alone and frightened, I mended the holes in my sail, pushing the big needle through the canvas, drawing it back again. Then, I heard voices nearby. **59** Major Gist stood there with an officer in a fine blue uniform. They asked me how deep the water was at this point between Brooklyn and Manhattan. They wanted to know if a British ship could sail between the two places. I told them that most ships could. **60** Only the fog was keeping the British men-of-war[9] from trapping Washington's army on Long Island.

The officer in the blue uniform thanked me. He and Major Gist walked away, looking thoughtful.

The next day the heavy rains continued. I spread the sail over the boat and slept

---

9. A *man-of-war* is a warship.

26 ~ Unit 1

GUIDING THE READING

LITERAL

Q: What does Major Mordecai Gist want Samuel to do?
A: He asks him to be his orderly and to march by his side.

Q: How does Samuel feel in Washington's camp?
A: He feels alone and frightened.

Q: What do Major Gist and the other officer ask Samuel?
A: They ask him how deep the water is between Brooklyn and Manhattan.

ANALYTICAL

Q: Why do you think Samuel feels alone and frightened?
A: Answers may vary.

Q: Why does the author say that only the fog is keeping the British from trapping Washington on Long Island?
A: Since the water is deep enough for the British men-of-war to navigate, the only explanation for their not having come is that the fog keeps them from sailing and from seeing Washington's camp.

SUMMING UP THE PLOT

- Samuel is awakened by Sana—the voice he misses more than anything in the world.
- Sana says he has made the right choice and shares her freedom bread with Samuel.

- Major Gist tells him that every boat is needed to carry Washington's army to Manhattan.
- That night the worst storm Samuel has ever seen blows up.
- The boats that are going to Manhattan need a rope to guide them against the wind and the current.

- Major Gist asks Samuel if he can get the boat across to Manhattan.
- Samuel tells Major Gist that he can take the rope across.

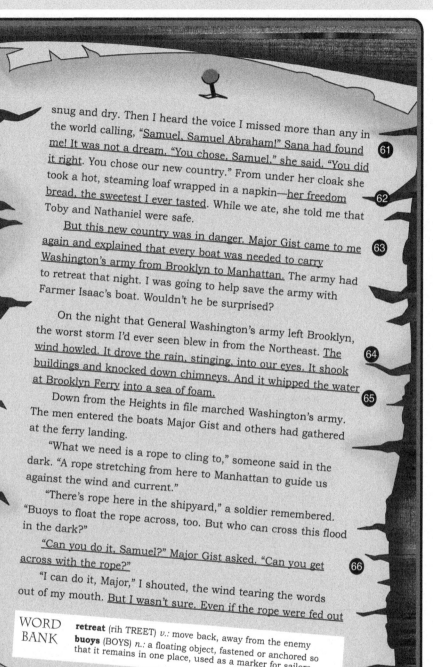

snug and dry. Then I heard the voice I missed more than any in the world calling, "Samuel, Samuel Abraham!" Sana had found me! It was not a dream. "You chose, Samuel," she said. "You did it right. You chose our new country." From under her cloak she took a hot, steaming loaf wrapped in a napkin—her freedom bread, the sweetest I ever tasted. While we ate, she told me that Toby and Nathaniel were safe.

But this new country was in danger. Major Gist came to me again and explained that every boat was needed to carry Washington's army from Brooklyn to Manhattan. The army had to retreat that night. I was going to help save the army with Farmer Isaac's boat. Wouldn't he be surprised?

On the night that General Washington's army left Brooklyn, the worst storm I'd ever seen blew in from the Northeast. The wind howled. It drove the rain, stinging, into our eyes. It shook buildings and knocked down chimneys. And it whipped the water at Brooklyn Ferry into a sea of foam.

Down from the Heights in file marched Washington's army. The men entered the boats Major Gist and others had gathered at the ferry landing.

"What we need is a rope to cling to," someone said in the dark. "A rope stretching from here to Manhattan to guide us against the wind and current."

"There's rope here in the shipyard," a soldier remembered. "Buoys to float the rope across, too. But who can cross this flood in the dark?"

"Can you do it, Samuel?" Major Gist asked. "Can you get across with the rope?"

"I can do it, Major," I shouted, the wind tearing the words out of my mouth. But I wasn't sure. Even if the rope were fed out

WORD BANK
retreat (rih TREET) *v.*: move back, away from the enemy
buoys (BOYS) *n.*: a floating object, fastened or anchored so that it remains in one place, used as a marker for sailors

Samuel's Choice ~ 27

LITERARY COMPONENTS

▶ **61. Rising Action; Characters Reunited; Theme:** Sana finds Samuel and tells him he has made the right choice.

▶ **62. Symbol; Theme; Metaphor:** Sana shares her freedom bread with Samuel. It is the sweetest he has ever tasted. Of course, what could be sweeter than freedom?

▶ **63. Rising Action; Suspense:** Every boat will be needed for Washington's retreat!

▶ **64. Setting; Onomatopoeia:** The wind *howls*. The storm is vividly described so that the reader can *feel* it.

▶ **65. Historical Reference:** Brooklyn Ferry (or as the actual ferry was later called, the Fulton Ferry) was a hamlet on the waterfront in early Brooklyn. It is now a small sector of musty, decaying buildings in the shadow of the Brooklyn Bridge. The settlement grew up around the ferry landing. Eventually, several boat lines fanned from both sides of the river. In 1839, all of the lines merged as the New York and Brooklyn Ferry Company. Before Robert Fulton presented a *steam* ferry in Nassau in 1814, all of the crossings were made by "row boats, flat scows with sprit sails, piraguas, and boats propelled by horses walking on treadmills." The last ferry stopped running in 1924.

▶ **66. Rising Action; Suspense:** Can Samuel save the day?

GUIDING THE READING

LITERAL

Q: Who awakens Samuel from his dream?
A: Samuel awakens to Sana's voice.

Q: What does Samuel say about Sana's freedom bread?
A: He says it is the sweetest bread he has ever tasted.

Q: What is the weather like the night the boats are to take Washington's army to Manhattan?
A: The wind is howling, there is driving rain,

the water at Brooklyn Ferry is being whipped into a sea of foam. Students may add other details.

ANALYTICAL

Q: How will the boats help Washington's army?
A: The boats are going to carry Washington's army across the river so that they can retreat to Manhattan instead of being trapped by the British.

Q: What are they going to do with the rope?
A: (This must be a very long and heavy rope.) The rope is going to run from Long Island to Manhattan over the water. It will apparently be secured at both ends, and the boats will use it as a guide—such as a banister is on a staircase—in the storm.

TE: Samuel's Choice ~ 27

SUMMING UP THE PLOT

- Samuel ties the rope to the mast of his boat.
- Sana jumps into the boat as Samuel shoves off into the swirling current.
- Samuel struggles with the rudder. Water crashes over the side. Sana bails.
- They are halfway across and the rope pulls them backward.
- Samuel heaves at the sail, the boom swings around, and they shoot forward at last.
- Over the roar of the storm, Samuel and
- Sana can hear the people on the far shore cheering them on.
- The boat is sinking.
- The mast breaks and is carried over the side.

LITERARY COMPONENTS

▸ **67. Rising Action; Suspense; Internal Dialogue:** Samuel is not sure he can make it. The rope may tear down the mast.

▸ **68. Characterization; Transformation; Theme:** Is this the same Samuel we met at the beginning of the story? Is this the Samuel who could not decide? This Samuel who is a free person is full of courage.

▸ **69. Conflict; Rising Suspense:** The storm and the struggle with the sea are good examples of an external conflict, one in which man struggles with forces of nature. Now they are halfway across to Manhattan and Sana cries out that she cannot swim.

▸ **70. Onomatopoeia:** The boom swings around with a *crack*.

▸ **71. Plot; Tension Building to Climax; Onomatopoeia:** This is the crisis that must lead up to a climax. The boat is sinking. The rope tears the mast out of the bottom, and breaks with a terrible *crash*. The bow *smashes*.

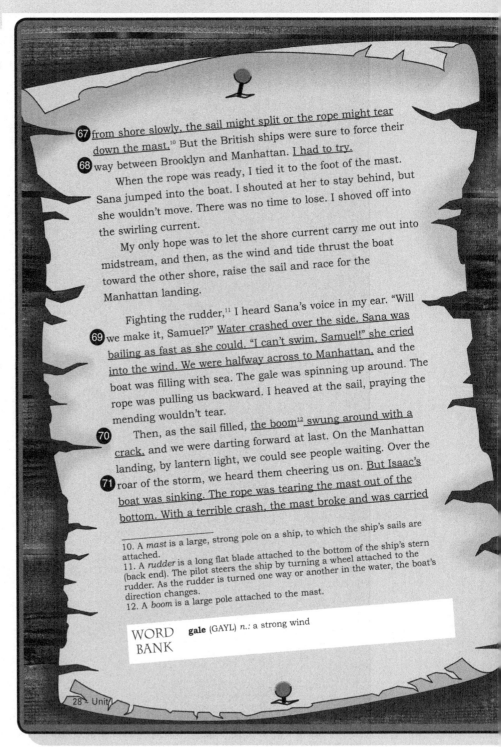

67 from shore slowly, the sail might split or the rope might tear down the mast.[10] But the British ships were sure to force their 68 way between Brooklyn and Manhattan. I had to try.

When the rope was ready, I tied it to the foot of the mast. Sana jumped into the boat. I shouted at her to stay behind, but she wouldn't move. There was no time to lose. I shoved off into the swirling current.

My only hope was to let the shore current carry me out into midstream, and then, as the wind and tide thrust the boat toward the other shore, raise the sail and race for the Manhattan landing.

Fighting the rudder,[11] I heard Sana's voice in my ear. "Will 69 we make it, Samuel?" Water crashed over the side. Sana was bailing as fast as she could. "I can't swim, Samuel!" she cried into the wind. We were halfway across to Manhattan, and the boat was filling with sea. The gale was spinning up around. The rope was pulling us backward. I heaved at the sail, praying the mending wouldn't tear.

70 Then, as the sail filled, the boom[12] swung around with a crack, and we were darting forward at last. On the Manhattan landing, by lantern light, we could see people waiting. Over the 71 roar of the storm, we heard them cheering us on. But Isaac's boat was sinking. The rope was tearing the mast out of the bottom. With a terrible crash, the mast broke and was carried

10. A *mast* is a large, strong pole on a ship, to which the ship's sails are attached.
11. A *rudder* is a long flat blade attached to the bottom of the ship's stern (back end). The pilot steers the ship by turning a wheel attached to the rudder. As the rudder is turned one way or another in the water, the boat's direction changes.
12. A *boom* is a large pole attached to the mast.

WORD BANK **gale** (GAYL) *n.*: a strong wind

28 ~ Unit 1

GUIDING THE READING

LITERAL

Q: Why does Samuel think he may not make it across with the rope?
A: He worries that the sail may split or the rope may tear down the mast.

Q: To what part of the boat is the rope tied?
A: The rope is tied to the mast. The mast is a long pole rising vertically from the deck of a ship that supports the boom. The boom is a long, rounded, solid piece of wood that is used to extend the bottom of the sail.

Q: What does Sana cry to Samuel, as the boat starts filling with water?
A: She tells him she cannot swim.

ANALYTICAL

Q: Why does Samuel feel he must try to get the rope across, even though he may not succeed?
A: He knows that the British will come. Washington's army will be trapped. He has to at least see if he can do it. He is a brave young man who cares about what happens to others.

SUMMING UP THE PLOT

- The bow smashes into a wharf.
- Samuel swims with one arm and clings to Sana with the other.
- They stumble ashore on Manhattan Island.

- The rope is across!
- All through the night, Washington's men follow the rope in boat after boat.

- Samuel writes that it would take many long years before they would beat the British king, but never again would he wonder what freedom is.

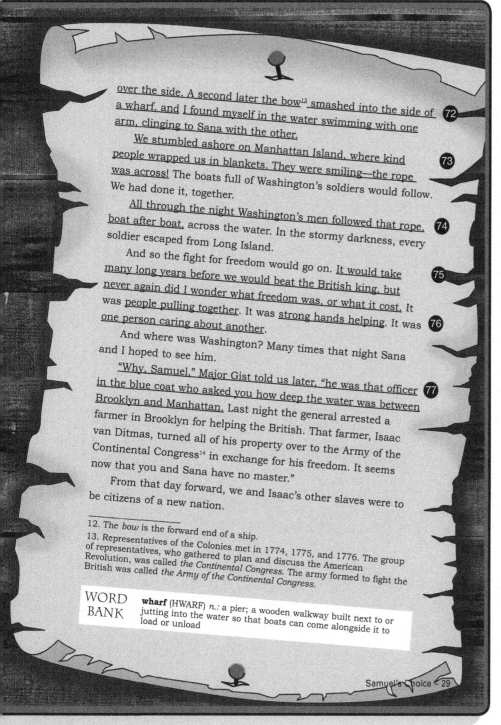

over the side. A second later the bow[13] smashed into the side of a wharf, and I found myself in the water swimming with one arm, clinging to Sana with the other.

We stumbled ashore on Manhattan Island, where kind people wrapped us in blankets. They were smiling—the rope was across! The boats full of Washington's soldiers would follow. We had done it, together.

All through the night Washington's men followed that rope, boat after boat, across the water. In the stormy darkness, every soldier escaped from Long Island.

And so the fight for freedom would go on. It would take many long years before we would beat the British king, but never again did I wonder what freedom was, or what it cost. It was people pulling together. It was strong hands helping. It was one person caring about another.

And where was Washington? Many times that night Sana and I hoped to see him.

"Why, Samuel," Major Gist told us later, "he was that officer in the blue coat who asked you how deep the water was between Brooklyn and Manhattan. Last night the general arrested a farmer in Brooklyn for helping the British. That farmer, Isaac van Ditmas, turned all of his property over to the Army of the Continental Congress[14] in exchange for his freedom. It seems now that you and Sana have no master."

From that day forward, we and Isaac's other slaves were to be citizens of a new nation.

---

12. The *bow* is the forward end of a ship.
13. Representatives of the Colonies met in 1774, 1775, and 1776. The group of representatives, who gathered to plan and discuss the American Revolution, was called *the Continental Congress.* The army formed to fight the British was called *the Army of the Continental Congress.*

WORD BANK   **wharf** (HWARF) *n.:* a pier; a wooden walkway built next to or jutting into the water so that boats can come alongside it to load or unload

Samuel's Choice ~ 29

LITERARY COMPONENTS

▶ **72. Characterization:** Samuel is swimming in the water with one arm and holding Sana with the other.

▶ **73. Climax:** Samuel and Sana stumble ashore on Manhattan Island. The rope is across!

▶ **74. Falling Action:** All night long Washington's men follow the rope in boat after boat.

▶ **75. Conclusion; Theme:** *It would take many long years before we would beat the British king, but never again did I wonder what freedom was, or what it cost.*

▶ **76. Theme:** Samuel says that *freedom* is "people pulling together"; "strong hands helping"; "one person caring about another."

▶ **77. Epilogue; Revelatory Ending:** This story has a revelatory ending—a surprise, like the punch line of a joke—that is appended as an epilogue. (An epilogue is the final part that rounds out or completes the design of a nondramatic literary work.)

GUIDING THE READING

LITERAL

Q: What happens when they stumble ashore on Manhattan Island?
A: People wrap them in blankets.

Q: Did the war end that night?
A: The war would not end for many long years.

Q: Did George Washington ever appear in the story?
A: Washington was the officer in the fine blue uniform who asked about the depth of the water.

ANALYTICAL

Q: When the boat finally smashes, how do they make it?
A: Samuel says that the bow smashed into the side of a wharf, which means they are almost there. (A wharf is any structure projecting from the shore that permits boats or ships to lie alongside for loading or unloading.) Samuel swims with one arm and holds Sana with the other.

5. Suggest that students reread the paragraphs below before trying to answer the question:

> Cannonballs were whizzing through the air. One crashed though the roof of the mill. Farmer Isaac was nowhere to be seen. Sana knelt by someone who had fallen beside the road. She tied a strip of petticoat around a bloody gash in his leg. He was soaked and shaking. When I looked at his face, I saw that he was Nathaniel, the boy with the empty canteen.
>
> "Stop staring," Sana shouted at me. "He's trembling. Wrap him in them empty sacks." Nathaniel told us how he swam across Gowanus Creek to escape from the British. But the tide was rising fast. Dozens of Americans were wounded and many couldn't swim. The army was trapped without boats in the swamps around the creek. Some were still fighting, but lots of soldiers were being shot like ducks in the marshes. Washington's men needed help badly.
>
> Sana's eyes pleaded with me. She knew I tied my boat in the reeds along the creek. Her look said, "It's up to you, Samuel."
>
> Nathaniel groaned. The small red spot on his bandage had begun to spread. Toby had come and was kneeling beside Sana. He shrugged. "You got the boat, Samuel. It's your choice."
>
> Sana and Toby got set to carry Nathaniel up the road into the American lines. Sana caught me looking at the bag on her shoulder.
>
> That's my freedom flour," she said. "I'm going where I can bake my freedom loaf." A moment later, more soldiers ran between us. When they had passed, Sana, Toby, and Nathaniel were gone.
>
> All at once the road was empty. From away in the distance came the roar of muskets. Isaac van Ditmas was gone. Sana was gone and the soldiers were, too. I was alone.
>
> Was this freedom? I thought about that boy Nathaniel from far away. How a lot more people just like him were trapped in the marshes along the creek.

From these paragraphs, it seems reasonable to suggest that freedom to Samuel represents all of the following: the whizzing of cannonballs and people being injured, even young people that he knew; seeing soldiers being either injured or killed in battle; being asked to do things by friends; being asked to take risks; being asked to think for himself, instead of always taking orders; being in a position to make a decision; seeing oneself as a person who could make a difference; feeling trapped; being alone. Students' answers are sure to vary.

6. Students will likely write several different answers. The story is exciting. It's about someone's making a difficult decision. It's about someone's learning the meaning of liberty. It's about the Revolutionary War. It's about a young slave's becoming free. It shows that American blacks fought in the war on the side of America—even though there was no guarantee they would find themselves free at its conclusion.

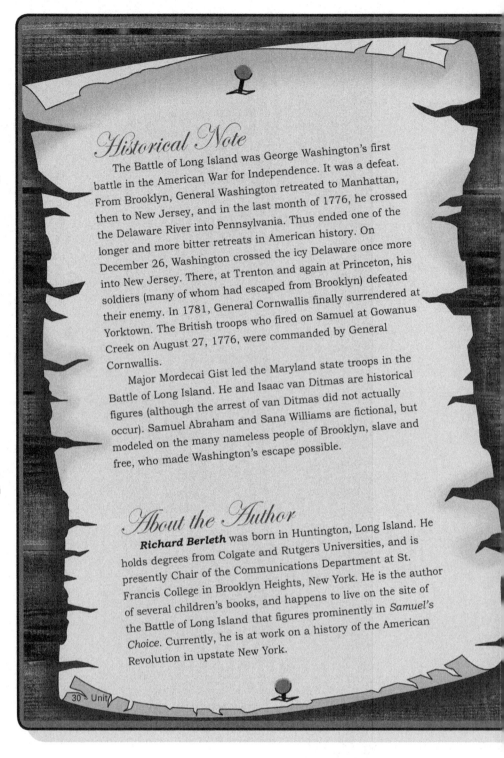

Historical Note

The Battle of Long Island was George Washington's first battle in the American War for Independence. It was a defeat. From Brooklyn, General Washington retreated to Manhattan, then to New Jersey, and in the last month of 1776, he crossed the Delaware River into Pennsylvania. Thus ended one of the longer and more bitter retreats in American history. On December 26, Washington crossed the icy Delaware once more into New Jersey. There, at Trenton and again at Princeton, his soldiers (many of whom had escaped from Brooklyn) defeated their enemy. In 1781, General Cornwallis finally surrendered at Yorktown. The British troops who fired on Samuel at Gowanus Creek on August 27, 1776, were commanded by General Cornwallis.

Major Mordecai Gist led the Maryland state troops in the Battle of Long Island. He and Isaac van Ditmas are historical figures (although the arrest of van Ditmas did not actually occur). Samuel Abraham and Sana Williams are fictional, but modeled on the many nameless people of Brooklyn, slave and free, who made Washington's escape possible.

About the Author

Richard Berleth was born in Huntington, Long Island. He holds degrees from Colgate and Rutgers Universities, and is presently Chair of the Communications Department at St. Francis College in Brooklyn Heights, New York. He is the author of several children's books, and happens to live on the site of the Battle of Long Island that figures prominently in *Samuel's Choice*. Currently, he is at work on a history of the American Revolution in upstate New York.

30 ~ Unit 1

FIRST IMPRESSIONS

Remind students that being free means being free to choose to act, to make a decision, to follow your own religious beliefs. Sometimes, we do what we believe is right and are faced with the disapproval of our friends or neighbors.

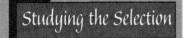

Studying the Selection

FIRST IMPRESSIONS

In the story, Sana says that "Nobody here's gonna be free unless they take the risk." Why does being free require taking a risk? Do you think this is still true today?

QUICK REVIEW

1. Write down two words or phrases that describe Isaac van Ditmas.

2. Why was Samuel hungry all of the time?

3. Why did Isaac teach Samuel about "the currents that flow between Brooklyn and Manhattan" and "setting a sail and holding a course"?

4. What does Samuel say about doing work you "do not choose to do"?

FOCUS

5. On page 24, Samuel finds himself alone. Everyone has gone. He asks himself, Is this freedom? Reread several paragraphs before this line in the story, and the paragraph that follows it. What do you think Samuel's question means?

6. In a short paragraph, explain why you think that *Samuel's Choice* is a good story.

CREATING & WRITING

7. Imagine that you are Samuel. Why do you decide to help the wounded soldiers?

8. You are Samuel. You have just met a soldier who wants to give up. He is tired, hungry, and discouraged. He does not believe the Colonists can win against the mighty British. How do you persuade him to stay and fight?

9. You are a slave. You are going to join a group of slaves in the center of Brooklyn to protest being kept in slavery. Each of you has made a sign with a message on it. Make your sign for the gathering.

Samuel's Choice ~ 31

CREATING & WRITING

7. Presumably students will say that Samuel was a good person. He knew what it was like to suffer. He sympathized with the soldier. And so forth.

8. The students may draw their answers from the story, from their general knowledge, and from their imaginations. Some possible answers are: the Colonists are fighting on and for their own land; freedom is worth fighting for; the British are not as invincible as they appear; we've learned a new way to fight from the Indians; when right is on your side you will win, etc.

9. Make certain students have poster board. After they have made their signs, allow them to hold "demonstrations" or protests for freedom in small groups (in the classroom).

QUICK REVIEW

1. We know from the story that Isaac van Ditmas is a slave holder. He believes that people can be purchased as property (*inhumane*). Isaac van Ditmas is also described as *strict* and *stingy* (page 18). Although he *does* teach Samuel how to use the boat (*willing to teach*), Samuel may only use it to transport Farmer Isaac's wife and daughters (*willing to teach only if it serves his own interest*). We learn that in spite of his owning a flour mill, his slaves are not even given bread to eat (*selfish, unfeeling, irresponsible*). We learn that his slaves don't get enough sleep (*thoughtless, uncaring*). On page 22, we see that van Ditmas does not agree with the revolution and is loyal to the King of England (some might say his is a *traitor;* a *royalist;* wanting things to stay the same). When the war comes closer to the farm, van Ditmas appears to have run away (page 23) (*cowardly*). On page 24, Samuel says that Isaac had *sneered* at soldiers who were trapped in the marshes (*arrogant; unfeeling*). At the end of the story, van Ditmas shows that he values his *own* freedom, by having turned all of his property over to the Army of the Continental Congress so that he does not become a prisoner of war (*smart; clever;* knows how to look out for his own interest).

2. Samuel was hungry all the time because his "owner" did not give him food. As a slave, he would have no access to food unless he stole it from the kitchen.

3. Farmer Isaac wanted Samuel to be able to take Mrs. van Ditmas and her daughters "over to Manhattan, or down the Brooklyn shore to Staten Island" (page 18)—and there were no bridges. He would not be able to navigate if he did not know about "the currents that flow between Brooklyn and Manhattan" or "setting a sail and holding a course."

4. Samuel says that work you do not choose to do is always tiring (page 18).

LESSON IN LITERATURE . . .

WHAT IS PLOT?

- The events that take place in a story make up the plot. Some of the events happen to the story's characters, and some are caused by the story's characters.

- The plot starts early in the story. As events unfold, a conflict arises for the main character. A conflict is a struggle to overcome some problem or challenge. If the plot is to hold our interest, there must be a conflict.

- At one point in the story, everything changes. The main character either overcomes the problem presented in the plot, or is defeated by it. This point in the story is called the story's climax.

- After the climax, the story comes to a conclusion. This is the part of the story where the reader feels that all has been explained, and the story is complete.

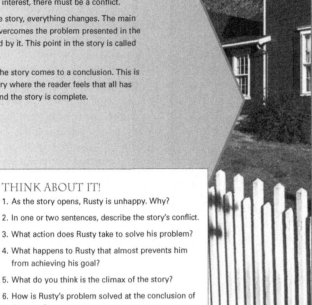

THINK ABOUT IT!

1. As the story opens, Rusty is unhappy. Why?

2. In one or two sentences, describe the story's conflict.

3. What action does Rusty take to solve his problem?

4. What happens to Rusty that almost prevents him from achieving his goal?

5. What do you think is the climax of the story?

6. How is Rusty's problem solved at the conclusion of the story?

New Kid

All alone in the fenced-in backyard, Rusty hurled the baseball as hard as he could into the air. When a gust of wind caught the ball, Rusty ran after it.

Just over the fence he could see the kite the kids next door had been trying all morning to keep in the air. Back home, if somebody had a kite, everybody had a kite. And the new kid wouldn't be left playing catch by himself for a whole week without somebody comin' over to say "Hey."

Suddenly, the wind slammed the kite right into a tree near the fence.

The neighbor, a redhead, appeared at the top of Rusty's fence. Rusty watched as the kid reached for the lowest hanging branch.

Rusty stepped closer. "Why don't you let me try?"

"You?"

"Lots of trees back home. Used to climb all the time."

The kid shrugged. Rusty climbed up the fence. On the other side a bunch of kids stared up at him.

"Give me a boost," Rusty ordered.

Pulling himself up on the lowest branch, Rusty climbed the next several branches as easily as he would a ladder, but he couldn't quite reach the kite.

"You guys got a broom?" he shouted down.

One of the younger boys raced off. An instant later he returned with a broom.

The moment Rusty nudged the kite free, the wind slammed it into a branch a little further out.

With his left hand he inched as far out along the branch as he could. With his right he reached out with the broom. The delicate material of the kite was caught in some twigs. One false move and there would be no kite to rescue. Using the stick end of the broom, he gently lifted the edge of the kite. It fell free.

When Rusty got down there were high fives all around.

The red-haired kid handed him the string. "You fly it first."

Rusty took off running. Behind him, climbing higher with each step, was the kite. On all sides, panting and shouting their delight, ran Rusty's new friends.

LESSON IN LITERATURE

1. Rusty has just moved into the neighborhood and he has no one to play with because no one is friendly.

2. The conflict is about whether the neighborhood kids will accept Rusty. This is paralleled in another conflict, which is whether or not Rusty will be able to save the kite.

3. Rusty offers to help save the kite.

4. The wind blows the kite out of Rusty's reach.

5. The climax of the story is when the kite falls free.

6. Both problems are solved: Rusty now has friends and the kite has been saved.

SELECTION VOCABULARY

achievement: something accomplished through great effort or skill

ambition: a strong desire for success, fame, wealth, or the like, and the willingness to work for it

beckoning: motioning to someone to come closer

congenial: agreeable; pleasant

drifted: slowly moved away

frantically: wildly and desperately

occasional: occurring once in a while

plaque: a metal plate engraved with the name of a person being honored

rarely: hardly ever

sympathetic: to have a positive or favorable feeling about something

---

| achievement | beckoning | drifting | occasional | rarely |
| ambition | congenial | frantically | plaque | sympathetic |

1. Mr. Hanson was a man who was comfortable with himself, his home, and his job. Some considered him a friendly, _____ (agreeable) man.

2. So what if he _____ (hardly ever) changed his routine! "He likes what he does each day," they said. "Why trouble trouble, 'til trouble troubles you?"

3. These thoughts were expressed by those who were _____ to (in agreement with) Mr. Hanson.

4. Others, though, criticized him, saying he lacked drive and _____ (desire for success).

5. These critics, seeing no new _____ (accomplishments), called him lazy, dull, and useless.

6. "Why, that man is so lazy," said Mrs. Brownley, "that if he were on a raft that was _____ (slowly moving) out to sea, he'd think it too much trouble to row for shore."

7. "And," added sharp-tongued Mrs. Dickens, "if the people on shore _____ (wildly) motioned to him, he'd probably give them no more than an _____ (once in a while) glance."

8. "Yes," snickered Ben Hufton, "he'd probably think they were just _____ (motioning to come closer) to him to come join them for a cold drink!"

9. "I do declare," exclaimed Mrs. Thomas. "That man deserves a _____ (an engraved plate given as an award) for being the most 'laid-back' man on the face of the earth!"

Workbook p. 7   Answer Guide p. 1

Would you. . .?

Answer the questions below in a few words. Then answer the 'why' in a complete sentence. If you are not sure what the vocabulary word means, check the glossary at the back of the workbook.

1. ...rather your mother be sympathetic or critical when you failed your math test? _sympathetic_ Why? _I study very hard for math so if I don't do well I feel terrible and need a little sympathy._

2. ...prefer a doctor who is congenial or businesslike? _____ Why? _____

3. ...search for a lost diamond ring frantically or calmly? _____ Why? _____

4. ...want to eat pizza occasionally or daily? _____ Why? _____

5. ...like to attend gym class often or rarely? _____ Why? _____

6. ...swim out after a beach ball that had drifted into deep water? _____ Why? _____

7. ...approach a stranger who was beckoning to you? _____ Why? _____

8. ...proudly display a plaque you had won ? _____ Why? _____

9. ...tell your parents about an achievement in school or keep it to yourself? _____ Why? _____

10. ...describe ambition as a positive or a negative trait? _____ Why? _____

Workbook p. 8   Answer Guide p. 1

BACKGROUND BYTES

This little story gives you the opportunity to begin a conversation with your students about caring for the environment—a conversation that will be developed and sustained throughout the year by other pieces in this anthology.

The focus on the turtle in *Slower Than the Rest*, and the tenderness with which the protagonist regards him, is a nice lead in to a discussion of what is happening to both our land and sea creatures. From the material that follows, take what you feel is appropriate for your 5th graders. These lessons are designed so that our children are aware of the world around them, and so that they grow up to help the world rather than hurt it.

For thousands of years, turtles were impervious to attack. Until the 20th century, the armor that turtles grew made them nearly invulnerable, no matter where they went. The turtle's hard shell could be cracked only by wolves and coyotes (and perhaps a few other predators). Then the automobile was invented.

In the United States, the turtle population has diminished dramatically. Scientists attribute their declining numbers more to automobiles and trucks than to loss of habitat. In fact, in the eastern regions where roads are so dense, there is a ten to twenty percent annual death rate among turtle adults from these vehicles.

"Some of the most threatened turtles are land turtles. Such turtles, including box turtles, wood turtles, spotted turtles and tortoises, plod between wetlands and drier regions during the year. Although most days turtles just lumber around, moving only 50 meters [164 feet] or so, about once a month they trek 500 meters [1,640 feet] or more. In many areas this means that the turtle crosses a road."

Consequently, wood turtles, Blandings turtles, and box turtles have nearly vanished from parts of the country. These turtles have not simply moved to safer areas. Unlike most other animals, turtles do not have babies until they are twelve to twenty years old. This means that under current circumstances most have not reproduced before they die. Turtles in captivity do not breed.

Nationally, it is believed that the death rate on the roads is nearly a million animals every day. Not all of these dead animals are observed, because many crawl off the road as they die. Any animal that moves slowly is most vulnerable.

There are no cars in the oceans, but sea turtles are equally threatened. Many formerly common species are on the brink of extinction. All over the world—but particularly in Hawaii—green sea turtles are dying from *fibropapilloma* (FY bro PAP il LO ma) tumors. These tumors are ugly white lumps that can grow as big as a head of cauliflower. Such big tumors are larger than the turtle. The tumors grow on all of the turtle's soft body parts. When tumors grow over the turtle's eyes, it is blind. If the tumors make it impossible to swim, the turtle starves.

Many countries and many industries behave as though the ocean is a garbage dump. Human and animal sewage is often washed into the sea. Oil spills from ocean liners affect ocean plant and animal life in ways we cannot even predict. Farmers use pesticides to kill insects. These chemicals are hazardous. When it rains, they are washed out of the soil. Then they enter ditches and streams. When pesticides drain into the sea, it is called run-off. Run-off poisons turtles.

Fibropapilloma tumors seem to be contagious. Turtles go to special places to get clean. In these places, there are fish that eat substances off of their shells and clean them. Here, turtles unwittingly spread the disease.

Marine turtles everywhere are dying because of things people do. Turtles are killed for their shells and their meat. Fishermen trap turtles in their nets and drown them. Turtle eggs are stolen by humans by the thousands. Turtles are killed so that their shells can be made into combs and art objects.

What does this mean for us? It means that there are lots of things that we must do to improve the situation. Our public officials need to know that we care about the land, we care about the ocean, and we even care about turtles.

Language Alert

then or than: *Than* is used in a comparison between one thing and another. The comparison shows that the word or phrase <u>before</u> the word *than* is different from, less *than*, or more *than* the word that follows it. The comparison shows a difference in kind, in identity, or in manner.

INTO "SLOWER THAN THE REST"

Slower Than the Rest has several themes. The most significant of these is that slower does not mean less than, nor does it mean undeserving. The story reminds us that we should pay attention to the world around us, so that we can see who needs help, whether a turtle or a boy. And that boy shows us that caring is nothing to laugh at.

Leo's behavior moves us because he is so loving and affectionate, and because *he lacks the usual prejudice against difference and slowness.* He wins, basically because he is a good, loving, and honest boy.

In Leo we see that isolation crushes the human spirit. But we also see that when a person is open and expressive, it may open the door to the world of the others.

For the teacher, this story, perhaps more than any other in the book, presents a challenge. The story may closely resemble a situation that individual students strongly identify with. Other students may make thoughtless or callous remarks during classroom discussion. We present here some thoughts on how the story should be taught and what we consider a healthy approach to the issue of children who are "slower than the rest."

Leo is a child who does not learn easily or quickly. For this reason, he has been placed in a class which will move at his pace of learning. Leo is mortified at what he considers a public humiliation. However, the real source of his sense of worthlessness is an oft-repeated comment of his father, that Leo is "slower than the rest."

Many very common obstacles to a child's happiness are described in this story, and any discussion of them must be guided by the teacher in a sensitive, mature, and positive way. Today, most classes either include some individual "slow learners," have a built-in tutorial which some of the children attend after class, are divided into several sections for subjects such as math or science, or are altogether divided according to academic ability. The students' attitudes to the group in which they are placed are vital to their success and happiness. Additionally, their attitudes to those at other levels (i.e. feelings of inferiority or of superiority) are important.

What is the ideal? Ideally, a child should be made to feel that the learning process, not the pace of learning, is what counts. Children should be taught that effort and persistence will result in success. A child should be provided with the means to achieve success, which often includes a separate class, a skilled teacher, and different teaching methods. This should be done by the school in a positive, matter-of-fact way. Young children will imitate the adults. If the slower children are treated with respect and acceptance, the children's peers will adopt the same attitude. Should the peers step out of line, the adults must immediately step in and correct their behavior. A laissez-faire policy is unacceptable in this area.

Let us return to the story. Point out to the children that there is only one fact in Leo's life that cannot be changed: that he finds learning difficult (but by no means impossible). Every other problem he has is caused by a flawed attitude. The worst attitude in the story is that of the father. The father tells Leo that he is slow. The father is probably not unkind, he is just insensitive or completely unaware of the terrible effect this comment has on his son. (People *do* make unfeeling remarks, and it might be of value to discuss with your students how to deal with such remarks.)

The second example of a mistaken, damaging attitude is Leo's own attitude to being placed in a separate class. Leo's feelings are not unnatural, but it is the adults' obligation to change those feelings. It should be explained to him that it is to his advantage to learn at his own pace. Moreover, he is far from unique—there is an entire group of children who learn at his pace. Most important, of course, is to point out that there are many talents, skills, and success stories that are unrelated to excellence in the classroom. Leo is a person first and a student second, and it is the duty of every adult in his life to make sure he knows that.

Leo's sense of inferiority harms his ability to function in another arena—socially. Leo's classmates are not unkind. They applaud him and are happy when he wins the award. It is his own dejection that prevents him from interacting with them. This is another very important lesson for your students. On the one hand, someone who feels inadequate should be coaxed, cajoled, pushed and whatever else it takes to reach out to others and see how well others will respond. On the other hand, those who see a classmate who appears to be a loner should be guided to reach out to that student.

The conclusion of *Slower Than the Rest* is instructive. As comforting as Charlie the turtle is it is the human recognition of his principal and classmates that bring Leo happiness. Our students can and should be taught to appreciate each other in a real, open, and generous way.

EYES ON...PLOT

It may be helpful to students to think of the word *plot* as just another word for story. The tale that is woven is the plot. The full definition of *plot* in Webster's Unabridged Collegiate Dictionary is "the plan or pattern of events or the main story of a literary work (as a novel, play, short story, or poem) comprising the gradual unfolding of a causally connected series of motivated incidents."

How to sum up the plot of *Slower Than the Rest*?
Exposition:

The story begins with a boy named Leo who spots a turtle on the highway as his family goes for a drive. He is allowed to keep the turtle, which he loves, and he calls the turtle, Charlie. We learn that Leo is ten and has few friends, because he is "slower than the rest." That's what his father says. Leo learns slowly at school. Leo has been put in a separate class for slow children and feels he will never be happy again.

The exposition introduces the following Characters:

Leo, his father, his mother, his two little sisters, and Charlie
Leo and Charlie are the **Main Characters**.
The exposition establishes the **Setting**: contemporary times, likely the United States.
The exposition also establishes the basic **Conflict**, which is Leo's conflict, both an **internal** one and an **external** one: his slowness, his being isolated by it, and his feeling compromised by the response of his father and the external world.

The exposition is followed by Rising Action, Further Characterization of Leo, and a sad and bitter statement of Leo's **Conflict** and the **Theme** in his comment about Charlie:

Charlie's entrance into Leo's life makes Leo happy. Leo takes good care of Charlie, takes him outside in the backyard every day after school to let him explore, and talks with him privately. Leo is loving, responsible, and delights in Charlie. Charlie is congenial and special. (Even though the story is written in the third person, Leo's inner voice is very clear here.) In addition to his other skills, Charlie "takes off as if no one ever told him how slow he was supposed to be." Charlie is the friend and confidante that Leo has never had.

Rising Action That Leads to the Turning Point; Rising Suspense:

Leo takes Charlie to school. It is Prevent Forest Fires week, and each student in Leo's class is supposed to make a report. (We see, here, that Leo is a creative thinker and capable of abstract thought.)

Turning Point for Leo; Rising Excitement; Conflict; Theme:

When it is Leo's turn to speak, he speaks powerfully. He takes Charlie out of the box. He says that in a forest fire the slow ones cannot escape, that it isn't fair for the slow ones.

Rising Action; Some Amelioration of the External Conflict; New Characters:

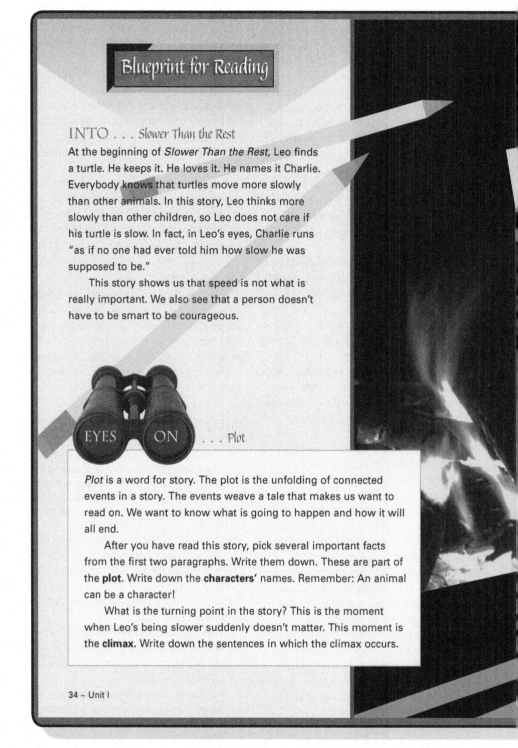

Blueprint for Reading

INTO . . . *Slower Than the Rest*
At the beginning of *Slower Than the Rest*, Leo finds a turtle. He keeps it. He loves it. He names it Charlie. Everybody knows that turtles move more slowly than other animals. In this story, Leo thinks more slowly than other children, so Leo does not care if his turtle is slow. In fact, in Leo's eyes, Charlie runs "as if no one had ever told him how slow he was supposed to be."

This story shows us that speed is not what is really important. We also see that a person doesn't have to be smart to be courageous.

EYES ON . . . Plot

Plot is a word for story. The plot is the unfolding of connected events in a story. The events weave a tale that makes us want to read on. We want to know what is going to happen and how it will all end.

After you have read this story, pick several important facts from the first two paragraphs. Write them down. These are part of the **plot**. Write down the **characters'** names. Remember: An animal can be a character!

What is the turning point in the story? This is the moment when Leo's being slower suddenly doesn't matter. This moment is the **climax**. Write down the sentences in which the climax occurs.

34 ~ Unit I

Leo talks about Charlie, about turtles in general, about Charlie the friend. His classmates and his teacher are very moved by his presentation.
Rising Action Approaching the Climax:
In the afternoon, the school gathers in the gymnasium to bring Fire Prevention week to a close. The school principal speaks, while Leo's thoughts wander. Someone whispers Leo's name, and the children around him are saying that Leo has won.

The Climax:
Leo is given an award for his presentation with

Charlie. This is the first time in his life Leo has won an award. He thinks his heart will explode with happiness.
Falling Action and **Resolution:**
That night, alone in his room with Charlie, Leo feels proud. He feels fast.

SUMMING UP THE PLOT

● Leo spots a turtle in the road as he and his family drive up Tyler Mountain.

● His mother is sympathetic toward turtles, so Leo is allowed to bring it home.

LITERARY COMPONENTS

▶ **1. Exposition:** Leo sees the turtle first, so he gets to keep it.

▶ **2. Setting:** Leo is with his family in the car, driving up Tyler Mountain.

▶ **3. Characters; Characterization:** His father grumbles, his mother is sympathetic.

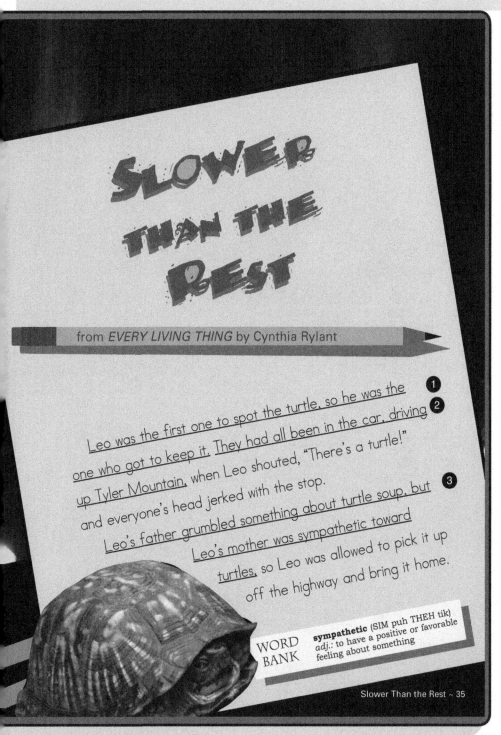

SLOWER THAN THE REST

from *EVERY LIVING THING* by Cynthia Rylant

Leo was the first one to spot the turtle, so he was the **①** one who got to keep it. They had all been in the car, driving **②** up Tyler Mountain, when Leo shouted, "There's a turtle!" and everyone's head jerked with the stop.

Leo's father grumbled something about turtle soup, but **③** Leo's mother was sympathetic toward turtles, so Leo was allowed to pick it up off the highway and bring it home.

WORD BANK — **sympathetic** (SIM puh THEH tik) *adj.:* to have a positive or favorable feeling about something

Slower Than the Rest ~ 35

GUIDING THE READING

LITERAL

Q: Who spots the turtle?
A: Leo is the first one to see it.

Q: Where is the turtle?
A: The turtle is on the highway.

Q: How do Leo's parents react?
A: Leo's father grumbles about turtle soup—as if he would make soup out of the turtle!—and Leo's mother is sympathetic to Leo's wanting the turtle.

ANALYTICAL

Q: Why do you think Leo's father stops the car, when Leo points out the turtle?
A: Answers will vary. Leo's father is responsive to a situation in which an animal needs assistance. Turtles are so slow, they are often killed by cars when they are crossing a road.

SUMMING UP THE PLOT

- His sisters are repelled by the turtle, but Leo loves it. He calls it Charlie.
- Leo settles Charlie in a cardboard box, with some lettuces and radishes. He declares himself a happy boy.
- Leo adores Charlie and hugs and kisses him. He carries him around on his shoulder.
- Leo is ten years old and hasn't many friends because he is slower than the rest.

LITERARY COMPONENTS

▶ **4. Characters; Characterization; Onomatopoeia:** His sisters *squeal* at the sight of the turtle.

▶ **5. Theme:** *Beauty is in the eyes of the beholder.* Leo's sisters fuss when they see the turtle's "ugly head" and horrifying claws. But Leo loves it from the start.

▶ **6. Character:** Leo calls the turtle Charlie.

▶ **7. Background Information; Humor; Characterization:** The dogs belong to Leo's father; the cat belongs to herself. Leo is grateful for a pet of his own.

▶ **8. Characterization:** Leo adores Charlie.

▶ **9. Characterization; Critical Background Information; Theme:** Leo doesn't have many friends because he is "slower than the rest." That's how his father puts it.

Leo loved Charlie from the very start.

4 5 Both his little sisters squealed when the animal stuck its ugly head out to look at them, and they thought its claws horrifying, but Leo loved it from the start. He named it Charlie.

6 The dogs at Leo's house had always belonged more to Leo's father than to anyone else, and the cat thought she belonged to no one but herself, so Leo was grateful for a pet of his own. He

7 settled Charlie in a cardboard box, threw in some lettuce and radishes, and declared himself a happy boy.

8 Leo adored Charlie, and the turtle was hugged and kissed as if he were a baby. Leo liked to fit Charlie's shell on his shoulder under his left ear, just as one might carry a cat, and Charlie would poke his head into Leo's neck now and then to keep them both entertained.

9 Leo was ten years old the year he found Charlie. He hadn't many friends because he was slower than the rest. That was the

36 ~ Unit I

GUIDING THE READING

LITERAL

Q: How do Leo's sisters react?
A: They squeal. From the way this is written, it is clear that they think the turtle is ugly and horrifying.

Q: Why does Leo want a pet, when the family has dogs and a cat?
A: The dogs belong more to Leo's father, and the cat belongs to herself.

Q: When Leo carries Charlie on his shoulder, what does Charlie do to entertain them?
A: Charlie pokes his head into Leo's neck now and then.

ANALYTICAL

Q: Why doesn't Leo realize that Charlie is ugly and horrifying?
A: A turtle is a turtle. Some people may find turtles unattractive and frightening, but others will find them beautiful. Class answers will vary.

Q: Do you think Charlie responds to all that love from Leo?
A: Answers will vary.

SUMMING UP THE PLOT

- Leo is slow in reading and numbers.
- Leo is slow in understanding nearly everything in class.
- In fourth grade, Leo was separated from his classmates and placed with other children who were as slow as he.
- He saw no way to be happy after that.
- But Charlie takes care of Leo's happiness.
- Charlie is the friendliest turtle anyone has ever seen.
- Put Charlie down, and he takes off as if no one has ever told him how slow he is supposed to be.
- Every day after school, Leo takes Charlie outside and lets him explore.
- Leo tells Charlie about what happens in fifth grade.
- Charlie has lines around his forehead, eyes, and mouth, and Leo thinks Charlie is wise the way old people are wise.
- Leo talks to him privately every day.
- It is Prevent Forest Fires week and the whole school is involved in related activities.

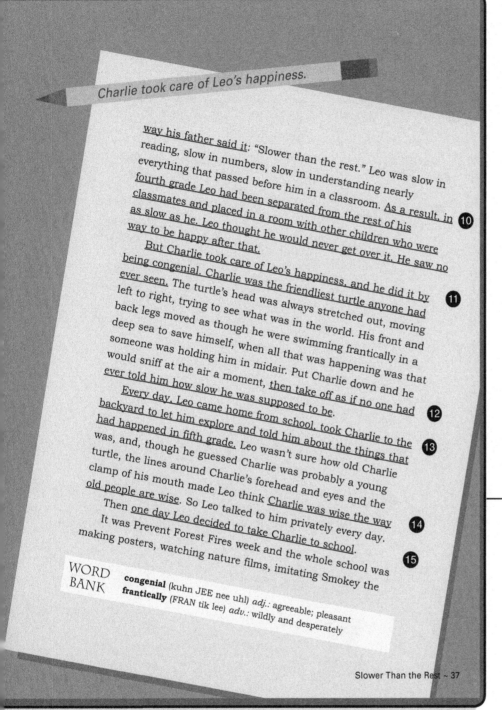

Charlie took care of Leo's happiness.

way his father said it: "Slower than the rest." Leo was slow in reading, slow in numbers, slow in understanding nearly everything that passed before him in a classroom. As a result, in **10** fourth grade Leo had been separated from the rest of his classmates and placed in a room with other children who were as slow as he. Leo thought he would never get over it. He saw no way to be happy after that.

But Charlie took care of Leo's happiness, and he did it by being congenial. Charlie was the friendliest turtle anyone had **11** ever seen. The turtle's head was always stretched out, moving left to right, trying to see what was in the world. His front and back legs moved as though he were swimming frantically in a deep sea to save himself, when all that was happening was that someone was holding him in midair. Put Charlie down and he would sniff at the air a moment, then take off as if no one had **12** ever told him how slow he was supposed to be.

Every day, Leo came home from school, took Charlie to the **13** backyard to let him explore and told him about the things that had happened in fifth grade. Leo wasn't sure how old Charlie was, and, though he guessed Charlie was probably a young turtle, the lines around Charlie's forehead and eyes and the clamp of his mouth made Leo think Charlie was wise the way **14** old people are wise. So Leo talked to him privately every day.

Then one day Leo decided to take Charlie to school. **15** It was Prevent Forest Fires week and the whole school was making posters, watching nature films, imitating Smokey the

WORD BANK **congenial** (kuhn JEE nee uhl) *adj.*: agreeable; pleasant
frantically (FRAN tik lee) *adv.*: wildly and desperately

Slower Than the Rest ~ 37

LITERARY COMPONENTS

▶ **10. Characterization; Conflict; Theme:** In fourth grade Leo had been separated from the rest of his classmates. He was placed in a room with other slow children. Leo thought he would never be happy again. His separation from others and the way that he is different crush his spirit.

▶ **11. Rising Action; Third-Person Point of View Is Charlie's View:** Charlie makes Leo happy because Charlie is friendly. Wonderfully and credibly, Leo perceives Charlie's turtle actions as being very special, as directed outwards towards others.

▶ **12. Theme; Characterization of Leo; Metaphor:** Charlie is bitter here—since his father and others have told him how slow he is supposed to be. The slow, ugly, lovable turtle is a metaphor for Charlie.

▶ **13. Rising Action; Characterization of Friendship:** Leo shares his life with Charlie. Leo is responsible in the care of his pet.

▶ **14. Theme:** Love is transforming. It transforms Leo who gives it and feels love in return. It transforms the turtle who to Leo seems very wise. The turtle is what he thinks it is.

▶ **15. Important Moment, Critical Rising Action:** Leo is bringing Charlie out into the world of people.

Q: How is Leo and Charlie's relationship like a friendship?
A: Leo talks to Charlie privately every day.

Q: What has Leo decided to do?
A: Leo has decided to take Charlie to school.

ANALYTICAL

Q: How would you feel if you were separated from your classmates and put in another, slower class? If this has happened to you, how did you feel?
A: Answers will vary.

Q: Unlike what has happened to Leo, what has no one ever told Charlie?
A: No one has ever told him how slow he is supposed to be.

Q: What is the result of no one's ever having told that to Charlie?
A: The result is that he really takes off—he must be fast. No one has ever told him he is slow, so he is not slow.

Q: Can you imagine Charlie as congenial?
A: Answers will vary.

Q: Can you imagine the turtle as wise?
A: Answers will vary.

Q: Does it matter if Charlie is really congenial or really wise?
A: Answers will vary.

GUIDING THE READING

LITERAL

Q: What happened to Leo in the fourth grade?
A: He was separated from his classmates and placed in a room with other children who were as slow as he.

Q: How does Leo react to this?
A: He feels he will never get over it. After this occurred, he saw no way to be happy again.

Q: How does Charlie take care of Leo's happiness?
A: Charlie does it by being congenial.

Q: When Charlie's head is stretched out, moving left to right, what is he trying to do?
A: He is trying to see what is in the world.

Q: What does Leo do every day when he comes home from school?
A: Every day after school, Leo takes Charlie to the backyard to let him explore. He also tells him things that have happened in the fifth grade.

Q: Why does Charlie seem wise?
A: Charlie has lines around his forehead and eyes and the clamp of his mouth. This makes Charlie look old. Leo says that old people are wise. Therefore, if Charlie is old, then he is wise.

SUMMING UP THE PLOT

- Every student has to make a report, and so Leo is bringing Charlie.
- On the school bus, Leo holds the covered box on his lap, relieved that turtles are quiet except for an occasional hiss.
- In the middle of the morning, the forest reports begin.
- Leo is bored with the reports.
- A boy says that if there were no forest, his father couldn't go hunting. Leo doesn't see the connection.
- Finally it is Leo's turn.
- Leo begins by saying, "when somebody throws a match in a forest, he is a murderer."
- Some animals are fast runners and get out, but other animals have no hope. They are too slow.
- Leo lifts Charlie out of the box and says that it isn't fair for the slow ones.

LITERARY COMPONENTS

▶ **16. Characterization:** Leo is no fool. He is going to use Charlie for his report.

▶ **17. Onomatopoeia; Charlie as a Person:** Charlie rarely *hissed* in the morning; he was a turtle who likes to sleep in.

▶ **18. Setting:** The windowsill in the classroom is wide and has geraniums on it.

▶ **19. Rising Action; Suspense:** The reports are being given. When will it be Charlie's turn?

▶ **20. Approaching the Turning Point; Suspense:** Finally it is Leo's turn to speak.

▶ **21. The Moment We Have Been Waiting for (But Not the Situational Climax); Characterization:** Leo speaks powerful words.

▶ **22. Identification; Metaphor; Characterization:** Leo identifies with the turtle. Leo knows what it's like to be slow. It isn't fair for the slow ones.

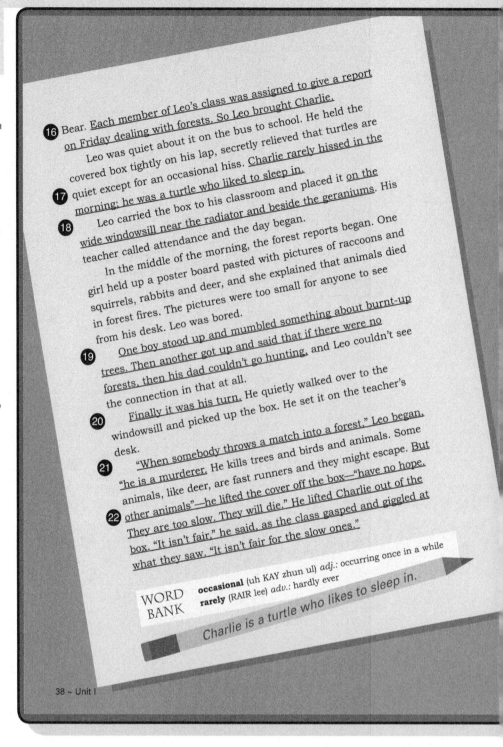

16 Bear. Each member of Leo's class was assigned to give a report on Friday dealing with forests. So Leo brought Charlie.

Leo was quiet about it on the bus to school. He held the covered box tightly on his lap, secretly relieved that turtles are

17 quiet except for an occasional hiss. Charlie rarely hissed in the morning; he was a turtle who liked to sleep in.

Leo carried the box to his classroom and placed it on the

18 wide windowsill near the radiator and beside the geraniums. His teacher called attendance and the day began.

In the middle of the morning, the forest reports began. One girl held up a poster board pasted with pictures of raccoons and squirrels, rabbits and deer, and she explained that animals died in forest fires. The pictures were too small for anyone to see from his desk. Leo was bored.

19 One boy stood up and mumbled something about burnt-up trees. Then another got up and said that if there were no forests, then his dad couldn't go hunting, and Leo couldn't see the connection in that at all.

20 Finally it was his turn. He quietly walked over to the windowsill and picked up the box. He set it on the teacher's desk.

21 "When somebody throws a match into a forest," Leo began, "he is a murderer. He kills trees and birds and animals. Some animals, like deer, are fast runners and they might escape. But

22 other animals"—he lifted the cover off the box—"have no hope. They are too slow. They will die." He lifted Charlie out of the box. "It isn't fair," he said, as the class gasped and giggled at what they saw. "It isn't fair for the slow ones."

WORD BANK **occasional** (uh KAY zhun ul) *adj.*: occurring once in a while
rarely (RAIR lee) *adv.*: hardly ever

Charlie is a turtle who likes to sleep in.

38 ~ Unit I

GUIDING THE READING

LITERAL

Q: Why is Leo taking Charlie to school?
A: He is going to use Charlie for his Prevent Forest Fires report.

Q: How does Leo feel during the other students' reports?
A: He is bored and he doesn't see the connection between hunting and wanting to prevent forest fires.

Q: What does Leo say about the animals who are caught in a forest fire and are too slow?
A: He says they have no hope and that they will die. He also adds that it isn't fair for the slow ones.

ANALYTICAL

Q: Leo's decision to bring Charlie for his report tells us something about him—something we might not expect from someone people say is slow. What does it tell us?
A: It tells us he is no dummy. On some level, Leo has thought about this. He has made the connection between what happens to woodland creatures and that his own turtle is one of them. If he loves his turtle, then he must care about the fate of the other animals. Ordinary people often don't make that sort of connection.

Q: Why does Leo say that a person who throws a match into a forest is a murderer?
A: The person who starts a forest fire kills animals—particularly those that are too slow to move quickly.

Q: How does Leo know so well that it isn't fair for the slow ones?
A: Leo himself is slow. School is hard for him. It seems unfair that he should have to struggle at what comes so easily to others.

SUMMING UP THE PLOT

- Leo talks about what turtles are like and what talents they possess, about Charlie the turtle and Charlie the friend.

- What Leo says makes everyone in the class love turtles and hate forest fires.

- That afternoon, the whole school assembles in the gymnasium as a conclusion to the special Prevent Forest Fire week.

- The school principal stands up and talks. Leo's thoughts drift off.

- Leo jumps when he hears the boy next to him shout, "Leo! It's you!"

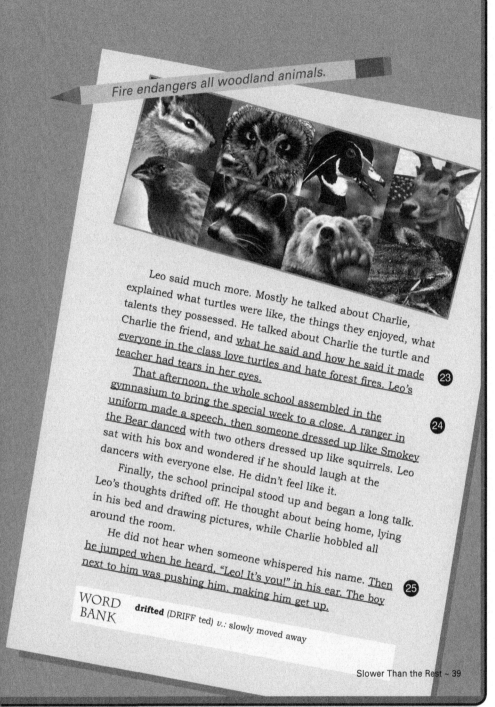

Fire endangers all woodland animals.

Leo said much more. Mostly he talked about Charlie, explained what turtles were like, the things they enjoyed, what talents they possessed. He talked about Charlie the turtle and Charlie the friend, and what he said and how he said it made everyone in the class love turtles and hate forest fires. Leo's teacher had tears in her eyes. ㉓

That afternoon, the whole school assembled in the gymnasium to bring the special week to a close. A ranger in uniform made a speech, then someone dressed up like Smokey the Bear danced with two others dressed up like squirrels. Leo sat with his box and wondered if he should laugh at the dancers with everyone else. He didn't feel like it. ㉔

Finally, the school principal stood up and began a long talk. Leo's thoughts drifted off. He thought about being home, lying in his bed and drawing pictures, while Charlie hobbled all around the room.

He did not hear when someone whispered his name. Then he jumped when he heard, "Leo! It's you!" in his ear. The boy next to him was pushing him, making him get up. ㉕

WORD BANK **drifted** (DRIFF ted) *v.*: slowly moved away

LITERARY COMPONENTS

▶ **23. Theme; Turning Point:** Leo has spoken openly and honestly, with love, compassion, and knowledge. He has shown everyone something they could not see before.

▶ **24. We Are Tricked into Thinking This Is the Falling Action:** The reports are done and it is afternoon. The school assembles in the gymnasium, etc., etc.

▶ **25. Climax:** Leo is roused by another boy. The students are shouting that he has won!

GUIDING THE READING

LITERAL
Q: What does Leo do while the principal is talking?
A: His thoughts drift off.

ANALYTICAL
Q: Why do you think Leo's teacher had tears in her eyes, and all the children loved turtles and hated forest fires, after Leo spoke?
A: Answers will vary. Students may talk about Leo's honesty, his first-hand knowledge, and the enthusiasm he expresses for Charlie.

SUMMING UP THE PLOT

- "You won!" all the students are saying. "Go on!"
- Leo is pushed onto the floor. He sees the principal smiling at him.
- His legs move like Charlie's—quickly and forward.

- He shakes the principal's hand and puts down Charlie's box to accept the award plaque.
- This is the first time Leo has won an award.

- Leo thinks his heart will explode with happiness.
- At night, alone in his room with Charlie on his shoulder, Leo feels proud. He feels fast.

LITERARY COMPONENTS

▶ **26. Theme:** Leo's legs move like Charlie's—quickly and forward. Charlie is supposed to be slow and he's not. Perhaps Leo is not slow, either.

▶ **27. Characterization; Resolution of Conflict:** Finally, Leo can be happy.

▶ **28. Falling Action; Resolution of Plot:** Leo and Charlie are alone in his room. Leo feels *fast*.

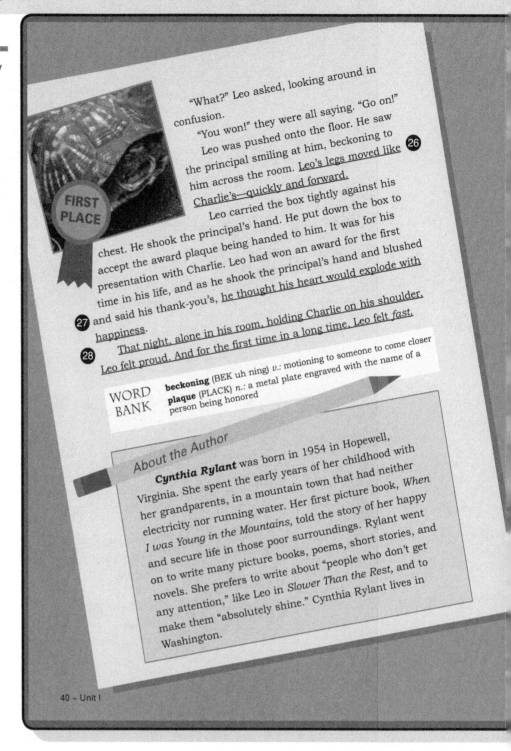

"What?" Leo asked, looking around in confusion.

"You won!" they were all saying. "Go on!"

Leo was pushed onto the floor. He saw the principal smiling at him, beckoning to him across the room. Leo's legs moved like Charlie's—quickly and forward. **26**

Leo carried the box tightly against his chest. He shook the principal's hand. He put down the box to accept the award plaque being handed to him. It was for his presentation with Charlie. Leo had won an award for the first time in his life, and as he shook the principal's hand and said his thank-you's, **27** he thought his heart would explode with happiness.

That night, alone in his room, holding Charlie on his shoulder, **28** Leo felt proud. And for the first time in a long time, Leo felt *fast*.

WORD BANK

beckoning (BEK uh ning) *v.*: motioning to someone to come closer
plaque (PLACK) *n.*: a metal plate engraved with the name of a person being honored

About the Author

Cynthia Rylant was born in 1954 in Hopewell, Virginia. She spent the early years of her childhood with her grandparents, in a mountain town that had neither electricity nor running water. Her first picture book, *When I was Young in the Mountains*, told the story of her happy and secure life in those poor surroundings. Rylant went on to write many picture books, poems, short stories, and novels. She prefers to write about "people who don't get any attention," like Leo in *Slower Than the Rest*, and to make them "absolutely shine." Cynthia Rylant lives in Washington.

GUIDING THE READING

LITERAL

Q: How does Leo walk up to the principal?
A: His legs move like Charlie's—quickly and forward.

Q: Has Leo ever won an award before?
A: No. This is the first time in his life he has won an award.

ANALYTICAL

Q: Why do you think Leo finally feels fast?
A: He feels fast because he is proud of himself. He has received an award, just as a non-slow person might.

Studying the Selection

FIRST IMPRESSIONS

What do you love, in the same way that Leo loves Charlie?

QUICK REVIEW

1. Where were Leo and his family, when he spotted the turtle?

2. What does Leo call the turtle?

3. Why doesn't Leo have many friends?

4. Where did the expression, "slower than the rest," come from?

FOCUS

5. How does Leo show that he has courage?

6. What is the climax of the story? Why is that moment so important?

CREATING & WRITING

7. It took courage for Leo to speak to his class about the suffering of animals that move slowly. He may have feared they would laugh at him and call *him* slow. But he did speak, and the class listened with great interest. Think about a time when you wanted to step forward and speak about something that you felt was wrong—but you just couldn't. It was too scary. Perhaps you waited too long and the moment had passed. Write about the experience in two paragraphs. In the first paragraph, explain what happened or what was said that you felt was wrong. In the next paragraph, write down what you wish you had said.

8. Leo and his family noticed the turtle on the highway. Then they rescued it and took it home to take care of it. Why do you think Leo's family did this? Think about it and write your answer in one or two paragraphs.

9. Create a turtle either by drawing one or making one from clay.

Slower Than the Rest ~ 41

QUICK REVIEW

1. Leo and his family are in the car, driving up Tyler Mountain, when Leo spots the turtle.

2. Leo names the turtle Charlie.

3. Leo doesn't have many friends because he is "slower than the rest."

4. The expression came from his father.

FOCUS

5. Many people are afraid to talk before a group. Leo has come to see that he is not as smart—not as fast—as other children who are his age. We would expect Leo to be even *more* afraid of speaking in front of others. Furthermore, many people cannot talk freely and openly about something or someone they love.

6. The climax occurs when someone whispers in Leo's ear, "Leo! It's you!" The sentences that follow sustain the moment.

> The boy next to him was pushing him, making him get up.
> "What?" Leo asked, looking around in confusion.
> "You won!" they were all saying. "Go on!"
> Leo was pushed onto the floor. He saw the principal smiling at him, beckoning to him across the room. Leo's legs moved like Charlie's—quickly and forward.

It is clear from the story that Leo has suffered from being told he is slower than the rest. He undoubtedly suffers from being slower—without anyone's having to point it out to him. Leo is a loving boy and he loves his turtle. He has had the courage to step forward and speak about his turtle and his relationship with his turtle. Now he is being recognized for this. At least for the time being, the conflict in the story is resolved.

CREATING & WRITING

7. Doing this assignment will teach the children the rudiments of outlining. Suggest that they think of the situation they wish to describe in the first paragraph and write down two or three words that reflect the core idea of what they will say. They should then do the same for the second paragraph. Next, they should return to the first paragraph and expand it into several full sentences. Finally, do the same for the second paragraph.

8. It is important for students to focus on what characterizes people who pay attention to the world around them, and who care about what they see. This is a way of stepping outside one's concern for oneself, and seeing the whole world and all its creatures as an individual and community responsibility.

9. It will be helpful to students if you can provide them with pictures.

WHAT IS CHARACTER?

- The people or animals in a story are its characters.
- Stories include main characters and secondary characters. The secondary characters are those who have a smaller part in the story.
- In some stories, the author talks mainly about what the characters *do*. In others, the focus is on what the characters *think* or *feel*.
- In some stories, the author describes a character's thoughts and actions in a positive or negative way. We understand that this is a "good" character or a "bad" character.
- Sometimes the author is careful not to express an opinion about a character. The author wishes the reader to form an opinion without help from the author.

THINK ABOUT IT!

1. Use three adjectives to describe Marie.

2. Although we are told only about Marie's actions, we can imagine what Marie was thinking and feeling as she took those actions. Describe Marie's thoughts and feelings as she packed Brady's lunch each day.

3. Do you prefer stories that tell you what to think about each character, or stories that force you to make up your own mind?

Just Like Mom

Before Mom died, Brady hardly paid any attention to his sister, Marie. Five years older than Brady, she seemed to live in an entirely separate world. After Mom died, Marie became the most important person in Brady's life.

Dad had a good job; he took good care of them. But it was Marie who got Brady up every morning and got him ready for school. She always packed his lunch for school, just like Mom had. And just like Mom, she never let him take "junk food" for lunch.

Every afternoon, Marie picked him up after school and walked him home, just like Mom had. And just like Mom, she never accepted "I don't know" or "Nothing" in response to the question "What did you do in school today?" She really wanted to know.

Every evening, Marie made dinner for Brady and Dad, just like Mom had. And just like Mom, she made everyone help clear the table while she did the dishes.

It wasn't until years later, when Brady was in high school and would microwave pizza for himself and Dad after football practice, that Brady realized something. He finally understood that in order for her to get him up and ready for school on time, Marie had had to get up that much earlier herself. And that in order to walk him home from school every day, Marie had had to give up the after-school sports and activities he took for granted. And that because she made dinner, cleaned up, helped him with his homework and helped him get ready for bed, Marie didn't get to start on her homework until after she was through taking care of him.

Marie was just like Mom, and now that Marie was off to college, he missed them both very much.

LESSON IN LITERATURE

1. Marie is kindhearted, generous, responsible, caring, thoughtful, mature, industrious, self-sacrificing, etc.

2. Perhaps Marie is thinking: I feel so sorry for little Brady. I had a mother as I was growing up—he doesn't. I'm going to do my best to make him feel cared for and loved.

3. Answers will vary.

SELECTION VOCABULARY

buffeting: repeated hitting and pushing

extinguish: put out (a light or a fire)

foreman: a person in charge of a department or group of workers, as in a factory

fragments: bits and pieces of something

hazards: dangers

lingered: stayed longer than usual

lull: a temporary calm or quiet

recede: return to a lower level; move back and further away

rugged: rough; rocky and hilly

timber: trees; an area of woodland or forest

| buffeting | foreman | hazards | lull | rugged |
| extinguish | fragments | lingered | recede | timber |

1. Real hikers are always looking for new and more _____ (*rough and rocky*) trails to conquer.

2. It was easy to pick out the _____ (*person in charge of a group of workers*) of the crew. He was wearing a bright yellow hard hat and a T-shirt that said "hail to the chief."

3. There is a warning on every box of cigarettes about the _____ (*dangers*) of smoking.

4. In European countries, where the first American settlers were born, wealthy people built their houses of stone. In America, a land blessed with forests, _____ (*trees used for construction*) was most often used.

5. I looked up from my desk. The noise in the playground had been so continuous that the sudden _____ (*temporary calm*) disturbed me.

6. It was my last day in Paris. I should have hurried home to pack, but I _____ (*stayed longer than necessary*) to say goodbye to the place I'd called home for five years.

7. The stewardess approached the passenger and quietly asked him to _____ (*put out*) his cigarette, as no smoking is allowed on planes.

8. The river flooded the town, destroying many homes and businesses, and taking the lives of pets and livestock, before the water began to _____ (*go back down*).

9. The archaeologist was thrilled. He held in his hand what appeared to be _____ (*bits and pieces*) of a three-thousand-year-old vase.

10. We watched in terror as the little boat struggled against the storm, wind, and rain _____ (*repeatedly hitting*) it from every side.

Workbook p. 13   Answer Guide p. 2

Sign of the Times

Make six "signs" using one vocabulary word in each, to warn or inform the reader of something. You may change the form of the word from singular to plural or from one tense to another. Funny signs are welcome!

Workbook p. 14   Answer Guide p. 2

BACKGROUND BYTES

One unnamed historical source tells us that Kate came to the United States with her parents, Michael and Norah Shelley, when she was nine months old. They had emigrated from Offaly County, Ireland. The Shelleys went west and settled on a plot of poor farming land. At the time, Moingona, Iowa was experiencing a coal mining boom. Michael started working as a section hand on the railroad. He built the house in which the family lived. The farmhouse was up the slope from Honey Creek, which was a tributary of the Des Moines River.

All of Kate's siblings were born in the cottage: Margaret, Mayme, Michael, Jr., and John. The Shelleys tilled the soil, and purchased a cow, some pigs, and chickens. Kate became "second-in-command" when her father was killed in a railroad accident and Michael, Jr. drowned in the Des Moines River. [Note, here, that this record calls the son "Michael, Jr." not James.]

The same record describes the July 6 accident at Honey Creek Bridge this way:

It was already after eleven o'clock when Kate and her mother heard the rumble of a train crossing the distant Des Moines River bridge. It was old No. 12 with Ed Wood, George Olmstead, Adam Agar, and Patrick Donahue on board. Their orders were to "run to Boone and return to Moingona regardless of all trains." The engine came backing down the track with the brakeman and section foreman standing on the running board behind the tender looking for washouts. They came in view of the Shelley house and then rolled out on the swaying Honey Creek bridge. Kate and her mother listened intently and twice heard the bell over the noise of the storm. Then, as she described it later, "came the horrible crash and the fierce hissing of steam" as the engine plunged down with her crew into twenty-five feet of rushing swirling waters.

[When Kate went out to the bluff] flashes of lightning showed her that Wood and Agar had somehow grabbed limbs of trees as they fought in the stream and had climbed up into the branches. They were safe for the time being, if the trees weren't washed away. She could see that one of the men was calling to her but his voice was drowned out by the roar of the torrent. No other men were in sight.

Regarding their rescue, the same "historian" writes that a rope was cast out to Wood, still perched in a tree, who fastened down the line and then came ashore, hand over hand. Agar couldn't be reached until the waters began to recede, but he was rescued after long exposure. Olmstead and Donahue drowned. One man's body was found in a cornfield. The other was never recovered.

The record tells that the lantern Kate clutched as she crawled across the Des Moines River Bridge is "in the Historical Museum at Des Moines today."

When Kate was finally up and about, a new world had opened before her.

The passengers of the train she saved collected a purse of a few hundred dollars for her; the school children of Dubuque gave her a medal; the state of Iowa gave her another and with it an award of $200; the Chicago and North Western Railroad presented her with $100, a half barrel of flour, half a load of coal and a lifetime pass. A gold watch and chain came from the Order of Railway Conductors. Letters poured into the Shelley cottage from all over the world.

Kate's heroism caught the fancy of the nation's poets. Eugene J. Hall wrote:

Ah, noble Kate Shelley, your mission is done;
Your deed that dark night will not fade from our gaze.
An endless renown you have worthily won;
Let the nation be just and accord you its praise.
Let your name, let your fame and your courage declare
What a woman can do and a woman can dare!

From Francis Schreiber of Havana, Illinois came these words

Up to the station her steps she bent
To state the doleful incident;
And when she'd done and knew no more
She swooned and reeled and hit the floor.

A well-known journalist-writer, MacKinlay Kantor, wrote *The Ballad of Kate Shelley*, which was published in 1930:

The midnight coaches from the west
Plunged in the ripping rain;
West of Moingona Ties were sound –
East was a broken train –
(East in the bile of Honey Creek
In one drowned, creaking curl,
Lay ninety tons of twisted steel)
Between them was a girl.

Kate even had a statue erected in her honor in Dubuque, and was provided the funds to attend Simpson College in Indianola, Iowa, which she attended for one term. Kate went back to living and working at the Shelley home, plowing and trying to make ends meet. She "passed her examinations for a teacher's certificate and started her career at a small school near her home. The monthly salary of $35 was the principal cash income for the Shelley household."

Eventually, the nation forgot about Kate. But in 1890, a Chicago newspaper learned that the Shelleys were unable to pay their mortgage. They were about to lose their home of twenty-three years. There was an immediate public response and an auction to raise money. The mortgage was paid off, cash gifts were raised, and the legislature of the state of Iowa voted to give Kate $5,000. A school textbook publisher gave an account of her heroism in a "Third Reader," which was subsequently used in Iowa schools.

The North Western railroad offered Kate a job, and in 1903 she became one of the few women station agents employed by the company. "Twice each day she made the trip between her home and the station on foot along the same route she traveled that fateful night in 1881." In 1900, the bridge she had crawled across was replaced by a new iron bridge. The new bridge was named the Kate Shelley Bridge.

Today there is no train track past the Shelley homestead. That track was originally the main line. But when the Des Moines River Bridge was reconstructed, a new route was laid, and it became a branch line. In 1933, the branch line was replaced by a road. The historian concludes by writing, "Even so there are those who say the spirit of Kate Shelley still visits the spot on dark and stormy nights, warning," as does MacKinlay Kantor:

Be sure to take a lantern flame
To keep your spirit warm
For there will be a phantom train,
And foggy whistle cries –
And in the lightning flare you'll see
Kate Shelley on the ties.

Language Alert

Make sure your students know what and where Iowa is, since geography has not traditionally been the strong suit of American institutions of learning.

Iowa became the 29th state on December 28, 1846. The capital city is Des Moines, which was founded as a military outpost at the confluence of the Des Moines and Raccoon rivers.

The word *Iowa* is an Anglicized form of *Ayuha,* a word the French heard from the Dakota tribe, who seem to have been enemies of these Ayuha. The Iowa tribe was pushed further and further westward as a result of white settlement and a series of treaties through which they ultimately lost all of their land and were moved onto a reservation in Nebraska.

Iowa is bordered by Wisconsin and Illinois on the east, Missouri on the south, Nebraska and South Dakota on the west, and Minnesota on the north.

The name *Des Moines* is also a French corruption of the name of a native tribe: the Moingwena. The Moingwena were a subdivision of native people called the Iliniwek (*ilini* meaning "man," *iw* meaning "is," and *ek* the plural ending). Iliniwek was changed by the French to *Illinois.* – *ois* is a French ending.

The story also makes clear the origin of the work *sidetracked*. We are accustomed to the later meaning, "to turn aside from a purpose; to divert (as from the main subject or action) into another and usually less important channel." But as the story shows, *sidetracked* originally meant "to transfer to a railroad siding from a main line."

INTO "KATE SHELLEY"

Kate Shelley is about a hardworking young woman who is accustomed to taking responsibility when someone is needed to do a job. She is modest and sees herself as an instrument of good: "I believe that G-d makes strong the weakest and makes the poorest of us able to do much for His merciful purposes." Whatever one's approach to matters "religious," this is the statement of one who credits a higher source for her very creditable actions.

The story really asks, or tries to pinpoint: what is it that made this 15-year-old behave with such enormous courage? The wonderful lesson of the story is not that we ourselves should emulate such behavior—since many of us simply could not do so—but to reveal the stunning beauty of a person who was inspired and driven to do so.

EYES ON...THE CHARACTER

Robert San Souci tells us about Kate Shelley by talking about all of the things she does. Then he shows us Kate Shelley as she decides it is her mission to "go help the men."

Through his vivid description of the storm and her passage over the Des Moines River Bridge, her courage emerges clearly. Only twice does he use a family member, her sister Mayme, to tell us about Kate, and then he is quoting Mayme's words at a later date. Not until the falling action and the resolution, after the storybook story has ended, do we learn about the response of the world to her heroism. That part of the tale is more formal, almost a summary, of what occurred after Wednesday, July 6, 1881, till her death. In his reconstruction of the events of that day, Robert San Souci allows Kate Shelley to take form just by herself.

Blueprint for Reading

INTO . . . *Kate Shelley*

Kate Shelley: Bound for Legend is about a girl who actually lived from 1866 to 1912 on an Iowa farm. As a child, she had heavy responsibilities. Farm families worked very hard and had little money. When Kate was nine, her father was killed in a railroad accident. Shortly afterwards, her oldest brother, Michael, drowned in the Des Moines River. (In the story, he is called James.)

Kate's mother was "broken in health and spirit." Kate's responsibilities at home grew and she could not go to school. *Kate Shelley* shows how this young girl, only fifteen years old, behaved with extraordinary courage in a great crisis. Why are such stories retold again and again?

EYES ON . . . *the Character*

Characters are the people in a story. The word *character* is usually used for the people in fictional stories, but it may also be used for a nonfiction account such as *Kate Shelley*.

In a short piece like a short story, we learn mostly about the main character. The author describes what the character does, says, and thinks. The author also teaches us about this person from the way other people in the story—the secondary characters—respond to the main character. Describing a character in these and other ways is called **characterization.**

The word *character* has other uses that are important to understand. Sometimes we ask about a person's *character,* meaning how that person usually behaves and thinks. Or we may state, "Kate Shelley is a person of strong character." What do we mean when we use the word this way?

44 ~ Unit I

- A railroad bridge crosses Honey Creek not far from Kate Shelley's farmhouse in Iowa.
- The trains that roar past bring a touch of excitement to 15-year-old Kate.

KATE SHELLEY: BOUND FOR LEGEND

Robert D. San Souci

A railroad bridge crossed Honey ❶ Creek not far from Kate Shelley's little Iowa farmhouse. Every day trains sped back and forth over the trestle,[1] heading east toward Chicago or west toward the long Des Moines River Bridge on the way to Salt Lake City. As they roared past, the trains ❷ brought a touch of excitement to fifteen-year-old Kate's life.

---

1. A *trestle* (TRESS uhl) is a framework of wood or steel beams that resembles a large sawhorse. This framework can support a *trestle bridge* on which railway tracks may be laid. In the story, the word trestle is used to mean trestle bridge.

Kate Shelley ~ 45

LITERARY COMPONENTS

▶ **1. Gradual Exposition:** The basic facts that we need, the introduction to the character, her family, the family history, and the setting, takes place over the first three paragraphs.

▶ **2. Characterization; Possible Character Motivation:** "...the trains brought a touch of excitement to fifteen-year-old Kate's life."

GUIDING THE READING

LITERAL
Q: Where does Kate Shelley live?
A: The Shelleys live on a farmhouse in Iowa.

ANALYTICAL
Q: Why do you think the trains bring a touch of excitement to Kate's life?
A: Student answers will vary. It is likely that Kate never goes anywhere. The trains mean travel to faraway places. Many people react that way to the whistle and the chug-a-chug-chug of trains. Trains make us feel wistful—full of longing to visit places we have never been.

SUMMING UP THE PLOT

- Kate's father had died three years earlier. He had worked for Chicago & North Western Railway.
- It's 1881, and the farm now supports the family.
- Because of her mother's poor health, Kate has taken charge of the family.
- She plows, plants, and with her sister Mayme, gathers firewood and tends the vegetable garden.
- She has taught herself to shoot to keep hawks away from the chickens.
- Kate sees her younger siblings—Margaret, Mayme, and John—off to school in the mornings and tucks them into bed at night.
- She keeps them away from the banks of Honey Creek, because they cannot swim.
- Kate's oldest brother, James, drowned shortly after Mr. Shelley's death.

LITERARY COMPONENTS

▶ **3. Characterization; Possible Character Motivation:** Kate's father worked as a section foreman on the Chicago & North Western Railway before his death.

▶ **4. Setting:** It is 1881. The farm is "a patch of pasture and timber set amid rugged hills in the heart of Iowa."

▶ **5. Characterization; Secondary Characters:** Kate takes care of her brother and sisters.

▶ **6. Characterization; Family History; Vivid Image:** Kate's brother drowned not long after her father died. She discovered his riderless horse.

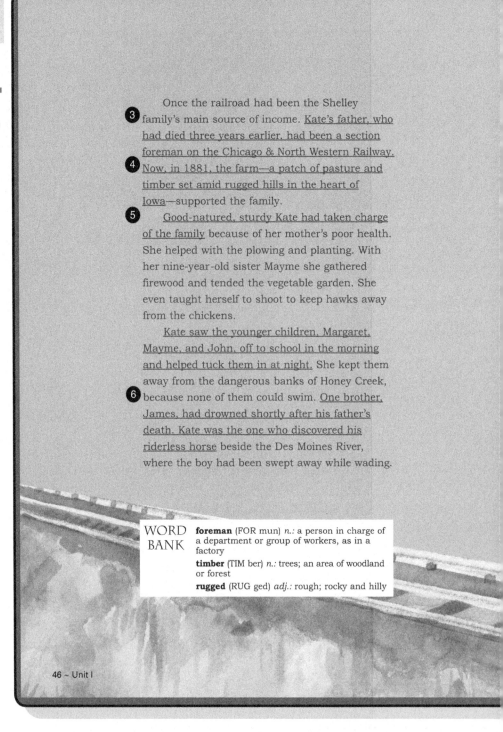

③ Once the railroad had been the Shelley family's main source of income. Kate's father, who had died three years earlier, had been a section foreman on the Chicago & North Western Railway. **④** Now, in 1881, the farm—a patch of pasture and timber set amid rugged hills in the heart of Iowa—supported the family.

⑤ Good-natured, sturdy Kate had taken charge of the family because of her mother's poor health. She helped with the plowing and planting. With her nine-year-old sister Mayme she gathered firewood and tended the vegetable garden. She even taught herself to shoot to keep hawks away from the chickens.

Kate saw the younger children, Margaret, Mayme, and John, off to school in the morning and helped tuck them in at night. She kept them away from the dangerous banks of Honey Creek, **⑥** because none of them could swim. One brother, James, had drowned shortly after his father's death. Kate was the one who discovered his riderless horse beside the Des Moines River, where the boy had been swept away while wading.

WORD BANK

foreman (FOR mun) *n.:* a person in charge of a department or group of workers, as in a factory

timber (TIM ber) *n.:* trees; an area of woodland or forest

rugged (RUG ged) *adj.:* rough; rocky and hilly

46 ~ Unit I

GUIDING THE READING

LITERAL

Q: How was the family supported before Mr. Shelley died?
A: Kate's father worked as a section foreman on the Chicago & North Western Railway.

Q: What chores does Kate take care of?
A: She helps with the plowing and planting, and with her sister, Mayme, she gathers firewood and tends the vegetable garden.

Q: How does Kate take care of her brother and sisters?
A: She sees them off to school in the morning, tucks them into bed at night, and keeps them away from the banks of Honey Creek.

Q: What are the children's names?
A: Their names are Margaret, Mayme, and John.

Q: What happened to her brother, James?
A: He had drowned in Honey Creek.

ANALYTICAL

Q: Is there a special reason why Kate helps out as much as she does?
A: Not only has her father died, but also, her mother is sick. She is obviously the oldest of the children, and she hardly sounds like someone who won't do her share.

- Between chores, Kate reads every book she can. She does not go to school.
- The railroad is her real love.

- When she goes on errands to the village of Moingona, she stops at the train station, and sometimes hears the urgent tapping of the telegraph.

- Kate's sister Mayme later recalls that Kate was "absolutely without fear."
- On July 6, 1881, Kate and her mother are taking laundry off the clothesline.

In moments between chores Kate read every book she could lay her hands on, to make up for her lack of schooling. She loved to ride bareback through the forests in autumn or row a skiff along the broad, smooth surface of the river in high summer.

But the railroad was her real love. When errands took her to the little coal mining village of Moingona, a mile away, she would stop by the train station. She would linger in the waiting room with its potbellied stove and high-backed bench. Sometimes she would hear urgent tapping from behind the ticket window as news came over the telegraph wire, or as the stationmaster sent word to distant stations to alert approaching trains of hazards.

Adventure appealed to Kate. "She was absolutely without fear," her sister Mayme would recall later in life. But her adventures were confined to farm and family for the first fifteen years of her life—until one July day in 1881.

When the eastbound freight from Moingona neared the Shelley farm on the afternoon of Wednesday, July 6, 1881, Kate and her mother were taking the wash off the clothesline. It had

| WORD BANK | **linger** (LING er) *v.:* stay longer than usual |
| | **hazards** (HAZZ erds) *n.:* dangers |

Kate Shelley ~ 47

LITERARY COMPONENTS

▶ **7. Characterization:** Kate is not only hardworking, she is driven to learn. She does not go to school.

▶ **8. Characterization; Foreshadowing:** It seems likely that something is going to happen in this story that has to do with trains!

▶ **9. Vivid Imagery; Onomatopoeia:** We can see the train station; we can hear the sounds.

▶ **10. Foreshadowing:** The stationmaster uses the telegraph wire "to alert approaching trains of hazards."

▶ **11. Indirect Characterization; Rising Action:** The author uses a quotation from Mayme to tell us about Kate. Also, telling us she is fearless suggests that something is up!

▶ **12. Creating Suspense; Setting as Time:** Kate's adventures were confined to the farm until July 1881.

GUIDING THE READING

LITERAL

Q: What did Kate do between chores?
A: She read every book she could get her hands on.

Q: What did Kate do in autumn?
A: She loved to ride a horse bareback through the forests.

Q: What did Kate's sister Mayme say about her, later in life?
A: Mayme said that Kate was "absolutely without fear."

ANALYTICAL

Q: How do we know that Kate doesn't go to school?
A: The first clue is that she sees the other children off to school, with no mention of her going herself. Then we are told that she reads a lot, to make up for her lack of schooling.

Q: What was the major industry of the village of Moingona?
A: The author calls it "the little coal mining village of Moingona."

Q: Why do you think Kate liked to stop at the train station, when she was on an errand in Moingona?
A: Answers will vary. Kate was never anywhere but at home. She didn't even go to school. The train station is a new environment. Also, it would be a good resting place between walking a mile there and walking a mile home. She might see and talk to other people besides those in her family. She may have liked the "atmosphere." Also, her father had worked for the trains and this may have allowed her to feel closer to him.

SUMMING UP THE PLOT

- It has been raining for a week, and black clouds are heaping up on the horizon.
- Kate stops to watch Engine 230, a pusher train, help a freight train climb the grade up to Honey Creek Bridge.
- Kate knows the schedules by heart, and can recognize each of the pushers by its whistle.
- The pusher trains are locomotives that sit on sidetracks until they are needed to push or pull heavy trains up the steep slope.
- As Kate and her mother take the laundry in, the sky becomes dark "as if a black curtain" has been "flung across the sun."

LITERARY COMPONENTS

▶ **13. Foreshadowing; Rising Action; External Conflict Between Man and Nature:** The weather threatens. We know something is going to happen. Terrible weather and its destructive power are the essence of Kate's conflict. She will struggle with a storm and the repercussions of raging wind and water.

▶ **14. Characterization; Rising Action; Suspense:** Kate has the information to recognize a crisis.

▶ **15. Special Knowledge:** This is information about the trains of that period, which the reader needs in order to understand the disaster that ensues.

▶ **16. Simile; Foreshadowing; Vivid Imagery:** As Kate and her mom take the laundry inside, the sky becomes dark, "as if a black curtain had been flung across the sun."

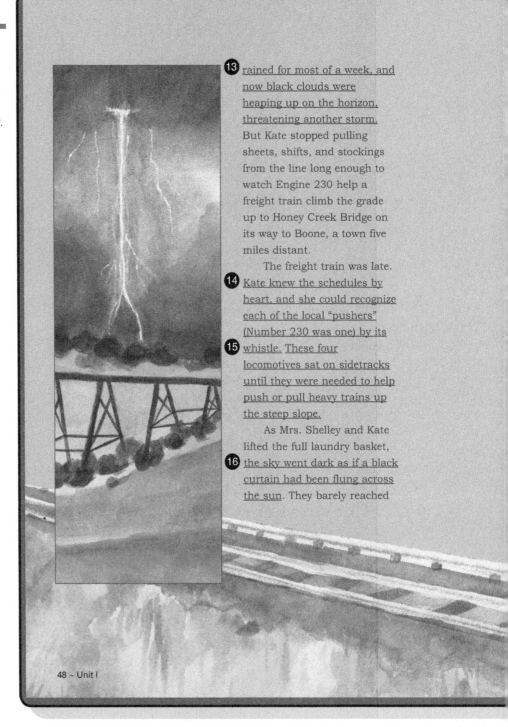

13 rained for most of a week, and now black clouds were heaping up on the horizon, threatening another storm. But Kate stopped pulling sheets, shifts, and stockings from the line long enough to watch Engine 230 help a freight train climb the grade up to Honey Creek Bridge on its way to Boone, a town five miles distant.

The freight train was late. **14** Kate knew the schedules by heart, and she could recognize each of the local "pushers" (Number 230 was one) by its **15** whistle. These four locomotives sat on sidetracks until they were needed to help push or pull heavy trains up the steep slope.

As Mrs. Shelley and Kate lifted the full laundry basket, **16** the sky went dark as if a black curtain had been flung across the sun. They barely reached

48 ~ Unit I

GUIDING THE READING

LITERAL
Q: Kate stops taking the laundry down from the line, in order to watch what?
A: She stops to watch Engine 230, a pusher locomotive, help a freight train climb the grade up to Honey Creek Bridge.

ANALYTICAL
Q: What are "pushers"?
A: Pushers are (or were) locomotives that sat on sidetracks, until they were needed to help push or pull heavy trains up a steep slope.

Q: At this place in the story, how does the description of the weather make it seem as though something bad is going to happen?
A: The clouds are described as black, "heaping up on the horizon, threatening another storm." Also, when Mrs. Shelley and Kate are about to go inside with the clean laundry, the sky becomes "dark as if a black curtain had been flung across the sun."

- The deadly storm breaks.
- Thunder rattles the windows and fierce wind hurls sheets of rain against the house.
- The waters of Honey Creek rise higher than Kate has ever seen them before.

- Kate fears for the safety of the animals in the barn and moves them to higher ground in an oat field.
- Drenched and chilled, she runs back into the house.

the back door of their two-story clapboard[2] house before the first heavy raindrops began to fall.

Soon the deadly storm broke. "You can only imagine what a fearful thing it is to see the heavens grow black and blacker until the light of day is all shut out," Kate later said, "to see the clouds torn into fragments by the fierce lightnings, and the torrents fall and swallow up the earth." **(17)**

Thunder rattled loose glass in the window frame, while fierce wind hurled sheets of rain against the house. Kate watched anxiously as Honey Creek's waters rose higher than she had ever seen them. **(18)** **(19)**

She soon began to fear for the safety of the animals in the barn on the slope below the house. Putting on an old coat and hat, she hurried to the barn through the ankle-deep water gushing down the hillside. **(20)**

The water was just as deep inside. The plow horses, cattle, and hogs were splashing nervously in their stalls and pens. Kate led each of them to higher ground in an oat field, then turned them loose.

By the time she returned to the barn for a last look around, the water had grown knee-deep. Hearing a terrified squealing, Kate discovered several piglets that had climbed onto an island of hay. She carried them to the safety of the oat field and tucked them under the sow. Then, drenched and chilled, she ran back to the house.

---

2. A *clapboard* is a long, thin board, thicker along one edge than another. A *clapboard house*, often called "a frame house," is covered with these overlapping boards.

WORD BANK **fragments** (FRAG ments) *n.*: bits and pieces of something

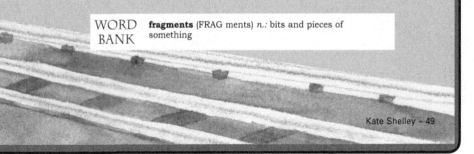

Kate Shelley ~ 49

LITERARY COMPONENTS

▶ **17. Dialogue:** In all likelihood, Kate's words were recorded by a reporter or someone else who earlier wrote about Kate Shelley. It is impossible to know if the words are Kate's specific language, but the description is vivid and poetic.

▶ **18. Rising Action; Vivid Imagery; Onomatopoeia:** Thunder *rattles* loose glass; a fierce wind hurls sheets of rain against the house.

▶ **19. Suspense:** The water in Honey Creek is higher than Kate has ever seen it previously.

▶ **20. Rising Action; Characterization:** Kate goes out to rescue the animals.

GUIDING THE READING

LITERAL

Q: What is different about Honey Creek's waters on this night?
A: Kate has never seen them rise so high.

Q: What does Kate do for the animals?
A: She takes them out of the barn and turns them loose in an oat field, which is on higher ground. She also finds squealing piglets, and takes them to the mother pig in the oat field.

ANALYTICAL

Q: Why does Kate take the animals out of the barn and turn them loose in a field?
A: The barn is located on lower land than the house. We know this from Kate's hurrying "down the hillside" to get to the barn. The water is rising in the barn. Kate believes that if she takes the animals to higher ground, they will be safer because there will be less flooding.

SUMMING UP THE PLOT

- Kate hears the noise of trees being uprooted by the gale, and feeds the children and puts them to bed.
- Even small trees are piling up against the straining supports of the trestle bridge.
- Kate begins to worry about the midnight express, and her mother says that "Surely no trains will be dispatched in this storm."

- It is past eleven o'clock when Kate hears the rumble of a pusher engine climbing the grade to Honey Creek Bridge.
- She hears a dreadful crash, and the awful hiss of steam as hot metal hits cold water.

- Kate and her mother stare at each other in horror.
- Kate says she must go to help the men. "If it were Father down there, we'd expect someone to help him."

LITERARY COMPONENTS

▶ **21. Rising Action:** With every lull in the downpour, Kate sees fences, walls, and trees pile up against the straining supports of the trestle.

▶ **22. Characterization of Mother:** The mother is largely absent from this story, presumably to simplify the tale—or because not so much is known about her. In any case, here she tries to soothe her daughter.

▶ **23. Rising Action; Suspense; Onomatopoeia:** This moment is a situational turning point that ups the ante and forces Kate to act. Honey Creek Bridge goes down. There is the awful *hiss* of steam, as the locomotive metal hits the water.

▶ **24. Theme; Motivation:** Kate makes the decision that will turn her into a national heroine. Kate remembers that if it were her father, they would expect him to be helped.

As she dried off by the kitchen stove, Kate heard the frightening noise of trees being uprooted by the gale. The younger children were fed and put to bed, but the effort

21 didn't take Kate's mind off raging Honey Creek. With every lull in the downpour, Kate saw picket fences, parts of walls, even small trees pile up against the straining supports of the trestle over the brimming stream.

As Kate noted the passing hours, she began to worry

22 about the midnight express. "Surely no trains will be dispatched in this storm," Margaret Shelley said to soothe her daughter.

It was well past eleven o'clock when Kate clearly heard the rumble of a pusher engine climbing the grade to Honey

23 Creek Bridge. She heard its bell clang twice. Then there was a dreadful crash, followed by an awful hiss of steam as hot metal hit cold water.

"Oh, Mother!" cried Kate, clutching Margaret's hand. "It's Number Eleven. They've gone down Honey Creek Bridge!"

For a moment the two stared at each other in horror, while Mayme, awakened by the sound, huddled in the kitchen door. Then Kate reached for her damp coat and

24 soggy straw hat hanging beside the stove. "I must go to help the men," Kate said.

Mrs. Shelley begged her not to go, but Kate insisted. "If that were Father down there," she said, "we'd expect

WORD BANK   **lull** *n.:* a temporary calm or quiet

50 ~ Unit I

GUIDING THE READING

LITERAL

Q: What does Kate see with every lull in the downpour?
A: She sees picket fences, parts of walls, even small trees pile up against the supports of the trestle.

Q: What does Kate begin to worry about as the hours pass?
A: She is worried about the safety of the midnight express.

Q: What is Kate's mother's first name?
A: It is Margaret. We read, "'Oh, Mother!' cried Kate, clutching Margaret's hand."

Q: Kate wants to help the men from Number Eleven, which has crashed. But what is an even graver danger?
A: The graver danger is the midnight express, bound for Chicago with hundreds of passengers, and headed for the collapsed Honey Creek Bridge.

ANALYTICAL

Q: Why is a violent storm so scary?
A: Answers will vary. Students may mention the noise of the wind, rain, and thunder; the lightning;

the darkness; the unpredictability of what is going to happen; seeing buildings, trees, and fences vulnerable to destruction.

Q: What can we tell about Mrs. Shelley when she talks to Kate, here?
A: Answers will vary. But she is loving, and trying to reassure her daughter. Because the story focuses on Kate, it probably diminishes Mrs. Shelley's active role in family life.

Q: What causes the awful hiss, when Honey Creek Bridge goes down?
A: The hiss is caused by the hot metal of the

locomotive—from the running of its engine—hitting the cold water. Students may have heard the same sound, when they have put a hot pot in water.

Q: Why do you think it is so hard for Kate's mother, to let Kate go?
A: Mrs. Shelley has lost a husband and a son. She surely does not want to lose her daughter. She may also feel bad that she is not in the condition to make the trek herself, and that it should be her job as the adult, not her daughter's.

- Kate is concerned about the greater danger of the midnight express, carrying hundreds of passengers to Chicago, and headed for the ruined Honey Creek Bridge.

- She tells her mother that she will go to Moingona Station to warn the stationmaster, so he can telegraph down the line.

- Her mother worries that she will be lost or hurt.

- Kate says she could never forgive herself if she didn't go.

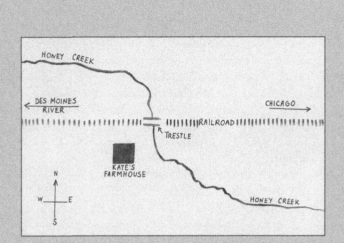

someone to help him." Then, mindful of a grave danger, she added, "And I must stop the midnight train from the west."

Hundreds of passengers bound for Chicago would be aboard the express train headed for the ruined Honey Creek Bridge. Kate told her mother that she would go to Moingona Station and have the stationmaster telegraph a warning down the line. If she couldn't reach the station in time, she would flag down the train herself.

Quickly she took her father's old railroad lantern and filled it with oil. There was no wick, so Kate grabbed an old flannel skirt and tore off a strip. In a moment she had lit the lamp.

"Kate, if you go out there, you'll be lost or hurt," her mother said in a last effort to make her stay.

"I could never forgive myself if I didn't," she replied.

Her mother sighed, "Go, then, in the name of G-d, and do what you can."

LITERARY COMPONENTS

▶ **25. Rising Action:** Hundreds of passengers are aboard the midnight train to Chicago. It is headed for the ruined Honey Creek Bridge.

▶ **26. Characterization of Mother:** Mrs. Shelley does not want her to go. She has already lost a husband and a son!

▶ **27. Characterization; Theme:** Kate has the character of a person who cannot just stand by while others are in jeopardy, even if it means she will endanger herself.

GUIDING THE READING

LITERAL
Q: When her mother asks her one last time to stay, what is Kate's response?
A: She says that she could never forgive herself if she didn't go.

ANALYTICAL
Q: What does Kate hope to do with her father's lantern?
A: She thinks that if she cannot reach the stationmaster in time, she can flag down the train herself with the lantern.

Q: Why does Kate go?
A: Certainly answers will vary. Her motivation comes from her caring and her taking personal responsibility, instead of waiting for someone else to come along and fix things. It surely seems to be more than identifying the men on the pusher engine with her father.

SUMMING UP THE PLOT

- Kate's mother runs after her, but slips in the water streaming down the hillside. Kate helps her to her feet and continues on her way.
- Kate comes to the bluff above Honey Creek. The bridge is no longer there.
- Amid broken timbers and pilings, a small rounded section of the steam engine juts out of the churning water.
- Kate waves her lantern from the cliff.

- Two men shout up to her.
- She can barely see them as they cling to branches above the raging water.

- The storm is so fierce that Kate cannot hear what the men in the water are shouting.
- She realizes that she can do nothing by herself for the men, and time is running out for the midnight express.

LITERARY COMPONENTS

▶ **28. Rising Action:** Kate gets to the bluff above Honey Creek and the bridge is gone.

▶ **29. Rising Action:** Kate moves along the cliff and waves her lantern. Two men shout up to her.

▶ **30. Rising Action; Suspense:** Kate realizes she cannot help the men by herself, and time is running out for the midnight express.

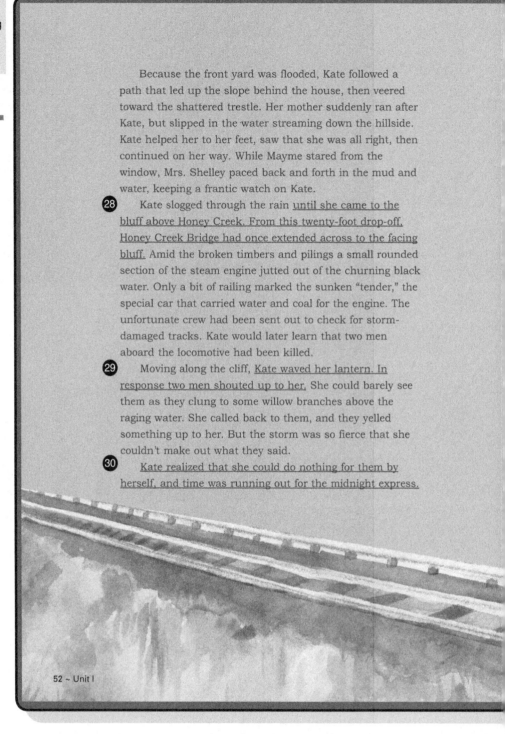

Because the front yard was flooded, Kate followed a path that led up the slope behind the house, then veered toward the shattered trestle. Her mother suddenly ran after Kate, but slipped in the water streaming down the hillside. Kate helped her to her feet, saw that she was all right, then continued on her way. While Mayme stared from the window, Mrs. Shelley paced back and forth in the mud and water, keeping a frantic watch on Kate.

28 Kate slogged through the rain until she came to the bluff above Honey Creek. From this twenty-foot drop-off, Honey Creek Bridge had once extended across to the facing bluff. Amid the broken timbers and pilings a small rounded section of the steam engine jutted out of the churning black water. Only a bit of railing marked the sunken "tender," the special car that carried water and coal for the engine. The unfortunate crew had been sent out to check for storm-damaged tracks. Kate would later learn that two men aboard the locomotive had been killed.

29 Moving along the cliff, Kate waved her lantern. In response two men shouted up to her. She could barely see them as they clung to some willow branches above the raging water. She called back to them, and they yelled something up to her. But the storm was so fierce that she couldn't make out what they said.

30 Kate realized that she could do nothing for them by herself, and time was running out for the midnight express.

52 ~ Unit I

GUIDING THE READING

LITERAL

Q: After Kate helps her up and continues on her way, what does Mrs. Shelley do? Where is Mayme?

A: Mrs. Shelley paces back and forth in the mud and water, "keeping a frantic watch" on Kate. Mayme stares from the window.

Q: What does Kate see when she comes to the bluff above Honey creek?

A: She sees that the bridge is gone.

Q: What had the crew of the steam engine been sent out to do?

A: They were sent out to check for storm-damaged tracks.

Q: What happened when Kate waved her lantern as she moved along the cliff?

A: Two men in the water shouted up to her.

Q: Why can't Kate hear what the men in the river are shouting?

A: She can't hear them because the storm is so fierce.

- Kate turns around and heads for the Des Moines River Bridge; Moingona Station is on the other side of the river, going in the opposite direction.

- The lightning is frightening, but it lights up the bridge.
- The approach to the bridge is steep. As she nears it, her lantern is extinguished by the wind.

LITERARY COMPONENTS

▶ **31. Rising Action:** Kate struggles against the rain and the bushes and brambles that snag her clothes.

She turned and headed for the Des Moines River Bridge. Moingona Station and its telegraph were on the other side. <u>Kate struggled on against the pelting rain as bushes and brambles snagged her clothes.</u> The lightning seemed a hundred times more frightening in the open, but it lit the long bridge that was her goal.

Inch by inch, Kate fought her way up the steep approach to the bridge. Though the span was normally a full fifty feet above the water, the angry river seemed only a short distance below her. Before she reached the bridge, the wind extinguished her feeble lamp, and she had no way to relight it.

Fearfully she peered into the dark, afraid that the midnight express might be speeding across the bridge. But

31

> WORD BANK **extinguished** (ex TING wishd) *v.*: put out (a light or a fire)

Kate Shelley ~ 53

GUIDING THE READING

LITERAL

Q: What does Kate have to cross to get to the Moingona Station?
A: She has to get across the Des Moines River Bridge.

Q: How does her lantern light become extinguished?
A: The wind blows it out.

ANALYTICAL

Q: What is Kate afraid of when her lantern goes out?
A: She is afraid that the midnight express will be coming down the track and they won't see her on the bridge. There is no place on the bridge for her to move over to the side, out of the path of the train, as there would be with ordinary train tracks.

SUMMING UP THE PLOT

- Kate is afraid that the midnight express may be coming down the track, but she hears no whistle and sees no headlamp.

- The bridge is studded with twisted spikes and nails.

- Kate remarks later that a misstep while crossing the bridge would have sent her down "into the flood that was boiling below."

- Kate begins to cross the bridge on her hands and knees.

- Shivering from wet and cold, Kate creeps along the bridge.

- Her clothing is repeatedly caught on a nail or spike or splinter.

- Her hands are cut and bleeding.

- Several times she nearly loses her hold on the ties, which are slick with rain water.

- She sees a great tree being swept along by the flood.

LITERARY COMPONENTS

▶ **32. Vivid Language; Onomatopoeia:** "But no whistle *knifed* through the *howling* wind; no engine's headlamp *hurtled* toward her."

▶ **33. Alliteration and Consonance:** The author's use of words that repeat the **s, t,** and **p** sounds vividly evoke the difficulty of the Des Moines River Bridge: *its splintery ties were studded with twisted spikes.*

▶ **34. Characterization; Rising Action:** We see how Kate is tested and what she endures—torn clothing, torn hands, rain-slicked ties.

▶ **35. Personification:** The river is described as *hungry.*

32 no whistle knifed through the howling wind; no engine's headlamp hurtled toward her.

Nearly seven hundred feet long, the Des Moines River Bridge was a ladder of cross ties, each nearly two feet apart. **33** Though Kate had crossed the bridge in good weather, its splintery ties were studded with twisted spikes and nails to discourage such foot traffic.

"Those who cross a railroad bridge on a swiftly moving train can form no conception of the sensation a traveler experiences who attempts to cross on foot," Kate later said. "A misstep would send me down below the ties into the flood that was boiling below. I got down on my hands and knees, carrying yet my useless lantern and guiding myself by the stretch of rail."

Shivering from the wet and cold, Kate crept along, avoiding the worst buffeting of the wind. She would reach her fingers out to locate the next tie, then cross to it with **34** the help of the iron track. Again and again, her skirt or coat sleeve caught on a nail or spike or splinter. Her hands and knees were cut and bleeding. Several times she nearly lost **35** her hold on the rain-slick ties. The hungry river was terrifying to Kate, who was near the spot where her brother James had drowned.

"Halfway over, a piercing flash of lightning showed me the angry flood more closely than ever," Kate would remember, "and swept along upon it a great tree—the earth still hanging to its roots—was racing for the bridge, and, it

> **WORD BANK** **buffeting** (BUFF ih ting) *n.:* repeated hitting and pushing

54 ~ Unit I

GUIDING THE READING

LITERAL

Q: How long is the Des Moines River Bridge?
A: The bridge is 700 feet long.

Q: How does Kate move across the bridge?
A: She crawls on her hands and knees.

Q: What happens to Kate's hands and clothing as she crosses the bridge?
A: Her clothing and hands catch on nails, spikes, and splinters.

Q: Why is it hard for her to hold on to the ties?
A: The ties are slippery with rain.

Q: What does she see in the flash of lightning?
A: She sees the flood closer—presumably higher—than ever, and a great tree being swept along with it.

ANALYTICAL

Q: Why is it hard to cross the bridge?
A: The cross ties are nearly two feet apart, which leaves space to fall through. The ties are splintery and studded with spikes and nails.

- As the tree moves towards the bridge, Kate clasps her hands in terror and prays.
- The tree sweeps between the pilings. Its branches grab and slap Kate through the ties, and she is spattered with water and foam.
- Kate is so tired she can only think of reaching the next tie and the next.

LITERARY COMPONENTS

▶ **36. Rising Action:** Kate braces for the crash of the great tree.

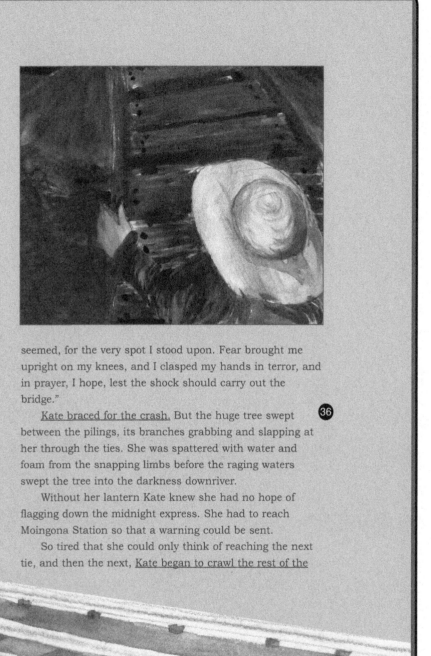

seemed, for the very spot I stood upon. Fear brought me upright on my knees, and I clasped my hands in terror, and in prayer, I hope, lest the shock should carry out the bridge."

Kate braced for the crash. But the huge tree swept **36** between the pilings, its branches grabbing and slapping at her through the ties. She was spattered with water and foam from the snapping limbs before the raging waters swept the tree into the darkness downriver.

Without her lantern Kate knew she had no hope of flagging down the midnight express. She had to reach Moingona Station so that a warning could be sent.

So tired that she could only think of reaching the next tie, and then the next, Kate began to crawl the rest of the

Kate Shelley ~ 55

GUIDING THE READING

LITERAL

Q: Why does Kate clasp her hands in terror and prayer?
A: She is afraid that the shock of the huge tree hitting the bridge will carry out the bridge.

SUMMING UP THE PLOT

- Kate takes heart when she sees the lights of the railway station in the distance.
- At last she reaches solid ground, and she runs the remaining half mile to the station.
- She bursts into the waiting room and several men are talking.
- Later she has no memory of how she told her tale, but one of the men says, "The girl is crazy."
- The station agent cries out that it's Kate Shelley, and she would know what she's talking about.
- Kate collapses.
- She learns the midnight express has not yet come through.

- Later Kate will learn that the midnight express was halted forty miles to the west, at the edge of the storm.
- Kate tells the men at the station that the crew from Number Eleven need help.

- She guides the rescue mission.
- Engine 230 is filled with volunteers carrying ropes and shovels.

LITERARY COMPONENTS

▶ **37. Rising Action:** Kate crawls the rest of the way across the bridge. She sees the lights of the railway station in the distance.

▶ **38. Climax:** This is her moment. This is what Kate has suffered so to make happen: "That's Kate Shelley and she would know if the bridge were out."

▶ **39. Falling Action:** Kate guides the rescue mission to save the men from Number Eleven.

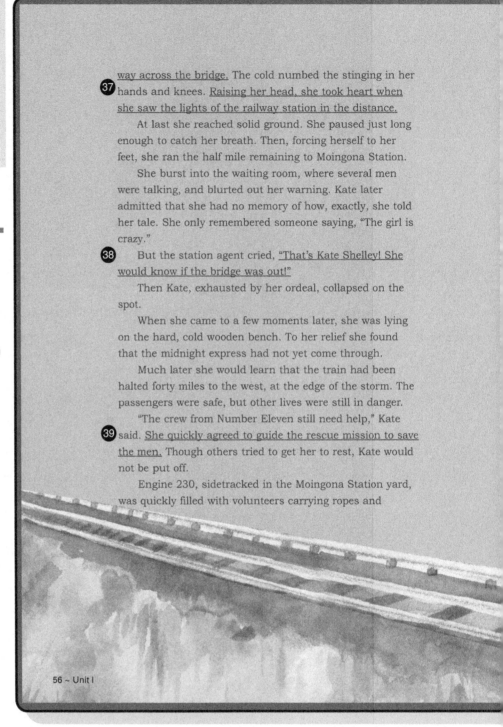

(37) way across the bridge. The cold numbed the stinging in her hands and knees. Raising her head, she took heart when she saw the lights of the railway station in the distance.

At last she reached solid ground. She paused just long enough to catch her breath. Then, forcing herself to her feet, she ran the half mile remaining to Moingona Station.

She burst into the waiting room, where several men were talking, and blurted out her warning. Kate later admitted that she had no memory of how, exactly, she told her tale. She only remembered someone saying, "The girl is crazy."

(38) But the station agent cried, "That's Kate Shelley! She would know if the bridge was out!"

Then Kate, exhausted by her ordeal, collapsed on the spot.

When she came to a few moments later, she was lying on the hard, cold wooden bench. To her relief she found that the midnight express had not yet come through.

Much later she would learn that the train had been halted forty miles to the west, at the edge of the storm. The passengers were safe, but other lives were still in danger.

"The crew from Number Eleven still need help," Kate
(39) said. She quickly agreed to guide the rescue mission to save the men. Though others tried to get her to rest, Kate would not be put off.

Engine 230, sidetracked in the Moingona Station yard, was quickly filled with volunteers carrying ropes and

56 ~ Unit I

GUIDING THE READING

LITERAL

Q: When does Kate "take heart"?
A: When she sees the lights of the railway station in the distance.

Q: How far is it from the bridge to the Moingona Station?
A: A half-mile.

Q: What does the station agent say, when Kate tells her story?
A: He cries, "That's Kate Shelley! She would know if the bridge was out!"

Q: What will Kate learn later about the midnight express?
A: She will learn that the train was halted forty miles to the west. The passengers were safe.

SUMMING UP THE PLOT

- The men from Number Eleven are still clinging to branches. There is no way for the rescuers to get down to the stream.

- Kate leads them into the hills behind her home. They do not reach the men until it is nearly dawn.

LITERARY COMPONENTS

▶ **40. Falling Action:** They cannot reach the two men from the bluff, so Kate shows them a different way.

shovels. As it headed for the fallen trestle, the engineer kept sounding the whistle to let the stranded men know that help was on the way.

Riding in the cab, Kate must have held her breath as the train eased across the Des Moines Bridge. But the structure proved solid, and the storm was quieting at last.

Exhausted yet determined, Kate guided the others to where she had seen the two crewmen in Honey Creek. The men, Number Eleven's engineer and brakeman, still clung to branches above the receding water, but there was no way for the rescuers to get down to the stream. <u>Kate had to lead</u> <u>them into the hills behind her home</u>—reversing the path she had traced earlier that evening—to an undamaged railroad bridge beyond the house.

| WORD BANK | **receding** (ree SEE ding) *adj.:* returning to a lower level; moving back and further away |

Kate Shelley ~ 57

GUIDING THE READING

LITERAL

Q: When the rescue mission cannot get down to the men, what does Kate do?
  A: She leads them to a path behind her house.

Q: What is Kate called in newspapers across the country?
  A: She is celebrated as "the Iowa heroine."

ANALYTICAL

Q: Why does the rescue mission in Engine 230 have to go by a back route to get to the men in the water?
  A: They cannot get down to the water from the cliff.

SUMMING UP THE PLOT

- Shaking with cold and weariness, Kate is brought home and put to bed.

- The story of her bravery is telegraphed all over the state and the nation. In newspapers, she is called "the Iowa heroine."

- Kate is too ill to care about the acclaim.

- Mrs. Shelley sends for the doctor.

LITERARY COMPONENTS

▶ **41. Falling Action:** Kate is brought home shaking with cold and weariness.

▶ **42. This Ought to Be the Resolution:** Kate's bravery is telegraphed across the nation and she is called "the Iowa heroine."

▶ **43. Rising Action Again:** Because this piece is biographical, it does not follow a simple exposition-rising action-climax-falling action-resolution format. Although Kate's bursting into the train station and telling her story is the climax of the action and the resolution of her struggle, now we are awaiting the outcome of her illness.

Only now could they follow the track back west to reach the stranded men. By the time they were brought to safety, the rain had almost ceased, and chilly gray dawn had begun to lighten the sky.

41 Shaking from cold and weariness, Kate was brought home. Her mother hugged her, then put her to bed, mounding the blankets above the shivering girl.

42 The story of Kate's bravery was telegraphed all over the state and across the nation. She was celebrated in countless newspapers as "the Iowa heroine."

43 But Kate was too sick to care. Over and over she repeated to Mayme, "I can still feel the cold rain on my face."

At one point her teeth began to chatter so loudly that Mrs. Shelley was forced to send for the doctor; but all he could do was whittle a peg from soft wood. He told Kate's mother, "Put this between her teeth to keep her from breaking them."

58 ~ Unit I

GUIDING THE READING

LITERAL

Q: Why doesn't Kate care about all the public attention?
A: She is too sick to care.

Q: How long does it take for Kate's strength to come back?
A: Nearly three months.

Q: What do the trains do when they pass Kate's house?
A: They blow their whistles.

SUMMING UP THE PLOT

- Strangers gather in the yard to look for "Our Kate."
- It is nearly three months before Kate regains her strength.
- During her time in bed, the trains blow their whistles when they pass the Shelley farmhouse.
- Finally, one afternoon Kate announces that she feels well enough to go outside.
- Escorted out onto the porch by her family, she hopes to catch a glimpse of the westbound train.
- The train stops in front of the house and the crew and passengers lean out to cheer her.
- Later, when she is able to go into town, the trains stop and carry her to Moingona.
- In the days that follow, many honors come to Kate.

Strangers gathered in the yard to look at "Our Kate," as they called her. Some even asked for a bit of her skirt or a lock of her hair. Mrs. Shelley shooed them away.

It was nearly three months before Kate's strength came back. During this time as she lay in bed, she was greeted by the trains that blew their whistles when they passed the Shelley farmhouse.

Finally, one afternoon she announced that she felt well enough to go outside. Escorted by her mother, sisters, and brother, Kate stepped out on the porch, hoping to catch a glimpse of the westbound train. To her surprise, the train stopped in front of the house, and crew and passengers leaned out to cheer her. Red-faced but delighted, she waved back to them.

Later, when she was able to go into town, the trains would stop and carry her to Moingona.

Many honors came to Kate in the days that followed. She received a medal from the state of Iowa, inscribed:

Presented by the State of Iowa, to Kate Shelley, with the thanks of the General Assembly in recognition of the Courage and Devotion of a child of fifteen years whom neither the fury of the elements, nor the fear of death could appall in her effort to save human life during the terrible storm and flood in the Des Moines Valley on the night of July 6th, 1881.

Kate Shelley ~ 59

LITERARY COMPONENTS

▶ **44. Resolution to the Crisis of Illness:** It is "nearly three months before Kate's strength" comes back. But it does come back.

▶ **45. Falling Action:** Kate is well enough to go outside onto the porch.

▶ **46. Theme; Conclusion:** The train stops and the crew and passengers cheer Kate.

▶ **47. Summing Up:** Here begins a summing up of the rest of Kate's life. It does not include anything deeply personal. We don't learn how Kate lived, thought, or felt.

▶ **48. Information from the Record:** The author includes the words inscribed on a medal Kate received from the state of Iowa.

GUIDING THE READING

LITERAL

Q: What happens when the train stops?
A: The crew and passengers lean out and cheer Kate.

Q: Later, what did the trains do for Kate?
A: The trains would stop in front of her house and carry her to Moingona.

ANALYTICAL

Q: Why do you think Mrs. Shelley shoos people away when they ask for a bit of Kate's skirt or a lock of her hair?
A: Mrs. Shelley disapproves of the idea that objects connected with Kate have any magical power. She is a modest, sensible person and does not want her daughter to be the object of superstition or undue hero worship.

Q: Why is Kate red-faced, when the crew and passengers cheer her?
A: She is embarrassed by all of the attention.

- Kate receives gifts and awards, and a lifetime pass on the railroad.

- In 1903 she becomes a station agent.

- She dies in 1912 at the age of 46.

- Kate was always modest when asked about her heroism.

- On the day of her funeral, a special train stops at the Shelley home to pick up her coffin and carry her to the Boone depot.

- She is buried in a cemetery on the edge of Boone.

There were other gifts and awards, but perhaps the most wonderful for Kate was a lifetime pass on the railroad. In the years that followed she attended Simpson College, and in 1903 became station agent at Moingona. She held this job until illness forced her to retire in 1911. She died the following year at the age of forty-six.

Always modest when asked about her heroic deed, Kate would say, "I believe that G-d makes strong the weakest and makes the poorest of us able to do much for His merciful purposes."

Kate's final train ride came on the day of her funeral. A special train stopped at the Shelley home to pick up her coffin and carry her to the Boone depot. Her resting place was in the peaceful cemetery on the edge of Boone.

ABOUT THE AUTHOR

Robert D. San Souci (SOO see) was born in San Francisco in 1946. He is best known for his use of folktales, stories, and legends in his stories. Although the majority of his books and stories are written for children, he has also written several books for adults. Many of his books are illustrated by his younger brother Dan, with whom he shares ideas, work, and a birthday— October 10! San Souci likes to work on several projects at once, and hopes to continue writing as long as there is "an audience...willing to listen." He lives in California.

60 ~ Unit I

GUIDING THE READING

LITERAL

Q: What does the author think is the most wonderful of the gifts Kate received?
  A: A lifetime pass on the railroad.

Q: How old was Kate when she died?
  A: Kate was 46.

FIRST IMPRESSIONS

You can begin the discussion by talking about what, if anything, would make *you* cross such a bridge under similar circumstances.

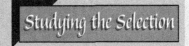

FIRST IMPRESSIONS

What would it take for you to crawl across a 700-foot bridge hanging over a raging river in the dark?

QUICK REVIEW

1. What is the name of the main character in the story?

2. How old was Kate when the incident of the train occurred?

3. At what place and time do the events occur?

4. What had happened to Mr. Shelley?

FOCUS

5. Why did this 15-year-old girl become a national heroine? Your answer should be no more than two or three sentences.

6. Who is the most important character in this story? Who do you think is the next most important character? Why?

CREATING & WRITING

7. In two or three paragraphs, describe the courageous actions of someone you know. If you don't know of any such actions, write about the courageous actions of a character in a book you have read, or a story you have heard.

8. It is 1881. You are the chairperson of an organization. Tonight you are having a dinner to honor Kate Shelley. She is attending the dinner. Write out the speech in which you introduce her to the members of the organization. Don't forget to give your organization a name!

9. With two to four other students, act out one of the scenes in the story. Remember to use dialogue. Rehearse your scene and practice, before presenting your drama to the class. Your presentation should last about five minutes.

Kate Shelley ~ 61

QUICK REVIEW

1. The main character is Kate Shelley.

2. Kate was 15 years old at the time of the incident with the train.

3. The location is the State of Iowa. The time is 1881. Students may add that the events occurred in a rural area or note that the family lived on a farm.

4. The story tells that Kate's father had died three years earlier. The curriculum indicates that he had been killed in a railroad accident.

FOCUS

5. Students answers may vary. However, the core of their answers should be that Kate behaved with extraordinary courage, whether or not her actions were needed to stop the midnight express. Moreover, she led the mission to rescue the surviving crew members of the pusher engine that had gone into the river when the Honey Creek Bridge went down.

6. This is an easy question to draw students into talking about **characters.** Kate is the most important character. Student answers may vary for the second question. Our vote goes to Mrs. Shelley.

CREATING & WRITING

7. You may want to remind students that a courageous act need not be as dramatic as crawling across a bridge at night in a storm.

8. Encourage students to be imaginative regarding such details as what their organization does, how far Kate Shelley traveled to be there, and so forth.

9. Help students form groups. They may also need advice regarding what qualifies as a scene. The possibilities are many, and include Kate and her sister Mayme gathering firewood, tending the garden, and shooting at hawks to keep them away from the chickens; Kate's putting the children to bed; Kate and her mother taking down the wash and anticipating the storm; Kate and Mrs. Shelley rushing outdoors after the train crashes; and so forth. The scene may include words and legitimate actions that are not in the story.

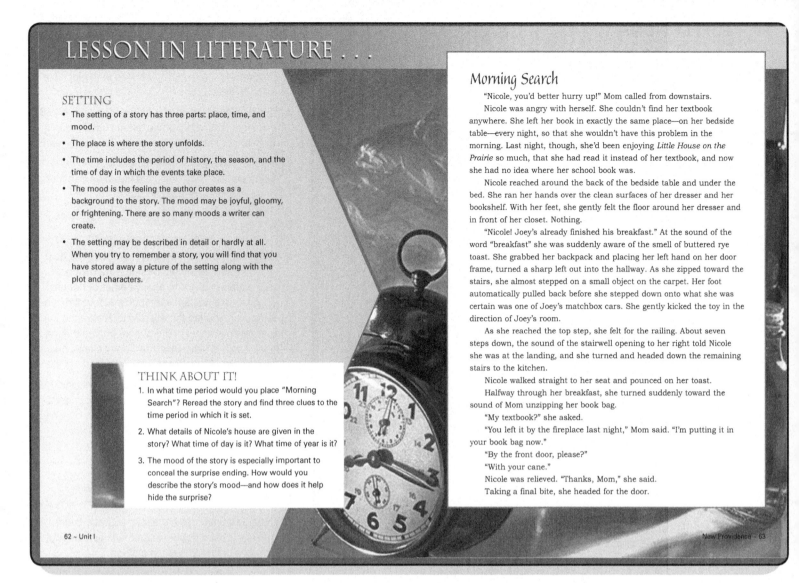

LESSON IN LITERATURE . . .

SETTING

- The setting of a story has three parts: place, time, and mood.

- The place is where the story unfolds.

- The time includes the period of history, the season, and the time of day in which the events take place.

- The mood is the feeling the author creates as a background to the story. The mood may be joyful, gloomy, or frightening. There are so many moods a writer can create.

- The setting may be described in detail or hardly at all. When you try to remember a story, you will find that you have stored away a picture of the setting along with the plot and characters.

THINK ABOUT IT!

1. In what time period would you place "Morning Search"? Reread the story and find three clues to the time period in which it is set.

2. What details of Nicole's house are given in the story? What time of day is it? What time of year is it?

3. The mood of the story is especially important to conceal the surprise ending. How would you describe the story's mood—and how does it help hide the surprise?

62 ~ Unit I

Morning Search

"Nicole, you'd better hurry up!" Mom called from downstairs.

Nicole was angry with herself. She couldn't find her textbook anywhere. She left her book in exactly the same place—on her bedside table—every night, so that she wouldn't have this problem in the morning. Last night, though, she'd been enjoying *Little House on the Prairie* so much, that she had read it instead of her textbook, and now she had no idea where her school book was.

Nicole reached around the back of the bedside table and under the bed. She ran her hands over the clean surfaces of her dresser and her bookshelf. With her feet, she gently felt the floor around her dresser and in front of her closet. Nothing.

"Nicole! Joey's already finished his breakfast." At the sound of the word "breakfast" she was suddenly aware of the smell of buttered rye toast. She grabbed her backpack and placing her left hand on her door frame, turned a sharp left out into the hallway. As she zipped toward the stairs, she almost stepped on a small object on the carpet. Her foot automatically pulled back before she stepped down onto what she was certain was one of Joey's matchbox cars. She gently kicked the toy in the direction of Joey's room.

As she reached the top step, she felt for the railing. About seven steps down, the sound of the stairwell opening to her right told Nicole she was at the landing, and she turned and headed down the remaining stairs to the kitchen.

Nicole walked straight to her seat and pounced on her toast.

Halfway through her breakfast, she turned suddenly toward the sound of Mom unzipping her book bag.

"My textbook?" she asked.

"You left it by the fireplace last night," Mom said. "I'm putting it in your book bag now."

"By the front door, please?"

"With your cane."

Nicole was relieved. "Thanks, Mom," she said.

Taking a final bite, she headed for the door.

New Providence ~ 63

SELECTION VOCABULARY

commemoration: in memory of some person or event

debris: the remains of anything destroyed; bits of old waste matter lying about

deteriorating: becoming worse in some or many ways

facade: the front of a building, especially a decorative one

graffiti: words or pictures painted illegally on public property

inscription: word or words carved on stone or other hard surface; brief dedication or note written by hand in a book, on a photo-graph, or similar item

renovated: restored to good condition as by repairing or remodeling

rural: characteristics of or having to do with the country

thriving: doing very well; prospering

vandalized: deliberately destroyed or damaged

---

commemorated façades debris renovate thriving
deteriorating graffiti inscription rural vandalized

1. New York City, like all the world's great cities, is a crazy quilt of beautiful and ugly, prosperous and failing, improving and _____ (*growing worse*).

2. On Fifth Avenue, one can spend hours window shopping, people watching, or enjoying some of the more interesting _____ (*decorative fronts*) on the older buildings.

3. Well-dressed people hurry to and fro, new cars crowd the streets; the city is _____ (*prospering*).

4. But walk a few blocks, turn a corner and, suddenly, the buildings are old and deserted, walls are covered with _____ (*illegal scrawling*), and the sidewalks are filled with dirt and _____ (*waste matter*).

5. In some spots, one can see cars that have been _____ (*damaged illegally and to no purpose*) and left to be towed to the junkyard.

6. A curious tourist might discover a nearly rubbed out _____ (*words engraved in stone*) on an old building, carved there in better times.

7. A historian might visit a crumbling monument in the area, and note what event it _____ (*honored the memory of*).

8. But, New Yorkers, being what they are, will not leave things in a rundown state forever. New York is alive. Build! Invest! _____! (*restore*) are the bywords.

9. For the person who loves all things urban, there is no place like New York. Of course, for those people who feel happier in a _____ (*country-like*) setting, New York will be too crowded, noisy, and dirty to feel like home.

Workbook p. 19   Answer Guide p. 2

Using Words in Context

The best way to learn words is to use them! Next to each word below, are two other words. Write a sentence using all three words. Your sentence should be at least six words long.

1. thriving — business — selling
   The roadside stand was doing a thriving business selling homegrown peaches.

2. commemoration — dinner — speech
   _____

3. inscription — book — grandfather
   _____

4. rural — horse — field
   _____

5. deteriorating — building — neighborhood
   _____

6. vandalized — cars — police
   _____

7. debris — streets — deserted
   _____

8. façade — ugly — attractive
   _____

9. grafitti — angry — spoil
   _____

10. renovated — modern — comfortable
    _____

Workbook p. 20   Answer Guide p. 2

LESSON IN LITERATURE

1. The story is set in modern times. Three clues are: a) Nicole is reading *Little House on the Prairie*, a popular book among today's teens which was not even published until the 20th century. b) She has a book bag; twenty or thirty years ago teens carried their books in their arms. c) Matchbox cars are modern toys.

2. Nicole has a bedside table, a bed, a dresser, a bookshelf, and a closet. The house has stairs, a railing on the stairs, a stairwell, a landing, a kitchen, and a fireplace, a front door. It is morning and, although we don't know whether it is fall, winter, or spring, it is not summer, as Nicole is going to school.

3. The mood is a cheerful, everyday mood. This helps conceal the surprise ending, as we think of Nicole as an ordinary school girl who cannot find her book. Had the mood been one of stress and anxiety, we would have immediately felt that Nicole had some problem other than a missing book.

BACKGROUND BYTES

In *New Providence: A Changing Cityscape,* we see a city thriving in 1900. We watch as it becomes less and less prosperous over the decades. In 1992, however, we see that the city has been restored to its original grandeur. As we read the selection, it is sad to see the decline of New Providence and exhilarating to see its renewal.

The cycle of cities throughout history has been much like New Providence, except of course that New Providence has not been attacked during war—the sad fate of many cities.

With their industries, traffic jams, and sleek buildings, cities are often seen as new developments in history. In fact, the origin of cities goes far back and passes through at least three distinct phases.

Cities have existed for several thousand years. The foundations of early cities have been uncovered in the great river valley civilizations of Mesopotamia, Egypt, India, and China. The ruins of the walls of many of these ancient cities can still be seen.

Early on, these were settlements that depended on agriculture and domesticated animals. As the civilizations grew in size, trade routes were developed and grew in number. The settlements became centers for merchants, craftspeople, and traders. Settlements need rules, and individuals became "public officials" in a variety of ways: through conquest, selection, or a rise to power. The difference between *town* and *country* and between *urban* and *rural* began. This process was repeated in other civilizations, such as Iranian, Roman, the Great Zimbabwe, and Mayan.

A second phase in the development of cities came much later, around the middle of the eighteenth century, with the industrial revolution in Europe. Factories needed a large labor force and urban centers grew rapidly. The increase in commercial activity created new opportunities for people in cities. Looking for employment and a better life, people moved from rural areas into cities in great numbers.

A third phase began after World War II. The largest and fastest growth in the world's urban population occurred after 1950. As the world economy became global, cities all over the world began to grow larger at a very fast pace. This growth was, and continues to be, explosive both in size and number. Most of it has been concentrated in Asia, Latin America, and Africa, although some cities in the United States—such as Phoenix and Los Angeles—have been growing equally fast. This process is called *urbanization*.

Today, the most rapid urbanization continues to take place in countries on the continents of Asia and Africa and on the North American subcontinent of Central America. Many businesses in the United States and other developed nations have moved to these countries, because there are no environmental regulations and fewer safety regulations to worry about, and they can pay their workers much less than they would in their own countries. The absence of environmental regulations—which makes production cheaper—and the fast growth of industry are the source of terrible problems of pollution.

Cities are becoming more and more important as their size and numbers grow. By the 21st century, it is estimated that half the world's population will be living in cities. Humankind needs to focus attention *now* on how to make big and growing cities better places, because these cities must provide services to millions of people who will suffer greatly without them.

No matter where people live, they need some essential things to survive: shelter (housing), food, and water. Wherever there are *lots* of people, a safe way of disposing of human waste is absolutely critical to avoid the spread of disease. If water in a city is not clean enough, the residents of the city will become ill. Life in a city also requires electricity for buildings and streets. Buildings must have running water, toilets, and heat. Garbage must be dealt with safely. A system of transportation is necessary if the city is large, so that people can get from one place to another. Citizens also need schools so that they can learn to read. Schools must teach many things, but literacy is essential to civilization. Unfortunately, where literacy is very low, infant mortality is very high.

Cities also require such institutions as libraries, hospitals, museums, parks, post offices, and government buildings. There must be stores or markets so that people can buy the food, clothing, and products that they need. A city must build roads and take care of them. A city needs a fire department and a police department.

None of these services and institutions just appear. They all need to be supported, just as the bricks or wood in our homes need strong beams to keep them up. Electricity needs electric lines, water needs plumbing, cars and buses need roads, schools need buildings, governments need elections and offices, hospitals need trained doctors and nurses and supplies, and so on. These are the city's *infrastructure.*

It is a tremendous task for a city to provide the necessary infrastructure and services to its citizens. Yet it is easier for these services to be provided to lots of people in a city than in the country, because of *population density*—in a city, people are living very close to each other. A single electric line on a single street can provide electricity to hundreds or thousands of people. But what happens when a city grows up without an infrastructure?

Today, the global population has grown so large that the cities need serious attention. Cities are now home to *half of mankind.* Cities have *always* had slums, but now the current worldwide slum population is one billion. The global slum population is expected to triple to three billion in the next fifty years. Cities are usually the hub of national production and consumption. These are the processes that generate wealth and opportunity. But cities also generate disease, crime, pollution, and poverty. More than half of the people living worldwide in slums have no access to shelter, water, or sanitation.

Between 1980 and 2000, Lagos (Nigeria), Dhaka (Bangladesh), Cairo (Egypt), Tianjin (China), and Hyderabad and Lahore (India) grew to populations of over 10 million. These are cities that are unable to provide the basic services that we associate with cities: health clinics, emergency medical service, schools for children, sewerage and sanitation services, water, gas, and electricity provision, shelter construction, building inspection, road building, and law enforcement. These are cities in which fewer than 50% of the adults can read. (The exception, here, may be China, which has had increasing literacy among women over the last several decades.)

The rise of these *mega-cities* (cities of 10 million or more people) in developing countries is a critically important, global issue. People have come together from all over the world to discuss urban problems. One solution has been for national governments to move their capitals. For example, in the African nation of Côte d'Ivoire (Ivory Coast), the government replaced Abidjan with Yamoussoukrou as the capital city. Assigning a new capital means transferring government offices, foreign embassies, and businesses to a smaller city in order to attract people away from overcrowded sites. Another such created capital city was Brasilia in Brazil.

Other healthy city strategies include

(1) Intensive recycling programs that require citizens to bag their cans, paper, plastic, and glass separately from garbage.

(2) Enabling squatters to build their own neighborhoods. The Community Contracts System developed by the National Housing Development Authority in Sri Lanka is an example. To upgrade a squatter settlement, the residents themselves were given the materials and the technical train-

ing and assistance to build footpaths, drains, wells, toilets. Slums were transformed into well-maintained communities. In many places, squatter settlements of homeless people are destroyed by the police on orders from the government, with no solution to the problem of homelessness.

(3) Public education films about public hygiene. Poor drainage, accumulation of garbage, and a lack of drinkable water were among the consequences of runaway population growth in Bamako, Mali. Informal discussion groups were held and films were shown, in a program aimed at women and adolescents. These focused on the importance of sanitation, proper waste disposal, and protection and treatment of drinking water. In addition to the public education campaign, unemployed secondary school graduates were organized in efforts to collect household garbage and to clean up sewage ditches.

These are just a few examples. But the work ahead will need to be massive in order to have an impact. Public education is the beginning.

Exercise for Students Using Table 1

Table 1: Largest cities in 1950 and 2015:
Population in millions

Column A:		Column B:	
City	**1950 Population**	**City**	**2015 Population**
Calcutta	4.4	Jakarta	21.2
Buenos Aires	5.0	Bombay	27.4
Tokyo	6.9	Mexico City	18.8
Paris	5.4	Shanghai	23.4
Moscow	5.4	Tokyo	28.7
New York	12.3	Dhaka	19.0
Essen	5.3	Karachi	20.6
London	8.7	Beijing	19.4
Chicago	4.9	Lagos	24.4
Shanghai	5.3	Sao Paulo	20.8

Look at Table 1. Column A represents the world's largest cities in 1950. Column B represents the world's largest cities in 2015. Make two tables, one for the cities in Column A and one for the cities in Column B. Your tables will be entitled The Largest Cities of the World in 1950 and The Largest Cities of the World in 2015.

Your tables should each have four columns with the headings: City, Country, Continent, and Population. (1) List the cities *in order of their population size*.

(2) Find out which country and continent each city is in and fill in the tables.

Blueprint for Reading

INTO . . . *New Providence*

This is the story of a city. It is written as though it were true. But the city of New Providence is imaginary. A group of historians and city designers created it from old designs and plans of actual cities.

This is a story of how a city changes over time. The story has no characters. There are many settings, but no action. We see the city change over time, because we are given snapshots: from 1910, 1935, 1955, 1970, 1980, and 1992.

The theme of the story can be expressed in a word: change. The detailed pictures show the changes and the text explains them. No opinion is offered as to whether the changes are good or bad. The story just presents the facts. It is left to the reader to form an opinion.

EYES   ON   . . . *Setting*

The **setting** is the physical background of a story. The setting tells the reader *when* the story takes place and *where* it takes place. Setting can also include the weather, the clothing people wear, the furniture and design of a house, the region—whether city or country—and other details that help the reader enter into the story. All the things we need when we are planning a play—props, costume, scenery, and makeup—are the setting.

New Providence: A Changing Cityscape is nearly all setting and theme. Notice that the descriptions are very clear and exact. None of the poetic language that we see in *Kate Shelley* is used to describe *New Providence*.

See if you can keep track of the changes to the cityscape as you read the selection.

64 ~ Unit I

For Teachers: The two tables are filled in for you, below.

Largest Cities of the World in 1950: Population in Millions

City	Country	Continent	Population
New York	U.S.A.	North America	12.3
London	England	Europe	8.7
Tokyo	Japan	Asia	6.9
Paris	France	Europe	5.4
Moscow	Russia	Europe/Asia	5.4
Essen	Germany	Europe	5.3
Shanghai	China	Asia	5.3
Buenos Aires	Argentina	South America	5.0
Chicago	U.S.A.	North America	4.9
Calcutta	India	Asia	4.4

Largest Cities of the World in 2015: Population in Millions

City	Country	Continent	Population
Tokyo	Japan	Asia	28.7
Bombay	India	Asia	27.4
Lagos	Nigeria	Africa	24.4
Shanghai	China	Asia	23.4
Jakarta	Indonesia	Asia	21.2
Sao Paulo	Brazil	S. America	20.8
Karachi	Pakistan	Asia	20.6
Beijing	China	Asia	19.4
Dhaka	Bangladesh	Asia	19.0
Mexico City	Mexico	N. America	18.8

In the annotations for *Samuel's Choice,* we said that the theme is usually what we react to most powerfully when we read a story. It is the source of the feelings we are left with when we are done reading. This is very clear in *New Providence: A Changing Cityscape.*

How do students feel when they read the text for each of the years? Do they feel good when the city is thriving and looks like a wonderful place to live? Do they feel bad as they watch it go downhill? How dreadful it is in 1980 when, even with the changes that have been made, the decline of this city seems inevitable. New Providence will continue to decline, until the wonderful relief offered by 1992!

Clearly, this selection is not a complex story. But it does elicit regret and a sense of loss—a yearning for times of yore when life may have been simpler. At the same time, it generates a sense of excitement about change and progress in an America that never gives up.

EYES ON...SETTING

How odd to have a story in which there is so much setting and so little metaphor! Nothing is compared with anything else. The physical features are simply recorded details. However, the theme emerges when the physical features are compared and contrasted across time.

The changes in time, and the alteration in details *over* time, bring this map of a city to life—as do the wonderful drawings. Here is literature that we see and hear: the story of a city in eight decades as told through changes in setting.

NEW PROVIDENCE
A CHANGING CITYSCAPE

CONCEIVED BY RENATA VON TSCHARNER AND RONALD LEE FLEMING ⁓ THE TOWNSCAPE INSTITUTE ⁓ ILLUSTRATIONS BY DENIS ORLOFF

New Providence ~ 65

Language Alert

The English word *city* comes from the Latin *civitas*, which meant a highly organized community such as the city-states of Ancient Greece. The selection mentions a statue of the fictional Chief Tenebo. In Latin, the word *tenebo* means I shall hold, keep, have, grasp, hold fast.

On page 68, we read that "the city has fallen on hard times." This is an idiom. Or it may be two idioms. In this context, *to fall on* means to encounter, to meet, to come together. *Hard times* are a period of difficulty or hardship, especially financial hardship. The entire expression, *to fall on hard times,* has been dated to a first use in English in the 1500s.

SUMMING UP THE PLOT

- It is 1910.
- The city is thriving and bustling with activity.
- There is a bandstand where concerts are held.
- A statue of an Indian chief is about to be unveiled.
- At the base of the fountain is an inscription: GOOD CITIZENS ARE THE RICHES OF A CITY.

LITERARY COMPONENTS

▶ **1. Exposition; Setting:** The city is New Providence and it is thriving in 1910.

▶ **2. Characterization:** There are no characters. Only the city is characterized: "New Providence is thriving. Cobblestone streets bustle with activity..."

▶ **3. Setting; Character of the City:** This is a city that has a fountain and a statue to commemorate a Native American from a local tribe.

▶ **4. Declaration; Theme:** "GOOD CITIZENS ARE THE RICHES OF A CITY." In other words, a city will be poor without good citizens.

Put the city up; tear the city down; put it up again; let us find a city.... —CARL SANDBURG

1910

❶
❷ New Providence is thriving. Cobblestone[1] streets bustle with activity—Model T Fords, streetcars, and horse-drawn carts carrying meat, milk, and ice. There is no concert in the bandstand today, but a crowd has gathered in the
❸ square in front of the Town Hall and the Tenebo County Courthouse. A fountain has been built in commemoration of Chief Tenebo, a Native American from a local tribe. The statue is about to be unveiled. Around the base of the fountain is an
❹ inscription: GOOD CITIZENS ARE THE RICHES OF A CITY.

---

1. *Cobblestones* are naturally rounded stones that were used to pave streets before asphalt came into use.

WORD BANK	**thriving** (THRY ving) *adj.:* doing very well; prospering **commemoration** (kuh MEM uh RAY shun) *n.:* in memory of some person or event **inscription** (in SKRIP shun) *n.:* a word or words carved on stone or other hard surface; a brief dedication or note written by hand in a book, on a photograph, or on a similar item

66 ~ Unit I

GUIDING THE READING

LITERAL

Q: What is the name of the city?
A: The city is called New Providence.

Q: What year is it?
A: It is 1910.

Q: In 1910, how is New Providence doing?
A: The city is thriving.

Q: After whom is the County Courthouse named?
A: Tenebo County Courthouse is named after Chief Tenebo, a Native American from a local tribe.

Q: According to the inscription on the base of the fountain, what are the riches of a city?
A: Good citizens are the riches of a city.

ANALYTICAL

Q: What sometimes happens at the bandstand, but not today?
A: On some days there are concerts.

Q: Why has a crowd gathered in front of the Town Hall?

A: The statue of Chief Tenebo is about to be unveiled.

Q: Why are good citizens the riches of a city?
A: Answers will vary. Without law-abiding, working citizens, no amount of beautiful buildings will make it a good city. It is ultimately the people who matter. Buildings come and go, but steadfast, productive citizens have real value.

SUMMING UP THE PLOT

- Women in long skirts and men in hats shop at Getz & McClure's—the largest store in town—and at the other New Providence stores; they have supper at Gilman's or the Butler House Café.

- Lush, rural hillsides surround the city and comfortable Victorian houses dot the landscape.

- The Bloom mill and worker housing are in the distance.

- A flock of birds flies peacefully overhead.

New Providence's good citizens—women in long skirts and men in hats—buy fruit **5** at the sidewalk stand in front of the grocery and most of their clothing and household items at Getz & McClure's, the largest store in town. They shop for shoes and jewelry and office supplies and have supper at Gilman's or at the Butler House Café.

The rural hillsides surrounding the city are lush, with comfortable Victorian **6** homes dotting the landscape and the Bloom mill and worker housing in the distance. The large red brick schoolhouse is attended by all school-age children in the region. A flock of birds flies peacefully overhead. **7**

New Providence is filled with a typical jumble of late-nineteenth-century architectural styles: Gothic, Classical, and Romanesque revivals, Queen Anne and Italianate Victorians. Pictured here is the Colonel Fleming House, which was built in the late eighteenth century and is the last single-family home left on the square.

WORD BANK	**rural** (RUH rul) *adj.*: characteristic of or having to do with the country (compare to *urban*: characteristic of or having to do with the city)

New Providence ~ 67

LITERARY COMPONENTS

▶ **5. Characterization of Citizens; Setting; Laying the Foundation for the Theme:** The citizens dress in the manner of the period. They are good citizens who do all of their shopping in town and eat supper at Gilman's or the Butler House Café. Many of the business establishments in the picture—which will change over time—are identified.

▶ **6. Setting; Theme:** The surrounding area is described as rural and lush, with comfortable (large; the seat of affluence) Victorian homes. A feature of the times in some regions of the country, such as Lowell, MA—worker housing for mill employees—is present.

▶ **7. Theme; Setting; Mood:** What is in the skies in 1910? A flock of birds flying *peacefully.*

ANALYTICAL

Q: What does the clothing of the men and women tell us about the times?
A: Answers will vary. But the women cover themselves—they are modest—and the men are more formally clothed.

Q: Are the surrounding hillsides like the city or like the country?
A: The surrounding hillsides are rural, which means of, relating to, associated with, or typical of the country.

Q: The hillsides are described as "lush." How does the word "lush" mirror what is happening in the town?
A: Lush means vigorously growing, producing an abundance of juicy green foliage; lush also means thriving, generous, plentiful, even prosperous. Although the land is undeveloped, which is why it is lush, it is similar to the town which is thriving as well.

Q: Have you ever heard of a factory or mill building housing for their workers?
A: Answers will vary. Ask students why this policy may have changed in the last century.

Q: What mood is conveyed about the setting when we read, "A flock of birds flies peacefully overhead"?
A: Answers will vary.

GUIDING THE READING

LITERAL

Q: What do the men and women wear in 1910 (in addition to their other clothing)?
A: The women wear long skirts; the men wear hats.

Q: Where do the citizens buy most of their clothing and household items?
A: The citizens buy clothing and household items at Getz & McClure's.

Q: What is the largest store in town?
A: The largest store in town is Getz & McClure's.

Q: What else is available at the stores in New Providence in 1910?
A: The citizens can buy shoes, jewelry, and office supplies.

Q: What can be seen in the distance?
A: The lush rural hillsides with Victorian homes; the Bloom mill and the mill worker housing.

Q: How many schools are in New Providence?
A: There is one school for all the school-age children in the region.

- It is 1935 and a mist rolls into town.
- The effects of the Great Depression can be seen—the city has fallen on hard times.

- Homeless men now huddle over makeshift fires in the courthouse square.
- Jobless men wait for free bread in lines outside the post office.

- But life goes on. People still go to concerts, drink coca cola, and buy cars.
- The Bloom mill is still in operation as are a shoe store and a jeweler's.

LITERARY COMPONENTS

▶ **8. Setting as Time; The Illustration Has Changed:** The picture doesn't look as pretty.

▶ **9. Characterization of the City; Mood; Theme:** A mist may feel cold, and its sensation unpleasant. As a metaphor, a mist may hide objects or concepts. A mist dims one's perceptions or understanding. What has happened to the city? How did it happen?

▶ **10. Historical Reference:** The Great Depression began with the crash of the New York Stock Market in 1929 and lasted until 1939. It was the longest and most severe economic depression of the Western world.

▶ **11. Idiom:** In this context, *to fall on* means to encounter, to meet, to come together. *Hard times* are a period of difficulty or hardship, especially financial hardship.

▶ **12. Mood; Theme:** Twenty-five years have passed, and the bandstand is gone. This is not a time when people gather together to listen to music. There are now people in the city who have no homes, who need fires from trash cans to get warm. The city is cold both literally and metaphorically.

▶ **13. Historical Reference:** *WPA* stands for Works Progress Administration, a program of Franklin Roosevelt's New Deal. The program was created in 1935. Its goal was to stimulate the economy during the Great Depression.

▶ **14. Setting; Characterization of the City:** Recall the inscription on the fountain that the riches of a city are its citizens. Now, many of the citizens have no jobs or money, and the city has lost much of its riches.

▶ **15. Characterization of the City and Its People:** Life goes on. What are the indications? A concert at the Strand Theater. An advertisement for Coca Cola—so someone must have the money to buy it.

▶ **16. Characterization of the City; Setting:** Now traffic lights tell cars when to go and when to stop.

▶ **17. Setting:** What has changed? What remains the same? Again, look at the pictures with your students.

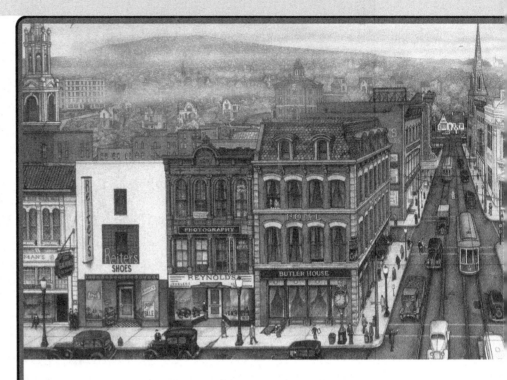

8

9 10
11 12 As a mist rolls into New Providence, effects of the Great Depression are visible; the city has fallen on hard times. Gone is the bandstand from the courthouse square, where homeless men now huddle over trash can fires for
13 warmth. A WPA sign publicizes the Works Progress Administration, a jobs program funded by the government. A line of jobless men waits for free bread outside the
14 post office, and hoboes[2] are taking a free ride out of the city on trains. Many buildings are in need of repair.
15 But even in times such as these, life goes on. There is a concert playing at the Strand Theater. A huge Coca-Cola advertisement goes up on the side of a building.
16 17 A streetlight now controls automobile traffic. The Bloom mill—expanded before the stock market crash—is still in operation, the grocery has become a shoe store, and the dry goods store, a jeweler's. The Colonel Fleming House now accommodates

---

2. *Hobo* is an old-fashioned word for a tramp or a jobless person who wanders from place to place.

68 ~ Unit I

GUIDING THE READING

LITERAL

Q: In 1935, the effects of what are visible?
A: The effects of the Great Depression are visible.

Q: According to the text, what has happened to the city financially?
A: The city has fallen on hard times.

Q: What are men waiting for outside the post office?

A: They are waiting for the distribution of free bread.

Q: How do we know that life goes on?
A: There is a concert at the Strand and a huge Coca Cola sign has been painted on a building.

ANALYTICAL

Q: What does it mean to fall on hard times?
A: To fall on hard times means to enter a period of financial hardship.

Q: Why do you think the city has not repaired its buildings?

A: Cities rely on taxes for public works. If many of its residents are not employed, they will not pay taxes. The city will not have the money to hire people and to buy materials to make repairs.

Q: Why do a concert and a Coca Cola sign show that life goes on?
A: Answers will vary, but listening to music shows that people are still interested in—and some are still able to pay for—the pleasure of hearing it. The sign shows that in spite of the Depression there are still potential customers out there.

SUMMING UP THE PLOT

- A new style of design called Art Deco dominates the cityscape.
- A modern apartment building squats on the hillside and biplanes and blimps appear

where birds once flew peacefully overhead.
- A biplane and a blimp cruise the skies.

three small businesses. <u>Art Deco</u> chrome and glass streamline some of the **(18)** storefronts, contrasting with the older styles of the upper stories. A modern yellow apartment building <u>squats</u> on the hillside, while a <u>biplane and a blimp cruise the</u> **(19)(20)** <u>skies</u>.

The house at the end of Main Street has been replaced by a cottage-style gas station.

A neoclassical granite post office has been constructed, revealing the train station in the distance.

New Providence ~ 69

LITERARY COMPONENTS

▶ **18. Historical Reference:** Art Deco refers to a popular architectural and decorative style of the 1920s and 1930s characterized especially by bold outlines and colors, by streamlined and geometric forms, and by the use of man made materials (such as chrome and glass). The etymology of the term is the French *Art Dutchéco*, from *Exposition Internationale des Arts Dutchécoratifs et Industriels Modernes*, an exposition of modern decorative and industrial arts held in Paris, France, in 1925. Here, *streamlined* means designed with flowing contours. An *exposition* such as this one is like a World's Fair: a display on a rather large scale.

▶ **19. Words Create Feelings:** The word *squat* surely has an ugly sound—which is certainly intended by the authors. Now a yellow apartment building appears to have replaced the Victorian homes that dotted the lush, rural hillsides. *Squat* means to crouch on the ground with legs fully drawn up before the body, but it also means to crouch close to the ground to escape observation or to settle on land without right or title.

▶ **20. Setting; Characterization of City and Sky:** Peaceful birds of 1910 have been replaced by a biplane (an airplane with two main supporting surfaces usually placed one above the other) and a blimp.

GUIDING THE READING

LITERAL

To the Teacher: Most of the questions below are based upon the illustrations. The students will need to compare the pictures of the city in 1910 and 1935 for the answers.

Q: What is on the top floor of the Getz & McClure building in 1935?
A: A printing business is located on the 5th floor.

Q: What has replaced the 1910 building

that housed the Market & Grocery and the Dentist?
A: A building with only two windows in the upper floors that houses Reiter's Shoes.

Q: What is different about the windows of the Butler Café and Hotel building?
A: The striped awnings have been removed.

Q: How is the post office different from the building it replaced?
A: The building it replaced had several more floors, with a shorter first floor. The 1910 building had a rounded, fancy corner part with

three narrow windows on the upper floors. Students may add to this discussion.

ANALYTICAL

Q: Comparing the 1910 and 1935 pictures of New Providence, what do you see that has changed?
A: Answers will vary. It may be helpful for students to make a list, since the changes are many and various.

SUMMING UP THE PLOT

- It is 1955.
- Although a postwar prosperity has settled over New Providence, the downtown is deteriorating.
- The night sky glows with neon lights and lights from advertising billboards.
- Part of the courthouse square has been paved with asphalt to make room for more and larger cars.
- Buses have replaced streetcars.
- Franchise businesses have moved into town.
- Traveling businessmen stay at the Alpine Motel.
- The New Providence Symphony Orchestra is performing at the Strand.

LITERARY COMPONENTS

▶ **21. Setting:** It is 1955.

▶ **22. Characterization of the City:** For the first time in the text, the word *downtown* is used. *Downtown* means the lower part or business center of a city. In 1910, New Providence was a place where people lived. Even if they resided in the Victorian houses on the hillsides in the distance, they were still part of the town. Now the picture is of a place *separate* from its citizens.

▶ **23. Rising Action; Theme:** The sky is lit by neon and the light of advertising billboards. The courthouse square is paved with asphalt to make room for more and larger cars. This is no longer a place where people will want to live. In the illustration, we see that a liquor store has replaced the beautiful Butler Café of 1910 and 1935.

▶ **24. Characterization of the City:** What happens when franchises come to town? Please make sure the students know that, in this context, a *franchise* is the right granted or sold to an individual, or group, to market a company's goods in a particular territory. When Rexall's or Woolworth's comes to town, they replace family-run businesses that cater to local tastes. Local businesses have a local character. Franchises and chains work because they do so much business across such a large territory (say, the United States) that they do not need to make so much profit on each item they sell. They can afford to sell their goods much more cheaply than the family-owned business. This is why the supermarkets put most of the family-owned grocery stores out of business.

▶ **25. Characterization; Theme:** A motel is a place where people stay briefly and cheaply. The word is a portmanteau word made from *motor* and *hotel.* The idea was/is that people could enter their rooms directly from the parking lot. A motel does not have the character of a hotel. Now the city becomes a place for transients, people who come and go and that no one in New Providence knows.

GUIDING THE READING

LITERAL

Q: In 1955, what has settled over New Providence?
A: A postwar prosperity has settled over New Providence.

Q: What does the night sky glow with?
A: The night sky glows with neon and holiday lights and the lights of advertising billboards.

Q: What has happened to the courthouse square?
A: Part of it has been paved with asphalt to make room for more and larger cars.

Q: Who stays at the Alpine Motel?
A: Traveling businessmen stay at the Alpine Motel.

1955

(21)

(22)
(23)
A postwar prosperity settles over New Providence, although there are signs that <u>downtown</u> is deteriorating.
<u>The night sky glows with neon, holiday lights, and lighted billboards advertising bread and used cars. Part of the courthouse square is now paved with asphalt to make room for more and larger cars.</u> Buses have replaced streetcars.
(24)(25) <u>Franchises[3] like Rexall's and Woolworth's have moved into town,</u> and <u>the Alpine Motel attracts traveling businessmen.</u> The New Providence Symphony Orchestra is performing at the Strand.

---

3. Sometimes companies, instead of doing their own marketing, sell the right to market their products or services to private individuals or groups. This right is called a *franchise* (FRAN chyz). The people who have bought the franchise use the name, advertisements, and products of the company, but privately own and run their own stores.

WORD BANK **deteriorating** (dee TEER ee uh RAYT ing) *v.:* becoming worse in some or many ways

70 ~ Unit I

ANALYTICAL

Q: How does the use of the word downtown show how much the city has changed since 1910?
A: Downtown suggests that this is not a place where people live any longer, that the daily lives of the citizens are not steeped in the daily life of the town.

Q: How does the feeling of the city change, when part of the courthouse square is paved with asphalt to create parking spaces for larger cars?
A: Answers will vary. Asphalt paving means fewer plants, less grass, fewer trees. Plants provide oxygen. Plants provide a softer mood. When the plants and trees disappear, so do the squirrels and the birds. More and larger cars mean more air pollution. At the same time, more cars could indicate more business, more activity, more prosperity, more excitement. In this case, it does not. Downtown has become a depressing, concrete wilderness.

Q: When a franchise such as Rexall's or Woolworth's replaces local businesses, what has the town lost?
A: The town and its citizens lose a family-run business that caters to local tastes.

- The elegant Butler House is now a liquor store and a boarding house for transients.
- The Victorian building next to it is being covered with prefabricated siding.

- Getz & McClure's has been sheathed with metal grillwork and a popular style of lettering.
- The old slate roof of the Town Hall has been replaced by asphalt shingles.

- A fire is raging at the train station, while citizens are shopping.

LITERARY COMPONENTS

▶ **26. Characterization of the City; Rising Action:** The elegant Butler House is replaced by a liquor store and a boarding house.

▶ **27. Characterization:** A series of architectural changes rob the city of its former elegance.

▶ **28. Rising Action:** Why are the citizens shopping when the train station is on fire? Where are the firemen? This is not clear in the story.

The elegant Butler House is now a liquor store and a boarding house for transients.[4] **26**
Next to it, a Victorian cast-iron building is being covered with prefabricated siding. **27**
Getz & McClure's has already been sheathed with stark metal grillwork and a
currently popular style of lettering. Two of the small businesses in the Colonel
Fleming House are boarded up. Behind it, a bland new building has been erected to
house Monarch Insurance. The old slate roof of the Town Hall has been replaced by **28**
asphalt shingles. A fire is raging at the train station, while the citizens of New
Providence go about their holiday shopping.

4. *Transients* (tran ZEE ints) are people, usually workers or salesmen, who stay in a city for a short time.

The nuclear age arrives: An air-raid siren has replaced the decorative ornament atop Town Hall, and the courthouse bears a fallout shelter sign.

The baby boom following World War II explains the new addition to the schoolhouse. The surrounding hills are gradually filling up with the ranch-style and split-level houses of suburbia.

New Providence ~ 71

GUIDING THE READING

LITERAL

Q: What has replaced the Butler House?
A: A liquor store and a boarding house for transients have replaced the Butler House.

Q: What has happened to Getz & McClure's?
A: The building has been encased in or covered with stark ("having no ornaments; appearing stripped") metal grillwork.

Q: What has happened to the business in the Colonel Fleming House?
A: Two of the businesses have been boarded up.

Q: What is happening as shoppers shop?
A: The train station is on fire.

ANALYTICAL

Q: Why are each of the architectural changes misguided?
A: A Victorian cast-iron building is a thing of beauty, an architectural legacy from the past, and a solidly made structure. Asphalt shingles do not have the permanence nor the beauty of a slate roof. If students compare the pictures,

they may be better able to articulate the reasons why the changes are not desirable.

Q: If citizens keep shopping when there is a fire raging, what may it suggest about life in the city?
A: Answers will vary. (1) The city may be so large now, that people do not know what is going on in another part of town. (2) It seems unlikely, but people may think it is more important to get their holiday shopping done than to be concerned about a fire. Presumably the authors took this event from the history of an actual city. But their point really is not clear.

- It is 1970, and downtown New Providence is an unattractive jumble of old and new buildings.

- To attract people from suburbia, part of Main Street has been converted into a pedestrian mall.

- A protest against the Vietnam War is taking place in front of the courthouse.

- The courthouse square is newly sunken and cemented.

- A mugging is in progress.

- The city is marred by graffiti and billboards.

- The post office and several other buildings have been demolished and turned into parking lots.

- The Bloom mill is for rent.

- The train station tower has not been restored.

LITERARY COMPONENTS

▶ **29. Setting; Rising Action:** It is 1970. The city is an architectural mess. No planning was involved in what the city has come to be today.

▶ **30. Theme; Characterization:** Attempts to attract people from "thriving suburbia" have thus far failed. New Providence is *not even a downtown* for the outer area associated with it. Suburbia, itself, is thriving and presumably does not need the town.

▶ **31. Characterization:** However, the demonstration against the Vietnam War shows that the town is still the legal and governmental brain for the people who are ordinarily so separated from it. The demonstration also shows that there are people living in the suburbs who are concerned about the actions of government. This may be a sign of hope for the city.

▶ **32. Characterization; Theme:** Advertising may presumably be good for business, but billboards don't do much for the environment.

▶ **33. Characterization; Rising Action:** The ugly city no longer needs the beautiful post office.

1970

㉙

㉚ B y 1970, downtown New Providence is an uninspired jumble of old and new. To attract people from thriving suburbia, part of Main Street has been converted into a pedestrian[5] mall, dominated by a harsh concrete fountain. But there is less traffic than ever in the city center, and fewer people actually live there.

㉛ A number of people in town today are gathered outside the courthouse, taking part in a protest march against the Vietnam War. Across the newly sunken and cemented ㉜ square, a mugging is in progress. Graffiti mars the area, as do more and more billboards, and an Army/Navy surplus[6] store. The post office and several other ㉝ buildings have been demolished and turned into parking lots, the Bloom mill is for rent, and the train station tower remains burnt out.

5. A *pedestrian* (puh DESS tree un) *mall* is a large area closed to traffic, used by people walking on foot.
6. *Surplus* is something extra or left over. *Army/navy surplus stores* sell leftover army and navy supplies.

| WORD BANK | **graffiti** (gruh FEE tee) *n.*: words or pictures painted illegally on public property |

72 ~ Unit I

GUIDING THE READING

LITERAL

Q: What has been done to attract people from the suburbs?
A: A pedestrian mall has been built over part of Main Street.

Q: What has been done to the courthouse square?
A: It has been sunken and cemented.

Q: What mars the area?
A: Graffiti and billboards make the town ugly.

Q: What has replaced the grand post office building?
A: A parking lot has replaced it.

ANALYTICAL

Q: Why is New Providence an "uninspired jumble of old and new" in 1970?

A: The city came to be as it is because it was buffeted about by the winds of time and fashion. As the city developed, there was no planning, no design. New businesses and developers had no respect for the architecture of the past. Students may have other answers.

Q: If suburbia is now thriving, what does that mean for the city?
A: It will be harder to draw people in from the suburbs. Why come into the city if there is a mall in the suburbs?

Q: What is your opinion of protest marches?

A: Answers will vary. A protest march shows that people care, and that they have the courage and discipline to plan an event and publicly express their feelings. A protest march can be abused if it turns violent or if it promotes prejudice or demagoguery. We are fortunate to live in a country where the government not only allows protest, but also defends the right of its citizens to protest.

Q: Why is the train station tower burnt out?
A: Apparently it was destroyed in the fire of 1955 and never fixed.

SUMMING UP THE PLOT

- The Alpine Motel has become a Holiday Inn and a Fotomat has opened.
- The Colonel Fleming House seems about to be rescued by a preservation group.
- The Victorian homes on the hills are making room for highways and look-alike suburban housing.
- A jet flies over the increasing number of power lines strung across the horizon.

The Alpine Motel is now a Holiday Inn, a Fotomat has opened, and a famous musician is playing at the Strand. A day school has opened, complete with colorful murals and giant toadstools. The Colonel Fleming House seems about to be rescued by a preservation group.[7] Victorian homes in the hills are disappearing to make room for highways, look-alike suburban housing, and another addition to the school. In the afternoon sky, a jet flies over the increasing number of powerlines strung across the horizon.

(34) **(35)** **(36)**

7. A *preservation group* is an organization that has been formed to save old buildings or sculptures that have historical value from being destroyed or changed.

An ordinary digital clock now hangs where there was once a quaint shoe sign, and the bank's classical architecture has recently been covered with mirrored glass.

The Butler House features trendy boutiques, a Day-Glo mural, and resident hippies. Space-age pavilions line the sidewalk.

New Providence ~ 73

LITERARY COMPONENTS

▶ **34. Are Change and Rescue on the Way?** A day school has opened! The Colonel Fleming House—whatever it once was—may be saved by a preservation society.

▶ **35. Theme:** But the beautiful Victorian houses are being demolished so that highways can come through. They will also make way for lots of look-alike housing. Of course highways, housing, and a school addition are necessary for a growing population.

▶ **36. Theme:** Now the sky reveals power lines and a jet.

GUIDING THE READING

LITERAL

Q: Who is performing at the Strand Theater?
A: A famous musician is performing.

Q: What has opened?
A: A day school with colorful murals and giant toadstools.

ANALYTICAL

Q: What does the program at the Strand Theater consistently show?
A: Fine, classical music sustains the culture of a city. It seems to be all that is left of the elegant, old New Providence.

Q: Why is it sad that the Victorian houses are being taken down?
A: These are big, old, beautiful houses.

Q: Why is it necessary for the Victorian houses to be taken down?
A: If their location is the only place the highways and needed middle-income housing can be built, they must make way for the people of the 1970s. It may also be that too few people are interested in buying them or can afford to heat them. Obviously, a greater supply of housing is necessary when the population

grows. A highway may also make it possible for people to travel to the city more easily. This will bring life and money to the city.

SUMMING UP THE PLOT

- The year is 1980.
- Downtown is sadly in need of recovery. But there are signs that help is on the way.
- Chief Tenebo's statue has been vandalized (in fact, the statue doesn't even seem to be there!).
- Debris and graffiti are everywhere and street lamps are smashed.
- The Colonel Fleming House has been moved across the street to the courthouse square.
- In its old place are a Cor-Ten steel sculpture and Monarch Insurance's new highrise—which has no architectural relationship to the buildings around it.
- But the streets seem more populated. People are again living downtown in the new red brick building next to McDonald's.

LITERARY COMPONENTS

▶ **37. Setting; Theme:** It is 1980. New Providence looks really dreadful. The text declares that there are signs that help is on the way, but one has to look hard at the picture to find them.

▶ **38. Powerful Use of Word:** The text tells us that *debris* blows around the statue's base and across the square. Although today debris is used as a synonym for trash, the word originally came from French and meant "the remains of something broken down or destroyed." This describes New Providence very well.

▶ **39. Repeated Reference; Architectural Reference:** Once again, we are given information about the Fleming House, the original function of which is obscure. In its old location is a Cor-Ten sculpture. In the last half of the 20th century, weathering steel (COR-TEN®) came to be widely used in city sculptures. COR-TEN® is a trademark of US Steel. Cor-Ten is a corrosion resistant low-alloy steel that forms a protective coating of rust (hydrated iron oxide) when exposed in natural climate. The authors' point seems to be that these sculptures are not welcoming. They make the city a stark people-less place of steel and glass.

▶ **40. Rising Action; Signs of Hope; Theme:** People have returned to live in the city. And we know what people are: Citizens are the riches of a city. (The word *Good* seems to have disappeared from the base of the fountain.)

1980

37

38

39

    Ten years later, there are signs that downtown New Providence is sadly in need of recovery—and also signs that help is on the way.

    Chief Tenebo's statue has been vandalized; debris blows around its dry base and across the square. Graffiti is everywhere, street lamps are smashed, and a police box has appeared. The Colonel Fleming House has been moved across the street, but its placement does not look permanent. In its old location are a Cor-Ten steel sculpture and Monarch Insurance's new highrise, which bears no architectural relationship to the buildings around it.

40

    But the streets seem more populated, and people are again living—even barbecuing—downtown in the new red brick infill structure[8] next to McDonald's.

WORD BANK	**vandalized** (VAN duh LYZD) *v.*: deliberately destroyed or damaged
	debris (duh BREE) *n.*: the remains of anything destroyed; bits of old waste matter lying about

74 ~ Unit I

GUIDING THE READING

LITERAL

Q: In 1980, what has been vandalized?
A: Chief Tenebo's statue has been vandalized. Since it is no longer there, hopefully it has not been destroyed but only removed for repairs.

Q: What blows across the square?
A: Debris blows across the square.

Q: What has happened to the street lamps?
A: The street lamps have been smashed.

Q: What has been done with the Colonel Fleming House?
A: It has been moved across the street from its original location to the courthouse square.

Q: What major change has occurred?
A: People are living again downtown.

Q: What are the riches of a city?
A: Good citizens are the riches of a city.

ANALYTICAL

Q: Why would a business build a new building that has no architectural relationship to the other buildings in the town?
A: Answers will vary.

- There is only one billboard in town and it advertises health food and a cultural event.
- A sign on the abandoned Butler House shows that rehabilitation is planned.
- A superhighway cuts through the hillside, which makes downtown more accessible to summer holiday travelers.

LITERARY COMPONENTS

▸ **41. Characterization of the City:** The single billboard advertises health food and a cultural event.

The only billboard in town advertises health food and a cultural event. The old Strand Theater is being expanded into a Cultural Center. And although the Butler House has been all but abandoned, a sign shows that rehabilitation is being planned. A superhighway now cuts through the hillside, making downtown more accessible to summer holiday travelers. A large parking structure has been built, and well-tended plantings soften the mall. **41**

---

8. An *infill structure* is a building placed so as to fill up the gap between two other buildings.

Graffiti and rusted steel girders indicate that citizens' groups have so far been able to prevent further construction of a highrise office tower on the old post office site.

A Health Center has replaced the Medical Offices, and New Providence has its first McDonald's.

New Providence ~ 75

GUIDING THE READING

LITERAL

Q: What does the only billboard in town advertise?
A: The billboard advertises health food and a cultural event.

Q: Has the old Butler House been completely abandoned?
A: No. The building has a Preservation/ Development sign posted on the second floor.

Q: How has the look of the pedestrian mall been "softened"?
A: The pedestrian mall looks less severe now, because of the planting of bushes and trees.

ANALYTICAL

Q: Look at the picture. Where the post office once was, where a parking lot was subsequently located, there is now a sign that reads "Save New Providence" and a picture of the proposed skyscraper. Scrawled on the fence are the words, "Stop the Tower." Why would people not want a skyscraper placed on that corner?
A: Answers will vary. But skyscrapers block the sky and block the horizon. They make a city stark and ugly. Skyscrapers also create wind tunnels.

SUMMING UP THE PLOT

- It is a sunny afternoon in 1992 and *a flock of birds* heads back to its winter home.

- All of the old building façades have been renovated, and the condition of the buildings is much as it was in 1910.

- The slate roof of the town hall has been restored.

LITERARY COMPONENTS

▶ **42. Setting; Coming Full Circle:** It is 1992 and once again there are birds in the sky! People have returned to the city. Just as in 1910, people are now living, shopping, working, and playing in New Providence.

▶ **43. The Importance of Language:** In the 1992 text, the word *downtown* is never used.

▶ **44. More Echoes of 1910:** Sidewalk vendors sell produce, the mall (and its plants) are gone, the busses look like old-fashioned trolley cars. The bandstand is back and people are sitting on the grass listening to a concert.

▶ **45. Building to a Climax; Rising Action:** All of the old building facades have been renovated.

It is wisdom to think the people are the city.... —CARL SANDBURG

1992

42 In the sunny afternoon sky a flock of birds heads back to its winter home. Below,
43 people have returned to the city—living, shopping, working, playing. New
44 Providence has never looked better. Sidewalk vendors sell their produce once more,
and traffic again flows through handsomely paved streets. Buses are made to look
like old-fashioned trolleys. Chief Tenebo has been restored, and the bandstand is back,
a concert in full swing. Gone are graffiti, billboards, and harsh sculptures. Plants and
fall flowers are everywhere—even the parking structure has been elegantly camouflaged.
45 All of the old building facades have been renovated, and the condition of most
buildings is strikingly similar to what it was in 1910. The Town Hall's slate roof has
been restored, and the air-raid siren is gone. Street furniture is comfortable and

| WORD | **facade** (fuh SOD) *n.:* the front of a building, especially a decorative one |
| BANK | **renovated** (REN uh VAY tuhd) *v.:* restored to good condition as by repairing or remodeling |

76 ~ Unit I

GUIDING THE READING

LITERAL

Q: On a sunny afternoon in 1992, what is in the sky over New Providence?
  A: A flock of birds is returning to its winter home.

Q: What has happened to the pedestrian mall?
  A: The mall has apparently been removed.

Q: What do the busses look like?
  A: The busses are made to look like old-fashioned trolleys.

Q: In 1992, what is everywhere in New Providence?
  A: Plants and fall flowers are everywhere.

Q: To what are the buildings now similar?
  A: The buildings are strikingly similar to what they were in 1910.

ANALYTICAL

Q: By bringing back the old architecture, handsomely paving the streets, restoring the bandstand, getting rid of billboards and harsh sculptures, and placing plants and flowers everywhere, what effect has been created?
  A: New Providence looks like a town, like a place that is not too big for people to live in. Answers may vary.

- The Butler House is beautifully refurbished.
- An arcaded building where people live and work occupies the site of the proposed tower.
- An atrium full of plants softens the look of the Monarch Insurance building.
- A Fitness Center has replaced a Health Center and an arts festival is in progress at the Strand.
- The good citizens of New Providence have worked hard to make the city livable again.

LITERARY COMPONENTS

▶ **46. Rising Action:** The clock is back and the Butler House is restored.

▶ **47. Climax; Theme:** Good, involved citizens are the riches of a city.

compatible with[9] the architecture. The circular clock is back in front of the Butler House, now beautifully refurbished. An arcaded building where people live and work occupies the site of the controversial tower, serving as an entry into the restored train station, and an atrium full of plants softens the Monarch Insurance skyscraper. A Fitness Center has replaced the Health Center, and an arts festival is in progress at the Strand Cultural Center. **(46)**

The good citizens of New Providence have worked hard to make the city livable again—and true to its heritage. **(47)**

---
9. *Compatible with* means that something fits in with the people, objects, or ideas around it.

The Colonel Fleming House has been carefully restored—not as a historical museum but as an outdoor restaurant.

New buildings and additions to existing structures have been designed to complement the medley of architectural styles in downtown New Providence.

New Providence ~ 77

GUIDING THE READING

LITERAL

Q: What was built in place of the controversial tower?
A: An arcaded building where people live and work.

Q: What softens the look of the Monarch Insurance skyscraper?
A: An atrium full of plants.

ANALYTICAL

Q: Which group of people may be adversely affected by the urban renewal we see in 1992?
A: Unfortunately, urban renewal is not always good for everyone. When slums are torn down and new properties built in their place, there is often no housing that lower-income working people can afford.

Q: Looking at the picture for 1992, we can see that the parking garage built in 1980 made what possible?

A: The parking garage made it possible to get rid of the parking spaces and expand the courthouse square.

New Providence, a small American city, will not be found on any map. It is the creation of a team of architectural historians and designers, and yet its fictional cityscape is truly authentic. The buildings, the signs, even the street furniture can be found somewhere in urban America. Almost every detail was discovered in old photographs and assembled by the design team at The Townscape Institute.

Baltimore, Maryland (McDonald's building and H_2O fountain); Binghamton, New York (courthouse lights); Boston, Massachusetts (church in center and 1970 concrete plaza); Brookline, Massachusetts (church); Cambridge, Massachusetts (signs); Chelsea, Massachusetts (storefront); Chicago, Illinois (metal awning on the Butler House); Cincinnati, Ohio (1987 City Identity System booth); Denver, Colorado (building across the street from courthouse in 1910); Eugene, Oregon (1970 modern concrete fountain); Flint, Michigan (1910 shoe sign and street awnings); Fresno, California (1970-1980 sculptural clock tower); Garland, Utah (Bloom mill); Grand Rapids, Michigan (City Hall); Heber City, Utah (water tower); Junction City, Kansas (corner bank); Knoxville, Tennessee (billboard); Los Angeles, California (Getz & McClure building); Milwaukee, Wisconsin (suburban villas); Montclair, New Jersey (Colonel Fleming House); Montgomery, Alabama (Victorian cast-iron building); New York, New York (Butler House and train station); Portland, Oregon (fountain base); Richmond, Virginia (signs on Reiter's shoe store); Salem, Ohio (cornice on Main Street); San Diego, California (circular clock); Scottsdale, Arizona (parking structure with plantings); Staunton, Virginia (stained glass in McDonald's building); Syracuse, New York (layout of courthouse square); Topeka, Kansas (Alpine Motel sign); Townsend, Massachusetts (bandstand); Traverse City, Michigan (mansard roof on Butler House); Upper Sandusky, Ohio (horse fountain and pavilion); Waltham, Massachusetts (bench); Washington, D.C. (Masonic building); Westerville, Ohio (gas station); Wilkes-Barre, Pennsylvania (park outline); Wilmington, Delaware (1970 metal Main Street shelters); Winooski, Vermont (Main Street building).

FIRST IMPRESSIONS

Answers will vary. Ask the students to explain their choice.

Studying the Selection

FIRST IMPRESSIONS

In which year do you think the city was most attractive?

QUICK REVIEW

1. What is the name of the city?

2. Which years of the city's existence are described?

3. What is the Butler House?

4. Whom does the fountain commemorate?

FOCUS

5. Select one change that stands out for you. Do you think it is a change for the better or for the worse? Why?

6. Choose a year and describe how New Providence looked that year. You may even choose a year in the future.

CREATING & WRITING

7. Choose one of the cityscapes described in the story, and write about what New Providence was like that year and why.

8. Choose a subject from 1910: cobblestone streets, Model T Fords, streetcars, horse-drawn carts, bandstand concerts, food shopping before there were supermarkets, or Victorian homes. Do you wish we had some of those things today, or are you thankful that we don't? Perhaps you have mixed feelings— you like the idea of, say, horse-drawn carts, but you know they would be slower and bumpier than a car. Write a paragraph about what life would be like if we still had the item you chose.

9. Draw a picture of one or several of the buildings in New Providence. In the caption, name the buildings and the year.

New Providence ~ 79

QUICK REVIEW

1. The city is called New Providence.

2. We see the city in 1910, 1935, 1955, 1970, 1980, and 1992.

3. Butler House is both a café and a hotel in 1910 and 1935. By 1955 it is a liquor store and a boarding house for transients. In 1970, the building houses Someplace Else Music, Amy's Boutique—and looks like apartments on the second and third floors. In 1992, the Butler House Café is back. Again it looks like apartments—albeit nicer ones—on the upper floors in that year.

4. The fountain commemorates Chief Tenebo, a Native American from a (probably) once-local tribe.

FOCUS

5. Answers will vary.

6. It will be especially interesting, if students pick years not in the selection, by extrapolating from those that are.

CREATING & WRITING

7. Answers will vary. Encourage students to use their imagination and try to go beyond what is in the selection.

8. Try to help the students see the pros and cons of modernization.

9. While the students should be able to choose the building or buildings of their choice, you may want to encourage a distribution of choices that will give you the opportunity to create the city along your wall, for several of the years described.

THEME

- The theme of a story is the idea that runs through the entire story.
- The idea that the author chooses for a theme is one that he thinks is true for all people, not just for the characters in the story.
- The plot, characters, and setting all help express the theme.
- Stories, poems, plays, and songs may express the same theme in different ways.

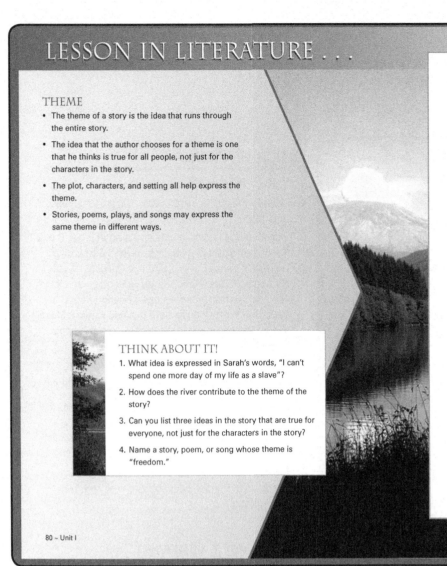

THINK ABOUT IT!

1. What idea is expressed in Sarah's words, "I can't spend one more day of my life as a slave"?
2. How does the river contribute to the theme of the story?
3. Can you list three ideas in the story that are true for everyone, not just for the characters in the story?
4. Name a story, poem, or song whose theme is "freedom."

No Turning Back

"Sarah, you can't swim across. You'll freeze."

The fear on Aunty's face didn't stop Sarah from taking the next step into the cold water of the river. "I can't spend one more day of my life as a slave, Aunty."

"We can try again tomorrow night," Aunty said.

Sarah turned her head around to face Aunty, but she kept her feet planted firmly in the direction of freedom. "Aunty, what is it you been saying to me these last two weeks when I get scared? When we hidin' in a swamp and feel the snakes swimmin' by our feet? When we hear those hounds baying in the distance?"

Aunty looked down. "'G-d will provide.'"

"'G-d will provide.' All my whole life, Aunty. When they sold Mama down to Alabama, you tell me G-d gonna provide. G-d got us this far. Why ain't He gonna provide right now?"

Aaaaaaaoooooo! The baying of the dogs was getting closer.

"No turning back now, Aunty," Sarah whispered fiercely. "C'mon."

Suddenly Aunty pointed downriver. A flat boat was being poled upriver by a white man in dark clothing. He was struggling against the current of the river, but he was headed straight for them.

"Tracker didn't say it was going to be a white man," said Aunty.

Sarah stood tall and proud. These weeks in the woods—this taste of freedom—had changed her. Either this white man was their ride to freedom, or she would dive in and outswim him to the other side.

About twenty feet from Sarah the man cupped a hand over his mouth.

"You folks sure ain't quiet," he shouted. "I heard you half a mile away."

Sarah held her breath.

The man drew to within fifteen feet. "Good thing, I guess. Rucker said you was *supposed* to cross down that way."

Sarah breathed a huge sigh of relief. "You Mr. Rucker's man?"

The man nodded. "Rucker will meet you at the barn," he said. "C'mon, get on before you freeze."

Barely aware of the chilly air, Sarah turned her eyes heavenward and mouthed the words, "Thank You."

SELECTION VOCABULARY

affidavit: a written statement made with the promise to tell the truth

alarmed: suddenly frightened or worried

credentials: documents showing that a person has privileges

legislators: lawmakers

lobby: to work at influencing lawmakers to vote a certain way

optimist: one who generally expects things to turn out well; a person with a positive, upbeat attitude

persistence: firmly keeping to a particular course of action in spite of opposition

petition: a written request signed by a large number of people

prejudice: an already formed opinion not pased on actual experience; an unreasoning like or dislike

struggle: a fight

---

affidavit	credentials	lobby	persistence	prejudice
alarmed	legislators	optimist	petition	struggle

1. A group of doctors have joined together in the _____ (*fight*) against disease, poverty, and ignorance in poor and war-torn countries. They call themselves "Doctors Without Borders."

2. The students respectfully handed the principal a _____ (*written request signed by many people*) requesting that they be given one no-homework night a week.

3. As I sat in the dentist's chair, I grew more and more nervous. What if he was a madman? What if he knew only how to drill? What if he wasn't really a dentist at all? "I should have checked his _____ (*evidence that he is entitled to the position he holds*) before I got into this chair," I thought, as I gripped the arms in fear.

4. Two people can look at a glass of water; the pessimist will say it is half empty, and the _____ (*one who views the world in a positive light*) will say it is half full.

5. A group representing the steelworker of America went to Washington, D C to _____ (*work at influencing lawmakers*) members of Congress.

6. The secret of success is not luck or talent—although they certainly help. It is hard work and _____ (*keeping to a course of action*).

7. The woman was driving home when she noticed an emergency truck ahead of her. When it stopped in front of her house, she became _____ (*frightened*).

8. Our social studies teacher arranged a trip to the state capital for our class, so that we could observe the state _____ (*lawmakers*) in session.

9. No matter what Jones, the clerk, did, the boss, Mr. Harcourt, found fault with him. Mr. Harcourt seemed to have a _____ (*unreasonable dislike*) against poor Jones.

10. The judge asked for an _____ (*written declaration*) stating that Mrs. Simson was the owner of the stolen painting.

Workbook p. 25   Answer Guide p. 3

Circle the correct answer. If you know what the vocabulary word means, you will know which answer makes no sense at all!

1. **Who** would be involved in a *struggle*?
   a. Two goldfish
   b. Two wrestlers

2. **Why** was the lady alarmed?
   a. She saw a fire engine racing towards her house.
   b. She heard her favorite song played on the radio.

3. **What** was written on the *affidavit*?
   a. Mrs. Hunter's grandmother's recipe for pumpkin pie
   b. Mrs. Hunter's grandmother's claim of ownership of the house

4. **Why** did they write a *petition*?
   a. To express appreciation for the pay raise
   b. To demand a pay raise

5. **Where** did the group lobby?
   a. In Washington, D C at the capitol building
   b. In the large front room of the hotel, where the desk and elevators were located

6. **What** do *legislators* write?
   a. laws
   b. traffic tickets

7. **When** might one need to show one's credentials?
   a. when applying for a position as chief surgeon at a hospital
   b. when purchasing fresh rolls at a bakery

8. **How** can we ensure that our children are free of *prejudice*?
   a. We inoculate them before they enter kindergarten.
   b. We can teach them about equality.

9. **Who** do you wish had less *persistence*?
   a. the Olympic runner who represents your country
   b. the telemarketer who calls once a week asking you to subscribe to a certain magazine

10. **What** would an *optimist* be more likely to say upon arising?
    a. I have a feeling things will go all wrong today.
    b. I have a feeling it's going to be a great day!

Workbook p. 26   Answer Guide p. 3

LESSON IN LITERATURE

1. The theme of the story is easiest expressed by quoting Patrick Henry: *Give me liberty or give me death!*

2. The river separates Sarah and her aunt from freedom. It is a tangible representation of the prison in which the slaves lived. The risk Sarah is willing to take to swim across it, dra-

matizes just how strong her yearning for freedom is.

3. Some examples are: freedom, kindness, crime and punishment, humility, goodness is rewarded in the end, and so on.

4. Answers will vary.

BACKGROUND BYTES

Jim Crow is not the name of a person. Jim Crow refers to a system of laws and customs that separated whites and blacks in the American South. Jim Crow laws and customs made it possible for white people to treat blacks as if they were inferior.

From the 1880s to the 1950s, the federal government did nothing to stop Jim Crow. The Southern states enacted a series of laws that guaranteed racial segregation and racial oppression. What is *segregation*? **Segregation** is the separation of an individual or a group of individuals from a larger group or from society. What is *oppression*? When people are **oppressed**, they are "crushed, burdened, or trampled down" by other people who have power or authority.

The name, *Jim Crow,* came from a popular 19th-century song that was performed by an actor wearing blackface in a traveling show. What is **blackface**? In order to appear as "Negroes," white men would smear their faces with soot from burned cork. This was called appearing in blackface. This was a form of "theatre" that was based on prejudice.

The Encyclopedia of New York City tells us that from the 1790s, blackface acts were common in traveling shows and circuses. The actors would walk and dance the way they imagined black people walked and danced. They told jokes in so-called "Negro" dialect.

In the 1820s, a white man named Thomas Rice "caused a nationwide sensation," when he wore blackface and danced and sang a song called "Jump Jim Crow." The title came from an old street singer from whom he learned the song.

Blacks were thought not smart enough to speak proper English. But when Africans were brought here as slaves, they were never taught English. It was illegal for slaves to learn to read and write, illegal for them to go to school, and they were punished if they spoke their own languages with each other.

Thus, in 1828, Jim Crow was born. Jim Crow was an "amusing" character and comedy act used over and over again in minstrel shows. Everyone knew the character Jim Crow. And Jim Crow also became the name for a system of legalized racism.

By the end of the Reconstruction period that followed the Civil War, the term Jim Crow became the name for the very complicated system of racial rules in the American South. These rules made it possible for whites to have power over blacks in their everyday lives, in their jobs or trades, in the amount of money they earned, with the police and in the courts, in the government, and in the laws.

Beginning in the late 1870s, Southern legislatures passed laws that required the separation of persons of color from white people on any type of public transportation. Anyone who was suspected of having any black ancestors, no matter how far back, was considered a person of color. The rules of segregation came to include public parks, cemeteries, restaurants, theatres, and blood banks—to make sure that blacks never appeared to be the same as white people.

Although black men had been given the vote during the Reconstruction era, Jim Crow practices made it nearly impossible for blacks to vote in the South for more than a century after the Civil War ended. On April 26, 1865, Union General William T. Sherman received the surrender of Confederate General Joseph Johnston, thereby ending the war. On August 6, 1965, President Lyndon Baynes Johnson signed the Voting Rights Act, which guaranteed the right to vote without penalties or poll taxes.

Finally, regarding the racial separation of blood in blood banks, an interesting and terrible story is told. Charles Drew (1904-1950) was black. Charles Drew discovered how blood could be preserved as blood plasma and reconstituted, which made possible the creation of blood banks. Dr. Drew was named director of the Red Cross Blood Bank and assistant director of the National Research Council. He was in charge of blood collection for the U.S. Armed Forces during World War II.

The Armed Forces had issued an order that blood was to be separated according to race. Dr. Drew spoke out against this policy, since there is no difference between the blood of whites and blacks. He knew soldiers and sailors might die waiting for the "right" blood.

On April 1, 1950, Dr. Drew was driving to give a lecture in Tuskegee, Alabama. His car ran off the road and turned over. Newspaper accounts said that the hospital closest to the accident refused to admit him because he was black. He had to be taken farther away to a black hospital. By the time he arrived there, he had lost too much blood to survive. The man who had made blood available for transfusions in medical emergencies did not have access to a transfusion when he needed one. He was 46.

Language Alert

Do your students know where Mississippi is? You will want to show them on a map of the United States. Mississippi is bordered by the Gulf of Mexico and Louisiana to its south, Louisiana and Arkansas to the west, Tennessee to the north, and Alabama to the East. The capital of Mississippi is Jackson.

Mississippi was first inhabited by three major tribes of indigenous (native) people: Chickasaws in the north, Choctaws in the central region and south, and Natchez in the southwest along the Mississippi River. Other tribes included the Biloxi, Houma, Pascagoula, Tunica, Chakchiuma/Chocchuma, and Yazoo.

The word, *Mississippi,* is a native word of Algonquian origin; akin to Ojibwa *Misisipi,* from *misi* big + *sipi* river. The Ojibwas were a tribe from the region around Lake Superior and westward. (Ojibwa, or *ojib-ubway,* referred to a moccasin with a puckered seam, which the Ojibwa traditionally wore. Literally the word meant to roast until puckered up.)

INTO "THE SILENT LOBBY"

It has been said, *Never doubt that a small group of committed citizens can change the world. It's the only thing that ever has.*

The Silent Lobby shows us that theme is not always clear-cut. Here we see the theme as the quote states; but we also see the theme of nonviolent struggle (as Papa says, without guns or bombs). Nonviolent struggle was one of the hallmarks of the civil rights movement of the 1950s and 1960s.

Perhaps more than any other single individual, Martin Luther King, Jr. was responsible for creating the events that led to social change and for sustaining their momentum. Dr. King (1929-1968) advocated nonviolent protest. His challenge to Jim Crow convinced many white Americans to support the cause. Others feared him, and he was assassinated in 1968.

These words of Martin Luther King are very famous, and come from the speech he gave at the 1963 March on Washington. On August 28, 1963, more than 200,000 ordinary white and black Americans gathered in Washington and listened to *I Have a Dream*—a speech that has entered into the annals of American history.

The excerpts below encapsulate—and even go beyond—the theme of *The Silent Lobby.* Have each student practice reading one or two "stanzas" and recite them before the class for the final exercise in the post-curriculum.

Excerpts from *I Have a Dream*
Go back to Mississippi, go back to Alabama, go back to South Carolina, go back to Georgia, go back to Louisiana, go back to the slums and ghettos of our northern cities, knowing that somehow this situation can and will be changed.

Let us not wallow in the valley of despair. I say to you today my friends—so even though we face the difficulties of today and tomorrow, I still have a dream. It is a dream deeply rooted in the American dream.

I have a dream that one day this nation will rise

up and live out the true meaning of its creed: "We hold these truths to be self-evident, that all men are created equal."

I have a dream that one day on the red hills of Georgia the sons of former slaves and the sons of former slave owners will be able to sit down together at the table of brotherhood.

I have a dream that one day even the state of Mississippi, a state sweltering with the heat of injustice, sweltering with the heat of oppression, will be transformed into an oasis of freedom and justice.

I have a dream that my four little children will one day live in a nation where they will not be judged by the color of their skin but by the content of their character.

I have a dream today....

I have a dream that one day every valley shall be exalted, and every hill and mountain shall be made low, the rough places will be made plain, and the crooked places will be made straight....

This is our hope...to hew out of the mountain of despair a stone of hope...

to transform the jangling discords of our nation into a beautiful symphony of brotherhood...to work together...to struggle together, to go to jail together, to stand up for freedom together, knowing that we will be free one day.

This will be the day, this will be the day when all... will be able to sing with new meaning "My country 'tis of thee, sweet land of liberty, of thee I sing. Land where my fathers died, land of the Pilgrim's pride, from every mountainside, let freedom ring!"

And if America is to be a great nation, this must become true. And so let freedom ring from the prodigious hilltops of New Hampshire. Let freedom ring from the mighty mountains of New York. Let freedom ring from the heightening Alleghenies of Pennsylvania.

Let freedom ring from the snow-capped Rockies of Colorado. Let freedom ring from the ...slopes of California.

But not only that; let freedom ring from Stone Mountain of Georgia.

Let freedom ring from Lookout Mountain of Tennessee.

Let freedom ring from every hill and molehill of Mississippi—from every mountainside.

Let freedom ring. And when this happens, and when we allow freedom to ring—when we let it ring from every village and every hamlet, from every state and every city, we will be able to speed up that day when all of our children...will be able to join hands and sing in the words of the old Negro spiritual: "Free at last! Free at last! Thank G-d Almighty, we are free at last!"

EYES ON...THEME

You may want to review or expand upon the discussion of theme in the Into section of *Samuel's Choice* (Teacher's Edition, page 15.)

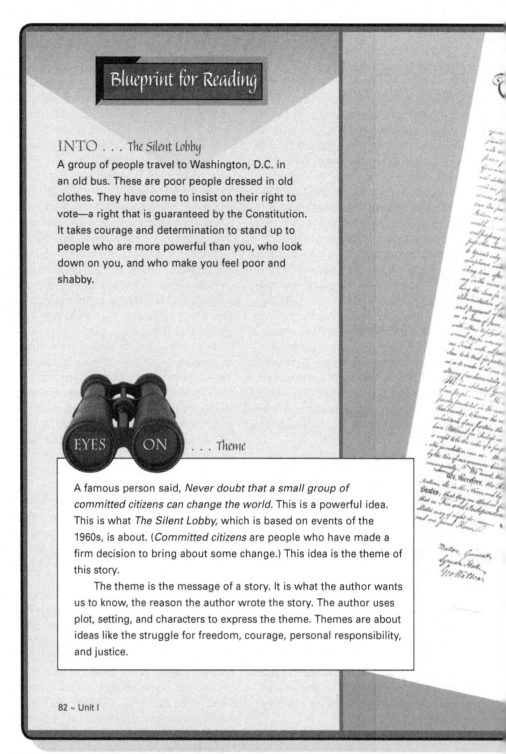

Blueprint for Reading

INTO . . . *The Silent Lobby*

A group of people travel to Washington, D.C. in an old bus. These are poor people dressed in old clothes. They have come to insist on their right to vote—a right that is guaranteed by the Constitution. It takes courage and determination to stand up to people who are more powerful than you, who look down on you, and who make you feel poor and shabby.

EYES ON . . . *Theme*

A famous person said, *Never doubt that a small group of committed citizens can change the world.* This is a powerful idea. This is what *The Silent Lobby,* which is based on events of the 1960s, is about. (*Committed citizens* are people who have made a firm decision to bring about some change.) This idea is the theme of this story.

The theme is the message of a story. It is what the author wants us to know, the reason the author wrote the story. The author uses plot, setting, and characters to express the theme. Themes are about ideas like the struggle for freedom, courage, personal responsibility, and justice.

82 ~ Unit I

GUIDING THE READING (P. 83)

LITERAL

Q: In which state is the bus traveling?
A: We know that the bus is in Mississippi, because the bus is traveling "along the Mississippi highway."

Q: Is the narrator traveling with both his parents?
A: No, he is traveling with his father ("just before me and Papa left . . .").

Q: How many other people are traveling with them?
A: Twenty other people. It is not clear whether this number includes a driver.

Q: What sound does the bus make?

A: The bus is chug-chug-chugging.

Q: Why didn't his mother want them to go?
A: She was afraid that it would be dangerous and that the bus might be bombed.

Q: What does Papa say people must have, if they are to have peace?
A: Papa says people must have freedom to have peace.

ANALYTICAL

Q: The narrator is both excited and fearful. Why?

A: He is excited to be going to Washington, D.C. He is afraid that the bus is going to stall again and they will never make it.

SUMMING UP THE PLOT

- An old bus chugs along, traveling from Mississippi to Washington, D.C.
- The narrator shivers from the wind and from excitement and fear.

- The narrator is excited about going to Washington, but afraid that the old bus will stall again and they won't make it.
- He cannot forget his parents' words just before he and his father left to pick up other people who are riding on the bus.

- He drifts back in his mind to events that occurred before the bus ride.
- His mother had said it was too dangerous for him to go with his father—the bus could be bombed.
- His father had said that their house could be bombed, for that matter.
- His mother responded by saying she doesn't want her husband to go. Why couldn't he just forget about voting and let them live in peace?
- Papa said there could be no peace without freedom.

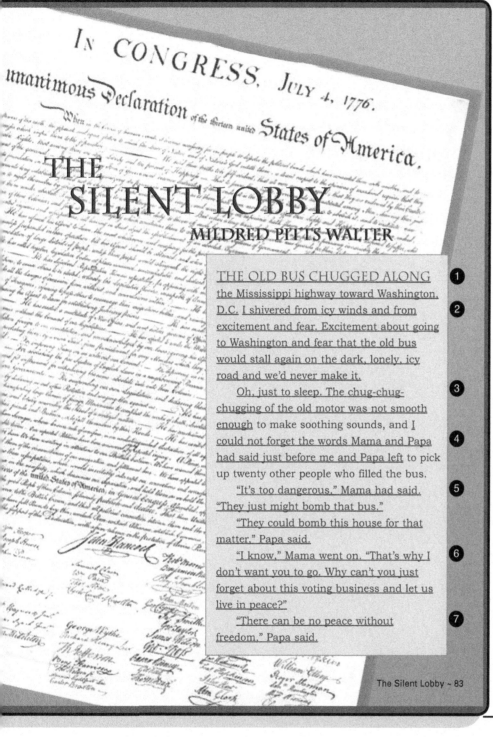

THE
SILENT LOBBY
MILDRED PITTS WALTER

THE OLD BUS CHUGGED ALONG **1**
the Mississippi highway toward Washington,
D.C. I shivered from icy winds and from **2**
excitement and fear. Excitement about going
to Washington and fear that the old bus
would stall again on the dark, lonely, icy
road and we'd never make it.

Oh, just to sleep. The chug-chug- **3**
chugging of the old motor was not smooth
enough to make soothing sounds, and I
could not forget the words Mama and Papa **4**
had said just before me and Papa left to pick
up twenty other people who filled the bus.

"It's too dangerous," Mama had said. **5**
"They just might bomb that bus."

"They could bomb this house for that
matter," Papa said.

"I know," Mama went on. "That's why I **6**
don't want you to go. Why can't you just
forget about this voting business and let us
live in peace?"

"There can be no peace without **7**
freedom," Papa said.

The Silent Lobby ~ 83

LITERARY COMPONENTS

▶ **1. Setting; Exposition:** The narrator is on an old bus that is chugging its way along a Mississippi highway. They are traveling to Washington, D.C. This should be established clearly in students' minds as the Present Time of the story. This will enable them to see the subplots, and to see how a writer can smoothly move back in time to events that occurred before the story began.

▶ **2. Setting; Motivation; Characterization of Narrator; Suspense; Clues:** The bus is cold—the narrator shivers from icy winds on the bus. He also shivers from excitement about going to Washington, and from fear that the bus will break down and they will never make it. Will they make it? Why are they using an old bus for something important?

▶ **3. Setting; Onomatopoeia:** The motor is old and makes *chug-chug-chugging* sounds that keep him from sleeping.

▶ **4. Exposition; Conflict; Narrator Begins Thinking About Past Events:** He cannot forget his parents' discussion before he and his dad departed. He says "just before me and Papa left..."

▶ **5. Dialogue; Suspense; Characterization of Narrator's Parents; Theme:** His mother said it was too dangerous to go. His father said, essentially, that life is always dangerous for them.

▶ **6. Characterization; Elaboration of Conflict; Theme:** The mother is afraid, protective of her family. She cares less about voting and more about her husband and son.

▶ **7. Theme; Emotional Setting:** The father cannot have peace if he doesn't have rights like other people. Here, freedom means the exercise of rights.

Q: Why can't he fall asleep?
A: He says that the chug-chug-chugging of the motor is not a soothing sound. Also, he cannot forget the conversation his parents had before he and his father left on the bus.

Q: Why do you think their discussion disturbed him?
A: Answers will vary. The most likely, however, are (1) their talking about the trip's potentially being dangerous; and (2) they do not agree on what is right to do.

Q: The narrator's father says, "They could bomb this house for that matter." What do you think he means by that?

A: Answers will vary, and students may need help with this. His response is like the proverbial, "Life is dangerous, for that matter." But since many people were killed during the struggle for black civil rights, he is not being flip. He really means that their life is dangerous. And their life has got to be dangerous, if they fight for their rights, because many whites in the South went to terrible lengths to maintain Jim Crow.

Q: Is the parents' discussion taking place during the present time of the story?
A: No. The narrator is remembering what

had occurred, as he travels on the bus. From the first paragraph of the story, we know that the present time is the bus ride—and whatever happens after the bus ride.

Q: What do you think Papa means by *freedom*?
A: Answers will vary. Certainly he means being able to exercise the right to vote. Given the violence towards blacks in the American South, he may also mean freedom from being hurt or threatened.

GUIDING THE READING (P. 85)

LITERAL

Q: What does Mama say Papa should do, instead of going to Washington?

A: She says that he should get a gun and protect them, instead of going to Washington.

Q: How old is the narrator of the story and what is his name?

A: Craig is eleven years old.

Q: How many years before does the narrator say "It had all started . . ."? What year was it?

A: He says it had all started two years earlier, in 1963.

Q: What had started?

A: His father had decided to go to register to vote—as had many other African Americans living in the south.

Q: What does Mr. Clem, Papa's boss, say?

A: He warns Papa not to try to register. He says that if he does, he will fire him from his job.

Q: Why doesn't his mother want his father to try to register to vote?

A: She says that "people have been arrested and beaten for going down there."

Q: Craig wants to go with his father, when he registers to vote. What does his father tell him to do?

A: Papa says that Craig should stay and look after his mother and the house until he returns.

Q: What is Papa's first name?

A: His name is Sylvester.

Q: Why wasn't Papa able to register?

A: He couldn't interpret the state constitution the way they wanted.

Q: Did this mean Papa wouldn't lose his job?

A: No. Papa would lose his job just for trying to register to vote.

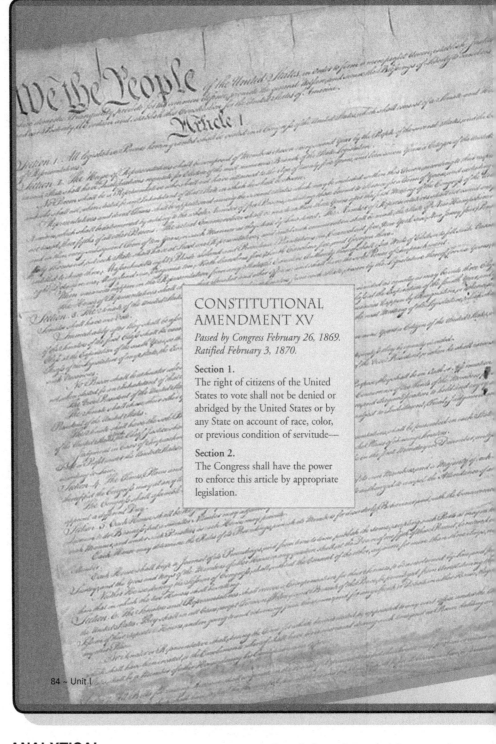

CONSTITUTIONAL
AMENDMENT XV

Passed by Congress February 26, 1869.
Ratified February 3, 1870.

Section 1.
The right of citizens of the United States to vote shall not be denied or abridged by the United States or by any State on account of race, color, or previous condition of servitude—

Section 2.
The Congress shall have the power to enforce this article by appropriate legislation.

84 ~ Unit I

ANALYTICAL

Q: When Mama asks Papa if he thinks someone is going to give him freedom, does she really expect an answer? What is she really saying?

A: This is what is called a rhetorical question. It is also a statement made in anger. She does not expect an answer. Also, she is saying that no matter what he does, it is not going to get them the vote or real equality.

Q: If Papa says you can win a struggle without bombs and guns, what kind of struggle does he believe in?

A: Papa believes in a nonviolent struggle—a struggle in which no one is physically harmed or threatened with physical harm.

Q: What does the narrator mean when he says "I knew"?

A: Answers may vary. His statement refers to his parents' discussion. He has lived there and has seen violence. He also knows what this struggle is about. He has witnessed the repercussions of his father's trying to register to vote. He may also be saying that he knows why it is important.

SUMMING UP THE PLOT

- Craig's mother asked, rhetorically, "You think someone is going to give you freedom?" She did not believe his going to Washington was going to make one whit of difference in their lives.

- She said her husband should get a gun to protect them, instead of going to Washington.

- Papa commented that a struggle can be won without bombs or guns.

- He said he was taking their son Craig with him. Craig "is old enough to know what this is all about."

- The narrator says that he knew (what this was all about).

- Two years earlier, in 1963, his father's boss had said that if he registered to vote, he would be fired from his job.

- His mother had said his father shouldn't go to register—he could be arrested and beaten.

- The narrator had said to his father, "Let me go with you, Papa."

- His father had told him to stay and look after his mother and the house, until he returned.

- Day had turned to night and his father had not returned.

- Mama and Craig waited, afraid, for Papa to return.

- When Papa got home, he told them that he had paid the poll tax and passed the literacy test, but that he hadn't interpreted the state constitution the way they had wanted. So they would not register him.

"And you think someone is going to give you freedom?" Mama asked with heat in her voice. "Instead of going to Washington, you should be getting a gun to protect us." **8**

"There are ways to win a struggle without bombs and guns. I'm going to Washington and Craig is going with me." **9**

"Craig is too young."

"He's eleven. That's old enough to know what this is all about," Papa insisted.

I KNEW. IT HAD ALL STARTED TWO YEARS AGO, IN 1963. **10 11** Papa was getting ready to go into town to register[1] to vote. Just as he was leaving, Mr. Clem, Papa's boss, came and warned Papa that he should not try to register.

"I intend to register," Papa said.

"If you do, I'll have to fire you." Mr. Clem drove away in a cloud of dust. **12**

"You ought not go," Mama said, alarmed. "You know that people have been arrested and beaten for going down there."

"I'm going," Papa insisted.

"Let me go with you, Papa." I was scared, too, and wanted to be with him if **13** he needed help.

"No, you stay and look after your mama and the house till I get back."

Day turned to night, and Papa had not returned. Mama paced the floor. **14** Was Papa in jail? Had he been beaten? We waited, afraid. Finally, I said, **15** "Mama, I'll go find him."

"Oh, no!" she cried. Her fear scared me more, and I felt angry because I couldn't do anything.

At last we heard Papa's footsteps. The look on his face let us know right **16** away that something was mighty wrong.

"What happened, Sylvester?" Mama asked.

"I paid the poll tax, passed the literacy test, but I didn't interpret the state constitution the way they wanted. So they wouldn't register me."

Feeling a sense of sad relief, I said, "Now you won't lose your job."

"Oh, but I will. I tried to register."

---

1. Before someone can vote in an election for the first time, the person must complete a form and send it into the local board of elections. The person's name will then be placed on the list of *registered voters* and, on election day, that person can vote.

WORD BANK	**struggle** (STRUH gul) *n.*: a fight **alarmed** (uh LARMD) *adj.*: suddenly frightened or worried

The Silent Lobby ~ 85

LITERARY COMPONENTS

▶ **8. Characterization:** The mother does not share the father's idealism. She is more grounded in the everyday realities. She wants to be protected and not to take chances given the history of violence towards blacks in the American South.

▶ **9. Characterization; Theme:** The father is committed to the struggle and to a nonviolent struggle. He is going to go to Washington and take his son with him.

▶ **10. Characterization; Emotional Setting:** Of course the narrator knows—whatever his parents are referring to. He has lived with this all of his life. When people are harmed for acting like equals, they always live with fear and anger: fear of reprisal and anger at the people who make them act in an unnatural way, who do not allow them to be true to themselves, and who mistreat them.

▶ **11. Background; Setting; Subplot:** The narrator describes what happened in 1963, when his father was going to register to vote.

▶ **12. Rising Action in Subplot:** His father's boss says he will fire him from his job. His mother is frightened, because of violence that has been done to others.

▶ **13. Characterization; Theme:** We learn that because the narrator is afraid, he *wants* to go with his father, in case he needs help. He is a courageous boy.

▶ **14. Rising Action; Suspense in Subplot:** Day turns to night and his father has not yet returned. What has happened to him?

▶ **15. Characterization; Theme:** Once again, Craig shows what a brave boy he is. He also demonstrates that he would rather risk danger to himself than remain in the dark about a situation.

▶ **16. Resolution of First Subplot:** Papa returns home (but doesn't explain why he is so late).

Q: Why does Mr. Clem say he will fire Papa for registering, when it is Papa's right to vote?

A: Answers will vary, and you may need to help students repeatedly with this kind of question. People in the American South did not want blacks to be able to vote, because they did not want them to feel equal and did not want them to have any power. They needed to feel that they were superior to the blacks and that they could control them. If blacks continued to be powerless, they would continue to provide cheap labor to the whites.

Q: Why didn't Mama want Craig to go look for his father?

A: She was afraid he would be hurt.

Q: Why did Craig feel angry, when Mama told him not to go looking for Papa?

A: He was angry, because he couldn't do anything to help his father or to find out what had happened.

Q: What would Papa have had to do, in order to register to vote?

A: Papa had to pay a poll tax, pass a literacy test, and explain the Mississippi constitution in a way that satisfied the person who was handling his registration.

SUMMING UP THE PLOT

- Papa still lost his job, but continued to want to vote.
- One day Papa heard about Mrs. Fannie Lou Hamer and the Mississippi Freedom Democratic Party.
- The Freedom Party registered people without charging a poll tax, or other restrictions.
- On Election Day in 1964, Papa voted for Mrs. Hamer and her colleagues.
- They were elected but Paul B. Johnson, Governor of Mississippi, declared all the votes illegal and gave certificates of election to three white men.
- The Freedom Party didn't give up, and lawyers came from all over the country to help them.
- People signed affidavits saying that when they tried to register to vote, they had lost their jobs, been beaten, had their homes burned, and had their businesses bombed.
- Craig returns to the present: He hears the old bus slowly grinding along.

LITERARY COMPONENTS

▶ **17. Historical Reference; Beginning of Second Subplot:** Mrs. Fannie Lou Hamer (October 6, 1917 to March 14, 1977) grew up in rural Montgomery County Mississippi, the twentieth child born to her parents, who were sharecroppers. In 1962, when she tried to register to vote, she was fired from her job—where she had worked and lived for eighteen years. She helped found and became vice chairperson of the Mississippi Freedom Democratic Party.

▶ **18. Historical Fiction:** Although "Papa" is not a specific real person as far as we know, this paragraph is replete with facts that come from history.

▶ **19. Theme:** Never give up!

▶ **20. Setting; Return to Plot:** We are returned to the present time of the story. Craig is riding the bus to Washington, which breaks down once again in the cold wind and icy drizzling rain.

▶ **21. Rising Action; Onomatopoeia:** A policeman demands they move the bus, which has broken down—seemingly permanently—once again. The use of the word *barked* to describe the policeman's tone is an example of onomatopoeia.

GUIDING THE READING

LITERAL

Q: Who was the person that Papa heard about one day?
A: Papa heard about Mrs. Fannie Lou Hamer.

Q: Which party made it possible for black people to register to vote in Mississippi?
A: The Mississippi Freedom Democratic Party registered black people.

Q: What was the name of the Governor of Mississippi who declared all of the black votes illegal?
A: The governor's name was Paul B. Johnson.

Q: What did the governor of Mississippi do after he declared the 83,000 votes illegal?
A: He gave certificates of election to three white men: William Colmer, John Williams, and a Mr. Whittier.

Q: What did the Mississippi Freedom Democratic Party do?

- The bus breaks down, and his father gets out in the cold wind and icy rain to look under the hood.
- People on the bus sing and pray.
- Soon they are moving along again.

- Craig wakes to hear a policeman shouting that they cannot stop the bus near the Capitol.
- Papa says the bus won't go.
- The policeman says that if they came all the way from Mississippi, they can go a little bit farther.

---

17   Even losing his job didn't stop Papa from wanting to vote. One day he heard about Mrs. Fannie Lou Hamer and the Mississippi Freedom Democratic Party. The Freedom Party registered people without charging a poll tax, without a literacy test, and without people having to tell what the Mississippi Constitution was about.

18   On election day in 1964, Papa proudly voted for Mrs. Hamer, Mrs. Victoria Grey, and Mrs. Annie Devine to represent the people of the Second Congressional District of Mississippi. Eighty-three thousand other black men and women voted that day, too. Great victory celebrations were held in homes and community centers. But the Governor of Mississippi, Paul B. Johnson, declared all of those eighty-three thousand votes of black people illegal. He gave certificates of election to three white men—William Colmer, John Williams, and a Mr. Whittier—to represent the mostly black Second Congressional District.

19   Members of the Freedom Party were like Papa—they didn't give up. They got busy when the governor threw out their votes. Lawyers from all over the country came to help. People signed affidavits saying that when they tried to register they lost their jobs, they were beaten, and their homes were burned and businesses bombed. More than ten thousand people signed petitions to the governor asking him to count their votes. There was never a word from the governor.

20   MY MIND RETURNED TO THE SOUND OF THE OLD BUS slowly grinding along. Suddenly the bus stopped. Not again! We'd never make it now. Papa got out in the cold wind and icy drizzling rain and raised the hood. While he worked, we sang and clapped our hands to keep warm. I could hear Sister Phyllis praying with all her might for our safety. After a while we were moving along again.

I must have finally fallen asleep, for a policeman's voice woke me. "You can't stop here near the Capitol," he shouted.

21   "Our bus won't go," Papa said.

"If you made it from Mississippi all the way to D.C., you'll make it from here," the policeman barked.

> WORD BANK
> **affidavit** (AH fih DAY vit) *n.*: a written statement made with the promise to tell the truth
> **petition** (puh TIH shun) *n.*: a written request signed by a large number of people

---

A: It registered black people without having them pay a poll tax, take a literacy test, or explain the Mississippi constitution.

Q: When the bus breaks down again, how does the policeman help?
A: The policeman does not help.

ANALYTICAL

Q: What was wrong with declaring the votes illegal?
A: The three men were not elected by the people of the congressional district.

Q: What did the members of the Freedom Party do after the election?

A: They didn't give up. Lawyers came to help them and they signed affidavits about their experiences trying to register to vote.

Q: Did Papa's attempt to register to vote happen during the time of the story?
A: No. Craig is telling about an event that had occurred two years earlier.

Q: Did the registration by the Freedom Party, and the election of Mrs. Fannie Lou Hamer, Mrs. Victoria Grey, and Mrs. Annie Devine occur during the present time of the story?
A: No. Craig is thinking about these events, which had occurred in the past, while riding on the bus to Washington.

SUMMING UP THE PLOT

- Craig wonders why his father doesn't tell the policeman that they will go as soon as the bus starts.
- He tries to start the bus and the engine dies.
- The policeman shouts, "I said get out of here."

- Papa says they will have to push the bus.
- Everyone gets off the bus and pushes.
- Passersby stop and stare, and form a crowd around them.

- Someone in the crowd says, "You mean they came all the way from Mississippi in that?"
- Suddenly the bus looks shabby to Craig.
- He lowers his head and becomes aware of how old his clothes are. He feels ashamed.
- A man asks what they've come to D.C. for.
- Papa explains that they want to see about seating the people they elected to Congress.
- A woman says, "So you've come to lobby," and the crowd laughs.
- Craig wonders why they are laughing. He knows that lobby means to try to get someone to decide for or against something.

At first the loud voice frightened me. Then, wide awake, sensing the policeman's impatience, I wondered why Papa didn't let him know that we would go as soon as the motor started. But Papa, knowing that old bus, said nothing. He stepped on the starter. The old motor growled and died. Again the policeman shouted, "I said get out of here."

"We'll have to push it," Papa said.

Everyone got off the bus and pushed. Passersby stopped and stared. Finally we were safe on a side street, away from the Capitol with a crowd gathered around us.

"You mean they came all the way from Mississippi in that?" someone in the crowd asked.

Suddenly the old bus looked shabby. I lowered my head and became aware of my clothes: my faded coat too small; my cotton pants too thin. With a feeling of shame, I wished those people would go away.

"What brings you all to the District?" a man called to us.

"We've come to see about seating the people we voted for and elected," Papa answered. "Down home they say our votes don't count, and up here they've gone ahead and seated men who don't represent us. We've come to talk about that."

"So you've come to lobby," a woman shouted. The crowd laughed.

Why were they laughing? I knew that to lobby meant to try to get someone to decide for or against something. Yes, that was why we had

WORD BANK — **lobby** (LAH bee) *v.:* to work at influencing lawmakers to vote a certain way

LITERARY COMPONENTS

▶ **22. Characterization of Papa; Contrast with His Son:** Papa has grown up black in America. He has spent his life in the South. He is surely not going to challenge a policeman. Craig thinks about it logically. If the bus won't start, how can the policeman tell them to move it? And why can't his father say this?

▶ **23. Rising Action; Suspense; Onomatopoeia:** The bus motor dies with a *growl*. The policeman repeats his demand that they get out of there.

▶ **24. Theme:** This is what the hardest parts of struggle are about: Facing up to people who, intentionally or unintentionally, are going to make you feel like a fool for trying.

▶ **25. Contrasting Settings and People; Characterization:** Now Craig sees himself and his friends through the eyes of people from a different world. He experiences shame based on one thing: material wealth. He is ashamed because he has less money—poor clothes and an old bus.

▶ **26. Summing Up the Conflict; Theme:** Papa makes a concise, public statement about what it is they are trying to do.

Q: What does the woman shout?
A: She says, "So you've come to lobby."

Q: What does Craig know about the word lobby?
A: He knows it means "to try to get someone to decide for or against something."

ANALYTICAL

Q: Why do you think Papa says so little to the policeman?
A: Answers will vary. Papa has been trained since early childhood not to talk back.

Q: Why do you think the policeman isn't more helpful?
A: Answers will vary.

Q: Someone in the crowd says, "You mean they came all the way from Mississippi in that?" Why do you think the person says that? Is it really a question? Do you think it is a mean thing to say?
A: Answers will vary.

Q: Craig says he feels ashamed. Does Craig have anything to be ashamed of?
A: Answers will vary.

GUIDING THE READING

LITERAL

Q: What happens when Papa steps on the starter?
A: The old motor growls and dies.

Q: What does Papa say to everyone on the bus, after the engine dies and the policeman says, once again, to move the bus?
A: He says they will have to push the bus.

Q: What do the passersby do?
A: They stop and stare and crowd around them.

Q: What does someone in the crowd say?
A: Someone in the crowd says, "You mean they came all the way from Mississippi in that?"

Q: What does Craig notice about his clothing?
A: He says that his coat is faded and too small; his cotton pants are too thin.

Q: Someone asks what brings them to the District of Columbia. What does Papa tell him?
A: Papa says that they have come to see about seating the people they voted for. (Students may well add more to this answer.)

CONSTITUTIONAL
AMENDMENT XXIV

Passed by Congress August 27, 1962.
Ratified January 23, 1964.

Section 1.
The right of citizens of the United
States to vote in any primary or
other election for President or Vice
President, for electors for President
or Vice President, or for Senator or
Representative in Congress, shall not
be denied or abridged by the United
States or any State by reason of
failure to pay poll tax or other tax.

Section 2.
The Congress shall have power to
enforce this article by appropriate
legislation.

SUMMING UP THE PLOT

- Craig wishes that he could have told the people that the suffering that brought them there was nothing to laugh about.
- Someone from the crowd says that they are too late to lobby on the issue. "The House of Representatives is going to vote on the issue this morning."
- Craig thinks, "too late." Had they come so far in the cold for nothing?
- Would the men chosen by the governor, rather than the representatives they had elected, be seated in the House of Representatives?
- The rain begins to fall again.
- Papa says that they cannot turn back. They have come too far.
- They rush against the cold wind back to the Capitol.
- A doorman stops them on the steps and asks for their passes.
- They have no passes. They doorman says they must have passes to be seated in the gallery.
- Papa says they must stay, even if they do no more than let the legislators see that they have come all of this way. He pleads with the doorman to let them in out of the cold.

come. I wished I could have said to those people who stood gawking at us that the suffering that brought us here was surely nothing to laugh about. **(27)**

The laughter from the crowd quieted when another woman shouted, "You're too late to lobby. The House of Representatives will vote on that issue this morning." **(28)**

Too late. That's what had worried me when the old bus kept breaking down. Had we come so far in this cold for nothing? Was it really too late to talk to members of the House of Representatives to persuade them to seat our representatives elected by the Freedom Party, not the ones chosen by the governor? **(29)**

JUST THEN RAIN BEGAN TO FALL. THE CROWD QUICKLY LEFT, and we climbed onto our bus. Papa and the others started to talk. What would we do now? Finally, Papa said, "We can't turn back now. We've done too much and come too far." **(30)**

After more talk we all agreed that we must try to do what we had come to do. Icy rain pelted us as we rushed against cold wind back to the Capitol.

A doorman stopped us on the steps. "May I have your passes?" **(31)**

"We don't have any," Papa replied.

"Sorry, you have to have passes for seats in the gallery." The doorman blocked the way.

"We're cold in this rain. Let us in," Sister Phyllis cried.

"Maybe we should just go on back home," someone suggested.

"Yes. We can't talk to the legislators now, anyway," another woman said impatiently.

"No," Papa said. "We must stay if we do no more than let them see that we have come all this way." **(32)**

"But we're getting soaking wet. We can't stand out here much longer," another protested. **(33)**

"Can't you just let us in out of this cold?" Papa pleaded with the doorman.

"Not without passes." The doorman still blocked the way. Then he said, "There's a tunnel underneath this building. You can go there to get out of the rain." **(34)**

WORD BANK **legislators** (LEH jiss LAY torz) *n.:* lawmakers

The Silent Lobby ~ 89

LITERARY COMPONENTS

▶ **27. Characterization; Theme:** Craig wishes he could tell the gawkers that the suffering that brought them there is nothing to laugh at.

▶ **28. Rising Action; Suspense:** A woman in the crowd tells them they are too late to lobby. What will they do now?

▶ **29. Theme:** Had they come for nothing?

▶ **30. Characterization; Theme:** Papa says they must continue.

▶ **31. Rising Action; Suspense:** The doorman says they need passes and they don't have passes.

▶ **32. Papa Speaks to the Essence of Lobbying; Foreshadowing:** "We must stay if we do no more than *let them see that we have come all this way.*"

▶ **33. Theme; Characterization:** People are discouraged. They don't know what to do. They don't know whether to give up and go home. Papa pushes one more time. "Can't you just let us in…?"

▶ **34. Rising Action; Turning Point:** The doorman relents. He tells them there is a tunnel underneath the building where they can go to get out of the rain. We see here that, as in life, a minor character can have a powerful impact.

GUIDING THE READING

LITERAL

Q: What have they come too late for?
A: They have come too late to lobby.

Q: Have the legislators already voted on the issue?
A: No. They are going to vote on the issue that very morning.

Q: Papa says that they must stay, even if they do no more than . . . what?
A: Papa says they must stay, even if they do no more than let the legislators see that they have come all this way.

ANALYTICAL

Q: If Craig could have told the people who stood gawking about the suffering that brought them there, what would he have said?
A: There are many possible answers: Students can talk about the problems with registering to vote, the racial abuse at home, the losing of jobs, the governor's declaring the election illegal and appointing his own people, the difficult bus trip, and so forth.

Q: How do you think the doorman feels about these people?
A: Answers will vary.

Q: Do you think the people who wanted to go back home after Sister Phyllis cried, "Let us in," were giving up too easily?
A: Answers will vary. Some students may say they were giving up too easily, because they finally did get in from Papa's persistence and the doorman's partially relenting. But given what they had already been through—registering to vote at home; possibly losing jobs or being arrested; leaving home to come to a strange place on a bus that kept breaking down; standing in the icy rain; perhaps feeling ashamed as Craig felt ashamed—they had already done more than most of us would have done.

Q: Why does Papa continue to plead with the doorman?
A: Answers will vary. This matters so much and this is a man who does not give up easily.

SUMMING UP THE PLOT

- The doorman tells them there is a tunnel under the building where they can get in out of the rain.
- They crowd into the tunnel and line up along the sides.
- They hear footsteps and voices. Craig fears it's a trap.
- The voices cease when the people come upon them and walk by.
- His father says that they are congressmen and congresswomen.
- They are dressed finely in warm coats and gleaming shoes.
- The passing legislators react in various ways to the people gathered there from Mississippi: Some frown; some glare; some sigh; some are scared; some surprised; and there are a few friendly smiles.
- Craig sees how poor his father and their friends look beside these well-dressed people. But they all stand straight and tall.
- Craig wants to shout, "Count my papa's vote! Let my people help make the laws!"
- Craig prays, "L-rd, let them hear us in this silence."

LITERARY COMPONENTS

▶ **35. Strong Sensory Images; Setting:** Throughout this and the next several paragraphs, when they are in the tunnel, the visual images are very strong. We can also feel Craig's being so chilled and then being warmed by the walls. Here, the author appeals to our physical senses.

▶ **36. Rising Action; Suspense; Characterization:** Some may think that Craig is overreacting, but this speaks to his experience living in Mississippi.

▶ **37. Minor Climax:** This is one of the most important moments in the story. This is the fulfillment of Papa's deep desire: that they just be seen!

▶ **38. Contrast:** The contrast between the affluence of the legislators and the poverty of these petitioners is very effective.

▶ **39. Characterization; Theme:** Craig sees how they look in comparison to the legislators—but he also sees that "they all stood straight and tall."

▶ **40. Characterization; Theme:** Craig wants to shout, "Count my papa's vote! Let my people help make laws, too." This is a child's plea, and very moving. It resounds in a way similar to the excerpt from Martin Luther King's *I Have a Dream* speech.

▶ **41. Characterization; Culture:** These are deeply religious people. The role of religion in the civil rights movement should not be underestimated.

▶ **42. Rising Action; New Characters:** Two congressmen stop in front of Papa and introduce themselves. One of the congressmen is black!

▶ **43. Rising Action:** They say they had little luck lobbying themselves and only expect fifty votes.

- Two congressmen stop in front of Papa and introduce themselves.
- Papa introduces himself and says that they are from Mississippi.
- Congressman Ryan from New York says they expected them much earlier.
- Papa explains their difficulties.
- The congressmen say that they lobbied late into the night, and didn't do very well.

---

35 WE CROWDED INTO THE TUNNEL AND LINED UP ALONG the sides. My chilled body and hands came to life pressed against the warm **36** walls. Then footsteps and voices echoed through the tunnel. Police. This tunnel...a trap! Would they do something to us for trying to get in without passes? I wanted to cry out to Papa, but I could not speak.

The footsteps came closer. Then many people began to walk by. When they came upon us, they suddenly stopped talking. Only the sound of their feet echoed in the tunnel. Where had they come from? What did they do? "Who are they, Papa?" I whispered.

37 "Congressmen and women." Papa spoke so softly, I hardly heard him, even in the silence.

38 They wore warm coats, some trimmed with fur. Their shoes gleamed. Some of them frowned at us. Others glared. Some sighed quickly as they walked by. Others looked at us, then turned their eyes to their shoes. I could tell by a sudden lift of the head and a certain look that some were surprised and scared. And there were a few whose friendly smiles seemed to say, Right on!

39 I glanced at Papa. How poor he and our friends looked beside those well-dressed people. Their clothes were damp, threadbare, and wrinkled; their shoes were worn and mud stained. But they all stood straight and tall.

40 My heart pounded. I wanted to call out to those men and women, "Count my Papa's vote! Let my people help make laws, too." But I didn't dare speak in that silence.

Could they hear my heart beating? Did they know what was on my mind? **41** "L-rd," I prayed, "let them hear us in this silence."

Then two congressmen stopped in front of Papa. I was frightened until I saw smiles on their faces.

42 "I'm Congressman Ryan from New York," one of them said. Then he introduced a black man: "This is Congressman Hawkins from California."

"I'm Sylvester Saunders. We are here from Mississippi," Papa said.

"We expected you much earlier," Congressman Ryan said.

"Our old bus and bad weather delayed us," Papa explained.

43 "That's unfortunate. You could've helped us a lot. We worked late into the night lobbying to get votes on your side. But maybe I should say on our side." Mr. Ryan smiled.

"And we didn't do very well," Congressman Hawkins said.

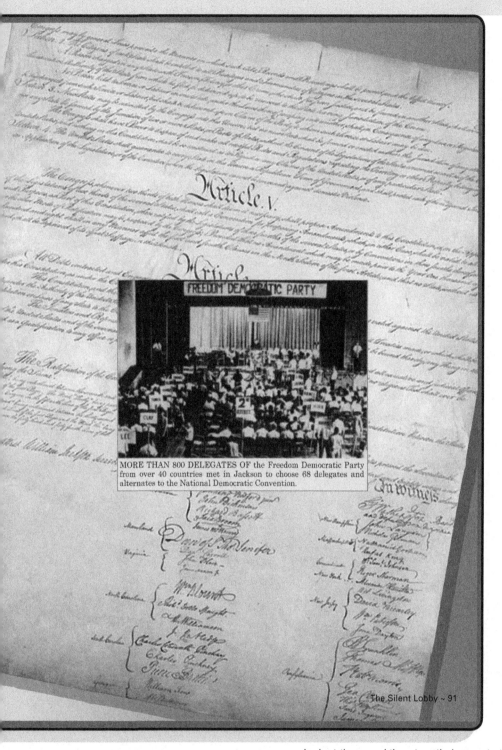

MORE THAN 800 DELEGATES OF the Freedom Democratic Party from over 40 countries met in Jackson to choose 68 delegates and alternates to the National Democratic Convention.

GUIDING THE READING (P. 90)

LITERAL

Q: Where does the doorman finally let them go?
A: He tells them that there is a tunnel underneath the building.

Q: Who are the people who pass them in the tunnel?
A: The people are congressmen and congresswomen.

Q: What are the different reactions the legislators have to these poor, wet brave people from Mississippi?
A: Some frown; some glare; and some sigh. Some look at them and then turn their eyes to their shoes. Some seem surprised and others seem scared. There are also a few friendly smiles.

Q: What does Craig want to call out to these men and women?
A: He wants to say, "Count my papa's vote! Let my people help make laws, too."

Q: Who are the two congressmen and where are they from?
A: Congressman Ryan is from New York and Congressman Hawkins is from California.

ANALYTICAL

Q: Why do you think the doorman tells them about the tunnel?
A: Answers will vary.

Q: Why does Craig think the tunnel is a trap when he hears footsteps and voices?
A: Answers will vary. Certainly he has heard about people's terrible experiences where he lives in Mississippi.

Q: Why do you think the legislators stop speaking when they see the people from Mississippi?
A: Answers will vary. They are probably shocked. They are seeing the real people who are deeply affected by their actions. They are seeing people who are poorer than many of them can imagine. Certainly, they don't expect to see these people at the House of Representatives in Washington, D.C. (If students have trouble with this one, encourage them to close their eyes and see the picture in the tunnel in their own minds.)

Q: What does Craig pray? What does he mean by this?
A: He says, "L-rd, let them hear us in this silence." Each group is shocked to see the other. The legislators are just walking through on the way to the House of Representatives session. Social protocol and lack of time keep the people from one group from speaking to people from the other group. But Craig hopes that the legislators will hear their inner voices speaking.

CONSTITUTIONAL
AMENDMENT XXVI

*Passed by Congress March 23, 1971.
Ratified July 1, 1971.*

Note: Amendment 14, section 2, of
the Constitution was modified by
section 1 of the 26th amendment.

Section 1.
The right of citizens of the United
States, who are eighteen years of age
or older, to vote shall not be denied
or abridged by the United States or
by any State on account of age.

Section 2.
The Congress shall have power to
enforce this article by appropriate
legislation.

GUIDING THE READING (P. 93)

LITERAL

Q: Which Congressman is speaking, who does not want Mrs. Hamer seated in the House?
A: The Congressman from Michigan, Gerald Ford.

Q: Which Congressman argues that sticking to the rules denies blacks the right to vote in the state of Mississippi?
A: Congressman Ryan.

Q: How many votes did Congressman Ryan think they would be lucky to get?
A: He thought they would be lucky to get fifty votes.

Q: How many Representatives are voting in the House?
A: 435.

Q: How does Craig feel with every yes vote?
A: He feels as though he can hardly keep from clapping his hands and shouting.

Q: What is the strange thing that happens?
A: Congressmen and congresswomen keep saying, "Yes. Yes. Yes."

ANALYTICAL

Q: What does Congressman Ford think is important?
A: He thinks that it is important to follow the rule that says that the only people who will be seated in Congress are people with credentials from their own states.

Q: What does he think will, in time, undo the wrongs done to black Americans?

A: He believes that the new civil rights act will undo the wrongs done to black Americans.

Q: Why do you think that he wants to seat the men chosen by Governor Johnson?
A: Answers will vary.

Q: Why can't the rules from segregated states justly apply in the United States Congress?
A: Answers will vary.

Q: Which petitions is Craig thinking of?
A: The petitions signed by more than 10,000 people and sent to Governor Paul Johnson of Mississippi, asking that he count their votes.

- Congressman Ryan invites them to come in and watch the session.
- A little later, as they find seats in the gallery, they watch Congressman Gerald Ford speak against seating the elected members of the Freedom Party.
- He says that, for now, the only "representatives" that should be seated are those who have credentials from their states.
- Congressman Ryan asks, How can Congress abide by the rules of Mississippi, a state that denies blacks the right to vote?
- Craig wonders if the men and women of the House of Representatives are listening to Congressman Ryan.
- He recalls that Congressman Ryan has said that they will be lucky to get fifty votes for seating Mrs. Hamer, Mrs. Victoria Grey, and Mrs. Annie Devine.
- At every yes vote, Craig can hardly keep from clapping his hands and shouting.

"We'll be lucky if we get fifty votes on our side today," Congressman Ryan **(43)** informed us. "Maybe you would like to come in and see us at work."

"We don't have passes," I said, surprised at my voice.

"We'll see about getting all of you in," Congressman Hawkins promised. **(44)**

A LITTLE LATER, AS WE FOUND SEATS IN THE GALLERY, **(45)** Congressman Gerald Ford[2] from the state of Michigan was speaking. He did not **(46)** want Mrs. Hamer and other fairly elected members of the Freedom Party seated in the House. He asked his fellow congressmen to stick to the rule of letting **(47)** only those with credentials from their states be seated in Congress. The new civil rights act would, in time, undo wrongs done to black Americans. But for now, Congress should let the men chosen by Governor Johnson keep their seats and get on with other business.

Then Congressman Ryan rose to speak. How could Congress stick to rules **(48)** that denied blacks their right to vote in the state of Mississippi? The rule of letting only those with credentials from a segregated[3] state have seats in the House could not justly apply here.

I looked down on those men and few women and wondered if they were listening. Did they know about the petitions? I remembered what Congressman **(49)** Ryan had said: "We'll be lucky if we get fifty...." Only 50 out of 435 elected to the House.

Finally the time came for Congress to vote. Those who wanted to seat Mrs. Hamer and members of the Freedom Democratic Party were to say, yes. Those who didn't want to seat Mrs. Hamer were to say, no.

At every yes vote I could hardly keep from clapping my hands and **(50)** shouting, "Yea! Yea!" But I kept quiet, counting: thirty, then forty, forty-eight...only two more. We would lose badly.

Then something strange happened. Congressmen and congresswomen kept **(51)** saying "Yes. Yes. Yes." On and on, "Yes." My heart pounded. Could we win? I sat

---

2. *Congressman Gerald Ford* later became the 38th president of the United States.
3. Prior to the Civil Rights Act of 1964, in some states, black Americans were kept separate from white Americans in many situations. For example, white children and black children were sent to separate schools. States where blacks and whites were kept separate by law were called *segregated* (SEG rih GAY tid) *states.*

WORD BANK	**credentials** (kruh DENN shulz) *n.*: documents showing that a person has privileges

LITERARY COMPONENTS

▶ **44. Rising Action:** They invite the group in to watch the vote.

▶ **45. Setting:** They are now sitting in the gallery of the Congress.

▶ **46. Historical Reference:** Congressman Gerald Ford of Michigan was elected to the House of Representatives in 1948 for the first of thirteen terms. From 1965 to 1973, he was House Minority Leader. He became the 38th President of the United States in 1974 through a very unusual set of circumstances. In 1972, Richard Nixon was reelected President. Spiro Agnew was his Vice President. Spiro Agnew was charged by the U.S. Dept. of Justice with having accepted bribes as Governor of Maryland. It was believed he continued to accept bribes as Vice President. Consequently, he resigned from office. President Nixon appointed Mr. Ford Vice President on December 6, 1973. This was the first time in U.S. history that procedures for filling such vacancies were used. (These procedures are outlined in the 25th Amendment to the Constitution.) When President Nixon, himself, was forced to resign on August 9, 1974—following the Watergate scandal—Gerald Ford became President.

▶ **47. Rising Action; Increased Tension:** Likely in his role as House Minority Leader, Congressman Ford is asking his fellow congressmen to follow a rule that will not allow the seating of the Freedom Party representatives. The rule stipulates that representatives to Congress must be elected according to the legal procedures of the state from which they come. (Of course, it is very important to have rules so that a country can be governed properly. But Jim Crow meant that blacks in the South were kept from voting and had no representation in Congress.) Congressman Ford says that in time, the new civil rights act will right these wrongs. (On June 29, 1964, President Lyndon Baines Johnson had signed the Omnibus Civil Rights Act. However another piece of legislation, the Voting Rights Act, needed to be passed on August 6, 1965, in order to guarantee the right to vote without penalties or poll taxes.)

▶ **48. Rising Action; Theme:** Congressman Ryan rises to speak. How can Congress obey rules that make it impossible for blacks to vote? Rules from a state that practices segregation *cannot justly apply here.*

▶ **49. Rising Action; Suspense; Important Data:** Congressman Ryan has said they will be lucky to get fifty votes. We learn that the total votes will be 435—from 435 elected representatives to the House. Fifty votes would be 11% of the total vote.

▶ **50. Characterization; Rising Action; Suspense:** At every yes vote, Craig can hardly keep from clapping his hands and shouting.

▶ **51. Rising Action:** *Then something strange happens.* Congressmen and congresswomen keep saying, "Yes. Yes. Yes."

SUMMING UP THE PLOT

- Everyone in their group is sitting on the edge of their seats.
- When the voting is over, 148 votes have been cast in their favor.
- Why have so many Representatives changed their minds?
- Papa introduces Craig to Congressman Hawkins.
- Congressman Hawkins asks Craig how they had known that some of the representatives would walk through the tunnel.

- Craig says that they had just been sent there to get out of the rain.
- The congressman says that their standing there silently made a difference in the vote.
- Craig feels proud.

- He thinks to himself that Papa was right when he told Mama that a struggle can be won without bombs and guns.
- They had lobbied in silence and they had been heard.

LITERARY COMPONENTS

▶ **52. Building to a Climax:** They look as if they can hardly keep from shouting as more yes votes ring from the floor.

▶ **53. Climax:** When the voting is over, 148 votes have been cast in their favor. *Why have so many changed their minds?*

▶ **54. Falling Action; Setting:** Later, presumably when they are no longer in the gallery (although their location is uncertain), Papa introduces Craig to Congressman Hawkins.

▶ **55. Falling Action:** The congressman remarks on the strange coincidence of their being in the tunnel—and the repercussions of that.

▶ **56. Characterization; Theme:** Craig feels proud. His father was right: A struggle can be won without violence.

▶ **57. Resolution; Moral of the Story; Title:** They have lobbied in silence and they have been *heard.*

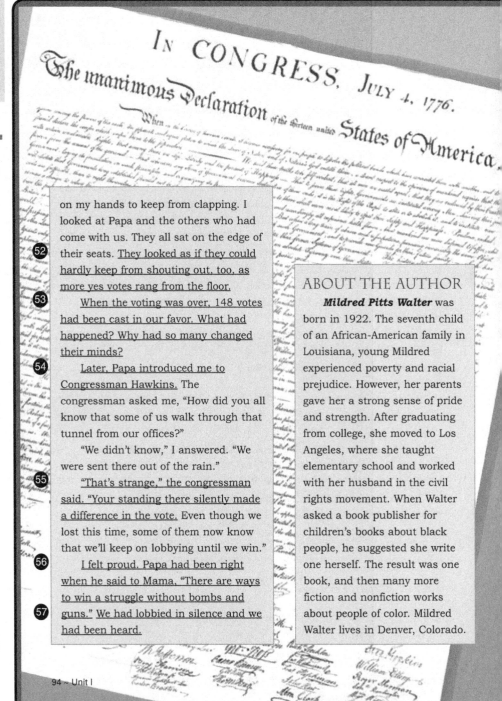

on my hands to keep from clapping. I looked at Papa and the others who had come with us. They all sat on the edge of their seats. **They looked as if they could hardly keep from shouting out, too, as more yes votes rang from the floor.**

When the voting was over, 148 votes had been cast in our favor. What had happened? Why had so many changed their minds?

Later, Papa introduced me to Congressman Hawkins. The congressman asked me, "How did you all know that some of us walk through that tunnel from our offices?"

"We didn't know," I answered. "We were sent there out of the rain."

"That's strange," the congressman said. "Your standing there silently made a difference in the vote. Even though we lost this time, some of them now know that we'll keep on lobbying until we win."

I felt proud. Papa had been right when he said to Mama, "There are ways to win a struggle without bombs and guns." We had lobbied in silence and we had been heard.

94 ~ Unit I

ABOUT THE AUTHOR

Mildred Pitts Walter was born in 1922. The seventh child of an African-American family in Louisiana, young Mildred experienced poverty and racial prejudice. However, her parents gave her a strong sense of pride and strength. After graduating from college, she moved to Los Angeles, where she taught elementary school and worked with her husband in the civil rights movement. When Walter asked a book publisher for children's books about black people, he suggested she write one herself. The result was one book, and then many more fiction and nonfiction works about people of color. Mildred Walter lives in Denver, Colorado.

GUIDING THE READING

LITERAL

Q: How are Papa and the others sitting?
A: They are all sitting on the edge of their seats.

Q: When the voting is over, how many congresspersons have voted to seat the representatives from the Freedom Party?
A: 148.

Q: To whom does Papa introduce Craig after the vote?
A: He introduces him to Congressman Hawkins, the black representative from California.

ANALYTICAL

Q: Why do so many congressmen and congresswomen chang their minds?
A: Answers will vary. Certainly actually seeing the people to whom this mattered so deeply, and perhaps seeing their poverty, would have been a very powerful experience.

Q: Do you know what percentage of the House voted in favor of seating the Freedom Party members?
A: To figure the percentage, students will need to divide 148 by 435. Thirty-four percent, or slightly more than one-third.

Q: What does Congressman Hawkins think is strange?
A: He thinks it is strange that the people from Mississippi were standing in the tunnel without even knowing that some of the representatives came through that way. And that is what made the difference in the vote.

Q: Why does Craig feel proud?
A: Answers will vary. But their presence had surely accomplished something, and he had been there.

Q: What kind of struggle does Papa believe in?
A: Papa believes in a nonviolent struggle, a struggle in which no one is hurt.

FIRST IMPRESSIONS

If students have difficulty with the question, ask them if they have ever been in a situation in which they felt unsure of themselves.

Studying the Selection

FIRST IMPRESSIONS

How would you have felt, standing in the tunnel, as the congressmen and women walked by?

QUICK REVIEW

1. Where is the old bus coming from and where is it going?

2. Who were the three people who had been elected by the people of the Second Congressional District?

3. What organization registered people without charging a poll tax, without a literacy test, and without people having to tell what the Mississippi Constitution was about?

4. What had Papa's boss said he would do, if Papa registered to vote?

FOCUS

5. Why does Papa insist that Craig go on the bus ride to Washington?

6. One of the themes of *The Silent Lobby* is the struggle for equality—black Americans are supposed to have the same rights as white Americans and they are struggling to get those rights. Why don't people want them to vote?

CREATING & WRITING

7. You are a member of Congress. You changed your vote, after seeing the people from Mississippi standing in the tunnel. Write a letter home to one of your grandparents, explaining why you did so.

8. Read through the story once again, and list some examples of actions that show that people from Mississippi don't give up. Make sure you give the page numbers in parentheses.

9. Study the stanza from the *I Have a Dream* speech that your teacher has provided. You and the rest of your classmates will recite the part assigned to you. Notice how some of the lines are repeated, making the speech almost like a song or a poem.

The Silent Lobby ~ 95

QUICK REVIEW

1. The bus is coming from Mississippi and going to Washington, D.C.

2. The people of the Second Congressional District of Mississippi had elected Mrs. Fannie Lou Hamer, Mrs. Victoria Grey, and Mrs. Annie Devine to represent them.

3. The Mississippi Freedom Democratic Party registered people without their paying poll tax, taking a literacy test, or giving an explanation of the Mississippi Constitution.

4. Papa's boss said he would fire Papa, if he registered to vote.

FOCUS

5. Papa believes that Craig is old enough to understand that blacks in Mississippi are being denied the right to vote, and that he is old enough to take responsibility for making change.

6. Answers will vary, and it will be interesting to see what students have to say. Partly, their ability to respond to the question will come out of your presenting the material in **Background Bytes,** and your talking about the social function of an underclass. Blacks provided a source of cheap house and field labor. By looking down on black people, white people—no matter how uneducated or poor themselves—could feel that they were superior to someone. Racial discrimination also meant that people didn't have to think about how horrible the enslavement of blacks had been.

CREATING & WRITING

7. Answers will vary.

8. Examples of the steadfastness of the blacks from Mississippi:

> They go on the bus, even though it is old. (p. 83)
>
> People consider it dangerous, but they go anyway. (p. 83)
>
> Papa says there is no peace without freedom. (p. 83)
>
> Papa insists Craig is old enough to know what the trip to Washington is all about. (p. 85)
>
> Papa tries to register to vote even though his boss threatens to fire him. (p. 85)
>
> Papa is turned down at the polls and loses his job, but he still wants to register with the Mississippi Freedom Democratic Party. (p. 86)
>
> After the Governor of Mississippi, Paul B. Johnson, declares 83,000 votes illegal, people don't give up: People sign affidavits describing what had happened to them. Ten thousand people sign petitions to the governor asking him to count their votes. (p. 86)
> And so forth.

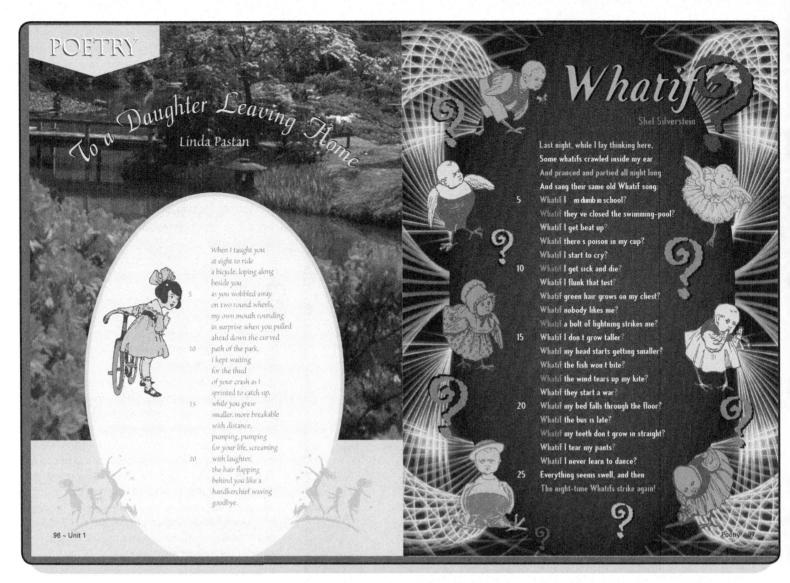

POETRY

To a Daughter Leaving Home
Linda Pastan

When I taught you
at eight to ride
a bicycle, loping along
beside you
5 as you wobbled away
on two round wheels,
my own mouth rounding
in surprise when you pulled
ahead down the curved
10 path of the park,
I kept waiting
for the thud
of your crash as I
sprinted to catch up,
15 while you grew
smaller, more breakable
with distance,
pumping, pumping
for your life, screaming
20 with laughter,
the hair flapping
behind you like a
handkerchief waving
goodbye.

96 ~ Unit 1

Whatif
Shel Silverstein

Last night, while I lay thinking here,
Some whatifs crawled inside my ear
And pranced and partied all night long
And sang their same old Whatif song:
5 Whatif I'm dumb in school?
Whatif they've closed the swimming-pool?
Whatif I get beat up?
Whatif there's poison in my cup?
Whatif I start to cry?
10 Whatif I get sick and die?
Whatif I flunk that test?
Whatif green hair grows on my chest?
Whatif nobody likes me?
Whatif a bolt of lightning strikes me?
15 Whatif I don't grow taller?
Whatif my head starts getting smaller?
Whatif the fish won't bite?
Whatif the wind tears up my kite?
Whatif they start a war?
20 Whatif my bed falls through the floor?
Whatif the bus is late?
Whatif my teeth don't grow in straight?
Whatif I tear my pants?
Whatif I never learn to dance?
25 Everything seems swell, and then
The night-time Whatifs strike again!

Poetry ~ 97

Talking About Poetry and *To a Daughter Leaving Home*

Lots of people are afraid of poetry. Some people have complaints about poetry: They don't understand it. It's too hard. They don't *get* it. (And, certainly, if a teacher is uncomfortable with poetry, it will be difficult *not* to communicate the feeling to the students!)

Oddly enough, poetry is closest to literary forms we love and to experiences we have that are comforting and entertaining: songs, lullabies, nursery rhymes, and tongue twisters. People ought to get a kick out of poetry.

One of the ways we begin to teach very little children to talk—without even being aware of it—is through the use of nursery rhymes and funny songs with funny sounds and animal noises. If older children learn to love poetry, to be unafraid of it, they will have a lifetime of pleasurable reading awaiting them. This is because like music, poetry is about sound. Poetry is also often about rhythm.

Poetry must be read out loud. Some poems just cry out to be memorized and performed! Human beings like to hear nice sounds. Human beings like dramatic performance.

Poetry is also a short way of expressing a feeling, relating an observation, or recounting a story. How does poetry do this with such brevity? One way is through the skillful use of *figures of speech*. A figure of speech is any language that is not meant to be taken literally. A telephone book contains no figures of speech because it is purely informational. A story, a poem, a speech—any language which speaks not only to our conscious minds but also to our senses, our emotions, our intuitions—may contain figures of speech. Figures of speech help us see in our mind's eye the story or event the poet is recounting. Some figures of speech help us *hear* the sounds of the story. And some figures of speech drive home the theme of the poem.

A figure of speech appears in the last four lines of *To a Daughter Leaving Home*. In the poem we read,

> the hair flapping
> behind you **like** a
> handkerchief waving
> goodbye.

(You may need to familiarize your students with the notion that women used to wave goodbye with their handkerchiefs. Since few people carry handkerchiefs, this social ritual may be unfamiliar to young readers—and even to young teachers.)

What specific type of figure of speech appears in the last four lines? A *simile* (SIM uh lee). A simile is a comparison between two things—two things that presumably are not alike. The comparison evokes in us the sense that they *are* alike in some (but not all) ways, after all. This is also the definition of a *metaphor* (MEHT uh fore). But a simile has one other condition: The comparison must use the words *like* or *as* or *as if* or *as though*.

Does the poet or the speaker of the poem *really* believe that the daughter's hair is a handkerchief? No, of course not. But what a wonderful picture this creates, a girl riding off on her bike, with her hair waving goodbye! More than that, the simile that closes the poem shows us that the whole poem, the whole story of the poem—a daughter riding off on her two-wheeler alone for the first time—is an anecdote taken from the past that in the mother's mind is a metaphor for the daughter's actually leaving home in the present time. Interestingly, the present time is established *only* by the title.

Does the poet or mother think that her daughter's actual leaving home is just the same as her bicycling off by herself when she was a little girl? Yes and no. She surely knows that her daughter won't be coming back right away. She surely knows that her daughter is older now and is (probably) not riding a bike to take her wherever she is going. But some of her feelings, some of the feelings she had when her daughter went biking off, are the *same* as today, when her daughter is moving out.

What about these two experiences is the same? That is a good question for your students. How are (1) a daughter's riding on a two-wheeler by herself for the first time and (2) a daughter's moving away from home as a young adult alike for a mom? Do these experiences also have similarities for the daughter?

More About Figures of Speech

Figures of speech have been called *dream language*. In dreams, events occur that represent events or feelings from our waking life. The dream is a kind of shorthand for a way we feel or a situation we have experienced. Figures of speech are also a kind of shorthand.

A95 ~ **Unit 1**

A figure of speech is a word or phrase that describes an object, idea, event, person, creature, or phenomenon in terms of another object, idea, event, person, creature, or phenomenon. The description or comparison is not meant to be taken as literally true. That means, it is not to be understood as a factual description or comparison nor to be interpreted as actually so.

Below, we shall briefly discuss five types of figures of speech. The first, **simile**, has been mentioned above. Its fraternal—but not identical—twin is **metaphor**, in which, like the simile, two unlike things are shown to share one or many traits.

A metaphor, however, is an *equation*, whereas a simile is an *approximation*. A simile—to be *like* something—retains the difference between the two things being compared. One can never be fully substituted for the other. But a metaphor is a substitution, an equation in principle.

Compare metaphor:

I fall upon the thorns of life,/ I bleed.(Shelley)
Her life was a bed of roses, until—
Thomas Edison was "the wizard of Menlo Park."

to simile:

A good book is like a good meal.
O lift me as a wave, a leaf, a cloud, (Shelley)
She walks in beauty like the night (Byron)

In addition to **metaphor** and **simile,** common figures of speech include

Hyperbole (hi PURR boh lee): an extravagant exaggeration that is often funny, because a reality is conveyed that is impossible. When a writer or speaker uses hyperbole, they express more than the truth, in order to make a vivid impression. Hyperbole is often used meanly to make fun of others—so we need to be careful with our examples.

I must have walked a thousand miles.
When I saw Roger's dog I was shocked: He was as big as a house!

Idiom (IHD ee ohm): a set and commonly understood phrase of two or more words that means something other than the literal definition of its words. A rule of thumb is that, although one can translate a simile or metaphor into another language and retain its sense, one cannot translate an idiom word for word. In another language, the words of the idiom will make no sense at all. One can only translate the *idea* that the idiom conveys. English has thousands of idioms.

I didn't want to be the one to break the news to her.
Done is done; Jim will have to face the music. He's not very bright.

Personification (purr SAHN if ick AY shun): A metaphor in which human qualities, feelings, action, or characteristics are given to inanimate (non-living) objects. Giving animals human qualities is **not** personification.

Kurt shivered as an angry wind blew across the field.

Jane had been working with the shovel for an hour, but the rock refused to budge. The sun smiled down on us as we embarked upon our journey.

Literary Devices Using Sound

Poets use sound to bring the reader into their poem. Some of these literary devices are just the repetition of letters. In fact there are three ways that poets repeat letters. (1) Repetition of the *initial* consonant sound of words; (2) Repetition of consonant sounds and consonant combinations *within* words; and (3) Repetition of the vowel sounds *within* words in a line or stanza.

Here are examples of each type:

(1) **between the black heads / bent below the heavy yoke** (see *Figures in the Field Against the Sky,* page 99)
(2) **A Niche in the Kitchen** (see page 199)
(3) **And the warm air / Carries the haunting sound** (see *The Whippoorwill Calls,* page 98)

The repetition of the same initial consonant sound within a poem or a passage of prose is called **alliteration.** Of course, tongue twisters use lots of alliteration. (**P**eter **P**iper **p**icked a **p**eck of **p**ickled **p**eppers.)

Another form of poetic repetition is the simple repetition of the same words. *To a Daughter Leaving Home* does this nicely with *pumping, pumping.* In *The Whippoorwill Calls,* Lines 1-6 of Stanza 2 mimic the words and construction of the same lines in Stanza 1.

Rhyme is the repetition of accented vowel sounds and all the sounds following them in words that are close together in a poem. Rhyme is the correspondence of the terminal sounds of two or more words or lines of verse. The poem, *Whatif,* is written in rhyming pairs of lines.

Another sound-based figure of speech is **onomatopoeia.** This is the use of a word whose sound imitates or suggests its meaning: the *clanging* of the bell; the *bubbling* brook; the *sizzling* hamburgers; the slow *hiss* of the air from a balloon.

What Else Makes Poetry Hard to Understand?

Poetry may be hard to understand, because it is not usually punctuated the way that prose is punctuated. Notice, in fact, that *To a Daughter Leaving Home* is only one sentence! When poetry does this, it may leave us breathless, amazed. Our first reaction to all of those words in one sustained breath—although we do get a break with some of the commas—is What?!

In fact, most poems are not just one sentence. This is a device the author uses deliberately in *To a Daughter Leaving Home.* You may wish to discuss this with your students. What effect does the single sentence format

of the poem have on its impact? How does the experience of reading this, especially reading it aloud, mirror the feelings of the writer, talking about her daughter bicycling away?

All of the words, without letup, from Line 7 (*my own mouth rounding*) to the poem's close, give a sense of propulsion, of the mother's *waiting for the thud of [her] crash,* of *pumping, pumping.*

Poetry can be difficult because thoughts are not completed on a single line—or two or three. The interruption of ideas, the splitting apart of events, ideas, or images by separating them, is a literary construction to which a reader must become accustomed and through which students may need to be guided. This sort of visual and mental training that poetry necessitates is worth the effort, because it makes it possible for the poet to give great emphasis to some words or pictures. It allows us to see and hear wonderful things. For example, *my own mouth rounding* is an image that lasts because it stands there by itself (and both words have the same internal vowel sound), not completed with *in surprise* until the next line. What is the effect of *pumping, pumping* on its own line? Or, *for your life, screaming*? Or the final word of the poem, *goodbye,* on its final line alone?

An Excellent Exercise for You and Your Students: Translating a Poem into Prose

Most people like puzzles. Poetry can be a puzzle that is fascinating to unravel. A good exercise, even with young students, is translating a poem into prose sentences. Here is our version of *To a Daughter Leaving Home:*

When you were eight, I taught you to ride a bicycle.
I loped along beside you, as you wobbled away on two round wheels.
My own mouth rounded in surprise, when you pulled ahead down the curved path of the park.
I kept waiting for the thud of your crash.
As I sprinted to catch up, you grew smaller, more breakable with distance.
There you were, pumping, pumping for your life.
You screamed with laughter, and your hair flapped behind you—like a handkerchief waving goodbye.

Some of these sentences may be too long for fifth graders. But you can break them down even more, into smaller pieces, as long as you have complete sentences, and as long as you don't change the meaning of the poem. Doing this enables students to understand the meaning of the poem, and also shows, by contrast, how much more vivid and powerful the poem is, as it has been written.

TO "TO A DAUGHTER LEAVING HOME"

The poem is about the excitement and terror the parent feels when the child embarks on a new experience and develops new skills. New experiences enable children to grow and mature.

Ultimately, most children will grow up and leave home. Parents know this but are not always thinking about it. Often, when children do something new it is, for their parents, a little bit like they are leaving. The more independent the child becomes, the less it seems

they need the parent. When the time comes for the child to leave, events of the past may suddenly be remembered. What is the theme? It is both very difficult and a source of pride when children leave home.

EYES ON...FREE VERSE AND THE FIRST-PERSON VOICE

We usually think of poetry as having a pattern of rhyme and rhythm. Poetry without meter, without a beat, without a regular pattern of end rhymes is called *free verse*. Free verse, however, may have *cadence*, which is the rhythmic recurrence of a sound, its rising and falling inflection. **Free verse usually relies more heavily than traditional poetry on the repetition of words, phrases, sentence structure, images, and even—especially—the repetition of consonant and vowel sounds.** Free verse may also pay special attention to the number of syllables in each word and the number of words per line. These are important guidelines to help you and your students appreciate and think about poetry.

The *I* of the poem is the mother of the daughter-leaving-home. The use of *I* by the speaker of the poem tells us that the poem is written in the first person.

LITERARY COMPONENTS

▶ **1. Title Establishes Extended Metaphor:** The title establishes the time of the telling of the story. The title is also essential to our understanding that the incident recounted in the poem resembles the event in the title for the mother, who is the speaker of the poem.

▶ **2. Syntactical Structure:** The poem is just one sentence.

▶ **3. Syllabification:** You may want to think about whether the following lines are more effective because they only use words of one syllable.
Line 1:   *When I taught you*
Line 2:   *at eight to ride*
Line 6:   *on two round wheels*
Line 10: *path of the park*
Line 12: *for the thud*
Line 13: *of your crash as I* etc.

▶ **4. Repetition of Letters:** In Lines 3-6, the *b*'s and the *w*'s are repeated at the beginning of and within words. *a **b**icycle, loping along*
> ***b**eside you*
> *as you **w**o**bb**led a**w**ay*
> *on two round **w**heels*

▶ **5. Repetition of Words:** In Lines 6 and 7, *round* is repeated.

▶ **6. Repetition of the –ing Ending:** Lines 3, 7, 11, 18, 19, 21, and 23 create a cadence with the repetition of –*ing* in *loping, rounding, waiting, pumping, screaming, flapping,* and *waving.*

▶ **7. Vivid Imagery; Appeals to Sense of Physical Experience; Repetition of Word:** Line 7: *My own mouth rounding...* is a very strong image. We see her mouth, shaped like an **O**. The image is all the stronger because of the carryover of the word *round* from the previous line (*round wheels*).

▶ **8. Repetition of Letters:** Look for the *p*'s in Lines 8 and 10 (and again in Line 18). *in surprise when you pulled...path of the park...pumping, pumping.*

▶ **9. Onomatopoeia:** Line 12, *thud;* Line 13, *crash.*

▶ **10. Emotional Climax of the Poem; Repetition of Words:** In Line 18, the poem peaks with *pumping, pumping.* The peak is created by the buildup of –*ing* words.

▶ **11. Ambiguous Meaning:** In Line 19, the *for your life, screaming* suggests excitement, but danger too.

▶ **12. Simile:** Lines 21-24 hold the crucial simile
> *the hair flapping*
> *behind you like a*
> *handkerchief waving*
> *goodbye.*

▶ **13. Poignant Conclusion:** Line 24, the last line of the poem, has only one word: *goodbye.* The daughter's hair waves goodbye blithely, her face turned towards the path that lies ahead. The mother, left behind, says the single word—perhaps unheard—goodbye.

POETRY

To a Daughter Leaving Home
Linda Pastan

> When I taught you
> at eight to ride
> a bicycle, loping along
> beside you
> 5 as you wobbled away
> on two round wheels,
> my own mouth rounding
> in surprise when you pulled
> ahead down the curved
> 10 path of the park,
> I kept waiting
> for the thud
> of your crash as I
> sprinted to catch up,
> 15 while you grew
> smaller, more breakable
> with distance,
> pumping, pumping
> for your life, screaming
> 20 with laughter,
> the hair flapping
> behind you like a
> handkerchief waving
> goodbye.

96 ~ Unit 1

ANALYZING THE POEM

To a Daughter Leaving Home is a one-sentence, free verse poem. A mother describes a past event—her eight-year-old daughter's going off on her two-wheeler alone for the first time. She thinks of that time, because her daughter is about to leave home. Interestingly, it is only the title that establishes the point of reference of the present time. The simile of the last four lines is the clincher for extended metaphor that is the entire poem.

The poem has poignancy. As her daughter rides away on her bike, the mother awaits the thud of her crash and sees her as smaller, increasingly fragile with distance; the daughter is screaming with laughter. The mother's recollection of that time is very tender.

INTO "WHATIF"

This is a poem about worries. The poet has even coined a new word, a *whatif,* a noun that means things that we worry will go wrong. The Whatifs come from our living in the future in our minds and our inability to just relax at night and go to sleep.

Ask your students what *they* think about when they go to sleep at night. Do any of them have the Whatifs? What are their Whatifs?

Whatif
Shel Silverstein

Last night, while I lay thinking here,
Some whatifs crawled inside my ear
And pranced and partied all night long
And sang their same old Whatif song:
5 Whatif I'm dumb in school?
Whatif they've closed the swimming-pool?
Whatif I get beat up?
Whatif there's poison in my cup?
Whatif I start to cry?
10 Whatif I get sick and die?
Whatif I flunk that test?
Whatif green hair grows on my chest?
Whatif nobody likes me?
Whatif a bolt of lightning strikes me?
15 Whatif I don't grow taller?
Whatif my head starts getting smaller?
Whatif the fish won't bite?
Whatif the wind tears up my kite?
Whatif they start a war?
20 Whatif my bed falls through the floor?
Whatif the bus is late?
Whatif my teeth don't grow in straight?
Whatif I tear my pants?
Whatif I never learn to dance?
25 Everything seems swell, and then
The night-time Whatifs strike again!

Poetry ~ 97

Shel Silverstein is a poet who can be relied upon for odd rhythms, odd words, and sometimes, odd poems. Largely because of the irregular rhythm, and certainly because of the very human subject, this is a good poem to have students recite in teams, a couplet per team. The lines are funny enough, with their woe-is-me-quality to get students started with dramatic and fun recitation. Have them use large arm and hand gestures. Try to get them over their public-speaking shyness with this funny poem that comes early in the book.

Student recitations need to be practiced a lot, precisely enunciated, and loudly declaimed. Make sure that each team knows exactly how many beats each of their lines has, and where the emphasis is.

This poem is also in the *I* or first-person voice. In contrast to *To a Daughter Leaving Home,* who is speaking in this poem?

LITERARY COMPONENTS

▶ **1. Personification:** The Whatifs *crawled, pranced, partied,* and *sang* (Lines 2, 3, and 4). The Whatifs even have their own song.

▶ **2. Repetition of Initial Consonants:** In Line 3 the Whatifs *pranced* and *partied;* in Line 4 they *sang their same old...song.*

▶ **3. Repetition of Word and Phrasing; Punctuation:** Lines 5 through 24 begin a question with the world *Whatif.* Make sure your students see that all of these lines are questions and end in question marks.

▶ **4. Change in Rhythmic Formulation:** Lines 25 begins with a metric foot that has emphasis on the *first* syllable (*EV ree **thing** seems **swell** and **then***). The line ends with a pause—and then what? This creates a wonderful waiting effect before the last line, which goes back to the original rhythm.

ANALYZING THE POEM

Whatif is a twenty-six line poem in near couplets. The couplets rhyme, but the rhythm—especially the number of feet—varies. Most of the lines are tetrameter or trimeter. Most of the feet have two syllables, with the emphasis on the second syllable (iambic tetrameter or iambic trimeter). Most of the lines are written as questions. A child lies in bed at night beleaguered by the Whatifs. The Whatifs are worries about what could go wrong. The poem is funny and a little sad. Like many of us, this child has an extensive list of Whatifs. Lines 5 through 24 begin with the word *Whatif* to give us a sense of just how repetitive and unrelenting this child's worries are.

INTO "THE WHIPPOORWILL CALLS"

Harriet Tubman moved silently and solitarily through the woods at night, like the whippoorwill. She called to her people and rescued them.

EYES ON…THE BRIEF BIOGRAPHICAL POEM, THE THIRD-PERSON VOICE, AND STANZAS

The Whippoorwill Calls is a free-verse biographical poem. However, this is not the story of a person's life. Rather, it is intended to convey the sense of a person, her character, her actions. We can tell it is in the third person, because there is no *I*. The poet speaks of a *haunting sound*. This poem, which is strongly evocative of the woods at night, is itself haunting. Harriet Tubman moved like a spirit through the night woods— the bounty hunters could never catch her.

Notice that unlike *To a Daughter Leaving Home* and *Whatif*, *The Whippoorwill Calls* has stanzas. Stanzas are like paragraphs in prose, separated by a blank line.

LITERARY COMPONENTS

▶ **1. Onomatopoeia:** The word, *whippoorwill,* comes from the sound of the bird's call.

▶ **2. Setting:** Setting is essential here to both the story and the mood of the poem.

▶ **3. Repetition of Rhythm, Cadence:** Notice the similarity of the structure, cadence, and rhythm of Stanza 1 and Stanza 2. Each stanza has eight lines. The first lines have 4 beats; the second lines, 2; the third, 3; the fourth, 2; the fifth, 4; the sixth, 4; and the seventh, 5. Only the eighth lines differ. Similarity is a form of repetition.

▶ **4. Repetition of Consonant:** In Stanza 1, the repetition of *w* in *woods, whippoorwill,* and *wings.*

▶ **5. Repetition of Wording:** Both Stanza 1 and Stanza 2 begin *No one…her.* Their second lines each have one word, a verb, ending *–ing.* Their third lines are the same: *Through the woods.* Their fifth and sixth lines read *For she is like / A whippoorwill.*

▶ **6. Echo and Mood:** When Stanza 2 echoes Stanza 1, it lends the poem a haunting quality.

▶ **7. Repetition of Vowel Sounds:** In Lines 5, 7, 9, 13, and 15, the long *–ee-* sound in *she, trees, sees, she,* and *leaves.*

▶ **8. Repetition of Vowel Sounds:** In Lines 19 and 20, the internal *–aw-* sound of *warm* and *haunting.*

The Whippoorwill Calls
(for Harriet Tubman)

No one hears her
Coming
Through the woods
At night
5   For she is like
A whippoorwill
Moving through the trees
On silent wings.

No one sees her
10   Hiding
In the woods
By day
For she is like
A whippoorwill
15   Blending into leaves
On the forest floor.

And one night
The whippoorwill calls
And the warm air
20   Carries the haunting sound
Across the fields
And into the small dark cabins.

And only the slaves know
It is Harriet.

Beverly McLoughland

ANALYZING THE POEM

The Whippoorwill Calls is a free verse poem in four stanzas. The poem itself has a haunting quality. In fact, the whippoorwill, here, *is* Harriet. This is a very simple sort of symbology. This is a good poem with which students can be introduced to the idea of symbols, the idea of one thing representing another.

The first and second stanzas of the poem mirror each other, both in terms of their content and their cadence. Line for line the second stanza replicates the first in terms of the number of beats. This sort of structural repetition has a hypnotic quality. This is a poem in which setting is essential.

INTO "FIGURES IN...SKY!"

The **imperative** case in grammar is accompanied by an exclamation point. What is the imperative case? It is expressive of a command, an entreaty, or an exhortation. Thus, both the title and the first line exhort the read-er, the person who is seeing this, to *behold*. Behold a woman and a man with their baby, cultivating the land in autumn, in the sunset.

This is literature that makes us feel, that resonates with power. But what does it make us feel? What is the poet writing about? What is the theme here? The stark appearance of two lone people against the vastness of the sky: the terrible toil of planting the land; a man and a woman, their oxen, and their baby, small against the hugeness of nature; the sun setting in a brilliant sky, as their shadow over the land grows huge.

What does the writer tell us? This is big, these two people trying to make their way. The oxen's heads are bent with the work. They are slow and the work is hard. The man plods. Nature has magnificence: clouds of flame, green fluid gold in the sunset. But man's shadow grows gigantic over the land.

Figures in the Field Against the Sky!

Antonio Machado

Figures in the field against the sky!

Two slow oxen plowing

a knoll in early autumn:

between the black heads

5 bent below the heavy yoke

hangs a basket made of broom and reed—

a child's cradle.

Behind the team

a man plows, leaning toward the earth;

10 a woman

throws seed in open furrows.

Under a cloud of flame and crimson

in the green fluid gold of sunset,

these shadows grow gigantic.

Poetry ~ 99

LITERARY COMPONENTS

Recall the earlier statement that free verse may rely very heavily on the repetition of consonant and vowel sounds. This not only binds the poem through the cadence of the words—it creates verse of consummate beauty.

▶ **1. Punctuation; Mood:** Exclamation point in title and first line makes these imperative statements with an implied verb. This establishes a mood of power: What the reader, viewer is being shown is important.

▶ **2. Setting:** Here is another poem (*The Whippoorwill Calls* is the other of the four in this unit) in which setting is crucial to the sweep and theme of the poem.

▶ **3. Repetition of Initial Consonants:** In the title and line one, we read, *Figures in the field...*

▶ **4. Repetition of Entire Sentence; Contrasting Cadence:** The repetition of the title in the first line makes this a definitive statement and establishes a rhythm. By contrast, the second line, *Two slow oxen plowing*, sounds plodding and slow.

▶ **5. Repetition of Internal Consonant:** We can almost taste the *l* in, *a knoll in early autumn.*

▶ **6. Repetition of Consonants:** In Lines 3-5, there is repetition of **b, l, h, y,** and **r: between** the **b**lack **h**eads / **b**ent **b**elow the **h**eavy **y**oke / **h**angs a **b**asket made of **b**room and **r**eed.

▶ **7. Repetition of Vowel Sounds:** In Lines 4 and 5, *head* and *heavy*; in Lines 6, 8, 9, and 13, *reed, team, leaning,* and *green.*

▶ **8. Double Meaning:** The word *plod* (Line 9) means walks heavily or slowly, but also means works laboriously and monotonously.

▶ **9. Emphasis Through Placement:** The words, *a woman*, stand alone on Line 10 for heightened effect.

▶ **10. Repetition of Vowel Sound:** This repetition is noticeable both to the eyes and the ears: Lines 11 and 14, the long *O* sound of *-ow-* in *throws, furrows, shadows,* and *grow*. Also, the long *O* sound of *open* (Line 11) and *gold* (Line 13) adds to the vowel repetitiveness.

▶ **11. Repetition of Consonant:** In Lines 11-13, look for *furrows, flame,* and *fluid;* in Line 12, *cloud* and *crimson;* in Lines 13-14, *green, gold, grow gigantic.*

EYES ON...REPETITION IN FREE VERSE

Free verse works without regular rhyme or rhythm. One of the "threads" that may bind a free-verse poem is the repetition of consonant and vowel sounds. Your students will learn a lot about how poetry works, if you review this literary device with them. Remind your students that this poem has been translated from Spanish to English.

Look for the repetition of initial consonants:
Figures in the field
between the black heads / bent below...

Look for the repetition of initial and internal consonants: *...heavy yoke*
hangs a basket of broom and reed
Look for the repetition of vowel sounds:
throws seed in open furrows
Students will be intrigued by the way that poetry is like a puzzle that can be deciphered.

ANALYZING THE POEM

Figures in the Field Against the Sky! is a free-verse poem translated from the original Spanish to English. The poem was written by the Spanish poet, Antonio Machado (1875 to 1939). Both the title of the poem and the first line finish with an exclamation point, as if to emphasize the importance of the picture Machado has shown us—as if he has commanded, *Behold! Look at this.*

The poet draws a picture of a man and a woman, their oxen, their suspended baby's cradle, as they plow the land upon a knoll and plant seed. They seem small against the vastness of sky and land. The sun is setting. The sunset is flame and fluid gold. The figures throw gigantic shadows. Setting is the foundation, here, of both the theme and the magnificence of the language.

STUDYING THE SELECTION

To a Daughter Leaving Home

1. Answers may vary. They should include the idea that the daughter is leaving now, which we learn from the title. The rest is the memory of a time when the mother experienced similar feelings. The mother remembers the time when the daughter first rode away alone on her two-wheel bicycle. At that time, mom was both excited and scared. In fact, the *pumping, pumping / for your life screaming* suggests that both of them were excited and scared.

2. *To a Daughter Leaving Home* is written in one sentence.

3. Refer to the introductory material above. Some categories include, letter repetition (**b, w, p,** for example), repetition of the **-ing** ending, and repetition of single-syllable words.

4. *Thud, crash,* and *screaming* are examples of onomatopoeia.

5. Students' answers will vary. Our own favorites are *wobbled away; my own mouth rounding; you grew smaller, more breakable; pumping, pumping; for your life, screaming; hair flapping...*

ABOUT THE AUTHORS

Linda Pastan, born in New York City in 1932, was already on her way to a promising career as a poet, when she dropped everything to marry and start a family. Once her children were in school, however, she resumed writing poetry. As we see in *To a Daughter Leaving Home,* she often drew upon her life as a wife and mother for subject matter. Pastan has written more than fifteen volumes of poetry. The Pastans live in Potomac, Maryland.

Shel Silverstein, born in 1930 in Chicago, Illinois, started drawing and writing in his early teens. After his service with the U.S. armed forces, he worked as a cartoonist until a well-known editor convinced him to write for children. He wrote and illustrated sixteen books for children, among them *A Light in the Attic*. He also wrote numerous songs. Shel Silverstein died in 1999 in Key West, Florida.

Beverly McLoughland, born in 1946 in New Jersey, was an elementary school teacher before deciding to pursue a career as a writer. Her poems have appeared in magazines and anthologies for young people. She has also published a collection of her own poems. Her wonder at human creativity and the natural world are the inspiration for many of her poems. She currently lives in Virginia.

Antonio Machado, born in 1875, was one of Spain's greatest 20th century poets. By the early 1900s he had begun writing poetry, taken a teaching position, and married. In 1912, one year following his wife's death, Machado published a volume of poems in her memory. After graduating from a Madrid university, he and his brother wrote several plays together. During his lifetime, Machado wrote more than twenty volumes of poetry, and nine plays.

Studying the Selection   POETRY

To a Daughter Leaving Home

1. What is this poem about? Give a short, simple answer in two or three sentences.

2. In how many sentences is the poem written?

3. Describe one kind of repetition the poet uses. Give examples from the poem.

4. Give an example of onomatopoeia from the poem.

5. What is the strongest picture you have in your mind from the poem? (There is no single correct answer to this question.)

100 ~ Unit 1

Whatif

1. What is a "whatif"?

2. This poem is different from the other three in several ways. In two sentences, describe two of the ways *Whatif* is different from *To a Daughter Leaving Home*, *The Whippoorwill Calls*, and *Figures in the Field Against the Sky!*

3. Pick one of the Whatifs and think about how a person could deal with such an event if it actually happened. After all, difficult events occur in all of our lives. Most of us, at some time, don't feel smart enough, brave enough, or liked enough by other children in school. How do we find courage? How do we get through embarrassing situations? Write one or two paragraphs. You may write something humorous if you wish.

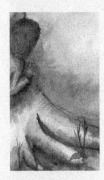

The Whippoorwill Calls

1. How is the second stanza like the first stanza?

2. In this poem, Harriet Tubman is compared to a whippoorwill. Write a three stanza poem, similar to this one, about another hero you know of. In the first two stanzas of your poem, compare the hero to a bird, animal, or insect. In the third stanza, let the reader know who the hero really is.

3. Choose one of the stanzas to memorize. Your teacher will organize groups for performance before the class.

Figures in a Field Against the Sky!

1. Why does the poet use an exclamation point?

2. Where does the poet repeat the letter *f*?
   Where does the poet repeat the letters *b, h,* and *k*?
   Where does the poet repeat the long *o* sound (don't forget to include –*ow*—where it sounds like *oh*)?
   Where does the poet repeat the letter *g*?

3. This poem has three sentences. Pick one and rewrite it in prose (regular sentences, not poetry). Use a dictionary if there are any words you don't understand.

Whatif

1. A Whatif is a worry about something bad that might happen in the future.

2. *Whatif* is different from the other three poems in that (1) it consists of rhyming couplets; (2) it has a rhythmic pattern of sorts; therefore it is not (3) free verse. Moreover (4) it certainly has more lines; (5) most of these lines are questions and end in question marks; (6) it seems to be written from the point of view of a child; (7) it is a little funny; and (8) it is written more informally. Students may find other differences.

3. Students may need some kindly guidance with this assignment. A Whatif is a worry about something bad that might happen in the future.

The Whippoorwill Calls

1. Both Stanza 1 and Stanza 2 begin *No one . . . her.* Their second lines each have one word, a verb, ending –*ing.* Their third lines are the same: *Through the woods.* Their fifth and sixth lines read *For she is like / A whippoorwill.* The number of beats for the respective lines of the stanzas are the same, except for the last.

2. In simple language, explain how metaphors are used. Encourage the students to write their poems using metaphors rather than similes. For example, the student could write a poem about how a fearless lion runs between the tall trees of the jungle. In the third stanza, the writer would explain that the lion is a brave fireman running between burning objects to rescue someone from the Twin Towers.

3. Stanza four should be said in unison, by all the members of each group.

Figures in a Field Against the Sky!

1. See your notes above regarding the imperative case, which is used to exhort or command.

2. See your **Literary Components** for *Figures in a Field Against the Sky!*

3. Please give individual students the help they need to do this, so that they will feel good about this sort of exercise. It is the basis for understanding poetry.

UNIT ONE WRAP-UP

Samuel's Choice • Slower Than the Rest • Kate Shelley
New Providence • The Silent Lobby

EXTRA! EXTRA! READ ALL ABOUT IT!

Create a Newspaper

1. You have read five selections in this unit: *Samuel's Choice, Slower Than the Rest, Kate Shelley, New Providence,* and *The Silent Lobby.* Pick one of the selections and make a table for your selection, using the column categories below. For *New Providence,* your **Who** will be The City. For *Slower Than the Rest,* you will have to make up your **When**—but it could just be the day before the date the newspaper is published.

Selection	Who	What	When	Where
Samuel's Choice				

2. Now, on a large sheet of paper, create your newspaper: its name, its motto, the date of publication. If you are not familiar with newspaper formats, ask your parents or teacher for a newspaper, so that you have an example to follow. A newspaper motto is something like, "All the News That's Fit to Print," "The Journal That Helps You Judge," or "More News Than You Need."

3. Now you are ready to create the headlines and write the copy (words) for your news story—the big story of the day, for example, **Samuel Makes Big Decision** or **Boy Brings Turtle to School** or **New Providence: Down in the Dumps.**

4. Make sure your news article includes the who, what, when, and where. Try to conclude your article with **Why**—why did the event occur.

THE MYSTERIOUS STORYTELLER
You Are a Stranger Who Has Come to Town to Tell a Story

1. Once more, pick one of the selections. Now, you are going to be one of the characters in the story you have selected. You may be a major character or one of the minor characters. You can even be one of the buildings in New Providence. Make or find some piece of clothing or a prop (such as a cane if you were an old person or a chimney if you were a building that had a chimney) that helps you look like the character. You can also—with help from a grownup or a sibling—put on makeup to help you get into character, when the time comes for your presentation.

2. Your presentation will be very simple. You will give your audience some biographical information about yourself. You will conclude by asking your class, "Who am I?" Biographical information could be something like, "I am a woman. I was born in Brooklyn, New York and lived from 1725 to 1810. During my life I have made a lot of buttermilk." And so forth. Give several facts about your life, so that your class can make a good guess. Don't be afraid to be funny.

3. Make notes on index cards for that moment when you are to be the mysterious stranger. Practice your presentation in front of your family to make sure it works smoothly. Good luck!

THE PLAY'S THE THING!
Acting and Teamwork

1. Your teacher will help you and your class form small groups.

2. You and your group are going to act out a scene from one of the five stories in which a small group of people is involved in the action. Will you be American soldiers fighting the British in a creek? Will you be the students listening to the turtle presentation? Will you be a group of homeless men standing over trash can fires during the Great Depression in New Providence? There are many possibilities.

3. You and your team will get together to work out a short script and rehearse your big scene.

4. Good luck with your presentation!

IT TAKES COURAGE TO WRITE

Your Favorite Courageous Character

1. What is courage? Look up the word in the dictionary and write down the definition(s). Now look up the word in a good thesaurus and write down some of the synonyms given for courage.

2. Think about the characters in each of the selections, including those in the poems. All of them have courage. But which one impressed you the most? Who did you think was most brave?

3. Now it's time to write several paragraphs. In your first paragraph, you are going to say what courage is. You are going to tell your reader what some of the synonyms are for courage, too. For the final sentence of your first paragraph you will write something like, "These words remind me of _____ *the hero or heroine* _____ in _____ *the name of the story or poem* _____, and I am going to write about (him or her)." Use your second paragraph to give examples of your hero's good qualities and actions. Use your third paragraph to conclude. Here is an example of a conclusion: "For all of these reasons, I picked this character as my favorite. I hope that I can be as brave if I ever have to face the situation my character faced."

unit 2

GROWING

CONFLICT

- Conflict means a struggle.
- A conflict can be *external* or *internal*.
- An *external* conflict is a struggle between a person and another person, a group of people, or a force of nature.
- An *internal* conflict is a conflict of ideas or feelings *within* a person.

THINK ABOUT IT!

1. What is the external conflict at the center of the story?
2. What did Ryan do to Ernie the last time they raced?
3. What do you think are Ryan's two internal conflicts in this race?
4. What is the outcome of Ryan's internal conflict?

The Race

Ernie's stomach was tight as he waited for the starter's pistol. He looked over at Ryan Douglas, the boy he had to beat. Ryan refused to make eye contact.

Bang!

Ernie lurched forward with the other runners, keeping a close eye on Ryan.

By the end of the first mile, the pack of runners had started to spread out. Ten or fifteen steps behind Ryan, Ernie didn't want to get any closer as they entered the woods. The last time he tried to pass Ryan in the woods, the other boy had stepped on his foot, sending him plunging to the ground and costing him the race.

Ryan left the woods for the final half-mile less than ten seconds ahead of Ernie, but when Ernie came out into the late summer sun, it seemed like Ryan had doubled the distance between them. He couldn't afford to start sprinting. Not yet. Picking up his pace slightly, he began slowly to whittle away the distance between them. Ryan never looked back, but each time Ernie got within a few steps, his opponent surged ahead.

Ernie refused to panic. He had time. Turning up his pace one more notch, he closed the gap between them to a single step and allowed himself to cruise at Ryan's pace.

A lump formed in Ernie's throat as he spotted the crowd at the finish line. His legs felt strong. His wind was good.

Ernie threw himself into high gear.

Breaking first gave him the edge he needed. Though he could feel the other boy's footsteps pounding the grass behind him, Ernie concentrated only on the finish line. The crowd, the coaches, the other racers all disappeared. From somewhere deep inside himself, Ernie drew an extra surge of energy and bolted across the finish line a full five strides ahead of Ryan.

Afterward, when Ernie was stretching, he heard a voice behind him say, "Great race."

Ernie turned around. It was Ryan.

"Thanks," Ernie said.

Ryan smiled. "I'll get you next time."

Ernie smiled back. "I'll be there."

LESSON IN LITERATURE

1. The external conflict is the boys' race against each other.

2. He cheated by stepping on Ryan's foot.

3. Ryan must choose whether or not to play fair and, if he loses, he must choose whether or not to be a good loser.

4. Ryan runs a fair race. This is the outcome of the first internal conflict. He also chooses to be a "good loser," not a jealous one. This is the outcome of the second internal conflict.

SELECTION VOCABULARY

ambled: walked slowly and casually

countered: answered a question with a question

desperation: a feeling of hopelessness

fitful: stopping and starting

hitched: fastened, tied

level: sensible; spoken in a calm, even voice

meditative: thoughtful

novelty: new experience

piercingly: sharply and knowingly

restraint: control, holding back

sinister: looking a bit frightening or threatening

stealthily: quietly, carefully and secretly so as not to be discovered

---

amble   desperation   meditative   piercingly   sinister
counter   level   novelty   restraint   stealthily

1. Sheriff Blake was not a _____ (*thoughtful*) man.

2. If a newcomer looked _____ (*threatening*), he liked to shoot first and ask questions later.

3. When it came to nabbing crooks, Sheriff Blake did not believe in using _____ (*holding back*).

4. If someone in town was seen moving _____ (*secretly and suspiciously*), Sheriff Blake would notice him instantly.

5. The sheriff would set his eyes on that man and look at him _____ (*sharply and knowingly*).

6. He would speak to him in a _____ (*calm, even*) voice.

7. He would _____ (*walk casually*) over to where the man had hitched his horse and unfasten the horse's reins.

8. Usually, the suspicious-looking stranger would yell, "Hey! Whatch'er doin'?" Sheriff Blake would _____ (*answer a question with a question*): 'and whut d'yer think yer doin'? I'm the sheriff in this here town and Ah don't like the looks of yer, yuh sneakin' skunk!"

9. Now, to most crooks, being spoken to like that was a _____ (*new experience*).

10. In _____ (*feeling of hopelessness*) they would grab the reins of their horse, jump on, and ride away into the dust, never to return.

Workbook p. 31   Answer Guide p. 4

Rhyme Time

Choose the correct word from the vocabulary words below.

ambled   fitful   sinister   novelty   desperation
firm   meditative   level   restraint   stealthily

1. He stole up to the cupboard and grabbed a chocolate _____
Because he'd solemnly promised his Mom he'd eat "healthily".

2. This man who claimed that he was the prime minister
Looked positively dangerous, absolutely _____.

3. I wanted to serve hot, these eggs that were scrambled,
But now they are cold because, instead of running, you _____.

4. "You know," he said, "the early bird catches the worm,"
"And you'll have to work hard to get ahead in this _____."

5. "Ah do declare! This feller looks pit'ful,"
"He's tired, cuz he's sick and his short sleep was _____."

6. She was so awfully upset, she almost did faint,
But when she finally calmed down, she spoke with _____.

7. "Oh, my!" I said, when I saw the date of expiration,
"This book's two years overdue—help!" I cried in _____.

8. He looked wild and mean—almost like a devil,
But he spoke in a voice that was surprisingly _____.

9. "I tell you," I said, "I'm not that creative!
I just can't find a rhyme for the word '_____'."

10. And we can't find anything that rhymes with *novelty*! For us, that is a *new experience*!

Workbook p. 32   Answer Guide p. 4

BACKGROUND BYTES

We are indebted to the Texas Longhorn Reference Library and to Alan Hoyt for much of the information below.

How the Great Plains Became the Violent Old West of Longhorn City

The children that grew up in the 1950s (perhaps the grandparents of some of your students) played cowboys and Indians. That was a time when people were more simplistic about the history of the United States. The cowboys and buffalo hunters were depicted in a generally positive light, while the Indians appeared as faceless, primitive, unreasoning enemies. Indians were portrayed simply as obstacles to be removed. No rights, no feelings, no reason for being on the land in the first place were ascribed to them.

Buffalo hunters, like Buffalo Bill Cody, were actually carrying out the unspoken policy of the United States government: extermination of the buffalo. Had the buffalo remained, the Texas Longhorns would have remained in Texas.

The buffalo hunters killed millions of buffalo. The buffalo meat, hide, and bones were good business for the railroads, which were suffering from an economic depression in the early 1870s. But the larger purpose of getting rid of the buffalo was to starve the Indians and to clear the Great Plains for railroads and the Texas Longhorns. When the white man arrived, buffalo roamed in herds hundreds of miles across, from South Texas to Canada. By the end of the 19th century, the buffalo was nearly extinct.

Thus, the Old West was founded on a lot of violence—violence to people, violence to animals. It was a harsh culture, and there were no laws and few law keepers.

In fact, it is surprising that the "good-guy" cowboys were usually good guys. These were uneducated men (with lots of "horse sense"), who had to work very hard. They were on the trail for long periods of time, frequently with terrible weather, bringing huge herds of Texas Longhorn cattle to such shipping points as Great Bend or Dodge City. Great Bend and Dodge City had loading pens and a railroad that ran through the middle of town.

Texas Longhorns were different from the beef steers of today. They had great stamina, and were able to travel 15 miles a day for up to 100 days—without losing weight. The cowboys had to ensure that no matter what the weather, the herd stayed together and kept up its pace. Depending upon where they were coming from, they lived on the trail for one to three months. They slept and dreamed under the stars.

Buyers of cattle came to Dodge City from all over the country, from New York to Wyoming. Once in Dodge, most of the cattle were put on trains and shipped to slaughterhouses. The remaining twenty percent of the cattle were used to start cattle breeding in other parts of the country. Breeder herds went from Dodge to Wyoming, Colorado, North and South Dakota, and Montana. The entire enormous enterprise of moving hundreds of thousands of heads of cattle each year and slaughtering them resulted in Americans becoming the biggest consumers of meat in history.

For ten years, Dodge City was the greatest cattle market in the world. The town was busy with buyers, ranchers, speculators, cowboys, and the railroad ten months a year. "During the peak season, 1,000 to 2,000 cowboys" could be found within the city limits. Once there, they might do branding or be responsible for holding cattle until they gained weight. As a consequence, cowboys often spent several months at a time in Dodge.

They received six to twelve months' pay once the cattle were sold. It is likely that most cowboys were illiterate. Although there was some traveling theatre, and surely some of them read, there was not a lot for them to do in town during their vacations. It is not surprising, then, that they played a lot of cards, maybe some checkers and even some chess, and that they gambled and drank too much. Apparently, they also liked to shoot their guns. But these gunslingers often shot in the air to create a ruckus. They did not shoot to kill people for the most part. At times, gambling thieves caused a lot of trouble in cattle towns, and their presence resulted in "bad blood" among both the cowboys and the ordinary citizens. It also resulted in spilled blood at times.

Two points should be made. Few cowboys were ruthless and rowdy. According to Alan Hoyt, they were loyal to their employers and brave. Cowboys died trying to save their herds during floods. During storms, cattle and horses would stampede, and the cattlemen had to go tearing after them and round them up. Cowboys were forced to adapt to a rough and wild life, living outside as they did most of the time. They had to be strong and in very good physical condition if they were to do their jobs.

When they came to town after being on the trail for months, they bathed, bought new clothes, ammunition, and perhaps a new gun. They met with friends, talked, played cards, and sometimes slept indoors. They ate and drank to their hearts' content. But these men were neither loafers nor desperadoes.

In much of the Old West, there was no law and no government. Often, a town that was desperate for control, in the face of train and bank robberies, would hire someone to be sheriff—and that someone might be the meanest, toughest man around. A number of villains were transformed into U.S. marshals. But that's not the sheriff in our story.

The Longhorn City of *Gold-Mounted Guns* is probably modeled after a city such as Dodge.

Language Alert

The author makes use of idioms that may not be as much in use today as they were in 1922, when the story was published.

All things being equal means "given the circumstances...I'd rather do __."

The young man says that he "can shoot the pips out of a ten-spot at ten paces." A *ten-spot* is a playing card that has ten *pips* on the face. *Pips* are the spots on dice, playing cards, and dominoes. So he is saying that if he walks the distance covered by ten steps, he can shoot the spots on a playing card that has ten spots.

After Mr. Sanderson realizes that the money has been stolen, he cries. His daughter implores him, "Daddy—Daddy—don't take on so—please don't." *To take on so* means "to display strong emotion." The popular idiom is the full phrase, *don't take on so*.

INTO "GOLD-MOUNTED GUNS"

Once again, we have a story with major and minor themes:

Crime does not pay.

If your behavior is not in keeping with the dictates of your conscience, you will experience great inner conflict.

It takes a great deal of courage to stand up for one's convictions. This is what Will Arblaster ultimately does, when he faces the man he believes to be Pecos Tommy, and announces that he is returning the money.

You can't tell a book by its cover. The hard-faced man is not hard inside: He's a caring person who wants the young man to learn a lesson and avoid a life of crime.

If we can show people who do bad things how their behavior affects other people, it may be a powerful incentive for helping them change.

People are capable of changing for the better.

It is important to help people learn by their mistakes—and thus become better people who change their behavior. It is clear at the end of the story that by giving Will the chance to see the consequences of his behavior, the sheriff ensures that the Sandersons get their money back and that Will's inclination to do good has a chance to assert itself over his inclination to do bad. This is far more positive than if, for example, the Sheriff had simply set a trap for Will, and then arrested him and had him punished.

EYES ON...CONFLICT

Gold-Mounted Guns begins with *external conflict.* We assume that it is external conflict that will dominate the story. After all, this is a story of the old West, the Wild West, of gunslingers and cowboys.

The story takes place in a town where there may be no written laws and likely no government. There may be few social institutions to influence people's behavior. Here there are few businesses, few settled families, very few women to lay a moral foundation, no schools, no places of worship.

We can make other assumptions: This is a town that offers few jobs. This is not a place where people are kept busy working. Most of the people who come through town are transients—people on the move—mostly cattle drivers and buffalo hunters.

There is a saloon, and where there is a saloon, there is alcohol and gambling and arguments. But surprisingly, this story becomes a story in which the internal conflict of one of the two main protagonists is much more important than the conflicts between people.

The transformation of external conflict to internal conflict is not the only surprise. This story has what is called a *revelatory* ending, a twist, when the identity (but not the name) of the mysterious hard-faced, lean man is revealed. So despite the story's being steeped in a serious moral turnabout, the disclosure of the last few paragraphs makes this story fun.

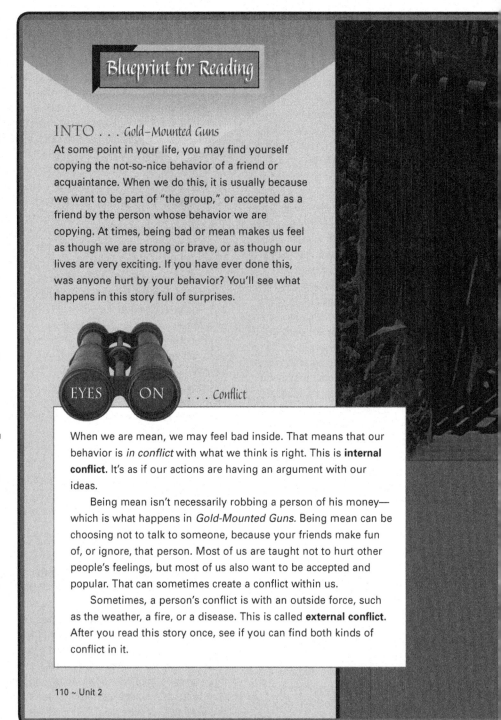

Blueprint for Reading

INTO . . . *Gold-Mounted Guns*

At some point in your life, you may find yourself copying the not-so-nice behavior of a friend or acquaintance. When we do this, it is usually because we want to be part of "the group," or accepted as a friend by the person whose behavior we are copying. At times, being bad or mean makes us feel as though we are strong or brave, or as though our lives are very exciting. If you have ever done this, was anyone hurt by your behavior? You'll see what happens in this story full of surprises.

EYES ON . . . *Conflict*

When we are mean, we may feel bad inside. That means that our behavior is *in conflict* with what we think is right. This is **internal conflict**. It's as if our actions are having an argument with our ideas.

Being mean isn't necessarily robbing a person of his money—which is what happens in *Gold-Mounted Guns.* Being mean can be choosing not to talk to someone, because your friends make fun of, or ignore, that person. Most of us are taught not to hurt other people's feelings, but most of us also want to be accepted and popular. That can sometimes create a conflict within us.

Sometimes, a person's conflict is with an outside force, such as the weather, a fire, or a disease. This is called **external conflict**. After you read this story once, see if you can find both kinds of conflict in it.

SUMMING UP THE PLOT

- It is evening in Longhorn City.
- A hard-faced man walks slowly down the main street and chooses one of the ponies hitched beside the general store.

Gold-Mounted Guns

F. R. Buckley

Evening had fallen on Longhorn City. To the south a lone star twinkled in the velvet sky. Soon *a hard-faced man ambled down the main street and chose a pony from the dozen hitched beside Tim Geogehan's[1] general store. The town was lit only by weak lights from the one store and one saloon,[2]* so it was *from the dark shadows that a voice came. It was calling to the hard-faced man.*

"Tommy!" the voice softly called.

1
2
3
4
5

---

1. *Geogehan's* (GAY gunz)
2. A *saloon* is a bar.

> **WORD BANK**
> **ambled** (AM buld) *v.:* walked slowly and casually
> **hitched** *v.:* fastened, tied

LITERARY COMPONENTS

▶ **1. Setting:** It's evening in Longhorn City.

▶ **2. Character; Characterization; Setting:** A *hard-faced* man *ambles* down the main street and takes one of the horses hitched beside the general store.

▶ **3. Setting:** The town is lit "only by weak lights from the one store and one saloon."

▶ **4. Setting; Character; Characterization; Suspense:** From the dark shadows, a voice calls to the *hard-faced man*.

▶ **5. Mistaken Identity of Protagonist Established:** "Tommy!" the voice calls. This is the beginning of setting the reader up for the surprise ending.

GUIDING THE READING

LITERAL

Q: When the story opens, what time of day is it?

A: It is evening.

Q: Where are we when the story opens?

A: We are in Longhorn City.

Q: By what name, does the soft voice in the shadows call the hard-faced man?

A: The voice calls softly, "Tommy!"

SUMMING UP THE PLOT

- "Tommy!" a voice calls softly.
- The hard-faced man draws his gun.
- A young man, with hands upraised, moves out into the light that shines from the general store.
- "I'm a friend," the young man says.
- The young man notes the sinister droop of a mustache over a hidden mouth, and shivers a little as his gaze meets a pair of steel-blue eyes.
- "What do you want?" asks the lean, hard-faced man.
- The boy asks whether he can put his hands down.

LITERARY COMPONENTS

▶ **6. Characterization:** The *hard-faced* man pulls his gun, when he hears the voice.

▶ **7. Relationship Between the Two Protagonists Begins; Exposition; Characterization:** The newcomer and the *hard-faced* man study each other with the steady eyes of *those who take chances of life and death.*

▶ **8. Characterization:** The man with the gun has a *sinister* droop to his gray mustache, which conceals his mouth. The young man shivers as he meets the steel-blue eyes of the gunman.

▶ **9. Character; Characterization:** The young man is boyish, handsome, and marked by "a certain desperation."

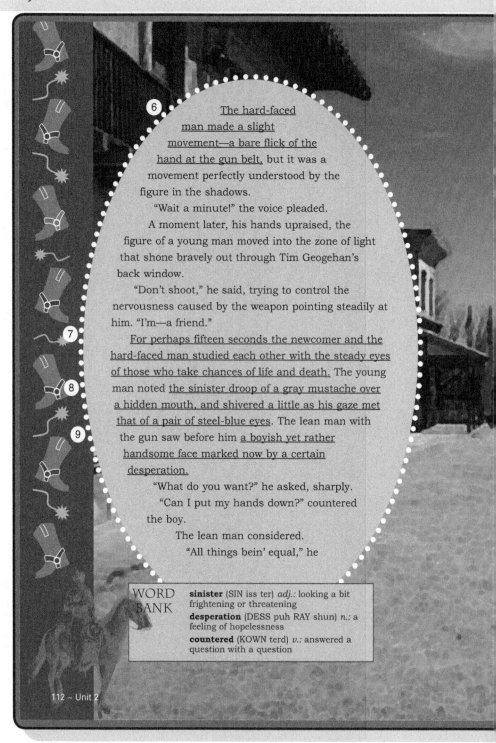

6
The hard-faced man made a slight movement—a bare flick of the hand at the gun belt, but it was a movement perfectly understood by the figure in the shadows.

"Wait a minute!" the voice pleaded.

A moment later, his hands upraised, the figure of a young man moved into the zone of light that shone bravely out through Tim Geogehan's back window.

"Don't shoot," he said, trying to control the nervousness caused by the weapon pointing steadily at him. "I'm—a friend."

7 For perhaps fifteen seconds the newcomer and the hard-faced man studied each other with the steady eyes of those who take chances of life and death. The young man noted 8 the sinister droop of a gray mustache over a hidden mouth, and shivered a little as his gaze met that of a pair of steel-blue eyes. The lean man with the gun saw before him 9 a boyish yet rather handsome face marked now by a certain desperation.

"What do you want?" he asked, sharply.

"Can I put my hands down?" countered the boy.

The lean man considered.

"All things bein' equal," he

WORD BANK

sinister (SIN iss ter) *adj.:* looking a bit frightening or threatening

desperation (DESS puh RAY shun) *n.:* a feeling of hopelessness

countered (KOWN terd) *v.:* answered a question with a question

112 ~ Unit 2

GUIDING THE READING

LITERAL
Q: What does the hard-faced man look like?
A: He has a gray mustache that hangs with a sinister droop over his mouth, which is hidden. He has steel-blue eyes. He is lean.

ANALYTICAL
Q: What is the effect of calling him "the hard-faced man" four times in the first seven paragraphs?
A: By using this phrase repeatedly, the author makes us think he's tough and mean.

Q: In the seventh paragraph, the author begins to use another, somewhat softer, phrase to describe the gun man. What is it?
A: Now he is the lean man.

Q: What is the young man's face marked by? What does this mean? (Encourage students to go beyond the definition in the book and to look up desperation in the dictionary.)
A: The young man's face is marked by "a certain desperation." People who are desperate may have no hope. They have an urgent need or desire (that may make them dangerous).

SUMMING UP THE PLOT

- The lean man says he wants to know first how he got around to calling him Tommy. Had he been asking people in the street?
- The boy says that he only got into town that afternoon. He knew he was Pecos Tommy because of the gold-mounted guns he's carrying.
- The man tells him to put his hands down and to tell him what he wants.
- The boy says that he wants to join him.
- The man says, "You want to *what?*"
- The boy says he knows his sidekick's in jail, and that he can ride and shoot "the pips out of a ten-spot at ten paces." He also has "a little job to bring into the firm to start with."

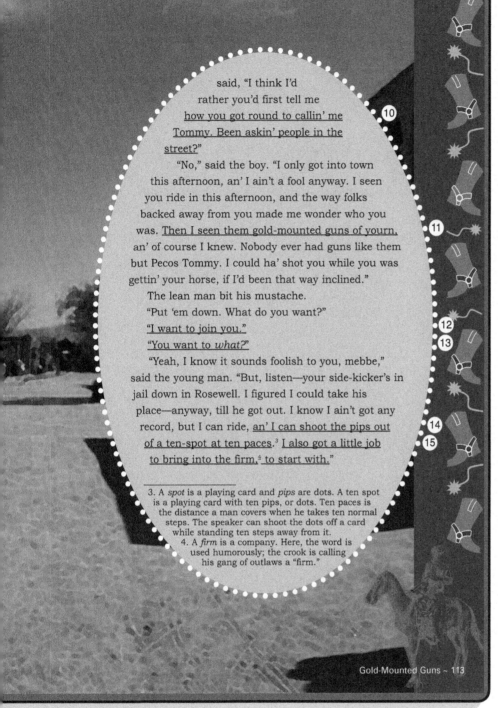

said, "I think I'd rather you'd first tell me how you got round to callin' me Tommy. Been askin' people in the street?"

"No," said the boy. "I only got into town this afternoon, an' I ain't a fool anyway. I seen you ride in this afternoon, and the way folks backed away from you made me wonder who you was. Then I seen them gold-mounted guns of yourn, an' of course I knew. Nobody ever had guns like them but Pecos Tommy. I could ha' shot you while you was gettin' your horse, if I'd been that way inclined."

The lean man bit his mustache.

"Put 'em down. What do you want?"

"I want to join you."

"You want to *what?*"

"Yeah, I know it sounds foolish to you, mebbe," said the young man. "But, listen—your side-kicker's in jail down in Rosewell. I figured I could take his place—anyway, till he got out. I know I ain't got any record, but I can ride, an' I can shoot the pips out of a ten-spot at ten paces.[3] I also got a little job to bring into the firm,[4] to start with."

_____

3. A *spot* is a playing card and *pips* are dots. A ten spot is a playing card with ten pips, or dots. Ten paces is the distance a man covers when he takes ten normal steps. The speaker can shoot the dots off a card while standing ten steps away from it.
4. A *firm* is a company. Here, the word is used humorously; the crook is calling his gang of outlaws a "firm."

LITERARY COMPONENTS

▶ **10. Dialogue That Sets up the Twist at the End:** (For discussion with students *after* they have read the story. You don't want to spoil the surprise for them!) The lean man asks why the boy called him Tommy. Then he says, "Been askin' people in the street?" The author purposely misleads the reader and the boy, here. Certainly, if the boy had asked people in town, he would know that the lean man *is not* Tommy Pecos.

▶ **11. Source of Title:** The boy says, "Then I seen them gold-mounted guns of yourn . . ."

▶ **12. Rising Action; Characterization:** The boy wants to join the man he thinks is Pecos Tommy in his career of robbing.

▶ **13. Characterization:** The lean man is shocked by the young man's desire.

▶ **14. Archaic Expression:** "I can shoot *the pips out of a ten-spot.*" See above in **Language Alert.**

▶ **15. Rising Action:** The young man says he has "got a little job to bring into the firm, to start with."

GUIDING THE READING

LITERAL

Q: When did the boy arrive in town?
A: That afternoon.

Q: What about the lean man makes the boy think he is Pecos Tommy?
A: The man is wearing Tommy's famous gold-mounted guns.

Q: What does the boy want from the man?
A: Because he believes that he is Pecos Tommy, he wants to join him.

Q: What does the boy say, to show that he can shoot accurately?

A: He says that he "can shoot the pips out of a ten-spot at ten paces."

ANALYTICAL

Q: [The next two questions come after students have read the story.] If the boy had asked people on the street about the hard-faced man, would they have said he was Pecos Tommy?
A: Of course not. He's the Sheriff of Longhorn City.

Q: Why do you think the author wrote the story that way? Why would he have the Sheriff make such a statement—and it is really a statement, not a question, since he knows the people in town would never have said he was Pecos Tommy—if the Sheriff knows it could not have happened that way?
A: There are two reasons. First, he may know the boy just arrived, and he may want to go along with the boy's belief that he is Pecos Tommy. Second, he wants the reader to be confused about his identity.

- The boy apologizes that the job he is bringing to the firm isn't what Pecos Tommy does as a rule.

- The man asks him why he quit cow punching.

- The boy says that he is sick of it, and he'd like a little fun in life.

LITERARY COMPONENTS

▶ **16. Idiom; Characterization:** *As a rule* means in general or usually. Pecos Tommy probably robs banks or trains or stagecoaches—not individuals, as the young man plans to do. Here, *straight* means *honest*— he does what he says and he's representing himself truthfully. He is a truthful robber.

▶ **17. Revealing Dialogue; Characterization; Motivation:** The questions the lean man asks here point to his *real* persona. Their conversation, during which the young man gives his reason for wanting to do this, may be precisely the moment when the sheriff decides to take him on to see if he's as rotten as he sounds.

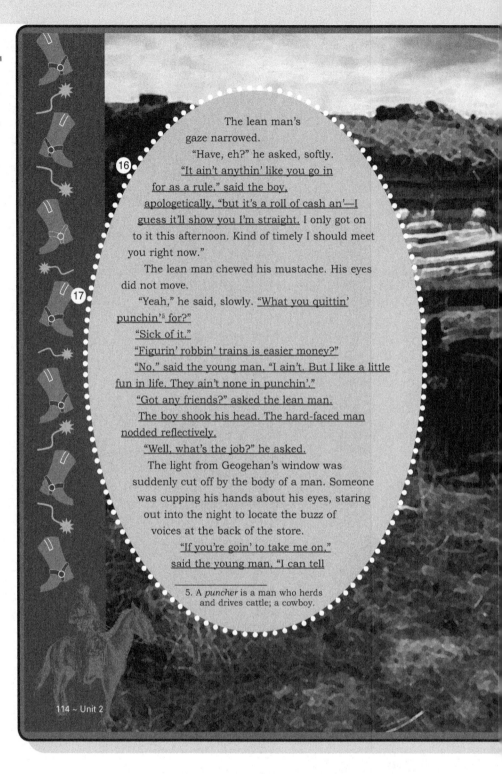

The lean man's gaze narrowed.

"Have, eh?" he asked, softly.

"It ain't anythin' like you go in for as a rule," said the boy, apologetically, "but it's a roll of cash an'—I guess it'll show you I'm straight. I only got on to it this afternoon. Kind of timely I should meet you right now."

The lean man chewed his mustache. His eyes did not move.

"Yeah," he said, slowly. "What you quittin' punchin's for?"

"Sick of it."

"Figurin' robbin' trains is easier money?"

"No," said the young man. "I ain't. But I like a little fun in life. They ain't none in punchin'."

"Got any friends?" asked the lean man.

The boy shook his head. The hard-faced man nodded reflectively.

"Well, what's the job?" he asked.

The light from Geogehan's window was suddenly cut off by the body of a man. Someone was cupping his hands about his eyes, staring out into the night to locate the buzz of voices at the back of the store.

"If you're goin' to take me on," said the young man, "I can tell

---
5. A *puncher* is a man who herds and drives cattle; a cowboy.

114 ~ Unit 2

GUIDING THE READING

LITERAL
Q: What does the boy think is true about robbing, that is not true about cow punching?
A: He thinks robbing will be fun.

ANALYTICAL
Q: [This question should be asked when students have finished the story.] Why would the job that the boy is "bringing to the firm" not be what Pecos Tommy goes in for as a rule?
A: It is likely that Pecos Tommy robbed banks, trains, and the stagecoach, not individuals.

Q: When the boy says that he wants the man to know he's straight, he's talking about something that is often called "honor among thieves." What do you think that means?
A: There are people who will rob a bank who insist that they would not think of robbing an individual. More to the point, people who work together on an illegal job may consider themselves very loyal and honest to the people with whom they are working. In reality, a dishonest person is just that—dishonest.

Under pressure, or as circumstances change, he cannot be relied upon to be loyal even to his fellow thief. As the complete saying goes, "there is no honor among thieves."

Q: Why do you think the lean man asks the boy why he quit cow punching? Why would he care?
A: This is one of the moments when the lean man reveals himself as a moral, caring person.

SUMMING UP THE PLOT

- The boy says that he will tell the man about the job if he's going to take him on—otherwise there's no point to it.
- The man says, "Come on," and they ride out of town.
- Will Arblaster (the boy) has given the unemotional man the details of the job.
- The man asks how he knows "the old guy's got the money."
- Will Arblaster says he saw him come out of the bank in the afternoon, grinning, and stuff-ing the money into his pants pocket.
- The boy asked who the man was, after he saw him. He says that his name is Sanderson and he lives in a cabin a mile away.
- The man is an "old geezer" who will give up the money easily, Arblaster says, when the lean man asks him for it.

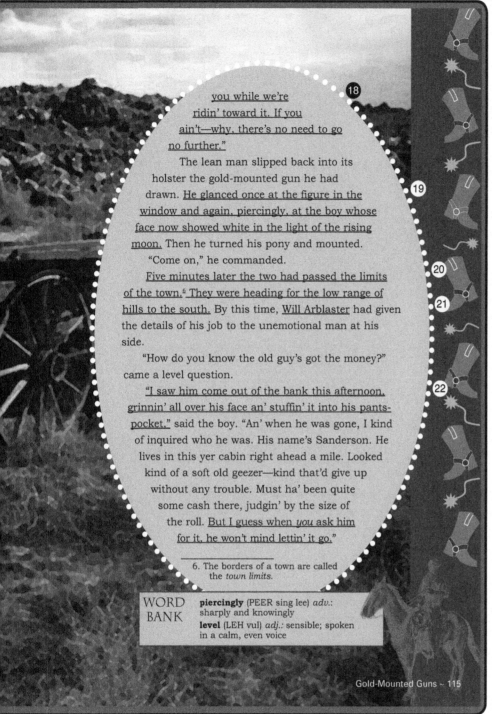

you while we're ridin' toward it. If you ain't—why, there's no need to go no further."

The lean man slipped back into its holster the gold-mounted gun he had drawn. He glanced once at the figure in the window and again, piercingly, at the boy whose face now showed white in the light of the rising moon. Then he turned his pony and mounted.

"Come on," he commanded.

Five minutes later the two had passed the limits of the town.[6] They were heading for the low range of hills to the south. By this time, Will Arblaster had given the details of his job to the unemotional man at his side.

"How do you know the old guy's got the money?" came a level question.

"I saw him come out of the bank this afternoon, grinnin' all over his face an' stuffin' it into his pants-pocket," said the boy. "An' when he was gone, I kind of inquired who he was. His name's Sanderson. He lives in this yer cabin right ahead a mile. Looked kind of a soft old geezer—kind that'd give up without any trouble. Must ha' been quite some cash there, judgin' by the size of the roll. But I guess when *you* ask him for it, he won't mind lettin' it go."

6. The borders of a town are called the *town limits*.

WORD BANK

piercingly (PEER sing lee) *adv.:* sharply and knowingly

level (LEH vul) *adj.:* sensible; spoken in a calm, even voice

Gold-Mounted Guns ~ 115

LITERARY COMPONENTS

▶ **18. Motivation; Rising Action:** The boy is not going to tell him about his plans unless he allows him to "join" him. Certainly, if he wants to prevent or undo the crime, he will have to follow through, and continue to act the role of Tommy Pecos.

▶ **19. Characterization; Strong Visual Image; Setting:** The lean man looks *piercingly* at the boy, as if he's trying to figure him out. The boy's face shows *white in the light of the rising moon*.

▶ **20. Rising Action:** The two ride out of town and head for the hills to the south.

▶ **21. Character:** Now the boy has a name, Will Arblaster. This is the beginning of the author's human-izing him.

▶ **22. Rising Action; Sympathetic Characterization of the Intended Victim:** The boy saw the man come out of the bank that afternoon. He describes him as grinning all over. He describes someone who is happy and who doesn't know he is going to suffer.

GUIDING THE READING

LITERAL

Q: Where do the man and the boy ride?
A: They pass the limits of the town and head for a low range of hills to the south.

Q: What is the boy's name?
A: The boy's name is Will Arblaster.

Q: How does the boy know the "old guy's got the money"?
A: He saw the man come out of the bank in the afternoon, stuffing the money in his pants pocket.

Q: How does Arblaster describe Mr. Sanderson?
A: He says that he lives in a cabin a mile ahead, and that he looks "kind of a soft old geezer," who will give up without any trouble.

ANALYTICAL

Q: What's a geezer?
A: A geezer is "an eccentric, elderly man." Eccentric means peculiar, odd—different from how one thinks people are usually.

SUMMING UP THE PLOT

- "I ain't going to ask him," says the lean man. "This is your job."

- The boy is hesitant, and asks if the lean man will take him along, if he does it right.

- "Yeah—I'll take you along."

- In the moonlight, they see a cabin with its windows unlit. The lean man chuckles. He says the old man is out.

- Arblaster says, "It's likely the money ain't."

- He creeps towards the house and the darkness swallows him.

- The lean man hears a rap of knuckles on the door, the rattle of the latch, and then a crash as the door is knocked down.

- The lean man's lips tighten.

LITERARY COMPONENTS

▶ **23. Characterization; Rising Action:** Arblaster presumes. Then he learns that the lean man is not going to do the robbery. This is an important moment dramatically.

▶ **24. Double Entendre:** After reading through the story once and going back over it, the lean man's line seems to have two meanings—the one that Arblaster wants (he'll take him along as a sidekick), and a second, that he'll take him right along to jail.

▶ **25. Confusing Characterization:** Why does the lean man chuckle? Presumably he's acting, to stay in the role of Pecos Tommy.

▶ **26. Vivid Image; Metaphor:** As Arblaster creeps towards the house, the moon goes "behind a cloud-bank," and the darkness *swallows* him.

▶ **27. Characterization:** The lean man's lips tighten, when he hears the crash of the door. He's not happy with what's happening.

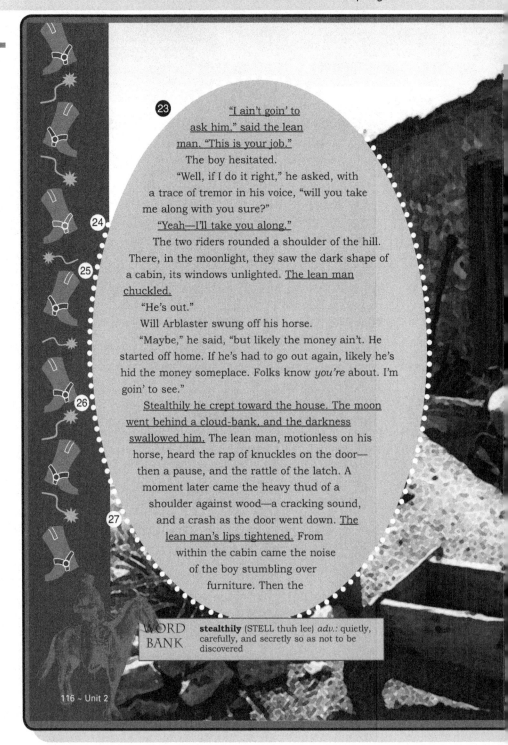

㉓ "I ain't goin' to ask him," said the lean man. "This is your job."

The boy hesitated.

"Well, if I do it right," he asked, with a trace of tremor in his voice, "will you take me along with you sure?"

"Yeah—I'll take you along."

The two riders rounded a shoulder of the hill. There, in the moonlight, they saw the dark shape of a cabin, its windows unlighted. The lean man chuckled.

"He's out."

Will Arblaster swung off his horse.

"Maybe," he said, "but likely the money ain't. He started off home. If he's had to go out again, likely he's hid the money someplace. Folks know *you're* about. I'm goin' to see."

Stealthily he crept toward the house. The moon went behind a cloud-bank, and the darkness swallowed him. The lean man, motionless on his horse, heard the rap of knuckles on the door—then a pause, and the rattle of the latch. A moment later came the heavy thud of a shoulder against wood—a cracking sound, and a crash as the door went down. The lean man's lips tightened. From within the cabin came the noise of the boy stumbling over furniture. Then the

WORD BANK | **stealthily** (STELL thuh lee) *adv.*: quietly, carefully, and secretly so as not to be discovered

116 ~ Unit 2

GUIDING THE READING

LITERAL

Q: When Arblaster says that the old man won't mind letting go of his cash when the lean man asks him for it, what does the lean man say?

A: He says that he ain't going to ask him—that this is Arblaster's job.

Q: Find five examples of onomatopoeia on page 116.

A: The words are rap, rattle, thud, cracking, crash, clumping, and rustle.

ANALYTICAL

Q: How does Arblaster react, when the lean man tells him that this is Arblaster's job?

A: He hesitates. He's probably nervous and surprised, since there's a tremor in his voice. After all, he has never done this before. He also asks the lean man if he will take him along, if he does all right.

Q: Why do you think the lean man's lips tighten as he hears Arblaster break down the door of the cabin?

A: Answers will vary. Presumably he's not comfortable with the damage being done to the old man's cabin.

- The lean man sees a lit match in the windows.
- He also hears the clumping of the young man's boots on the rough board floor of the cabin.

- The lean man hears a cry of triumph.
- Running feet pad across the grass and Will Arblaster says, "Got it!"
- The lean man reaches down and takes the roll of money. He says, "I guess I'll carry it."

- The lean man's hand seems to hesitate over the butt of his gold-mounted gun, but as "Willie" smiles and nods, the hand moves away.

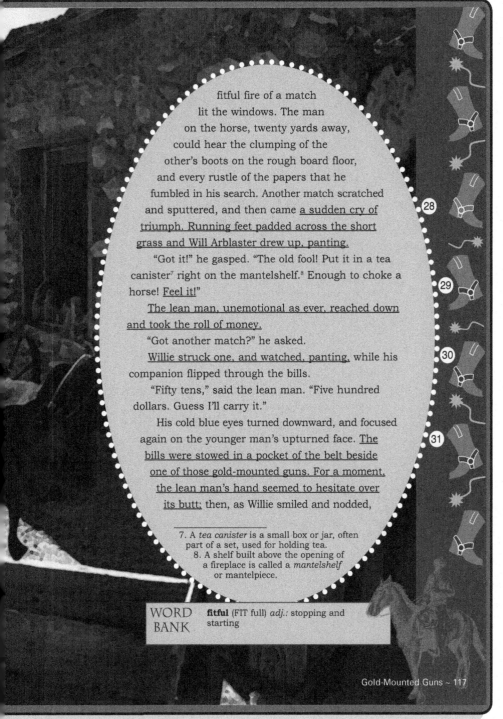

fitful fire of a match lit the windows. The man on the horse, twenty yards away, could hear the clumping of the other's boots on the rough board floor, and every rustle of the papers that he fumbled in his search. Another match scratched and sputtered, and then came a sudden cry of triumph. Running feet padded across the short grass and Will Arblaster drew up, panting.

"Got it!" he gasped. "The old fool! Put it in a tea canister[7] right on the mantelshelf.[8] Enough to choke a horse! Feel it!"

The lean man, unemotional as ever, reached down and took the roll of money.

"Got another match?" he asked.

Willie struck one, and watched, panting, while his companion flipped through the bills.

"Fifty tens," said the lean man. "Five hundred dollars. Guess I'll carry it."

His cold blue eyes turned downward, and focused again on the younger man's upturned face. The bills were stowed in a pocket of the belt beside one of those gold-mounted guns. For a moment, the lean man's hand seemed to hesitate over its butt; then, as Willie smiled and nodded,

7. A *tea canister* is a small box or jar, often part of a set, used for holding tea.
8. A shelf built above the opening of a fireplace is called a *mantelshelf* or mantelpiece.

WORD BANK **fitful** (FIT full) *adj.:* stopping and starting

Gold-Mounted Guns ~ 117

LITERARY COMPONENTS

▶ **28. Rising Action:** There is a cry of triumph, and Will Arblaster runs back with the money.

▶ **29. Interesting Turn of Events:** Will tells the lean man to feel the roll of money, and the lean man reaches down and takes it (and keeps it).

▶ **30. Characterization:** The author begins to refer to Arblaster as "Willie." Perhaps this is to make him seem younger, simpler, vulnerable, more sympathetic.

▶ **31. Rising Action; Suspense:** The lean man has put the roll of bills in a pocket beside one of the gold-mounted guns. (Is he a thief who is going to steal the money? Is he a good guy who is going to return the money?) His hand hesitates for a moment over his gun. (Is he going to shoot Arblaster and take the money himself? Is he going to arrest Arblaster?)

GUIDING THE READING

LITERAL

Q: Where does Will Arblaster find the roll of bills?
A: He finds it in a tea canister on the mantelpiece.

Q: How much money is it?
A: It's fifty ten dollar bills, or five hundred dollars.

ANALYTICAL

Q: Why do you think the lean man says he will carry the money?
A: Answers will vary. He is protecting the money—either to keep it for himself or to return it to the people.

Q: Why does the author start calling Arblaster Willie at this point?
A: Answers will vary.

Q: What do you think the lean man is thinking, when his hand hesitates over his gun butt?

A: Answers will vary.

Q: What effect does it have, to know that when the man and his daughter return they are happy and laughing?
A: Answers will vary. This makes us feel for them, because their happiness is about to be destroyed, and they sound so carefree.

- "Willie" says they should get out of there. The lean man wants him to get on his hawss and set still awhile.

- The young man asks, "What's the idea?"

- The lean man says that this is a novelty to him. Robbing trains, he doesn't get the chance to see what happens. He wants to see what the old man does when he finds the money gone. "Ought to be amusin'!"

- Two riders come, a man and a girl. They are laughing as they ride up to their broken-down old stable.

LITERARY COMPONENTS

▶ **32. Rising Action; Characterization; Theme:** The lean man doesn't want them to leave now that they have the money. He wants to stay and watch the reaction of the victim. He says that it ought to be amusing. (Is he a monster that he wants to see someone suffer? But after reading the story through, we know that he is doing this to teach the kid a lesson. No doubt, he also wants to return the money to the people.)

▶ **33. Rising Action; Characters; Characterization of Victims Begins:** The old man and his daughter come riding home. They are laughing, happy. Their stable is broken down, which shows us how poor they are.

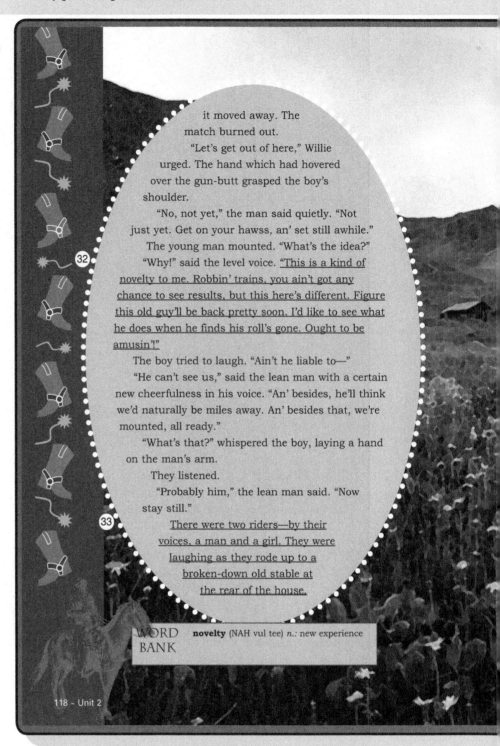

it moved away. The match burned out.

"Let's get out of here," Willie urged. The hand which had hovered over the gun-butt grasped the boy's shoulder.

"No, not yet," the man said quietly. "Not just yet. Get on your hawss, an' set still awhile."

The young man mounted. "What's the idea?"

"Why!" said the level voice. "This is a kind of novelty to me. Robbin' trains, you ain't got any chance to see results, but this here's different. Figure this old guy'll be back pretty soon. I'd like to see what he does when he finds his roll's gone. Ought to be amusin'!"

The boy tried to laugh. "Ain't he liable to—"

"He can't see us," said the lean man with a certain new cheerfulness in his voice. "An' besides, he'll think we'd naturally be miles away. An' besides that, we're mounted, all ready."

"What's that?" whispered the boy, laying a hand on the man's arm.

They listened.

"Probably him," the lean man said. "Now stay still."

There were two riders—by their voices, a man and a girl. They were laughing as they rode up to a broken-down old stable at the rear of the house.

WORD BANK   **novelty** (NAH vul tee) *n.:* new experience

118 ~ Unit 2

GUIDING THE READING

LITERAL

Q: Why does the lean man want them to wait for the old man to get back?
A: In his Pecos Tommy role, this is a novelty for him. Pecos Tommy just robs trains. He says it should be amusing. If students have read the story through, they will know that he wants "Willie" to see the repercussions of his behavior.

ANALYTICAL

Q: What effect does it have that their stable is described as old and broken down?
A: It makes us feel especially bad, because we know they are very poor.

SUMMING UP THE PLOT

- As the man and his daughter walk to the door, their words become clear to Will Arblaster and the lean man.

- The daughter says that she feels bad about her father's continuing to live there while—

- He interrupts her to say that Aunt Elviry gave her half the money to go to college, and that she had worked to earn the rest.

- He cannot find the key. There is a silence. Then she asks if he left the money in the

house. She tells him that the door is broken down.

- There is a hoarse cry. The old man stumbles across the floor boards and a match flares.

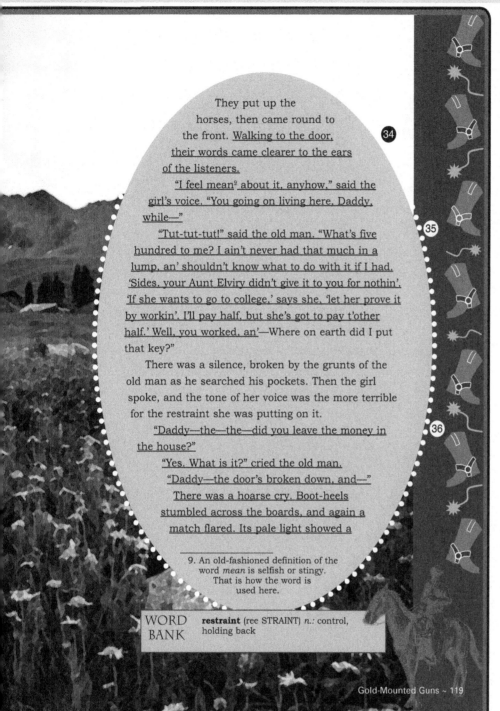

They put up the horses, then came round to the front. Walking to the door, their words came clearer to the ears of the listeners.

"I feel mean[9] about it, anyhow," said the girl's voice. "You going on living here, Daddy, while—"

"Tut-tut-tut!" said the old man. "What's five hundred to me? I ain't never had that much in a lump, an' shouldn't know what to do with it if I had. 'Sides, your Aunt Elviry didn't give it to you for nothin'. 'If she wants to go to college,' says she, 'let her prove it by workin'. I'll pay half, but she's got to pay t'other half.' Well, you worked, an'—Where on earth did I put that key?"

There was a silence, broken by the grunts of the old man as he searched his pockets. Then the girl spoke, and the tone of her voice was the more terrible for the restraint she was putting on it.

"Daddy—the—the—did you leave the money in the house?"

"Yes. What is it?" cried the old man.

"Daddy—the door's broken down, and—"

There was a hoarse cry. Boot-heels stumbled across the boards, and again a match flared. Its pale light showed a

---

9. An old-fashioned definition of the word *mean* is selfish or stingy. That is how the word is used here.

> WORD BANK **restraint** (ree STRAINT) *n.:* control, holding back

LITERARY COMPONENTS

▶ **34. Point of View:** The entire scene that follows is described as though it is being listened to by other ears and watched by other eyes. This is very effective.

▶ **35. Characterization:** Both father and daughter sound like selfless, hardworking people, devoted to each other. She worries about going to college and leaving him living there, even though she has earned half the money, and he just wants her to have the life before her. He is a person who has never had $500 all at once.

▶ **36. Rising Action; Suspense; Characterization:** The daughter asks if he left the money in the house. Then she tells him that the door is broken down. Notice her restraint here. She doesn't yell at him and call him a fool—she is hesitating because she knows this will break him.

GUIDING THE READING

LITERAL

Q: What does Pa Sanderson say about the $500?

A: He says that it is nothing to him. He has never had that much money at one time and wouldn't know what to do with it if he had it.

Q: Where did the money come from?

A: One-half came from Aunt Elviry and the other half the daughter earned.

SUMMING UP THE PLOT

- Pa Sanderson totters away from the mantelpiece. He holds a flickering match in one hand and a tin box in the other. "Gone!" he cries. "Gone!"

- Willie Arblaster draws a breath through his teeth

and moves uneasily in his saddle. A lean, strong hand with a grip like steel falls on his wrist. The lean man chuckles. He says, "Listen!"

- The old man is hunched in his seat by the fireplace, his face in his hands.

- The daughter throws her arms around his neck and pleads, "Now, Daddy, it's all right. Don't take on so. It's all right."

- Pa Sanderson will not be comforted. "I can't replace it!" he cries.

LITERARY COMPONENTS

▶ **37. Vivid, Poignant Scene; Metaphor:** He cries hoarsely. He stumbles across the boards. A match flares, revealing the girl as she stands in the door-way with her hands clasped. The door is not the only wreckage. He is bent, with silver hair. He totters.

▶ **38. Characterization; Onomatopoeia:** Arblaster reacts, but the lean man forces him to watch. When he *chuckles*, it puts the scene in starker contrast. Their pain vs. his apparent amusement.

▶ **39. Powerful Dialogue; Characterization; Another Vivid Tableau:** Her trying to comfort him is done very well, very convincingly. It is desperately sad. She seems not to think at all of her lost college education, and her years of work, but to be focused exclusively on her father who seems broken by this. We can see what the men outside on their horses see: *. . . she forced the old man into his seat by the fireplace. He hunched there, his face in his hands. . . .*

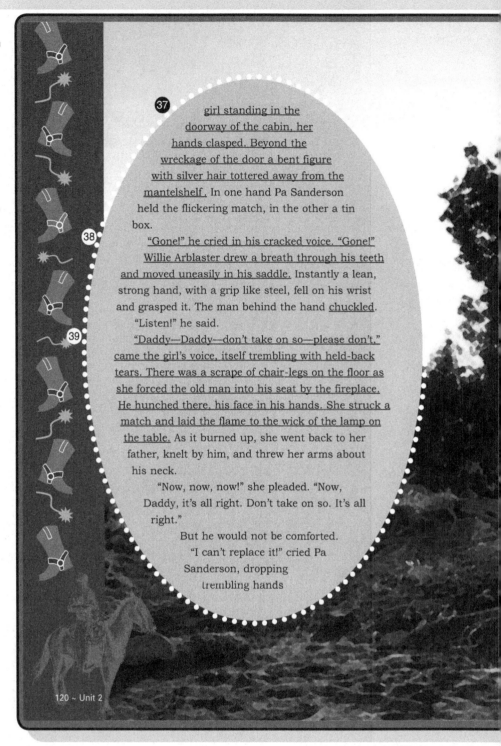

37 girl standing in the doorway of the cabin, her hands clasped. Beyond the wreckage of the door a bent figure with silver hair tottered away from the mantelshelf. In one hand Pa Sanderson held the flickering match, in the other a tin box.

"Gone!" he cried in his cracked voice. "Gone!"

38 Willie Arblaster drew a breath through his teeth and moved uneasily in his saddle. Instantly a lean, strong hand, with a grip like steel, fell on his wrist and grasped it. The man behind the hand chuckled.

"Listen!" he said.

39 "Daddy—Daddy—don't take on so—please don't," came the girl's voice, itself trembling with held-back tears. There was a scrape of chair-legs on the floor as she forced the old man into his seat by the fireplace. He hunched there, his face in his hands. She struck a match and laid the flame to the wick of the lamp on the table. As it burned up, she went back to her father, knelt by him, and threw her arms about his neck.

"Now, now, now!" she pleaded. "Now, Daddy, it's all right. Don't take on so. It's all right."

But he would not be comforted.

"I can't replace it!" cried Pa Sanderson, dropping trembling hands

120 ~ Unit 2

GUIDING THE READING

LITERAL

Q: When Pa lights a match, what can be seen in its pale light?

A: Its pale light shows the girl standing in the door-way of the cabin, her hands clasped.

Q: How does Arblaster react when he hears Pa Sanderson cry, "Gone! Gone!"

A: He draws a breath through his teeth and moves uneasily in his saddle.

ANALYTICAL

Q: Describe the relationship of the father and the daughter.

A: They are devoted to each other, each placing the other's needs first.

Q: What does the wreckage of the door symbolize or represent?

A: The wreckage of the door is the wreckage of their home and their lives. They have been intruded on violently.

Q: What is the effect of the lean man's chuckling?

A: Answers will vary. His apparent cruelty is in such stark contrast to the suffering and beauty of these two people, that it may make Arblaster shake his head at such monstrous behavior and want to distance himself from it.

SUMMING UP THE PLOT

- The old man says that his daughter was away from him for two years, slaving in a store. "And now I've—"

- She begs him to hush. "Now Daddy, —it's all right. I can go on working, and—"

- He cries out, "Curse him! Whoever it is, curse him!" He says that their happiness has been wiped out in a minute by a low sneaking thief.

- Gently, like a mother with a little child, the daughter leads her heartbroken father out of the watchers' line of vision.

- With heartbreaking distinctness, the sounds of weeping can still be heard.

- The lean man chuckles and says, "Some circus!" he starts to move away.

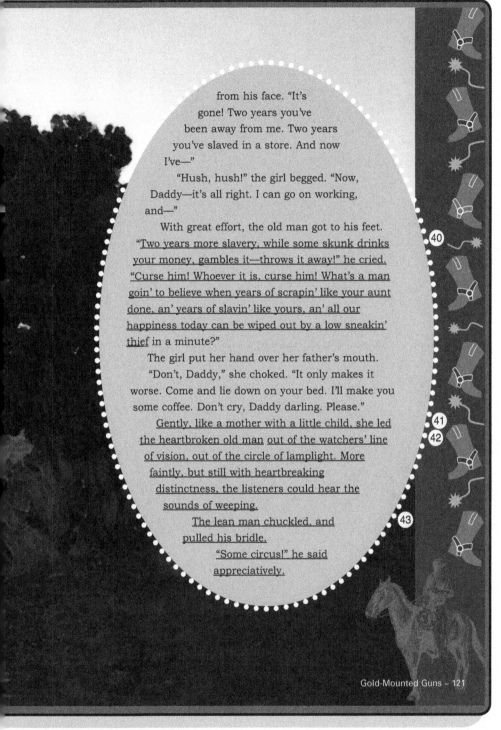

from his face. "It's gone! Two years you've been away from me. Two years you've slaved in a store. And now I've—"

"Hush, hush!" the girl begged. "Now, Daddy—it's all right. I can go on working, and—"

With great effort, the old man got to his feet. "Two years more slavery, while some skunk drinks your money, gambles it—throws it away!" he cried. "Curse him! Whoever it is, curse him! What's a man goin' to believe when years of scrapin' like your aunt done, an' years of slavin' like yours, an' all our happiness today can be wiped out by a low sneakin' thief in a minute?"

The girl put her hand over her father's mouth. "Don't, Daddy," she choked. "It only makes it worse. Come and lie down on your bed. I'll make you some coffee. Don't cry, Daddy darling. Please."

Gently, like a mother with a little child, she led the heartbroken old man out of the watchers' line of vision, out of the circle of lamplight. More faintly, but still with heartbreaking distinctness, the listeners could hear the sounds of weeping.

The lean man chuckled, and pulled his bridle.

"Some circus!" he said appreciatively.

Gold-Mounted Guns ~ 121

LITERARY COMPONENTS

▶ **40. Dialogue Rises in a Crescendo; Theme:** The old man utters a powerful invocation, cursing Will Arblaster, calling him a skunk and a low sneaking thief.

▶ **41. Characterization:** How children should treat their parents at such times. The daughter is now like a mother, trying to console her father.

▶ **42. Point of View:** We are reminded that this scene has been presented through the eyes of watchers. They can no longer see them, "but still with heartbreaking distinctness, the listeners could hear the sounds of weeping."

▶ **43. Rising Tension:** The lean man as Pecos Tommy chuckles and calls the tragedy a circus. He is pushing Arblaster to behave with decency.

GUIDING THE READING

LITERAL

Q: How long had it taken Miss Sanderson to earn $250?
A: It had taken her two years.

Q: What does Pa Sanderson call the man who stole the money?
A: He calls him a skunk and a low sneaking thief.

Q: What is the lean man's reaction to the crying in the cabin?
A: He chuckles, calls it a circus, and acts as though he is ready to leave.

ANALYTICAL

Q: Why does the old man blame himself?
A: Answers may vary. He has been careless with the money that both Aunt Elviry and his daughter slaved for years to earn.

Q: Why is the daughter more concerned with her father than with the fact that she has lost her chance for a college education?
A: Answers will vary.

Q: Why does the author write about the man and his daughter as witnessed and heard by Arblaster and the lean man?
A: Answers will vary. This is an interesting tool. Their reaction to the tragedy that has befallen them is given eyes and ears by the presence of the men who are responsible for the tragedy.

SUMMING UP THE PLOT

- "Ain't you comin'?" the lean man asks Arblaster.

- Arblaster says, "No. An'—an' I ain't goin' to take that money, neither."

- He says that he never thought about old men crying.

- Will says that he is going to take the money back.

- The lean man says, "Suppose I say I won't let go of it?"

- Arblaster says that he will blow the lean man's head off and take the money.

LITERARY COMPONENTS

▶ **44. Emotional Turning Point; Emotional Climax:** Arblaster says he's not going with the lean man and that he's not going to take the money.

▶ **45. Theme; Motivation; Characterization:** Arblaster talks about how he'd thought this was a game. "Kind of fun, at that." But he'd "Never thought 'bout—old men cryin'."

▶ **46. Moral Climax; Theme:** Will says he's going to take the money back.

▶ **47. Suspense:** The lean man allows that he might not let him have the money.

▶ **48. Characterization:** Arblaster says he's taking the money (or he'll shoot the lean man).

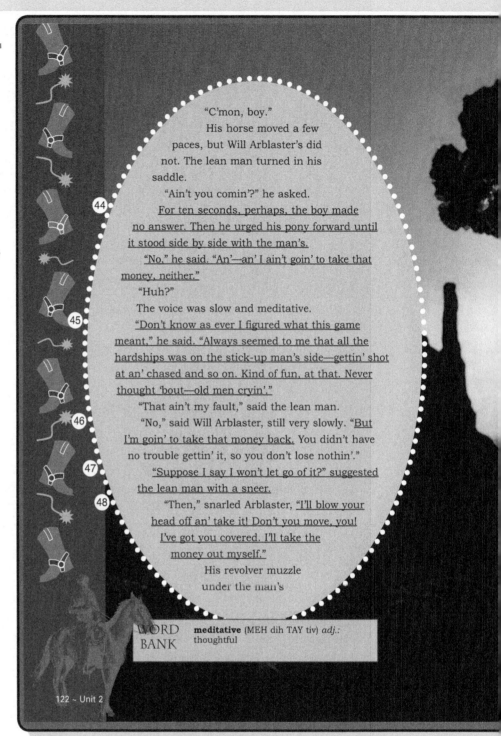

"C'mon, boy."

His horse moved a few paces, but Will Arblaster's did not. The lean man turned in his saddle.

"Ain't you comin'?" he asked.

(44) For ten seconds, perhaps, the boy made no answer. Then he urged his pony forward until it stood side by side with the man's.

"No," he said. "An'—an' I ain't goin' to take that money, neither."

"Huh?"

The voice was slow and meditative.

(45) "Don't know as ever I figured what this game meant," he said. "Always seemed to me that all the hardships was on the stick-up man's side—gettin' shot at an' chased and so on. Kind of fun, at that. Never thought 'bout—old men cryin'."

"That ain't my fault," said the lean man.

(46) "No," said Will Arblaster, still very slowly. "But I'm goin' to take that money back. You didn't have no trouble gettin' it, so you don't lose nothin'."

(47) "Suppose I say I won't let go of it?" suggested the lean man with a sneer.

(48) "Then," snarled Arblaster, "I'll blow your head off an' take it! Don't you move, you! I've got you covered. I'll take the money out myself."

His revolver muzzle under the man's

WORD BANK **meditative** (MEH dih TAY tiv) *adj.:* thoughtful

122 ~ Unit 2

GUIDING THE READING

LITERAL

Q: What does Will Arblaster say he will do if the lean man won't let go of the money?
A: He says he will blow his head off and take it.

ANALYTICAL

Q: Why had Will Arblaster thought that the life of a stick-up man was fun?
A: Answers will vary.

SUMMING UP THE PLOT

- Will holds his revolver under the man's nose and takes the roll of bills from the pocket in his belt.
- With determined steps, Arblaster walks to the lighted doorway of the cabin.
- The lean man sits perfectly still, listening.
- Soon there is the sound of surprise and joy from the cabin.
- It is a full ten minutes before Will Arblaster appears in the doorway.
- He tells the lean man he's sorry.
- The lean man says, "I ain't."
- He asks Arblaster, "What do you think I made you stay an' watch for?"
- The boy's mouth drops open. "Ain't you Pecos Tommy?"
- The lean man laughs.
- The boy says that he's got Pecos' guns. "If you ain't him, who are you?"

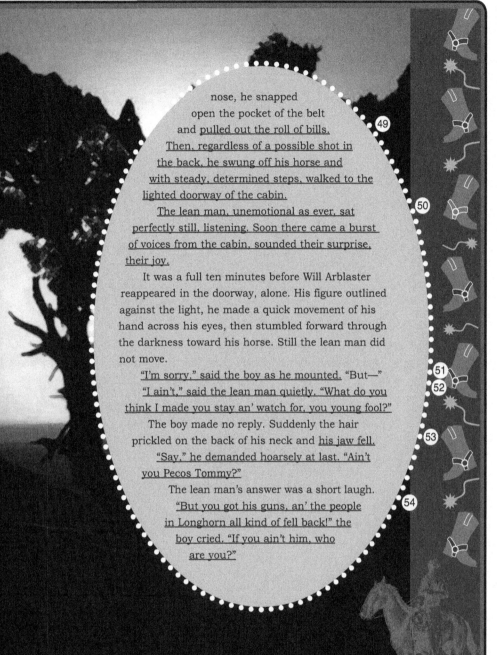

nose, he snapped open the pocket of the belt and pulled out the roll of bills. Then, regardless of a possible shot in the back, he swung off his horse and with steady, determined steps, walked to the lighted doorway of the cabin.

The lean man, unemotional as ever, sat perfectly still, listening. Soon there came a burst of voices from the cabin, sounded their surprise, their joy.

It was a full ten minutes before Will Arblaster reappeared in the doorway, alone. His figure outlined against the light, he made a quick movement of his hand across his eyes, then stumbled forward through the darkness toward his horse. Still the lean man did not move.

"I'm sorry," said the boy as he mounted. "But—"

"I ain't," said the lean man quietly. "What do you think I made you stay an' watch for, you young fool?"

The boy made no reply. Suddenly the hair prickled on the back of his neck and his jaw fell.

"Say," he demanded hoarsely at last. "Ain't you Pecos Tommy?"

The lean man's answer was a short laugh.

"But you got his guns, an' the people in Longhorn all kind of fell back!" the boy cried. "If you ain't him, who are you?"

Gold-Mounted Guns ~ 123

LITERARY COMPONENTS

▶ **49. Falling Action:** Arblaster takes the money from the lean man and walks towards the lighted doorway.

▶ **50. Emotional Resolution; Viewpoint:** Through the lean man's ears, we are privy to sounds of joy and surprise in the cabin.

▶ **51. Characterization; Falling Action:** Arblaster apologizes to the lean man.

▶ **52. Building to the Revelatory Ending:** The lean man says that he's not sorry. He asks Will why he thinks he made him stay and watch.

▶ **53. Dawning Realization; Characterization:** Will asks, "Ain't you Pecos Tommy?"

▶ **54. Suspense; Building to the Disclosure:** Will says, "But you got his guns…If you ain't him, who are you?"

GUIDING THE READING

LITERAL

Q: How does Will get the money?
A: He puts a gun to the lean man's nose, snaps open the pocket of his belt, and pulls out the roll of bills.

Q: After Will enters the cabin, what does the lean man hear as he sits there listening?
A: He hears a burst of voices sounding their surprise and joy.

Q: How long was Will in the cabin?
A: Ten minutes.

ANALYTICAL

Q: How do we know that Will Arblaster is really determined to return the money?
A: He threatens to shoot the lean man. He puts a gun to his nose and takes the money from the pocket of his belt. He walks towards the cabin with steady, determined steps, even though he could be shot in the back by the man he believes to be Pecos Tommy.

Q: What do you think Will said to the Sandersons?
A: Answers will vary.

Q: Why do you think Will apologizes to the lean man?
A: Answers will vary.

SUMMING UP THE PLOT

- The lean man says, "I'm the sheriff that killed him yesterday."

LITERARY COMPONENTS

▶ **55. Vivid Image; Making Us Wait for the Moment of Truth:** This is beautifully written: "The moon had drifted from behind a cloud and flung a ray of light across the face of the lean man..."

▶ **56. Surprise!:** The lean man says, dryly, "Why I'm the sheriff that killed him yesterday."

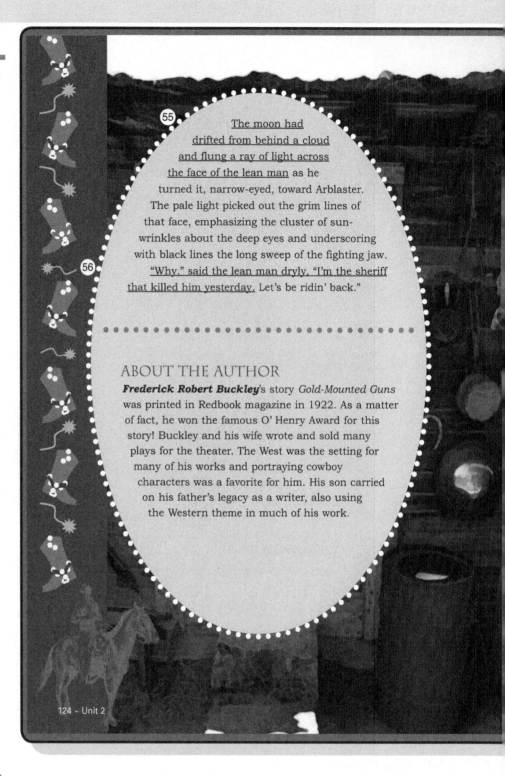

(55) The moon had drifted from behind a cloud and flung a ray of light across the face of the lean man as he turned it, narrow-eyed, toward Arblaster. The pale light picked out the grim lines of that face, emphasizing the cluster of sun-wrinkles about the deep eyes and underscoring with black lines the long sweep of the fighting jaw. (56) "Why," said the lean man dryly, "I'm the sheriff that killed him yesterday. Let's be ridin' back."

ABOUT THE AUTHOR

Frederick Robert Buckley's story *Gold-Mounted Guns* was printed in Redbook magazine in 1922. As a matter of fact, he won the famous O' Henry Award for this story! Buckley and his wife wrote and sold many plays for the theater. The West was the setting for many of his works and portraying cowboy characters was a favorite for him. His son carried on his father's legacy as a writer, also using the Western theme in much of his work.

124 ~ Unit 2

GUIDING THE READING

LITERAL

Q: Who is the lean man?
A: He's the sheriff of Longhorn City.

Q: How did he get the guns?
A: He killed Pecos Tommy.

ANALYTICAL

Q: Were you surprised?
A: Answers will vary.

FIRST IMPRESSIONS

If students say they were surprised, have them say more about *what it was* that surprised them. If students say they were not surprised by the ending, try to get them to expand on their answer. Were there any clues in the story to suggest that the "hard-faced man" was a good guy and not a bad guy?

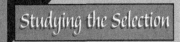

Studying the Selection

FIRST IMPRESSIONS
Were you surprised by the ending?

QUICK REVIEW

1. When the story opens, in which city do we find the characters?

2. What time of day is it?

3. How long has "the boy" lived in town? What is his name?

4. Do we ever learn the name of the "hard-faced man"?

FOCUS

5. Look up the word *conscience* in the dictionary. Write down the definition. How do we know that Will Arblaster has a conscience?

6. After Will takes the money, he tells the "hard-faced man" that they should "'get out of here.'" But the man says, "'Not just yet. Get on your hawss, an' set still awhile.'" Why does the hard-faced man say this?

CREATING & WRITING

7. In one or two paragraphs, describe what you think is the story's lesson.

8. In *Gold-Mounted Guns,* we see that Will Arblaster has an inner conflict after he robs Mr. Sanderson. In one paragraph, tell how the story lets us know that he feels bad. In a second paragraph, describe what he does about it.

9. Create a collage of images and words that paint a picture of what life was like in Longhorn City.

Gold-Mounted Guns ~ 125

QUICK REVIEW

1. The city is Longhorn City. (This is an imaginary city.)

2. The story opens with the sentence, "Evening had fallen on Longhorn City."

3. The boy has just arrived in town that afternoon (p. 113). We learn his name is Will Arblaster (p. 115).

4. We never learn his name. He remains mysterious. We only learn that he is the sheriff and that he killed Pecos Tommy the day before.

FOCUS

5. *Conscience* is the inner sense of what is right or wrong in one's conduct or motives, moving one toward right action. We know that Will Arblaster has a conscience because he has trouble listening to the suffering of the girl and her father, because he stands up to the lean man and insists he give him the money, and he returns the money.

6. The hard-faced man forces Will to wait, because he wants him to see the consequences of his behavior. He is testing Will and is waiting to see if Will will pass the test. He is giving Will a chance to make up for his bad act.

CREATING & WRITING

7. The answer should come out of your earlier discussion of theme with the students. Certainly the story teaches that crime is not exciting. Robbing people loses its "thrill"—if robbing people has a thrill—when the robber hears them crying afterwards. This is one way that crime does not pay. The story also shows that it takes courage to stand up for one's convictions, as Will Arblaster ultimately does. *Gold-Mounted Guns* also shows that "you can't tell a book by its cover." The hard-faced man is not hard inside: He's a caring person who wants the young man to learn a lesson and avoid a life of crime. Interestingly, he is not interested in trapping and punishing Will as long as it is clear to him that Will can be reformed. He is intent on helping Will to learn by his mistakes and become a better person.

8. Students can draw on the passages that describe Will's reaction to hearing the despair of the girl and her father: He "drew a breath through his teeth and moved uneasily in his saddle." After Will has heard more, he does not move his horse. For ten seconds, he does not respond to "the lean man." Then he says, "Don't know as ever I figured what this game meant… Always seemed to me that all the hardships was on the stick-up man's side …. Never about old men cryin'." To resolve his conflict, Will takes the money back. He even threatens to kill the lean man, if he tries to prevent him from returning the money.

9. Make sure students have enough material cut out from magazines and newspapers, if they are unable to get such materials at home. The cow cities of the old West were "tough"—although certainly people conducted business there and there were ordinary residents. Students will be able to handle this assignment well from your discussion of **Background Bytes.**

SEQUENCE

- Sequence means the order in which events occur.
- In a nonfiction story, the sequence of events is part of the true reporting of the facts. A change in sequence means the story is, in part, untrue.
- In a mystery, the solution will often depend on the order, or sequence, of events.
- Some stories are purposely written out of sequence. An author may use flashbacks, mixing present and past events, or may hide some past event only to reveal it later on in the story.

THINK ABOUT IT!

1. When Angela was little, how did she and her grandfather spend Sunday afternoons?

2. How does Papa behave after his stroke?

3. In this story, some events take place in the present, some, in the recent past, and some, in the more distant past. When did the stroke take place? When did Angela's grandfather make spaghetti and meatballs? When did Angela make pizzelles by herself? Are the story's events told in sequence?

4. List in sequence the six steps of pizzelle making that are mentioned in the story.

Angela and Papa

Sunday afternoons meant Papa's famous homemade spaghetti and meatballs. It also meant cousins. The best part, though, was making pizzelles—the flat, Italian cookies Papa made on a special waffle iron. Ever since Angela was little, she'd been her grandfather's "official stacker," going over early on Sundays to help Papa mix the batter and stack the cookies on the metal cooling racks.

Then came Papa's stroke. Papa was not the same. He could not move his left arm or leg, and he seemed very sad, staring blankly from his armchair.

One day, while visiting Papa, Angela got an idea.

In eleven years of making pizzelles, Angela and Papa had discussed many things—school, friends, her parents, missing Nana—but they'd never discussed the recipe. It was time to put all that watching and helping to use.

"Eggs!" she shouted as she cracked four eggs into the glass bowl they'd always used.

She thought she saw Papa turn his head when she shouted "Vanilla!" He always said vanilla was the secret to good pizzelles.

When the batter was mixed, she plugged in the griddle and went to get Papa. Helping him to take very slow steps, Angela got Papa seated at the table just as the light indicated the griddle was hot.

Opening the lid, she placed a drop of batter on each of two flower-shaped griddles and pressed down gently.

"Very hot," she said as she placed the first two steaming pizzelles on the cooling rack. "No tasting yet." Papa's exact words.

In a short while, Angela spread a clean dish towel in front of Papa. "Ready, stacker?" she asked, mimicking Papa's ship-captain tone. "Commence stacking."

Gently taking Papa's right hand in hers, she helped him to pick up one cookie and move it to the towel. Then another.

"You seem to have a knack for this," she said. "I'd say you should be moving up to chief cook in no time."

Slowly, a smile appeared on Papa's face. It wasn't a big smile, but it was the first she'd seen in a long time.

LESSON IN LITERATURE

1. They spent the afternoon cooking and eating spaghetti, meatballs, and pizelles.

2. He sits listlessly in his chair.

3. In the recent past, Papa had a stroke. In the more distant past, Papa would cook an Italian dinner every Sunday afternoon. In the present, Angela bakes pizelles in an effort to engage her father's interest. The story's events are related in chronological sequence.

4. a) crack 4 eggs into a glass bowl b) add vanilla c) mix batter d) plug in griddle e) place a drop of batter on the griddle and press down f) remove the pizelle

SELECTION VOCABULARY

amateur: not professional or expert; a person who is unskilled or inexperienced in a particular activity

analyze: to examine each part of something in a careful, logical way

edging: moving slowly and cautiously

enigma: a puzzling occurrence; a mystery that seems unsolvable

evacuate: leave

heists: robberies or holdups

loner: a person who has little to do with other people

milling: moving aimlessly

peddling: selling

sleuth: detective

---

amateur   edging   evacuate   loner   peddling
analyze   enigma   heists   milling   sleuth

1. One of the most famous literary figures of all times was the British _____ (detective) Sherlock Holmes.

2. He started out as an _____ (not professional), a man who simply loved to apply his mind to solving problems.

3. He was something of a _____ (a person who has little to do with others). His only friend was Dr. Watson.

4. In the Sherlock Holmes stories, the chief of Scotland Yard, England's F.B.I., often asks Holmes to help him catch a criminal or to help him _____ (examine each part carefully) a crime.

5. Holmes was not interested in simple thefts or _____ (robberies).

6. He preferred a challenge, a deep mystery, an _____ (deep mystery) so great it seemed unsolvable.

7. Holmes used many disguises. Often, he pretended to be part of a crowd that was _____ (moving aimlessly) about.

8. At other times, he would take a pushcart and pretend to be _____ (selling) some simple goods.

9. In one of the stories, the criminal is caught just as he is _____ (moving cautiously) away from the police.

10. In another story, Holmes solves a mystery by starting a small fire, which forces the thief who lives there to _____ (leave) the house. Through this ruse, he is able to discover where the thief has hidden the stolen goods.

Workbook p. 37   Answer Guide p. 5

Unscramble

Unscramble the ten words below, placing one letter in each square. When you are finished, arrange the circled letters to form the answer to the riddle.

ITESH

PLEDED

GEGDIN

ZANELAY

HUTELS

ELRON

AVEETUAC

GAMEIN

GLIMLIN

EURATAM

CIRCUS-CIRCUS

Riddle:
What did the animals have that enabled them to escape from their locked cages?

Answer:
T H E Y ◯◯◯ ◯ ◯◯◯◯ K ◯◯

Workbook p. 38   Answer Guide p. 5

BACKGROUND BYTES

We are indebted to ClassicCrimeFiction, Wikipedia, and Donna Goldthwaite for much of the material below.

Perhaps more than any other type of fiction, mysteries are about problem solving and about understanding the sequence of events that holds the key to the mystery.

Edgar Allan Poe was the first person to write detective fiction. *The Murders in the Rue Morgue* appeared in 1841. The story, and another two Poe works that followed (*The Mystery of Marie Roget* and *The Purloined Letter*), were skillfully written and included the two primary components of detective fiction: a crime that baffles and an ingenious detective whose intelligence enables him to solve the crime. The Poe stories also included the detective's colleague or friend who records the case, similar to Sherlock Holmes' Doctor Watson—who came forty-five years later. Unlike the detective in our story (Larry's father, not Larry), Poe's detective works privately and is treated with contempt by the police—who are stunned and apologetic when he solves the case. In spite of his success, the detective remains an outsider.

Although the word *detective* was not known at the time that Edgar Allan Poe was writing, Poe is considered by mystery buffs to be "the father of the detective story." Poe uses

• an "eccentric detective and his sidekick"
• a "least-likely suspect"
• the locked room mystery (how could anyone have gotten in the room? how could anyone have gotten out of the room?)
• "armchair detection"—the detective sits and thinks about what has occurred (he just uses his "little grey cells")
• "hiding in plain sight"

The next great writer in the genre was Wilkie Collins. His 1859 classic, *The Woman in White,* has a fascination even for the modern reader. There was a lot of bad mystery and crime writing, but other fine writers followed: Victor Hugo with *Les Miserables* [lay miz uh ROB] (1862); Emile Gaboriau with the first detective novel in 1866; Wilkie Collins again in 1868 with *The Moonstone*; and Charles Dickens' *The Mystery of Edwin Drood* (1870). In 1878, Anna Katharine Green, dubbed the "mother of the American detective story," appeared on the literary scene.

Interestingly, the development of the crime story coincided with the establishment of police forces around the world in the nineteenth century.

Then came the greatest detective of all time: Arthur Conan Doyle's "Sherlock Holmes, the greatest detective that never lived and who will never die!" Sherlock Holmes, in fact, is believed to be the most famous literary character around the globe.

Based on Joseph Bell, Conan Doyle's real life professor at the medical college of Edinburgh University, Sherlock Holmes became the gold standard against which all fictional detectives, past and future, were measured. The Sherlock Holmes stories appeared between the years 1887-1927, but those published in the Strand Magazine in 1891 are generally considered the best. The following year, they were published as a book entitled "The Adventures of Sherlock Holmes." The reasons for the immense and time-less popularity of these stories are many. One of the reasons probably lies in the stories' setting—the orderly world of Victorian England where, at least in theory, everything had its proper place. When only one thing—the crime—is askew in a very predictable pattern, it can readily be solved through logic. As the world lurched from World War I to World War II, the average person yearned for a universe in which all things were identifiable as good or evil, where a tall thin man and his companionable friend could make the world safe—at least for as long as it took to read a good story on a cold night next to a warm fire.

The years between 1920 and 1939 were the "Golden Age" of detective fiction. The finest writers of the time were largely British, and the most famous among them included Agatha Christie (1890-1976), Dorothy L. Sayers (1893-1957), Josephine Tey (1895-1952), and John Dickson Carr (who was American, but who sounded British). Many of these novels were set in an English country house peopled by upper-class Englishmen and their well-mannered servants. The victim himself and his murder existed only as a focal point for the author's real interest: the suspects, the English setting, the detective, and, above all, the psychology of crime. Few readers of Agatha Christie will remember the names of any of her fictional victims or their manners of death, but Miss Marple, Hercule Poirot, and the many keen insights into human nature woven into the stories are unforgettable.

In the late 1930s, a new form of detective novel emerged: hard-boiled crime fiction writing. Many of these stories were written in the first person and were narrated by the hero-detective. He was a loner, a tough guy, a private eye, who drank a lot of coffee, carried a gun, and smoked a lot of cigarettes. He was very American in his radical individualism. He worked in the big city, with danger lurking in every shadow. Cases that seem easy "often turn out to be quite complicated, forcing him to embark on an odyssey through the urban landscape"—the mean streets of Los Angeles, New York, or Chicago. These writers included Dashiell Hammett (1894-1961), Raymond Chandler (1888-1959), and Mickey Spillane (born 1918).

In the past 25 years, "the number of detective stories published annually has reached astronomical proportions, as have the range and variety of these fictions (and nonfictions)." Recent crime fiction tends to be as much concerned with people and what drives them, as it is with events. Victims, perpetrators, and the detectives themselves are gradually revealed to answer the question, "what makes them tick?"

INTO "THE DISAPPEARING MAN"

There is no deep theme to this story. (In fact, this story is a bit of a spoof—a light, humorous parody— of detective and mystery stories.) What we do see in *The Disappearing Man* is that the protagonist, a fourteen-year-old boy, notices what is going on around him, and is capable of fairly sophisticated deductive thinking—of the sort that Sherlock Holmes first made popular. The boy arrives at his conclusion from reasoning logically, in steps—in fact, in sequence.

So what can we say about the theme? Try these:
• If you look, listen, and reason carefully, you will develop the capacity to *think* and draw accurate conclusions.
• Crime does not pay.
• Never underestimate the capacity of younger folks to think and act wisely.

EYES ON...SEQUENCE

What is a sequence? Sequence refers to a continuous, uninterrupted, or connected series; the order of succession (the act or process of following in order); the continuity of progression.

How do we say this in simple English? The sequence of events is the order in which they occurred. Event **a** in our story: "I was coming home from the library that afternoon." Event **b** in our story: "...a man dashed by me and ran into an alley between two buildings." And, finally, Larry tells his parents how he knew a man was Stockton.

Certainly, students can practice sequencing just by describing what happened between getting up for school in the morning and arriving at school (or any similar ordinary event).

Discuss the potential difficulty in recalling the sequence of statements in a conversation or an argument. Also, you may want to talk about the difficulty inherent in picking out the most important points to include when trying to outline the sequence of events in a story.

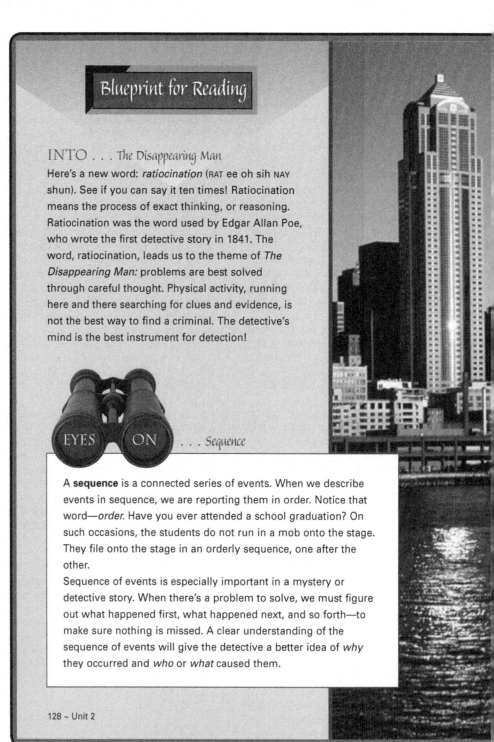

Blueprint for Reading

INTO . . . The Disappearing Man

Here's a new word: *ratiocination* (RAT ee oh sih NAY shun). See if you can say it ten times! Ratiocination means the process of exact thinking, or reasoning. Ratiocination was the word used by Edgar Allan Poe, who wrote the first detective story in 1841. The word, ratiocination, leads us to the theme of *The Disappearing Man:* problems are best solved through careful thought. Physical activity, running here and there searching for clues and evidence, is not the best way to find a criminal. The detective's mind is the best instrument for detection!

EYES ON . . . Sequence

A **sequence** is a connected series of events. When we describe events in sequence, we are reporting them in order. Notice that word—*order.* Have you ever attended a school graduation? On such occasions, the students do not run in a mob onto the stage. They file onto the stage in an orderly sequence, one after the other.

Sequence of events is especially important in a mystery or detective story. When there's a problem to solve, we must figure out what happened first, what happened next, and so forth—to make sure nothing is missed. A clear understanding of the sequence of events will give the detective a better idea of *why* they occurred and *who* or *what* caused them.

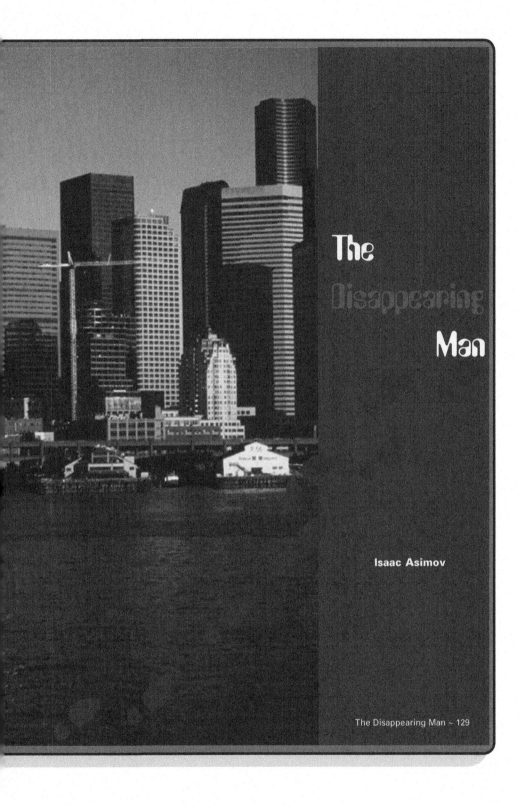

The
Disappearing
Man

Isaac Asimov

- The narrator declares that he is not often on the spot when his father is on one of his cases, but couldn't help being there that day.
- He was coming home from the library, and a man dashed by him and ran into an alleyway.
- In less than a minute, two police officers came running.
- "He went in there," the narrator directed them.
- Three police cars drove up.

LITERARY COMPONENTS

▶ **1. Character; Characterization; Point of View:** This first-person narration is told by the son of a detective. He explains that he couldn't help being where he was at the time.

▶ **2. Exposition; Setting:** He was walking home from the library when a man dashed full speed in front of him and into an alley between two buildings.

▶ **3. Characterization; Humor:** We learn more about the relationship between father and son, and that the narrator is fourteen years old, with his recollection of this humorous line from Dad.

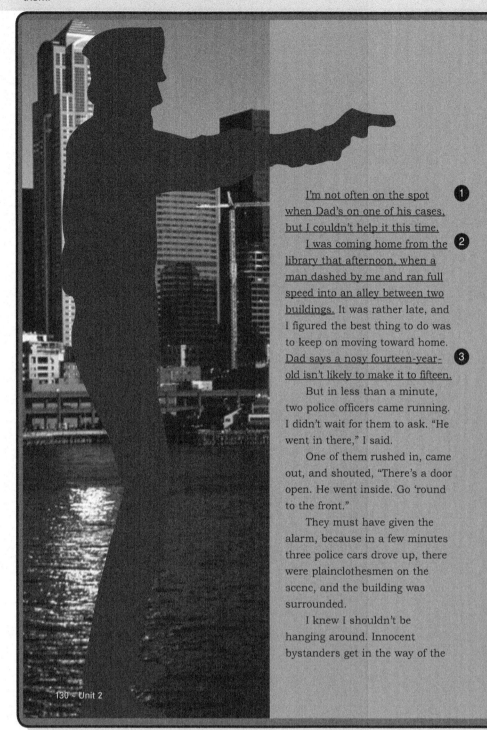

130 ~ Unit 2

<u>I'm not often on the spot when Dad's on one of his cases, but I couldn't help it this time.</u> ❶

<u>I was coming home from the library that afternoon, when a man dashed by me and ran full speed into an alley between two buildings.</u> ❷ It was rather late, and I figured the best thing to do was to keep on moving toward home. <u>Dad says a nosy fourteen-year-old isn't likely to make it to fifteen.</u> ❸

But in less than a minute, two police officers came running. I didn't wait for them to ask. "He went in there," I said.

One of them rushed in, came out, and shouted, "There's a door open. He went inside. Go 'round to the front."

They must have given the alarm, because in a few minutes three police cars drove up, there were plainclothesmen on the scene, and the building was surrounded.

I knew I shouldn't be hanging around. Innocent bystanders get in the way of the

GUIDING THE READING

LITERAL

Q: How did the narrator happen to be at the scene of the crime?

A: He was walking home from the library.

Q: What does his father say will happen to a nosy fourteen-year-old?

A: Dad says a nosy fourteen-year-old isn't likely to make it to fifteen.

- From what he could hear the police saying, the narrator knew they were after Stockton. He knew about Stockton, because his father was a detective and he had been working on the case.

- In his earlier discussion with his dad, the narrator had pointed out that Stockton couldn't work alone. He would have to have a fence to sell the jewels he stole. His father had suggested he get back to his homework.

- The alley Stockton ran into was closed on all sides but the street, and he hadn't come out.

- The boy notices that the door to the building in the alley is open, and figures that Stockton must have gone inside.

police. Just the same, I was there when it started and, <u>from what I heard the police saying, I knew they were after this man, Stockton. He was a loner who'd pulled off some pretty spectacular jewel robberies over the last few months.</u> I knew about it because Dad is a detective on the force, and he was on the case.

"Slippery fellow," he said, "but when you work alone, there's no one to double-cross you."

I said, <u>"Doesn't he have to work with someone, Dad? He's got to have a fence[1]—someone to peddle the jewels."</u>

"If he has," said Dad, "we haven't located him. And why don't you get on with your homework?" (He always says that when he thinks I'm getting too interested in his cases.)

Well, they had him now. Some jeweler must have pushed the alarm button.

<u>The alley he ran into was closed on all sides but the street, and he hadn't come out.</u> There was a door there that was open, so he must have gone in. The police had the possible

1. A *fence* is a person who receives stolen goods from a thief and finds a buyer for them.

WORD BANK	**loner** (LO ner) *n.:* a person who has little to do with other people **peddle** (PED dl) *v.:* sell

The Disappearing Man ~ 131

LITERARY COMPONENTS

▶ **4. Rising Action; Type of Mystery:** Unlike many mysteries or detective stories, in this one we know right from the start who the guilty party is.

▶ **5. Characterization:** Here's a good example of the narrator's deductive abilities. A young Sherlock, he is.

▶ **6. Type of Mystery:** We see that the story uses a variation of the "locked room" mystery. A locked room or a "hermetically sealed chamber" is ordinarily the room in which the murder is committed—a room that, at the time of the murder, no one could have entered or exited. The alley is closed on all sides but the street and Stockton hasn't come out. Ultimately, the reader will ask, "well where is he, if the police can't find him in the building?"

GUIDING THE READING

LITERAL
Q: What is the name of the fleeing thief? What does he like to steal?
A: His name is Stockton, and he likes to steal jewelry.

Q: What does the boy's father say when he thinks his son is getting too involved in his cases?
A: He says, "Why don't you get on with your homework?"

ANALYTICAL
Q: Why does the boy say that Stockton has to be working with someone?
A: He's a clever lad, and he knows that Stockton needs someone to sell his stolen goods.

Q: Why couldn't Stockton have run out of the other end of the alley?
A: The alley has no other end. It is closed on all sides but the street.

Q: Who is the disappearing man?
A: The disappearing man is Stockton, the jewel thief.

SUMMING UP THE PLOT

- The boy's father arrives on the scene and asks what he is doing there.

- Both his father and his father's driver tell him he should go home. He says he will leave in a minute.

- He reasons that Stockton must have a key, if the door into the alley is open, since nobody leaves doors open in New York City. There hasn't been time for Stockton to pick the lock.

LITERARY COMPONENTS

▶ **7. Rising Action; Characterization:** Larry's dad arrives (that's how we know his name is Larry). He wants Larry to go home.

▶ **8. Characterization; Ratiocination in Progress:** Larry doesn't leave. He wants to do some thinking. Quick on the uptake, Larry figures out that Stockton must have a key. No one leaves a door open in New York City, and Stockton hasn't had time to jimmy the lock. That also means he works out of the building.

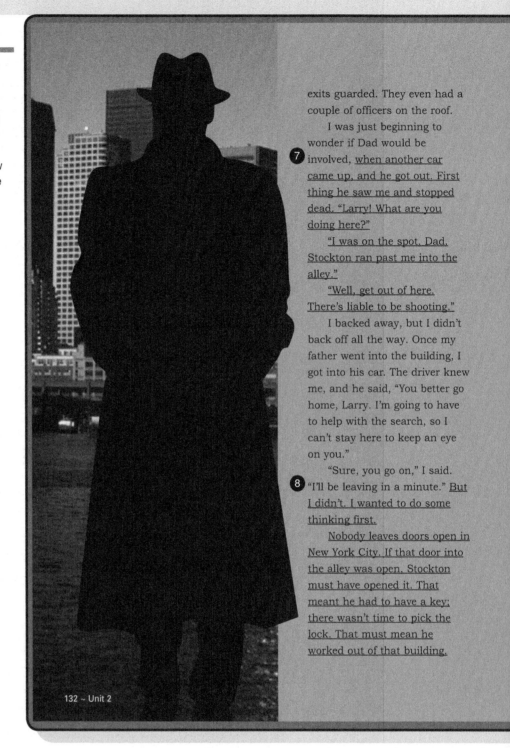

exits guarded. They even had a couple of officers on the roof.

I was just beginning to wonder if Dad would be

7 involved, <u>when another car came up, and he got out. First thing he saw me and stopped dead. "Larry! What are you doing here?"</u>

"<u>I was on the spot, Dad. Stockton ran past me into the alley.</u>"

"<u>Well, get out of here. There's liable to be shooting.</u>"

I backed away, but I didn't back off all the way. Once my father went into the building, I got into his car. The driver knew me, and he said, "You better go home, Larry. I'm going to have to help with the search, so I can't stay here to keep an eye on you."

"Sure, you go on," I said.

8 "I'll be leaving in a minute." <u>But I didn't. I wanted to do some thinking first.</u>

<u>Nobody leaves doors open in New York City. If that door into the alley was open, Stockton must have opened it. That meant he had to have a key; there wasn't time to pick the lock. That must mean he worked out of that building.</u>

132 ~ Unit 2

GUIDING THE READING

LITERAL

Q: What does Larry's father tell him to do when he arrives?

A: He tells him to leave, since there's liable to be some shooting.

ANALYTICAL

Q: Why does Larry remain there, after his father and his father's driver tell him he should go home?

A: He is unable to resist thinking about the problem and trying to solve it.

SUMMING UP THE PLOT

- Larry looks at the building and sees that a tailor is on the second floor, a theatrical costumer is on the third, and a jeweler on the fourth. He quickly decides that Stockton works with the jeweler.

- He gets tired of waiting, and moves quickly to the building entrance. He wants to see Stockton.

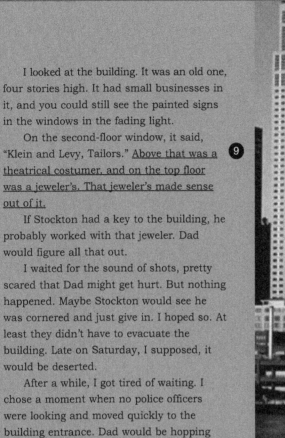

I looked at the building. It was an old one, four stories high. It had small businesses in it, and you could still see the painted signs in the windows in the fading light.

On the second-floor window, it said, "Klein and Levy, Tailors." <u>Above that was a theatrical costumer, and on the top floor was a jeweler's. That jeweler's made sense out of it.</u>

If Stockton had a key to the building, he probably worked with that jeweler. Dad would figure all that out.

I waited for the sound of shots, pretty scared that Dad might get hurt. But nothing happened. Maybe Stockton would see he was cornered and just give in. I hoped so. At least they didn't have to evacuate the building. Late on Saturday, I supposed, it would be deserted.

After a while, I got tired of waiting. I chose a moment when no police officers were looking and moved quickly to the building entrance. Dad would be hopping mad when he saw me, but I was curious. I figured they had Stockton, and I wanted to see him.

They didn't have him.

There was a fat man in a vest in the lobby. He looked scared, and I guess he was the watchman. He kept saying, "I didn't see *any*body."

> **WORD BANK** **evacuate** (ee VAK yoo AYT) *v.:* leave

LITERARY COMPONENTS

▶ **9. Foreshadowing; Aha!:** Larry sees a costumer on the third floor and a jeweler's on the top floor.

GUIDING THE READING

LITERAL
Q: How many stories does the building have?
A: Four stories.

Q: What types of businesses are on the second, third, and fourth floors?
A: Respectively, a tailor, a theatrical costumer, and a jeweler's.

ANALYTICAL
Q: Why does Larry think that Stockton has a key?

A: Stockton went into the building through the doorway in the alley. The door is still open. Since nobody leaves a door open in New York City, and there wasn't time for Stockton to pick the lock, he must have a key.

Q: What does Larry think is the significance of a jeweler's presence in the building?
A: He has already determined that Stockton would need someone to sell his stolen jewels, and here is someone who could do just that. Moreover, Stockton's working with someone in the building is suggested by the fact that he has a key.

TE: The Disappearing Man ~ 133

SUMMING UP THE PLOT

- Police officers are coming down the stairs and shaking their heads. Larry's father says, "No one has anything?"
- A policeman says that no one has climbed out on the roof, and all the doors and windows are covered.
- His father says that if he hasn't gotten out, then he's in the building.
- The sergeant says, "We can't find him."

- A policeman says, "He's nowhere inside."
- Larry's father says that it isn't a big building.
- The policemen say that they have looked everywhere.

- Larry's father says, "Then how do we know he went into the building in the first place? Who saw him go in?"
- Larry says, "I did, Dad."

LITERARY COMPONENTS

▶ **10. Rising Action; Growing Suspense:** Nobody can find Stockton. Has he disappeared?

▶ **11. Dialogue:** The dialogue between Larry's father and policemen reveals that they can't find Stockton in the building.

10 Police officers were coming down the stairs and out of the old elevator, all shaking their heads.

My father was pretty angry. He said, "No one has anything?"

A police sergeant said, "Donovan said no one got out on the roof. All the doors and windows are covered."

"If he didn't get out," said my father, in a low voice that carried, "then he's in the building."

"We can't find him," said the **11** sergeant. "He's nowhere inside."

My father said, "It isn't a big building—"

"We had the watchman's keys. We've looked everywhere."

"Then how do we know he went into the building in the first place? Who saw him go in?"

There was a silence. A lot of police officers were milling about the lobby now, but no one said anything. So I spoke up. "I did, Dad."

Dad whirled around and looked at me and made a funny sound in the back of his throat

WORD BANK	**milling** (MILL ing) v.: moving aimlessly

- His father says that Larry saw him run into the alley—that's not the same thing.
- Larry says, "He didn't come out, Dad."
- Larry says that there was nowhere else for Stockton to go.

- His father says, "But you didn't actually see him go in, did you?"
- Larry responds, "He couldn't go up the side of the building."
- His dad says, "Did *anyone* actually see him go in?"

- Larry is afraid his dad is going to call the whole pursuit off—and then when they get home he will get the talking-to of his life.
- The thought of the talking-to stimulates his brain.
- Larry says, "But, Dad, he *did* go into the building, and he didn't disappear. There he is right now. That man there." He points to the man and drops down and rolls out of the way.
- The man he points to makes a dash for it.
- A policeman who has been knocked down grabs Stockton's leg and everyone piles on top of him.

that meant I was in for it for still being there. "You said you saw him run into the alley," he said. "That's not the same thing."

"He didn't come out, Dad. There was no place else for him to go."

"But you didn't actually see him go in, did you?"

"He couldn't go up the side of the building. There wouldn't have been time for him to reach the roof before the police—"

But Dad wasn't listening. "Did *anyone* actually see him go in?"

Of course no one said anything, and I could see my father was going to call the whole thing off, and then when he got me home I was going to get the talking-to of my life. **12**

The thought of that talking-to must have stimulated my brain, I guess. I looked about the lobby desperately and said, "But, Dad, he *did* go into the building, and he didn't disappear. There he is right now. That **13** man there." I pointed, and then I dropped down and rolled out of the way.

There wasn't any shooting. The man I pointed to was close to the door—he must have been edging toward it—and now he made a dash for it. He almost made it, but a **14** police officer who had been knocked down grabbed his leg and then everyone piled on him. Later they had the jeweler, too.

WORD BANK	**edging** (EDJ ing) *v.*: moving slowly and cautiously

The Disappearing Man ~ 135

LITERARY COMPONENTS

▶ **12. Rising Action; Characterization; Idiom:** Larry is afraid his father will call off the pursuit. The thought of the talking-to he will get at home stimulates his brain. *Talking-to* is an idiom that means a scolding or a reprimand.

▶ **13. Situational Climax of the Story:** Larry points: "There he is right now. That man there."

▶ **14. Falling Action:** The criminal is caught.

GUIDING THE READING

LITERAL
Q: When Larry's dad makes a funny sound in the back of his throat, what does it mean?
A: It means that Larry is "in for it"—certain to face trouble or punishment— for still being there.

Q: When Larry's dad says, "But you didn't actually see him go in, did you?" what does Larry say in response?
A: He says that Stockton couldn't have gone up the side of the building.

Q: What stimulates Larry's brain and helps him identify the criminal?
A: He is afraid his father will call off the chase and give him the talking-to of his life when he gets home.

ANALYTICAL
Q: Larry's father insists that seeing Stockton go into the alley is not the same thing as seeing him go into the building. Do you agree?
A: Answers will vary.

Q: How did Larry identify the criminal?
A: He looked for a policeman in an ill-fitting uniform.

SUMMING UP THE PLOT

- When Larry's father gets home much later, he says something about Larry's risking his life, but he also says, "You got onto that theatrical costume bit very nicely, Larry."

- Larry's mother asks, "But how did you know which police officer it was?"

- Larry says that when he saw a police officer whose trouser legs stopped above his ankles, he knew it was Stockton.

LITERARY COMPONENTS

▶ **15. Falling Action; Characterization:** Indeed, Larry's father chastises him when he comes home, but he also compliments him.

▶ **16. Resolution; Emotional Climax; Type of Mystery:** Larry explains how he figured it out. Stockton's trick is called "hiding in plain sight."

I went home after Stockton was caught, and when my father got **(15)** home much later, <u>he did have some things to say about my risking my life. But he also said, "You got onto that theatrical costume bit very nicely, Larry."</u>

I said, "Well, I was sure he went into the building and was familiar with it. He could get into the costumer's if he had to, and they would be bound to have police uniforms. I figured if he could dump his jacket and pants and get into a uniform quickly, he could just walk out of the building."

Dad said, "You're right. Even after he got outside, he could pretend he was dealing with the crowd and then just walk away."

Mom said, "But how did you know which police officer it was, Larry? Don't tell me you know everyone by sight."

"I didn't have to, Mom," I said. "I figured if he got a police uniform at the costumer's, he had to work fast and grab any one he saw. And they wouldn't have much of an **(16)** assortment of sizes anyway. <u>So I just looked around for a police officer whose uniform didn't fit, and, when I saw one with trouser legs stopping above his ankles, I knew he was Stockton."</u>

ABOUT THE AUTHOR

Born in Russia in 1920, ***Isaac Asimov*** immigrated to the U.S. with his family in 1923. They settled in Brooklyn, New York, where Isaac later attended Columbia University, earning a Ph.D. in chemistry in 1948. Although he started out as a professor, his true love was writing: "Me and my typewriter, that's all there is in the world," he told an interviewer. Asimov was best known for his works of science fiction, but he also wrote books on a variety of other subjects. He worked every day from 7:30 a.m. until 10:00 p.m., typing 90 words a minute and hardly ever rewriting anything. In total, he wrote 467 books before his death in 1992.

Answers will vary.

Studying the Selection

FIRST IMPRESSIONS
If you had been there, do you think you could have figured it out?

QUICK REVIEW

1. How old is the boy who narrates the story?

2. What does his father do for a living?

3. What is the boy's first name?

4. What kind of business is on the third floor of the building?

FOCUS

5. There is an expression, "it's all in the details." Larry solves the mystery by noticing details and drawing conclusions. Make a list of all the details Larry sees or hears that lead him to the discovery of the criminal.

6. Without logical thinking, even Larry's ability to notice details would not have helped him solve the mystery. Take each detail that you listed in question #1 and write next to it what conclusion you think Larry drew from each one.

CREATING & WRITING

7. You are writing your first detective story. What is the mystery or the "crime"? In a few sentences, describe the mystery or crime, how it will be "covered up," and how it will be solved.

8. Now that you have settled on the crime, invent an interesting detective. Give him or her (or them) a name, and tell us how he, she, or they look. Next, describe the setting in which the mystery takes place. This should include the place, approximate year, time of day, and some added details, such as the weather and the lighting.

9. You are publishing a detective magazine. Use the title the class made up in their discussion of the story—or make up a new title. Then, draw a cover that you think will make people want to read the stories inside. You may wish to write the story you outlined in the questions above, and place it under the cover.

The Disappearing Man ~ 137

QUICK REVIEW

1. The boy is fourteen. (In paragraph two, we read "Dad says a nosy fourteen-year-old isn't likely to make it to fifteen.")

2. His father is a police detective.

3. The boy's first name is Larry. (We learn this when his father arrives and says, "Larry! What are you doing here?")

4. "On the second-floor window, it said, 'Klein and Levy, Tailors.' Above that was a *theatrical costumer...*"

FOCUS

5. Larry sees a man dash by into an alley between two buildings.
   Larry sees that the alley is closed on all sides but the street.
   Larry notices that the door is ajar.
   He sees that no one has come out of the building through the door.
   He observes that the building houses a tailor, a costumer, and a jeweler.
   He hears the police sergeant say that no one got out on the roof or through the doors or windows.
   He notices that the uniform of one of the policemen does not fit properly.

6. Larry thinks the man is suspicious-looking and is perhaps the thief his father described to him earlier.
   He concludes that if the man comes back out , it will have to be into the street where Larry is standing.
   He concludes two things: a) the man went through the door and b) the man had a key, because he could not have picked the door's lock that quickly.
   He concludes that the man must be inside or on the roof.
   He deduces that the jeweler is the fence for the jewels that Stockton steals.
   He concludes that Stockton must be inside the building.
   He deduces that the uniform was stolen from the costumer.

CREATING & WRITING

7. Answers will vary. Stress that the mystery does not necessarily have to be a crime.

8. Encourage students to give complete, colorful descriptions. You may wish to help them by writing a list of sample adjectives on the board.

9. Make sure students have the supplies they need to do the job!

LESSON IN LITERATURE . . .

CAUSE AND EFFECT

- A **cause** is any action, speech, or thought that causes something to happen.
- An **effect** is the result of that action, speech, or thought.
- A fiction or nonfiction story will usually present the cause first and the effect second.
- A mystery or detective story will often give the effect first; revealing the cause, is what the rest of the story is all about.

THINK ABOUT IT!

1. Michael did not make the basketball team. What was the cause?

2. Rodney Everett had been injured in the war. What was the immediate effect?

3. Rodney Everett *did* play again. What do you think was the cause?

4. Michael wants a certain "effect" very much. What is that effect? How will he cause it to happen?

What a Difference

Failing to make the school basketball team was the most embarrassing experience of Michael's life. Especially because he was the tallest kid in the school.

"A bit too slow," Coach Gregory said.

"Just doesn't make the shots," Coach Johnson said.

"Forget basketball," Michael said.

Michael's father didn't say much about Michael's not making the team, but one night a few weeks later, he brought a guest home for dinner, a guy he'd served with in the war. Michael had never met the man before, but he sure knew who he was.

Rodney Everett had been a football player when the war broke out. Putting his football career on hold to serve in the army, he returned to the U.S. after less than a year with injuries so severe his doctors told him he might never walk again. He went on not only to walk, but to play again, leading his team to two championships.

Michael couldn't believe he was talking to Rodney Everett right here in his own kitchen! And when Mr. Everett said, "Your dad tells me you're pretty disappointed about basketball this year," Michael found himself saying, "Yeah, but I'm going to work real hard in the off season to get ready for next year."

Even before the weather warmed up in the spring, Michael started spending every afternoon after school at his basketball hoop. He practiced dribbling. He practiced lay-ups. He practiced his jump shot. And he always ended with free throws, refusing to go inside until he could hit five in a row without a miss.

Michael worked hard on his skills all spring and summer. In addition, he started running as well, alternating between long, slow runs to work on endurance and shorter, faster runs to improve his speed.

Michael's hard work paid off. By the time tryouts came in November, there was no question Michael would make the team.

"With his height—and his quickness—this guy's going to be a team leader," Coach Gregory said.

"You see that jump shot?" said Coach Johnson. "What a difference a year makes."

LESSON IN LITERATURE

1. He was too slow and didn't make the shots.

2. Doctors said he would never play again.

3. He worked very hard to overcome his injuries.

4. He wants to make the team in the fall. He will work on his skills all summer.

SELECTION VOCABULARY

aristocratic: belonging to a class of people who are educated, wealthy and "well-born"

brocades: expensive fabrics with raised designs, often woven with gold or silver threads

genteel: well-bred; polite (today, used to mean overly polite)

heirloom: a family possession handed down from one generation to another

hoarded: hid and carefully guarded a supply of something; often, money or food

laboriously: with much difficulty and effort

litany: a long prayer in which many of the lines are repeated

miserly: stingy

omen: a sign that something will happen; an omen can be "good" or "evil"

prominent: standing out so as to be easily seen

| aristocratic | genteel | hoarded | litany | omens |
| brocades | heirlooms | laboriously | miserly | prominent |

1. In eighteenth century France, some people were very rich, others, very poor. Among the rich were the king, queen, and _____ (a class of people who are wealthy and well-born) people who were of noble birth.

2. These people dressed in expensive clothes. They wore plush velvets and rich _____ (expensive fabrics with raised designs).

3. Their castles and palaces stood in _____ (easily seen, noticeable) places in the cities, towns and countryside.

4. These palaces were filled with expensive furniture, paintings, and _____ (family possessions handed down), handed down from generation to generation.

5. Extravagant as they were for themselves, many of these noblemen were _____ (stingy) when it came to helping the poor.

6. They _____ (carefully guarded) their money, not sharing a penny of it with the hungry peasants.

7. Towards the second half of the eighteenth century, the peasants became angrier and angrier. There were many signs that a revolution was coming, but few aristocrats noticed the many _____ (signs) that their end was near.

8. The planners of the revolution would stir up the peasants with a _____ (a long prayer in which many lines are repeated, or a speech which sounds like such a prayer) of the cruel deeds of the aristocrats.

9. A very few well-bred, _____ (polite) people remained calm, but most of the hungry peasants became even more enraged as they listened.

10. The organizers of the revolution worked _____ (with much effort) at planning the revolution. Finally, in 1789, the French Revolution took place. The king, queen, and hundreds of aristocrats were killed by the revolutionaries.

Workbook p. 43   Answer Guide p. 5

What's Wrong With This Sentence?

In each of the sentences below, the vocabulary word has been used incorrectly. Explain why the word is wrong for the sentence.

Example: The **miserly** man gave his last few dollars to the beggar.
             A miser would not give away his money.

1. Jason **hoarded** his bread, throwing big pieces to the birds every morning.

2. "Come in and see this beautiful **heirloom** we bought at Wal-Mart last week!"

3. The weatherman, after studying all sorts of maps and charts, declared the next day a good one to launch the rocket. "There are good **omens** for tomorrow," said the scientist.

4. The picture had been given such a **prominent** place on the wall that we hardly noticed it.

5. Miss Wilson, a **genteel** young lady, shouted insults as she rudely elbowed her way to the front of the line.

6. The baker's son, Ed Thomas, looked truly **aristocratic** in his secondhand suit, shabby hat, and worn-out shoes.

7. The children came in from playing in the sandbox. "My, your clothes are dirty," said their mother, as she took off their **brocade** playclothes and threw them in the washing machine.

8. The ice skater seemed to fly over the ice, gracefully, swiftly, and **laboriously**.

Workbook p. 44   Answer Guide p. 5

BACKGROUND BYTES

We are indebted to Dr. Marilyn H. Stouffer for material included below.

When we think of folktales, we may think only of stories for children, stories that begin, "Once upon a time." (In fact, this phrase opens many folktales, and it points to one of their defining features: in folktales, the period in which the action occurs—and often the country—is not specified.) But there are many kinds of folk expressions. The voice of the folk can be heard in songs, lullabies, dance games, jumping rope formulas, poetry, jokes, folktales, riddles, proverbs, myths, and special sayings.

There are folk activities carried on exclusively by children—passed from one group of children to the next—that seem oddly meaningless, but are nonetheless repeated: Ring Around the Rosy and London Bridge Is Falling Down are good examples.

What Are the Characteristic Components of Folktales?

The **plot** of a folktale opens with a *brief* exposition that describes the **setting** (once upon a time in a palace, hut, forest, or peasant home) and introduces the main **characters.**

Even the leading **characters** are not very complex in folktales. The characters often symbolize human qualities: They are good. They are bad. They are stupid. They are foolish.

Theme is where folktales are really grounded. In folktales, good is almost always rewarded; evil or selfishness is punished. Often, the good people are poor people, who end up with material reward so that their suffering is diminished. Folktales are about what it means to be human, our frailties and foibles.

Recurring Motifs

A motif is a dominant idea or a recurring thematic element. Folktales often have a wicked stepmother, an evil witch, a stupid boy, an uncaring father, a handsome prince, a woodcutter, a donkey, or a giant. Forests, huts, and palaces are recurring settings. There may be glass slippers, magical tablecloths, spinning wheels, dangerous needles. There may be palace balls, a journey embarked upon, animals that talk, riddles to answer, and seemingly impossible deeds to be performed. People may fall into a deep sleep, only to be awakened by the arrival of a special person.

Types of Folktales

The broad class of folktales includes **fairy tales,** which usually involve magical or supernatural acts: these are events that simply could not occur in our own lives.

A second type of folktale is the **noodlehead story**, in which a seemingly silly person ends up outwitting an opponent.

A third variety of folktale explains *how* something came to be or *why* something happens. These stories often involve the natural world or the weather and are called **pourquoi stories.** *Pourquoi* is the French word for *why*. Myths are a type of pourquoi story.

In **talking animal tales,** the animals behave much like human beings, and individual animals may symbolize particular human characteristics. Animal tales in which a point or moral is briefly made are called **fables.**

Realistic tales have greater complexity and finer detail than many other folktales. Except for the exaggeration, most of the story could have occurred. *The Speckled Hen's Egg* is a good example of this genre.

Legends are told about quasi-historical figures, such as King Arthur and Robin Hood. These stories are told as historical truth and are associated with a particular time and place. They are based on a kernel of truth, a person who likely lived. But it is hard for us to separate fact from the fiction that has grown up around these figures over the centuries.

Students who are familiar with folktales may be able to recall stories they have read (or that were read to them when they were younger) that match each category. Remind them that the categories were invented by people who study folktales. The categories came long after most folktales were told and written down. Categories are supposed to make thinking about a large body of information easier, but they are sometimes confusing. Many folktales fit into more than one category.

INTO "THE SPECKLED HEN'S EGG"

"Folktales satisfy our sense of justice and morality because good is usually rewarded and evil punished." Folktales are also satisfying, when a person has the opportunity to change for the good. Madame Roberge is rescued from the fate of the flat character, because she ultimately emerges from her disillusionment as a gentler version of her self.

She is certainly transformed when she believes that she is descended from nobility. That behavior is thematically interesting, because it shows us that people can be what they believe themselves to be. Their self-image persuades others. Therefore, when Madame believes herself to be a marquise (mar KAY zah) as she travels to Quebec, she is treated royally by the peasants whose hospitality she enjoys— her old horse and cart notwithstanding. Although Madame Roberge's values may be shallow here, the thematic importance of *the power of belief* stands nonetheless.

Because of her harshness and miserliness as the story opens and her increased sense of self-worth once she believes herself an aristocrat, the lovely resolution at the end is surprising: with her return to selling eggs, and to scrubbing and cooking, she becomes friendlier and more generous (although not to the hen). What does this tell us? The loss of foolish dreams may be humbling and softening.

EYES ON...CAUSE AND EFFECT

Talk with students about the way that literature helps us develop the ability to analyze situations. Why did a particular event occur? Whose behavior, attitude, or words contributed to it? What was really at the root of a series of events? Tell your students that thinking about cause and effect helps us to understand what we read. Developing these analytical skills gives us training that has practical application in our own lives.

The phrase, *cause and effect*, may be confusing to students. But *cause* simply means the reasons for some action or some event's occurring, as in "the cause of the argument."

A *cause* can be an action a person takes which causes something else to happen.

A *cause* can also be something that occurs by itself.

A *cause* produces a specific result. That result is called the *effect*.

Thus, the *effect* is the consequence of the *cause*.

Examples of cause and effect can be found in all the stories your students have read in the book so far.

Blueprint for Reading

INTO . . . *The Speckled Hen's Egg*

In folktales, characters believe things that seem very silly to us today. If you found a mark on the outside of an egg, would you believe it had an important, secret meaning? Do you believe that people have special, "noble" blood in their veins, if their parents or grandparents or great-grandparents were members of royalty? Do you believe in omens— "signs" that tell us what is going to occur in the future? Well, Madame Roberge does, in *The Speckled Hen's Egg*. But then again, Madame Roberge lived "once in another time," once upon a time.

EYES ON . . . *Cause and Effect*

Have you ever heard the expression "cause and effect"? It means the reason something happened—the cause, and what actually *did* happen—the effect.

Here's a simple example of cause and effect: Jim was hungry, so he ate an apple.

The cause: Jim was hungry. The effect: he ate an apple.

Every story includes at least one cause and its effect. Some stories start with the cause and then describe the effect. Other stories start with the effect and then reveal the cause. When you have read *The Speckled Hen's Egg*, ask yourself: which came first in this story, the cause or the effect?

SUMMING UP THE PLOT

- Once in another time, a strange thing happens to Madame Roberge.
- Madame Roberge sells her chickens' eggs for a good price.
- She is stingy with her egg money and keeps it in a closet in a silver bowl.
- The bowl is shaped like a fan, and was brought from Quebec in the long ago by her great-grandfather.
- She is proud of the bowl and the coins from her eggs, so it is fitting that the coins are saved in the bowl.

The Speckled Hen's Egg

Natalie Savage Carlson

Once in another time, a very strange thing happened to Madame Roberge.[1] ①

Madame gave great care to her chickens because they laid well, and she sold their eggs at the store for a good price.

She was miserly with her egg money and hoarded it in the closet ② in a fluted[2] silver bowl which was an heirloom. It was shaped something like a fan, and one said that it had been brought from Quebec in the ③ long ago by her great-grandfather, Lazare Proutte.[3]

Madame was very proud of the bowl and she was also proud of ④ all the coins that her eggs made for her. So it was fitting that the coins should be saved in the silver bowl.

---
1. *Madame Roberge* (Muh DAHM roe BAIRZH)
2. A *fluted* bowl is one whose sides have decorative grooves.
3. *Lazare Proutte* (lah ZARR PROOT)

WORD BANK	**miserly** (MY zer lee) *adv.*: stingy
	hoarded (HOHRD ed) *v.*: hid and carefully guarded a supply of something—often, money or food
	heirloom (AIR loom) *n.*: a family possession handed down from one generation to another

The Speckled Hen's Egg ~ 141

LITERARY COMPONENTS

▶ **1. Folktale Introductory Formula:** "Once in another time..." which is similar to "Once upon a time..."

▶ **2. Characterization; Theme:** Madame Roberge is miserly and *hoards* the money. The verb *hoard* means "to lay up a hoard." A hoard is a supply or fund stored up and often hidden away. In fact, *hoard* is etymologically related to the word *hide*. It has negative connotations that imply selfishness.

▶ **3. Essential Background:** The bowl had been brought from Quebec in the long ago by a great-grandfather, Lazare Proutte.

▶ **4. Characterization:** Madame Roberge is proud of her egg money and she is proud of her bowl.

GUIDING THE READING

LITERAL

Q: How does Madame Roberge make money?
A: She sells the eggs that her chickens lay.

Q: What does she do with the egg money?
A: She "hoards" it in the closet in a silver bowl.

Q: What kind of shape does the bowl have?
A: The bowl is shaped like a fan.

Q: What is the bowl made of?
A: The bowl is silver.

Q: Where did the bowl come from?
A: The bowl is said to have come from Quebec.

Q: Who was the original owner of the bowl?
A: The bowl was owned by her great-grandfather, Lazare Proutte.

Q: What makes Madame feel proud?
A: She is proud of the bowl and she is proud of the coins.

ANALYTICAL

Q: How would you describe Madame Roberge? What kind of person is she?
A: Answers will vary. Certainly, she is industrious and thrifty. But there are several negative implications: She is stingy; she is selfish (she hoards); and she is proud (too proud) of material possessions.

TE: The Speckled Hen's Egg ~ 141

- One day Madame picks up an egg that has a picture on the shell!

- When she went to the store in the village, she took the unusual one with her.

LITERARY COMPONENTS

▶ **5. Rising Action:** Madame Roberge goes out to the henhouse to gather eggs.

▶ **6. Onomatopoeia:** She *shoos* the hen who *flaps* her wings and *cackles puck-puck…..*

▶ **7. Rising Action; Event Central to This Folktale:** She notices that the egg has a picture on it.

▶ **8. Rising Action:** Madame Roberge takes the egg to the store with her.

5
6 One day when Madame went out to her henhouse to gather the eggs, the scrawny old speckled hen was on the nest. Madame shooed her with her lips and a fling of her skirts. The hen jumped off the nest and ran away, flapping her wings and cackling puck-puck-puck-a-a-puck-puck-a-a.

Madame was displeased to see that there was only one egg in the nest.

"That worthless creature!" said Madame Roberge. "This is the first egg she has laid in a week. She is no longer worth her feed. I will put her in my stewpot Sunday."

7 Madame was about to drop the egg into her apron when she noticed a strange thing about it. There was a picture on the egg, just as surely as if it had been painted there. She studied it carefully. Yes, the picture on the egg was certainly of something. But what?

8 The next time she went to the store in the village with her eggs, she took the unusual one with her.

142 ~ Unit 2

GUIDING THE READING

LITERAL

Q: Why does Madame Roberge threaten her hen with the stew pot?
A: The hen has laid only one egg, and therefore Madame Roberge thinks she is a worthless creature.

Q: What is strange about the egg?
A: The egg has a picture on the shell.

SUMMING UP THE PLOT

- Madame tells the storekeeper the egg is not for sale.
- She shows the egg to the others in the store.
- Andre Drouillard says the picture on the egg is surely an omen.

"This one is not for sale," Madame told Henri Dupuis,[4] the storekeeper. "It is a very strange egg laid by my old speckled hen. See, there is a picture on it. What would you say it is?"

Henri Dupuis looked at the egg closely. Others who were in the store gathered around.

"Perhaps you aren't feeding your hens the right food," said Henri. "Now I have a new kind of chicken feed that—"

But André Drouillard,[5] who had taken the egg in his own hands, interrupted.

"It is surely some omen," he said. "See those long lines that curve like feathers—like an Indian war bonnet?"

_____
4. *Henri Dupuis* (on REE dew PWEE)
5. *Andre Drouillard* (on REE drew YARR)

WORD BANK	**omen** (OH mun) *n.*: a sign that something will happen; an omen can be "good" or "evil"

GUIDING THE READING

LITERAL

Q: What does the storekeeper say, when Madame Roberge shows him the egg?

A: He suggests that perhaps she isn't feeding her hens the right food.

Q: What does Andre Drouillard think of the picture?

A: He believes it is an omen, and that it looks like an Indian war bonnet.

SUMMING UP THE PLOT

- Eusible Latrop believes that the picture is a crown. "Perhaps it means that Madame Roberge has noble blood in her veins . . . "
- Madam Roberge immediately believes this explanation because it sounds close to the truth.
- Madame Roberge remarks that her great-grandfather was a rich man, and that everyone thought it strange that he had nothing to say of his life before he came here.
- She postulates that her great-grandfather must have displeased the King and so had to hide in the New World.
- He had always been uncomfortable around strangers.

- Madame returns home and places the egg in a place of prominence on her parlor table.
- She makes a pet of the hen who laid the egg.
- A change comes over Madame. She behaves as though she is a noblewoman. She hires an orphan girl and engages in embroidery, the pastime of the rich.
- She walks about with her nose held high and with a la-la-de-da air.

LITERARY COMPONENTS

▶ **9. Rising Tension; Theme:** Eusible Latrop believes the picture is a crown, and points to Madame Roberge's noble blood.

▶ **10. Subtle Humor; Characterization:** Madame Roberge thinks this explanation sounds closer to the truth. Well, of course, why not?

▶ **11. Foreshadowing:** Madame Roberge remarks about her great-grandfather, that everyone thought it strange that "he had nothing to say about his life before he came here."

▶ **12. Characterization:** Madame has a great imagination.

▶ **13. Foreshadowing:** Great-grandfather was uneasy in the presence of strangers. Why?

▶ **14. Characterization:** Madame is a woman of extremes. This hen never knows what to expect!

▶ **15. Characterization; Rising Action:** Madame's nobility increases daily. Spelled **la-di-da** in our dictionary, the word means affectedly refined in manners or tastes, pretentious.

"Perhaps there will be an Indian uprising," cried Angéline Meloche[6] in terror, "and a massacre! Oh, my poor husband on the road somewhere and my unprotected children picking berries in the woods!"

But the pop-eyed Eusibe Latrop[7] must have his say.

9 "You are all wrong," he said. "This is a crown on the egg. See! A royal crown. Perhaps it means that Madame Roberge has noble blood in her veins and does not know it."

10 Madame immediately believed this explanation because it sounded closer to the truth.

"My great-grandfather, Lazare Proutte, was a rich man," she remembered, **11** "but everyone thought it strange that he had nothing to say of his life before **12** he came here. Perhaps he was a *comte*[8] or a *duc*[8] in disguise. No doubt the King was displeased with him over some matter and he had to hide in the **13** New World. Yes, I am sure of it. One said he always seemed a little uneasy when strangers were around."

Madame proudly went home and put the wonderful egg in a prominent place on her parlor table. **14** Instead of stewing the speckled hen, she made a special pet of her and build her a runway all for herself. She planted flowers in it and saw that the water dish and feed bowl were always full.

Then a great change came over Madame. She no longer sold eggs at the store because she said that was quite beneath a noblewoman. She took in an orphan girl to do her work so that she would have more time for her embroidery, which was a genteel pastime. She even began to call herself Madame de Roberge, which had a more aristocratic sound, even though the crown on the egg had nothing to do with her husband's family.

15 She took to walking about with the wart on her nose so high she no longer could see many of her old friends. She walked about with a la-la-de-da air and carried her handkerchief, so!

---

6. *Angeline Meloche* (on zhay LEEN may LOSH)
7. *Eusibe Latrop* (uh ZEEB lah TROP)
8. A *comte* (KOMT) is a count. A *duc* (DUK) is a duke.

WORD BANK	**prominent** (PRAH mih nent) *adj.*: standing out so as to be easily seen
	genteel (jen TEEL) *adj.*: well-bred; polite (today, used to mean overly polite)
	aristocratic (uh RISS tuh KRATT ik) *adj.*: belonging to a class of people who are educated, wealthy, and "well-born"

GUIDING THE READING

LITERAL

Q: What does Madame Roberge imagine is the reason for her great-grandfather's coming to the New World?
A: She imagines that he had displeased the King over some matter and had to hide in the New World.

Q: How does Madame Roberge treat the speckled hen now?
A: She makes a special pet of her, builds her a runway with flowers, and makes sure her water and feed bowl are always full.

Q: To what does she change her name? Why?
A: She changes her name to Madame de Roberge, because she thinks it has a more aristocratic sound.

ANALYTICAL

Q: Why does Eusible Latrop think the picture on the egg shows that Madame Roberge has royal blood?
A: He believes the picture is a crown, a royal crown. Also, he is foolish.

Q: Why does Madame think that Latrop's explanation is closer to the truth?
A: She thinks that because she believes that she is someone special, an aristocrat.

Q: Why do you think Madame's great-grandfather might have said little about his earlier life and have been uneasy in the presence of strangers?
A: Answers will vary.

Q: Why would it be beneath a noblewoman to sell eggs at a store?
A: Answers will vary.

Q: Imitate Madame de Roberge as she walks about with her nose held high, with a la-la-de-da air, and carries her handkerchief, so!
A: Imitations will vary!

SUMMING UP THE PLOT

- Madam muses that perhaps she is really a comtesse or a marquise or even a princesse.
- She believes that the laying of the egg and *that* day is an omen.

- Madame Roberge muses that omens often have to do with death. Death in noble families means money and castles and titles changing hands.
- It must be that some high and rich relative of

hers in France has died.

- The crown on the egg means that it is time for her to claim her inheritance.

Sometimes her needle would snag in the fancy handkerchief she was embroidering and her eyes would have a faraway look.

"Perhaps I am really a *comtesse* or a *marquise*[9] or even a *princesse*," she would dream to herself. "If only Great-grandpére[10] Proutte had not made such a secret of his life before he came here!"

She began to wonder why the egg with the crown had been laid on that certain day—no sooner, no later. It was an omen all right. But what did it mean?

Omens often had to do with death. Perhaps the death of some important person back in old France. Death in noble families meant money and castles and titles changing hands.

Perhaps—could it be—was it possible? Yes, that was it! Some high and rich relative in France had died. The crown on the egg meant that it was time for her to claim her inheritance.

She puzzled over this for a few days. Then she made up her mind. <u>She would take her egg money and make the long trip to the big records hall in</u>

---

9. A *comtesse* (kum TESS) is a countess. A *marquise* (mar KEES) is the wife of a marquis, who ranks below a duke and above a count.
10. *Great-grandpere* (grahn PAIR) is great-grandfather.

The Speckled Hen's Egg ~ 145

GUIDING THE READING

LITERAL
Q: Madame Roberge believes that omens often have to do with...
 A: ...death.

ANALYTICAL
Q: Why does the idea of being a noble-woman start to grow on Madame Roberge? Why does she become preoccupied with the idea?
 A: Answers will vary.

Q: If omens have to do with death, what does Madame Roberge think this egg omen will mean for her?
 A: She thinks that a high and rich relative in France has died. The crown on the egg is a special communication to her (from where? from whom?!) that it is time for her to claim her inheritance.

- Madam decides to make the long trip to the records hall in Quebec, where documents and records of the past are kept.

- She hitches her wheezy horse to a two-wheeled cart and sets forth. She is in high spirits.

- It is as if the cart pulled by her horse, Coquin, is a fine coach drawn by four white horses. Madame the Marquise rides forth in silks, brocades, and jewels.

LITERARY COMPONENTS

▶ **16. Rising Action; Turning Point in the Action; Foreshadowing; Dramatic Irony:** Madame decides she will go to Quebec to the hall of records. She will learn the secret of her noble blood.

▶ **17. Characterization:** For all her foibles, Madame is a gutsy person, willing to set off on an adventure.

▶ **18. Folktale:** This is a folktale, but in the mind of Madame Roberge, it is also a fairy tale!

---

16 Quebec where they kept the documents and records of the past. She would learn the secret of her noble blood.

She hitched Coquin,[11] the wheezy horse, to the two-wheeled cart and set forth on the trip to Quebec. She would go to the old clerk and have him look up the family record of the Prouttes. Her egg money would be spent for food and lodging along the way.

17 Madame de Roberge set off in high spirit. She sat straight on the edge of the hard seat, with the reins in her hands and her wart in the air, so!

18 It was as if the two-wheeled cart pulled by the wheezy Coquin had become a fine coach drawn by four spirited white horses. And Madame the Marquise rode forth in silks and brocades and jewels.

---

11. *Coquin* (co KAH)

WORD BANK	**brocades** (broe KAYDZ) *n.*: expensive fabrics with raised designs, often woven with gold or silver threads

GUIDING THE READING

LITERAL

Q: What is Madame going to use her egg money for now?
 A: She is going to use it to pay for food and lodging along the way to Quebec.

Q: How does Madame Roberge imagine herself, her cart, and Coquin as she sets off on her journey to Quebec?
 A: She imagines herself in a fine coach drawn by four spirited white horses; she, the Marquise, wears silks, brocades, and jewels.

ANALYTICAL

Q: What do you think it says about Madame Roberge, that she is going off on a long trip with a wheezy horse and an old cart, but nonetheless, she sets off in "high spirits"?
 A: Answers will vary. But try to guide students to realizing that in spite of her fantasies and all the nonsense, she really is a person of some courage.

SUMMING UP THE PLOT

- Madame Roberge nods royally to the peasants as she passes them on her journey to Quebec.
- At night she is invited to stay in the farmhouses of peasants awed by Madame and honored to have the noblewoman grace their humble homes.
- Ever the penny-pincher, Madame is glad to have free lodging.
- Madame drives proudly through the streets of Quebec to the records hall.
- The clerk takes Madame down to the musty cellar where all the old papers and records are kept.

From time to time, she passed people on the road. To them she gave a stiff little bow of the head and half a smile, as if saluting her humble peasants.

At night Madame sought shelter in farmhouses, where the owners were overcome with awe and hospitality when they learned that their guest was a distinguished noblewoman riding to Quebec to claim an inheritance across the sea. They would not even accept payment for food and lodging, so honored were they. And the Marquise still had enough of the peasant left in her to be glad that she could hold fast to her egg money. **19**

When Madame drove Coquin down the cobbled streets[12] of Quebec to the big records hall, she had no feeling of the country bumpkin come to the city. Rather she sat proudly erect, with her la-la-de-da air and her wart high in the air, so! **20**

She twirled her embroidered handkerchief daintily as she told the clerk that she had come to seek records of the noble Proutte family so that she could rightfully claim an inheritance in France.

He led her into a cellar beneath the building where all the old papers and records were kept. He pulled out drawers, fussed through yellow papers and

---

12. *Cobbled streets* are paved with round stones called cobblestones.

The Speckled Hen's Egg ~ 147

LITERARY COMPONENTS

▶ **19. Theme; Rising Action:** So convinced is Madame of her nobility, that what she projects persuades the peasants as well.

▶ **20. Rising Action; Characterization:** Madame has come to the big city. She is still feeling herself to be the aristocrat.

GUIDING THE READING

LITERAL
Q: What does Madame Roberge tell the clerk?
A: She says that she has come to seek records of the noble Proutte family, so that she can rightfully claim an inheritance in France.

ANALYTICAL
Q: What do you think it means to say that Madame Roberge "still had enough of the peasant left in her to be glad that she could hold fast to her egg money"?
A: The suggestion is that nobles don't worry about money or try to hold on to it. Answers will vary.

SUMMING UP THE PLOT

- The clerk discovers a record of one Guillaume Proutte.

- The clerk tells Madame Roberge that, alas, a Guillaume Proutte was released from a Paris pris-on on the condition that he sail to the New World and turn over a new leaf.

LITERARY COMPONENTS

▶ **21. Foreshadowing; Rising Action; Idiom:** The clerk tells her that a Guillaume Proutte was released from a Paris prison on the condition that he sail for the new world and turn over a new leaf. The idiom *turn over a new leaf* means "to make a fresh start; to change one's conduct or attitude for the better." You may want to tell your students that Guillaume is the French version of the English William.

adjusted his spectacles on his Roman nose. So old were most of the documents that fine, dry dust blew from the drawers and Madame must from time to time use her fancy handkerchief with a vigor that was not so la-la-de-da.

"Proutte, Proutte, Proutte," chanted the clerk as if he were saying his litany. "Ah, here we have him. Guillaume Proutte, who came to the New World with Champlain."

"Yes, yes," cried Madame impatiently, "that must be the one. Was he a *duc* or a *marquis?*"

The clerk pinched his eyebrows together and popped the tip of his tongue out of his lips. He studied the fine handwriting. He shook his head sadly.

㉑ "Alas!" he said. "This Guillaume Proutte was released from a <u>Paris prison on condition that he sail to the New World and turn over a new leaf</u>."

Madame hastily leaned over his shoulder and strained her own eyes on the handwriting.

> WORD BANK   **litany** (LITT uh nee) *n.:* a long prayer in which many of the lines are repeated

SUMMING UP THE PLOT

- Madame says that that must be some other family of Prouttes. She asks the clerk to look further, for Lazare Proutte.
- The clerk reads a document that says that Lazare Proutte disappeared from Quebec at the same time as the silver bowl of the Sieur de Mare disappeared.

"Tut! Tut!" said the clerk. "It seems that Guillaume did not turn his leaf over, for he was up before the council three times for stealing beaver skins from the Indians. And you must know, my daughter, that beaver skins were the coin of the country in those days."

"How disgusting!" exclaimed Madame. "That must be some other family of Prouttes. Look further, my man. What about Lazare Proutte?"

The clerk dug through some more documents.

"Here is another Proutte," he said. "Yes, it is your Lazare."

"That's the one!" exclaimed Madame. "He was my great-grandfather."

The clerk slowly and laboriously read the document. He mumbled from time to time. Certain phrases crawled into Madame's ears like stinging ants.

"Apprenticed to Març Nadie, the silversmith. Disappeared from Quebec at the same time as the silver plate of the Sieur de Mare, which had been left with the smith for polishing."

WORD BANK	laboriously (luh BORR ee us LEE) *adv.*: with much difficulty and effort

The Speckled Hen's Egg ~ 149

LITERARY COMPONENTS

▶ **22. Turning Point; Approaching the Climax:** The clerk determines the origin of the silver bowl, Madame's prized possession, and reveals that great-grandfather Proutte was a thief.

GUIDING THE READING

LITERAL

Q: What is Madame's reaction to the information about Guillaume Proutte?
A: She responds, "How disgusting!" and declares that he must have come from some other family of Prouttes. Then she asks the clerk to search further.

Q: What happened at the same time that Lazare Proutte disappeared from Quebec?
A: The silver bowl of the Sieur de Mare also disappeared from the silversmith's, where it had been left for polishing.

SUMMING UP THE PLOT

- Madame stammers that there must be some mistake.
- She tells the clerk about the wonderful egg with the crown on it that the speckled hen had laid.
- She removes the egg from her bag, and shows it to him.
- "See," she says, "a distinct crown. It must mean something."
- The clerk says, "But Madame is looking at it upside down. Turn it around—like this! Now what does it look like to you?"
- Madame Roberge stammers that the picture on the egg now looks like the silver bowl that her great-grandfather . . . the bowl in which she keeps her egg money.
- The clerk concludes that the picture on the egg is a warning that a person of Proutte blood should never let money get too strong a hold on her.

LITERARY COMPONENTS

▶ **23. One Step from the Climax:** The clerk also believes the mark on the egg legitimately signifies something of importance. Only he turns the egg over!

▶ **24. Climax:** At the clerk's insistence, Madame perceives the crown on the egg as the stolen silver bowl of her great-grandfather.

▶ **25. Moral of the Story; Theme:** Delivered by the clerk: we should not let money get too strong a hold on us.

"But—but there must be some mistake," Madame stammered.

Then she told the clerk about the wonderful egg with the crown on it which her speckled hen had laid.

"I have it here in my bag," she said, "wrapped in a piece of musquash[13] fur." She carefully took it out of the fur and held it up.

"See," she said, "a distinct crown. It must mean something."

The clerk pinched his brows together again and pushed his glasses higher on his Roman nose.

23 "But Madame is looking at it upside down," he said. "Turn it around—like this! Now what does it look like to you?"

24 "It—it looks like the fluted silver bowl my great-grandfather, Lazare—er—ah—the bowl I keep my egg money in."

25 "There, you have it, my lady," said the clerk with a twinkle in his eye. "The sign on the egg is a warning that one of Proutte blood should never let money get too strong a hold on her."

---

13. A *musquash* is a muskrat, which is a large rodent resembling a beaver. Its fur is brown and thick.

GUIDING THE READING

LITERAL

Q: How had Madame carried the egg with her?
A: She had carried it in her bag, wrapped in a piece of Musquash fur.

Q: What does the picture on the egg look like when the egg is turned right side up (or is it upside down?)?
A: The picture looks like the silver bowl Madame's great-grandfather stole.

ANALYTICAL

Q: What is the difference between the way that Madame looks at the egg and the way that the clerk looks at the egg?
A: He turns the egg over, and says that she has been looking at it upside down.

SUMMING UP THE PLOT

- So when Madame Roberge makes the journey back from Quebec, the two-wheeled cart is no longer a coach, and Coquin is no longer four white steeds.
- Much of Madame's egg money is used up

on the return trip, because it is a nuisance for peasants to have ordinary persons turning in from the road requiring food and a bed.

- Madame Roberge's la-la-de-da manner is gone, and her handkerchief has been left

behind with the Marquise in the records cellar in Quebec.

- After her return, she goes back to her own scrubbing, cooking, and the selling of eggs.
- She speaks in a friendly manner to everyone and she is a bit more charitable, except to the speckled hen, who ended up in the stewpot.

So when Madame drove back to her village, the two-wheeled cart was no longer a coach and Coquin no longer divided himself into four prancing white steeds. And Madame the Marquise had been left behind in the dusty records cellar. The return trip dug quite deeply into the egg money, too, for while it is a rare privilege to entertain a *marquise*, it is nothing but a nuisance to have ordinary persons turning in from the road to crowd one's table and beds.

Madame Roberge's wart came down, her la-la-de-da manner was gone and her handkerchief had been left where it fell in the cellar of the big hall in Quebec. She found a position for the orphan girl and went back to her own scrubbing and cooking.

LITERARY COMPONENTS

▶ **26. Falling Action:** Madame journeys home, no longer a marquise.

▶ **27. Resolution:** Madame resumes her "proper station" in life and becomes friendlier and more generous.

She began to sell eggs at the store again, and spoke in a friendly manner to everyone. It was noticed that she became a bit more generous with her charity, and she no longer took pleasure in hoarding money. Perhaps this was because she no longer had a fine bowl to save it in, since the silver one was turned into a water pan for the chickens. And the old speckled hen disappeared from the fancy runway only to find herself in the stewpot one Sunday.

The Speckled Hen's Egg ~ 151

GUIDING THE READING

LITERAL

Q: What happened to Madame's handkerchief?
A: She left it in the cellar of the records hall.

Q: How does Madame Roberge's manner of speaking change when she returns home?
A: She begins to speak in a friendly manner.

So you see, my friends, it is not a good thing to hold one's nose high and go about with a la-la-de-da air, for a turn of the egg can easily change a crown into a stolen bowl.

The End

ABOUT THE AUTHOR

Natalie Savage Carlson wrote more than forty novels and picture books for children. Born in Virginia in 1906, Natalie was raised on a farm in Maryland. As a child, she was enchanted by the legends and folktales told by her French-Canadian mother. In the late 1920s, Natalie married Daniel Carlson, a member of the U.S. navy. His career took the couple to many places, including Paris, France. Mrs. Carlson's love of folktales and her vivid memories of France can be seen in *The Speckled Hen's Egg*. She died in 1997.

FIRST IMPRESSIONS

That she is friendlier and more generous seems to suggest she is happier. What does your class think?

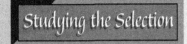

FIRST IMPRESSIONS

Does it make sense to you that Madame Roberge became more friendly and generous at the end of the story, when she had to go back to the hard work of scrubbing and cooking?

QUICK REVIEW

1. What is the main character's name? Make sure you can pronounce it properly.

2. Give the name of her great-grandfather. Make sure you can pronounce it properly.

3. Where does she keep her egg money?

4. What is the picture on the egg?

FOCUS

5. Why does Madame Roberge feel superior to other people, when she believes she has "royal blood" in her veins?

6. Why does Madame Roberge travel to Quebec?

CREATING & WRITING

7. You are Madame Roberge. Earlier today, you learned that your great-grandfather was a thief. You are in a barn, where a farmer's family has invited you to spend the night. Tomorrow, you will drive home, but right now, you wish to put down your thoughts in your journal. What do you write about? How do you feel? What are your plans for when you arrive home? Don't forget to refer to yourself as **I**.

8. Have you ever owned a thing: clothing, jewelry, or a special book, for example, that made you feel better about yourself? Write about it in two or three paragraphs.

9. Draw a picture of the famous egg with the crown (or silver bowl). Don't forget to give your picture a caption, as it is to be hung in a museum.

The Speckled Hen's Egg ~ 153

QUICK REVIEW

1. The main character's name is Madame Roberge. Please make certain that your students can pronounce the French words and are not afraid to say them.

2. Her great-grandfather was Lazare Proutte.

3. She keeps her egg money in a silver bowl in the closet.

4. Andre Drouillard thinks the picture on the egg looks like a native war bonnet. It looks like a crown to Eusible Latrop—which Madame believes because "it sounded closer to the truth." But the clerk (in conjunction with Madame Roberge) seems to believe that it looks like a bowl—the stolen silver bowl.

FOCUS

5. Answers will vary. Students will need to think somewhat analytically about why being a member of a privileged group makes us feel truly superior to others.

6. Madame Roberge travels to Quebec in order to "learn the secret of her noble blood." In Quebec records of families are kept by civil and religious authorities.

CREATING & WRITING

7. Make certain students know that they are writing in the first-person voice and in the present tense. They do not need to know the meaning of those terms— they simply need to follow your example. What they write should show how Madame Roberge went from being a once-miserly snooty aristocrat to the friendly, more generous person she becomes when she returns to town. How does she react to the information about her great-grandfather? Why does this make her want to be a better person?

8. Remind students that nearly all of us associate wealth with status. It is a great human failing. See if you can gently get your students to be honest. You may want to give an example from your own life.

9. Make sure the pictures are at least 8 1/2 x 11.

PREDICTING

- Predicting is a form of guessing what will happen in the future.
- Good predictions are based on the facts that we have been given combined with our own experience.
- In a story, the author often provides many facts or clues to help us *predict* what will happen, but not enough to make us *sure* of what will happen.
- In stories with surprise endings, the readers' predictions often turn out to be wrong!

THINK ABOUT IT!

1. In Part I of "Camping Trip," the author describes one weekend in the life of a family. Write down three facts about the family. Then, make two predictions based on the facts in the story and what your own experience has taught you.

2. Look back at the story and review the events it describes. Write down three events. Even small, seemingly unimportant actions, may be included.

3. Think again about the action in the story. Is there any action that might be a clue to a future event? What is it, and what is your prediction?

Camping Trip, Part 1

As Mom and Dad packed the car for the camping trip, little Sally lay on the ground, her body a landing pad for the maple helicopters fluttering to the ground like a gentle green snow. Baby John sat contentedly in his car seat, looking out the window and babbling happily. The packing completed, Dad nosed the car out of the driveway and headed down the two-lane highway that connected the family's five acres to the rest of the world.

After miles and miles of fields and farmhouses, Dad turned into a gas station to check his directions. On the other corner sat a country store, but there was no need to cross the street for refreshments. Mom had thought of everything. Opening the trunk to pour some lemonade, she noticed a cluster of green maple helicopters, and with one swipe, scooped them out and tossed them into the grass nearby. Delighted, Sally rescued a handful of the seeds and put them into her pocket.

"Perfect," Dad said, back from his chat with the gas station attendant. "It's just down this road here. Let's go."

More fields, more farms, and suddenly a small wooden sign announcing "Monhegan State Park." Dad turned right onto a dirt road that wound through a meadow that seemed to Sally to go on forever.

"Guess I expected a few more campers," Mom said. "You think it'll be alright?"

Dad nodded. "We've got the place to ourselves."

While Mom and Dad pitched the tent, it was Sally's job to keep an eye on the baby. She took the maple helicopters from her pocket. Sally stood straight and tall, the only "tree" on this flat stretch of grass. Sally reached way up high and, one at a time, let the helicopter go. As the blade of each seed fluttered to the ground, the baby, on his back on a blanket, squealed in delight.

SELECTION VOCABULARY

altered: changed

descended: came down

diminished: lessened

eerie: strange, mysterious, and somewhat frightening

elated: immensely happy

hectic: rushed and confused

monotonously: dully and boringly

quota: fixed amount

ruthless: without pity; cruel

savage: wild; fierce

---

altered	diminish	elated	monotonously	ruthless
descended	eerie	hectic	quota	savage

1. As we _____ (*came down*) into the cavern, it got darker and darker.

2. The damp air and small amount of greenish light gave the cavern an _____ (*strange and frightening*) feeling.

3. As our ability to see continued to _____ (*lessen*), we became a bit frightened.

4. The guide, who seemed completely unaffected by the darkness, droned on _____ (*boringly*) about stalactites and stalagmites.

5. Only yesterday I had been working at my usual _____ (*rushed*) job.

6. I had been _____ (*overjoyed*) when my boss handed me tickets for a tour of "Haunted Caverns" and given me today off.

7. But now I was chilled and scared. My active imagination pictured a _____ (*wild, fierce*) animal lurking in the shadows.

8. Or worse, I pictured a _____ (*cruel*) killer waiting to jump on us from behind.

9. My life had certainly been _____ (*changed*) from one day to the next.

10. Whew! We were coming back out into the sunshine. As I wiped my brow, I decided I'd had my _____ (*fixed amount; number something can hold*) of caverns for the year!

Workbook p. 49 Answer Guide p. 5

How Would You Describe. . .

Choose the best answer.

1. ...a dark cave?
   - a. ruthless
   - b. eerie

2. ...a very busy day?
   - a. hectic
   - b. altered

3. ...your bank account after a shopping spree?
   - a. altered
   - b. diminished

4. ...a lecture on the habits of the snail?
   - a. ruthless
   - b. monotonous

5. ...the number of tickets to the opening game that each person may purchase?
   - a. quota
   - b. eerie

6. ...an angry python?
   - a. hectic
   - b. savage

7. ...someone's appearance after plastic surgery?
   - a. altered
   - b. descended

8. ...what the submarine did when it got out to sea?
   - a. descended
   - b. diminished

9. ...a criminal who had no mercy?
   - a. ruthless
   - b. elated

10. ...your feeling on the last day of school?
    - a. altered
    - b. elated

Workbook p. 50   Answer Guide p. 5

LESSON IN LITERATURE

1. Some facts about the family include: The family has a mother and father. The family has two children, a little girl, Sally, and a baby. The family owns a car and lives on a five-acre farm. The family lives in an area where there are many maple trees. The father likes camping. The family is happy and peaceful.

   Predictions based on the facts given in the story and my experience could include: The two children will grow up to be good friends, as they seem to be friendly in the story. Something usually goes wrong on camping trips! Perhaps the story will include some "disaster." Children get tired of babysitting. The story may include Sally's "rebellion" against this job. The story will be about all the members of the family, as the author seems interested in acquainting us with each of them. The baby's squeals of delight will soon change to cries of hunger, wetness, or boredom.

2. Some events in the story include: Mom and Dad pack the car. The family sets out on a camping trip. Dad stops at a gas station to ask for directions. Mom serves the family lemonade. Sally puts a handful of maple helicopters in her pocket. Mom and Dad pitch the tent. Sally entertains the baby by throwing maple tree seeds to the ground.

3. The clue is the maple helicopters that flutter to the ground. The prediction is that they will grow into maple trees. For your students: some "clues" to discovering clues in stories are: the repetition of or stress on some seemingly minor detail, the insertion of a detail that doesn't really seem necessary to the plot. Veteran readers of mysteries are quick to notice these clues. For everyone else, the clues will be recognized for what they are only at the end of the story.

BACKGROUND BYTES

The black stallion of The Black Stallion is one of the most famous horses of fiction. The horse who narrates Black Beauty, which was written by Anna Sewell and published in 1877, is another. Both books, especially Black Beauty, were catalysts for changing people's attitudes towards animals in general and towards horses specifically. Black Beauty is particularly heartrending, because the horse himself describes terrible abuse of horses (although it does have a happy ending).

Horses have been very important to man from early times. Old cave paintings of horses have been found in France. It is believed that in North America, changes in climate and hunting led to the extinction of horses. But in the steppes of central Asia, horses were domesticated. Horses were first kept for milk and meat. As human beings traveled longer distances, horses began to be used as pack animals. There is also archaeological evidence that vehicles drawn by horses began to be used sometime later.

The word equid is the name of the animal family that includes the domestic horse. The other equids are three groups of wild mammal species: the zebra, which is native to Africa; the ass, which includes the kiang and onager of Asia and the wild ass of Africa; and Przewalski's (sha VAL ski's) horse, which is native to Asia. Przewalski's is the only surviving true wild horse. These horses, in fact, were hunted to extinction in the wild. The species is now being bred in captivity and is gradually being reintroduced to the wild. Other so-called wild horses are descendants of domestic horses that have reverted to the wild state.

The most distinctive physical characteristic of the modern horse is that it has only one toe on each of its four feet. That is why scientists call it a perissodactyl. The word, perissodactyl, comes from Greek: dactylos means "finger," and perissos means "odd in number." Other perissodactyls are the rhinoceros and the tapir.

The horse's toe corresponds to the middle finger of the human hand. Only on the horse, this "finger" is very large and is protected by a horny hoof. The hoof surrounds the toe in a semicircle. Bony "swellings" (called splints) are located on each side of the foot above the hoof. These cor-

respond to second and forth fingers or toes.

Archaeological evidence indicates that horses were brought to Babylonia several millennia ago. Shortly after, they were introduced into Egypt. The Egyptian and Babylonian horses were bred for speed and endurance and were the forerunners of the swift Arabian breeds.

Another strain of horses, however, was domesticated by man in Europe. These were larger, more powerful, native horses that were bred for strength. From the early centuries b.c.e. until the 1600s, the European horses were used for cavalry and for carrying and pulling heavy loads.

The smaller, faster Arabian horses were brought to Spain in the eighth century with the Muslim conquest. These horses continued to be bred in Spain, and word of their speed and endurance traveled far and wide. The English and the Europeans were purchasing them as early as the twelfth century.

It is these horses that were brought to the Americas by Spanish conquistadores. Both the brutal Hernan Cortes, who descended upon Mexico, and Hernando de Soto who "found" the Mississippi River, lost or left some of their horses. The herds of wild horses that were once found in various parts of the western United States are believed to be the descendants of these horses. Horses left by the Spanish also ran wild on the pampas of South America around the Río de la Plata.

The Przewalski Horse is also called the Asiatic Wild Horse, Mongolian Wild Horse, Mongolian Tarpan, and the Taki. Until a decade ago, the Przewalski was extinct in the wild, exterminated by hunters. But the Przewalski Foundation in the Netherlands worked with the staff of breeding preserves in the Ukraine. They combined two breeding groups of Przewalski horses. Some of these horses were reintroduced to Mongolia. The ultimate goal is to have the animals run free on the open steppe.

The Przewalski horse has fascinated biologists. They have determined that it is actually a different species from the domesticated horse. Przewalskis have 66 chromosomes. Domestic

horses have 64. When the Przewalski breeds with the domestic horse, their babies usually have 65 chromosomes. These babies also can have babies. This is important, because when species crossbreed, as with the horse and the donkey, the mules that are born are usually sterile. Like zebras, only a few Przewalski horses are tamable.

INTO "THE BLACK STALLION"

The Black Stallion is a wonderful teaching piece, because it is exciting, beautifully written, and emphasizes the important value of kindness towards animals. In this instance, the lead character also shows what it means to be frightened and brave simultaneously. Some of us have difficulty managing that combination.

How is Alexander Ramsay able to be brave in spite of the fear the black stallion elicits? His deep appreciation of the species makes it possible, as well as Alec's maturity. By maturity, here, we mean the ability to see oneself and others—whether human or animal—as valuable parts of the whole. Here, the idea of *dominion* over animals means responsibility and kindness rather than tyranny and slaughter.

Alec puts the stallion before his fear for himself—even when the ship is foundering in the storm. This is not a conscious decision he makes. He is not thinking about any reward he will receive. He just *does* it. And in so doing, he saves himself.

How can the theme be stated? Here are some possibilities:

What is hateful to you, do not do to other living things.

In happiness and suffering, regard all creatures as you would regard your own self.

The language of kindness is understood by all creatures.

EYES ON...PREDICTING

It will be important to point out to your students the wonderful descriptions in The Black Stallion. This is a subject in and of itself, but it is also true that some of the descriptions are integral to the clues the author provides regarding the outcome of the events. The descriptions tell us what is important to Alec, what stays with him. What stays with him, stays with us until the conclusion.

Predicting, by definition, is not just guessing or having a feeling—it is supposed to be based on clues that we read, hear, observe, or experience. However, it is also the case, that we sometimes have a sense of things, we are guided "unconsciously" by something we cannot quite put our fingers on. As you discuss the story and make predictions, guide your students in looking for the author's clues, and encourage them to articulate their "intuitions."

Clues *foreshadow*. Foreshadow means to represent or indicate before hand. A fancier word is *adumbrate*, which basically has the same meaning, and comes from the Latin word *umbra*, which means *shadow*. To foreshadow is to *prefigure*. Prefigure means to show, suggest, or announce by an antecedent (preceding, prior) type, image, or likeness; to picture or imagine beforehand.

The best way to teach predicting is by example. Find all of the clues the author offers with your students. A clue is present when we say at the end of the story, "I *knew* that was going to happen. Remember earlier in the story, when it says..." The clue is the *when it says*. Another short story with lots of clues is *Gold-Mounted Guns*.

Blueprint for Reading

INTO . . . The Black Stallion

Alexander Ramsay is going home on a tramp steamer that is traveling from India to England. When the *Drake* docks at a small Arabian port, a terrified black stallion is dragged aboard ship and locked into a small makeshift stall on deck. The horse is beautiful, powerful, and frightening. Alexander is the only passenger aboard the *Drake* that befriends the horse. Even though Alec is afraid of the horse's strength and wildness, he is drawn to him and wants to help him. When the ship sinks, he tries to save the horse. As it turns out, the horse saves *him!*

EYES ON . . . Predicting

What is *predicting? Predicting* is guessing what is going to happen before it happens. Usually, predicting is based on what we see, what we know, or what we ourselves have experienced. When you read a story, you may be able to predict what will happen at the end, from clues that the author has put in the story. Predicting can be fun, but it can also spoil the fun of reading. A good author will give you enough information to keep you guessing, but not enough to ruin the ending for you.

From THE BLACK STALLION

Walter Farley

The tramp steamer[1] *Drake* plowed away from the coast of India and pushed its blunt prow[2] into the Arabian Sea, homeward bound. Slowly it made its way west toward the Gulf of Aden. Its hold[3] was loaded with coffee, rice, tea, oilseeds, and jute. Black smoke poured from its one stack, darkening the hot cloudless sky.

1. A *tramp steamer* is a vessel that can be rented to take a load of goods from one port to another.
2. The *prow* (PROW) of a ship is the front part of it, also called "the bow."
3. The *hold* of a ship is the "basement" of the ship. It is a space below the lower deck used for cargo.

The Black Stallion ~ 157

LITERARY COMPONENTS

▶ **1. Exposition; Setting; Very Specific Terms; Wonderful Descriptions; Vivid Images:** The cast is onboard a "tramp steamer." A steamer is a ship propelled by steam. A tramp steamer is a commercial boat that differs from an ocean liner in that it has no set schedule; it does not make regular trips but takes cargo when and where it offers and to any port. Make sure students know where the coast of India, the Arabian Sea, and the Gulf of Aden are. We can picture the hold with its cargo—which generates an atmosphere of far away and exotic places. *Jute* is a glossy plant fiber that is used primarily for making sacking, burlap, and twine.

GUIDING THE READING

LITERAL

Q: What is the name of the tramp steamer?
A: It is called the *Drake.*

Q: Which country has the *Drake* just left?
A: The tramp steamer has just left India.

Q: What is in the hold of the *Drake*?
A: Its hold is loaded with coffee, rice, tea, oilseeds, and jute.

- Alexander Ramsay, whose friends back home in New York City call him Alec, looks back towards the fast-disappearing shore.

- His two months in India with his Uncle Ralph were fun.

- He will even miss the screams of the panthers and the eerie sounds of the jungle night.

LITERARY COMPONENTS

▶ **2. Protagonist:** Alexander Ramsay comes from New York City. His nickname is Alec.

▶ **3. Careful Description; Metaphor:** His hair is red and *blazes,* as if it is fire; "his tanned elbows" rest "heavily"; "his freckled face" looks back towards "the fast-disappearing shore."

▶ **4. Background; Description:** He has spent two months in India and will miss his uncle. Careful description brings his memories alive: "the screams of the panthers and the many eerie sounds of the jungle night."

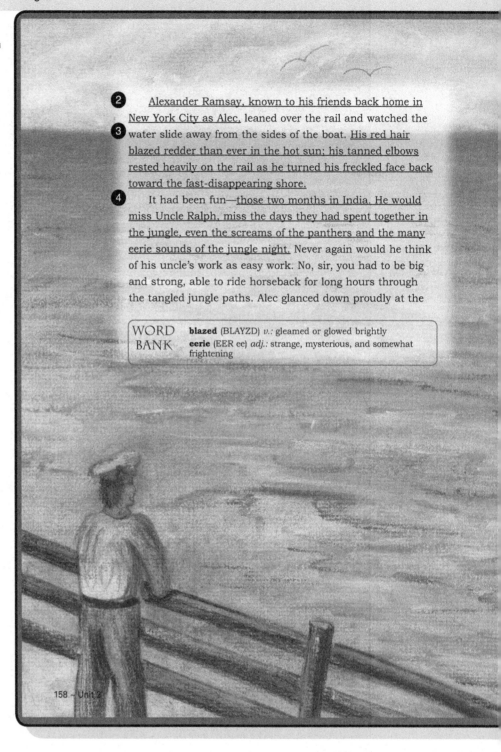

2   Alexander Ramsay, known to his friends back home in New York City as Alec, leaned over the rail and watched the **3** water slide away from the sides of the boat. His red hair blazed redder than ever in the hot sun; his tanned elbows rested heavily on the rail as he turned his freckled face back toward the fast-disappearing shore.

4   It had been fun—those two months in India. He would miss Uncle Ralph, miss the days they had spent together in the jungle, even the screams of the panthers and the many eerie sounds of the jungle night. Never again would he think of his uncle's work as easy work. No, sir, you had to be big and strong, able to ride horseback for long hours through the tangled jungle paths. Alec glanced down proudly at the

WORD BANK
  blazed (BLAYZD) *v.:* gleamed or glowed brightly
  eerie (EER ee) *adj.:* strange, mysterious, and somewhat frightening

158 ~ Unit 2

GUIDING THE READING

LITERAL
Q: What is the name of the young man on the boat?
  A: He is Alexander Ramsay.

Q: What was he doing in India?
  A: He had been visiting his Uncle Ralph.

ANALYTICAL
Q: When the author writes that Alec's hair blazed, what does he mean? Doesn't blaze mean to be in flames, to burn brightly?

A: Alexander's red hair looks so red in the hot sun, that it looks like flames. The author is using a metaphor and comparing the way his hair looks with fire.

Q: Why do you think Alec will miss the screams of the panthers and the eerie jungle sounds?
  A: Answers will vary. We become accustomed to the places where we spend time. The atmosphere in India must have been surprising when he first arrived, exotic and strange, but now he has grown used to India and has

special memories associated with his time there.

- Alec glances down at the hard muscles in his arms. Uncle Ralph had taught him how to ride—the one thing in the world he had always wanted to do. Rides back home would be few.

- Alec lovingly surveys the pearl pocketknife his uncle gave him for his birthday.

- He recalls that his uncle had said, "A knife, Alec, comes in handy sometimes."

- The captain of the *Drake* greets him. "Well,

m'boy, you're on your way home."

- Alec points out that he will still have to sail from England to New York on the *Majestic*.

- The captain says that it is about four weeks' sailing altogether, but that Alec looks like a good sailor.

- Alec tells the captain that school opens next month and he has to be there.

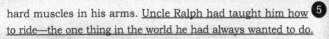

hard muscles in his arms. Uncle Ralph had taught him how ⑤ to ride—the one thing in the world he had always wanted to do.

But it was all over now. Rides back home would be few.

His fist opened. Lovingly he surveyed the pearl ⑥ pocketknife he held there. The inscription on it was in gold: *To Alec on his birthday, Bombay, India.* He remembered, too, ⑦ his uncle's words: "A knife, Alec, comes in handy sometimes."

Suddenly a large hand descended on his shoulder. "Well, ⑧ m'boy, you're on your way home," a gruff voice said, with a decidedly English accent.

Alec looked up into the captain's wrinkled, wind-tanned face. "Hello, Captain Watson," he answered. "It's rather a long way home, though, sir. To England with you and then to New York on the *Majestic*."

"About four weeks' sailing, all in all, lad, but you look like a pretty good sailor."

"I am, sir. I wasn't sick once all the way over and we had a rough crossing, too," Alec said proudly.

"When'd you come over, lad?"

"In June, sir, with some friends of my father's. They left me with my uncle in Bombay. You know my Uncle Ralph, don't you? He came aboard with me and spoke to you."

"Yes, I know your Uncle Ralph. A fine man, too....And now you're going home alone?"

"Yes, sir! School opens next month and I have to be there."

The captain smiled and took Alec by the arm. "Come along," he said. "I'll show you how we steer this ship and what makes it go."

WORD BANK	**surveyed** (sur VAYD) *v.:* looked at; inspected
	descended (dee SEND ed) *v.:* came down

LITERARY COMPONENTS

▶ **5. Background; Foreshadowing:** Uncle Ralph taught him to ride. Moreover, it was *the one thing in the world he had always wanted to do.*

▶ **6. Characterization; Background:** We can tell he loves his uncle, because he has such fond memories. We can also tell that the gift meant a great deal to Alec, who looks at it *lovingly.*

▶ **7. Foreshadowing:** This is one of those clues: *a knife, Alec, comes in handy sometimes.* And will it ever.

▶ **8. Strong Images; Careful Description; Characterization of the Captain:** Look in this paragraph and the next, for the phrases that bring the scene and the characters alive: *Suddenly a large hand descended on his shoulder; a gruff voice; the captain's wrinkled, wind-tanned face.*

GUIDING THE READING

LITERAL

Q: Who has taught Alec how to ride a horse? Where was Alec at the time?
A: His Uncle Ralph taught him to ride during his visit to India.

Q: What had his uncle given him for a birthday present?
A: Uncle Ralph had given him a pearl-handled pocketknife.

Q: How long is Alec's trip home to New York, all together?
A: The trip is four weeks' sailing.

Q: In which city does Alec's uncle live?
A: Uncle Ralph lives in Bombay.

ANALYTICAL

Q: Why do you think his uncle had had words inscribed on the pocketknife?
A: Answers will vary and may include (1) to commemorate the occasion; (2) to remind Alec of his wonderful summer in India; and (3) to remind Alec of his wonderful uncle.

Q: How do we know that Alec will stop in England?

A: We know that the tramp steamer he is on is called the *Drake*. We also see that Alec says to the captain that he will be traveling with him to England and then going on to New York on a ship called the *Majestic*. He will have to stop, even very briefly, to get on the other ship.

SUMMING UP THE PLOT

- The days pass monotonously for Alec as the *Drake* steams its way through the Gulf of Aden and into the Red Sea.
- As they pass miles of endless desert shore on the coast of Arabia, Alec thinks about how the greatest horses in the world are bred there.
- To him, the horse is the greatest animal in the world.
- One day, the *Drake* stops at a small Arabian port.

LITERARY COMPONENTS

▶ **9. Geography:** Fiction must always be accurate when it comes to facts. Thus, fiction is a vehicle for teaching people about the real world. Make sure you can show your students the path of the *Drake* on the map. This is also a chance to say something about the Suez Canal. Without the Canal, the tramp steamer would have had to travel all the way around the southern tip of Africa to get to the Atlantic.

The Suez Canal is west of the Sinai Peninsula and forms a 101 mile (163 km) ship canal in Egypt between Port Said on the Mediterranean and Suez on the Red Sea. The canal makes it possible to travel by water from Asia to Europe without circumnavigating Africa. Before the construction of the canal, sometimes ships were offloaded and their goods were taken overland between the Mediterranean and the Red Sea. The Canal was built by a French company between April 1850 and 1869. The first ship passed through the canal on November 17, 1869. It is estimated that 1.5 million Egyptians worked on the canal and that 125,000 died, many from cholera.

▶ **10. Setting; Vivid Description:** Notice the passages that describe setting in this and the following paragraph: *tropic sun beat down mercilessly; endless miles of barren desert shore; the scorching sand.*

▶ **11. Characterization; Foreshadowing:** Alec *really* likes horses, and as we know, it sure is a good thing he does.

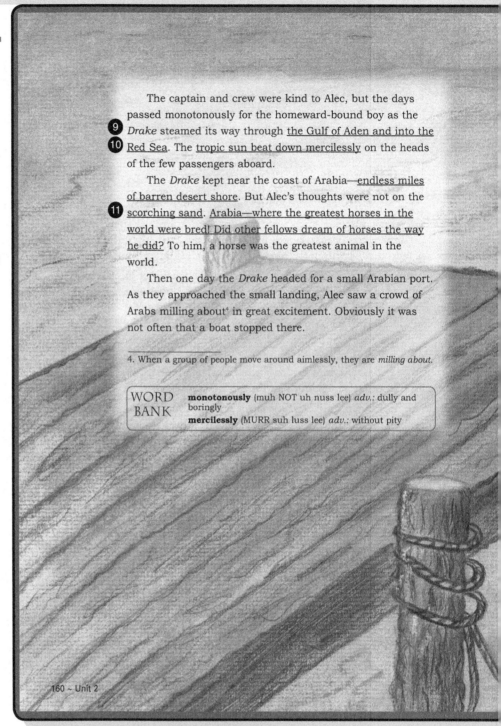

The captain and crew were kind to Alec, but the days passed monotonously for the homeward-bound boy as the **9** *Drake* steamed its way through <u>the Gulf of Aden and into the</u> **10** <u>Red Sea</u>. The <u>tropic sun beat down mercilessly</u> on the heads of the few passengers aboard.

The *Drake* kept near the coast of Arabia—<u>endless miles of barren desert shore</u>. But Alec's thoughts were not on the **11** <u>scorching sand</u>. <u>Arabia—where the greatest horses in the world were bred! Did other fellows dream of horses the way he did?</u> To him, a horse was the greatest animal in the world.

Then one day the *Drake* headed for a small Arabian port. As they approached the small landing, Alec saw a crowd of Arabs milling about[4] in great excitement. Obviously it was not often that a boat stopped there.

---

4. When a group of people move around aimlessly, they are *milling about.*

WORD BANK | **monotonously** (muh NOT uh nuss lee) *adv.:* dully and boringly
mercilessly (MURR suh luss lee) *adv.:* without pity

160 ~ Unit 2

GUIDING THE READING

LITERAL

Q: What is the coast of Arabia like?
A: The coast of Arabia is endless miles of barren desert shore.

Q: Where does the steamer stop?
A: The steamer stops at a small Arabian port.

ANALYTICAL

Q: Why doesn't the *Drake* have to go around Cape Agulhas (the geographic southern tip of the African continent—not Cape of Good Hope, as it happens!) to get to the Atlantic Ocean?

A: The *Drake* is going to use the Suez Canal and get to the Atlantic by traveling the length of the Mediterranean Sea.

Q: Why isn't Alec paying attention to the miles of barren desert shore and to the scorching sands?
A: Alec is recalling that Arabia is the place where the greatest horses in the world are bred. He is dreaming of horses.

160 ~ **Unit 2**

SUMMING UP THE PLOT

- Alec sees a crowd of men and hears a shrill whistle—unlike anything he has heard before.
- He sees a mighty black horse that rears on its hind legs and strikes out with its forelegs. The crowd breaks and runs.
- The horse's mouth is open, his teeth bared. White lather runs from his body. He is a giant of a horse, glistening black.
- His neck is long and slender. He has a savagely beautiful head.
- This is a stallion born wild—and it is beautiful, savage, and splendid.

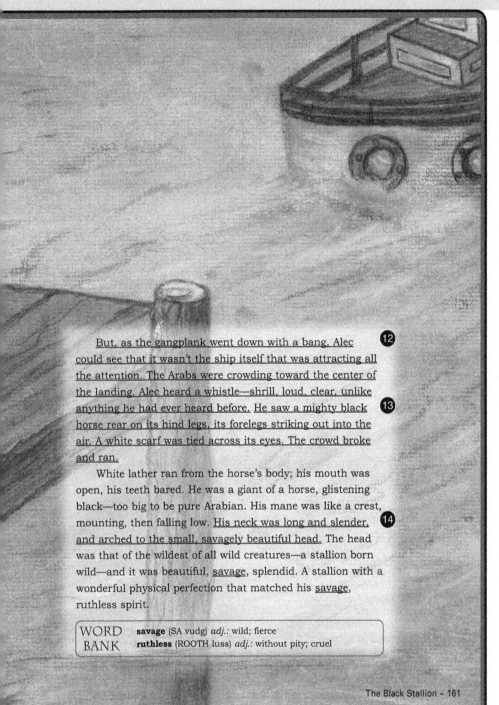

But, as the gangplank went down with a bang, Alec could see that it wasn't the ship itself that was attracting all the attention. The Arabs were crowding toward the center of the landing. Alec heard a whistle—shrill, loud, clear, unlike anything he had ever heard before. He saw a mighty black horse rear on its hind legs, its forelegs striking out into the air. A white scarf was tied across its eyes. The crowd broke and ran.

White lather ran from the horse's body; his mouth was open, his teeth bared. He was a giant of a horse, glistening black—too big to be pure Arabian. His mane was like a crest, mounting, then falling low. His neck was long and slender, and arched to the small, savagely beautiful head. The head was that of the wildest of all wild creatures—a stallion born wild—and it was beautiful, savage, splendid. A stallion with a wonderful physical perfection that matched his savage, ruthless spirit.

> WORD BANK
> **savage** (SA vudg) *adj.*: wild; fierce
> **ruthless** (ROOTH luss) *adj.*: without pity; cruel

The Black Stallion ~ 161

LITERARY COMPONENTS

▶ **12. Rising Action; Onomatopoeia:** Something important is about to happen. The scene comes alive with sound: *bang, whistle, shrill.*

▶ **13. The Black Stallion Makes Its First Appearance:** He is mighty, he rears on his hind legs, his forelegs strike out. The crowd watching him breaks and runs!

▶ **14. Characterization of Black Stallion; Characterization of Alec:** You may want to discuss with your class why Alec is so drawn to the horse. Three times in this short paragraph, the author uses the word *savage(ly).* What about this quality gives the horse meaning for the boy? The word *savage* can mean "not domesticated or under human control; untamed." It may be that, without realizing it, Alec associates savage—unspoiled by people or by civilization—with innocence. This horse has not yet been touched by any person. It would be extremely gratifying to Alec if such a horse were to come to him willingly, of its own choice. Perhaps Alec imagines winning over such a horse.

GUIDING THE READING

LITERAL

Q: What sound does Alec hear that is unlike anything he has ever heard before?
A: He hears a whistle that is shrill, loud, and clear.

Q: In a few sentences, describe the horse that Alec sees in the port.
A: It is a mighty black horse. It is rearing up on its hind legs and striking out with its forelegs. A white scarf is tied across its eyes. White lather runs from the horse's body. His mouth is open and his teeth are bared. He is a giant of a horse, glistening. His mane is like a crest.

ANALYTICAL

Q: Why does the crowd of men break and run?
A: Apparently they are afraid of the horse, a giant of a horse. He is rearing on his hind legs and striking out with his forelegs.

- Alec realizes that this is a wild stallion—unbroken, such as he has read and dreamed about!

LITERARY COMPONENTS

▶ **15. Characterization; Idiom:** This has been on Alec's mind for a long time; this horse is the sort of horse he has dreamt about. An *unbroken* horse is one that has not yet been trained to accept a rider. When a horse is *broken,* it is trained to accept a harness and a rider, and to accept a metal bit in its mouth. Some horse trainers today respect a horse's unwillingness to yield to pressure, and they employ much kinder methods than were used in the past.

Once again the Black screamed and rose on his hind legs. Alec could hardly believe his eyes and ears—a stallion, a wild stallion—unbroken, such as he had read and dreamed about!

Two ropes led from the halter on the horse's head, and four men were attempting to pull the stallion toward the gangplank. They were

162 ~ Unit 2

GUIDING THE READING

LITERAL

Q: How many men attempt to pull the stallion toward the gangplank?
A: Four men try to pull him using two ropes attached to the halter on the horse's head.

ANALYTICAL

Q: What is an unbroken horse?
A: An unbroken horse is one that has not been trained to accept a rider and a harness and a bit.

Q: Why do you think the idea of a wild stallion has such appeal for Alec?
A: Answers will vary. As we have written above in the Literary Components, savage may mean "not domesticated." It may be that, without realizing it, Alec sees a savage horse as one that is unspoiled and innocent. This horse has not yet been touched by any person. It would be extremely gratifying to Alec if such a horse were to come to him willingly. Perhaps Alec imagines winning over such a horse.

- Four men struggle to put the stallion on the ship. A dark-skinned man wearing European dress and a white turban strikes the horse hard with a whip.
- The horse is on board!

- Alec observes a makeshift stall on the deck, into which they are attempting to get the Black.
- Finally they have the horse in front of the stall. The white scarf is pulled off the stal-

lion's eyes and the man in the turban hits the horse again with the whip.

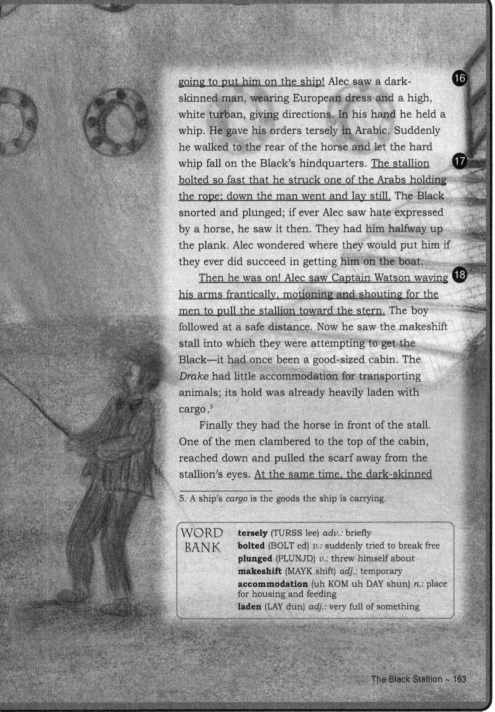

going to put him on the ship! Alec saw a dark-skinned man, wearing European dress and a high, white turban, giving directions. In his hand he held a whip. He gave his orders tersely in Arabic. Suddenly he walked to the rear of the horse and let the hard whip fall on the Black's hindquarters. The stallion bolted so fast that he struck one of the Arabs holding the rope; down the man went and lay still. The Black snorted and plunged; if ever Alec saw hate expressed by a horse, he saw it then. They had him halfway up the plank. Alec wondered where they would put him if they ever did succeed in getting him on the boat.

Then he was on! Alec saw Captain Watson waving his arms frantically, motioning and shouting for the men to pull the stallion toward the stern. The boy followed at a safe distance. Now he saw the makeshift stall into which they were attempting to get the Black—it had once been a good-sized cabin. The *Drake* had little accommodation for transporting animals; its hold was already heavily laden with cargo.[5]

Finally they had the horse in front of the stall. One of the men clambered to the top of the cabin, reached down and pulled the scarf away from the stallion's eyes. At the same time, the dark-skinned

---

5. A ship's *cargo* is the goods the ship is carrying.

WORD BANK	
tersely (TURSS lee) *adv.:* briefly
bolted (BOLT ed) *v.:* suddenly tried to break free
plunged (PLUNJD) *v.:* threw himself about
makeshift (MAYK shift) *adj.:* temporary
accommodation (uh KOM uh DAY shun) *n.:* place for housing and feeding
laden (LAY dun) *adj.:* very full of something

The Black Stallion ~ 163

LITERARY COMPONENTS

▶ **16. Rising Action; Foreshadowing:** The horse is going to be put on the ship!

▶ **17. Rising Action; Tension:** Now we see that the horse can really be dangerous. Later, when Alec tries to befriend the horse, his actions, juxtaposed with this scene, show how brave and good Alec is.

▶ **18. Rising Action:** The horse is *aboard*.

GUIDING THE READING

LITERAL

Q: What does the man wearing a white turban do?
A: He whips the horse hard on its hindquarters.

Q: What happens when the stallion bolts?
A: He knocks down one of the men holding the rope. The man does not move.

Q: Where do they put the horse, once they have gotten him on board?
A: They put him in a makeshift stall at the stern of the deck that had once been a "good-sized" cabin.

SUMMING UP THE PLOT

- After he has been struck with the whip, the horse bolts into the stall.
- He tears into the wood and sends it flying; thunder rolls from under his hoofs; his powerful legs crash

into the sides of the cabin.

- Captain Watson talks angrily with the dark-skinned, white turbaned man. He had never expected to ship such a cargo!
- The man gives him money. The Captain

shrugs his shoulders and walks away.

- As the *Drake* departs, Alec looks back at the shore and sees the group of workers gathered around the inert form of the man who was kicked by the Black.

LITERARY COMPONENTS

▶ **19. Rising Action; Moral Tension; Characterization:** The horse is being treated cruelly, and probably has been treated cruelly in the past.

▶ **20. Characterization of Boy and Horse; Setting:** Alec feels compassion for the newly imprisoned horse.

▶ **21. Plot; Characterization:** Captain Watson is angry with the man who has brought the horse, but his feelings are assuaged when the man gives him money.

---

(19) man again hit the horse on the hindquarters and he bolted inside. Alec thought the stall would never be strong enough to hold him. The stallion tore into the wood and sent it flying; thunder rolled from under his hoofs; his powerful legs crashed into the sides of the cabin; his wild, shrill, high-**(20)** pitched whistle filled the air. Alec felt a deep pity steal over him, for here was a wild stallion used to the open range imprisoned in a stall in which he was hardly able to turn.

(21) Captain Watson was conversing angrily with the dark-skinned man; the captain had probably never expected to ship a cargo such as this! Then the man pulled a thick wallet from inside his coat; he counted the bills off and handed them to the captain. Captain Watson looked at the bills and then at the stall; he took the money, shrugged his shoulders and walked away. The dark-skinned man gathered the Arabs who had helped bring the stallion aboard, gave them bills from his wallet, and they departed down the gangplank.

Soon the *Drake* was again under way. Alec gazed back at the port, watching the group gathered around the inert form of the Arab who had gone down under the Black's mighty hoofs; then he turned to the stall. The dark-skinned man had gone to his cabin, and only the excited passengers were standing around outside the stall. The black horse was still fighting madly inside.

The days that followed were hectic ones for Alec, passengers, and crew. He had never dreamed a horse could

| WORD BANK | **inert** (in URT) *adj.*: still; unmoving |
| | **hectic** (HEK tik) *adj.*: rushed and confused |

GUIDING THE READING

LITERAL

Q: What does the stallion do when it is put in the stall?

A: He tears into the wood and sends it flying. His powerful legs crash into the sides of the cabin. His shrill whistle fills the air.

Q: What does Alec see on shore as the steamer pulls out to sea?

A: He sees the group of Arab workers gathered around the unmoving body of the man who was knocked down by the Black's "mighty hoofs."

ANALYTICAL

Q: Why does Alec feel pity for the stallion?

A: Answers will vary. The stallion is suffering. It is used to the open range and now it is enclosed in a tiny stall. Alec is a compassionate person.

Q: Why is Captain Watson angry about the situation?

A: Apparently, he had never expected to be taking a wild horse on board ship. (He must have been expecting a horse, since a stall was built.)

Q: Why does the money make Captain Watson feel better?

A: Answers will vary.

- In the days that follow, Alec is struck by the spirit of the horse. The ship resounds into the night with the blows struck by the horse's powerful legs.
- The boat steams through the Suez into the Mediterranean.
- That night, Alec steals onto the deck.
- Alec listens carefully. The Black is quiet.
- Alec walks towards the stall and sees the pink-colored nostrils of the Black, who is sticking his head out of the window.
- Alec puts his hand in his pocket to see if the lumps of sugar he took from the dinner table are still there.
- Alec watches the Black. He cannot turn his eyes away. He cannot believe that such a perfect animal exists.
- The stallion sees Alec, emits a piercing whistle that fills the night air, and disappears into the stall.
- Alec leaves the sugar on the window sill of the stall and goes to his cabin.

---

have such spirit, be so untamable. The ship resounded far into the night from the blows struck by those powerful legs. **(22)** The outside of the stall was now covered with reinforcements. The dark-skinned man became more mysterious than ever—always alone, and never talking to anyone but the captain. **(23)**

The *Drake* steamed through the Suez into the Mediterranean. **(24)**

That night Alec stole out upon deck, leaving the rest of the passengers playing cards. He listened carefully. The Black was quiet tonight. Quickly he walked in the direction of the stall. At first he couldn't see or hear anything. Then as his eyes became accustomed to the darkness, he made out the pink-colored nostrils of the Black, who was sticking his head out of the window.

Alec walked slowly toward him; he put one hand in his pocket to see if the lumps of sugar he had taken from the dinner table were still there. The wind was blowing against him, carrying his scent away. He was quite close now. The Black was looking out on the open sea; his ears pricked forward, his thin-skinned nostrils quivering, his black mane flowing like windswept flame. Alec could not turn his eyes away; he could not believe such a perfect animal existed.

The stallion turned and looked directly at him—his black eyes blazed. Once again that piercing whistle filled the night air, and he disappeared into the stall. Alec took the sugar out of his pocket and left it on the window sill. **(25)** He went to

> WORD BANK   **resounded** (ree ZOWND ed) *v.:* echoed

The Black Stallion ~ 165

LITERARY COMPONENTS

▶ **22. Characterization:** The horse refuses to yield in the days that follow. Alec is increasingly taken with the horse.

▶ **23. Red Herring:** The dark-skinned man is characterized as "more mysterious than ever" in the days that follow, but as we see, he just drowns and doesn't appear to have any further part to play.

▶ **24. Change in Setting and Alec Takes Action:** They are now in the Mediterranean, and Alec steals out on deck at night.

▶ **25. Rising Action; Turning Point in Plot; Characterization:** Alec leaves sugar for the Black for the first time. He will do so every night thereafter.

ANALYTICAL

Q: Here, the word steal (or the past tense *stole*) means to come or go secretly, unobtrusively, gradually, or unexpectedly. Why do you think Alec keeps his visits to the horse a secret?

A: Answers will vary. He may think the captain would disapprove, because the horse can be dangerous. He may think the man who is shipping the horse would interfere. He certainly wants things to be calm and wants no one around so that the horse can relax. Above all, he wants a personal, one on one relationship with this magnificent horse.

Q: Why does Alec bring the sugar, if he doesn't even get to see the horse?

A: Answers will vary. If Alec wants friendship of some kind from the horse, it will take a long time and a lot of patience. For Alec, just seeing the horse accept his offering is gratifying; it represents the first glimmerings of a connection.

GUIDING THE READING

LITERAL

Q: In the days that follow, does the horse calm down?

A: No. The ship resounds far into the night with the blows struck by the horse's powerful legs.

Q: Where is the *Drake* after it steams through the Suez Canal?

A: It is on the Mediterranean Sea.

Q: What does Alec do that night?

A: He steals out on deck.

Q: What are the other passengers doing, when Alec goes up onto the deck?

A: They are playing cards.

Q: After his eyes become accustomed to the dark, what can Alec see of the horse?

A: He can see that the Black is sticking his head out the window of the stall, and he can make out his pink-colored nostrils.

Q: What does the Black do when it sees Alec?

A: His eyes blaze. He emits a piercing whistle that fills the night air and backs into the stall.

SUMMING UP THE PLOT

- Later Alec returns and sees that the sugar is gone.
- Every night thereafter, Alec steals up to the stall and leaves sugar and departs.
- Sometimes he sees the Black and at other times he only hears the ring of his hoofs against the floor.
- The *Drake* stops at Alexandria, Bengasi, Tripoli, Tunis, and Algiers; it passes the Rock of Gibraltar and turns north up the coast of Portugal. Now they are off Cape Finisterre on the coast of Spain.
- Captain Watson tells Alec they will be in England in a few days.
- That night, Alec makes his usual trip to the stall with the lumps of sugar.
- The Black whistles when he sees Alec, and then faces the water.
- Alec feels elated—it's the first time the stallion hasn't drawn back into the stall at the sight of him.
- Alec moves closer, extending his arm with the sugar in his palm.

- Neither he nor anyone else has been this close to the stallion since he came on board.
- But Alec doesn't care to get any closer to the bared teeth and the curled nostrils.

- Alec places the sugar on the sill of the stall window.
- The Black looks at it, looks back at Alec, and begins to eat the sugar.

LITERARY COMPONENTS

▶ **26. Characterization:** Alec is realistic about this process. It is a long one that requires great patience. There will be no immediate response to his kindness. Or, perhaps, he is simply doing it for the horse, to diminish his suffering.

▶ **27. Geographical References:** Make sure you look at a map with your students and locate Alexandria (Egypt), Bengasi (also Bengazi *or* Benghazi) (northeastern Libya), Tripoli (northwestern Libya), Tunis (northeastern Tunisia), Algiers (northwestern Algeria), the Rock of Gibraltar, Portugal, and Cape Finisterre (Spain).

▶ **28. Rising Action; A Gradual Shift in the Relationship of Boy and Horse:** The horse has seen Alec, who has come to bring sugar. This is the first time the horse has not backed into his stall at the sight of the boy.

▶ **29. Characterization of Horse and Boy:** The Black eats the sugar in the presence of the boy. Alec watches him, satisfied.

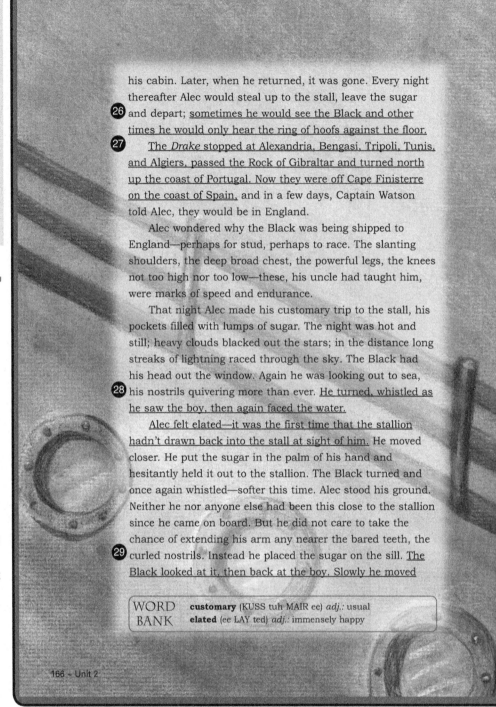

his cabin. Later, when he returned, it was gone. Every night thereafter Alec would steal up to the stall, leave the sugar ㉖ and depart; sometimes he would see the Black and other times he would only hear the ring of hoofs against the floor.

㉗ The *Drake* stopped at Alexandria, Bengasi, Tripoli, Tunis, and Algiers, passed the Rock of Gibraltar and turned north up the coast of Portugal. Now they were off Cape Finisterre on the coast of Spain, and in a few days, Captain Watson told Alec, they would be in England.

Alec wondered why the Black was being shipped to England—perhaps for stud, perhaps to race. The slanting shoulders, the deep broad chest, the powerful legs, the knees not too high nor too low—these, his uncle had taught him, were marks of speed and endurance.

That night Alec made his customary trip to the stall, his pockets filled with lumps of sugar. The night was hot and still; heavy clouds blacked out the stars; in the distance long streaks of lightning raced through the sky. The Black had his head out the window. Again he was looking out to sea, ㉘ his nostrils quivering more than ever. He turned, whistled as he saw the boy, then again faced the water.

Alec felt elated—it was the first time that the stallion hadn't drawn back into the stall at sight of him. He moved closer. He put the sugar in the palm of his hand and hesitantly held it out to the stallion. The Black turned and once again whistled—softer this time. Alec stood his ground. Neither he nor anyone else had been this close to the stallion since he came on board. But he did not care to take the chance of extending his arm any nearer the bared teeth, the ㉙ curled nostrils. Instead he placed the sugar on the sill. The Black looked at it, then back at the boy. Slowly he moved

> WORD BANK
> **customary** (KUSS tuh MAIR ee) *adj.:* usual
> **elated** (ee LAY ted) *adj.:* immensely happy

166 ~ Unit 2

GUIDING THE READING

LITERAL

Q: Name the places where the Drake stops.
A: The *Drake* stops at Alexandria, Bengasi, Tripoli, Tunis, and Algiers.

Q: Where are they, when Captain Watson tells Alec they will be in England in a few days?
A: They are off Cape Finisterre on the coast of Spain.

ANALYTICAL

Q: How do you think Alec feels when he returns and sees that the horse has eaten the sugar?
A: Answers will vary.

Q: Why is Alec elated, when the stallion does not back into the stall at the sight of him?
A: Answers will vary. This is a wild horse, and Alec is winning him over through his kind attentions.

SUMMING UP THE PLOT

- Alec is awakened suddenly in the middle of the night. The *Drake* is lurching crazily, and he is thrown onto the floor.
- This is Alec's first storm at sea!
- A flash of lightning illuminates the cabin—the floor is covered with broken glass.
- Alec dresses and puts on a life jacket.

LITERARY COMPONENTS

▶ **30. Rising Action; First Sign of Crisis:** Alec is awakened in the night. The *Drake* is lurching and he is thrown onto the floor.

▶ **31. Strong Visual Image:** The cabin is illuminated by a flash of lightning.

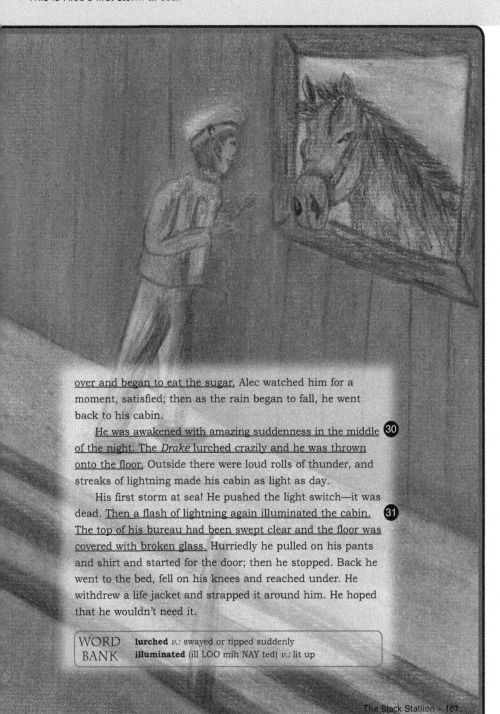

over and began to eat the sugar. Alec watched him for a moment, satisfied; then as the rain began to fall, he went back to his cabin.

He was awakened with amazing suddenness in the middle **30** of the night. The *Drake* lurched crazily and he was thrown onto the floor. Outside there were loud rolls of thunder, and streaks of lightning made his cabin as light as day.

His first storm at sea! He pushed the light switch—it was dead. Then a flash of lightning again illuminated the cabin. **31** The top of his bureau had been swept clear and the floor was covered with broken glass. Hurriedly he pulled on his pants and shirt and started for the door; then he stopped. Back he went to the bed, fell on his knees and reached under. He withdrew a life jacket and strapped it around him. He hoped that he wouldn't need it.

> WORD BANK
> **lurched** *v.*: swayed or tipped suddenly
> **illuminated** (ill LOO mih NAY ted) *v.*: lit up

The Black Stallion ~ 187

GUIDING THE READING

LITERAL

Q: What does the stallion do this time with the sugar that hasn't happened before?
A: He eats the sugar while Alec is still there.

Q: Why does Alec awaken in the middle of the night?
A: There is a storm, and the boat is lurching.

SUMMING UP THE PLOT

- Staggering to the deck, Alec can hear the shouts of Captain Watson and the crew faintly above the roar of the wind.
- Huge waves are sweeping from one end of the *Drake* to the other. Hysterical passengers crowd the corridor.
- For what seems hours, the *Drake* plows through wave after wave.
- As Alec watches, a huge wave sweeps a member of the crew overboard.
- Alec feels new hope as the storm seems to subside, but then the ship is struck by a bolt of lightning.

LITERARY COMPONENTS

▶ **32. Rising Action:** Alec makes his way, staggering, to the deck.

▶ **33. Rising Tension; Storm Becomes More Serious:** Alec watches as a huge wave sweeps on board and takes a sailor overboard.

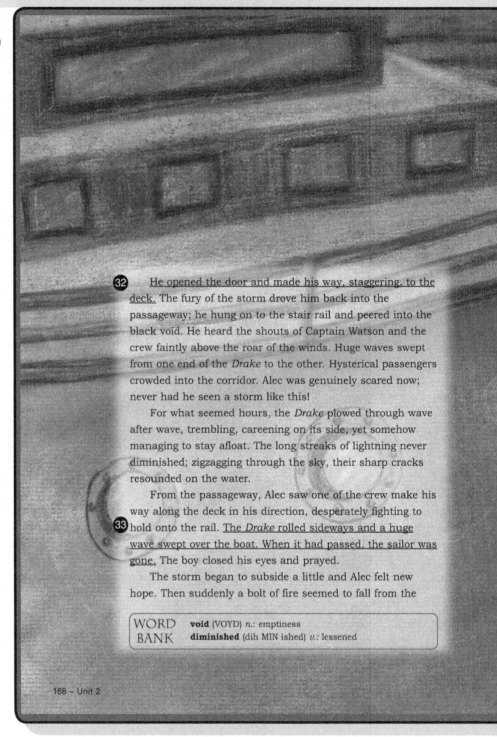

③② He opened the door and made his way, staggering, to the deck. The fury of the storm drove him back into the passageway; he hung on to the stair rail and peered into the black void. He heard the shouts of Captain Watson and the crew faintly above the roar of the winds. Huge waves swept from one end of the *Drake* to the other. Hysterical passengers crowded into the corridor. Alec was genuinely scared now; never had he seen a storm like this!

For what seemed hours, the *Drake* plowed through wave after wave, trembling, careening on its side, yet somehow managing to stay afloat. The long streaks of lightning never diminished; zigzagging through the sky, their sharp cracks resounded on the water.

From the passageway, Alec saw one of the crew make his way along the deck in his direction, desperately fighting to ③③ hold onto the rail. The *Drake* rolled sideways and a huge wave swept over the boat. When it had passed, the sailor was gone. The boy closed his eyes and prayed.

The storm began to subside a little and Alec felt new hope. Then suddenly a bolt of fire seemed to fall from the

> WORD BANK
> **void** (VOYD) *n*.: emptiness
> **diminished** (dih MIN ished) *v*.: lessened

168 ~ Unit 2

GUIDING THE READING

LITERAL

Q: Does Alec remain in his cabin after he straps on the life jacket?

A: No. He dresses and makes his way, staggering, to the deck.

ANALYTICAL

Q: Why does Alec pray?

A: Answers will vary, but he has just seen a sailor wash overboard.

SUMMING UP THE PLOT

- Alec is knocked to the floor.
- When he regains consciousness, his face is covered with blood.
- Passengers are yelling and screaming, crawling and climbing over Alec.
- The engines of the *Drake* are dead.
- The boat is sinking.
- A lifeboat is lowered into the sea. It is struck by a large wave and its occupants disappear into the sea.

LITERARY COMPONENTS

▶ **34. Rising Action:** The ship is struck by lightning.

▶ **35. Heightened Tension:** The engines are dead, and pandemonium ensues. The boat begins to sink!

▶ **36. The Crisis Worsens:** The occupants of the first lifeboat disappear into the sea when the boat over-turns.

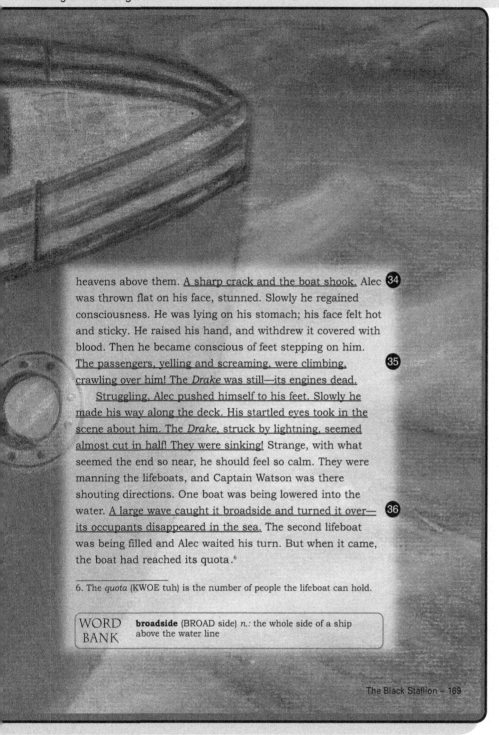

heavens above them. A sharp crack and the boat shook. Alec **34** was thrown flat on his face, stunned. Slowly he regained consciousness. He was lying on his stomach; his face felt hot and sticky. He raised his hand, and withdrew it covered with blood. Then he became conscious of feet stepping on him. The passengers, yelling and screaming, were climbing, **35** crawling over him! The *Drake* was still—its engines dead.

Struggling, Alec pushed himself to his feet. Slowly he made his way along the deck. His startled eyes took in the scene about him. The *Drake*, struck by lightning, seemed almost cut in half! They were sinking! Strange, with what seemed the end so near, he should feel so calm. They were manning the lifeboats, and Captain Watson was there shouting directions. One boat was being lowered into the water. A large wave caught it broadside and turned it over— **36** its occupants disappeared in the sea. The second lifeboat was being filled and Alec waited his turn. But when it came, the boat had reached its quota.[6]

---

6. The *quota* (KWOE tuh) is the number of people the lifeboat can hold.

> **WORD BANK** **broadside** (BROAD side) *n.*: the whole side of a ship above the water line

The Black Stallion ~ 169

GUIDING THE READING

LITERAL

Q: Why does Alec's face feel hot and sticky?
A: He is bleeding from a wound.

Q: What happens to the ship from the sharp crack of lightning?
A: To Alec, the ship looks nearly cut in half. The engines are dead. The ship is sinking.

Q: What happens to the people in the first lifeboat?
A: The boat is caught broadside by a wave and the people disappear into the sea.

ANALYTICAL

Q: What kind of person is the Captain, that he makes certain all of the passengers are in lifeboats before he himself can leave— and the boat is sinking!?
A: Answers will vary. But he certainly is very brave. He is ready to die.

SUMMING UP THE PLOT

- As Alec and the Captain watch the second lifeboat being lowered, the dark-skinned man rushes up to the captain babbling hysterically.
- The Captain shouts, "It's under the bed, under the bed!"
- Alec sees that the dark-skinned man has no life jacket.
- The man attacks Alec and tries to take his life jacket.
- The man sees that a lifeboat is being lowered. He climbs over the rail to jump into the boat. He falls into the sea and disappears.
- His drowning reminds Alec of the Black.
- Alec fights his way out of line and toward the stern. If the stallion is alive, he is going to set him free and give him his chance to fight for life.
- Alec lifts the heavy bar at the stall door and swings it open.
- For a second the mighty hoofs stop pounding. Alec backs slowly away.
- The Black snorts and plunges straight for the rail and Alec.

LITERARY COMPONENTS

▶ **37. High Drama:** The dark-skinned man tries to take Alec's lifejacket. In the paragraph that follows, he tries to jump into the lifeboat, loses his balance, and falls into the sea.

▶ **38. The Black!:** Alec comes to his senses! What is happening to the horse?

▶ **39. Characterization; Values; Foreshadowing:** If the stallion is alive, Alec is going to set him free and give him his chance to fight for life.

"Wait for the next one, Alec," Captain Watson said sternly. He put his arm on the boy's shoulder, softening the harshness of his words.

As they watched the second lifeboat being lowered, the dark-skinned man appeared and rushed up to the captain, waving his arms and babbling hysterically.

"It's under the bed, under the bed!" Captain Watson shouted at him.

Then Alec saw the man had no life jacket. Terror in his eyes, he turned away from the captain toward Alec. **(37)** Frantically he rushed at the boy and tried to tear the life jacket from his back. Alec struggled, but he was no match for the half-crazed man. Then Captain Watson had his hands on the man and threw him against the rail. Alec saw the man's eyes turn to the lifeboat that was being lowered. Before the captain could stop him, he was climbing over the rail. He was going to jump into the boat! Suddenly the *Drake* lurched. The man lost his balance and, screaming, fell into the water. He never rose to the surface.

(38) The dark-skinned man had drowned. Immediately Alec thought of the Black. What was happening to him? Was he still in his stall? Alec fought his way out of line and toward **(39)** the stern[7] of the boat. If the stallion was alive, he was going to set him free and give him his chance to fight for life.

The stall was still standing. Alec heard a shrill whistle rise above the storm. He rushed to the door, lifted the heavy bar and swung it open. For a second the mighty hoofs stopped pounding and there was silence. Alec backed slowly away.

Then he saw the Black, his head held high, his nostrils blown out with excitement. Suddenly he snorted and plunged straight for the rail and Alec. Alec was paralyzed, he couldn't move. One hand was on the rail, which was broken at this point, leaving nothing between him and the open water. The Black swerved as he came near him, and the boy

---

7. *The stern* of the ship is the back end of the ship.

GUIDING THE READING

LITERAL

Q: What does the dark-skinned man want from Alec?
A: He wants his life jacket.

Q: What happens to the dark-skinned man?
A: He sees that a lifeboat is being lowered, steps over the rail, with the intention of jumping in the boat. The ship lurches, and he falls into the sea and drowns.

Q: What does his death remind Alec of?
A: Alec thinks of the horse, who is presumably owned by the man who is now dead.

Q: What does the Black do once the door is open?
A: He snorts and then he heads for the hole in the rail.

ANALYTICAL

Q: Why does Alec set the stallion free?
A: Answers will vary. But Alec believes it is better to have a chance to struggle, than to be a prisoner and die without a fight.

The Black Stallion ~ 171

SUMMING UP THE PLOT

- The horse heads for a break in the railing.
- He grazes Alec with his shoulder, and Alec flies into space. He feels the water close over his head.
- When he surfaces, he hears an explosion. The *Drake* settles deep into the water.
- There are no lifeboats in sight.
- Then he sees the Black swimming not more than ten yards away.
- Something swishes by Alec. It is the rope that is attached to the Black's halter!
- Without thinking about it, Alec grabs hold of it.
- He is pulled through the water, into the oncoming seas.

LITERARY COMPONENTS

▶ **40. More High Drama:** The horse makes for the hole in the railing, grazes Alec with his shoulder, and Alec flies into space.

▶ **41. Rising Tension; Suspense; Aha!:** Alec surfaces but he sees no lifeboat. But then he sees the Black only ten yards away!

▶ **42. Foreshadowing Come Full Circle:** Alex grabs hold of the rope attached to the horse's halter.

40 realized that the stallion was making for the hole. The horse's shoulder grazed him as he swerved, and Alec went flying into space. He felt the water close over his head.

When he came up, his first thought was of the ship; then he heard an explosion, and he saw the *Drake* settling deep **41** into the water. Frantically he looked around for a lifeboat, but there was none in sight. Then he saw the Black swimming not more than ten yards away. Something swished by him—a rope, and it was attached to the Black's **42** halter! The same rope that they had used to bring the stallion aboard the boat, and which they had never been able to get close enough to the horse to untie. Without stopping to think, Alec grabbed hold of it. Then he was pulled through the water, into the oncoming seas.

172 ~ Unit 2

GUIDING THE READING

LITERAL

Q: How does Alec get knocked into the water?
A: As the Black makes for the opening, he grazes the boy with his shoulder, and Alec goes flying into space.

Q: What does Alec grab hold of in the water?
A: He grabs onto the rope that is attached to the Black's halter.

ANALYTICAL

Q: What do you think has happened to the lifeboats?
A: Answers will vary.

SUMMING UP THE PLOT

- If he is to die, Alec would rather die with the mighty stallion than alone.
- For hours Alec battles the waves. He has tied the rope securely around his waist.

LITERARY COMPONENTS

▶ **43. Characterization; Connection Between Boy and Horse:** Alec is brave, but finds great comfort in one of his fellow creatures.

The waves were still large, but with the aid of his life jacket, Alec was able to stay on top. He was too tired now to give much thought to what he had done. He only knew that he had had his choice of remaining in the water alone or being pulled by the Black. <u>If he was to die, he would rather die with the mighty stallion than alone.</u> **43** He took one last look behind and saw the *Drake* sink into the depths.

For hours Alec battled the waves. He had tied the rope securely around his waist. He could hardly hold his head up. Suddenly he felt the rope slacken. The Black had stopped swimming! Alec anxiously waited; peering into the darkness he could just make out the head of the stallion. The Black's whistle pierced the air! After a few minutes, the rope became taut again. The horse had changed his direction. Another

The Black Stallion ~ 173

GUIDING THE READING

ANALYTICAL
Q: How do you understand Alec's feeling that he prefers to die with the stallion than to die alone?
A: Answers will vary.

SUMMING UP THE PLOT

- The first streaks of dawn appear on the horizon.

- Was the stallion's wild instinct leading him to land?

- As the sun rises, Alec feels he can hold out no longer. But he looks at the horse, struggling and fighting, and new courage comes to him.

- Suddenly Alec realizes that they are going *with* the waves, not *against* them.

- Yes, they are riding in. They must be approaching land!

- Alec sees it, about a quarter mile away: a small island.

- They approach the white sand of the island, faster and faster.

- They are in the breakers! The Black is able to walk.

- Suddenly Alec realizes that he is in danger. If he does not untie the rope, he will be dragged to his death over the sand!

- Frantically, he works on the knot.

LITERARY COMPONENTS

▶ **44. Connection Between Boy and Horse:** The horse has not given up, so neither will Alec.

▶ **45. Their Luck Turns:** This moment, when Alec realizes that they are going with the tide, is a mini-climax.

▶ **46. Rising Excitement; Moving Towards the Climax:** Yes, they are approaching land!

▶ **47. Dawning Intelligence:** Alec remembers that he is tied to the horse.

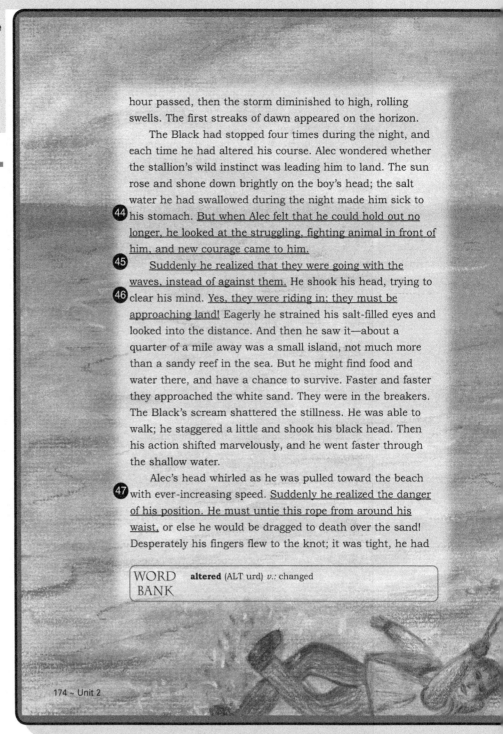

hour passed, then the storm diminished to high, rolling swells. The first streaks of dawn appeared on the horizon.

The Black had stopped four times during the night, and each time he had altered his course. Alec wondered whether the stallion's wild instinct was leading him to land. The sun rose and shone down brightly on the boy's head; the salt water he had swallowed during the night made him sick to

(44) his stomach. But when Alec felt that he could hold out no longer, he looked at the struggling, fighting animal in front of him, and new courage came to him.

(45) Suddenly he realized that they were going with the waves, instead of against them. He shook his head, trying to

(46) clear his mind. Yes, they were riding in; they must be approaching land! Eagerly he strained his salt-filled eyes and looked into the distance. And then he saw it—about a quarter of a mile away was a small island, not much more than a sandy reef in the sea. But he might find food and water there, and have a chance to survive. Faster and faster they approached the white sand. They were in the breakers. The Black's scream shattered the stillness. He was able to walk; he staggered a little and shook his black head. Then his action shifted marvelously, and he went faster through the shallow water.

Alec's head whirled as he was pulled toward the beach

(47) with ever-increasing speed. Suddenly he realized the danger of his position. He must untie this rope from around his waist, or else he would be dragged to death over the sand! Desperately his fingers flew to the knot; it was tight, he had

> **WORD BANK** **altered** (ALT urd) *v.:* changed

174 ~ Unit 2

GUIDING THE READING

LITERAL

Q: What land does the Black reach?
A: It is a small island, little more than a sandy reef in the sea.

Q: Why is Alec in such danger, as the Black approaches the shore?
A: He is tied by the waist to the horse. He will be dragged to his death in the sand, once the horse starts to run on shore.

ANALYTICAL

Q: Again, how do you explain Alec's renewed courage, when he sees the horse struggling to live?
A: Answers will vary.

Q: What does it mean that they are going with the waves instead of against them?
A: They are going with the tide, towards land.

SUMMING UP THE PLOT

- The Black is on the beach. Alec cannot untie the knot!

- He remembers the pocketknife. Is it still there?

made sure of that. Frantically he worked on it as the shore drew closer and closer.

The Black was now on the beach. Thunder began to roll from beneath his hoofs as he broke out of the water. Hours in the water had swelled the knot—Alec couldn't untie it! Then he remembered his pocketknife. Could it still be there? ⓐ Alec's hand darted to his rear pants pocket. His fingers reached inside and came out with the knife.

The Black Stallion ~ 175

LITERARY COMPONENTS

▶ **48. Rising Tension; Foreshadowing Come Full Circle:** He cannot untie the knot. He remembers the knife!

SUMMING UP THE PLOT

- Alec is on the beach being dragged by the stallion.
- He opens the knife and begins to cut the rope.
- Madly, he saws away at the rope.
- With one final thrust he is through!
- He murmurs, "Yes—Uncle Ralph—it did—come in handy."

LITERARY COMPONENTS

▶ **49. Vivid Image, Appealing to the Physical Sense of Touch:** Alec is trying to cut the rope as his body *burns from the sand.* His clothes are being torn off him.

▶ **50. Climax; Coming Full Circle:** He does it. He cuts through the rope. And he repeats his uncle's words to him.

He was now on the beach being dragged by the **(49)** stallion; the sand flew in his face. Quickly he opened the knife and began to cut the rope. His body burned from the sand, his clothes were being torn off of him! His speed was increasing every **(50)** second! Madly he sawed away at the rope. With one final thrust he was through! His outflung hands caressed the sand. As he closed his eyes, his parched lips murmured, "Yes—Uncle Ralph—it did—come in handy."

ABOUT THE AUTHOR

"There is no way to explain the magic that some people have with horses," said **Walter Farley**, who loved horses and wrote about them throughout his life. At age eleven, he was writing stories about horses, and in high school, he wrote the first draft of his best-selling novel, *The Black Stallion*. Born in Syracuse, New York in 1915, Farley's youth was filled with horses. In addition to befriending the horses owned by his neighbors, he spent many hours visiting horses at nearby race tracks. Farley went on to write 16 Black Stallion books. Active until his death, Farley died in 1989.

GUIDING THE READING

LITERAL

Q: What does Alec use to cut the rope?
 A: He uses the pocketknife that his uncle had given him.

Answers will vary.

Studying the Selection

> **FIRST IMPRESSIONS**
> Were you surprised by the horse's strength?

QUICK REVIEW

1. Where does Alexander Ramsay normally live?

2. With whom has he spent the last two months? What will he miss?

3. What has his uncle given him as a gift? What is inscribed on it?

4. What is the name of the ship Alec will be taking from England to New York?

FOCUS

5. Why does Alexander visit the horse and bring him sugar?

6. Describe an incident or an object that is mentioned early in the story that is important for the way the story ends. Did you suspect that this was going to be a part of the story's ending? Did you do any predicting while you were reading the story?

CREATING & WRITING

7. What is the theme of this story? Remember, a theme is not an event or character in the story. It is the *idea* of the story, which the reader understands better and better as the story unfolds.

8. Your assignment is to do some research about horses and to write a two-page report. There are many topics you could choose. Some examples are: Horse Anatomy, Horse Behavior, How Horses Have Helped Human Beings Throughout History, How Horses Came to the Americas, Different Kinds of Horse Training. There are more than one hundred breeds of horses. You may choose a particular breed to write about. You may also write about the horse of a famous person.

9. Using your favorite medium (pencil, pen, crayons, pastels, paint, or clay), create a horse to go with your report.

The Black Stallion ~ 177

QUICK REVIEW

1. Alexander Ramsay normally lives in New York City.

2. He has spent the last two months with his Uncle Ralph. He will miss "the days they spent together in the jungle, even the screams of the panthers and the many eerie sounds of the jungle night." He also will miss the rides on horseback.

3. His uncle had given him a pearl pocketknife. The words on it are inscribed in gold: *To Alec on his birthday, Bombay, India.*

4. The ship that Alec will be taking from England to New York is called the *Majestic.*

FOCUS

5. Answers will vary. The author never says explicitly. Earlier, when Alec is recalling his time in India, we read, "Uncle Ralph had taught him how to ride—the one thing in the world he had always wanted to do." If the boy likes to ride, he probably likes horses. The description of the horse as it is brought on board the ship is certainly sympathetic—it makes the reader wince. That scene (like the others) is witnessed through Alec's eyes. "Alec could hardly believe his eyes and ears—a stallion, a wild stallion—unbroken, such as he had read and dreamed about." Alec sympathizes with the horse. The horse is wild, and Alec wants to be the one to win him.

6. The pocketknife that saves him as the horse gallops onto the beach is the one that his uncle had given him for his birthday. "Lovingly he surveyed the pearl pocketknife he held there. " His uncle's words at the time of the gift were, "A knife, Alec, comes in handy sometimes."

   Horses have been important to Alec. Riding was "the one thing in the world he had always wanted to do." When he leaves sugar cubes for the horse, it is likely that an important bond is being forged.

   Students may have other examples. Certainly, these are the two most important.

CREATING & WRITING

7. Answers will vary. The story's themes include:

   Selfless love as represented by Alec

   The mystical connection that some people feel to some animals and vice versa

   Good deeds will eventually bear fruit

   Courage and perseverance, again as seen in Alec's approach to the Black

   The awesome power of the natural world as seen in the sea, the storm, and the horse

8. Help your students pick topics and provide them with good resources, so that everyone doesn't write about the same thing.

LESSON IN LITERATURE . . .

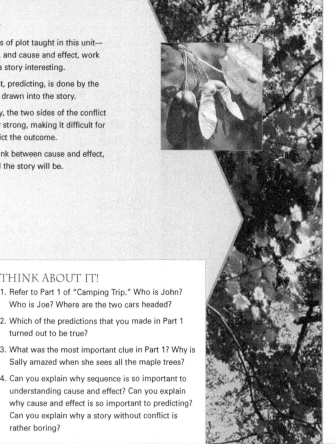

UNIT REVIEW
- The three elements of plot taught in this unit—conflict, sequence, and cause and effect, work together to make a story interesting.
- The fourth element, predicting, is done by the reader as they are drawn into the story.
- In an exciting story, the two sides of the conflict are almost equally strong, making it difficult for the reader to predict the outcome.
- The stronger the link between cause and effect, the more powerful the story will be.

THINK ABOUT IT!
1. Refer to Part 1 of "Camping Trip." Who is John? Who is Joe? Where are the two cars headed?

2. Which of the predictions that you made in Part 1 turned out to be true?

3. What was the most important clue in Part 1? Why is Sally amazed when she sees all the maple trees?

4. Can you explain why sequence is so important to understanding cause and effect? Can you explain why cause and effect is so important to predicting? Can you explain why a story without conflict is rather boring?

Camping Trip, Part 2

Pointing at a crumpled sheet of directions scrawled thirty years earlier, John poked his head in the window of his sister's car. "I'm telling you, Sal, the interstate gets us there twice as fast."

In the car ahead, John, his wife, and his three kids sat in the rush-hour traffic they'd hoped to avoid, fifteen feet ahead of Sally, Joe, and their two kids.

Sally sighed. "If you're sure you're going to be able to find the town."

John just smiled and shot back into his car.

An hour later John put on his turn signal, and Sally followed him off the highway. At the bottom of the exit ramp was a crowded intersection, with car dealerships on three corners. When they pulled into a gas station with a SuperMart, Joe said, "I'll go get us some snacks."

The kids poured out of both cars, and headed for the patch of grass next to the station. While the girls threw a Frisbee, the boys climbed the large maple tree next to the parking lot.

John was back, a state map in his hand. "The attendant says we turn right here. It's down on the right just past the mall."

"Mall?" Sally said, looking around at the intersection. "This doesn't look anything like—"

"I know. It's a four-lane highway now," John explained.

Everyone piled back into the cars and they headed down the highway past new housing developments and, on the right, a mall.

They almost missed the green painted metal sign at the park entrance.

They drove down the paved, single-lane road that wound through the campground until John pulled into a numbered campsite.

He approached Sally's car with a puzzled look on his face. "I think this is the right place," he said. "But I don't remember all these trees. You remember these trees, Sal?"

Sally looked around in amazement at all the maple trees. She had a far-off look on her face, as if she were remembering a time long past.

"Yeah, actually. I do remember them, now that you ask."

178 ~ Unit 2

By the Shores of Silver Lake ~ 179

LESSON IN LITERATURE

1. John is the baby. Joe is Sally's husband. They are headed to the old camping ground.

2. Answers will vary.

3. The maple helicopters are the most important clue. Sally is amazed when she sees the result of her little game of throwing down maple helicopters.

4. a) A cause must, by definition, precede an effect. Sometimes the only way to discover the cause of an effect is by carefully reviewing the sequence of events. b) When one views an event as a cause, one can predict what the effect will be. If cause and effect did not exist, predicting would be impossible. c) A sequence of events with no conflict is more of a report than a story. The reader may feel some slight curiosity, but not the delicious tension created by a really strong conflict.

SELECTION VOCABULARY

bank: the slope or high ground next to a river

desolate: empty, deserted, and lonely

earnestly: seriously, sincerely

glass: mirror

motionless: not moving, still

mourned: said in a sad, sorrowful tone

mufflers: scarves

radiance: shining brightness

shimmered: glowed and softly shone with a flickering light

steadying: calming

| bank | earnestly | motionless | mufflers | shimmered |
| desolate | glass | mourned | radiance | steadying |

1. "Wear your _____ (scarves)!" called their mother, as the children hurriedly dressed to go sledding.

2. The boy emerged from the river, shaking, chilled and scared. The man put a _____ (calming) hand on his shoulder and said: "Let's warm you up before you tell us what happened."

3. The little boy looked in his _____ (mirror) and said, "Mirror, Mirror on the wall, couldn't you teach me to play ball?"

4. The deer stood _____ (still) in the meadow, listening for the sounds of danger.

5. As the road wound up the mountain, the countryside looked more and more lonely and _____ (deserted).

6. "My Grampa's gone home," she _____ (said sadly). "He lives across the ocean, and I don't know if I'll ever see him again."

7. All summer long, the children would play on the river _____ (slope next to a river), watching the sailboats as they glided by.

8. As the coal miners stepped out of the elevators that had brought them up from the dark mines, they blinked in the _____ (shining brightness) of the sun.

9. The lake _____ (glowed) in the heat; nothing moved under the surface except for some lazy goldfish.

10. The little girl put a coin into the beggar's hand and said _____ (sincerely), "Here, Sir. I do hope this will help."

Workbook p. 55   Answer Guide p. 6

Why oh Why oh Why?

Match the silly answer to the silly question. Choose your answer from the list of answers and write it on the line below the question.

1. Why don't turtles wear mufflers?

2. What did the sun say about the radiance of the moon?

3. When is a two-year-old motionless?

4. What kind of money would you find in a riverbank?

5. Why was the jello shimmering?

6. What kind of glass doesn't hold water?

7. Why was Eve mourning?

8. Why did the tightrope walker need steadying?

Answers:
a. Because it is a light dessert.
b. Because he'd had a milkshake for breakfast.
c. Send dollars.
d. They prefer to wear turtleneck sweaters.
e. A looking glass.
f. "That feller's really taken a shine (likes) to me."
g. She longed for days gone by.
h. When she's asleep.

Workbook p. 56   Answer Guide p. 6

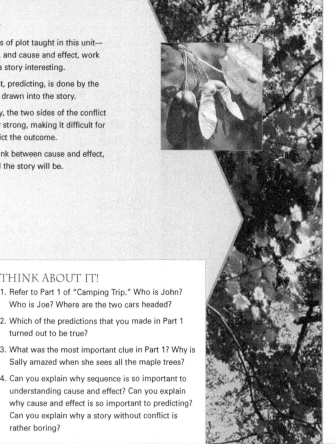

178 ~ **Unit 2**

BACKGROUND BYTES

The material below comes from the Defenders of Wildlife. Defenders of Wildlife is an organization dedicated to protecting wild animals and plants in the places where they live and grow naturally. Defenders of Wildlife considers two environmental threats most serious: (1) the increasing rate at which various species are becoming extinct; and (2) the expanding destruction of the places these species need in order to live.

Defenders of Wildlife is concerned with entire ecosystems. The word *ecosystem* is used to remind us that, in a given natural environment, everything that is there works together with everything else that is there. If one species is eliminated, the balance of nature changes for the worse. This means that predators *must* be preserved, because *their* presence is essential to the health of any ecosystem in which they are found. A *predator* is an animal that must kill other animals for food in order to survive.

Little Red Riding Hood Lied! Several Myths about Wolves

Myth: Wolves are dangerous to humans.

Fact: You are more likely to be hit by a meteorite than killed by a wolf. Although wolves are large and powerful animals, and they *could* kill human beings, they do *not*. Dr. L. David Mech, a wolf expert, says there is not a single documented instance of a healthy wild wolf killing a human in North America. By contrast, more than twenty people are killed, and three million attacked, by man's best friend (the dog) each year.

Myth: If the number of wolves increases, they will devastate populations of those species they prey upon.

Fact: Wolves and large grazing animals lived side-by-side for millennia, before Europeans arrived. Except for their being slaughtered by man, the numbers of wolves has always been controlled by the weather and the availability of food. When the animals that wolves eat are scarce (because it's very cold, there's been a long drought, or they've been over-hunted by man), wolves have smaller or no litters, and they may even starve to death. Wolves make the stock of animals that they prey upon genetically stronger, because they catch the weak and sick animals. This means that only the strongest animals have babies.

Talking about Defenders of Wildlife Is a Good Way to Talk about Wolves

Defenders of Wildlife has guided wolf conservation since wolves were placed on the U.S. endangered species list. In recent years, Defenders helped reintroduce wolves to the Northern Rockies. They also helped restore gray wolves to the Southwest and red wolves to the Southeast. In 1987, Defenders of Wildlife created a trust fund to compensate ranchers in the U.S. Northern Rockies for all proven losses of livestock to wolves. This fund has grown as wolves have been reintroduced in several regions of the United States.

Why does Defenders do this? The most respected biologists have shown that if we protect the habitat for predators that roam great distances—wolves, grizzly bears, and mountain lions—ninety percent of other plant and animal species are saved as well. The gray wolf has the greatest natural range of any living terrestrial mammal other than *Homo sapiens*.

This is how it works. Red meat is a really rich source of nutrition and energy. Bears, for example, can eat berries, nuts, and seeds to survive, but if a bear has protein and fat, it does not hibernate in winter. Fat is also very important for birds. The fatter a raven is, for example, the higher quality its egg will be. "The better its egg, the stronger the chick. The stronger the chick, the more likely it is to survive."

Birds and mammals eat meat—and *need* it, but before wolves were brought back to Yellowstone National Park, the only time that meat was available for the coyotes, grizzlies, ravens, magpies, and eagles living there, was when elk and bison died during harsh winters. The situation has now changed, because when wolves kill an elk or a bison, they are not the only ones who eat it. The food from the carcass trickles down to other animals.

Grizzly bears, by themselves, can only kill elk calves, and only for a few weeks in early summer. Now that wolves are back in Yellowstone, the grizzly bears, with their keen sense of smell, know when a wolf pack has killed an animal. They can smell a carcass more than a mile away. Not long after wolves were reintroduced to the Park, bears began to follow the wolf packs just to take over their kills. Park researchers saw nine wolves in a pack challenge an adult grizzly who wanted their kill. The bear lay down on the elk and refused to move! So the wolves gave up and left to make another kill.

Yellowstone researchers have seen as many as 43 ravens on one wolf kill, after the wolves had left. Moreover, ravens not only consume meat directly but store it in trees for a later meal. These small packages make protein available to many other creatures.

Bluebirds have been seen in Yellowstone as well, thirty at a time, crowded on the ribs of an elk carcass, picking fly larvae out of the rotting meat. The bluebirds who migrate to Yellowstone from their winter habitat have lost their body fat. This high-quality food—and lots of it—from the carcasses wolves leave, enables bluebirds to get into top shape to have their babies.

Healthy grizzlies, coyotes, ravens, magpie, and eagles, in turn, have a positive effect on many other plants and animals.

Large Predators Control Smaller Predators

In 1988, a man named Michael Soulé found that when wolves are removed from a region through hunting, there is a tremendous increase in smaller predators. This explains the national explosion in the coyote population. With the near extinction of wolves in the United States, coyotes moved west and east into states where they were never previously seen.

Much of the wolf killing was sponsored by ranchers, who were concerned for their cattle. They also conducted widespread killing of coyotes on the prairie. This was good for foxes and bad for ducks. (The coyotes didn't like it much, either.) The increase in foxes meant that the number of ducklings who survived into adulthood decreased by 15%.

When red wolves disappeared from the Southeast, the coyotes moved in and the numbers of raccoons increased. In Mississippi this threatened wild turkeys, whose numbers went down dramatically.

When wolves are brought back to an area where they once lived, there may be a fifty percent reduction in the artificially swollen coyote population. This can lead to a significant increase in small mammals, such as ground squirrels and pocket gophers. That, in turn, may result in an increase in hawks, owls, and eagles.

Without wolves, there are too many elk. Without bears there are too many deer. Thousands of elk and deer starve as a consequence.

With wolves, there is a "faster cycling of nutrients, because animals don't live as long." Without wolves, a few young animals are killed in the spring. With wolves, there is a steady trickle of meat and fat through the year, which makes the entire ecosystem stronger.

Public opinion about wolves has changed a lot for the better in recent years. Such new attitudes towards wolves are needed to guide predator management, conservation, and restoration policies.

INTO "BY THE SHORES OF SILVER LAKE"

For many of us, it is very uncomfortable to have feelings and attitudes that are different from those of the people around us. In *By the Shores of Silver Lake*, Laura remains true to her feelings—she keeps them. That takes courage. Moreover, even though her feelings about the wolf are not shared, she does not challenge her parents. She understands that her parents have far more experience than she does. She understands that it would be irresponsible on her father's part to ignore the fact that a fierce wolf was roaming near their house. Still, something inside her feels sympathy to the wolf, and she clings to the hope that the wolf will escape her father's gun.

Have the courage to believe in your feelings. Have patience and a broad view, so that you don't have to argue with others or persuade them to your view.

Pa finds the homestead when he goes after the wolves.

The path to a positive turn in life may appear in the guise of a threatening or upsetting event.

If we admire Laura for the respect she feels for the wolf and for her wanting to treat him as he treated her, we should remember for ourselves that our special feelings *and our sense of justice* are worth preserving.

Repay kindness with kindness.

EYES ON...PULLING IT ALL TOGETHER

Here is an opportunity to show students that, in most stories, several literary components are present. We choose a specific story to demonstrate a specific literary component *only for the purposes of teaching and analysis*.

You may want to point out to your students that *By the Shores of Silver Lake* reads just like a piece of fiction, but is a *memoir*. A memoir is an autobiographical account that is often anecdotal, or intimate in tone, that focuses on the persons, events, or times known to the writer.

(1)   Review the literary components of Unit 2 with your students, identifying and defining or describing them. Recall the respective story that was used as a showcase for each one:
Conflict: *Gold-Mounted Guns*
Sequence: *The Disappearing Man*
Cause/Effect: *The Speckled Hen's Egg*
Predicting: *The Black Stallion*
(2)   Talk about how you will be looking for each of these components following a first read-through of *By the Shores of Silver Lake.*

You may want to emphasize throughout the year that the first time we read a story it's just for pleasure. The analytical work should only begin with a second reading.

Literary components are present in a given story to a greater or lesser degree. For instance, *By the Shores of Silver Lake* does not lend itself well to a discussion of predicting. Certainly it's possible to have such a discussion, as we have done below, but it really is a bit of a stretch. You and your students may also find that you would have used different stories than the ones we selected for showcasing a

Blueprint for Reading

INTO . . . *By the Shores of Silver Lake*
Does the natural world play a part in your life? Do you look at the moon and stars in the night sky, or fill with excitement as you watch the snowflakes fall? How does it feel when the wind blows through the trees? What do we mean when we exclaim, "Oh what a beautiful day!"?

By the Shores of Silver Lake was written about a time when wolves roamed freely in the wilderness. In the story, two little girls are frightened when they see a wolf watching them. The older girl, Laura, cannot quite say why, but she does not want her father to kill the wolf she saw. Delicately, she expresses her feelings for an animal that never did her harm.

EYES   ON   *. . . Pulling It All Together*

When we *pull it all together,* we look for each of the literary components in a single story, and see how they work together in that story.

In *Gold-Mounted Guns,* we talked about **conflict**. Remember that conflict can take place inside a person or outside a person. What is Laura's inner struggle or conflict? The *external* conflict for the characters in *By the Shores of Silver Lake* is the presence of a wolf that might hurt someone.

In *The Disappearing Man,* we talked about **sequence**. Sequence is the order in which events occur. What is the sequence of events in *By the Shores of Silver Lake?*

In *The Speckled Hen's Egg,* we focused on **cause and effect**. The **cause** is what happened that results in the **effect**. In *By the Shores of Silver Lake,* what occurs that results in Mr. Ingalls' finding a homestead?

In *The Black Stallion,* we looked at **predicting**. While reading a story, we try to figure out what will happen at the end. Can you predict the end of *By the Shores of Silver Lake?*

given literary component. For example, *Gold-Mounted Guns* would be a very good story for predicting. We used it for conflict.

What are the **conflicts** in this story?

When Laura sees the wolf and the children flee, there is an *external* conflict of **man vs. nature**. She has an *internal* conflict, because she does not want the wolf to be killed, but she is only a child—there's little she can do to stop it—and she respects her father's decision. She is fairly quiet about this, because there is a potential for external conflict with her mother and father (a conflict of **man vs**. **man**). One cannot imagine Laura

arguing with them.

What is the **sequence of events** in this story?

Here, the task is to list the procession of events in the order in which they occur in the story. (We have found that it is difficult not to get carried away with the number of events. We tried to limit ourselves to fifteen, and did not succeed.) Remind students that feelings can be important events, because—as we see in the next literary component—they become *causes.*

Here is our list, with emotional events in bold:

Laura is feeling restless and needs physical activity.

By the Shores of Silver Lake

Laura Ingalls Wilder

started on a long journey and knew where they were going.

He says he wouldn't wonder that those are the last buffalo wolves that'll ever be seen in this part of the country. There's no more buffalo.

Laura says, "Oh, Pa, the poor wolves."

Laura's mom says there's enough to be sorry for without being sorry for wild beasts.

Then Pa tells them that he has found their homestead while he was out looking for the wolves.

Feelings, more than physical events, drive characters to do what they do (which leads us to **cause and effect**). And it is the *feelings* of the characters that establish the **theme**.

What causes people and animals to do what they do in the story? This is looking at **cause and effect.**

Remind students that what the people or animals *do* is the **effect.** Why they do it is the **cause** or reason. (Of course, what they do may also be the **cause** of another result or **effect.**)

Again, here is our list—which is abbreviated. There are certainly other causes and their respective effects in the story.

Cause: It is a winter night.
Effects: It's icy out; there's a moonpath that can be traveled on the lake; it's as light as day; the girls can play outside.
Cause: Laura is restless.
Effect: The girls play outside.
Cause: The girls play outside at night and travel the moonpath.
Effect: Laura sees a wolf.
Cause: The wolf looks at Laura and she at him. The wind fluffs his fur, and it looks as though the moonlight moves in and out of his fur.
Effect: [Inferred] Laura is moved by the majesty of the wolf.
Cause: [Inferred] Laura is a responsible older sister.
Effect: She doesn't want to alarm Carrie by mentioning the wolf.
Cause: The wolf does not chase the girls.
Effect: Laura thinks it would be unfair to kill the wolf.
Cause: [Inferred] Pa is worried for his family.
Effect: He goes out the next morning to track and kill the wolf.
Cause: The wolf and its mate leave the area, traveling all night and going a great distance.
Effect: Pa does not get the wolf.
Cause: Pa travels far while pursuing the wolf and sees places he hasn't seen before.
Effect: Pa finds the perfect spot for a homestead.

Could we **predict** the end of the story? Are there clues that point to the conclusion?

Since the Ingalls are living in a surveyor's house, it's possible the story will end with their finding a homestead.

The wolf is dignified and not gratuitously violent. Laura does not want it hurt. Some students may realize that Pa will not kill the wolf, because such an ending to the story would go against Laura's deep feelings.

Laura and her sister Carrie go outside at night and go sliding on the ice.

They follow the moonpath and go farther and farther from their side of the lake.

Laura looks up at the bank on the far shore, and in the moonlight stands a great wolf!

He is looking toward her; she sees the wind stir his fur and the moonlight seems to run in and out of it.

Laura does not tell her sister, but suggests they race home; the wolf does not follow them.

They arrive home breathless and tell their parents about the wolf.

Laura tells her father that she hopes he doesn't find the wolf, because the wolf didn't chase them.

The next morning Pa goes out to track the wolf.

When he returns, he starts to tell them what occurred.

Laura is eating and cannot swallow the smallest mouthful of food.

Pa says he found the wolves' den—the den of two big buffalo wolves.

He followed the tracks of two wolves trotting side by side for ten miles; as if they

- On this night, the moonlight shines silver clear. The earth is endless white.

- Laura can not settle down to anything.

- Suddenly she exclaims, "Carrie! Let's go slide on the ice!"

- She reassures her mother that it's almost as light as day outdoors.

- Pa tells mother that it will be all right—as long as they don't stay out too long in the cold and freeze.

- Laura and Carrie dress to go outside.

LITERARY COMPONENTS

▶ **1. Setting; Poetic Images:** It is nighttime, it is winter. The earth is endless white.

▶ **2. Metaphor:** The sky is a curve of light.

▶ **3. Characters; Characterization; Exposition:** In this paragraph and the next two, we meet Laura (who is restless), Pa (who plays the fiddle), Carrie (she's probably a sister—Laura wants to go outside and play with her), and their mother (whose name is Caroline). Because Laura is restless, and it is almost as light as day outside, and Pa thinks it's safe, Laura and Carrie are going to go outside to slide on the ice.

▶ **4. Setting as Costume:** The description of Laura and Carrie's clothing tells us a lot about the time.

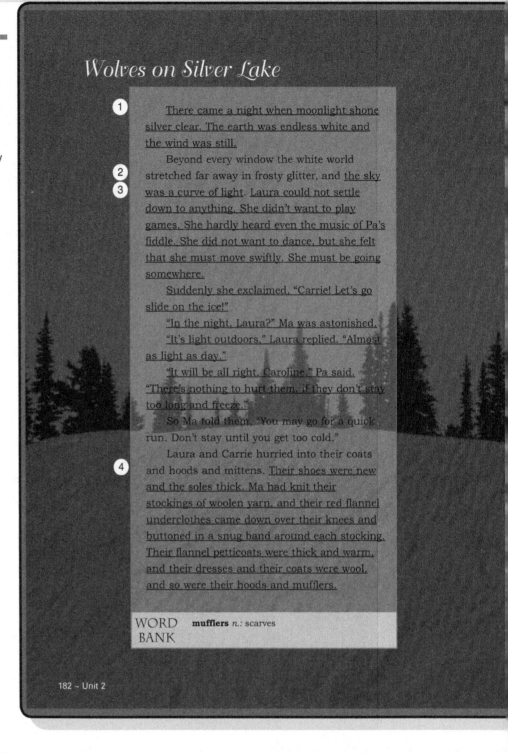

Wolves on Silver Lake

① There came a night when moonlight shone silver clear. The earth was endless white and the wind was still.

② Beyond every window the white world stretched far away in frosty glitter, and the sky ③ was a curve of light. Laura could not settle down to anything. She didn't want to play games. She hardly heard even the music of Pa's fiddle. She did not want to dance, but she felt that she must move swiftly. She must be going somewhere.

Suddenly she exclaimed, "Carrie! Let's go slide on the ice!"

"In the night, Laura?" Ma was astonished.

"It's light outdoors," Laura replied. "Almost as light as day."

"It will be all right, Caroline," Pa said. "There's nothing to hurt them, if they don't stay too long and freeze."

So Ma told them, "You may go for a quick run. Don't stay until you get too cold."

④ Laura and Carrie hurried into their coats and hoods and mittens. Their shoes were new and the soles thick. Ma had knit their stockings of woolen yarn, and their red flannel underclothes came down over their knees and buttoned in a snug band around each stocking. Their flannel petticoats were thick and warm, and their dresses and their coats were wool, and so were their hoods and mufflers.

WORD
BANK   **mufflers** *n.:* scarves

182 ~ Unit 2

GUIDING THE READING

LITERAL

Q: Describe the setting outside the surveyor's house.
A: It's nighttime; there's moonlight; there must be snow and ice (the earth is endless white); and the wind is still. Students may say more.

Q: What does Laura suggest to Carrie that they do?
A: She suggests that they go slide on the ice.

Q: Who in the family plays a musical instrument?
A: Pa plays the fiddle.

Q: Ma and Pa caution Carrie and Laura not to stay...
A: ...so long outside that they freeze (or get too cold).

ANALYTICAL

Q: Why might Laura be restless?
A: Answers will vary.

Q: Where do you think the girls get their clothes?
A: Answers will vary. Certainly, Ma knits their stockings and their mittens. She probably

makes their red flannel underclothes from material that she buys, as well as their petticoats and their dresses. Likely, they go into town for their shoes or buy them from a catalogue. As for coats—we're not sure!

- Out of the warm house the girls burst into the breathtaking air. It tingles with cold.
- Laura leads Carrie along the lake shore to avoid the water hole for the horses and the cow.
- It is so beautiful they hardly breathe.
- Carrie whispers, "How still it is. Listen how still it is."

Out of the warm house they burst into the breathtaking air that tingled with cold. They ran a race on the snowy path down the low hill to the stables. Then they followed the path that the horses and the cow had made when Pa led them through the snow to water at the hole he had cut in the lake ice.

"We mustn't go near the water hole," Laura said, and she led Carrie along the lake shore until they were well away from it. Then they stopped and looked at the night.

It was so beautiful that they hardly breathed. The great round moon hung in the sky and its radiance poured over a silvery world. Far, far away in every direction stretched motionless flatness, softly shining as if it were made of soft light. In the midst lay the dark, smooth lake, and a glittering moonpath stretched across it. Tall grass stood up in black lines from the snow drifted in the sloughs.[1]

The stable lay low and dark near the shore, and on the low hill stood the dark, small, surveyors' house, with the yellow light in the window twinkling from its darkness.

"How still it is," Carrie whispered. "Listen how still it is."

Laura's heart swelled. She felt herself a part of the wide land, of the far deep sky and

---

1. *Sloughs* (SLOOS) are areas of soft, muddy ground, similar to swamps.

WORD BANK
radiance (RAY dee unts) *n.*: shining brightness
motionless (MO shun luss) *adj.*: not moving, still

By the Shores of Silver Lake ~ 183

LITERARY COMPONENTS

▶ **5. Characterization; Background Information:** Laura is protective of Carrie. We also learn how farm animals get water in winter.

▶ **6. Setting; Characterization:** We see the outdoors in powerful visual images. Also, this is told as *their* perception, so we know that the children are profoundly affected by the beauty of the winter.

GUIDING THE READING

LITERAL

Q: What is it that stretches across the dark, smooth lake?
A: The glittering moonpath stretches across the frozen lake.

Q: Where is the stable in relation to the house?
A: The stable is near the shore of the lake, and the house is on a low hill.

ANALYTICAL

Q: Why does Laura steer clear of the hole Pa had cut in the ice for the animals?
A: They could both fall into the icy water.

Q: Why do you think the children so much appreciate the beauty of the outdoors?
A: Answers will vary.

SUMMING UP THE PLOT

- Laura takes Carrie's hand and says, "Let's slide. Come on, run!"

- "On the moonpath, Carrie! Let's follow the moonpath!" Laura cries.

- They slide farther and farther from the shore, toward the high bank on the other side.

- The girls swoop and almost seem to fly.

- They stop close to the farther shore. Laura looks up to the top of the bank.

LITERARY COMPONENTS

▶ **7. Characterization:** Laura will not do what is not good for her sister.

▶ **8. Repetition; Foreshadowing:** The repetition of the word *moonpath* almost weaves a spell. It is the moonpath that ultimately leads to the homestead.

▶ **9. Foreshadowing; Rising Action:** The girls are moving "farther and farther from shore." They are moving away from home and safety, toward "the high bank on the other side."

▶ **10. Characterization of Their Relationship:** These girls work together.

▶ **11. Terrifying Moment; Plot:** Laura sees a wolf!

▶ **12. Characterization of Wolf and of Laura; Simile:** Laura's ability to see the wolf's beauty tells us as much about her as it does about him. The moonlight *seems to run in and out of his fur.*

▶ **13. Characterization of the Girls' Relationship:** Once again Laura protects Carrie. She tries to distract her with a race. This girl keeps her head no matter what's up.

- There, dark against the moonlight, stands a great wolf!

- He is looking toward her. The wind stirs his fur and the moonlight seems to run in and out of it.

- Laura turns, taking Carrie with her. She says they should go back.

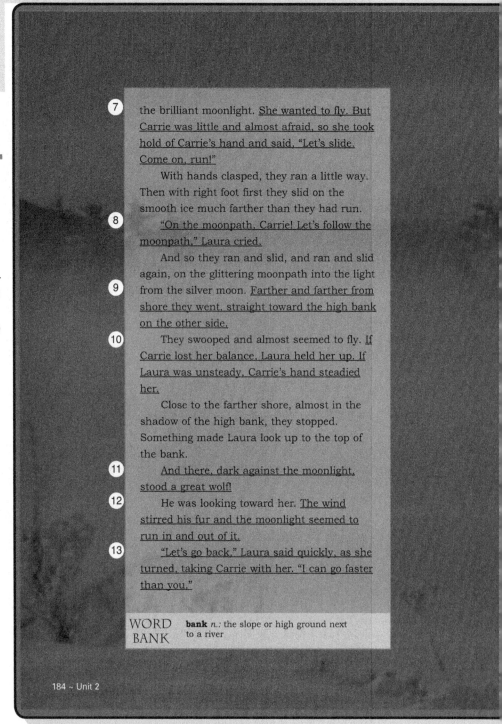

7   the brilliant moonlight. She wanted to fly. But Carrie was little and almost afraid, so she took hold of Carrie's hand and said, "Let's slide. Come on, run!"

With hands clasped, they ran a little way. Then with right foot first they slid on the smooth ice much farther than they had run.

8   "On the moonpath, Carrie! Let's follow the moonpath," Laura cried.

And so they ran and slid, and ran and slid again, on the glittering moonpath into the light from the silver moon.

9   Farther and farther from shore they went, straight toward the high bank on the other side.

10   They swooped and almost seemed to fly. If Carrie lost her balance, Laura held her up. If Laura was unsteady, Carrie's hand steadied her.

Close to the farther shore, almost in the shadow of the high bank, they stopped. Something made Laura look up to the top of the bank.

11   And there, dark against the moonlight, stood a great wolf!

12   He was looking toward her. The wind stirred his fur and the moonlight seemed to run in and out of it.

13   "Let's go back." Laura said quickly, as she turned, taking Carrie with her. "I can go faster than you."

WORD BANK   **bank** *n.:* the slope or high ground next to a river

GUIDING THE READING

LITERAL

Q: Why doesn't Laura fly?
A: Carrie is little and Laura feels she is almost afraid, so she takes her hand.

Q: What does Laura cry out to Carrie?
A: "On the moonpath, Carrie! Let's follow the moonpath."

Q: How do the girls behave towards each other when they are sliding across the ice?
A: They take care of each other, each one steadying the other.

Q: What does Laura see at the top of the bank?
A: A great wolf!

Q: What is the wolf doing?
A: It is standing (or sitting) there, dark against the moonlight. It is looking toward Laura.

ANALYTICAL

Q: What do you think is the effect of the repetition of the word *moonpath*?
A: Answers will vary.

Q: When the girls go farther and farther from shore, does that suggest anything to you?
A: Answers will vary. But those words set the stage for the next exciting move towards the climax!

Q: What do you think makes Laura look up to the top of the bank?
A: Answers will vary. But did you ever feel as though something or someone is looking at you? We seem to have a sixth sense...

Q: Does the way that Laura sees the wolf tell you anything about her?
A: Even when she is terrified, she sees the beauty of this creature.

Q: Why does Laura say to Carrie, "I can go faster than you"?
A: She is trying to distract her, so that Carrie won't even see the wolf and be frightened.

- Laura runs as fast as she can, but Carrie keeps up with her.
- Carrie pants that she saw it too.
- As they run and slide on the ice, Laura listens for a sound behind them, but there is none.

- They burst through the door into the front room and slam it behind them.
- "It was a wolf, Pa," Laura gulps.
- Pa asks where the wolf is.

- Laura says she doesn't know, it's gone.

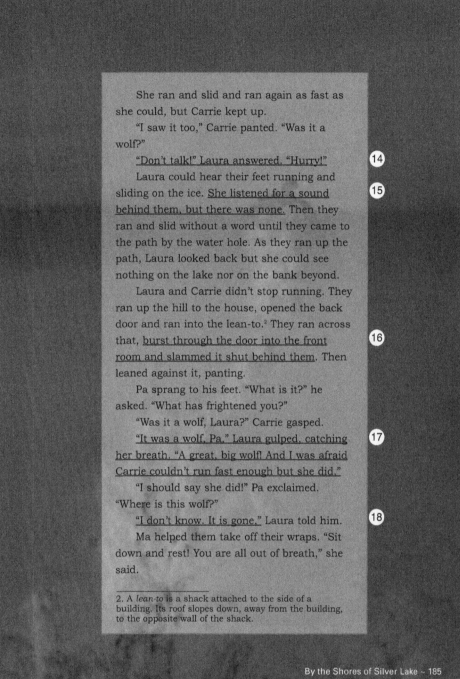

She ran and slid and ran again as fast as she could, but Carrie kept up.

"I saw it too," Carrie panted. "Was it a wolf?"

"Don't talk!" Laura answered. "Hurry!" 14

Laura could hear their feet running and sliding on the ice. She listened for a sound behind them, but there was none. Then they 15 ran and slid without a word until they came to the path by the water hole. As they ran up the path, Laura looked back but she could see nothing on the lake nor on the bank beyond.

Laura and Carrie didn't stop running. They ran up the hill to the house, opened the back door and ran into the lean-to.[2] They ran across that, burst through the door into the front 16 room and slammed it shut behind them. Then leaned against it, panting.

Pa sprang to his feet. "What is it?" he asked. "What has frightened you?"

"Was it a wolf, Laura?" Carrie gasped.

"It was a wolf, Pa." Laura gulped, catching 17 her breath. "A great, big wolf! And I was afraid Carrie couldn't run fast enough but she did."

"I should say she did!" Pa exclaimed. "Where is this wolf?"

"I don't know. It is gone." Laura told him. 18

Ma helped them take off their wraps. "Sit down and rest! You are all out of breath," she said.

---

2. A *lean-to* is a shack attached to the side of a building. Its roof slopes down, away from the building, to the opposite wall of the shack.

By the Shores of Silver Lake ~ 185

LITERARY COMPONENTS

▶ **14. Rising Tension:** Laura tells Carrie not to talk. "Hurry!"

▶ **15. Rising Tension; Plot:** She listens for a sound behind them, but there is none!

▶ **16. Resolution of Tension:** The girls burst through the door into the front room.

▶ **17. Plot:** The girls tell Pa and Ma what has happened.

▶ **18. Characterization:** Laura is reluctant to tell Pa of the wolf's whereabouts.

GUIDING THE READING

ANALYTICAL

Q: Do you think it has any special meaning that Laura tells Pa she doesn't know where the wolf is and that it is gone?

A: Answers will vary.

SUMMING UP THE PLOT

- Pa asks again, and Carrie says, "Up on the bank." Laura adds, "Across the lake."

- "We followed the moonpath," Laura tells him.

- Pa says he thought the wolves had gone. He will hunt them tomorrow.

- Laura tells him that she hopes he doesn't find the wolf. The wolf didn't chase them and he could have caught them.

LITERARY COMPONENTS

▶ **19. Characterization; Rising Action:** Pa blames himself and announces he will go hunt the wolves tomorrow.

▶ **20. New Character:** Their sister, Mary, is introduced for the first time in this scene.

▶ **21. Characterization:** Laura thinks to herself that if anything had happened to Carrie, it would have been her fault for taking her so far across the ice. In this family, *everyone* takes responsibility.

▶ **22. Repetition of Image of a Decent, Majestic Wolf:** Once again, we see the wolf through Laura's eyes.

▶ **23. Laura's Important Feelings; Theme:** "I hope you don't find the wolf, Pa."

▶ **24. Characterization of Ma:** Ma is just a no-nonsense person. "Why ever not?"

"Where was the wolf?" Pa wanted to know.

"Up on the bank," Carrie said, and Laura added, "The high bank across the lake."

"Did you girls go clear there?" Pa asked in surprise. "And ran all the way back after you saw him! I had no idea you would go so far. It is a good half-mile."

"We followed the moonpath," Laura told him. Pa looked at her strangely. "You would!" he said. (19) <u>"I thought those wolves had gone. It was careless of me. I'll hunt them tomorrow."</u>

(20) <u>Mary sat still, but her face was white.</u> "Oh, girls," she almost whispered. "Suppose he had caught you!"

Then they all sat silent while Laura and Carrie rested.

Laura was glad to be safe in the warm room with the desolate prairie shut out. (21) <u>If anything had happened to Carrie, it would have been her fault for taking her so far across the lake.</u>

(22) But nothing had happened. <u>She could almost see again the great wolf with the wind ruffling the moonlight on his fur.</u>

"Pa!" she said in a low voice.

"Yes, Laura?" Pa answered.

(23) <u>"I hope you don't find the wolf, Pa."</u> Laura said.

(24) <u>"Why ever not?" Ma wondered.</u>

"Because he didn't chase us," Laura told

WORD BANK **desolate** (DEH suh lut) *adj.*: empty, deserted, and lonely

186 ~ Unit 2

GUIDING THE READING

LITERAL

Q: Who tells Pa where they saw the wolf the second time he asks?
A: Carrie does. Then Laura explains further.

Q: What does Pa say he is going to do about the wolf?
A: He says he is going to go out tomorrow and hunt it.

Q: Which new character appears in this scene?
A: Mary, another sister, speaks for the first time.

ANALYTICAL

Q: Why/how does Pa blame himself?
A: He says he was careless to have assumed that the wolves were gone. Also, he is a person that takes responsibility.

Q: Why does Laura think it would have been her fault if anything had happened to Carrie?
A: Carrie is her younger sister, and so Laura is responsible for her well-being when they are alone together. It was Laura who took Carrie across the lake to the other bank. Also, Laura is a person who takes responsibility.

- A long, wild, wolf howl rises and fades away on the stillness. Another answers it.
- Laura's heart seems to turn over with a sickening flop.
- Ma tells the girls it's bedtime and gives them their hot flatirons to warm their bed.

LITERARY COMPONENTS

▶ **25. Characterization of Laura; Theme:** *Treat Others as They Have Treated You.* The wolf did not bother them and they shouldn't bother the wolf.

▶ **26. Poignant Moment; Onomatopoeia:** A long, wild wolf *howl* is answered by its mate. These wolves are old, loyal companions.

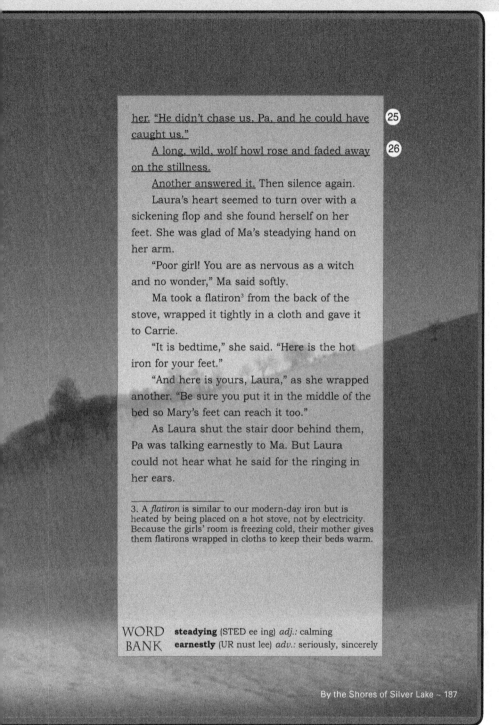

her. "He didn't chase us, Pa, and he could have caught us." **25**

A long, wild, wolf howl rose and faded away on the stillness. **26**

Another answered it. Then silence again.

Laura's heart seemed to turn over with a sickening flop and she found herself on her feet. She was glad of Ma's steadying hand on her arm.

"Poor girl! You are as nervous as a witch and no wonder," Ma said softly.

Ma took a flatiron³ from the back of the stove, wrapped it tightly in a cloth and gave it to Carrie.

"It is bedtime," she said. "Here is the hot iron for your feet."

"And here is yours, Laura," as she wrapped another. "Be sure you put it in the middle of the bed so Mary's feet can reach it too."

As Laura shut the stair door behind them, Pa was talking earnestly to Ma. But Laura could not hear what he said for the ringing in her ears.

---

3. A *flatiron* is similar to our modern-day iron but is heated by being placed on a hot stove, not by electricity. Because the girls' room is freezing cold, their mother gives them flatirons wrapped in cloths to keep their beds warm.

WORD BANK
steadying (STED ee ing) *adj.*: calming
earnestly (UR nust lee) *adv.*: seriously, sincerely

By the Shores of Silver Lake ~ 187

GUIDING THE READING

LITERAL
Q: After they talk with their parents about meeting the wolf, what do the girls do?
A: They go to bed.

ANALYTICAL
Q: Why does Laura say she hopes her father doesn't find the wolf?
A: The wolf could have chased them and caught them and it didn't.

Q: Do you think Laura has another reason for not wanting the wolf killed?
A: Answers will vary. Laura is very taken with the wolf. He has made a strong impression on her. She feels a sense of connection with the wolf. There is something about the wolf that she understands and that does not bear articulating.

SUMMING UP THE PLOT

- After breakfast the next morning, Pa takes his gun and sets out.
- All that morning, Laura is listening for a shot and not wanting to hear it.
- All that morning she remembers the great wolf sitting quietly in the moonlight that shimmered through his thick fur.
- Pa returns late for dinner. He apologizes and says he went farther than he had intended.
- Mary asks how far he went, and he says better than ten miles—the wolf tracks led him a chase.

LITERARY COMPONENTS

▶ **27. Rising Tension; Characterization; Theme; Image:** All morning Laura listens for the shot that she does not want to hear. Once again she remembers "the great wolf sitting quiet in the moonlight that shimmered through his thick fur." There are important and wonderful words in this passage, that increase our liking of the wolf: *great, quiet, shimmer,* and *thick.* This is how writers weave a spell and move their readers.

▶ **28. Rising Tension; Literary Ploy:** After Pa comes home, it takes a whole paragraph for him to settle in, while we (and Laura) are waiting to hear what happened.

Pa Finds The Homestead[4]

27 After breakfast next morning Pa took his gun and set out. All that morning Laura was listening for a shot and not wanting to hear it. All morning she remembered the great wolf sitting quiet in the moonlight that shimmered through his thick fur.

28 Pa was late for dinner. It was long past noon when he stamped the snow from his feet in the lean-to. He came in and put his gun on the wall, and hung his cap and coat on their nail. His mittens he hung, by their thumbs, to dry on the line behind the stove. Then he washed his face and hands in the tin basin on the bench, and before the small glass that hung above it he combed his hair and his beard.

"Sorry I kept dinner waiting, Caroline," he said. "I was gone longer than I thought. Went farther than I intended."

"It doesn't matter, Charles; I've kept dinner warm," Ma replied. "Come to the table, girls! Don't keep Pa waiting."

"How far did you go, Pa?" Mary asked.

"Better than ten miles, all told," said Pa. "Those wolf tracks led me a chase."

"Did you get the wolf, Pa?" Carrie wanted to know. Laura did not say anything.

---

4. A *homestead* is a piece of land on which a house can be built. In 1862, President Abraham Lincoln signed the Homestead Act. According to this new law, anyone who lived and worked on an area of government-owned land could become its owner. A settler was given 160 acres of land to farm in return for living on the land for five years.

WORD BANK — **shimmered** *v.*: glowed and softly shone with a flickering light
glass *n.*: mirror

188 ~ Unit 2

GUIDING THE READING

LITERAL
Q: What does Laura wait for all morning?
A: She waits for the gunshot that she doesn't want to hear.

Q: What does Mary ask Pa? What does he answer?
A: She asks how far he went. He tells her better than ten miles.

ANALYTICAL
Q: Why do you think the author devotes so much attention to what Pa does when he gets home?
A: She is slowing things down, making us wait for what we want to know. Although she is giving us interesting information and making the story fuller, she is deliberately creating suspense.

SUMMING UP THE PLOT

- "You found the wolf," Carrie says confidently. Laura's food is choking her. She can hardly swallow the smallest mouthful.

- "I found the wolves' *den*," says Pa. And the biggest wolf tracks he's ever seen.

- Pa tells the family that "there were two big buffalo wolves at that den last night."

- He says that their tracks were fresh, and

- from their size he figures they are not young wolves.

- The den is an old one that they must have lived in for years. However, they had not been living there this winter.

- He says that the wolves came down from the northwest yesterday evening and went straight to the den. They stayed till this morning.

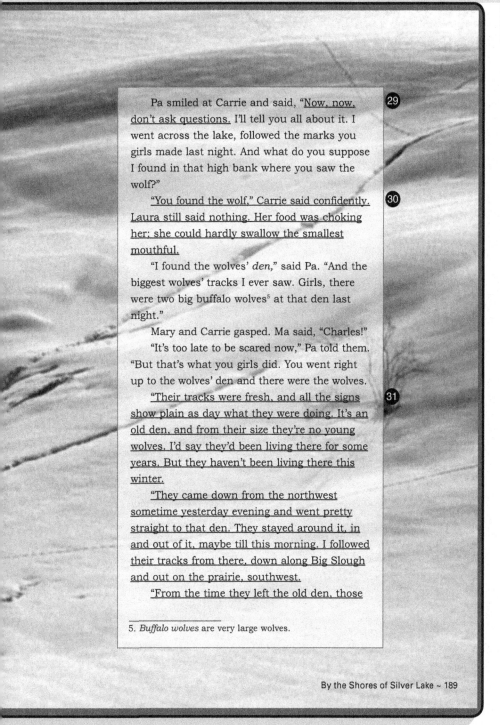

Pa smiled at Carrie and said, "Now, now, don't ask questions. I'll tell you all about it. I went across the lake, followed the marks you girls made last night. And what do you suppose I found in that high bank where you saw the wolf?"

"You found the wolf," Carrie said confidently. Laura still said nothing. Her food was choking her; she could hardly swallow the smallest mouthful.

"I found the wolves' *den*," said Pa. "And the biggest wolves' tracks I ever saw. Girls, there were two big buffalo wolves⁵ at that den last night."

Mary and Carrie gasped. Ma said, "Charles!"

"It's too late to be scared now," Pa told them. "But that's what you girls did. You went right up to the wolves' den and there were the wolves.

"Their tracks were fresh, and all the signs show plain as day what they were doing. It's an old den, and from their size they're no young wolves. I'd say they'd been living there for some years. But they haven't been living there this winter.

"They came down from the northwest sometime yesterday evening and went pretty straight to that den. They stayed around it, in and out of it, maybe till this morning. I followed their tracks from there, down along Big Slough and out on the prairie, southwest.

"From the time they left the old den, those

---
5. *Buffalo wolves* are very large wolves.

By the Shores of Silver Lake ~ 189

LITERARY COMPONENTS

▶ **29. Rising Tension; Drawing Out the Moment:** Even when Carrie finally asks, Pa tells her not to ask questions!

▶ **30. Contrast Between Carrie and Laura; Rising Tension; Image:** Carrie just wants to know and is enthusiastic about whatever information Pa brings. Laura cannot swallow. Her not being able to swallow her food very powerfully conveys her deep feelings about this.

▶ **31. Solving the Mystery of the Wolves, a Subplot:** Pa fills us in about the wolves for the next three paragraphs.

GUIDING THE READING

LITERAL

Q: As Pa begins the story, Laura is eating. What happens to her?
A: Her food is choking her and she can hardly swallow—even the smallest mouthful.

Q: What did Pa find in the high bank where the girls saw the wolf?
A: He found the wolves' den.

Q: Which kind of wolves does Pa say these wolves were?
A: He says that they were buffalo wolves.

Q: Were the wolves living in the den the evening before, when Laura saw the wolf? Explain. How long did they remain in the vicinity of the den?
A: No, they had not been living there. According to Pa, they may have lived there before. But the wolves had come down from the northwest last night, the night that Laura and the wolf saw each other, stayed until the morning, and left.

SUMMING UP THE PLOT

- Pa continues his story. "I followed their tracks from there.... From the time they left the old den, those wolves never stopped. They trotted along side by side...."

- He says he followed them far enough to be sure he couldn't get a shot at them. "They've left for good."

- Laura takes a deep breath, as though she has forgotten to breathe until now.

- Ma wonders what they were doing at that old den.

- Pa believes they used to live there before the hunters killed the last buffalo.

- Pa says that buffalo wolves were all over the country once, but there are not many left now.

- He says that those two wolves came straight from the west and went straight back west. They stopped for one night at the old den.

LITERARY COMPONENTS

▶ **32. Emotional Turning Point:** Laura breathes a sigh of relief.

▶ **33. Mystery Remains:** Pa's answer really doesn't solve the double mystery of the wolves' return, and their returning for only one night, but provides some sad information regarding an ecosystem.

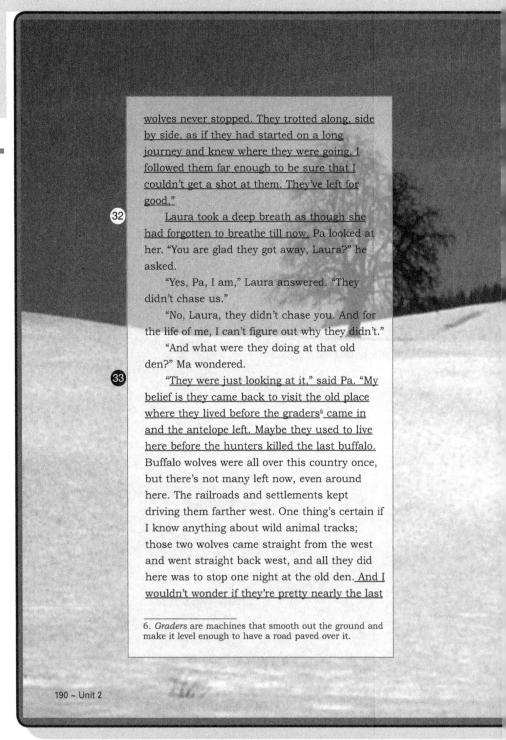

wolves never stopped. They trotted along, side by side, as if they had started on a long journey and knew where they were going. I followed them far enough to be sure that I couldn't get a shot at them. They've left for good."

(32)   Laura took a deep breath as though she had forgotten to breathe till now. Pa looked at her. "You are glad they got away, Laura?" he asked.

"Yes, Pa, I am," Laura answered. "They didn't chase us."

"No, Laura, they didn't chase you. And for the life of me, I can't figure out why they didn't."

"And what were they doing at that old den?" Ma wondered.

(33)   "They were just looking at it," said Pa. "My belief is they came back to visit the old place where they lived before the graders[6] came in and the antelope left. Maybe they used to live here before the hunters killed the last buffalo. Buffalo wolves were all over this country once, but there's not many left now, even around here. The railroads and settlements kept driving them farther west. One thing's certain if I know anything about wild animal tracks; those two wolves came straight from the west and went straight back west, and all they did here was to stop one night at the old den. And I wouldn't wonder if they're pretty nearly the last

---

6. *Graders* are machines that smooth out the ground and make it level enough to have a road paved over it.

190 ~ Unit 2

GUIDING THE READING

LITERAL

Q: What does Laura say, when Pa asks if she is glad the wolves got away?
A: She says that she is, that the wolves hadn't chased them.

Q: According to Pa, what kept driving the wolves farther west?
A: The railroads and the settlements.

ANALYTICAL

Q: Why did the wolves originally leave the region?
A: They left because the hunters killed all of the buffalo and the antelope were forced out by the graders.

- The wolves may be the last buffalo wolves that will ever be seen in this part of the country.
- Laura mourns, "Oh, Pa, the poor wolves."

- Ma says that there is enough to be sorry for, without being sorry for the feelings of wild beasts.
- Pa says he's got some news. While tracking the wolves, he found their homestead.

- Mary and Laura and Carrie ask, excited, "Oh, where, Pa!?"
- Pa tells them that it is just right in every way.
- There's a rise in the prairie to the south of the slough that will make a nice place to build. And it's near the townsite, so the girls can go to school.
- Ma says, "I'm glad, Charles."

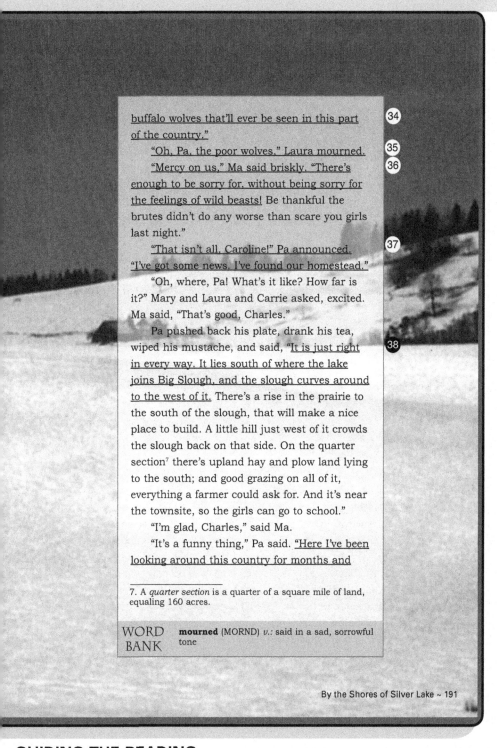

buffalo wolves that'll ever be seen in this part of the country." ③④

"Oh, Pa, the poor wolves," Laura mourned. ③⑤

"Mercy on us," Ma said briskly. "There's ③⑥ enough to be sorry for, without being sorry for the feelings of wild beasts! Be thankful the brutes didn't do any worse than scare you girls last night."

"That isn't all, Caroline!" Pa announced. ③⑦ "I've got some news. I've found our homestead."

"Oh, where, Pa! What's it like? How far is it?" Mary and Laura and Carrie asked, excited. Ma said, "That's good, Charles."

Pa pushed back his plate, drank his tea, wiped his mustache, and said, "It is just right ③⑧ in every way. It lies south of where the lake joins Big Slough, and the slough curves around to the west of it. There's a rise in the prairie to the south of the slough, that will make a nice place to build. A little hill just west of it crowds the slough back on that side. On the quarter section[7] there's upland hay and plow land lying to the south; and good grazing on all of it, everything a farmer could ask for. And it's near the townsite, so the girls can go to school."

"I'm glad, Charles," said Ma.

"It's a funny thing," Pa said. "Here I've been looking around this country for months and

---

7. A *quarter section* is a quarter of a square mile of land, equaling 160 acres.

WORD BANK — **mourned** (MORND) *v.:* said in a sad, sorrowful tone

By the Shores of Silver Lake ~ 191

LITERARY COMPONENTS

▶ **34. Eco Information:** Pa says he wouldn't wonder if they're the last buffalo wolves that will ever be seen in this part of the country. According to the Defenders of Wildlife, "When Europeans first set foot on North America, the gray wolf ranged across the continent from Mexico's Central Plateau to Canada and Alaska's low Arctic, and from the Pacific Ocean to the Atlantic Coast." The red wolf lived in forests from southern Pennsylvania to Florida and from the Mississippi delta to the Atlantic. It is estimated that prior to European contact, their populations together numbered 400,000. By the 1970s, "three centuries of hunting had eliminated wolves of both species from the wild *everywhere* in the contiguous United States except in northeastern Minnesota, where fewer than 1000 gray wolves remained."

▶ **35. Characterization; Theme:** Laura mourns for the wolves.

▶ **36. Characterization:** Ma is a no-nonsense person. Their lifestyle, living in those times, means that she works very hard, long hours, and must be very disciplined.

▶ **37. Climax; Plot:** Pa has found a homestead.

▶ **38. Resolution:** The story comes to resolution in Pa's description of the homestead for which they have apparently all waited.

GUIDING THE READING

LITERAL

Q: What does Pa announce?
A: He says he has found a homestead.

Q: Where is the homestead?
A: It lies south of where the lake joins Big Slough, and the slough curves around to the west of it.

ANALYTICAL

Q: Why does Laura mourn?
A: Laura expresses deep regret and sorrow when Pa says, "I wouldn't wonder if they're pretty nearly the last buffalo wolves that'll ever be seen in this part of the country."

Q: Why isn't Ma more sympathetic to the wolves?
A: Answers will vary.

SUMMING UP THE PLOT

- Pa says that here he'd been looking for a homestead for months, and there was a quarter section that exactly suited him all the time.

- He says he probably wouldn't have come across

it at all, if the wolf chase hadn't taken him across the lake and down along the slough on that side.

LITERARY COMPONENTS

▶ **39. Theme:** Pa says it's a funny thing that he's been looking for months and there it was, lying there all the time. "I wouldn't have come across it at all, if this wolf chase hadn't taken me across the lake and down the slough on that side."

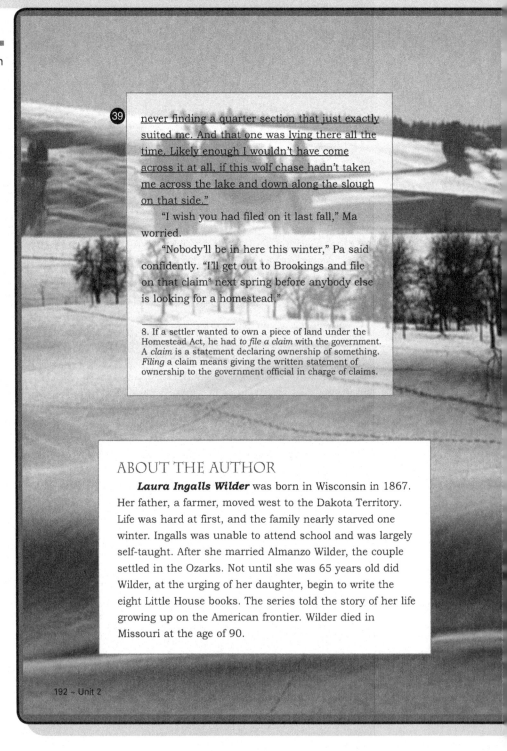

39 never finding a quarter section that just exactly suited me. And that one was lying there all the time. Likely enough I wouldn't have come across it at all, if this wolf chase hadn't taken me across the lake and down along the slough on that side."

"I wish you had filed on it last fall," Ma worried.

"Nobody'll be in here this winter," Pa said confidently. "I'll get out to Brookings and file on that claim⁸ next spring before anybody else is looking for a homestead."

8. If a settler wanted to own a piece of land under the Homestead Act, he had *to file a claim* with the government. A *claim* is a statement declaring ownership of something. *Filing* a claim means giving the written statement of ownership to the government official in charge of claims.

ABOUT THE AUTHOR

Laura Ingalls Wilder was born in Wisconsin in 1867. Her father, a farmer, moved west to the Dakota Territory. Life was hard at first, and the family nearly starved one winter. Ingalls was unable to attend school and was largely self-taught. After she married Almanzo Wilder, the couple settled in the Ozarks. Not until she was 65 years old did Wilder, at the urging of her daughter, begin to write the eight Little House books. The series told the story of her life growing up on the American frontier. Wilder died in Missouri at the age of 90.

192 ~ Unit 2

CREATING & WRITING (P. 193)

7. Student answers will vary.

8. Give students the guidance they need for a short research paper. You may want to have students select different topics, so everyone doesn't write about the same short wolf summary. You may want to contact Defenders of Wildlife ahead of time, and have them send you materials. They can also refer you to other sources.

9. Have the students write their lists and jot down notes next to each item. Call on several of the students to read their lists and ask them to explain why they have chosen these items. A discussion of what things children of those days were likely to own would be interesting. Also, the children may wish to comment on what items would hold up or be of use in the wilderness.

FIRST IMPRESSIONS

Ask your students what would be the good features and what they would not like.

QUICK REVIEW

1. The Ingalls live in the largely unsettled Dakota Territory, far from any other people. The time is the late 1800s. It is winter and it is nighttime.

2. The Ingalls family includes Ma (Caroline Ingalls) and Pa (Charles Ingalls), and Laura, Mary, and Carrie, their daughters.

3. Pa plays the fiddle.

4. Laura and Carrie wear wool coats, wool hoods, wool mittens, wool mufflers, and wool dresses. They have new shoes with thick soles. Their stockings are knit from woolen yarn. They are also wearing red flannel underclothes that come down over their knees and are buttoned around each stocking. Their petticoats are made of thick flannel.

Studying the Selection

FIRST IMPRESSIONS

Would you like to live as the Ingalls family lives?

QUICK REVIEW

1. What is the setting of the story? Setting includes the place and the time. Give the approximate year, the season, and the time of day.

2. Who are the characters?

3. What does *this* family do when they want to hear music?

4. Which clothes do Laura and Carrie wear outside in the cold?

FOCUS

5. Explain in several sentences why Laura does not want her father to kill the wolf.

6. Choose one of the literary components we studied in Unit Two and answer one of the following questions:

   • What are the conflicts in the story? (conflict)

   • List the sequence of events. Try to limit yourself to ten events. (sequence)

   • Which events led the father to their future homestead? (cause and effect)

   • Did you predict the end of the story? Which clues pointed to it? (predicting)

CREATING & WRITING

7. In one or two paragraphs, write what lesson you think the story teaches.

8. Wolves are fascinating animals. They have a very strong family unit. The mother and father who lead a wolf pack remain together for all of their lives. Find out about wolves. Write a two-paragraph report.

9. Your family is moving West in a covered wagon. Your parents have loaded furniture and household goods onto the wagon. You may choose five items to take along. Write a list and explain why these things are special to you.

By the Shores of Silver Lake ~ 193

FOCUS

5. Answers will vary. She and the wolf have looked at each other. This means that the wolf is real to her, not just something she has heard about. She sees that he is a "great" wolf, and that "the moonlight seem[s] to run in and out of" his coat. She may think he is beautiful and have respect or regard for him as a living creature.

   The wolf did not chase them. It let them go, when it could have killed them. Perhaps she thinks that the wolf should not be punished for simply being there. More to the point, why should the wolf be punished when it did not hurt them? How can that be just?

   Finally, if the wolf is killed, then Laura may feel it will be her fault, because she told her father where he was.

6. Answer one of the following questions.

   • What are the conflicts in the story? (**conflict**) When Laura sees the wolf and the children flee, there is an external conflict of man vs. nature. She has an internal conflict, because she does not want the wolf to be killed, but she is only a child—there's little she could do to stop it—and she respects her father's decision. She is fairly quiet about this, because there certainly is a potential for an external conflict with her mother and father (a conflict of man vs. man). One cannot imagine Laura arguing with them.

   • List the **sequence of events**. Try to limit yourself to fifteen events. These events also include important emotional events.

   Laura and her sister Carrie go outside at night and go sliding on the ice. They follow the moonpath and go farther and farther from their side of the lake. Laura looks up at the bank on the far shore, and in the moonlight stands a great wolf! The children race home, but the wolf does not follow them. They arrive home breathless and tell their parents about the wolf. Laura tells her father that she hopes he

doesn't find the wolf, because he didn't chase them. The next morning Pa goes out to track the wolf. When he returns, he starts to tell them what occurred. Laura is eating and cannot swallow the smallest mouthful. Pa says he found the wolves' den—the den of two big buffalo wolves. He followed the tracks of the two wolves trotting side by side for ten miles; as if they started on a long journey and knew where they were going. He says he wouldn't wonder that those are the last buffalo wolves that'll ever be seen in this part of the country. There's no more buffalo. Laura says, "Oh,

Pa, the poor wolves." Her mother says there's enough to be sorry for without being sorry for wild beasts. Then Pa tells them that he has found their homestead while he was out looking for the wolves.

   • Which events lead the father to their future homestead? (**cause and effect**) The girls play outside. They see a wolf. Pa goes hunting for the wolf to kill it. The wolf and its mate have traveled all night and gone a great distance. While following their tracks, Pa finds the perfect spot for a homestead. Students do not have to give the entire train

of events, as above. They may just say something like, "Pa has to go out and track a wolf. Because the wolf has traveled far, Pa comes across a place he has not seen before."

   • Did you predict the end of the story? Which clues pointed to it? (**predicting**) Some students may figure that the story would end with finding a homestead, since they are living in a surveyor's house. Some students may realize that Pa will not kill the wolf, because such an ending to the story would go against Laura's deep feelings. Students may have other answers and clues.

A NICHE IN THE KITCHEN

Ouida Sebestyen

Some days my mother asks me,
How can she possibly cook
With me underfoot, and her
Cookbook full of pressed flowers,
5 And clay on the rolling-pin
From projects I'm doing at all hours
There in her kitchen?

She says, how can she move around
Anymore, surrounded by hobbies
10 And models and crafts and
Tools and messes, no matter
Which end she works in?

I tell her I don't know.
it's just more fun when I'm
15 Larking around in the kitchen,
Working where she's working and
Making things while she's baking things.

She says, yes, but where can she stand
Without standing in the spot where,
20 For instance, I'm sanding a new bird-feeder?
I tell her I don't know, but
I need her a lot. For company.
I keep saying I'd rather be
There where she's dicing carrots
25 And icing éclairs, in the kitchen,
Than making things upstairs.
Or anywhere.

She just glares.

So I say, can't I have even one
30 Little niche in the kitchen?
Even if I'm a bother? Please?
Even when I'm not helping? I say,
I don't mind getting down on my knees
To pick up any split peas that scatter,
35 (Won't they make a beanbag?) while she
Lets the hamburgers spatter
And tries to answer the phone.

GETTING STARTED

Group your class into teams. Each team is going to make as many words as it can from the word *kitchen*. Make sure each group has the word written down, as it will be easier to mentally manipulate the letters. Their words must have a minimum of two letters. Whichever team comes up with the most words wins. You will have to figure out what exactly the winning team wins! The point of the exercise is for students to see, with your help if need be, that *niche* is one of those words. We came up with 38 and have probably missed some.

chin	chink	chit
etch	he	hen
hick	hike	hint
hit	ice	ick
in	inch	ink
it	itch	ken
kin	kit	kite
kith	knit	neck
niche	nice	nick
net	tech	ten
the	then	thick
thicken	tic	tick

tike (variant spelling of *tyke*, a small child)
tine

Reusing consonants in a different order than the one in which they first appear is a form of repetition. Partial anagrams can be a lot of fun, both to make and to find. Using *niche* near *kitchen* is an example.

Language Alert: Poetry Is Hard Enough for Some Folks! Make Sure Your Students Know What *Every* Word in the Poem Means!

Have students read the poem through, as you read it aloud to them. Their job, at this point, is to find each word they are not absolutely certain of, and to write it down. Either in class or for homework, have them look up each of the mystery words, and write down the definition. After the students have made their lists, talk about which words were confusing to members of the class, and what their definitions are. Do your students feel truly comfortable with the words now?

Keep in mind that sometimes people know what individual words mean, but they don't know what is being talked about. For example, the speaker of the poem mentions *pressed flowers* in Line 4. Do your students know what pressed flowers are? Have they ever pressed any flowers?

• Does everyone know what a *rolling-pin* is?
• Does everyone know what you do when you *sand* a new bird-feeder? (Smooth by grinding or rubbing with an abrasive; to rub or polish with sandpaper. *Abrasives* are natural or manufactured substances used to grind, wear down, rub away, smooth, scour, clean, or polish.)
• What do carrots look like after they are *diced*? (Clue: a *die* is a small cube)
• Has everyone eaten an *éclair* at one point or another?

Here are some of our words:
niche, which comes from Latin, through French, and originally meant *a nest*. A *niche* is a recess in a wall; a hiding place or retreat resembling a niche in its formation or privacy; *also,* a site or habitat supplying all that is needed for the successful existence of an organism or species. We like this last best for the speaker of this poem.

larking means behaving in a mischievous way or *sportively* (in such a way as to make oneself—and hopefully others—merry)

tooling leather is ornamenting it in various ways: attaching other things to the surface of the leather or decorating it by painting, cutting, or stamping

crewelwork is a type of embroidery

Literary Devices

Poets use sound to bring the reader into their poem. Some of these literary devices are just the repetition of letters. In fact there are three ways that poets repeat letters. (1) Repetition of the *initial* consonant sound of words; (2) repetition of consonant sounds and consonant combinations *within* words; and (3) repetition of the vowel sounds *within* words in a line or stanza.

As we have said above, reusing consonants in a different order than the one in which they first appear is a form of repetition. In a compound word such as *underfoot* or *cookbook*, the first letter of the second word of the compound (*foot* and *book* in this instance) can be considered an initial consonant.

Here are examples of each type from the first stanza:
(1) *With me underfoot, and her / Cookbook full of pressed flowers ...*
(2) *Cookbook full of pressed flowers, / And clay on the rolling pin / From projects I'm doing at all hours*
(3) *How can she possibly cook, With me underfoot, and her / Cookbook full of...*

The repetition of the same initial consonant sound within a poem or a passage of prose is called **alliteration.** The repetition of internal consonants is called **consonance.** The repetition of internal vowel sounds is called **assonance**. We supply these terms for your own use. You class may not be at a high enough level for you to use such terms with your students. But the names of these things are not important. Being able to perceive them *is.*

Another form of poetic repetition is the simple repetition of the same words. We see this in *cook / With me underfoot, and her / Cookbook...* (Lines 2-4) and in *Working where she's working and . . .* (Line 16). The plain repetition is nicely juxtaposed with actual rhymes that just pop up any old place!

Remember that **rhyme** is the repetition of accented vowel sounds and all the sounds following them in words that are close together in a poem. In this poem, they may not be so close together. Rhyme is the correspondence of the terminal sounds of two or more words or lines of verse. *A Niche in the Kitchen* is characterized by overlapping rhymes. For example, take Lines 23-28:

> *I keep saying I'd rather be*
> *There where she's dicing carrots*
> *And icing éclairs in the kitchen,*
> *Than making things upstairs,*
> *Or anywhere.*
> *She just glares.*

The rhyming groups are *there, where, anywhere; dicing, icing; éclairs, upstairs, glares.* The third group begins with *éclairs* before the first group finishes with *anywhere.* If we consider the first and third groups one group—with the words ending in **s** an imperfect or slant rhyme—then there is even greater overlap with group two stuck right in the middle.

INTO "A NICHE IN THE KITCHEN"

This poem is about the way it feels to work in the kitchen when your mom is there preparing food. And it's about the way it feels to be a mom or dad working in the kitchen with your children there also working, interfering with what you are doing, irritating you and giving you great pleasure.

For many of us, the kitchen is what we remember about childhood—not the living room, the den, or the dining room. The kitchen is the location of good smells—powerful drivers of intense memories and intense feelings.

In the poem, mom wants her child to get out of her way so she can get done what she needs to get done. But then it turns out that, on reflection, mom doesn't really want her child to go—"that time will come soon enough" (meaning, *too soon*).

Some may find this kid a little too creative to be true. Not to spoil the poem for anyone, but, after all, how many kids perform all of these operations in such quick succession: pressing flowers (in a cook book); rolling clay (with a rolling pin); making models; sanding a new bird-feeder (which this child has no doubt made him- or herself); making a wallet with a leather kit; stringing beads; gluing seeds to plaques; illustrating books; squashing papier-mâché in a tray; baking a mask in the oven; and drying a poster.

This mom also takes on a lot at once. (Maybe that's where the kid got it.) She's dicing carrots, frying hamburgers, making a cookie batter, slicing bologna, spicing applesauce, doing something with tomato paste, stringing beans, preparing a layer cake, shaking steak in flour, frying bacon, and baking bread, apparently simultaneously.

This child is also wonderfully expressive of the love it feels for its mother.

I tell her I don't know.
It's just more fun when I'm
Larking around in the kitchen,
Working where she's working . . . (Lines 13-16)

I tell her I don't know, but
I need her a lot. For company. (Lines 21-22)

I explain to her, well, it's just nicer
Knowing she's right on my heels
Behind me... (Lines 44-46)

A Niche in the Kitchen is about the way that loving relationships between parents and children provide a *biological* niche for children, one in which they get all the food and drink and oxygen and love they need to be healthy plants.

POETRY

A NICHE IN THE KITCHEN

Ouida Sebestyen

Some days my mother asks me,
How can she possibly cook
With me underfoot, and her
Cookbook full of pressed flowers,
5 And clay on the rolling-pin
From projects I'm doing at all hours
There in her kitchen?

She says, how can she move around
Anymore, surrounded by hobbies
10 And models and crafts and
Tools and messes, no matter
Which end she works in?

I tell her I don't know.
It's just more fun when I'm
15 Larking around in the kitchen,
Working where she's working and
Making things while she's baking things.

She says, yes, but where can she stand
Without standing in the spot where,
20 For instance, I'm sanding a new bird-feeder?
I tell her I don't know, but
I need her a lot. For company.
I keep saying I'd rather be
There where she's dicing carrots
25 And icing éclairs, in the kitchen,
Than making things upstairs.
Or anywhere.

She just glares.

So I say, can't I have even one
30 Little niche in the kitchen?
Even if I'm a bother? Please?
Even when I'm not helping? I say,
I don't mind getting down on my knees
To pick up any split peas that scatter,
35 (Won't they make a beanbag?) while she
Lets the hamburgers spatter
And tries to answer the phone.

A Niche in the Kitchen ~ 195

LITERARY COMPONENTS

▶ **1. Exposition; Characters; Plot; Conflict; Syntactical Structure:** In Lines 1-7, we meet the narrator and his mother. The setting is the present time (the narrator uses the present tense), and the action is set in a kitchen. We are introduced to the basic conflict: The narrator wants to be in the kitchen "at all hours," working on all kinds of projects, and how can mother cook, if the narrator is underfoot. Lines 1-7 are one sentence, a question mother asks.

▶ **2. Assonance (Internal Vowel Sounds):** The sound of the double **oo** is replicated in *cook, underfoot,* and *cookbook.*

▶ **3. End Rhymes:** In Lines 4 and 6, *flowers* rhymes with *hours.* In Lines 5 and 7, *-pin* rhymes with *kit-chen.*

▶ **4. Syntactical Structure; Repetition of Word Root:** Lines 8-12 are one sentence—again a question mother asks. In Lines 8-9 we read, *She says, how can she move ar**ound** / Anymore, surr**ound**ed by hobbies.* The repeated use of the word *and* in Lines 10-11 makes these obstacles really add up for mom.

▶ **5. Characterization; Theme; Syntax:** This kid likes mom (Lines 13-17). S/he answers her in two sentences.

▶ **6. New Expression:** *Larking around* means fooling around, playing, being mischievous (Line 15).

▶ **7. Repetition; Rhyme:** In Lines 16-17, ***Working*** *where she's* ***working*** *and /* ***Making*** *things while she's* ***baking*** *things.*

▶ **8. Rising Action; Syntax; Repetition of Word; Rhyme:** She answers, again, in one sentence that's a question.... *where can she* ***stand*** */ Without* ***stand**ing in the spot where, / For instance, I'm* ***sand**ing...*

▶ **9. Characterization; Theme; Syntax:** This is a child who has the integrity and courage to discuss feelings (Lines 21-22). Notice the break and new sentence, *For company.* It is not a complete sentence and it is powerful.

▶ **10. Alliteration & Consonance:** In Lines 22-25, notice the k sound of *company, keep, carrots, éclairs, kitchen.*

▶ **11. Rhymes:** In Lines 24-28, *There where* with *anywhere; dicing* and *icing;* and *éclairs* with *upstairs* and *glares.*

▶ **12. Syntax:** Notice that when Line 28 is set off by itself, it really stands out, as if the line itself were glaring (at us!).

▶ **13. Rising Action; Center of Poem:** Here the narrator pleads with mother. That makes this stanza (Lines 29-41) different from all the others.

▶ **14. Interwoven Rhymes; Assonance:** *Please* (Line 31) with *knees* (Line 33) and *peas* (Line 34), which have the same internal vowel sound as *beanbag* (Line 35), are the first group. *Scatter* (Line 34) with *spatter* (Line 36) and *batter* (all the way down at Line 40) are the second group. Then *phone* (Line 37) with *alone* (Line 41) and *Joan* (next stanza, Line 43).

▶ **15. Double Entendre:** Line 33 has ambiguity in meaning because the narrator is begging and then says *I don't mind getting down on my knees.* Well, that's what people do when they are begging someone else for something. But then the narrator finishes that thought on the next line with *To pick up any split peas that scatter.*

LITERARY COMPONENTS

▶ **16. Slang:** Kids may not use it today, but the word *neater* as used here (Line 38) means more wonderful, finer.

▶ **17. Characterization; Theme:** In Lines 44-51, the kid tells mom that it's just nicer to be with her, with her doing whatever she's doing.

▶ **18. Rhyme:** There's lots of rhyme here, some of it end rhyme (Lines 45-55) that goes beyond the stanza: *heels* with *feels*; *slicing* with *spicing*; *applesauce* with *boss*; *stuff* with *enough* and back to *stuff*; and *go* with *no*.

▶ **19. Turning Point of Poem:** Mom says that time will come soon enough.

▶ **20. Rhyme, Assonance, Consonance; Repetition:** In Lines 57-67, the following words rhyme or share vowel or consonant sounds: *taste* with *paste* and *lace*, *tooling* and *cooling*, *bea*ds and *bea*ns and *seed*s, and *plaques* with *racks*. For repetition of words there is *string* and *strings*.

▶ **21. Play on Words:** *I string beads / While she strings beans.*

▶ **22. Subplot:** Mom recalls what it was like when she was young. (Lines 68-76)

ANALYZING THE POEM

A Niche in the Kitchen is a free verse poem with lots of seemingly random pairs or sets of rhyming words. It is written in the present tense, from the first-person point of view: The speaker is both the narrator and one of the two main characters.

The poem is a narrative poem and tells the story of how the narrator wants to work on projects in the kitchen while his or her mother cooks. This poem is longer than one would have expected, and both child and mother are carrying on bravely and magically with their many tasks. The mother is preparing an extraordinary number of dishes. The child (and this is one child who will *never* be bored) is juggling projects sufficient in number to fill several weeks or months.

Both child and mother express a great and wonderful love for each other. Thus, we could *even* call this poem a **romance**, as the word was used in medieval times: This tale has as its basis and theme chivalric love.

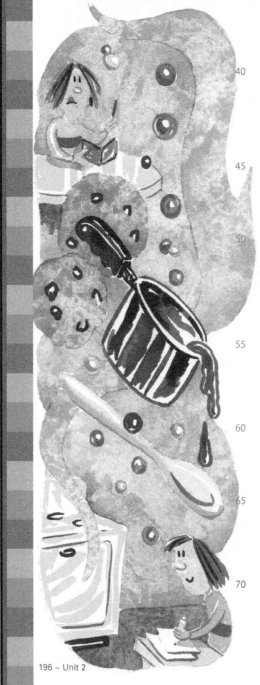

I say it's neater,
Smelling what's cooking and
Looking for raisins in the cookie batter,   40
Than playing alone.

She says, what's wrong with your room,
Or the yard, or playing with Joan?

I explain to her, well, it's just nicer
Knowing she's right on my heels   45
Behind me, slicing bologna
Or spicing the applesauce.
But she's the boss,
And if that's how she feels
I'd better just gather my stuff up   50
And go.

She says, well…no.

I say, no?

She says, no, that time will come soon enough.
Too soon. So just bring your stuff   55
Back into the kitchen.

She smiles and gives me a taste of
Tomato paste and makes more room
On the counter beside her, so I can lace
The pieces of wallet from my leather kit   60
Or do some tooling.
Working together like that for a bit
Is great. I string beads
While she strings beans,
Or I glue seeds to plaques,   65
Or illustrate books between
Racks of cake-layers cooling.

My mother says, when she was young
A kitchen was where everyone hung around
Telling what happened that day   70
And feeling at home.
She says it had a table for schoolwork
And mending and crewel, and

A stool for cutting hair,
75   And not so much chrome.
She liked it there.

I say I like it here, too, in this kitchen,
And I'm glad it's okay if I stay.
We get on with whatever we're making—
80   Shaking the steak in flour and
Squashing papier-mâché in a tray—
Feeling like artists
And getting in each other's way.
She doesn't scream
85   When she opens the oven and
Steam pours out of the mouth
Of the scary mask I'm baking.
She only sighs when the poster I'm drying
Falls into the meat she's frying.

90   Every once in a while
She tells me it probably would be grand
To have a kitchen no bigger than a minute—
So small that only one person could fit in it.
But then she folds a slice of warm bread
95   And puts my favorite jam between,
And I know she doesn't mean it.

I know when she laughs and
Gives my hair a muss,
And swipes the counter to clear a spot,
100   She's saying our kitchen will always be
Large enough for both of us—
For her, and the things she likes a lot,
And the things I like a lot,
And me.

A Niche in the Kitchen ~ 197

EYES ON...FREE VERSE, FIRST PERSON, NARRATIVE POETRY

Poetry without meter, without a beat, without a regular pattern of end rhymes is called *free verse*. *A Niche in the Kitchen* is surely free verse, and it will be interesting to see how students do with their memorizing and recitation.

This is a story poem or *narrative poem* (of sorts), with irregular rhythm, irregular cadence, and irregular rhyme. The rhyming is funny, since it often takes us by surprise. The rhyme is bolstered by a repetition of vowel sounds (as in Lines 31-35, where *please, knees,* and *peas* are followed by *beanbag*). Make sure that your students are aware of all these repetition of sounds, as they practice their assigned parts.

LITERARY COMPONENTS

▶ **23. Rhymes and Alliteration:** In Lines 68-69, *young* with *hung;* in Lines 71 and 75, *home* and *chrome;* in Lines 72-74, *school-, crewel,* and *stool;* and Lines 74 and 76, *hair* and *there.* There is alliteration with **cr**ewel, **c**utting, and **ch**rome.

▶ **24. Characterization; Echo of Mom's Life:** This child is warm-hearted: *I say I like it here, too, in this kitchen.*

▶ **25. Lots of Rhyme; Some Alliteration:** In Lines 77-89, look for *okay* with *stay* and *papier-mâché* and *tray;* making—/*Shaking* and *baking,* and the vowels sounds of *steak; scream* with *Steam; sighs* and *drying* and *frying.* There's alliteration in Line 79 with **W**e get on **w**ith **wh**atever **w**e're...

▶ **26. Characterization of Mother; Metaphor:** *Every once in a while / She tells me it probably would be grand / To have a kitchen **no bigger than a minute.***

▶ **27. Climax:** Lines 94-96 read, *But then she folds a slice of warm bread / And puts my favorite jam between...*

▶ **28. Rhymes:** Check out *minute* with *fit in it,* and *between* with *mean.*

▶ **29. Conclusion; Resolution:** The child knows that she really cares.

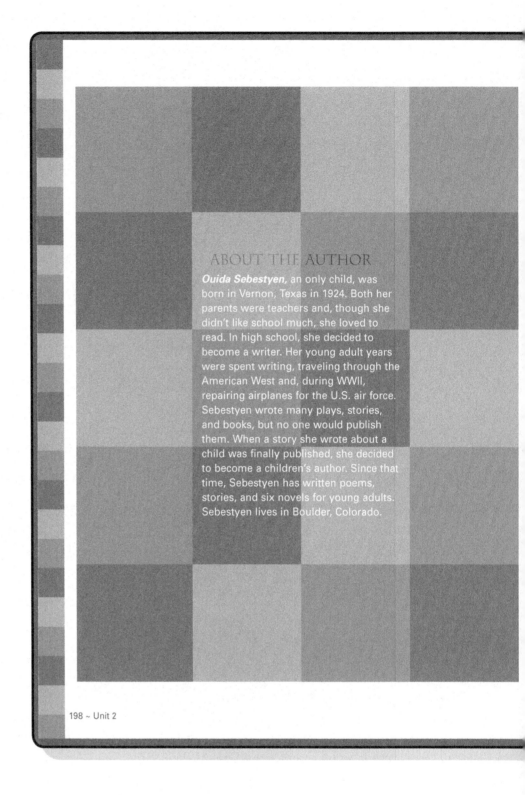

ABOUT THE AUTHOR

Ouida Sebestyen, an only child, was born in Vernon, Texas in 1924. Both her parents were teachers and, though she didn't like school much, she loved to read. In high school, she decided to become a writer. Her young adult years were spent writing, traveling through the American West and, during WWII, repairing airplanes for the U.S. air force. Sebestyen wrote many plays, stories, and books, but no one would publish them. When a story she wrote about a child was finally published, she decided to become a children's author. Since that time, Sebestyen has written poems, stories, and six novels for young adults. Sebestyen lives in Boulder, Colorado.

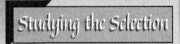 POETRY

1. What is a *niche*?

2. What are you doing, when you *tool* leather?

3. What is this poem about? Just give a short, simple answer in two or three sentences.

4. How many sentences are in the first stanza?

5. Give five rhyming pairs or sets of words in the poem.

6. Describe four activities the child is involved in. Describe four activities the mom is involved in.

7. Where do you like to play or do homework? Why?

STUDYING THE SELECTION

1. Students should know that it is all right to copy a definition word for word from a dictionary. That is not plagiarism—it is what dictionaries are for. However, they need to understand what the definition means, and you may need to help them with that. Student answers should include one or all of the following ideas. A *niche* is a recess in a wall; a hiding place or retreat resembling a niche in its formation or privacy; *also*, a site or habitat supplying all that is needed for the successful existence of an organism or species. Students may very well find other definitions in the dictionary.

2. Tooling leather means (using tools to) ornament something made of leather by attaching other things to the surface of the leather or decorating it by painting, cutting, or stamping.

3. The poem is about a child who likes to work on projects in the kitchen while his or her mom is preparing food there. The child wants to be with mom. Initially mom feels the speaker is underfoot, and then she relents, saying, that time will come soon enough.

4. The first stanza is made from one sentence.

5. *cook, (cook)book; flowers, hours; rolling-pin, kitchen, in; making things, baking things; standing, sanding; (bird)-feeder, (I) need her; there, anywhere; dicing, icing; éclairs, upstairs; please, knees, peas; scatter, spatter, batter; phone, alone, Joan; heels, feels; slicing, spicing; (apple)sauce, boss; go, no; enough, stuff; taste, paste; kit, bit; tooling, cooling, plaques, racks; young, hung; home, chrome; school-, crewel, stool, hair, there; okay, stay; making, shaking, baking; papier-mâché, tray, way; scream, steam, drying, frying,* and so forth.

6. The child presses flowers, makes things from clay, sands a birdfeeder, laces up or tools leather, strings beads, glues seeds to plaques, illustrates books, makes papier-mâché, bakes a voodoo mask, and so forth.

   The mother dices carrots, ices éclairs, fries hamburgers, makes cookie batter, slices bologna, spices applesauce, and so forth.

7. Answers will vary.

UNIT TWO WRAP-UP

Gold-Mounted Guns • The Disappearing Man • The Speckled Hen's Egg • The Black Stallion • By the Shores of Silver Lake

DO CHARACTERS HAVE DREAMS?

1. Pick one of the main characters from *Gold-Mounted Guns, The Disappearing Man, The Speckled Hen's Egg, The Black Stallion,* or *By the Shores of Silver Lake*. You are going to write down your character's dreams. For this, you will create a booklet with eight pages inside a cover. Fold a piece of 8½" x 11" colored paper in half across the middle, to create the front and back covers. Then fold two pieces of 8 ½" x 11" white paper in half and turn them sideways inside the cover. The cover of your booklet should say *My Character Book*. Don't forget to number your pages, using both the front and back of each piece of paper.

2. Pages 1 and 2 will be called **Vital Statistics**. On these pages, you write the name of the character, the character's age, whether the character is a boy or girl or a man or woman, and what your character looks like. Tell also where the character lives.

3. Pages 3 and 4 will be called **Family, Friends, Acquaintances, and Neighbors**. There, you will list the people who are important to the character in the story.

4. Pages 5 and 6 will be called **The Things I Like**. Make a list of the things you think the character likes based on your sense of the character as a person.

5. Pages 7 and 8 will be called **A Dream I Had**. This is a dream that you imagine your character had while he or she was sleeping. The dream should make sense in terms of the events of the character's life.

I CAN'T FIND MY STORY!
The Lost Character

1. You are one of the characters in one of the Unit 2 stories. You may be a major character or a minor character. You can even be an animal from *Gold-Mounted Guns, The Speckled Hen's Egg, The Black Stallion,* or *By the Shores of Silver Lake.* You should make or find some piece of clothing or a prop that helps you look like the character. You can also—with help from a grownup or a sibling—put on makeup to help you get into character, when the time comes for your presentation.

2. As it turns out, you can't remember who you are or which story (or poem) in Unit 2 you belong in. After you make your presentation to your class, it will be their job to tell you which story (or poem) you should go back to. But they can only do it if you give them the right information.
   - Begin by saying, *Help! I can't find my story! Can you help me?* Then you give the following information.
   - If you have a name, you will give your name, if you can remember it!
   - Then describe the setting, where and when you were living when you were in the story.
   - Tell who your friends or family are, if you have friends or family. Or, if you are an animal, who "owns" you.
   - Next, say what you like, what you don't like, and, maybe, what you eat.

- Finally, tell your class what the last thing you remember is, before you popped out of the story into the here and now. What you remember can be more detailed than what is in the story, but it must be based on the situation in the story.
- Conclude by asking your class, "Where do I belong? Which story should I go back to?" Your presentation can be serious or funny.

3. Make notes on index cards for that moment when you are to be "The Lost Character." Practice your presentation. Don't forget to speak up so everyone in the classroom can hear you!

THE ANIMAL'S THE THING!
Learning as a Team / Teaching by Acting

1. Your teacher will help you and your class form small groups or teams.

2. Each group is going to choose from a list of animals that are in trouble. Your teacher will help, so that each team picks a different animal for a mascot. A *mascot* is an emblem or symbol of a team. Here are the animals you can choose from:

- Dolphins
- Polar Bears
- Whales
- American Black Bears
- Florida Panther

- Manatees
- Owls
- The California Condor
- Sea Otters
- The Sonoran Pronghorn

3. Each team, with the help of the teacher, should write a short letter to The Wildlife Conservation Society, asking for information about their animal. Their address is:

The Wildlife Conservation Society
2300 Southern Boulevard
Bronx, New York 10460

4. From the information they receive, each group should write a scene about the life of their animal. The team will rehearse together to act out the scene, with each team member assigned a part.

5. Each team must write an introduction and a conclusion for the scene. The introduction will be read aloud to the audience before the scene, by a team narrator. The conclusion will be read aloud after the scene, by a team narrator.

6. Do a good job with your presentation!

CHARACTER DEVELOPMENT

1. Think about the characters in each of the selections, including those in the poetry section.

2. In literature, some characters change and develop throughout the story or poem. Other characters remain the same from beginning to end.

    a. What are two examples of characters who do not change?
    b. What are two examples of characters who do change in some way?

3. Describe the characters who do not change. Choose the main trait that each one displays. Bring examples from the beginning and end of the story and poem to show how the character has not changed.

4. Describe the characters that do change. Choose the main trait that has changed in each one during the story or poem. Bring examples from the beginning and end of the story or poem to show how the character has changed.

unit 3

AIMING
HIGH

CHARACTER

- The easiest way for us to know about a character is for the author to describe the character's looks, personality, and character traits.
- A more interesting way to learn about a character is to pay close attention to what the character says and does.
- At times, an author will let us in on a character's thoughts or feelings.
- In many stories, we learn about one character from another character.

THINK ABOUT IT!

1. Read the first paragraph of "We Love Our Marine." What are four facts that you have learned about PFC Escobar?

2. Read the rest of the story. What are two emotions PFC Escobar experiences in the story? How do you know this?

3. Does the author describe the physical appearance of Alejandro or Alicia? Does this add to or take away from the story?

4. What is one thing you learned about Mom from what she *says*? What is one thing you learned about Mom from what she *does*?

We Love Our Marine

Private First Class Alejandro Escobar stood on the sidewalk in the early morning sunlight. "We Love Our Marine!" the banner shouted to the world from the second story of his tiny house. Escobar walked up the short path to the front door. He started to knock, then looked at his watch. He should wait. Mom and Dad and his baby sister would still be sleeping. Despite all the pictures Mom had sent, in his mind Alicia had remained the mischievous two year old he'd left 17 months ago. Standing at his front door, he realized that Alicia was now a three and a half year old with little memory of her big brother.

Escobar looked in the picture window. Not even an extra folding chair in the small living room remained as evidence of last night's party. Mom, tired as she was, would never let herself go to sleep with the house a mess. Nonetheless, he knew it had been a big party. He could hear that when he had called. The music, the laughter, the noise.

"Don't say it's me," he instructed her. "Take the phone somewhere you can talk."

She did as he asked. There was fear in her voice when she finally spoke. "Alejandro? Where are you?"

"I just can't face the crowd tonight," he explained. "It's just a lot to get used to all of a sudden."

"Where are you," she asked again. This time he wasn't sure if it was fear or irritation in her voice.

"My bus got in a few hours ago. I've just been walking for a while."

"Everyone's been waiting," was all she said.

Escobar started to knock again, then stepped away from the door and sat down on a porch swing. He was so happy to be home, but he was nervous, too.

The front door swung open. Mom. She smiled at her son, then, without a word, she hugged him. A moment later, Dad held him in a hug so tight it almost took his breath away. No one spoke as Mom, Dad, and even Alejandro wiped tears away. Then, all three began to laugh. This was the welcome home party he needed. Escobar breathed a deep sigh of relief. Everything was going to be okay.

SELECTION VOCABULARY

chap: fellow, guy

cross: angry

curtly: briefly and a bit rudely

feeble: weak

persisted: continued to make a point in spite of opposition

premises: a building and its grounds

raucous: loud and harsh

rigmarole: confused or meaningless talk

scarlet: deep red

site: area or exact place where something is to be located or built

| chap | curtly | persisted | raucous | scarlet |
| cross | feeble | premises | rigmarole | site |

1. He looked old and _____ (weak), but he had a fierce temper.

2. When he saw the boys trespassing on the _____ (where something is to be built) of his new garage, he ran outside.

3. "Get off these _____ (grounds)," he shouted, his face turning _____ (deep red).

4. "Begging your pardon, sir," said one of the boys, "but we _____ (boys) just wanted to cut through your yard to the park. We don't mean any harm."

5. "What is all this _____ (meaningless talk)?" shouted the old man. "What's all this fancy talk?"

6. "Please let us use this short cut," _____ (continued to make his point) the boy.

7. "I will not!" yelled the man in a _____ (harsh) voice. "I'll not have you young whippersnappers traipsing across my property."

8. Another boy, less polite than the first, said, "We're sorry you're _____ (angry)."

9. _____ (briefly and rudely) they said goodbye to the angry man and ran out of his yard, as he watched to make sure they left.

Workbook p. 61   Answer Guide p. 6

Build a Sentence

Words are the tools of a writer. Nouns, verbs, adjectives and adverbs are used to "build" sentences. Below each of the tools in the tool cart there are lines for words. Choosing from your vocabulary list, put four nouns under the saw, one verb under the hammer, one adverb under the pliers, and four adjectives under the wrench.

Workbook p. 62   Answer Guide p. 6

LESSON IN LITERATURE

1. We know that PFC Escobar:
   Lives with his Mom and Dad
   Has a baby sister
   Lives in a house
   Has been gone for seventeen months

2. He feels overwhelmed by the idea of facing a crowd. Children might call this shy or afraid of people. We know this because he *says*, "I just can't face the crowd tonight." He is happy to be home, and he is nervous, too. We know that because *the author tells us* so. He feels satisfied and peaceful. We know that because the *author tells us* that "this was the welcome home party he needed." We also *see* him sigh in relief.

3. We are given no description of either Alejandro's or Mom's physical appearance. From his name, we might guess that he is of Latino or Hispanic background, but that is all. As to whether this lack of description is a plus or a minus, it will depend on how freely the reader likes to use his or her imagination.

4. Mom is wise. We know that from what she *says*. Instead of asking a lot of questions, or angrily criticizing her son for ruining her party, she asks one, brief question: "Where are you?" Her question also tells us she is concerned about her son. Mom is kind, sympathetic and loving. We know that from what she *does*. When she sees Alejandro, she asks nothing, she says nothing—she just smiles in welcome. We also know that she is neat and hardworking, because the house has been completely straightened up after the party.

BACKGROUND BYTES

This is an opportunity to continue your discussion of what happens to older people in "modern" society. Of course, you will want to begin by telling your students that the discussion is connected with the story they are about to read. When a family moves from a house to an apartment building, one of the family members—the most senior—suddenly finds himself stripped of the activities and role that made him the paterfamilias. Paterfamilias comes from Latin and literally means the father of the family, or the head of the family.

The material below is merely a suggestion, and our discussion is brief. You may want to set this discussion within the social, cultural, and ethical values that are given emphasis in your own community.

In most cultures across the globe, old age has traditionally been considered a virtue and a blessing. In some languages, the words for "old" and "wise" are interchangeable. Elderly people are respected because they have endured the hardship, gained the skill and experience, acquired the knowledge, and gained the compassion that comes only with many years. Therefore, a person's value grows with each new day.

But in the Western world of the 21st century, old age is no longer an asset. In fact, it is a great liability. People who are old are considered by many—and consider themselves—an inconvenience. Increasingly, in popular practice and thinking, dependence of any kind is suspect, despised. Today, we are supposed to take care of ourselves. If you ask for too much help, you have two problems: First, people don't like to be bothered; second, there's something wrong with you for needing help. When we can't take care of ourselves *and* we are old, it's time to go to a nursing home. Many families are just too busy to take care of the elderly parents who raised them. (It is also true that people live longer now and sometimes develop Alzheimer's Disease and really cannot be taken care of by their families.)

Today, "youth is seen as the highest credential." Getting a job after 50, a job that suits one's skills, is tough. After 60, it may be nearly impossible. People's homes in high-rise apartments may need special architecture for people who are older. Is it possible for the elderly people you know to get to the library, if they should want to read a new book? Could they do it without family? How does an elderly person go food shopping?

As our elderly population grows, we must acknowledge *as a society,* that a lot more of us are going to be having trouble getting around as we get on in years. Otherwise it is inevitable that an entire segment of society will be disenfranchised. Should growing old be "a descent into boredom, futility, and despair"?

Modern society seems to require that our later years be a time of inactivity and decline. Suddenly all the expertise and wisdom gained over the years are of little value.

We need to recall that working is human nature for all of us. If we are blessed, each one of us will age. How can we prepare for the future—our own future? This is a complex question whose answer will vary from individual to individual. A writer can write at any age, whereas a factory worker will be forced into retirement at 60 or 65. A wise person will cultivate interests outside of work as retirement age nears. The more spiritual, intellectual, and sociable a person is, the less burdensome old age will be.

It is reasonable to expect that, at one point, an elderly person will become at least partially dependent on his or her children or on society as a whole. Parents need to teach their children to respect the elderly and to have compassion for the helpless.

Related to our youth-oriented society are the utilitarian underpinnings of our society. The "me-first" attitude so many children are permitted to adopt, and which is overtly encouraged by our society, will hardly foster the devotion and self-sacrifice often needed to care for an aging or ailing parent.

In sum, we will reap what we sow. If we toil now to raise responsible, respectful, self-effacing children, if, in short, we swim against the current, we can hope for a more compassionate society in the future.

INTO "GRAMP"

What is remarkable about this story? A young boy cannot stand to see his grandfather suffer. He cannot endure seeing his grandfather with nothing to do. Gramp can no longer be himself—the independent, hardworking breadwinner upon whom the entire family depends. Gramp has changed, and the change in their relationship that results from his grandfather's misery is intolerable to the boy. He and his grandfather no longer share activities and conversation as they did before the move to the apartment house.

Simon, the boy, does not simply accustom himself to the change. He does not simply say, well, grandfather is old now so it's to be expected. In the face of his parents' apparent acceptance of the situation, and in spite of the ridicule he endures when he tries to find a place for his grandfather, he keeps going. After an unpleasant discussion with his mother, a less-than-satisfactory interchange with an ultimately sympathetic yard foreman, and a dreadful experience with factory gatekeepers, he nonetheless tries once more with the building superintendent. This is a good, courageous boy, and he *does* aim high.

Have your students also discuss how Gramp changes when there is nothing for him to do, and how he is transformed after he has the bench. See page 232: "Each day, Gramp seemed a little younger, a little quicker. Each day he moved a little more quickly."

The adage, that man's job is to toil, points to a crucial feature of human nature. This is another, no less important, theme of the piece.

EYES ON...CHARACTER

What impressions do your students have of each of the characters in the story? Make a list of the characters on the board.
- Simon
- Gramp
- Mum
- the greengrocer (whom we never meet, but hear about)
- Dad (whom we also never meet)
- the yard foreman
- the man with the peaked cap in the factory gatehouse
- the other man, Jim, in the factory gatehouse
- Mr. Gideon

Ask your class about a character. When the class has described its reaction to him or her, track that character through the story with your class. Simon and Gramp may be mentioned too frequently to do this in every instance, but it will be very instructive with the others, who are used more sparingly.

When you have finished going through the list of characters, ask your students, *how* they got to know each of these people. Was it from the
- **Adjectives** the author used in the narrative?
- the **Dialogue**?
- the **Character's Thoughts** (also called **Internal Dialogue**)?
- the **Character's Actions**?

Working together with the story, you and the class will be able to make these determinations.

Blueprint for Reading

INTO . . . *Gramp*

Do you have grandparents or great-grandparents? Are you close with them? What do your grandparents or great-grandparents do each day? Have you ever thought about what it is like to be a very old person?

Many older people continue to work at their jobs and live in their own homes. But others are unable to do many of the things they used to do and are unable to live alone. If they live in a place for older people, they must obey the rules of the place where they live. They may not even be able to have a dog or a cat for company. Sometimes, older people feel that they cannot be themselves any longer and have lost control of their lives.

EYES ON . . . *Character*

In our everyday lives, we usually get to know people little by little. Often, we may have an intuition—a sense or a feeling—about a person. We can *sense* the person's character. However, we ordinarily form our opinions based on what someone says and does.

We get to know a character in a book the same way. We learn quite a lot about the character, because we see them in a variety of situations. What's more, in a story, we are often told what the character is thinking. Because of this, we may feel as though we know a fictional character better than we know some of our own friends.

If the story is a good one, we will feel that, even though the character is imaginary, they have very important lessons to teach us.

GRAMP

From the book
Luke's Garden and Gramp

JOAN TATE

Gramp ~ 209

SUMMING UP THE PLOT

- That summer Simon is ten and life is full of new things.
- The apartment to which the family has moved is becoming home for him.
- Simon even likes going up and down in the elevator or sometimes running the whole way down the stairs.
- Gramp has fixed up a place for Simon's guinea pigs in the shed in the yard.

LITERARY COMPONENTS

▶ **1. Exposition; Setting; Characters; Characterization:** We are introduced to Simon, and told his age. It is summer and the family has moved from a house to an apartment that is "in the sky." We are introduced to Mum and Gramp. We see that Simon has spirit and energy.

▶ **2. Characterization:** Simon has guinea pigs that he takes care of. Gramp has fixed up a place for the guinea pigs.

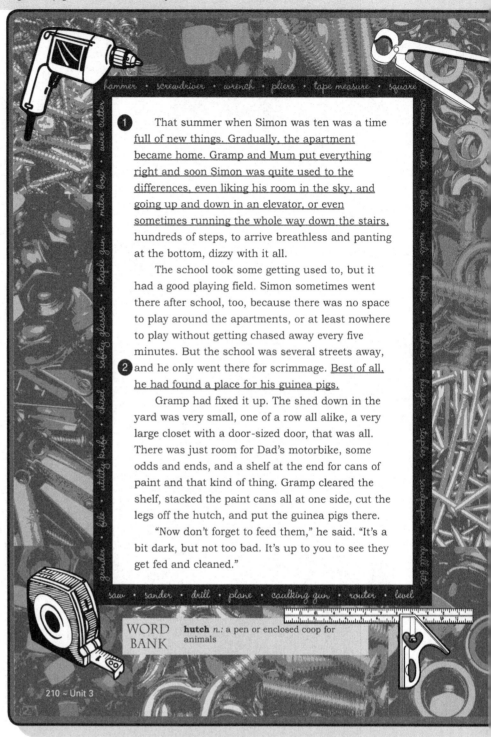

① That summer when Simon was ten was a time full of new things. Gradually, the apartment became home. Gramp and Mum put everything right and soon Simon was quite used to the differences, even liking his room in the sky, and going up and down in an elevator, or even sometimes running the whole way down the stairs, hundreds of steps, to arrive breathless and panting at the bottom, dizzy with it all.

The school took some getting used to, but it had a good playing field. Simon sometimes went there after school, too, because there was no space to play around the apartments, or at least nowhere to play without getting chased away every five minutes. But the school was several streets away, **②** and he only went there for scrimmage. Best of all, he had found a place for his guinea pigs.

Gramp had fixed it up. The shed down in the yard was very small, one of a row all alike, a very large closet with a door-sized door, that was all. There was just room for Dad's motorbike, some odds and ends, and a shelf at the end for cans of paint and that kind of thing. Gramp cleared the shelf, stacked the paint cans all at one side, cut the legs off the hutch, and put the guinea pigs there.

"Now don't forget to feed them," he said. "It's a bit dark, but not too bad. It's up to you to see they get fed and cleaned."

WORD BANK · **hutch** *n.:* a pen or enclosed coop for animals

210 ~ Unit 3

GUIDING THE READING

LITERAL

Q: When the story opens, what season is it?
A: It is summer.

Q: What has just changed for Simon and his family?
A: They have moved from a house to an apartment.

Q: What has Gramp just done for Simon?
A: He has fixed up a place for Simon's guinea pigs.

ANALYTICAL

Q: What does Simon like at the apartment building?
A: He likes his room in the sky, going up and down in the elevator, and running the whole way down the stairs. Best of all, he has found a place for his guinea pigs.

Q: What does having guinea pigs tell us about Simon?
A: Answers will vary. But he is a person who wants to have a pet to love and he takes care of them responsibly.

SUMMING UP THE PLOT

- Every day after school, Simon takes leftover greens to the guinea pigs.
- Sometimes he wanders all over the building sites down the road.
- For Gramp it is not the same at the apartment.
- At first there was a lot to do to help Mum organize the apartment.
- But then the apartment was finished and easy to look after, easier than the house had been.
- Mum got a part-time job, and Gramp is alone a lot.
- He sits in his room staring out the window at nothing, not even smoking his pipe.

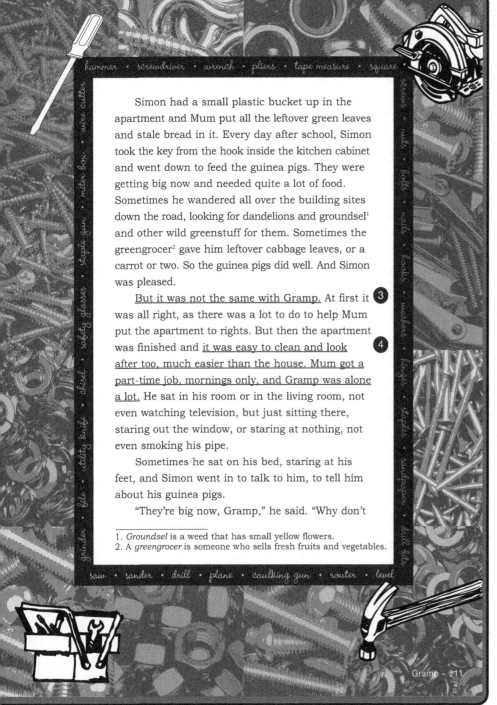

Simon had a small plastic bucket up in the apartment and Mum put all the leftover green leaves and stale bread in it. Every day after school, Simon took the key from the hook inside the kitchen cabinet and went down to feed the guinea pigs. They were getting big now and needed quite a lot of food. Sometimes he wandered all over the building sites down the road, looking for dandelions and groundsel[1] and other wild greenstuff for them. Sometimes the greengrocer[2] gave him leftover cabbage leaves, or a carrot or two. So the guinea pigs did well. And Simon was pleased.

But it was not the same with Gramp. At first it 3 was all right, as there was a lot to do to help Mum put the apartment to rights. But then the apartment was finished and it was easy to clean and look 4 after too, much easier than the house. Mum got a part-time job, mornings only, and Gramp was alone a lot. He sat in his room or in the living room, not even watching television, but just sitting there, staring out the window, or staring at nothing, not even smoking his pipe.

Sometimes he sat on his bed, staring at his feet, and Simon went in to talk to him, to tell him about his guinea pigs.

"They're big now, Gramp," he said. "Why don't

1. *Groundsel* is a weed that has small yellow flowers.
2. A *greengrocer* is someone who sells fresh fruits and vegetables.

LITERARY COMPONENTS

▶ **3. Basic Conflict Introduced:** At the apartment, "it was not the same with Gramp." The apartment is not big enough for Gramp's accustomed lifestyle. This is an external conflict for Gramp, a conflict of man vs. society. Because of "social forces," this family has moved from a house with space and privacy (and more work) to an apartment where there is no garage or shed for a carpentry area. This external conflict is going to become an internal conflict, as Gramp struggles within himself to keep his dignity and his equilibrium.

▶ **4. Compounding the Conflict:** It seems to be the case that since the apartment requires less housekeeping than did the house, Mum now has the time for a part-time job. So Gramp not only has nothing meaningful to do, he's alone much more.

GUIDING THE READING

LITERAL
Q: Why was the situation okay for Gramp when they first moved to the apartment?
A: A lot of things needed doing when they first moved, and he helped Mum put the apartment to rights.

ANALYTICAL
Q: Why do you think Gramp just stares out the window at nothing and doesn't even smoke his pipe?
A: Answers will vary. He is now unable to make a contribution to the family. He has now completely lost his role as father and provider.

SUMMING UP THE PLOT

- Simon asks, "What's the matter with you, Gramp?"
- Gramp says, "Nothing's the matter. Nothing, that's it."
- Simon says, "You mean you've nothing to do?"
- Simon suggests that Gramp build a workbench in the apartment.
- Gramp says "In here? There's not room."
- Simon says he could have a small one.

LITERARY COMPONENTS

▶ **5. Dialogue; Problem Revealed to Simon; Crux of Problem:** Since Gramp has no interest in going downstairs, Simon asks him what is wrong. Gramp has nothing to do. The realization dawns on Simon that Gramp needs a workbench.

▶ **6. Characterization of Setting:** When Gramp says there's not enough room, it is symbolic as well as literal. There is not enough room in the apartment for a full emotional life. There is not enough room to be a productive person.

▶ **7. Characterization of Mum:** Gramp's reaction suggests that Mum can't stand disorder.

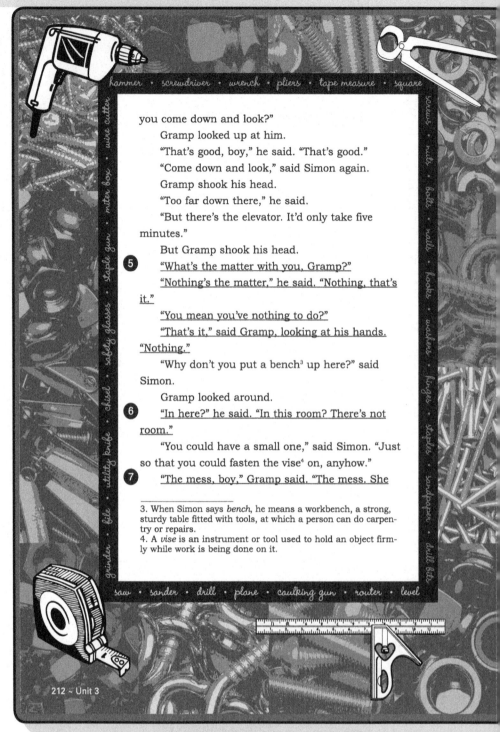

you come down and look?"

Gramp looked up at him.

"That's good, boy," he said. "That's good."

"Come down and look," said Simon again.

Gramp shook his head.

"Too far down there," he said.

"But there's the elevator. It'd only take five minutes."

But Gramp shook his head.

5 "What's the matter with you, Gramp?"

"Nothing's the matter," he said. "Nothing, that's it."

"You mean you've nothing to do?"

"That's it," said Gramp, looking at his hands. "Nothing."

"Why don't you put a bench[3] up here?" said Simon.

Gramp looked around.

6 "In here?" he said. "In this room? There's not room."

"You could have a small one," said Simon. "Just so that you could fasten the vise[4] on, anyhow."

7 "The mess, boy," Gramp said. "The mess. She

---

3. When Simon says *bench*, he means a workbench, a strong, sturdy table fitted with tools, at which a person can do carpentry or repairs.
4. A *vise* is an instrument or tool used to hold an object firmly while work is being done on it.

saw · sander · drill · plane · caulking gun · router · level

212 ~ Unit 3

GUIDING THE READING

LITERAL

Q: What does Simon invite Gramp to do?
A: He invites him to come down and look at the guinea pigs.

Q: What does Gramp say when Simon asks him?
A: He says it's too far down there.

Q: What type of workbench does Simon suggest that Gramp get?
A: Simon suggests he get a small one.

SUMMING UP THE PLOT

- Gramp says that Mum would never tolerate the mess.

- Simon says they could keep the work area clean, and Gramp tells him he doesn't know what he's talking about.

- Gramp turns his head away and refuses to talk any longer.

- Gramp gradually becomes more and more silent and does not speak to any of them for days on end.

- He sits in his chair all day long by the window, with a small hammer in his hands. He turns the hammer over and over again.

- Simon cannot bear to see him sit there that way.

- Mum tells Simon that Gramp is getting old and not to bother him.

- Simon protests that Gramp has always been old, and he has never minded his bothering him.

- Mum says, "Older, then."

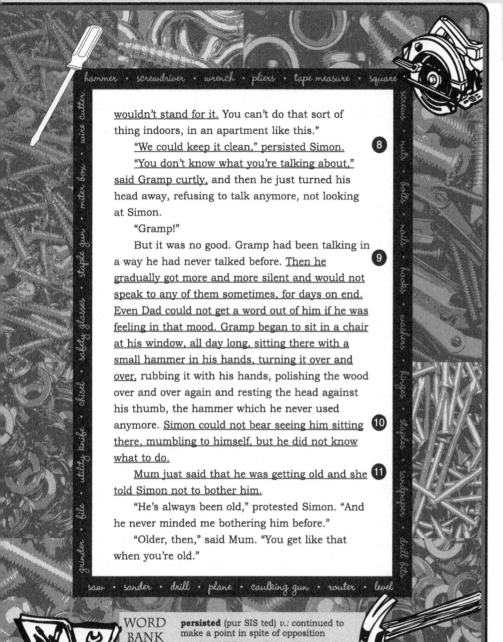

wouldn't stand for it. You can't do that sort of thing indoors, in an apartment like this."

"We could keep it clean," persisted Simon. **8**

"You don't know what you're talking about," said Gramp curtly, and then he just turned his head away, refusing to talk anymore, not looking at Simon.

"Gramp!"

But it was no good. Gramp had been talking in a way he had never talked before. Then he **9** gradually got more and more silent and would not speak to any of them sometimes, for days on end. Even Dad could not get a word out of him if he was feeling in that mood. Gramp began to sit in a chair at his window, all day long, sitting there with a small hammer in his hands, turning it over and over, rubbing it with his hands, polishing the wood over and over again and resting the head against his thumb, the hammer which he never used anymore. Simon could not bear seeing him sitting **10** there, mumbling to himself, but he did not know what to do.

Mum just said that he was getting old and she **11** told Simon not to bother him.

"He's always been old," protested Simon. "And he never minded me bothering him before."

"Older, then," said Mum. "You get like that when you're old."

WORD BANK

persisted (pur SIS ted) *v.*: continued to make a point in spite of opposition

curtly (KURT lee) *adv.*: briefly and a bit rudely

Gramp ~ 213

LITERARY COMPONENTS

▶ **8. Characterization:** When Simon persists in debating it, Gramp tells him he doesn't know what he's talking about. Simon is an idealist and he loves Gramp. He wants to make things okay. Gramp is curt because he probably knows better, and this is so painful for him.

▶ **9. Rising Action; Dad Introduced:** It is rising action as Gramp's spirits fall lower and lower. When the author writes, "Even Dad could not get a word out of him…," we can infer that Dad has a special relationship with Gramp.

▶ **10. Rising Action; Crisis; Motivation:** The crisis for Gramp is becoming a crisis for Simon.

▶ **11. Characterization:** Mum just cannot deal with it.

GUIDING THE READING

LITERAL

Q: Why couldn't Gramp have even a small workbench in the apartment?
A: He couldn't have one because Mum would not stand for the mess.

Q: How did Gramp's behavior gradually change?
A: He gradually became quieter. He sat by the window all day doing nothing.

Q: What was Mum's explanation for this behavior?
A: She said Gramp was getting old.

Q: What was Simon's answer to this?
A: Simon said Gramp has always been old.

ANALYTICAL

Q: Why do you think Gramp is curt, when Simon persists in talking about a workbench in the apartment?
A: Answers will vary. He probably knows Mum better than Simon might.

Q: Why does Gramp stop talking to everyone?

A: Answers will vary. Gramp may be angry that no one is helping him and that the only one who seems to be paying attention to the problem is Simon.

Q: Why do you think Mum just dismisses Gramp's behavior?
A: Answers will vary. It will be important to stress with students that when people feel overwhelmed by a problem or helpless to solve it, because it is so painful they sometimes deny to others that the problem exists.

SUMMING UP THE PLOT

- Simon asks, you get like what, when you are older?
- Mum says, "Like Grandpa."
- Simon says Gramp wasn't like that before they moved to the apartment.
- Mum says, "What d'you mean?" She says that Gramp is better off here than where they were

before. It's warmer and lighter and cleaner.

- Simon concludes that his mother does not understand. He says that Gramp would be okay if he had a bench, like Mum does (in the kitchen).

- Mum says, "Oh, you and Grandpa and that bench! Where can you find a workbench in a place like this?"
- Simon says, "We could try."

LITERARY COMPONENTS

▶ **12. Rising Action; Characterization; Dialogue:** The only way you can talk about Mum's denial is through how difficult this must be for her—which we see in her concluding statement. She wants this to be a *better* place for Gramp, because she cares about him.

▶ **13. Characterization:** Simon is resentful. His Mum has a place to work, but Gramp does not. He knows his saying this will make her angry.

▶ **14. Theme:** Simon says, "We could try." And that's what Simon and this story are about: trying. Making wishes come true.

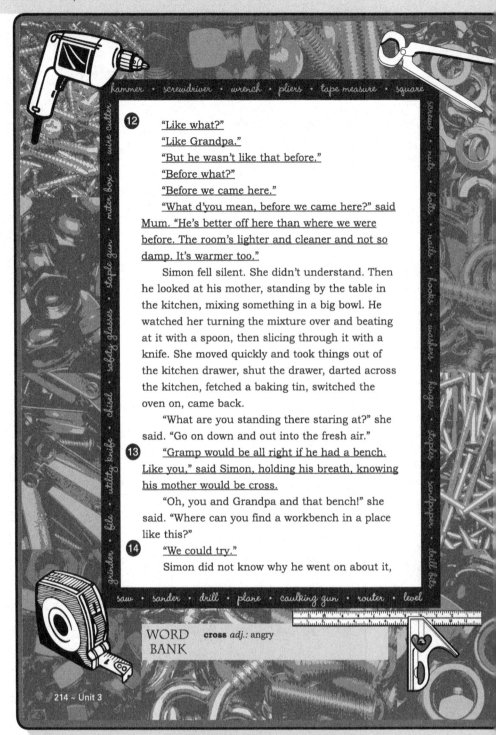

hammer · screwdriver · wrench · pliers · tape measure · square

12 "Like what?"

"Like Grandpa."

"But he wasn't like that before."

"Before what?"

"Before we came here."

"What d'you mean, before we came here?" said Mum. "He's better off here than where we were before. The room's lighter and cleaner and not so damp. It's warmer too."

Simon fell silent. She didn't understand. Then he looked at his mother, standing by the table in the kitchen, mixing something in a big bowl. He watched her turning the mixture over and beating at it with a spoon, then slicing through it with a knife. She moved quickly and took things out of the kitchen drawer, shut the drawer, darted across the kitchen, fetched a baking tin, switched the oven on, came back.

"What are you standing there staring at?" she said. "Go on down and out into the fresh air."

13 "Gramp would be all right if he had a bench. Like you," said Simon, holding his breath, knowing his mother would be cross.

"Oh, you and Grandpa and that bench!" she said. "Where can you find a workbench in a place like this?"

14 "We could try."

Simon did not know why he went on about it,

saw · sander · drill · plane · caulking gun · router · level

WORD BANK **cross** *adj.:* angry

214 ~ Unit 3

GUIDING THE READING

LITERAL

Q: Why does Mum think Gramp is better off at the apartment?

A: As she sees it, his room is lighter and cleaner and dryer and warmer. He is more comfortable physically.

Q: When Mum says, "Where can you find a workbench in a place like this?" how does Simon respond?

A: Simon says, "We could try."

- Simon does not know why he keeps going on about it, since he knows his mother is right. But still he keeps thinking of the way Gramp used to talk and work. Now it has all gone.

- Simon has no one to talk to and Gramp doesn't like the situation either.

- Mum knocks a small bowl on the floor by mistake and it breaks.

- She is upset. Controlling her anger, she challenges Simon to find Gramp a bench.

- Reluctantly, but with growing determination, Simon says he will find Gramp a bench.

- Simon wonders out loud if everyone is just too busy to care about Gramp any longer.

- Mum tells him that he knows that's not true and to say he is sorry.

- Unconvinced, Simon dashes out of the apartment.

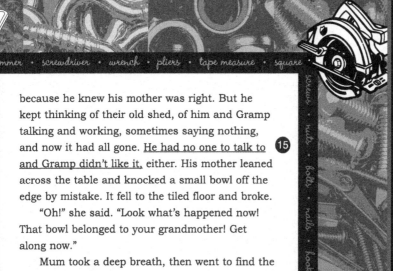

because he knew his mother was right. But he kept thinking of their old shed, of him and Gramp talking and working, sometimes saying nothing, and now it had all gone. He had no one to talk to and Gramp didn't like it, either. His mother leaned across the table and knocked a small bowl off the edge by mistake. It fell to the tiled floor and broke.

"Oh!" she said. "Look what's happened now! That bowl belonged to your grandmother! Get along now."

Mum took a deep breath, then went to find the broom. She swept the floor in short, sharp movements. After every sliver of china had been picked up, she straightened up and said, "If it's that important to you, why don't you go out and find him a bench yourself? Go on, go and find him one for yourself!"

"All right," said Simon slowly. "All right," he repeated with more conviction. "I *will* find him one," he said, his voice strong and determined. "You've all got things to do and maybe you just don't have time to worry about him, too."

"Now you know that's not true," said Mum. "You know it. Just you say you're sorry now."

But Simon felt it *was* true. Without a word, he dashed out of the kitchen. He felt hot and impatient and he couldn't wait for the elevator. He began stamping down the stairs, crashing his feet

Gramp ~ 215

LITERARY COMPONENTS

▶ **15. Characterization:** The loss for Simon is also very great. He has no one to be close with any longer.

▶ **16. Rising Action; Moral Lesson:** The exchange between Simon and his Mum shows that a problem in a family cannot just be pretended out of existence.

GUIDING THE READING

LITERAL
Q: **What happens while Simon is talking to his mother?**
A: She accidentally breaks a bowl that belonged to her mother.

ANALYTICAL
Q: **What will Simon lose, if Gramp stops speaking?**

A: Probably, he will lose his one close friendship.

Q: **Why does Mum break the bowl?**
A: Answers will vary.

Q: **Is Mum realistic, when she says that if the bench is that important, ten-year-old Simon should go out and find one himself?**
A: Answers will vary.

SUMMING UP THE PLOT

- Simon is intent on finding Gramp a workbench. Where could he look? Where do people do odd jobs if they live in apartments? Maybe they don't have odd jobs to do.

- Perhaps Gramp is too old. Perhaps they will put him in a home like Ken's granddad, who'd hated it.

- If Gramp went to a home, who would teach him to use tools?

- Dad isn't interested in tools. No one in the whole world uses tools as well as Gramp does.

LITERARY COMPONENTS

▶ **17. Motivation; Characterization; Theme:** Simon is angry and his Mum has said that *he* should find a workbench. So now he is going to figure out just how to do that.

▶ **18. Social Backdrop; Conflict:** Simon is tempted to blame the problem on Gramp's age, but he knows better. He sums up the social problem very succinctly when he thinks, "Where did people do their odd jobs when they lived in apartments? Perhaps they didn't have odd jobs to do.... Perhaps they would put him in a home next." When people move off the land into cities, when they move into high-rise dwellings, the lives of individuals and families are forever changed. And it is harder for older people to go outside. In contemporary society, people are less likely to repair things in any case. We just throw things out and buy new.

▶ **19. Characterization; Relationship; Theme:** Simon doesn't just want to get Gramp a bench to restore their closeness, nor does he pity Gramp. He *admires* Gramp and sees him as a teacher, wiser at his trade than anyone else.

▶ **20. Social and Historical Background; Characterization:** Simon sees a changing world. All of these buildings are growing up, and the author has him realize that soon they will "all be full of people."

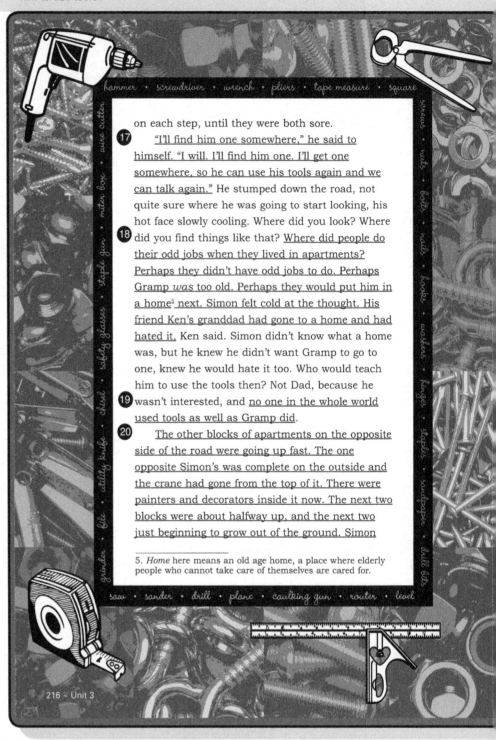

on each step, until they were both sore.

17 "I'll find him one somewhere," he said to himself. "I will. I'll find him one. I'll get one somewhere, so he can use his tools again and we can talk again." He stumped down the road, not quite sure where he was going to start looking, his hot face slowly cooling. Where did you look? Where

18 did you find things like that? Where did people do their odd jobs when they lived in apartments? Perhaps they didn't have odd jobs to do. Perhaps Gramp *was* too old. Perhaps they would put him in a home[5] next. Simon felt cold at the thought. His friend Ken's granddad had gone to a home and had hated it, Ken said. Simon didn't know what a home was, but he knew he didn't want Gramp to go to one, knew he would hate it too. Who would teach him to use the tools then? Not Dad, because he

19 wasn't interested, and no one in the whole world used tools as well as Gramp did.

20 The other blocks of apartments on the opposite side of the road were going up fast. The one opposite Simon's was complete on the outside and the crane had gone from the top of it. There were painters and decorators inside it now. The next two blocks were about halfway up, and the next two just beginning to grow out of the ground. Simon

---

5. *Home* here means an old age home, a place where elderly people who cannot take care of themselves are cared for.

216 ~ Unit 3

GUIDING THE READING

LITERAL

Q: When Simon leaves the apartment he is hot and impatient. How does he go down the stairs?
A: He stamps down the stairs, crashing his feet on each step, until both his feet are sore.

Q: How had Ken's granddad felt about living in a "home"?
A: He had hated it.

Q: Who does Simon think uses tools best in the whole world?
A: He thinks his grandfather does.

ANALYTICAL

Q: How do people who live in apartments do "odd jobs"?
A: Answers will vary.

Q: Simon thinks to himself that if Gramp went to a home, who would teach him to use tools? What are the roles that Gramp plays in Simon's life?
A: Answers will vary. Gramp is a parent, a friend, and a teacher. Gramp helps him out when he needs something done—like making a place for the guinea pigs.

- Simon sees apartment buildings rising in different stages—opposite his building, and stretching for blocks down the street. He realizes that soon they will be full of people.

- He stops and looks at the sheds through the fence at one site. Surely there would be room in one shed for a bench for Gramp.

- He goes inside the fence and walks toward one of the huts. It is big and roomy inside,

but filled with a desk and chairs, like an office.

- He begins to walk toward the next one.

LITERARY COMPONENTS

▶ **21. Dichotomy in Characterization:** Simon's caring, his persistence, and his initiative are admirable, mature qualities. But he is only ten, when he thinks so innocently about the world.

saw them every day from his window, and on his way to school, and each day they were a little higher. Soon they would all be full of people.

He stopped and looked through the gap in the fencing. The site was dry and dusty and the doors of all the builders' sheds were open in the sunlight. There were workers standing about everywhere, as it was payday and they were just getting off work.

The sheds?

They were fine sheds, wooden and sturdy, much larger than the shed they had had at home. In fact, some of them were almost as large as a small house. Surely one of them would have enough room inside for a bench for Gramp? Surely he wouldn't be in the way there? And he might even be useful, mending and making things for the men and the engineers.

Simon moved inside the fence. He knew you weren't supposed to go in, but no one seemed to notice him. He waited until the workers had gone away and then he moved over toward one of the huts.

It was big and roomy and had a kind of desk inside it. There were charts and papers all over the walls, and papers everywhere. There were chairs against the desk, just like an office. There wasn't much room for anything else. He turned around and began to walk toward the next one.

WORD BANK — **gap** *n.:* a break or opening in a row of objects or in a wall

Gramp ~ 217

GUIDING THE READING

ANALYTICAL

Q: What does Simon think of when he looks at all of the apartment buildings going up?
A: He thinks that soon they will all be full of people.

Q: Does it make sense to you that Simon thinks that surely one of the sheds would have room for Gramp?
A: Answers will vary. It will be interesting to see if your students think Simon is being realistic or if they think he is being naïve.

SUMMING UP THE PLOT

- A man shouts, "Get on out of there! You've no business here. Beat it!"
- Simon walks towards him slowly and thinks that if he runs away now, he'll never find a place for Gramp.
- He says that he was just looking, and the man says that he's trespassing.
- Simon boldly asks if it wouldn't be possible for his grandpa to have a bench anywhere there.
- He explains a little further.
- Now the man looks puzzled and he reminds Simon of his dad.

LITERARY COMPONENTS

▶ **22. Dialogue Reveals Character:** What the man says to Simon is so frightening, and yet Simon has the courage and the conviction to follow through.

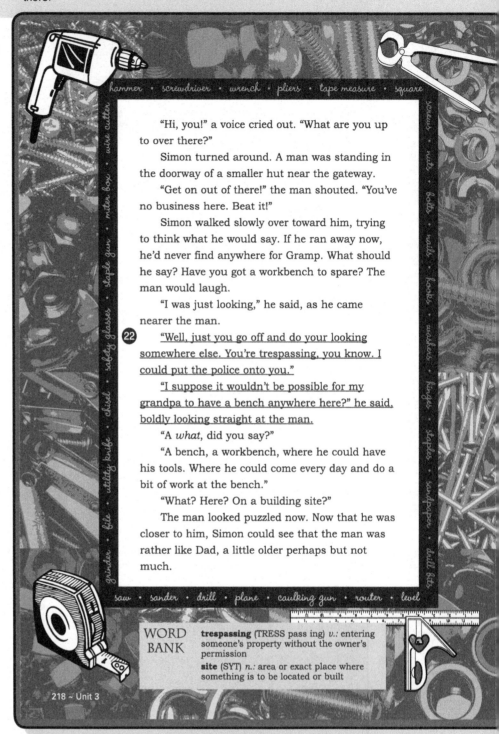

"Hi, you!" a voice cried out. "What are you up to over there?"

Simon turned around. A man was standing in the doorway of a smaller hut near the gateway.

"Get on out of there!" the man shouted. "You've no business here. Beat it!"

Simon walked slowly over toward him, trying to think what he would say. If he ran away now, he'd never find anywhere for Gramp. What should he say? Have you got a workbench to spare? The man would laugh.

"I was just looking," he said, as he came nearer the man.

22 "Well, just you go off and do your looking somewhere else. You're trespassing, you know. I could put the police onto you."

"I suppose it wouldn't be possible for my grandpa to have a bench anywhere here?" he said, boldly looking straight at the man.

"A *what*, did you say?"

"A bench, a workbench, where he could have his tools. Where he could come every day and do a bit of work at the bench."

"What? Here? On a building site?"

The man looked puzzled now. Now that he was closer to him, Simon could see that the man was rather like Dad, a little older perhaps but not much.

WORD BANK

trespassing (TRESS pass ing) *v.*: entering someone's property without the owner's permission

site (SYT) *n.*: area or exact place where something is to be located or built

218 ~ Unit 3

GUIDING THE READING

LITERAL

Q: What does the man shout at Simon?
A: He shouts, "Get on out of there! You've no business here. Beat it!"

Q: What does Simon say to the man?
A: He asks whether there might be a workbench for Gramp, where he could come every day and do a bit of work at the bench.

ANALYTICAL

Q: When the man first shouts at him, do you think he is unnecessarily rude?
A: Answers will vary.

Q: Why does Simon continue to speak to the man when he is so nasty?
A: Answers will vary. First, Simon is a brave kid. Second, he thinks to himself that if he just runs away, he will never find a place for Gramp.

SUMMING UP THE PLOT

- Simon explains, "We've come to live in the apartments... And Gramp hasn't got a shed for his tools and a bench."
- He falters as tears come into his eyes.
- As Simon wipes away his tears, all he can think of is how Gramp sits in a chair and rubs his hands up and down the handle of a small hammer.
- He tells the man he is looking for a place for him, where he can put his bench. "He's got all his tools and nowhere to use them."
- The man shakes his head and says that he knows what he means, but he can't help him.

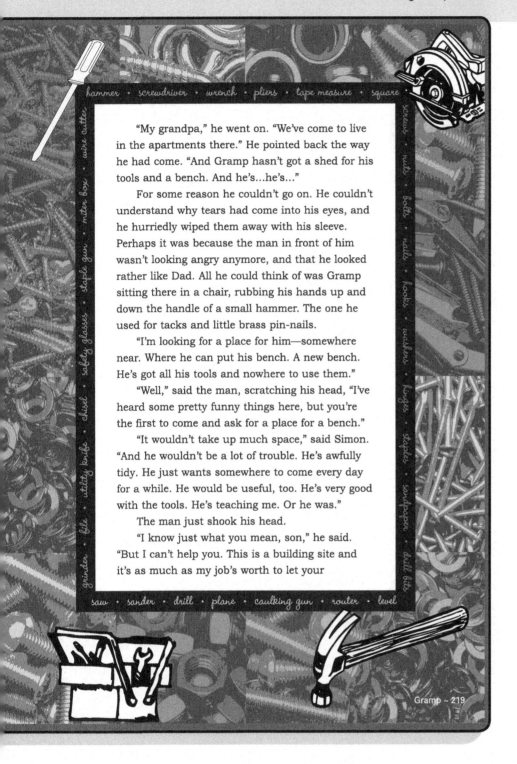

hammer · screwdriver · wrench · pliers · tape measure · square

screws · nuts · bolts · nails · hooks · washers · hinges · staples · sandpaper · drill bits

grinder · file · utility knife · chisel · safety glasses · staple gun · miter box · wire cutters

"My grandpa," he went on. "We've come to live in the apartments there." He pointed back the way he had come. "And Gramp hasn't got a shed for his tools and a bench. And he's...he's..."

For some reason he couldn't go on. He couldn't understand why tears had come into his eyes, and he hurriedly wiped them away with his sleeve. Perhaps it was because the man in front of him wasn't looking angry anymore, and that he looked rather like Dad. All he could think of was Gramp sitting there in a chair, rubbing his hands up and down the handle of a small hammer. The one he used for tacks and little brass pin-nails.

"I'm looking for a place for him—somewhere near. Where he can put his bench. A new bench. He's got all his tools and nowhere to use them."

"Well," said the man, scratching his head, "I've heard some pretty funny things here, but you're the first to come and ask for a place for a bench."

"It wouldn't take up much space," said Simon. "And he wouldn't be a lot of trouble. He's awfully tidy. He just wants somewhere to come every day for a while. He would be useful, too. He's very good with the tools. He's teaching me. Or he was."

The man just shook his head.

"I know just what you mean, son," he said. "But I can't help you. This is a building site and it's as much as my job's worth to let your

saw · sander · drill · plane · caulking gun · router · level

Gramp ~ 219

- The man says that he knows what Simon means. The old ones, he says, never like the apartments.

- He tells Simon to scat and get back to his Mum.

- Simon goes home expecting a row with his moth-er. But she only says, "Tell Grandpa his tea's ready, will you?"

- He tells Gramp, but the old man doesn't even turn his head.

- Simon dreams that night that he finds a bench for Gramp at one of the factories at the end of the road.

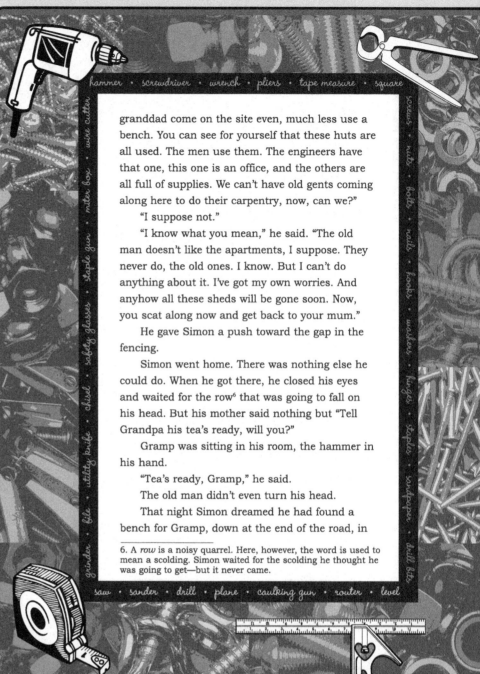

granddad come on the site even, much less use a bench. You can see for yourself that these huts are all used. The men use them. The engineers have that one, this one is an office, and the others are all full of supplies. We can't have old gents coming along here to do their carpentry, now, can we?"

"I suppose not."

"I know what you mean," he said. "The old man doesn't like the apartments, I suppose. They never do, the old ones. I know. But I can't do anything about it. I've got my own worries. And anyhow all these sheds will be gone soon. Now, you scat along now and get back to your mum."

He gave Simon a push toward the gap in the fencing.

Simon went home. There was nothing else he could do. When he got there, he closed his eyes and waited for the row[6] that was going to fall on his head. But his mother said nothing but "Tell Grandpa his tea's ready, will you?"

Gramp was sitting in his room, the hammer in his hand.

"Tea's ready, Gramp," he said.

The old man didn't even turn his head.

That night Simon dreamed he had found a bench for Gramp, down at the end of the road, in

---

6. A *row* is a noisy quarrel. Here, however, the word is used to mean a scolding. Simon waited for the scolding he thought he was going to get—but it never came.

GUIDING THE READING

LITERAL

Q: What does the man say about old people and the apartments?

A: He says that the old ones never like the apartments.

Q: How does Gramp respond when Simon calls him to tea?

A: Gramp does not even turn his head.

- The dream was so real, that the next day Simon walked straight down the road to the far end and turned in at the factory gate.
- For the first time, Simon hesitates, suddenly not so hopeful.
- The man at the factory gate says, "Looking for a job, are you?" Simon sees him wink at someone on the other side of the room.
- Simon draws a deep breath. It is not easy to explain.
- Simon begins by telling the man in the gatehouse that he's come to live in the new apartments.

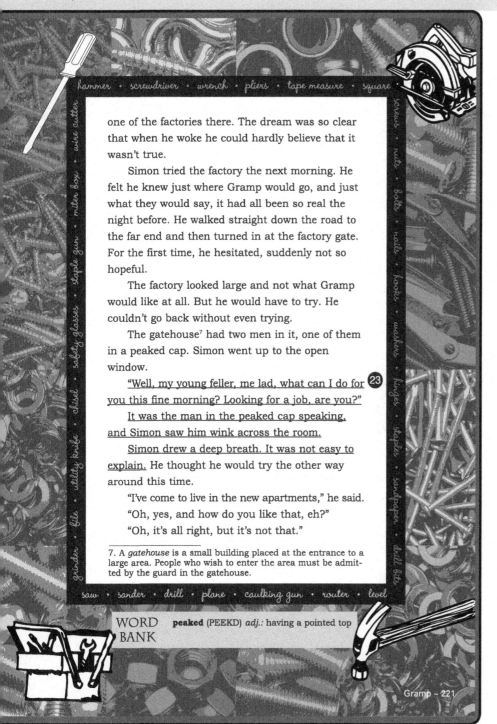

one of the factories there. The dream was so clear that when he woke he could hardly believe that it wasn't true.

Simon tried the factory the next morning. He felt he knew just where Gramp would go, and just what they would say, it had all been so real the night before. He walked straight down the road to the far end and then turned in at the factory gate. For the first time, he hesitated, suddenly not so hopeful.

The factory looked large and not what Gramp would like at all. But he would have to try. He couldn't go back without even trying.

The gatehouse[7] had two men in it, one of them in a peaked cap. Simon went up to the open window.

"Well, my young feller, me lad, what can I do for ㉓ you this fine morning? Looking for a job, are you?"

It was the man in the peaked cap speaking, and Simon saw him wink across the room.

Simon drew a deep breath. It was not easy to explain. He thought he would try the other way around this time.

"I've come to live in the new apartments," he said.

"Oh, yes, and how do you like that, eh?"

"Oh, it's all right, but it's not that."

---

7. A *gatehouse* is a small building placed at the entrance to a large area. People who wish to enter the area must be admitted by the guard in the gatehouse.

WORD BANK **peaked** (PEEKD) *adj.:* having a pointed top

Gramp ~ 221

LITERARY COMPONENTS

▶ **23. Rising Action; Characterization; Theme:** Simon is about to make his second attempt at asking about a bench for his grandfather. The author makes it clear that the gatekeepers are making fun of Simon. As Simon draws a deep breath, so do we, waiting to see just how mean they will be.

GUIDING THE READING

LITERAL

Q: What does Simon dream that night?
A: He dreams that he finds a bench for Gramp down at the end of the road, in one of the factories there.

Q: What does the man in the gatehouse say to Simon?
A: He asks him if he is looking for a job.

ANALYTICAL

Q: Why does Simon hesitate when he gets to the factory?
A: Answers will vary. It may be because the factory looks large and not what Gramp would like at all. He may be afraid of how his explanation will be responded to.

Q: What does it mean when someone winks at someone when they are speaking?
A: It means that they don't mean what they are saying.

SUMMING UP THE PLOT

- Simon goes on to say that he's come about his grandfather.

- At their old place, he tells the gatekeeper, they used to have a bit of garden and a shed. Gramp used the shed all the time and had his bench and tools in it.

- The gatekeeper says to another man in the gatehouse, "Here, come and listen to this, Jim. Here's someone with some rigmarole about his granddad."

- They both lean out the open window and look down at Simon. They ask if his granddad wants a job.

- Simon says no, that his granddad just needs a place where he can put his bench and tools.

- "Is that all?" says the second man. "...Smart young chap you are, aren't you?"

- Simon's hopes begin to rise. He begins to explain how his grandfather wouldn't be a nuisance and he wouldn't be in the way.

LITERARY COMPONENTS

▶ **24. Rising Tension:** In spite of their obvious unkindness, Simon gets pulled in by these two. Tension grows, because we are just waiting for their reaction.

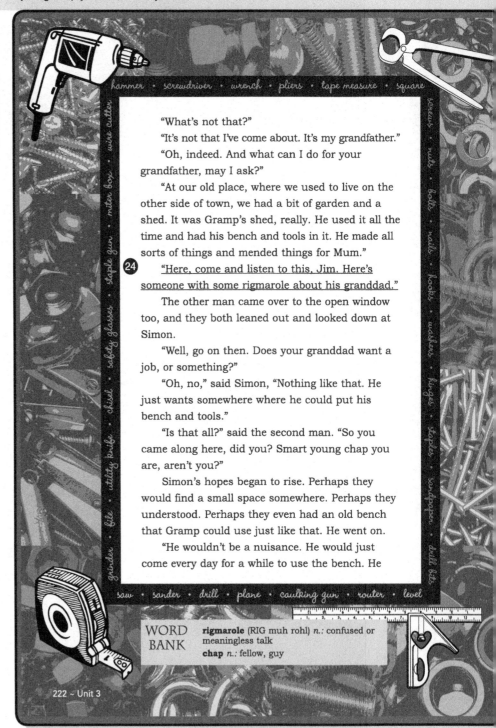

"What's not that?"

"It's not that I've come about. It's my grandfather."

"Oh, indeed. And what can I do for your grandfather, may I ask?"

"At our old place, where we used to live on the other side of town, we had a bit of garden and a shed. It was Gramp's shed, really. He used it all the time and had his bench and tools in it. He made all sorts of things and mended things for Mum."

(24) "Here, come and listen to this, Jim. Here's someone with some rigmarole about his granddad."

The other man came over to the open window too, and they both leaned out and looked down at Simon.

"Well, go on then. Does your granddad want a job, or something?"

"Oh, no," said Simon, "Nothing like that. He just wants somewhere where he could put his bench and tools."

"Is that all?" said the second man. "So you came along here, did you? Smart young chap you are, aren't you?"

Simon's hopes began to rise. Perhaps they would find a small space somewhere. Perhaps they understood. Perhaps they even had an old bench that Gramp could use just like that. He went on.

"He wouldn't be a nuisance. He would just come every day for a while to use the bench. He

WORD BANK

rigmarole (RIG muh rohl) *n.:* confused or meaningless talk
chap *n.:* fellow, guy

222 ~ Unit 3

GUIDING THE READING

ANALYTICAL

Q: When Simon tells the man in the gatehouse about his grandfather and how things used to be at their old place, the gatekeeper refers to his words as "some rigmarole about his granddad." How does that make you feel?

A: Answers will vary.

Q: When the gatekeeper calls Simon a "smart young chap," does he mean it?

A: He does not mean it. He's drawing Simon in further, so that he can humiliate him.

- Simon finishes his story by saying, "You can't have workbenches in those apartments."
- One of the men says, "You're dead right there."

- Simon says, "There isn't room, you see."
- The man says, "And so you came along here to see if we had a bench to spare for your poor old granddad eh? Is that it?"
- Simon says, "Yes, please," and the two men

burst into loud raucous laughter. "Old people's home," one says, "that's what we'd be in no time at all."
- The men stop laughing and the first man tells Simon, "Just you get cracking and get off these premises. If you think this is a place to dump your old granddad, then you're dead wrong, see?"

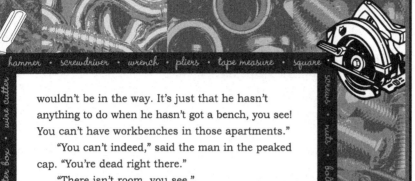

wouldn't be in the way. It's just that he hasn't anything to do when he hasn't got a bench, you see! You can't have workbenches in those apartments."

"You can't indeed," said the man in the peaked cap. "You're dead right there."

"There isn't room, you see."

"Yes, indeed I see," said the peaked cap man again. "And so you came along here to see if we had a bench to spare for your poor old granddad eh? Is that it?"

"Yes, please."

Both men suddenly burst out into loud raucous laughter, loud laughs which rained down over Simon's ears like hailstones.

"Oh, my, I've not heard such a good one for a right long time," gasped one of the men. "Old people's home, that's what we'd be in no time at all. Lor' help us, just imagine, every old person for miles traipsing in through the gate for their little bit of workshop!"

Both the men stopped laughing and the man in the peaked cap frowned.

"Now, look here, my lad," he said. "Just you get cracking and get off these premises. If you think this is a place to dump your granddad, then you're dead wrong, see? This is a factory, and a couple of thousand men work here for their living, see? Just think what'd happen if every granddad

WORD BANK
raucous (RAW kus) *adj.*: loud and harsh
traipsing (TRAYPS ing) *v.*: tramping through
premises (PREH mi suz) *n.*: a building and its grounds

Gramp ~ 223

LITERARY COMPONENTS

▶ **25. Simile:** *Both men suddenly burst out into loud raucous laughter, loud laughs which rained down over Simon's ears like hailstones.*

GUIDING THE READING

LITERAL
Q: What is the men's reaction to Simon's story about his grandfather and the apartment?

A: They burst into laughter. Students may want to describe the rest of what they say.

SUMMING UP THE PLOT

- Simon has already turned around to go. He feels hot and uncomfortable and he hates the two men.

- He feels like a fool, and thinks that perhaps Mum was right when she had said, "What can I do about it?"

- Perhaps Mum knew that Gramp was miserable. She hadn't asked to move. She had been sent to the apartment.

- Simon walks slowly back to the apartments. He doesn't want Gramp and Mum and Dad to see that he hasn't been able to do anything for Gramp.

- He doesn't want them to laugh at him.

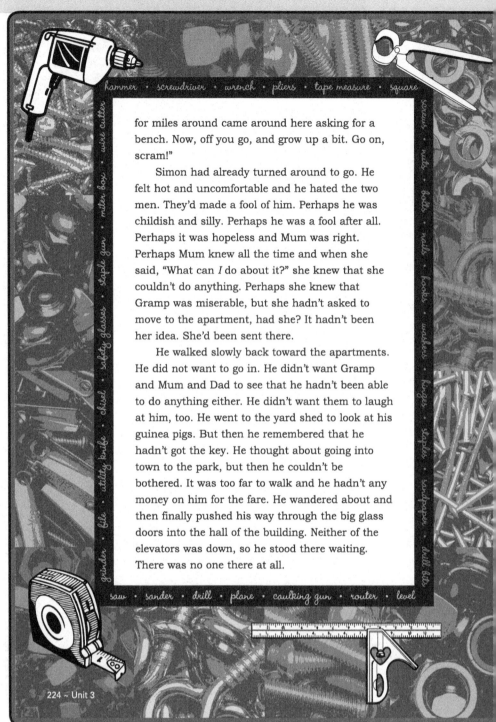

for miles around came around here asking for a bench. Now, off you go, and grow up a bit. Go on, scram!"

Simon had already turned around to go. He felt hot and uncomfortable and he hated the two men. They'd made a fool of him. Perhaps he was childish and silly. Perhaps he was a fool after all. Perhaps it was hopeless and Mum was right. Perhaps Mum knew all the time and when she said, "What can *I* do about it?" she knew that she couldn't do anything. Perhaps she knew that Gramp was miserable, but she hadn't asked to move to the apartment, had she? It hadn't been her idea. She'd been sent there.

He walked slowly back toward the apartments. He did not want to go in. He didn't want Gramp and Mum and Dad to see that he hadn't been able to do anything either. He didn't want them to laugh at him, too. He went to the yard shed to look at his guinea pigs. But then he remembered that he hadn't got the key. He thought about going into town to the park, but then he couldn't be bothered. It was too far to walk and he hadn't any money on him for the fare. He wandered about and then finally pushed his way through the big glass doors into the hall of the building. Neither of the elevators was down, so he stood there waiting. There was no one there at all.

GUIDING THE READING

ANALYTICAL

Q: What does Simon begin to think after his awful experience with the gatekeepers at the factory?

A: He thinks that perhaps he is childish and silly and a fool. He thinks that perhaps it is hopeless and that his mother was right. She didn't know what to do about it and perhaps there was nothing that could be done.

Q: Why doesn't Simon want to go back to the apartment?

A: He doesn't want Mum and Dad and Gramp to see that he hasn't been able to do anything about Gramp's workbench. He doesn't want them to laugh at him. (Students may have other things to say, as well.)

- As Simon waits for the elevator, Mr. Gideon, the caretaker, comes in through the main doors and heads for the stairs down to the basement.

- Mr. Gideon greets him and asks him why he has such a long face.
- He says he has some greens for Simon's guinea pigs.

- Mr. Gideon stops and asks Simon if he'd like to have a look around the basement.
- Simon is surprised by the invitation.

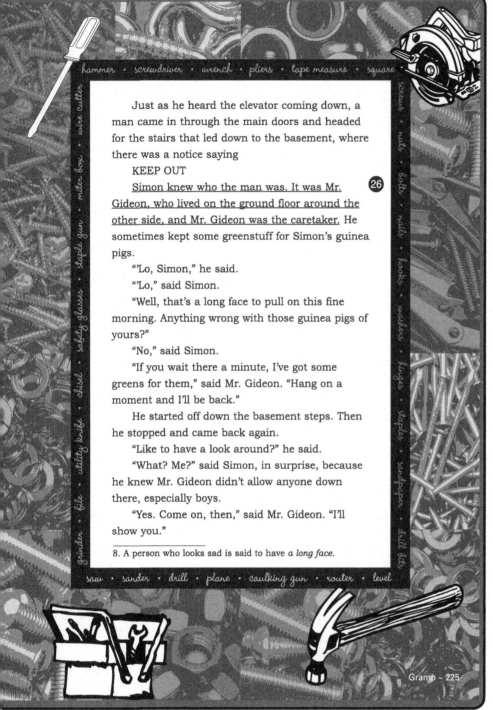

Just as he heard the elevator coming down, a man came in through the main doors and headed for the stairs that led down to the basement, where there was a notice saying

KEEP OUT

Simon knew who the man was. It was Mr. Gideon, who lived on the ground floor around the other side, and Mr. Gideon was the caretaker. He sometimes kept some greenstuff for Simon's guinea pigs.

"'Lo, Simon," he said.

"'Lo," said Simon.

"Well, that's a long face to pull on this fine morning. Anything wrong with those guinea pigs of yours?"

"No," said Simon.

"If you wait there a minute, I've got some greens for them," said Mr. Gideon. "Hang on a moment and I'll be back."

He started off down the basement steps. Then he stopped and came back again.

"Like to have a look around?" he said.

"What? Me?" said Simon, in surprise, because he knew Mr. Gideon didn't allow anyone down there, especially boys.

"Yes. Come on, then," said Mr. Gideon. "I'll show you."

8. A person who looks sad is said to have *a long face*.

Gramp ~ 225

LITERARY COMPONENTS

▶ **26. Introduction to Pivotal Character:** At this point, Simon has really reached the end of possibilities. He doesn't even know anyone to ask—as far as the reader is aware. Then, in walks Mr. Gideon, who just might save the day!

GUIDING THE READING

LITERAL

Q: Who is Mr. Gideon?
 A: Mr. Gideon is the caretaker of the building, or the building superintendent.

Q: What does Mr. Gideon offer to do?
 A: He is going to get some greens for Simon's guinea pigs.

Q: What does Mr. Gideon say that surprises Simon?
 A: He asks Simon if he'd like to have a look around the basement.

SUMMING UP THE PLOT

- In the basement, Simon feels they are in a different world altogether. "This was where the heating of the whole building came from and Mr. Gideon was in charge of it all."

- Mr. Gideon takes Simon around the basement and shows him how the heating system works.

LITERARY COMPONENTS

▶ **27. Setting; Characterization; Regal Importance!:** "Suddenly they were in a different world altogether." This is where the heat for the building comes from, and Mr. Gideon, like a minor ruler, is in charge of it all!

▶ **28. Setting:** The author describes the basement in detail through Simon's eyes. It is even clean. Why, this could be a place where miracles occur!

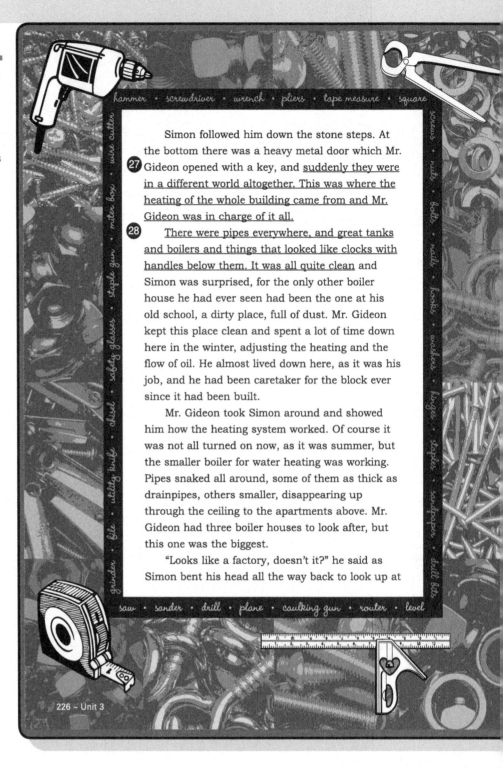

Simon followed him down the stone steps. At the bottom there was a heavy metal door which Mr. Gideon opened with a key, and suddenly they were in a different world altogether. This was where the heating of the whole building came from and Mr. Gideon was in charge of it all.

There were pipes everywhere, and great tanks and boilers and things that looked like clocks with handles below them. It was all quite clean and Simon was surprised, for the only other boiler house he had ever seen had been the one at his old school, a dirty place, full of dust. Mr. Gideon kept this place clean and spent a lot of time down here in the winter, adjusting the heating and the flow of oil. He almost lived down here, as it was his job, and he had been caretaker for the block ever since it had been built.

Mr. Gideon took Simon around and showed him how the heating system worked. Of course it was not all turned on now, as it was summer, but the smaller boiler for water heating was working. Pipes snaked all around, some of them as thick as drainpipes, others smaller, disappearing up through the ceiling to the apartments above. Mr. Gideon had three boiler houses to look after, but this one was the biggest.

"Looks like a factory, doesn't it?" he said as Simon bent his head all the way back to look up at

226 ~ Unit 3

GUIDING THE READING

LITERAL

Q: What does Simon feel happens suddenly, when Mr. Gideon opens the heavy metal door to the basement?

A: Simon feels as though suddenly they are in a different world altogether.

Q: What does Simon see in the basement?

A: He sees pipes everywhere, great tanks, boilers, and things that look like clocks with handles below them. It is clean.

ANALYTICAL

Q: Can you guess why the author makes the basement "a different world altogether?" If the basement is the opposite of the regular world, where Gramp has nothing to do, what might possibly happen in this basement?

A: Answers will vary. But probably most important is that if the basement is a different world, different from the world in which Simon has been having all of these unpleasant experiences, the world in which Gramp has nothing

to do, perhaps the basement is a place where just the opposite will be true. Try to guide your students to this realization.

SUMMING UP THE PLOT

- Alongside one of the storage tanks is a long rack of wrenches, each one slightly bigger than the last.
- Simon stares at the wrenches.

- Simon continues to stare as Mr. Gideon sweeps and wipes all the clock faces.
- Simon is so quiet that Mr. Gideon says, "What's up with you today?"
- Simon continues to stare, and Mr. Gideon

asks him what he is staring at.
- Simon points at an ordinary wooden workbench against the wall.

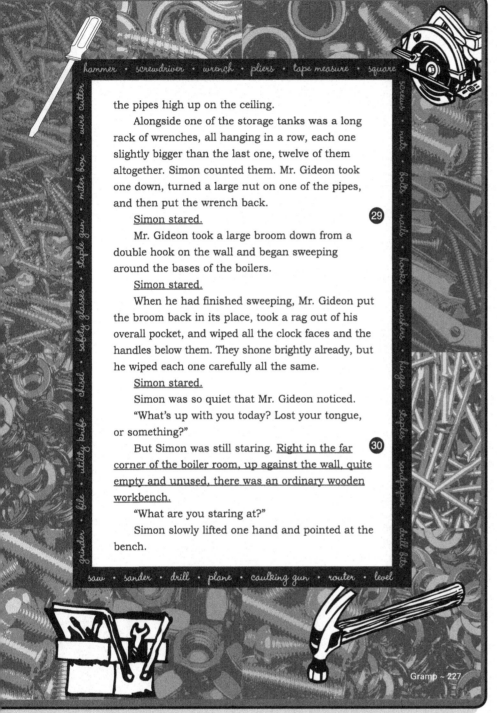

the pipes high up on the ceiling.

Alongside one of the storage tanks was a long rack of wrenches, all hanging in a row, each one slightly bigger than the last one, twelve of them altogether. Simon counted them. Mr. Gideon took one down, turned a large nut on one of the pipes, and then put the wrench back.

Simon stared. **29**

Mr. Gideon took a large broom down from a double hook on the wall and began sweeping around the bases of the boilers.

Simon stared.

When he had finished sweeping, Mr. Gideon put the broom back in its place, took a rag out of his overall pocket, and wiped all the clock faces and the handles below them. They shone brightly already, but he wiped each one carefully all the same.

Simon stared.

Simon was so quiet that Mr. Gideon noticed.

"What's up with you today? Lost your tongue, or something?"

But Simon was still staring. Right in the far **30** corner of the boiler room, up against the wall, quite empty and unused, there was an ordinary wooden workbench.

"What are you staring at?"

Simon slowly lifted one hand and pointed at the bench.

Gramp ~ 227

hammer • screwdriver • wrench • pliers • tape measure • square
saw • sander • drill • plane • caulking gun • router • level

LITERARY COMPONENTS

▸ **29. Repetition; Rising Action:** Each time we read, "Simon stared," we know something's up!

▸ **30. The Tide Turns:** When we read the magic word, *workbench,* we know a miracle is about to occur.

GUIDING THE READING

LITERAL
Q: What has Simon seen in the far corner of the boiler room, up against the wall?

A: He sees an empty and unused, ordinary wooden workbench.

ANALYTICAL
Q: What is the effect of the author's repeating the words, *Simon stared*?

A: Answers will vary. Students may say to increase suspense, to focus the attention of the reader on the fact that something is about to occur, and to give us a sense of how Simon feels.

SUMMING UP THE PLOT

- Simon asks if the workbench belongs to Mr. Gideon.

- Mr. Gideon says that he only uses it now and again.

- Simon asks if he knows his granddad.

- Mr. Gideon says that he didn't even know Simon had a granddad.

- Simon reminds Mr. Gideon that he had told him that his granddad had helped him make the hutch for the guinea pigs.

- Simon tells Mr. Gideon that his granddad doesn't like living at the apartments and doesn't go out

any longer. "He's lost his workbench and has nothing to do."

- Mr. Gideon agrees that "That's bad."

- Simon says that he's been out for two days looking for a place for Gramp to have a work-

bench. "He used to have one in the garden shed, you see? And now he's got...nowhere to put [his tools]. He couldn't...he couldn't ...?"

- Mr. Gideon turned and looked at the bench.

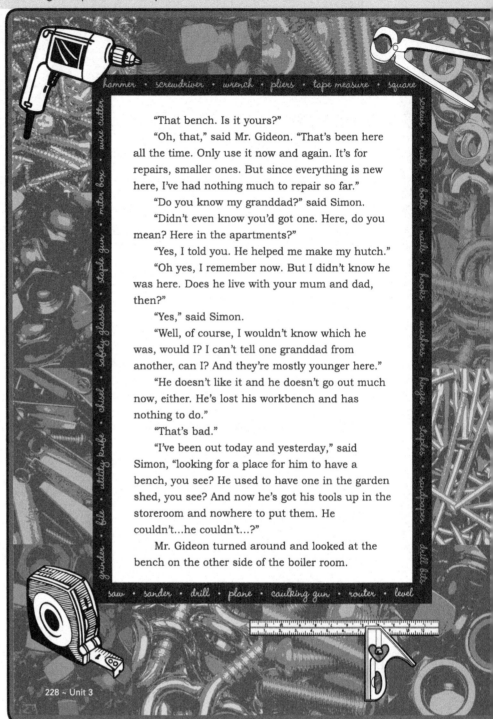

"That bench. Is it yours?"

"Oh, that," said Mr. Gideon. "That's been here all the time. Only use it now and again. It's for repairs, smaller ones. But since everything is new here, I've had nothing much to repair so far."

"Do you know my granddad?" said Simon.

"Didn't even know you'd got one. Here, do you mean? Here in the apartments?"

"Yes, I told you. He helped me make my hutch."

"Oh yes, I remember now. But I didn't know he was here. Does he live with your mum and dad, then?"

"Yes," said Simon.

"Well, of course, I wouldn't know which he was, would I? I can't tell one granddad from another, can I? And they're mostly younger here."

"He doesn't like it and he doesn't go out much now, either. He's lost his workbench and has nothing to do."

"That's bad."

"I've been out today and yesterday," said Simon, "looking for a place for him to have a bench, you see? He used to have one in the garden shed, you see? And now he's got his tools up in the storeroom and nowhere to put them. He couldn't...he couldn't...?"

Mr. Gideon turned around and looked at the bench on the other side of the boiler room.

228 ~ Unit 3

GUIDING THE READING

LITERAL

Q: What does Simon tell Mr. Gideon about how Gramp feels living in the apartment?

A: He says that he doesn't like it and doesn't go out much now, either. "He's lost his workbench and has nothing to do."

SUMMING UP THE PLOT

- Mr. Gideon says, "So that's what it's all about, is it?"

- "Well, no one uses it...I don't see why not. Bring him down one day and we'll see what we can do."

- Simon says, "You mean he could? Can I go and get him down now?"

- Mr. Gideon says, "If you like. No time like the present."

- Simon runs as he has never run before. He can't wait for the elevators and begins running up the stairs.

- He is so excited he can hardly get the key in the lock.

- No one is home but Gramp.

- Simon rushes into Gramp's room.

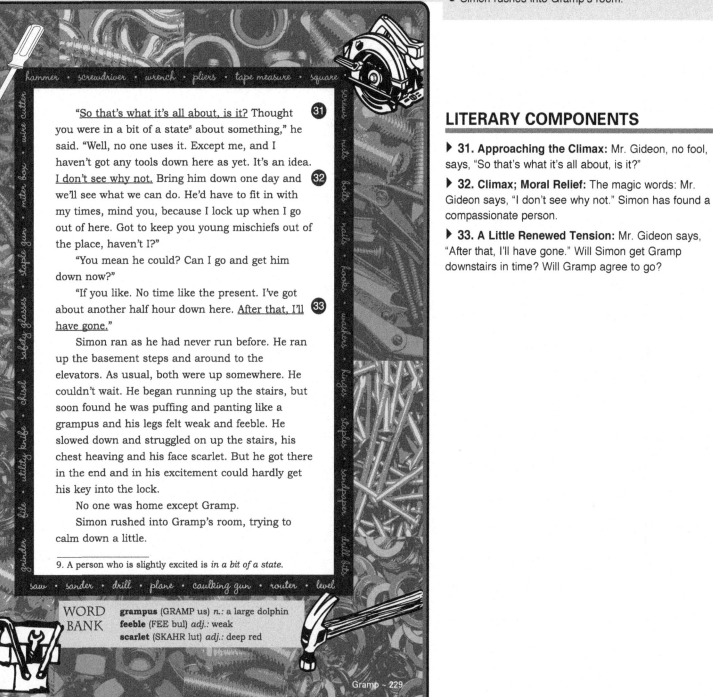

"So that's what it's all about, is it? Thought you were in a bit of a state[9] about something," he said. "Well, no one uses it. Except me, and I haven't got any tools down here as yet. It's an idea. I don't see why not. Bring him down one day and we'll see what we can do. He'd have to fit in with my times, mind you, because I lock up when I go out of here. Got to keep you young mischiefs out of the place, haven't I?"

"You mean he could? Can I go and get him down now?"

"If you like. No time like the present. I've got about another half hour down here. After that, I'll have gone."

Simon ran as he had never run before. He ran up the basement steps and around to the elevators. As usual, both were up somewhere. He couldn't wait. He began running up the stairs, but soon found he was puffing and panting like a grampus and his legs felt weak and feeble. He slowed down and struggled on up the stairs, his chest heaving and his face scarlet. But he got there in the end and in his excitement could hardly get his key into the lock.

No one was home except Gramp.

Simon rushed into Gramp's room, trying to calm down a little.

9. A person who is slightly excited is *in a bit of a state*.

WORD BANK
grampus (GRAMP us) *n.:* a large dolphin
feeble (FEE bul) *adj.:* weak
scarlet (SKAHR lut) *adj.:* deep red

Gramp ~ 229

LITERARY COMPONENTS

▶ **31. Approaching the Climax:** Mr. Gideon, no fool, says, "So that's what it's all about, is it?"

▶ **32. Climax; Moral Relief:** The magic words: Mr. Gideon says, "I don't see why not." Simon has found a compassionate person.

▶ **33. A Little Renewed Tension:** Mr. Gideon says, "After that, I'll have gone." Will Simon get Gramp downstairs in time? Will Gramp agree to go?

GUIDING THE READING

LITERAL
Q: How does Simon get up to the apartment from the basement?
A: He can't wait for the elevators, so he goes up the stairs. He begins by running.

ANALYTICAL
Q: What are the most important words in Mr. Gideon's response to Simon's barely uttered request?
A: Answers will vary. Our choice is, "I don't see why not."

Q: Why is it hard for him to get the key into the lock?
A: He is so excited—he's probably trembling.

SUMMING UP THE PLOT

- "I've found a bench for you."
- "What did you say?'
- "I've found a bench and a place for your tools."
- "A bench? Where?"
- "Come with me. I'll show you."

LITERARY COMPONENTS

▶ **34. But Maybe *This* Is the Climax:** Gramp says, "Come on, then, out with it. What's the excitement?" "*I've found a bench for you.*"

▶ **35. Characterization:** Simon still gives Gramp the room to be his own person. He grants him dignity as well, by not acting as though Gramp will just jump at the chance. This is an important value to discuss with the kids.

▶ **36. Idiom:** One of many in the story: *Are you pulling my leg* means Are you playing a joke on me or teasing me?

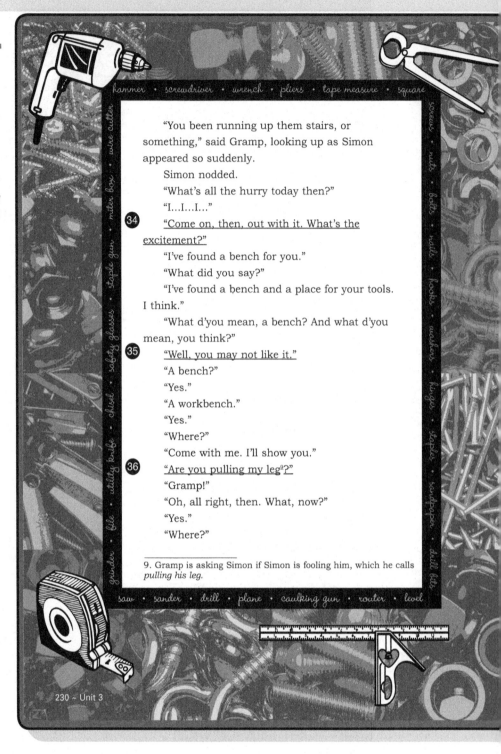

"You been running up them stairs, or something," said Gramp, looking up as Simon appeared so suddenly.

Simon nodded.

"What's all the hurry today then?"

"I...I...I..."

(34) "Come on, then, out with it. What's the excitement?"

"I've found a bench for you."

"What did you say?"

"I've found a bench and a place for your tools. I think."

"What d'you mean, a bench? And what d'you mean, you think?"

(35) "Well, you may not like it."

"A bench?"

"Yes."

"A workbench."

"Yes."

"Where?"

"Come with me. I'll show you."

(36) "Are you pulling my leg⁹?"

"Gramp!"

"Oh, all right, then. What, now?"

"Yes."

"Where?"

---

9. Gramp is asking Simon if Simon is fooling him, which he calls *pulling his leg.*

230 ~ Unit 3

GUIDING THE READING

ANALYTICAL

Q: Why do you think Gramp thinks this is a joke?

A: Answers may vary. He probably thought it was impossible to get a bench, himself. It is hard to believe his young grandson has managed to do what no one else could do. It is too good to be true and he doesn't want to be disappointed. This is so important to him.

- It takes a long time to get Gramp down to the basement.
- Simon is afraid Mr. Gideon will have left.
- But they get there and Mr. Gideon is still there.

- Gramp and Mr. Gideon talk and look at the workbench and talk again.
- Gramp says, "I could make a rack to go on the wall there."
- Simon agrees.

- Gramp adds, "Perhaps I could do a job or two for you, Mr. Gideon?"
- They continue to talk and it is arranged.

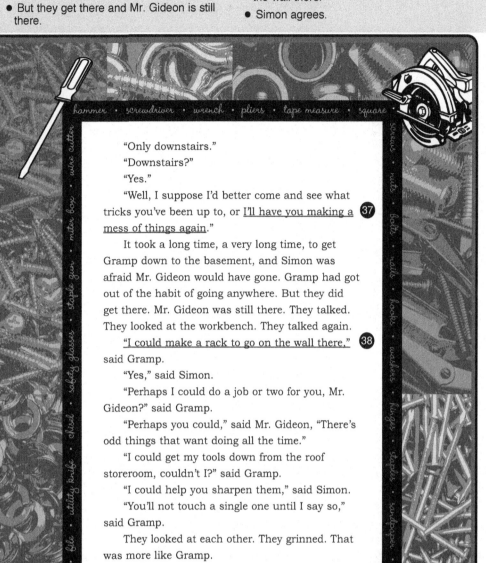

"Only downstairs."

"Downstairs?"

"Yes."

"Well, I suppose I'd better come and see what tricks you've been up to, or <u>I'll have you making a mess of things again</u>." 37

It took a long time, a very long time, to get Gramp down to the basement, and Simon was afraid Mr. Gideon would have gone. Gramp had got out of the habit of going anywhere. But they did get there. Mr. Gideon was still there. They talked. They looked at the workbench. They talked again.

<u>"I could make a rack to go on the wall there,"</u> 38 said Gramp.

"Yes," said Simon.

"Perhaps I could do a job or two for you, Mr. Gideon?" said Gramp.

"Perhaps you could," said Mr. Gideon, "There's odd things that want doing all the time."

"I could get my tools down from the roof storeroom, couldn't I?" said Gramp.

"I could help you sharpen them," said Simon.

"You'll not touch a single one until I say so," said Gramp.

They looked at each other. They grinned. That was more like Gramp.

So it was arranged.

It took a long time. Gramp's tools had to be got

Gramp ~ 231

LITERARY COMPONENTS

▶ **37. Relationship; Characterization:** Gramp reestablishes the balance of power when he says, "...or I'll have you making a mess of things again." Perhaps not the best way to thank someone.

▶ **38. Falling Action:** Gramp and Mr. Gideon negotiate the arrangement.

GUIDING THE READING

LITERAL

Q: Why is it difficult for Gramp to get down to the basement?

A: Answers may vary. But Gramp has gotten out of the habit of going anywhere, and if you don't move, you get stiff.

Q: What does Gramp have to do, before he can hang up his tools in the basement?

A: He has to make a rack for them, and then he has to clean and sharpen all of them.

SUMMING UP THE PLOT

- It takes Gramp a while to make a rack for his tools and to get them ready. Gramp has gotten a little slow.
- But each day Gramp seems a little younger, a little quicker.
- Each day Gramp tells the family what he has done.
- One night long afterward, Simon says to his mother, "I found Gramp a shed in the end, didn't I, Mum?"
- She says, "You certainly did."
- Dad says, "You certainly did. Some shed, too."
- Gramp adds, "You certainly did."

LITERARY COMPONENTS

▶ **39. Falling Action; Conclusion; Theme:** Gramp is transformed by his toil. His familial role is restored.

▶ **40. Continuing Conclusion:** The family acknowledges Simon's success.

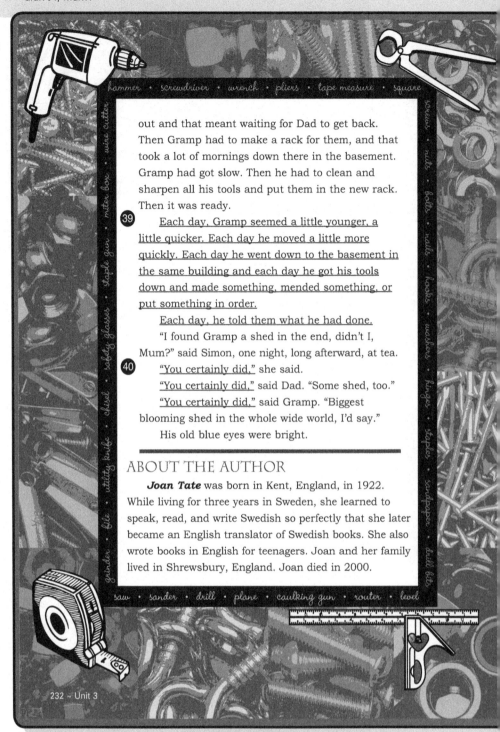

out and that meant waiting for Dad to get back. Then Gramp had to make a rack for them, and that took a lot of mornings down there in the basement. Gramp had got slow. Then he had to clean and sharpen all his tools and put them in the new rack. Then it was ready.

39 Each day, Gramp seemed a little younger, a little quicker. Each day he moved a little more quickly. Each day he went down to the basement in the same building and each day he got his tools down and made something, mended something, or put something in order.

Each day, he told them what he had done.

"I found Gramp a shed in the end, didn't I, Mum?" said Simon, one night, long afterward, at tea.

40 "You certainly did," she said.

"You certainly did," said Dad. "Some shed, too."

"You certainly did," said Gramp. "Biggest blooming shed in the whole wide world, I'd say."

His old blue eyes were bright.

ABOUT THE AUTHOR

Joan Tate was born in Kent, England, in 1922. While living for three years in Sweden, she learned to speak, read, and write Swedish so perfectly that she later became an English translator of Swedish books. She also wrote books in English for teenagers. Joan and her family lived in Shrewsbury, England. Joan died in 2000.

GUIDING THE READING

LITERAL

Q: What does Gramp say about the shed?
A: He says it's the biggest blooming shed in the whole wide world.

ANALYTICAL

Q: Why does Mum sound so different now?
A: Mum is no longer suffering over Gramp's misery and her inability to help him.

Q: Why is what Dad and Gramp say to Simon important?
A: Answers will vary. It is very important to each of us to have our good works and accomplishments acknowledged by our families.

FIRST IMPRESSIONS

Answers will vary. We think it's unusual for *anyone* to try that hard in the face of seemingly overwhelming odds.

Studying the Selection

FIRST IMPRESSIONS
Do you think it is unusual for a person Simon's age to try so hard to find a solution to his grandfather's problem?

QUICK REVIEW

1. When the story opens, what major event has recently taken place in the lives of the characters?

2. What was "best of all" for Simon, in the new situation?

3. How had Gramp helped Simon with the guinea pigs?

4. How does Simon feed his guinea pigs?

FOCUS

5. Is it easy for Simon to try to find a workbench for Gramp?

6. Simon encounters several different types of people as he tries to help his grandfather. Which person did you like the least? Why? Which did you like the most? What was there about his behavior that made you like him?

CREATING & WRITING

7. When Simon finds Gramp a workbench, Gramp is not the only one whose life improves. In several short paragraphs, write about who is helped and how.

   - *Your first paragraph* can be something like, "When Simon helps Gramp, he also helps . . . . *Your second* can be about how this helps Simon, himself. *The third* could be about how it helps his Mum. *The fourth* could be about how it helps Mr. Gideon, or Simon's Dad. (You choose the people or situations.) *In the final paragraph* write how we are all helped when another person is no longer suffering.

8. What do you know about Gramp? Imagine that he keeps a diary. What does he write in his diary after he learns about the workbench in the basement?

9. Make a collage about growing old.

Gramp ~ 233

QUICK REVIEW

1. The family has moved from a house to a(n) (high-rise) apartment building.

2. The last sentence of the second paragraph reads, "Best of all, he had found a place for his guinea pigs."

3. Gramp had arranged things in the shed, so that there was room for the guinea pigs' hutch, once he had cut the legs off it.

4. He keeps a small plastic bucket in their apartment and his mother puts leftover green leaves and stale bread in it. He also gets leftover cabbage leaves and an occasional carrot from the greengrocer and Mr. Gideon, the building caretaker.

FOCUS

5. Answers will vary. But students need to make the point that it is *not* easy. It's not easy to go talk to strangers. It's not easy to be ridiculed. It's not easy to try to do something that others say can not be done and should simply be accepted as an inevitable reality. All these points do not have to be made here, as we explore this issue in greater detail in the workbook.

6. Answers will vary on the least liked, but most children will like Mr. Gideon the most. He's patient, he listens, he treats Simon like an equal, he treats Gramp with respect, and so forth.

CREATING & WRITING

7. Answers will vary. If students can follow the suggested format but vary it somewhat with their own ideas, they will learn the basic logic of writing papers: introduction, example, example, example, conclusion. It is more important at this point for them to learn the formula than for them to be completely original.

8. Answers will vary. Remind students to write in the first-person voice and use I to refer to themselves (as Gramp) in the diary.

9. Try to make certain that students have enough material cut from magazines, if their access to magazines is limited.

CONFLICT

- A conflict is a clash of ideas, emotions, or forces.
- An *external* conflict is a conflict between a person and something outside of the person.
- An *internal* conflict is a conflict that takes place entirely inside a person's mind and emotions.
- In a story, the conflict makes the story interesting and exciting. A story without a conflict is hardly a story at all!

THINK ABOUT IT!

1. What is Jake's reaction the first time Bobby teases the new boy?
   What is his reaction the second time? What are his conflicting feelings towards Bobby?

2. What changes in Jake's reaction the third time Bobby is mean to Charles?
   Why didn't Jake act the first two times? How do you think he felt about himself each time he remained silent?

3. When Jake picks up his tray to move next to Charles, he probably is experiencing several conflicting emotions. Can you think of three things he is probably feeling?

4. What effect does Jake's action have on Bobby? Did you expect this reaction? Why or why not?

An Old Camp Trick

As Bobby and Jake left their cabin for the swimming pool, they practically bumped into the new kid.

"Watch yourself, Four Eyes," Bobby said.

Jake could hardly believe his ears. He and Bobby had been best friends at camp every summer since they were eight, and in all those years, Jake had never known Bobby to say a mean word. Jake didn't say anything, but he felt bad for the new kid.

Later, on their way into the dining hall for lunch, Jake saw Bobby stick out his foot at the last minute and trip the new kid. Jake was getting madder, but still he said nothing. What Bobby was doing was wrong, but Jake didn't want to lose his best friend.

At dinner that night, the new kid sat by himself at the end of the table where Jake and Bobby were sitting with their friends. When the boy got up to get something, Bobby grinned mischievously and shot quickly over to the new boy's tray, pouring salt and hot sauce into his milk.

Jake's face burned.

When the boy returned to his seat, the others watched as he took a bite of his food. Jake's friends giggled. The new boy looked up. His eyes met Jake's. Jake said nothing. Jake looked away, as angry with himself for saying nothing as he was with Bobby for playing this mean trick.

Finally, the new boy picked up his milk.

Jake couldn't hold back any longer. "Don't!"

The boy looked up uneasily.

"We put some stuff in your milk," he said. He looked at Bobby. Bobby stared back in disbelief. "It's an old camp trick. Don't drink it."

The boy looked confused, but he set the glass down.

Jake grabbed his tray and moved down next to the new boy.

"I'm Jake," he said.

"I'm Charles," the boy said, pushing up his glasses. "I'm from Evanston."

"Hey, Bobby's from Evanston." Jake looked over at his friend and gestured toward himself and the new boy.

Bobby looked at the other guys, then at Jake. He picked up his tray and moved toward Jake and Charles. "C'mon, guys," he said.

LESSON IN LITERATURE

1. Jake is amazed that his formerly kindhearted friend is being so mean. The second time, Jake is angry at Bobby. On the other hand, he feels loyal to him and does not want to lose his friendship.

2. The third time, Jake decides to defend Charles, instead of just feeling sympathy for him. Jake didn't do this the first two times because he was afraid of losing Bobby's friendship. He was probably disappointed and angry at himself.

3. He is probably angry at Bobby; afraid that his move to Charles will make him the object of ridicule; proud of himself; relieved that he has finally acted according to his conscience.

4. Bobby finally comes around and decides to be friendly to Charles. Those who expected this may have based their expectation on the point made at the beginning of the story that Bobby had always been a nice person. Those who didn't expect it probably judged Bobby by his forays into "bullyism."

SELECTION VOCABULARY

cajoling: persuading; coaxing

despondent: extremely discouraged; feeling hopeless

dictated: say or read aloud words so that they can be written down, typed, or recorded

distracted: draw someone's attention away

forlorn: lonely and sad

interceded: helped or defended someone by pleading or arguing on his behalf with another person

naive: lacking in experience, judgment or information

relish: great enjoyment

ridiculed: made fun of

triumphant: expressing joy over a success or victory

| cajoling | dictated | forlorn | naive | ridiculed |
| despondent | distracted | interceded | relish | triumphant |

1. The substitute teacher was inexperienced and _____ (lacking in judgment).

2. Through the store window, I saw the saleslady _____ (coaxing) Mrs. Anderson to try on an expensive fur coat.

3. Each morning, my Mom drinks her steaming hot cup of coffee with great _____ (enjoyment).

4. The president of the company _____ (read aloud) a letter to his secretary and instructed her to send a copy of it to the mayor.

5. Tracie was _____ (joyful over a victory) when, in spite of a strained muscle, she won the championship.

6. When Clara's life savings were stolen, she was _____ (extremely discouraged), for she saw no way to save up that amount of money again.

7. The lawyer _____ (pleaded for someone) on behalf of Mr. Jackson at the courthouse.

8. Sitting all alone in the playground, clutching a stuffed animal and crying softly, the little boy looked _____ (lonely and sad).

9. Tammy was _____ (attention drawn away) during school by the birds on the windowsill outside.

10. The candidate _____ (made fun of) his opponent at every opportunity.

Workbook p. 67   Answer Guide p. 7

How Do You Feel?

Each of the four words in the chart below describes how a person might feel. Draw a face in the box below representing that word.

Triumphant	Despondent	Naive	Forlorn

There are no wrong or right answers to the questions below. Answer each question, and next to "Why," explain your answer.

1. Is it better to distract a forlorn person or to ridicule him? _____
   Why? _____

2. Would it be easier for you to dictate a letter or to write it yourself? _____
   Why? _____

3. Is it better to cajole a child to eat, or to let her skip a meal? _____
   Why? _____

4. If someone in your class is angry at one of your friends, is it better to intercede on your friend's behalf, or to stay out of the argument? _____
   Why? _____

5. Do you eat leftovers with relish or reluctance? _____
   Why? _____

Workbook p. 68   Answer Guide p. 7

BACKGROUND BYTES

Two things stand out in *After School*. First, it is very well written. It is spare. No word is wasted. It is short. Yet, it is a very powerful story. The author shows us how painful it can be to be a child, and also what a difference another person can make.

The second thing that stands out in the story is that the children's parents "went far away." What does this mean? Why would both parents go far away?

Under the Communist regime (in which this story is set), the Soviet government regarded disagreement as very dangerous. If a person thought that the policies of the government were wrong and said so, or even *seemed* to say so, that person was considered a threat to the state. Such people were "taken away."

To ensure that the government knew who was expressing ideas that were a threat, the KGB, a secret police force, was formed. The job of the secret police was to make sure everyone conformed to Communist party rules. In order to squelch any dissent, the secret police spied on private citizens. People were encouraged to inform on their neighbors. Children were encouraged to inform on their parents. The job of the secret police, to crush or snuff out dangerous ideas, included crushing or snuffing out people.

Originally, as Karl Marx had it, "communism" had some well-intended ideas about sharing wealth and property. But when Communism didn't work, the failures were never attributed to the system itself. It was always the fault of another person or another way of thinking.

From the start, religious belief was outlawed. Moreover, every so often, the history books had to be officially revised to suit the party leaders of the time. Books and magazines that were not politically acceptable were removed from libraries. The media was controlled by the state. The "iron curtain" that kept out all foreign ideas or influences, was drawn tightly around the Soviet Union.

If people spoke up for human rights and freedom of speech, they were arrested. Actors performing in plays deemed dangerous, were arrested and killed. Scientists, writers, artists, composers, and poets whose work was critical of Soviet policy, were systematically persecuted and brought to trial. They were convicted as enemies of the state and imprisoned, or determined to be insane and put in mental hospitals. Some were executed. People simply disappeared. Needless to say, the Soviet Union was not the only place where this happened. There are places in the world today where it is still happening.

Thanks to a variety of complex political and economic factors, not the least of which was the tough stance taken by U.S. President Ronald Reagan against the USSR, the Soviet Union changed dramatically in the latter half of the 1980s and finally dissolved altogether in 1991.

The history of the Soviet Union is long and complicated. We have provided a very abbreviated version of events as a likely explanation of the disappearance of the children's parents. In all likelihood, the parents were taken away for "dis-sident activities."

What makes this story even more interesting to an adult reader, is the "story within a story" that it comprises. Who is V. Zhelznikov, the story's author, and what is he or she telling us about Soviet children? The real, intractable problem of the story, the "elephant in the room," is the disappearance of the parents. Where have they gone, and why? Does the young author accept the "leaving" of presumably loving parents as a normal part of life? Is the author subtly crying out to the world to notice this travesty? Does the truth lie somewhere in between? It is impossible to know. But reading about the petty arguments and slights of small children against the monumental backdrop of the "Evil Empire," makes the children's problems all the more poignant. Wondering whether the parents will receive the children's letter, and whether parents and children will ever be reunited, adds a powerful streak of *angst* to what is, on the surface, an inconsequential, if well-crafted, story.

INTO "AFTER SCHOOL"

Once again, we see that the theme reveals both glorious and devastating universal human truths: People suffer, but some people are very good. There are many hardships growing up: the hardships of embarrassment, of failure, of fear, and of loneliness may be the worst. No matter what the situation, no child, no person, is completely spared.

People are inexplicably cruel, and children do terrible things to other children. Fortunately, it is also true that some people stride through life, both men and women, both adults and children, like knights in shining armor.

EYES ON...INTERNAL AND EXTERNAL CONFLICT

As you review the story with students, make sure you discuss the internal and external conflicts of each of the characters. Explain to your students that we put things in categories like "external" and "internal" conflicts to help us isolate single qualities, ideas, events, and so forth. Once isolated, these can be more readily analyzed and compared to other qualities, ideas, etc. Analysis and comparison give us a clearer understanding of each individual thing we are talking about.

It is important to understand, however, that life does not really fit into neat categories. Real life people and events have a way of spilling over boundaries and demarcations. For example, an internal conflict can actually be the source of an external one. A person who is "conflicted" over a decision he must make, may cause an external conflict by losing his temper with the first person he encounters. Conversely, a person in the middle of an external conflict, may become embroiled in an internal one. A woman racing against the clock to get to work on time (an external conflict), may hear her toddler crying for her and face the internal—and eternal—conflict of whether to let the babysitter handle the problem or to go back and comfort her child.

Having advised you of the limitations of categorizing, we present you with a chart to be used as an aid in the analysis and comparison of the various internal and external conflicts in the story.

Character	Internal Conflicts	External Conflicts
Narrator (Yurik)	He is hungry and wants to go home, but he feels he cannot leave the little girl. His conscience nags him when he leaves the little girl and, so, he returns to her. He walks next to her even though he fears his friends will ridicule him.	He attempts to get the little girl to talk. He wants to draw her out; she remains stubbornly silent. The girl is broken-hearted and disappointed; he struggles to comfort and reassure her. The little boy is stubborn and young; the narrator struggles to explain that the little girl did not mean to fool him. The narrator struggles with the nasty neighbor's teasing.
Little Girl	She would like to go home, but feels terrible about facing her brother with disappointing news.	She expects to stay in school, but is faced with the narrator's urging and persuasiveness. She struggles to make her brother understand that she did not purposely mislead him.
Seryozha	He misses his parents but struggles against his loneliness by writing a letter to them in his mind.	He clings to the anger he feels towards his sister, but is slowly persuaded by the narrator to forgive her. He argues with the neighbor in defense of his sister and himself.
Neighbor Boy	Perhaps his sheer nastiness is attributable to some deep internal conflict.	He creates conflict by teasing and baiting Seryozha.

Blueprint for Reading

INTO . . . *After School*

Often, we think that it is the *events* of our lives that are important. When we write a letter, and nothing exciting has taken place, we write, "I don't have much to say. Nothing has happened lately." However, as we shall see in *After School,* most of "what happens" in our lives is our thoughts, our feelings, our friendships, and how we deal with other people.

Close your eyes. Focus on your breathing, in and out, in and out. How long can you do that with your mind turned off? How soon do the thoughts begin? Does it seem as though your mind has a life of its own? Thinking is almost as natural as breathing. It is the central activity of our lives.

EYES ON . . . *Conflict*

A **conflict** is a struggle. It can be a struggle between different ideas, needs, or emotions. It can also be a struggle between people and nature. It is what every story is about. Conflict is what makes a story suspenseful.

A conflict with anything that is outside, or *external* to, a person, is called an **external conflict**. A sailor caught in a storm at sea has an external conflict. He must battle the waves and the wind. Will he sink or survive? The conflict creates a suspenseful tale.

A struggle that takes place entirely *inside* a person's *mind* is called an **internal conflict**. When what we want to do is not what we ought to do, we experience an internal struggle. There are many combinations of thoughts and feelings that can create internal conflict. Can you think of some?

SUMMING UP THE PLOT

- When school is dismissed, the narrator goes to the classroom for first graders.
- He is looking after the son of his neighbor.
- It is the first of September and the first day of school.
- The narrator finds the classroom empty except for a little girl.

After School
V. Zheleznikov

When school was dismissed, I went to the classroom for first ❶ graders. I would not have gone there but our neighbor had asked me to look after her little son when school was over. After all, it was the first of September ❷ and the first day of school.

I ran into the classroom and found it empty. Everyone had already left. I was about to ❸ turn around and go on my way when I noticed someone sitting in the last row. Very little of her could be seen above her desk.

After School ~ 237

LITERARY COMPONENTS

▶ **1. Main Character/Narrator; Characterization:** The narrator is a character in the story, which is written in the first person. He is probably an elementary school child, since he visits a first grade classroom in the same building after school. We learn he is decent and responsible, since his neighbor has asked him to look after her little boy after school, and he is trying to do that.

▶ **2. Setting:** It is September, the first day of school. It is probably late afternoon, since school has been dismissed.

▶ **3. Exposition; Another Character; Characterization:** "I was about to turn around when I noticed someone . . ." The narrator sees the little girl. Her littleness is emphasized by his hardly being able to see her above her desk.

GUIDING THE READING

LITERAL

Q: What time of day is it?
A: Probably late afternoon, since it is after school.

Q: Who is telling the story?
A: The main character is narrating the story.

Q: Why has he gone to a first grade classroom?
A: He has promised his neighbor to look after her son who is in the first grade, since it is the first day of school.

Q: What does the narrator find when he looks in the first grade classroom?
A: The neighbor's boy is not there, and the room is empty except for a little girl.

ANALYTICAL

Q: What can we tell about the age of the narrator and his character?
A: Usually, high schools are not combined with elementary school classrooms, so it is likely that he is also of elementary school age. He is probably a responsible child, since his neighbor asked him to look after her little boy—which he is trying to do.

- It is odd for the little girl to be sitting there alone. All the other children are gone and probably home eating soup or jello and telling their family members about the wonders of school.

- The narrator asks her why she doesn't go home, but she doesn't answer.
- He draws a picture of a girl eating her dinner on the blackboard.

LITERARY COMPONENTS

▶ **4. Background Culture:** All the other children will have gone home and are eating soup or jello after school. They will be talking to their parents and "the other members of the family circle." The food is very specific (and certainly not necessarily what children in other countries might have), and it is clear that members of an extended family may live together.

▶ **5. Basic Conflict Introduced; Characterization:** The narrator asks the little girl why she doesn't go home. She doesn't answer easily. This is the beginning of the story. Also, he asks instead of just leaving.

▶ **6. Simile; Characterization:** The girl remains silent and sits there *like a stone statue.*

▶ **7. Strong Visual Image; Culture:** It is surprising, his drawing a picture on the board to amuse her. Both her grandmothers are there and she is eating with relish.

It was a little girl—and not at all the little boy for whom I had come. As is the custom for girl first graders on the first day of school, she wore a white apron and white bows in her hair—big ones.

It was strange for her to be

4 sitting there alone. All the other children had gone home and were probably already eating soup or jello while they were telling their parents and other members of the family circle about the wonders of school. But this one sat there waiting for heaven knew what.

5 "Little girl," I said, "why don't you go home?"

No answer.

"Have you lost something?"

She continued her silence and

6 sat there like a stone statue.

I didn't know what to do. I tried to think of a way to make this "stone statue" move. I went to the blackboard and began to draw.

I drew a first-grade girl who had come home from school and was

7 having her dinner. Then I drew a mommie, a daddy, and two grandmas. The girl was eating with relish, both cheeks bulging with

> WORD BANK **relish** (RELL ish) *n.*: great enjoyment

GUIDING THE READING

LITERAL

Q: What do first grade girls wear on the first day of school?

A: Girls wear a white apron and white bows in their hair.

Q: What does the narrator do to try to get a reaction from this "stone statue"?

A: He draws a picture on the blackboard of a mommie, a daddy, and two grandmas with a first-grade girl whose cheeks are bulging as she eats with relish.

ANALYTICAL

Q: What can you tell about life at home in Russia from the narrator's using the words "other members of the family circle" and from the fact that his drawing includes two grandmas?

A: People in Russia at that time live with their extended families.

Q: Why would people live with their extended families?

A: Answers will vary. But certainly, it is related to people's having less money. Family members do not own their own home or have the money to pay rent separately. Also, if grandmothers live with the family, there is someone to take care of the children if the mother works outside the home.

- The narrator reminds the girl that the two of them are hungry—isn't it time for them to go home, too?

- She says that she will not go home! Her voice is low and sad.

- He decides that she is a strange one and leaves the room.

- Then his conscience begins to nag and he goes back.

- He tells her he will call the school doctor and that then there will be an ambulance, the siren, and a trip to the hospital. He has decided to scare her a little.

- He, himself, is scared of the school doctor.

LITERARY COMPONENTS

▶ **8. Characterization; Simile; Onomatopoeia:** The little girl is sad and her voice is *like a mosquito. **buzz**.* In the next paragraph there is onomatopoeia, also, when his stomach begins to *rumble*.

▶ **9. Characterization; Theme:** The narrator decides she is strange and leaves, but then his *conscience begins to nag,* and he goes back.

▶ **10. Simile:** The doctor's thermometer is *as cold as an icicle.*

some delicious food, while the others were looking at her, straight into her mouth. It turned out to be an amusing picture.

"You and I," I said, "are hungry. Isn't it time for us, too, to go home?"

"No," she replied. "I'll not go home!"

"I suppose you're going to sleep here all night?"

"I don't know."

Her voice was sad and low, more like a mosquito buzz than a human voice. **8**

I looked again at my picture and my stomach began to rumble. I was getting very hungry.

"Well, too bad, she is a strange one," I said to myself. I left the room and was on my way to the exit when my conscience began to nag, and I turned back. **9**

"Listen," I said to her, "If you don't tell me why you are sitting there, I'll call the school doctor. And he—one, two, three,—he'll call 'Emergency,' there will be an ambulance, the siren, and off to the hospital you'll go." I decided to scare her a little. I am scared of the school doctor myself. He forever says: "Breathe, don't breathe...," and he sticks the thermometer under your arm. It is as cold as an icicle. **10**

"All right," she blurted out, "so

GUIDING THE READING

LITERAL

Q: What does the little girl say when he asks if it isn't time for them to go home?

A: She says she will not go home.

Q: What does the narrator remember about a visit to the doctor?

A: The doctor forever says, "Breathe, don't breathe . . . " and the thermometer is as cold as an icicle.

ANALYTICAL

Q: Why does his conscience nag him when he leaves the little girl? What do you imagine he is thinking?

A: Answers will vary.

Q: Why does he say he will call the school doctor?

A: The school doctor scares him. He figures if it scares him, it will scare her. Then he will get a reaction out of her and find out why she won't leave.

SUMMING UP THE PLOT

- The narrator asks the girl if she can't tell him what has happened.

- The little girl says that her brother is waiting for her in the yard, and that she promised to teach him all of the letters of the alphabet today.

- The narrator suggests that she makes big promises. "In one day—the whole alphabet?" Maybe she is planning to finish the whole school in one year.

- He tells her it takes weeks to learn to write all the letters.

- The little girl tells him that her mother and father went far away and that her brother, Seryozha, misses them terribly.

- She had told him that when she started school she would learn all the letters and then they would write to Mommie and Daddy.

- She says that all they wrote all day in class were sticks!

LITERARY COMPONENTS

▶ **11. Characterization; Theme:** The narrator cares very much and is very persistent. Can't the girl tell him what has happened?

▶ **12. Explaining the Conflict; Character:** Her brother is waiting for her in the yard. (And if she is so little, imagine how little *he* is!)

▶ **13. Strong Visual Image; Character:** The narrator looks out the window and a little boy is sitting there on a bench. Otherwise, the yard is deserted.

▶ **14. Explaining the Conflict; Characterization of Girl:** She had promised she would teach her brother all of the letters of the alphabet today.

▶ **15. Characterization; Theme:** He says she is quite a liar. But she says she just didn't know. He can see she is about to cry. He can see that because he pays attention and he is mature enough to be sympathetic.

▶ **16. Problem Revealed; Crux of Problem; Characterization; Theme:** Their parents have gone away. The little girl is not so little that she doesn't see how her brother suffers. She cares about his suffering. She has made a promise to help diminish his suffering.

▶ **17. Rising Action:** Her brother has already told the other boys on the street that she is going to teach him the alphabet today—but all they made that day were sticks!

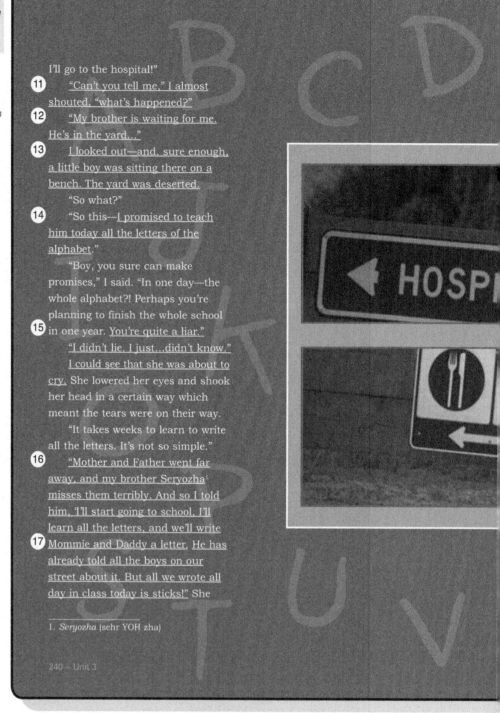

I'll go to the hospital!"

(11) "Can't you tell me," I almost shouted, "what's happened?"

(12) "My brother is waiting for me. He's in the yard..."

(13) I looked out—and, sure enough, a little boy was sitting there on a bench. The yard was deserted.

"So what?"

(14) "So this—I promised to teach him today all the letters of the alphabet."

"Boy, you sure can make promises," I said. "In one day—the whole alphabet?! Perhaps you're planning to finish the whole school

(15) in one year. You're quite a liar."

"I didn't lie. I just...didn't know." I could see that she was about to cry. She lowered her eyes and shook her head in a certain way which meant the tears were on their way.

"It takes weeks to learn to write all the letters. It's not so simple."

(16) "Mother and Father went far away, and my brother Seryozha[1] misses them terribly. And so I told him, 'I'll start going to school, I'll learn all the letters, and we'll write

(17) Mommie and Daddy a letter. He has already told all the boys on our street about it. But all we wrote all day in class today is sticks!" She

---

1. *Seryozha* (sehr YOH zha)

240 ~ Unit 3

GUIDING THE READING

LITERAL

Q: Where is the little girl's brother?
A: He is waiting out in the deserted schoolyard, sitting on a bench.

Q: What has the little girl promised her brother?
A: She has promised to teach him all of the letters of the alphabet, today.

Q: What does the little girl tell the narrator about what has happened in her family?
A: She says that her mother and father went far away and that her brother misses them terribly.

Q: What is the little brother's name?
A: His name is Seryozha.

Q: The little girl says that all they wrote in school all day was . . .
A: ...sticks.

ANALYTICAL

Q: Was the little girl lying when she told her brother she would teach him all of the letters of the alphabet the first day of school?
A: No. She had no idea how long it would take to learn the alphabet. She also wanted to reassure her brother and give him something to hope for.

Q: What will her knowing the alphabet do for the little boy?
A: If his sister knows all the letters of the alphabet, they will be able to write to their mother and father.

Q: Why is it helpful to write a letter to someone you miss?
A: Answers will vary. It helps us feel close to them, as if they are there.

Q: Why is the little girl near tears when she reports that all they wrote in class was "sticks"?
A: She is frustrated that she cannot fulfill the promise that she made in good faith.

240 ~ **Unit 3**

- The narrator says they should go to her brother and that he will explain everything to him.

- He takes her hand and they walk together to where her brother is waiting.

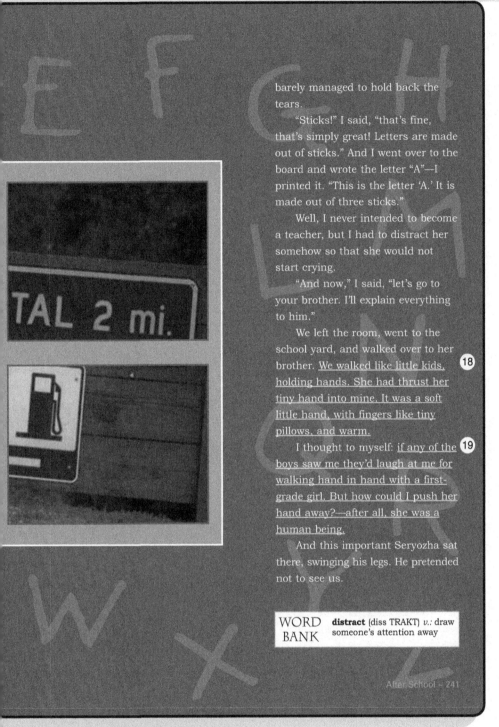

barely managed to hold back the tears.

"Sticks!" I said, "that's fine, that's simply great! Letters are made out of sticks." And I went over to the board and wrote the letter "A"—I printed it. "This is the letter 'A.' It is made out of three sticks."

Well, I never intended to become a teacher, but I had to distract her somehow so that she would not start crying.

"And now," I said, "let's go to your brother. I'll explain everything to him."

We left the room, went to the school yard, and walked over to her brother. We walked like little kids, holding hands. She had thrust her tiny hand into mine. It was a soft little hand, with fingers like tiny pillows, and warm. **18**

I thought to myself: if any of the boys saw me they'd laugh at me for walking hand in hand with a first-grade girl. But how could I push her hand away?—after all, she was a human being. **19**

And this important Seryozha sat there, swinging his legs. He pretended not to see us.

WORD BANK	**distract** (diss TRAKT) _v._: draw someone's attention away

After School ~ 241

LITERARY COMPONENTS

▶ **18. Strong, Nice Visual Image; Similes:** The narrator says that they walk _like little kids_. He describes her fingers as being _like little pillows_.

▶ **19. Characterization; Theme:** He imagines that his friends would laugh if they saw him walking with a first-grade girl. But he cannot push her hand away—after all, she's a human being.

GUIDING THE READING

LITERAL
Q: What does the narrator think the boys would do if they saw him walking with her?
A: He thinks the boys would laugh at him.

SUMMING UP THE PLOT

- The narrator tells the little brother that it takes a whole year to learn the whole alphabet.
- The little boy says, "That means she didn't learn it!" and looks at his sister with scorn.
- The little boy gets up from the bench, lowers his head, and shoves off "like a duck." He pays no attention to the narrator.
- The narrator is now tired of the entire affair. He always seems to get mixed up in other people's business.
- He catches up with the brother and tells him that he cannot blame his sister. That learning is complicated. Does he think that the astronauts Gagarin and Titov mastered the whole alphabet in one day?
- The little boy says that all day he has been memorizing the letter he was going to write to his mommie.

LITERARY COMPONENTS

▶ **20. Characterization; Simile:** Seryozha is not interested in explanations. He gets off the bench, and shoves off *like a duck.*

▶ **21. Characterization; Theme:** The narrator is getting tired of this. He always seems to get mixed up in other people's business—because he is a person who is aware and who cares.

▶ **22. Historical Reference:** The people of the Soviet Union called **Yuri Gagarin**, the Columbus of the Cosmos. Major Yuri A. Gagarin was the first man to orbit Earth. His epic 108-minute Earth orbital flight on April 12,1961, was man's first encounter with space and the beginning of our journey to the stars. As pilot of the spaceship *Vostok* 1, he showed that we can endure the rigors of lift-off, re-entry, and weightlessness. Yuri Gagarin was born March 9, 1934. He died in an airplane crash on March 27, 1968 at the age of 34. He was on a training flight in a MiG-15 aircraft. **Colonel Vladimir Georgievich Titov** was born January 1, 1947. He was selected to join the Russian cosmonaut team in 1976. He has spent a total of 387 days in space. He spent more than a year on the Soviet space station Mir 1.

▶ **23. Characterization; Informal Language:** The use of the word *Mommie* makes this poignant and heartbreaking. He is no longer an obnoxious little boy being mean to his sister.

"Listen, fellow," I said to him. "I want to explain something to you. ... You know, it takes almost a whole year to learn the whole alphabet. It's not so easy...."

"That means she didn't learn it!" he said and looked at his sister with scorn. "Then she didn't have to promise."

"We wrote only sticks all day," the little girl said desperately, "but letters are made out of sticks."

20 He didn't even listen to her. <u>He rose from the bench, put his hands in his pockets, lowered his head, and shoved off like a duck.</u> He had **21** paid no attention to me. <u>I got tired of the whole affair. I always seemed to get mixed up in other people's business.</u>

"I did learn the letter 'A'!" his sister cried after him. But he didn't even turn around.

I caught up with him.

"Listen," I said. "You can't blame her. Learning is complicated. When you start school you'll find out. Do **22** you think that <u>the astronauts Gagarin and Titov</u> mastered the whole alphabet in one day? They, too, sweated it out. And you complain..."

23 <u>"All day I've been memorizing the letter I was going to write my Mommie,"</u> he said.

242 ~ Unit 3

GUIDING THE READING

LITERAL
Q: What was the little brother doing all day?
A: He was memorizing the letter he was going to write to his mother.

ANALYTICAL
Q: Why do you think the narrator always gets involved in other people's business?
A: Answers will vary. But he is an aware, sensitive, caring person.

Q: Who are Gagarin and Titov?
A: See Literary Component 22.

- The narrator tells the boy not to worry—that he will come over after supper and will write down his letter.
- Seryozha says he will wait for him.
- After the narrator sees them enter their courtyard, he hears a loud, teasing voice.
- A boy says, "Well, Seryozha, did your sister learn the whole alphabet today?"
- Seryozha shouts that it takes a whole year to learn the whole alphabet.

LITERARY COMPONENTS

▶ **24. Rising Action; Theme; Characterization; Turning Point in Conflict:** The narrator says he will come to write down the letter. He is like a knight in shining armor.

▶ **25. Rising Action; Suspense; Characterization of Evil Villain:** A nasty neighbor boy teases Seryozha and his sister.

▶ **26. Characterization:** The little boy has learned something, *and* he stands up for his sister.

His face looked so gloomy that I thought it was wrong of his mother to have left him behind. If parents go off to distant places, let them take their children along. Children don't get scared of long trips or fierce frosts.

"Don't worry," I said to him. **24** "I'll come over after supper, and I'll write everything down just as you dictate it."

"Good!" the little girl said. "We live in that house behind the iron fence. Won't that be good, Seryozha?"

"All right," Seryozha nodded, "I'll wait for you."

I saw them enter their courtyard. Their little figures soon began to disappear behind the iron fence and some bushes.

Then I heard a loud voice, the **25** teasing voice of a boy: "Well, Seryozha, did your sister learn the whole alphabet today?"

Seryozha stopped, and his sister ran into the house.

"Do you know how long it takes **26** to learn the whole alphabet? It takes a whole year!" Seryozha shouted.

WORD BANK	**dictate** (DIK tayt) *v.:* say or read aloud words so that they can be written down, typed, or recorded

GUIDING THE READING

LITERAL
Q: What does the narrator tell the little brother and sister he will do?
  A: He says he will come over after supper and write down the letter to their parents.

SUMMING UP THE PLOT

- The nasty boy says that then Seryozha's letter will have to wait a whole year—and his parents, too.
- Seryozha says he has a friend who is coming that evening to write his letter.

- The boy says he is lying. "Can you tell me his name?"
- There is silence and then the narrator sticks his head through the bars of the iron fence. "It's Yurik," he says.

- The narrator jumps off the ledge and starts for home. He is in a pretty good mood, he says. He even feels like singing.

LITERARY COMPONENTS

▶ **27. Climax; Identity of Narrator:** This is a satisfying moment—the villain thwarted! Also, it is the moment we have all been waiting for, the name of the narrator.

▶ **28. Characterization; Theme:** He feels good—he's a good person, who makes people happy! He has solved the little girl's problem.

"Oh, is that so? Then your letter will have to wait a whole year—and your parents, too," the other boy said in a nasty way.

"No, I have a friend. He finished the first grade long ago, and he will come this evening and write my letter!"

"You're lying," the other boy said. "You're a big liar! Can you tell me his name?"

Silence.

In another second I expected to hear the triumphant cry of the tease, but I didn't let this happen. I climbed up to the stone ledge below the iron fence and stuck my

head through the bars.

"Do you want to know his name? It's Yurik," I said. ㉗

The tease's mouth fell open with surprise. Seryozha said nothing. He was not the kind to kick someone who was down.

I jumped off the ledge and started for home.

I didn't know why, but I was ㉘ in a pretty good mood. I even felt like singing.

| WORD BANK | **triumphant** (try UMF unt) *adj.:* expressing joy over a success or victory |

244 ~ Unit 3

GUIDING THE READING

LITERAL
Q: What is the narrator's name?
  A: His name is Yurik.

ANALYTICAL
Q: Why does the neighbor boy act the way he does?
  A: Answers will vary.

Q: Why does Yurik feel good at the end of the story?
  A: Answers will vary.

FIRST IMPRESSIONS

Talk with the class about times they may have helped out a younger child.

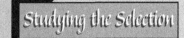

FIRST IMPRESSIONS
Are you surprised that the narrator, a young person himself, cares so much about what happens to other people?

QUICK REVIEW

1. Why does the narrator go to the classroom for first graders when school is dismissed?

2. What does he find when he goes to the classroom?

3. Who is waiting for the little girl in the school yard?

4. When do we learn the narrator's name?

FOCUS

5. Why does the narrator threaten the little girl by saying that he will call the school doctor?

6. Although the story tells of many small problems and conflicts, the children face a real problem, which casts a shadow over everything they do. What is that problem?

CREATING & WRITING

7. Why do you think the narrator helps the girl? What does he mean when he says that he was on his way to the exit "when my conscience began to nag, and I turned back"?

8. You are Yurik. Write out the letter that the little girl and her brother, Seryozha, dictate to you for their parents. Begin: *Dear Mommie and Daddy...*

9. Where is Russia? Using a globe or an atlas, draw your own map of Russia. Label the map to show the names of the countries that are on Russia's borders.

QUICK REVIEW

1. The narrator goes to the first grade classroom after school, because he has promised a neighbor that he will look after her son after school. As he explains, it is the first day of school.

2. When he goes to the classroom, he finds the room empty except for a little girl sitting in the last row.

3. The little girl's younger brother is waiting for her in the school yard.

4. We learn the narrator's name four short paragraphs from the end. It's Yurik.

FOCUS

5. The narrator tells us "I decided to scare her a little. I am scared of the school doctor myself…" He can't think of any other way to get her to tell him why she won't go home.

6. The problem is that their parents have gone away. If you haven't talked about Communist Russia yet (see Background Bytes), now would be a good time to do so. You might ask the students why this problem is only hinted at, why it is in the background and not the foreground of the story. There are many answers to this question. The children probably do not know why or where their parents have gone. A child's world is small and immediate; he can understand a teasing neighborhood boy, but he cannot grapple with Soviet ideology or KGB thuggery. The story is written from a child's point of view.

In addition, this story was written during the Communist era. The author, like the children in the story, is a victim of the Soviet regime. He or she cannot write openly about parents being transported. The author can only hint at this part of Soviet life, and in the most neutral way. Notice that there is no speculation as to where or why the parents have gone, and only the slightest, childish peeve, "If parents go off to distant places, let them take their children along." Is the reader to believe the parents have gone on some mysterious business trip or vacation? Or is the reader to "get the hint" that the parents have been transported? The author, it appears, must deflect criticism of the government and direct it towards the parents, pretending it is their fault the children have been left behind. If he does not, one would guess that the author himself, like the parents in the story, might find himself vacationing in Siberia.

An alternative interpretation would be that the parents, indeed, went on some trip, but that the author does not wish to focus on them at all, so barely discusses where or why they have gone. You, the teacher, will choose the interpretation that you find to be truest to the author's intention, and teach the story from that point of view.

CREATING & WRITING

7. The narrator is clearly a good person who cares about others. Every good person— each one of you—has a conscience that does not allow him or her to ignore a person in need.

8. Letters will vary. Encourage students to imagine (with restraint) that they are in the role of either the little girl or her brother.

9. Make sure that students have a map to copy. If you can distribute a map, that would be best. If students want to trace the map, that is fine. They will still learn about the shape and size of Russia and its neighboring countries.

LESSON IN LITERATURE . . .

DIALOGUE

- Dialogue is the conversation between the characters of a story, book, or play.

- The word, "dialogue," indicates that two or more people are speaking to one another. (The prefix *di* means "two.") A speech by a single character is called a "monologue." (The prefix *mono* means "one.")

- Dialogue tells the reader about the characters, and may be used to move the plot along.

- All dialogue is placed inside quotation marks.

THINK ABOUT IT!

1. How are the two speakers in the dialogue related?

2. What do we learn about the younger speaker from what is said?

3. How can the reader tell when a new speaker is speaking?

4. Without using any dialogue, describe, in two or three sentences, what is happening in the story.

CARPOOL

"Daddy, why do you think Ben is taking so long to get here?"

"I bet he's getting into his car seat to come pick you up right now."

"What if they forget to pick me up today?"

"If they forget to pick you up, I'll take you to school today."

"If you drove me, maybe our car would break down—by the zoo!"

"If the car broke down, we'd have to catch a city bus to get you to school."

"Maybe the bus would take us to Grandma's house instead!"

"If the bus took us to Grandma's house, we'd have to take an airplane to get you to school."

"Maybe the airplane would take us to Australia instead!"

"If the airplane took us to Australia, we'd have to charter a boat to get you to school."

"But Daddy, what if the boat took us to a lost city deep beneath the sea?"

"Oh, that's easy. We'd simply take the tunnel that leads from the lost city deep beneath the sea . . . directly into your classroom."

"Oh."

[Car pool arrives.]

"Hey, Ben's here. Time to go to school."

"Okay."

"Have a great day."

"You too, Daddy."

"Hey Sweetie—nice try."

"Thanks, Daddy."

LESSON IN LITERATURE

1. They are father and child. (It is unclear whether the speaker is a girl or boy.)

2. We learn that this child does *not* want to go to school.

3. Whenever there is a new speaker, a new line is started and new quotation marks are opened.

4. A father and child are waiting for the child's carpool. The child suggests many possible destinations other than school, indicating he/she would rather go just about anywhere than school. The father firmly lets the child know that the child must go to school. Finally, the car arrives and the two part on a friendly note.

RELATED VOCABULARY

A kick out of anything: pleasure

Bawls me out: criticizing loudly

Blow the whistle: reporting that another person is doing something wrong

Egging him on: encouraging someone to behave badly

I've got no kick coming: "I've got no reason to be angry or resentful."

Needle me: annoy or provoke

On my neck: criticizing

Rooming house: a building divided into furnished rooms or apartments for rent

Steam a kid up: trying to make someone angry

The brass: slang for authorities or people in power

A kick out of anything	Needle me
Bawls me out	On my neck
Blow the whistle	Rooming house
Egging him on	Steam a kid up
I've got no kick coming	The brass

Dear Sis,

I've been here in the big city for only a few weeks, but I have a lot to report. Last week I found a nice place to live: an old-fashioned _____ (building divided into rooms or apartments for rent) with a nice land-lady and good heating. That's the good news. Now for the rest.

Monday morning. I show up bright and early for my new job at the bank. Within an hour, I know I'm in for a rough ride. My boss doesn't wait even one day to get _____ (criticize me). He starts making comments designed to _____ (annoy me). His assistant stands there _____ (encouraging him to behave badly). Let me tell you, this guy knows just what to say to _____ (make a kid angry). He seems not to get _____ (a thrill) except criticizing the workers. Before the day is over, I am so nervous that I make a mistake counting the money, put it in the wrong place, and generally make a mess of things. The boss _____ (criticizes me loudly) and threatens to _____ (report that I have done something wrong) on me. Well, by that time, I'd had it. I tell him I'll go to _____ (the authorities) myself and complain about him- which I do. What I do not know is, "the brass" are his father and two uncles! I get fired on the spot! But _____ (I've got no reason to be angry), I'm glad to be out of there. Maybe I'll look for a job teaching proper English—there's a great need for that out there!

Love, Your Kid Brother

Workbook p. 73   Answer Guide p. 7

---

in a pickle	_____
the fuzz	_____
the horn	_____
the iron curtain	_____
a beatnik	_____
tickled pink	_____
raise the roof	_____
groovy	_____
dullsville	_____
a pad	_____

Ring Out the Old and Bring in the New

Every generation has its slang expressions. The ones in *One Throw* are quite old, and most are out of use. In the typewriter is a list of expressions from both your parents' and grandparents' generation. Do you know what these expressions mean? If you don't, ask a parent. If your parent doesn't know, it is probably one your grandparents used!

In the computer monitor on the right, write a list of five expressions used by your generation, whose meanings your grandparents may not know.

Workbook p. 74   Answer Guide p. 7

BACKGROUND BYTES

Baseball is considered the most popular sport in the United States. For those who may not know or who are unsure, here are the basics:

Baseball is played on a diamond-shaped field, with four bases: first, second, third, and home plate. A baseball team has nine players:

- pitcher
- catcher
- first baseman
- second baseman
- third baseman
- shortstop
- left field
- center field
- right field

The pitcher stands on the pitcher's mound, at the center of the diamond. The catcher squats behind home plate, at which the batters of the opposing team stand to hit the ball. (There are also umpires, men who rule on the plays, deciding, for example, whether a pitch is a *ball* or a *strike*. They do not work for either team.)

Each baseman covers his own base and tags players from the other team out if he is able. The shortstop defends the infield area on the third-base side of second base. The three fielders play in the outfield—the area around the infield, outside of the bases.

When the pitcher pitches a ball over home plate, a player on the opposing team tries to hit the ball with a bat. If he hits the ball and it is caught without touching the ground, he is out. If he hits it and it bounces on the ground, he can try to make it to first base without being tagged out. If he hits it really well, or if one of the outfielders fumbles the ball, he may even make it to second base (a double) or third base (a triple). If he hits it into the stands, no one on the opposing team can catch it and it is a home run—he runs past all three bases to home plate. When he does this he scores a run. If there are other players from his team on any of the bases, and they can make it to home plate on his hit, each of them scores a run. If there is a player on each of the bases, the bases are "loaded." If a home run is hit when the bases are loaded, it is called *a grand slam* and four runs are scored.

When a player is at bat, he is allowed to miss a good pitch only twice. These are called strikes. If he misses a third good pitch, he is out. The umpire determines whether the pitch is good or whether it is a *ball*. A strike is any ball which crosses the plate between the batter's shoulders and his knees and is not hit by the batter. A ball is any pitched ball which is outside this strike zone and is not swung at by the batter. The batter is allowed to walk to first base if the pitcher throws four balls.

Each team bats until it gets three outs. An inning is a division of a baseball game in which each team has a turn at bat and has gotten three outs. A game is nine innings unless the score is tied at the end of nine innings. Then extra innings are played, until one team has more runs at the end of the extra innings.

Two grand slams hit by one player in a single game

Believe it or not, this has happened twelve times. The last time was by Bill Mueller of the Boston Red Sox in 2003. He hit one in the 7th inning and one in the 8th inning.

Four home runs hit by one player in a single game

This has happened fifteen times. In 2003, this was done by Shawn Green of the Los Angeles Dodgers and Carlos Delgado of Toronto.

Nine pitches, nine strikes, side retired

Only 36 pitchers have done this in the history of baseball. In 2002, Pedro Martinez (Boston Red Sox), Jason Isringhausen (St. Louis Cardinals), Byrung-Hyon Kim (Arizona Diamondbacks), and Brian Lawrence (San Diego Padres); and in 2004, Ben Sheets (Milwaukee Brewers), Brandon Backe (Houston Astros), and LaTroy Hawkins (Chicago Cubs). Nolan Ryan did this twice, once in 1968 for the National League and once in 1972 for the American League. Two other pitchers have done this twice: Sandy Koufax of the Brooklyn Dodgers and Lefty Grove of the Philadelphia Athletics.

If there is enthusiasm and time for the activity, have students bring in their own fabulous baseball feats.

Language Alert

Since this story is about baseball, we can assume that the word *Throw* in the title refers to tossing or hurling a ball. But *throw* has two very different meanings in this story. What does it mean to *throw a game*? When a person *throws a game,* he or she allows an opponent to win; he or she loses the game intentionally or deliberately.

Pete says that he doesn't get along with Al, because he is "on his neck" all the time. This expression could be from one of the following idioms:

breathe down someone's neck:
(1) pursue someone closely; pose a threat to one;
(2) Watch or supervise someone very closely.

millstone around one's neck:
a heavy burden

Students are asked to explain the following paragraph in **Comprehension Questions, In-depth Thinking, #2.** It will be important for you to go through this with them. The passage is full of lingo, most of which is outdated. It does have a certain poetry to it, a sort of American rhythm, unique in all the world.

The kid was off for it when the ball started. He made a backhand stab and grabbed it. He was deep now, and he turned in the air and fired. If it goes over the first baseman's head, it's two runs in and a panic—but it's the prettiest throw you'd want to see. It's right on a line, and the runner goes out by a step, and it's the ball game.

(1) The first way to approach such a challenge is to make a list of all of the phrases, words, or sentences that are not understood. By understood, we mean *in the context within which it is used.* We all know what *deep* means, but do we know what *He was in deep now* means?

(2) The next step is the dictionary, and **writing down** the meanings that seem relevant next to each of the mystery words or phrases.

(3) Of course, most people don't have a dictionary of idioms. There are thousands and thousands of idioms in every language, in fact, and students may not be familiar with many of them.

(4) Finally, if it's not in the regular dictionary and it's not in a handbook of idioms, we just have to use our noodles and come up with the meaning that makes the most sense. This call to students to *rely on their own resources* is powerful training for life.

Our List, with each item followed by what we accomplished by trying steps (2), (3), and (4):

The kid was off for it when the ball started:
The kid was already *going after it,* as soon as the ball started moving after contact with the bat.

backhand: in baseball, a catch made on the side of the body that is opposite the hand being used. For example, if you used your right hand to catch a ball on the left side of your body, your right arm would cross in front of you and be turned so that the palm of the right hand would be facing forwards to catch a ball. (This is an example of doing the hard work of describing a physical movement with which many students may already be familiar.)

stab: an attempt, a go

he was deep now: We assume this means, he *was far advanced into the action* of doing what he was doing.

he turned in the air and fired: to propel from or as if from a gun; also, *hurl*

If it goes over the first baseman's head, it's two runs in and a panic ...:
In this story, if the ball flies over the first baseman's head, it will mean that Pete deliberately threw the game, because he is a good enough player not to do that. At this point in the story, the bases are *loaded*, which means that there is a player on each of all three bases. Since there are already two outs, if the player who has hit the ball is tagged out running from home plate to first base, no one can score. But if he is not tagged out, the likelihood is that at least the players on second and third base will make it to home plate and score two runs. This would mean that the visiting team would win by 4-3. The ninth inning is the end of the game unless there is a tie. So there would be a *panic. A panic* is a *sudden widespread fright.*

it's right on a line: it's right on target and follows imaginary line right to the first baseman

the runner goes out by a step: it takes just one step by the first baseman to tag him out; or the runner is one step away from the base before he is tagged by the first baseman—and it's the ball game:

Game's over: it's the end of the ball game, because it has been won.

INTO "ONE THROW"

Pete Maneri, "the kid," is an outstanding baseball player. He does everything right. He works hard, doesn't complain, and patiently waits to be noticed. Yet, Al Dall, the manager picks on him. He never praises his good work, but criticizes him loudly for mistakes. The Yankees, who promised to keep an eye on him, seem to have forgotten him.

Pete's story is not unusual. Most people, at one time or another in their lives, find themselves unnoticed, unappreciated, or worse, criticized or ridiculed. How should a person in such a situation react to the unfair treatment? In much of fiction, the hero remains silent, courageously soldiering on in the face of all kinds of unpleasant comments, demands, and bullying. At the other extreme, our modern-day person can be heard raucously demanding his rights and threatening lawsuits at the first hint of a perceived slight. Is there a golden medium? There may be, but it takes wisdom and maturity to find it. When and how to object to unfair treatment (if it is, indeed, unfair) is a topic worthy of discussion.

But the main point of the story is the deeper response provoked by Harry Franklin. Although Pete has been (in his eyes) unfairly treated, he refuses to compromise his personal ethic. This is called integrity. What someone else does is not in one's control; a person may protest it or not as he sees fit, with no guarantee of results either way. What the person *can* control is his own response, and what that response is, will reflect the true, inner character of that person.

EYES ON...DIALOGUE

What do your students think they know about "Harry Franklin," Nick, and Pete Maneri from the first two pages of the story? Also, does the dialogue in this passage introduce us to the characters *and* to the basic conflict?

Go through the dialogue in the passage as each character speaks, and talk with the students about what they learn. Our own list follows.
- The man at the hotel lobby desk thinks Maneri's a pretty good ballplayer.
- Maneri has been compared with Phil Rizzuto.
- There is a basic conflict: Why is he playing *here*, if he's so good?
- The man at the desk thinks Maneri is a nice kid who plays good ball.
- The man at the desk is a sympathetic person ("I feel sorry for him . . .").
- According to the man at the desk, Maneri is feeling down because he hasn't been picked up by the Yankees yet.
- Maneri's first name is Pete, and he lives at the hotel with a couple of other young players.
- The name of the man at the desk is Nick.
- There is no mail for Pete today (probably meaning no one has gotten in touch to tell him that the Yankees want him).

And so forth. Only talk about the information you gather from words within the quotation marks that indicate someone is speaking.

You may also talk with your students about the many verbs associated with vocal expression. *One Throw* uses only the word *said!* So you will want to introduce your students to the English language. It goes without saying—although you should say it—that the verb that is used by the writer must have something to do with the content and the emotion of the speaker's words.

"What do you want?" she asked.

"I just wanted to know if you have a pencil," she answered.

"I'd be glad to go to the store for you," Tess responded.

"I will *never* do that again," Kurt vowed.

"I've been shot!" he moaned.

"I need help!" Betsy shouted.

"I did so badly on the test," she sobbed.

"Come quickly," Walt urged.

"Oh, you are so funny!" Katharine laughed.

"I never meant to hurt your feelings," he apologized.

He leaned over and whispered in my ear, "Please be on your best behavior this afternoon."

"I know what I am talking about," Sue argued.

"Mom, please forgive me," she begged.

"I will do what you asked," he promised.

Perhaps your students can make up dialogue for

gasped, uttered, exclaimed, screamed, sighed, insisted, announced, declared, stated,

and any another verbs you and they can come up with.

- The narrator has checked into the Olympia hotel, the only hotel in town.
- He begins talking to the guy at the desk about a kid named Maneri who plays ball.

I checked into a hotel called the Olympia, which is right ❶ on the main street and the only hotel in the town. After lunch I was hanging around the lobby, and I got to talking to the guy at the desk. I asked him if this wasn't the town where that kid named Maneri played ball.

W. C. Heinz

One Throw ~ 249

LITERARY COMPONENTS

▶ **1. Characters; Setting; Beginning of Story:** We are introduced to the narrator, who tells the story in the first-person voice, and the person who is manning the desk in the lobby of the *only hotel in the town.* We can infer that it's a small hotel and a small town. The story begins when he asks about a kid named Maneri who plays ball.

GUIDING THE READING

LITERAL
Q: What does the narrator tell us about the Olympia Hotel?
  A: He says it's on the main street and that it's the only hotel in town.

ANALYTICAL
Q: When the narrator tells us that the Olympia is the only hotel in town, what does that tell us about the town?
  A: It tells us that it is a small town.

SUMMING UP THE PLOT

- The narrator remarks that he's read Maneri is the new Phil Rizzuto.
- The narrator asks what the matter is with this Maneri—he's such a good ballplayer, why is he in this league?
- The guy at the desk says that the Yankees must know what they're doing. He tells the narrator that Maneri is a nice kid who plays good ball. But he feels sorry for him. He thought he'd be playing for the Yankees soon, and "you can see it's got him down."
- He tells the narrator that Pete (Maneri) lives at the hotel.

LITERARY COMPONENTS

▶ **2. Metaphor; Historical Reference:** This boy Maneri is considered *the new Phil Rizzuto.* Phil Francis Rizzuto was born September 25, 1917. He played his first game with the Yankees April 15, 1941. He was only 5'6" and weighed 160 pounds. He was the American League's Most Valuable Player in 1950. He was a five time All Star. He played his final game August 16, 1956 and became a sports radio announcer. He was inducted into the Baseball Hall of Fame in 1994. Rizzuto played shortstop and threw right-handed. The famous Yankee coach, Casey Stengel, once told him he was too short and should go out and shine shoes! In fact, he helped the Yankees win seven of nine World Series games during his thirteen seasons. He helped "anchor a Yankee dynasty."

▶ **3. Opposite of Foreshadowing; Deliberately Misleading the Reader; Laying the Foundation for the Surprise Ending:** Here, the very man who turns out to be a Yankee scout asks a question he would never ask, since he's the only one who could actually answer the question.

▶ **4. Basic Conflict; Characterization:** Pete Maneri plays good ball and is a good kid. So why haven't the Yankees picked him up? The guy at the desk says that you can see it's got him down.

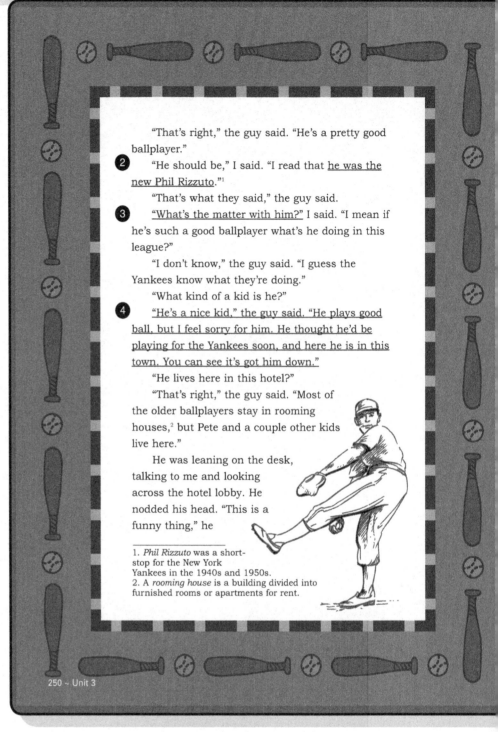

"That's right," the guy said. "He's a pretty good ballplayer."

❷ "He should be," I said. "I read that <u>he was the new Phil Rizzuto.</u>"[1]

"That's what they said," the guy said.

❸ <u>"What's the matter with him?"</u> I said. "I mean if he's such a good ballplayer what's he doing in this league?"

"I don't know," the guy said. "I guess the Yankees know what they're doing."

"What kind of a kid is he?"

❹ <u>"He's a nice kid," the guy said. "He plays good ball, but I feel sorry for him. He thought he'd be playing for the Yankees soon, and here he is in this town. You can see it's got him down."</u>

"He lives here in this hotel?"

"That's right," the guy said. "Most of the older ballplayers stay in rooming houses,[2] but Pete and a couple other kids live here."

He was leaning on the desk, talking to me and looking across the hotel lobby. He nodded his head. "This is a funny thing," he

1. *Phil Rizzuto* was a shortstop for the New York Yankees in the 1940s and 1950s.
2. A *rooming house* is a building divided into furnished rooms or apartments for rent.

GUIDING THE READING

LITERAL
Q: What is "the kid's" full name?
 A: His name is Pete Maneri.

ANALYTICAL
Q: The man at the desk says that the kid is feeling down. Why is he feeling down?
 A: Maneri is a good ballplayer. He thought he'd be playing for the Yankees by this time, so he's depressed about it.

- The narrator can see why the kid reminded people of Phil Rizzuto—he looks just like him.
- Pete Maneri says hello to the man at the desk, whose name is Nick.

- Nick introduces the narrator, Harry Franklin, to Pete Maneri.
- Harry Franklin says he recognizes Pete from pictures. Nick says that Pete's a good ballplayer.

- "Not very," Pete says.

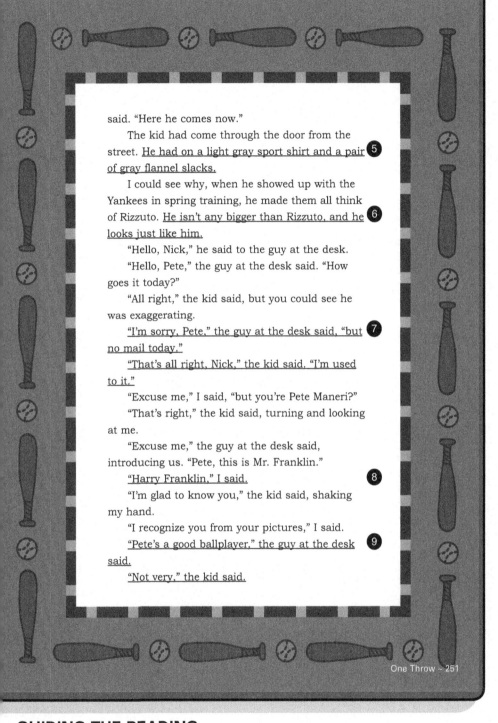

said. "Here he comes now."

The kid had come through the door from the street. He had on a light gray sport shirt and a pair of gray flannel slacks. **5**

I could see why, when he showed up with the Yankees in spring training, he made them all think of Rizzuto. He isn't any bigger than Rizzuto, and he looks just like him. **6**

"Hello, Nick," he said to the guy at the desk.

"Hello, Pete," the guy at the desk said. "How goes it today?"

"All right," the kid said, but you could see he was exaggerating.

"I'm sorry, Pete," the guy at the desk said, "but no mail today." **7**

"That's all right, Nick," the kid said. "I'm used to it."

"Excuse me," I said, "but you're Pete Maneri?"

"That's right," the kid said, turning and looking at me.

"Excuse me," the guy at the desk said, introducing us. "Pete, this is Mr. Franklin."

"Harry Franklin," I said. **8**

"I'm glad to know you," the kid said, shaking my hand.

"I recognize you from your pictures," I said.

"Pete's a good ballplayer," the guy at the desk said. **9**

"Not very," the kid said.

One Throw ~ 251

LITERARY COMPONENTS

▶ **5. Characterization:** Here comes Pete Maneri wearing a light gray sport shirt and a pair of gray flannel slacks.

▶ **6. Characterization:** The narrator says that Pete is small, just like Rizzuto.

▶ **7. Conflict:** Nick tells Pete that there is no mail and Pete says he is used to that. Presumably he is talking about a letter from the Yankees.

▶ **8. Characterization:** The narrator introduces himself to Pete as Harry Franklin.

▶ **9. Characterization:** When Nick says to Harry that Pete's a good ballplayer, Pete responds by saying, "Not very." We can see he is feeling bad about himself because he is still playing in a minor league.

GUIDING THE READING

LITERAL

Q: What is Pete wearing when he walks into the hotel lobby?

A: He has on a light gray sport shirt and a pair of gray flannel slacks.

Q: In what way does Pete seem to resemble Phil Rizzuto?

A: They are both short.

Q: What is the narrator's name?

A: He introduces himself as Harry Franklin.

Q: What does the guy at the desk say about Pete?

A: That he's a good baseball player.

ANALYTICAL

Q: Why do you think that Nick says he's sorry when he says there is no mail for Pete? Why does Pete say that he is used to it?

A: Presumably, they are not talking about letters from family and friends, but about mail that concerns his status as a baseball player. Since the story is not about any conflict Pete has with his family, or about his not having family, we have to assume that his concern about correspondence is a professional not familial one.

Q: Why do you think Pete says, "Not very," when Nick tells Harry Franklin that he's a good ballplayer?

A: Answers may vary, but he says this because it is hard for him to believe in his abilities, if he hasn't been picked up by a major league team.

SUMMING UP THE PLOT

- Mr. Franklin asks if they are playing that night. He says he's a great ball fan.

- Pete says they're playing two games, and Nick adds that the first one is at six o'clock.

- Mr. Franklin says he will be there. "I used to play a little ball myself."

- Mr. Franklin says that he played with Columbus twenty years ago.

- That's the way he gets talking with the kid in the pine-paneled taproom in the basement of the hotel. He has "a couple" and the kid has a soda. The boy is a good listener.

LITERARY COMPONENTS

▶ **10. Rising Action:** Harry manages to set things up so that he's going to see a game and he's going to get the kid to sit down and talk with him.

▶ **11. Setting; Characterization:** They are sitting talking in "one of those pine-paneled taprooms in the basement of the hotel." Harry has "a couple" (presumably this is liquor) and Pete has a soda. Harry says the boy is a good listener.

▶ **12. Setup for the Surprise Ending:** Harry Franklin tells the boy and us that he is a hardware salesman.

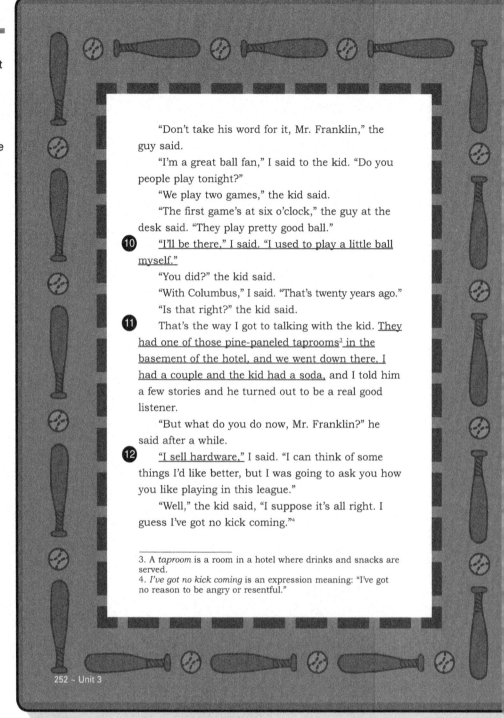

"Don't take his word for it, Mr. Franklin," the guy said.

"I'm a great ball fan," I said to the kid. "Do you people play tonight?"

"We play two games," the kid said.

"The first game's at six o'clock," the guy at the desk said. "They play pretty good ball."

❿ "I'll be there," I said. "I used to play a little ball myself."

"You did?" the kid said.

"With Columbus," I said. "That's twenty years ago."

"Is that right?" the kid said.

⓫ That's the way I got to talking with the kid. They had one of those pine-paneled taprooms[3] in the basement of the hotel, and we went down there. I had a couple and the kid had a soda, and I told him a few stories and he turned out to be a real good listener.

"But what do you do now, Mr. Franklin?" he said after a while.

⓬ "I sell hardware," I said. "I can think of some things I'd like better, but I was going to ask you how you like playing in this league."

"Well," the kid said, "I suppose it's all right. I guess I've got no kick coming."[4]

---

3. A *taproom* is a room in a hotel where drinks and snacks are served.
4. *I've got no kick coming* is an expression meaning: "I've got no reason to be angry or resentful."

GUIDING THE READING

LITERAL

Q. Is there a ball game tonight?
A. There are two games tonight.

Q: With which team did Harry Franklin play ball at one time?
A: He says he played with Columbus.

ANALYTICAL

Q: What does Harry Franklin say to Pete that is likely to get Pete interested in talking with him?
A: He says that he used to play a little ball himself.

- Pete asks him what he does now and Harry says he sells hardware.
- Harry says that he understands that Pete is too good for the league he's playing in. "What are they trying to do to you?"

- The kid says he doesn't understand it. He's hitting .365 and leads the league in stolen bases. But who cares?
- Harry asks who manages the ball club and the kid says it is Al Dall.

- Pete says he does not get along with him.
- Harry helpfully suggests that in the minors that's how they are sometimes: concerned about their ball clubs. "He's not worried about you."

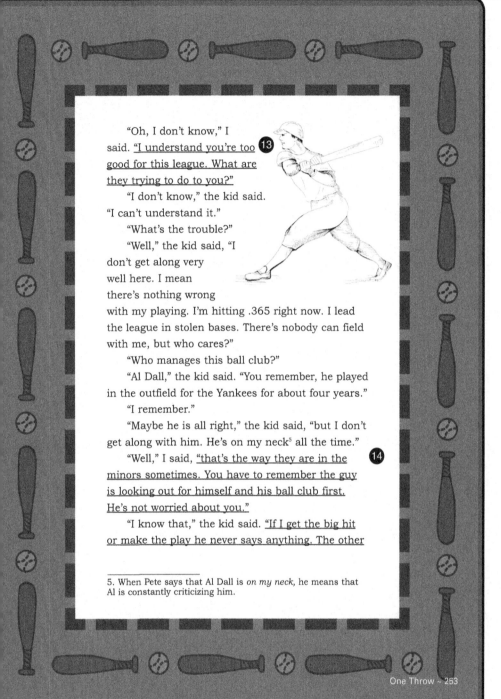

"Oh, I don't know," I said. "I understand you're too **13** good for this league. What are they trying to do to you?"

"I don't know," the kid said. "I can't understand it."

"What's the trouble?"

"Well," the kid said, "I don't get along very well here. I mean there's nothing wrong with my playing. I'm hitting .365 right now. I lead the league in stolen bases. There's nobody can field with me, but who cares?"

"Who manages this ball club?"

"Al Dall," the kid said. "You remember, he played in the outfield for the Yankees for about four years."

"I remember."

"Maybe he is all right," the kid said, "but I don't get along with him. He's on my neck[5] all the time."

"Well," I said, "that's the way they are in the **14** minors sometimes. You have to remember the guy is looking out for himself and his ball club first. He's not worried about you."

"I know that," the kid said. "If I get the big hit or make the play he never says anything. The other

5. When Pete says that Al Dall is *on my neck,* he means that Al is constantly criticizing him.

One Throw ~ 253

LITERARY COMPONENTS

▶ **13. Characterization; Exacerbation of Conflict:**
Harry tells Pete that he understands that he is too good for the league and asks what they are trying to do to him. Of course, in retrospect this is absurd, since it is the Yankees who had not sent someone yet, and now that that someone has arrived, he is pretending not to be himself.

▶ **14. Rising Action; Exacerbation of Conflict:**
Harry is continuing to try to make Pete *really* angry.

GUIDING THE READING

LITERAL
Q: What is Pete Maneri hitting now?
  A: He is hitting .365.

Q: What does Pete say Al Dall does if he gets a big hit or makes the play?
  A: He says that Al Dall never says anything.

ANALYTICAL
Q: What is the first indication that Harry Franklin is trying to egg Pete on?
  A: Franklin says that he understands that Pete is too good for this league and asks what they are trying to do to him.

Q: How does Harry explain why Al Dall may not be doing the right thing for Pete?
  A: He says that in the minors the manager is just looking out for himself and his ball club. Presumably, he doesn't want to lose a good player. He's not worried about Pete's career, but about his team's success.

SUMMING UP THE PLOT

- Pete says that when he makes a big hit or makes a play, Dall says nothing, but if he makes a mistake, Dall bawls him out in front of everyone.

- He says there is nothing that he can do.

- Harry says that Dall is probably a guy who knows he's got a good thing in Pete and is looking to keep him around. He doesn't want to lose him to Columbus or the Yankees.

- Pete says, "That's what I mean." The Yankees had said they would keep an eye on him, but (he assumes) Dall never sends a good report on him.

- What chance does he have that a guy like Eddie Brown will come down to see him?

- Harry reminds him that he has to remember that Eddie Brown is a big shot, a great Yankee scout.

LITERARY COMPONENTS

▶ **15. Characterization; Conflict:** Pete says that Al Dall doesn't compliment him when he's good, but demeans him when he's less good.

▶ **16. Rising Action; Setup for Surprise Ending:** Pete asks what chance there is that a guy like Eddie Brown will come down to see him.

▶ **17. Irony:** Eddie Brown, aka Harry Franklin, tells Pete that he has to remember that Eddie Brown is a big shot!

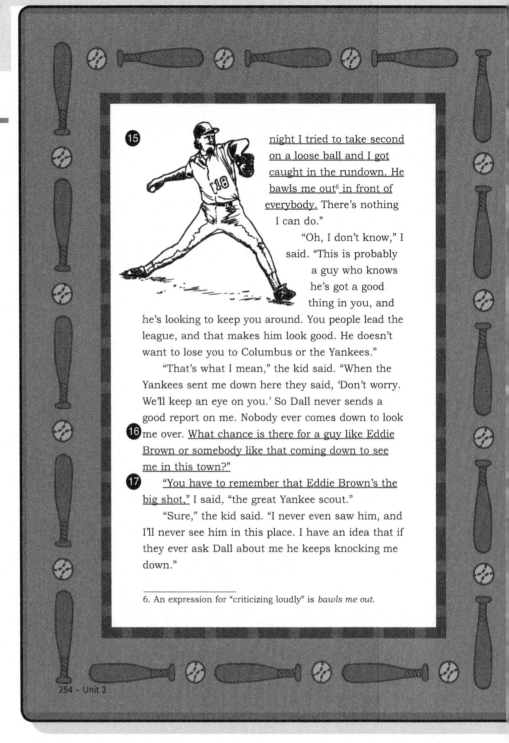

⑮ night I tried to take second on a loose ball and I got caught in the rundown. He bawls me out[6] in front of everybody. There's nothing I can do."

"Oh, I don't know," I said. "This is probably a guy who knows he's got a good thing in you, and he's looking to keep you around. You people lead the league, and that makes him look good. He doesn't want to lose you to Columbus or the Yankees."

"That's what I mean," the kid said. "When the Yankees sent me down here they said, 'Don't worry. We'll keep an eye on you.' So Dall never sends a good report on me. Nobody ever comes down to look **⑯** me over. What chance is there for a guy like Eddie Brown or somebody like that coming down to see me in this town?"

⑰ "You have to remember that Eddie Brown's the big shot," I said, "the great Yankee scout."

"Sure," the kid said. "I never even saw him, and I'll never see him in this place. I have an idea that if they ever ask Dall about me he keeps knocking me down."

---

6. An expression for "criticizing loudly" is *bawls me out.*

254 ~ Unit 3

GUIDING THE READING

LITERAL

Q: What does he say Al Dall does if he makes a mistake?

A: Pete says that then Al bawls him out in front of everyone.

Q: What is the name of the man who's a great Yankee scout (in the story)?

A: His name is Eddie Brown.

- Harry asks Pete why he doesn't go after Dall.
- He tells a story about how when he was playing for Columbus and had trouble like that, he threw a couple of games. The manager blew the whistle on him and so the brass got curious and sent someone down to see what was wrong.
- What happened? Two weeks later he was playing with Columbus.
- Harry eggs Pete on and tells him he has nothing to lose.
- The kid says he might try it tonight if the spot comes up.

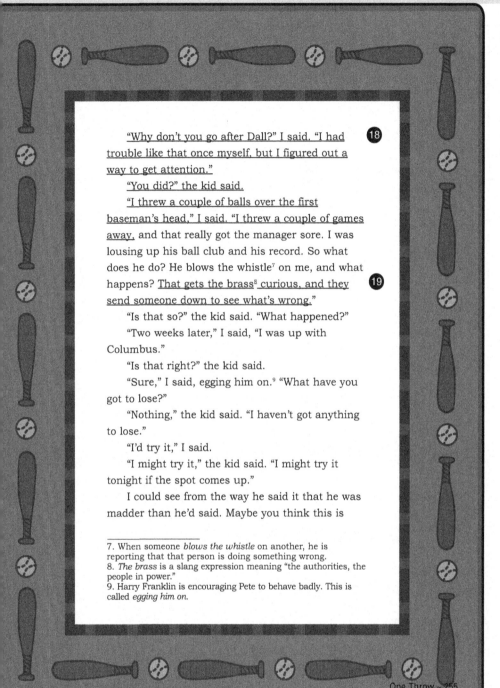

"Why don't you go after Dall?" I said. "I had trouble like that once myself, but I figured out a way to get attention." **18**

"You did?" the kid said.

"I threw a couple of balls over the first baseman's head," I said. "I threw a couple of games away, and that really got the manager sore. I was lousing up his ball club and his record. So what does he do? He blows the whistle[7] on me, and what happens? That gets the brass[8] curious, and they send someone down to see what's wrong." **19**

"Is that so?" the kid said. "What happened?"

"Two weeks later," I said, "I was up with Columbus."

"Is that right?" the kid said.

"Sure," I said, egging him on.[9] "What have you got to lose?"

"Nothing," the kid said. "I haven't got anything to lose."

"I'd try it," I said.

"I might try it," the kid said. "I might try it tonight if the spot comes up."

I could see from the way he said it that he was madder than he'd said. Maybe you think this is

_____

7. When someone *blows the whistle* on another, he is reporting that that person is doing something wrong.
8. *The brass* is a slang expression meaning "the authorities, the people in power."
9. Harry Franklin is encouraging Pete to behave badly. This is called *egging him on.*

One Throw ~ 255

LITERARY COMPONENTS

▶ **18. Beginning of Setup for the Moral Test:** Harry says to Pete, "Why don't you go after Dall?" He tells him that he threw a couple of games away by throwing balls *over the first baseman's head.*

▶ **19. Justification; Making It Seem Like It Wouldn't Be So Bad:** Well, that got the brass down there! Except that the scenario doesn't make sense. He would have been kicked out on his ear. No brass would have come to see what was going on. Would Pete believe such a story?

GUIDING THE READING

ANALYTICAL

Q: Harry Franklin tells the story about what happened when he threw a game when he was playing in the minors. Does the story make sense?

A: Answers will vary.

Q: Why is Harry Franklin trying to get Pete to throw a game?

A: He wants to see if Pete's character is as good as his baseball skills. [This story hearkens back to a time when baseball players were expected to be role models for American boys and girls.]

SUMMING UP THE PLOT

- Harry says, "Take over. Don't let this guy ruin your career."

- Pete asks Harry if he is coming out to the game that night.

- Harry says that he wouldn't miss it, and adds that *this will be better than making out route sheets and sales orders.*

- Harry says it's not much of a ball park in the town and that the first game wasn't much either. Pete's team had won 8 to 1.

- He can see the kid is a ballplayer, with a double and a couple of walks and a lot of speed.

- But the second game is different. At the top of

the ninth inning, the home team is leading 3-2. There are two outs, but the pitching has begun to fall apart and the bases are loaded.

- Harry is trying to wish the ball down to the kid, just to see what he will do.

- Just then, the batter drives the ball to the kid's right.

- He's off for it, makes a backhand stab, and grabs it.

LITERARY COMPONENTS

▶ **20. Theme; Rising Action; Suspense:** Why is Eddie Brown trying to do this to him? Your guess is as good as ours. But it is really diabolical when once more he says, "Take over. Don't let this guy ruin your career." Of course, if Pete acted on Harry's advice, that is precisely what would happen. His career would be ruined.

▶ **21. Rising Action; Suspense; Self-Characterization; Theme:** The kid says he will try it!!!

▶ **22. Rising Action; Suspense:** It's the top of the ninth. The home team has a one run lead, there are two outs, but now the bases are loaded.

▶ **23. Plot; Moral Test:** Evil Eddie is trying to wish the ball down to the kid to see what he will do and he gets his wish: the batter drives a ball to the kid's right!

▶ **24. Rising Action; Suspense:** The kid makes a backhand stab and grabs the ball. He's in deep now. If it goes over the first baseman's head . . .

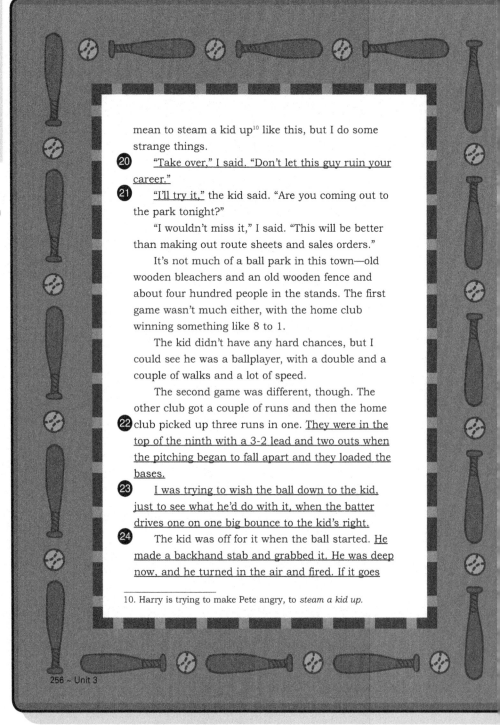

mean to steam a kid up[10] like this, but I do some strange things.

20   "Take over," I said. "Don't let this guy ruin your career."

21   "I'll try it," the kid said. "Are you coming out to the park tonight?"

"I wouldn't miss it," I said. "This will be better than making out route sheets and sales orders."

It's not much of a ball park in this town—old wooden bleachers and an old wooden fence and about four hundred people in the stands. The first game wasn't much either, with the home club winning something like 8 to 1.

The kid didn't have any hard chances, but I could see he was a ballplayer, with a double and a couple of walks and a lot of speed.

The second game was different, though. The other club got a couple of runs and then the home

22 club picked up three runs in one. They were in the top of the ninth with a 3-2 lead and two outs when the pitching began to fall apart and they loaded the bases.

23   I was trying to wish the ball down to the kid, just to see what he'd do with it, when the batter drives one on one big bounce to the kid's right.

24   The kid was off for it when the ball started. He made a backhand stab and grabbed it. He was deep now, and he turned in the air and fired. If it goes

---

10. Harry is trying to make Pete angry, to *steam a kid up.*

256 ~ Unit 3

GUIDING THE READING

LITERAL
Q: What is the kid's response to Harry Franklin's telling him to take over?
  A: Pete says "I'll try it."

Q: What is the situation at the top of the ninth inning?
  A: The home team is leading 3-2, and there are two outs, but the bases are loaded.

ANALYTICAL
Q: Why does Harry Franklin wish the ball down to the kid?
  A: He wants to see what Pete will do.

SUMMING UP THE PLOT

- If it goes over the first baseman's head, the home team may lose the game.
- But it's the prettiest throw you'd want to see.
- The runner goes out by a step, and it's the ball game.

- Harry Franklin walks back to the hotel after the game and sits in the lobby, waiting for Pete to come in.
- When Pete arrives, Harry can see he doesn't want to talk but offers him a soda.

- Pete says he's going to bed.
- Harry tells him that he did the right thing. "Have a soda."
- They are sitting in the taproom and Harry asks him why he didn't throw the ball away.
- Pete says he doesn't know. He had it in his mind to do it, but he couldn't.
- Harry asks him why and Pete says he doesn't know why.
- Harry says that he (Harry) knows why.
- He tells Pete that he couldn't throw the ball away, because he's going to be a major-league ballplayer someday.

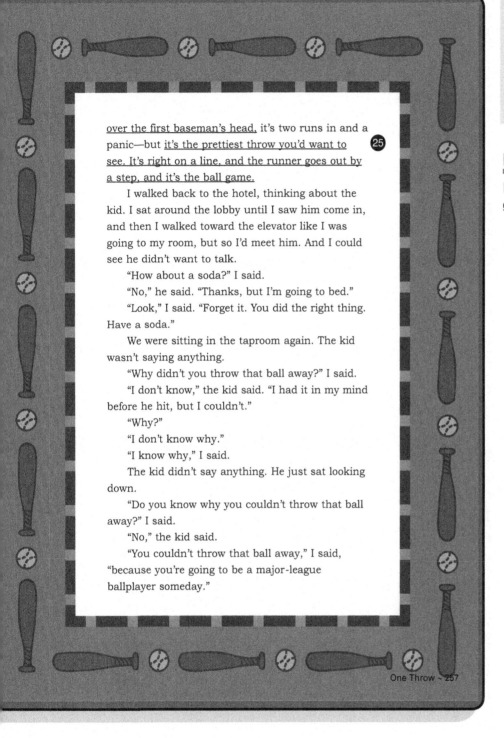

over the first baseman's head, it's two runs in and a panic—but it's the prettiest throw you'd want to see. It's right on a line, and the runner goes out by a step, and it's the ball game.

I walked back to the hotel, thinking about the kid. I sat around the lobby until I saw him come in, and then I walked toward the elevator like I was going to my room, but so I'd meet him. And I could see he didn't want to talk.

"How about a soda?" I said.

"No," he said. "Thanks, but I'm going to bed."

"Look," I said. "Forget it. You did the right thing. Have a soda."

We were sitting in the taproom again. The kid wasn't saying anything.

"Why didn't you throw that ball away?" I said.

"I don't know," the kid said. "I had it in my mind before he hit, but I couldn't."

"Why?"

"I don't know why."

"I know why," I said.

The kid didn't say anything. He just sat looking down.

"Do you know why you couldn't throw that ball away?" I said.

"No," the kid said.

"You couldn't throw that ball away," I said, "because you're going to be a major-league ballplayer someday."

One Throw ~ 257

LITERARY COMPONENTS

▶ **25. Climax; Theme:** Pete Maneri doesn't throw ball games, and "it's the prettiest throw you'd want to see."

SUMMING UP THE PLOT

- Pete just looks at him, looking angry.
- Harry says, "You're going to be a major-league ballplayer, because you couldn't throw that ball away, and because I'm not a hardware salesman and my name's not Harry Franklin."
- Pete says, "What do you mean?"
- "Harry" says, "I mean that I tried to needle you into throwing that ball away because I'm Eddie Brown."

LITERARY COMPONENTS

▶ **26. Denouement:** Everything is revealed at this moment. All our understandings are turned on their head. This is the final outcome, the main dramatic complication of this story. Here is our surprise ending, nicely done!

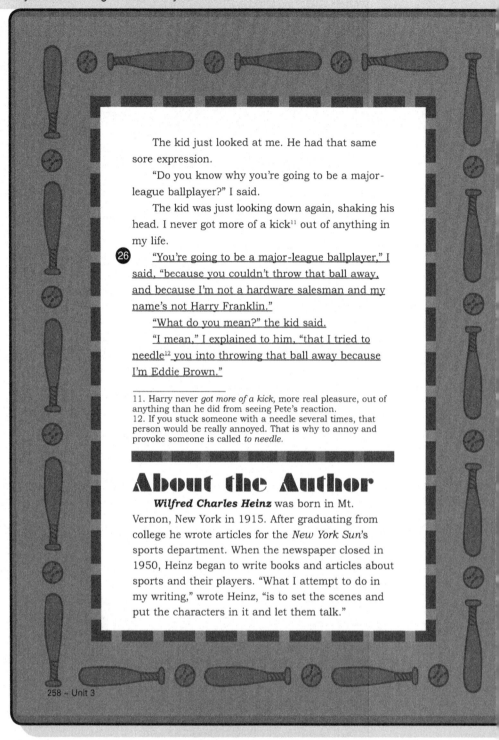

The kid just looked at me. He had that same sore expression.

"Do you know why you're going to be a major-league ballplayer?" I said.

The kid was just looking down again, shaking his head. I never got more of a kick[11] out of anything in my life.

26 "You're going to be a major-league ballplayer," I said, "because you couldn't throw that ball away, and because I'm not a hardware salesman and my name's not Harry Franklin."

"What do you mean?" the kid said.

"I mean," I explained to him, "that I tried to needle[12] you into throwing that ball away because I'm Eddie Brown."

---

11. Harry never *got more of a kick,* more real pleasure, out of anything than he did from seeing Pete's reaction.
12. If you stuck someone with a needle several times, that person would be really annoyed. That is why to annoy and provoke someone is called *to needle.*

About the Author

Wilfred Charles Heinz was born in Mt. Vernon, New York in 1915. After graduating from college he wrote articles for the *New York Sun*'s sports department. When the newspaper closed in 1950, Heinz began to write books and articles about sports and their players. "What I attempt to do in my writing," wrote Heinz, "is to set the scenes and put the characters in it and let them talk."

GUIDING THE READING

LITERAL

Q: Who is Harry Franklin?
A: Harry Franklin is really Eddie Brown, the big shot Yankee scout.

FIRST IMPRESSIONS

After students give their own reactions, talk with them about whether there were any clues to the surprise ending.

Studying the Selection

FIRST IMPRESSIONS
Were you surprised by the ending?

QUICK REVIEW

1. Where in the story do you first see the "kid's" last name? What is his last name? Where do you first see his first name? What is his first name?

2. When the narrator first sees the kid, what is he wearing?

3. When the kid played with the Yankees in spring training, who did he remind them all of?

4. What is the first name of the man working at the front desk of the hotel?

FOCUS

5. Why doesn't the kid throw the game?

6. To understand the way dialogue is written in a story, copy the paragraphs on page 254 in which the kid tells Harry Franklin why he is so upset with Al Dall, the manager of the ball club.

CREATING & WRITING

7. Imagine that the kid *did* throw the game. What would he and "Harry Franklin" talk about after the game? How would their conversation go? Write down their dialogue, as you imagine it would have been. Does Eddie still offer him a job with the Yankees?

8. You are Eddie Brown. Explain why you pretended to be someone other than who you *really* are, and why you tried to get the kid to throw the game. Tell us what you have learned about the kid that makes you want him for your team.

9. Draw a World Series scoreboard. Decide what two teams are playing, how many runs have already been scored, what inning it is, and who's at bat. If you want, you can even draw a company's ad above the scoreboard.

One Throw ~ 259

QUICK REVIEW

1. The kid's last name, *Maneri,* is in the very first paragraph. His first name is in paragraph 10, when the man at the desk says, "'Most of the older ballplayers stay in rooming houses, but *Pete* and a couple other kids live here.'"

2. In paragraph 12 we read, "He had on a light gray sport shirt and a pair of gray flannel slacks."

3. In paragraph 13 we read, "I could see why, when he showed up with the Yankees in spring training, he made them all think of Rizzuto. He isn't any bigger than Rizzuto, and he looks just like him." In paragraph 3 the narrator says, "'He should be,' I said. 'I read that he was the new Phil Rizzuto.'"

4. In paragraph 14, we read, "'Hello, Nick,' he said to the guy at the desk."

FOCUS

5. Answers will vary. Pete Maneri is honest. He has character. He has integrity. He respects baseball and knows there is no game if people cheat. He's a true sportsman. He doesn't want to turn into a second class player.

6. The passage we are thinking of is on page 254 and runs from "'Al Dall,' the kid said. 'You remember,...'" to "'...There's nothing I can do.'" When the students have copied the dialogue, ask if they have started a new line for each speaker, if they have put their quotation marks in the right places, if they have noticed the comma at the end of each person's dialogue, except where there is no narration following. Point out that sometimes narration breaks up a sentence and that the quotation marks are, likewise, broken up.

CREATING & WRITING

7. Help students with proper format. Try to make certain that the dialogue deals with a concrete response by Harry Franklin to the kid's yielding to temptation.

8. Answers will vary.

9. Please make certain that students have access to sufficient material to do their drawings. It is all right if they trace or copy.

A CHARACTER'S INNER THOUGHTS

- We learn about a character's inner thoughts from the story's dialogue.
- We learn about a character's inner thoughts from the character's actions.
- We learn about a character's inner thoughts from the story's narration.
- As in real life, it may take us time to fully understand a character's inner thoughts.

THINK ABOUT IT!

1. How do we know that Matt had not meant to hurt Frankie?
   - From his words
   - From his actions
   - From what the story's narration tells us
   - All of the above

2. How does Matt *feel* when he hears that Frankie has been taken to the hospital?

3. What does Matt *do* to express how sorry he is?

4. What are two feelings that Frankie had towards Matt before Matt gave him the card?

Friends

Matt hadn't meant to hurt his friend. It all happened so fast. One minute he and Frankie were playing; the next, Frankie's father was rushing Frankie to the hospital.

Frankie was pretty sure he knew what happened. They had been playing soldiers, tossing sticks and stones at pretend enemies in the woods behind Frankie's house. In the fading light of the evening, it was getting harder and harder to see. Frankie's eye must have been hurt by something Matt threw. A sickish feeling, like a tight fist, began to form in his stomach.

The next morning, Mom opened the curtains of Matt's room early. "Frankie's home," she said. "He'll have a patch on his eye for a while, but he's going to be fine."

Matt felt like an enormous weight had been lifted from him. Still, he knew he had to tell Frankie the truth. He quickly went to his house.

When he arrived at Frankie's, his friend was on the couch.

"That's a big bandage," Matt said. "Does it hurt?"

"A little," said Frankie.

He gave Frankie a get-well card. Inside was a single baseball card, the card Frankie had been trying to trade him for all summer.

"Wow!" Frankie exclaimed. "Now I've got the whole set! Thanks, Matt."

Matt was glad the baseball card made Frankie happy, but the sick feeling in Matt's stomach wasn't going away.

Matt took a deep breath. "Last night, when your eye got hurt...I'm pretty sure it was a stick I threw that hurt your eye."

Frankie said nothing.

"I'm sorry," Matt continued. "I didn't mean to hurt you."

"You know, I kind of thought that's what happened," Frankie said.

"You did?" Matt asked. "Why didn't you say anything?"

"Same reason you didn't. I'd feel terrible if I threw the stick."

"I do feel terrible. Will you still be my friend?" he asked.

"That's a silly question," said Frankie. "Of course I will." Then he added, "Can I still keep the baseball card?"

"It's yours," Matt said.

Frankie smiled, and the sick feeling in Matt's stomach began to go away.

LESSON IN LITERATURE

1. d. All of the above.

2. Matt had a sickish feeling.

3. Matt went to visit Frankie. He also gave Frankie a baseball card.

4. Frankie had several feelings. He was angry or hurt that perhaps Matt had hit him with the stick on purpose. On the other hand, he thought perhaps it had been an accident. If it was an accident, he felt sympathy for the guilt Matt might be experiencing. Either way, he seems to have felt a real liking for Matt.

SELECTION VOCABULARY

belligerent: argumentative; displaying an eagerness to fight

conspicuous: noticeable; standing out

flitted: flew swiftly from one place to another, settling only for a moment

incubating: sitting on eggs for the purpose of hatching

melodically: tunefully; with a beautiful melody

preened: trimmed or smoothed feathers with the beak or tongue

purling: flowing with a curling or rippling motion, as a shallow stream over stones

sapling: a young tree

serenely: calmly; peacefully

thicket: a dense growth of bush or small trees

---

belligerent	flitted	melodically	purling	serenely
conspicuous	incubating	preened	sapling	thicket

It was a gorgeous October day as we set out to hike through the enormous park. We passed a _____ (dense growth of bushes), then entered a woods through which a trail wound. Above us, birds _____ (flew from one place to another), resting on the branch of this tree or that _____ (young tree), only to fly off to perch somewhere else. The air was filled with the sweet sounds of birds singing _____ (tunefully). In the distance, we heard the burbling of a _____ (flowing with a rippling motion) stream. A _____ (argumentative) blue jay screamed at an unseen foe, while a pigeon stood _____ (calmly) in the pattern of shade and sunlight that filtered through the leaves. It was the wrong season for finding mother birds _____ (sitting on eggs) their eggs, but we did see an old, empty nest, which the birds had long forgotten. A cardinal hopped across our path, his bright feathers making him very _____ (noticeable) indeed! He _____ (smoothed feathers) his feathers for a moment, then flew off in a blaze of color.

Workbook p. 79   Answer Guide p. 8

Tongue-Tied Tim

Tongue-Tied Tim is a fifth grader with a very tiny vocabulary. Every sentence ends with "I mean," "you know," or just trails off...because Tim knows so few words. Can you help Tim? Replace his little baby words with some nice, juicy adult words from your vocabulary list. Then, eliminate all his "y'know"s and "like"s, correct the grammar, and rewrite his sentences on the line provided.

1. I don't like that guy. He's always looking for a fight, I mean, like, really a fighter.

2. Hey—she's a good teacher. I mean like, she talks you know- calm, soft...

3. That butterfly there...I been watching it. It you know—jumped from flower to flower—cool!

4. Meet me under that, uh, bush? Little tree? You know—it's like not a real tree yet.

5. That there is a, I don't know, like bubbling little river?

6. I found this wallet in the middle of like, you know, a lot of bushes.

7. I like watching those birds in the zoo like, cleaning their feathers, uh, they kind of use their mouth thing to smooth their feathers...

8. Yeah, I saw that boy! He kind of stuck out because you know, funny hair and like, well he was real noticeable.

9. On the farm, we watched those hens on their nest things. Really dull. Bo-ring. They were just sitting on those eggs.

10. He's a real good singer. His voice is like, good and he sings uh, cool, you know, good-sounding songs

Workbook p. 80   Answer Guide p. 8

BACKGROUND BYTES

This is a true story about a family in Washington State. The Allensons live about two miles from the nearest town, a town that consists of a post office and three houses. Mr. Allenson's name is Wankatya, which means in English *up above*. Mr. Allenson's father, who is also Mr. Allenson, translates Wankatya into English as *Brushes the Sky*. His father calls him that partly because Wankatya is 6'4". Mrs. Allenson is Tahcasca, or White Deer. The Allensons have two children, a boy and a girl. Mr. Allenson, or Brushes the Sky, is a Lakota (or Sioux), and he is a retired professor of English. Mrs. Allenson's great-great grandparents were Cherokee. The word, *Lakota,* means *considered* (*la*) *friends* (*kota*).

The Allensons live near the forest, although Mr. Allenson writes that most of the privately owned forest has been "logged off," and even the federal land—which is not supposed to be touched—has been thinned recently. "There is now a Song Sparrow in every available space. Song Sparrows need approximately one square mile each; that means one per square mile. However, they all overlap because of the loss of habitat. Plus, they all sneak into Spot's square mile to eat at the bird feeder." Spot is the Song Sparrow who resides in the Allenson's backyard. Spot is so named, because of the markings on his chest and because he follows Mr. Allenson and his son around like a dog.

"The song of the Song Sparrow is especially beautiful, which is why they were given that name, I guess. If you get a chance to listen to them sing, take it.

Mrs. Allenson, or White Deer, writes that "Watching a female Spotted Towhee taking care of a baby Song Sparrow, provided me with one example of the behavior of Song Sparrows, specifically, parental care—or the lack thereof. This is just one instance of cross-species parenting that I have seen at my bird feeder and in my backyard. Besides parenting (or not), the birds that flock to our feeder most clearly demonstrate such categories of animal behavior as territoriality and social interaction.

"One example is our resident female American Robin, whose nest is on our electric meter every other year—the same cycle as the blooming cycle for the rhododendrons that block her nest from view. Robins are usually not territorial. However, when she nests here, our robin will suffer no intrusions of any kind.

She will even chase the slightly larger Steller Jays, who are among the most notorious nest robbers in the region.

"Normal bird conflicts are like street fights among humans: name calling, chest puffing, and a series of feints and retreats. But during motherhood, our non-territorial American Robin not only chases other birds but tries to attack. One or both birds may be seriously injured as a consequence.

"Unlike Robins, Song Sparrows are territorial all year long, but presumably only towards other males of their species. However, on several occasions, Spot has assisted my husband in locating European Starlings and chasing them away from nesting sites around our property (which is also Spot's and the Robin's territory).

"According to my husband, Spot sings a particular song for each direction, as well as songs for up and down, far and close. My husband, who is an amateur ornithologist, even claims that Spot can sing, 'I love you,' and, 'I'm happy to see you!'

"The Purple Finch queen at our feeder assumes that her position of dominance extends to the entire feeder flock—not just to other finches—as well as to the chipmunks. She is queen and all others are not.

"On the other hand, the Junco and the Chickadee groups within the feeder flock each have their own intra-flock hierarchy. For Juncos and Chickadees, each member of the flock has a specific status. This is where we get the expression, *a pecking order*. Dominance is clearly to do with who eats how much, and with who is going to marry whom. Sometimes, it is hard to watch birds (or other animals) hurt or treat cruelly other birds (or animals), especially when their behavior is related to how they take care of their babies.

"Song Sparrows, for example, take great care making a nest and guarding it after the egg(s) are laid. Oddly, twelve to 36 hours after the eggs are laid, at least one, and usually both, parents desert the baby. At our feeder two years ago, a deserted baby Song Sparrow (who was to become our Spot), fixed its attention on a female Purple Finch. That Song Sparrow ate sunflower seeds, like a finch, instead of the food that its genetic parents had eaten.

"This year, that baby became a father to his own baby. But Spot learned parenting from a Finch, so he took care of it. (My husband claims that *he*, not the Finch, taught Spot good parenting.) The baby is a month old now, and Spot and his wife are still taking care of it. The new baby, Spot Jr., eats sunflower seeds with his father at the feeder, and wild bird food with his mother on the ground.

"Another common occurrence at our bird feeders is that the birds demand to be fed. One Black-Capped Chickadee clings to the window sill of our bay windows and pecks at the glass until the feeder is filled. The Purple Finch queen lands on the hummingbird feeder at the windowpane, and beats her wings against the glass until we respond. It is not clear how the birds figured out to tap on the glass the first time, since, after all, they do not reason as humans do. But it is the *humans* here that have been conditioned like Pavlov's dogs. When the birds tap on the glass, we feed them.

"An unnatural society has formed at the plentiful food source represented by our feeders. Species that normally would not interact, such as Purple Finch and Red-Breasted Nuthatches, do so (although with tension when their paths cross). This impromptu flock has both a static population—birds that remain here all year—as well as a dynamic population—one governed by migratory patterns.

"Our feeder flock uses *communal* strategies to provide food and maintain public safety. Among birds, communication is essential for the organization of the flock and for integrating individual and group behaviors. Bird communication is also essential to survival. All of our flock, no matter what their species, respond to the Black-Capped Chickadee's calls that mean *FOOD* and *ALL CLEAR*."

Some Added Notes:

Among northern Song Sparrows, there are both migratory and nonmigratory birds. Apparently, the decision to migrate is an individual one; it is a choice, not an inherited behavior.

First-year Song Sparrows sing a low, warbling song in autumn that sounds like a Purple Finch. Typically, the Song Sparrow sings a three-part song when he is courting or defending his territory. The song has a rhythmic beginning. The central part is trilled. It concludes with a short, irregular series of notes. Incredibly, every male Song Sparrow sings a half dozen to two dozen different songs! Each one is repeated several times before the individual goes on to the next one. Song Sparrows usually sing perched seven to 15 feet above the ground. Although they do so less in winter, Song Sparrows sing year round. They have a *tseep* to indicate alarm, and "a distinctive and recognizable call note, *tchenk*."

INTO "THE BIRDS' PEACE"

The major thing that occurs in this story is that Kristy goes from the painful feeling of her father's absence (which has an immediacy that is almost unbearable) to being able to keep him in her mind and talk to him there. Letter writing will help her do this. Talk to your students about this. It is one of the most important aspects of maturation and it is endlessly helpful to people in dealing with loss and tragedy. When we are feeling alone or lonely, we can close our eyes and visualize the people who love us and ourselves loving them back. They do not have to be physically present for us to draw comfort from them. We have told students (in *After School*) that their thoughts will be the most important events in their lives. Here, again, our thoughts create goodness and comfort.

EYES ON...WHEN A CHARACTER SPEAKS TO SOMEONE WHO CAN'T ANSWER

It is interesting to see how simply verbalizing one's thoughts is curative. Although expressing one's doubts and fears aloud does not always lead to a solution, it almost always helps one to clarify, analyze, and unravel the problem. Spoken words are a lot slower than panicky thoughts, and putting a problem into words starts out with the advantage of forcing the worrier to slow down and think more rationally.

In *The Birds' Peace*, the author uses an interesting device to achieve two effects. The device is what we shall call "the one-person-dialogue": Kristy talking to a songbird, something like Annie talking to Sandy, or Christopher Robin talking to Winnie-the-Pooh. (In each case, the "human's" lines differ from a monologue, in that a monologue is a long, formal speech to the audience or world at large, whereas a "one-person-dialogue" is a "conversation" with a nonverbal listener.) The first effect is to reveal the character's thoughts in a more dynamic way than could a first or second-person narrative. The second effect is to set the stage for a revelation on the part of the speaker, arrived at through the process of verbalizing the problem and perceiving (or projecting) some solution to it, in the behavior of the listener.

What part of what we have said is relevant to a fifth grader? The helpfulness of verbalizing a turbulent mix of emotion and anxiety should be emphasized. The notion of a mild, non-judgmental listener is appealing to children as well as to adults. A child who finds himself or herself on the listening end of a friend's problem should bear this in mind. Also, the idea that often we ourselves can be a source of solutions to our own inner turmoil, should be pointed out.

Blueprint for Reading

INTO . . . The Birds' Peace

When terrible things happen to people, they sometimes feel as though they can no longer be themselves. They know they must change to handle what has happened.

Kristy's father has left to fight in a war. How can this be? He doesn't even know how to shoot a gun! Her father is gone! This cannot be happening to her!

Kristy runs outside to a place where she and her father spent time together. As she weeps, she grows calmer and begins to notice the world around her. She hears the song sparrow. She listens and watches him. He seems to be in trouble. She tells him that she feels the way he feels. She watches again and learns something new.

EYES ON . . . When a Character Speaks to Someone Who Can't Answer

When a character speaks out loud, the words are put in quotation marks. A character's spoken lines are usually part of a *dialogue*, a conversation between two or more characters. In *The Birds' Peace*, there is only one speaker—Kristy, but her lines are treated as though they are part of a dialogue.

At times, a character's *thoughts* are placed in quotation marks. It may be difficult for the reader to decide whether the character is thinking these words or actually speaking them. In real life, there is a great difference between the way we think and the way we speak. Our thoughts are lightning quick, and not expressed in complete sentences. Our speech, however, must be in words that another person can understand. That is why the thoughts expressed in a story are written more like spoken language than the language of thought.

262 ~ Unit 3

The BIRDS' PEACE

Jean Craighead George

The Birds' Peace ~ 263

SUMMING UP THE PLOT

- It is the day Kristy's father has gone off to the war.
- She bursts out the back door and runs down the path to the woods.
- Her eyes hurt and her chest burns.
- She runs into the lean-to she and her father have built at the edge of the meadow.
- Kristy drops to her knees, covers her face with both hands, and sobs.
- She hears a bird sing.
- Kristy looks up and recognizes Fluter, the busy

LITERARY COMPONENTS

▶ **1. Exposition; Character; Setting:** Kristy's father has gone off to war.

▶ **2. Setting:** She runs down the path to the woods.

▶ **3. Characterization:** Her eyes hurt, her chest burns.

▶ **4. Setting; Characterization; Motivation:** The lean-to is a place she and her father have shared.

▶ **5. Rising Action:** Kristy falls to her knees and cries.

▶ **6. Intervention; Character (of Sorts):** A bird sings.

▶ **7. Motivation:** Kristy responds to Fluter.

▶ **8. Learn about Character Through Her Words:** Kristy is scared, because her father is going to war.

---

little song sparrow who lives in the bushes at the edge of the meadow.

- He seems to be in trouble. His song is loud and belligerent.
- Kristy says, "I'm in trouble, too. My father

had to go into the army. He's going to war. And I am scared."

- Fluter goes on singing. After a few moments he flies across the meadow and boldly sings from a raspberry patch.

On the day Kristy's father went off to war, she burst out the back ❶ door and ran down the path to the woods. Her eyes hurt. Her chest ❷ ❸ burned. She crossed the bridge over the purling stream and dashed into the lean-to she and her father ❹ had built near the edge of the flower-filled woodland meadow.

She dropped to her knees, then to her belly. ❺ Covering her face with both hands, she sobbed from the deepest well of her being.

Tears did not help. The pain went on and on. A bird sang. ❻

Kristy lifted her head. She recognized Fluter, the busy ❼ little song sparrow who lived in the bushes at the edge of the meadow. He seemed to be in trouble. His melodious song was loud and belligerent.

"I'm in trouble, too," she said. "My father had to go into ❽ the army. He's going to war. And I am scared." Fluter ignored her and sang on. From across the meadow, a strange song sparrow sang clearly and loudly. Kristy barely heard him.

"Daddy doesn't even know how to shoot a gun." Fluter flew to a sumac bush, thrust out his spotted tan breast, and sang again.

"Suppose bombs fall on him." Kristy began to cry again. "Or an enemy tank shoots at him."

Fluter went on singing. After a few moments he flew across the meadow and boldly sang from a raspberry patch.

Dulce, his mate, flew off their nest in the thicket, where she had been

WORD BANK

purling (PURR ling) *adj.*: flowing with a curling or rippling motion, as a shallow stream over stones
melodious (muh LOE dee us) *adj.*: tuneful; sweet-sounding
belligerent (buh LIJ urr int) *adj.*: argumentative; displaying an eagerness to fight
thicket (THIK et) *n.*: a dense growth of bushes or small trees
incubating (IN kyew BAY ting) *v.*: sitting on (eggs) for the purpose of hatching

264 ~ Unit 3

GUIDING THE READING

LITERAL

Q: Where is Kristy's father?
A: He has gone off to war.

Q: Where had Kristy and her father built the lean-to?
A: The lean-to is at the edge of a flower-filled woodland meadow.

Q: What does Kristy tell Fluter?
A: She tells him that she is in trouble, too, because her dad has gone off to war and she's scared. Dad doesn't even know how to shoot a gun. What if bombs fall on him or an enemy tank shoots at him?

Q: What is Fluter's wife's name?
A: Her name is Dulce.

ANALYTICAL

Q: Why do you think Kristy rushes outside and runs to the lean-to?
A: She may feel like she needs to escape from the house because her feelings overwhelm her. She may be soothed by being outdoors. She and her father have obviously spent time together there and have built the lean-to together. Being there probably makes her feel his presence.

Q: Why do you think Kristy stops crying when she hears the bird sing?

A: Perhaps she is all cried out. People, especially children, cannot weep forever. When they have expressed the worst of their grief, they can be distracted by outside events. Also, Kristy feels Fluter is echoing her own sense of being in trouble.

Q: Is Fluter's song a happy song?
A: Answers may vary, but the author tells us he sounds loud and belligerent. Make sure students know what the word belligerent means.

SUMMING UP THE PLOT

- Dulce, his mate, flies off their nest, where she has been incubating their eggs.
- She eats some bristlegrass seed, preens her feather, and seems quite at ease.

- Fluter is not.
- He flicks his tail and raises his crest and flies to the bracken fern.
- Fluter flits briskly to the sugar maple and sings from a conspicuous twig.

- He flies to the dogwood tree and sings from a high limb.
- He flies and he sings.
- Kristy becomes aware of what he is doing. He is making a circle, an invisible fence of song around his meadow and his nest in the thicket.
- Suddenly Fluter makes the sound that Kristy's dad had said were notes of warning. Dulce becomes alarmed and flies silently back to their nest.
- Kristy looks to see what is the matter. There is a strange song sparrow in Fluter's raspberry bush!
- Fluter crouches as if he is going to fly at the stranger, but instead he sings.
- The stranger departs when he hears Fluter's "stay-off-my-property" song.
- He alights on his own sapling and sings back to Fluter.

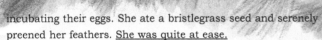

incubating their eggs. She ate a bristlegrass seed and serenely preened her feathers. <u>She was quite at ease.</u> ⑨

    <u>Fluter was not.</u> He turned this way and that. He flicked his tail and raised his crest, then flew to the bracken fern and sang. <u>He</u> ⑩ <u>flitted briskly to the sugar maple limb and sang from a conspicuous twig. He winged to the dogwood tree and sang from a high limb. As he flew and sang,</u> Kristy became aware of what he was doing. He ⑪ <u>was making a circle, an invisible fence of song around his meadow</u> and his nest in the thicket.

    Suddenly Fluter clicked out what Kristy's father had told her were notes of warning. Dulce became alarmed. She flattened her feathers to her body and flew silently back to their nest.

    Kristy checked to see what was the matter. The strange song sparrow was in Fluter's raspberry bush. He was pointing his bill at Fluter, who crouched as if he were going to fly at the stranger. But he did not. Instead, he sang.

    The stranger heard Fluter's "stay-off-my-property" song and swiftly departed. He flew over Fluter's invisible fence of song and alighted on his own sapling. Then he sang at Fluter.

> **WORD BANK**
> **serenely** (suh REEN lee) *adv.*: calmly; peacefully
> **preened** *v.*: trimmed or smoothed feathers with the beak or tongue
> **flitted** (FLITT ed) *v.*: flew swiftly from one place to another, settling only for a moment
> **conspicuous** (kun SPIK yoo us) *adj.*: noticeable; standing out
> **sapling** (SAPP ling) *n.*: a young tree

The Birds' Peace ~ 265

LITERARY COMPONENTS

▶ **9. The Plot Thickens; Rising Action:** Fluter has a mate who leaves the nest, and he is worried.

▶ **10. Rising Action:** Fluter flies and sings. Something is disturbing him.

▶ **11. Setting; Characterization; Dawning Realization; Metaphor:** Kristy realizes what is happening. She notices. Fluter is making *an invisible fence of song.* That's nice.

GUIDING THE READING

LITERAL

Q: What does Dulce do while Fluter flies around and boldly sings?
A: She takes a break. She leaves the nest, eats some bristlegrass seed, and preens her feathers.

Q: As Fluter flies and sings, what does Kristy realize he is doing?
A: He is making a circle, an invisible fence of song around his meadow and his nest in the thicket.

Q: According to the story, what kind of song does Fluter sing to the stranger?
A: Fluter sings a "stay-off-my-property" song.

SUMMING UP THE PLOT

- Fluter flies to the sugar maple on the border of his territory and sings right back to the stranger.

- The stranger answers with his own flood of melody from his trees and bushes.

- When they understand where each other's territory lies, they rest and preen their feathers.

- Kristy is fascinated. "Even Daddy doesn't know about this," she says.

- She watches the birds until the day's long shadows tells her she must go home.

- Fluter does not fly beyond the raspberry bush, and the stranger does not come back to Fluter's territory.

- But sing they do, as their mates sit serenely on their eggs.

- That night Kristy writes, *Dear Daddy, I know how the birds keep the peace.*

LITERARY COMPONENTS

▶ **12. Setting; Metaphor; Science:** The stranger sings back to Fluter from his own trees and bushes. He answers Fluter with *a flood of melody.*

▶ **13. Emotional Turning Point; Theme:** This is a wonderful moment, when Kristy's curiosity, her ability to pay attention to things other than herself, and her analytical skills save her from crushing grief. She is no longer the abandoned child, but a young adult person who has something new to share with her father. She is experiencing *wonder.*

▶ **14. Climax; Tone; Theme; Metaphor:** The climax comes in the last line of the story, when Kristy writes to her dad. Closing with Kristy's own words, with her move into maturity, with the metaphor of the birds, makes this a lovely, powerful ending.

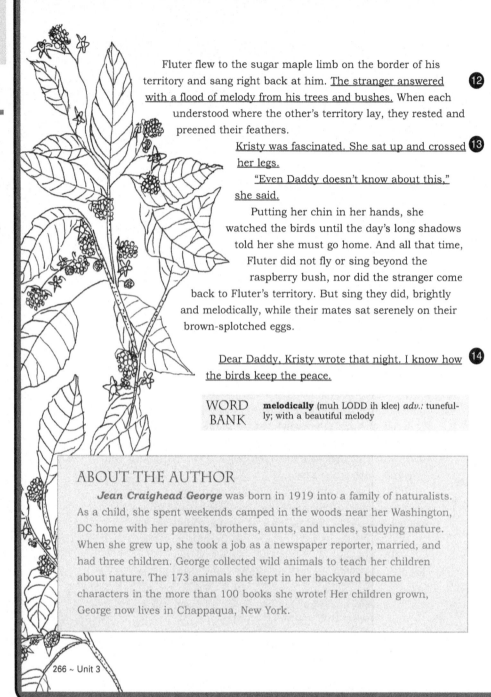

Fluter flew to the sugar maple limb on the border of his territory and sang right back at him. The stranger answered with a flood of melody from his trees and bushes. When each understood where the other's territory lay, they rested and preened their feathers. **12**

Kristy was fascinated. She sat up and crossed her legs. **13**

"Even Daddy doesn't know about this," she said.

Putting her chin in her hands, she watched the birds until the day's long shadows told her she must go home. And all that time, Fluter did not fly or sing beyond the raspberry bush, nor did the stranger come back to Fluter's territory. But sing they did, brightly and melodically, while their mates sat serenely on their brown-splotched eggs.

Dear Daddy, Kristy wrote that night. I know how the birds keep the peace. **14**

WORD BANK   **melodically** (muh LODD ih klee) *adv.:* tunefully; with a beautiful melody

ABOUT THE AUTHOR

Jean Craighead George was born in 1919 into a family of naturalists. As a child, she spent weekends camped in the woods near her Washington, DC home with her parents, brothers, aunts, and uncles, studying nature. When she grew up, she took a job as a newspaper reporter, married, and had three children. George collected wild animals to teach her children about nature. The 173 animals she kept in her backyard became characters in the more than 100 books she wrote! Her children grown, George now lives in Chappaqua, New York.

266 ~ Unit 3

GUIDING THE READING

LITERAL

Q: What do Fluter and the stranger do when they stopped communicating with each other?
A: They rest and preen their feathers.

Q: What do Fluter and the stranger's mates do as the men folk sing brightly and melodically?
A: They sit serenely on their eggs.

Q: What is the color of the eggs of song sparrows?
A: The eggs are brown-splotched.

ANALYTICAL

Q: What do Fluter and the stranger-sparrow each understand from their singing back and forth to each other?
A: They each understand where the other's territory lies.

Q: How do you think Kristy feels when she says, "Even Daddy doesn't know about this"?
A: She doesn't sound sad (although some students may think she does), primarily because of the word Even. If the sentence were,

"Daddy doesn't know about this" or "Daddy doesn't even know about this," then whether Kristy was feeling grief or wonder would be arguable. But that even makes her sound proud. She has learned something new. It is that something new that balances out her grief. Also, she is going to share this with her father. She will have something special, something of the intellect, to tell him.

FIRST IMPRESSIONS

The story is satisfying in that Kristy comes full circle with her feelings. At the outset, she feels abandoned and scared. But by the end of the story, she has reconnected with her father, this time in a new way, with new knowledge.

FIRST IMPRESSIONS
Did you find the ending of the story satisfying?

QUICK REVIEW

1. What happened to Kristy's father?

2. Two sentences describe physical feelings she has, as she runs out the back door that day. Which sentences are they?

3. What is it that gets Kristy's attention as she kneels in the grass sobbing?

4. What are Kristy's two fears for her father?

FOCUS

5. Why do you think Kristy stops sobbing when she hears the song sparrow sing?

6. When Kristy talks to Fluter, she is able to express her feelings. What does she tell Fluter? Describe the feelings and thoughts she shares with him. Don't write this as dialogue.

CREATING & WRITING

7. In the story, Kristy grows up a little. How does she grow up?

8. Write the dialogue that you imagine takes place between Fluter and the intruder sparrow. For this you will use dialogue format, with quotation marks. Use the usual "he said /she said" format, but remember they can squawk, cheep, chirp, or sing their words. Remember to use a new paragraph every time the speaker changes. If you wish, Dulce, Fluter's mate, can also be part of this discussion.

9. Make a mobile on a hanger with the three sparrows hanging at different levels.

The Birds' Peace ~ 267

QUICK REVIEW

1. Kristy's father has had to go into the army to go to war.

2. Her eyes hurt. Her chest burns.

3. A bird sings.

4. Bombs may fall on him or an enemy tank may shoot him. Students may also mention that he does not know how to shoot a gun—so how will he be prepared for this and how can he protect himself.

FOCUS

5. Perhaps Fluter feels like a friend to her, since she knows him well enough to call him by name. Like most children, once she has vented her grief, she becomes aware of the world around her. In addition, she views Fluter's singing as an echo of her own sense of being in trouble.

6. Kristy tells Fluter that she is in trouble, too. She says that her father had to go into the army, and that he is going to war. Kristy says to him that she is scared. Her daddy doesn't even know how to shoot a gun. What if bombs fall on him or an enemy tank shoots at him?

CREATING & WRITING

7. She observes something on her own. She comes to a sound conclusion about what the birds' behavior means. She stops crying over the loss of her father. She finds a new way to connect to him and begins a letter in which she will share with him her new knowledge.

8. If students need you to, review dialogue format.

9. Please bring in a sufficient number of hangers for your students to use for their mobiles.

POINT OF VIEW AND NARRATION

- The point of view of a story depends on who is telling the story.

- If the story is told by a character in the story, it is told in the first person and the character is the "I" of the story.

- If the story is told by a narrator, it is told in the third person with the pronouns he, she, they, and it.

- Sometimes an author will have different characters take part in the storytelling to show the different ways the same story could be told.

THINK ABOUT IT!

1. Who is telling the story? What is he called in the story?

2. When do the first and last sentence take place? Do you think the speaker is a child or an adult?

3. When does the middle of the story take place? Whose point of view does the storyteller try to express?

4. Why does Harold expect his father to be angry at him for playing the organ?

The Old Parlor Organ

An antique dealer came today to haul away the old parlor organ. The organ belonged to my grandfather's mother, who died the winter my grandfather turned nine. Harold, my grandfather, was a silent man. His silence was due in part to his having lost his hearing as an adult, but I imagine the silence began much earlier. Harold was an only child; he must have felt very lonely growing up on the farm after his mother died. Sometimes, staring at the old parlor organ in our basement, I try to imagine what it was like for him.

I picture Harold, perhaps seven, sitting next to his mother on the organ bench. A fire in the fireplace makes the little parlor glow with warmth against the cold Ohio winter. With her feet, his mother pumps the pedals that breathe air through the organ. Harold taps his toe to the tune, his face aglow with firelight and love. His world is complete.

Later, I imagine a hot afternoon the summer after Harold's mother died. Having worked in the fields with his father since sunrise, he's come inside to make lunch. For some reason, he feels drawn today to the parlor, to the silent organ. No one has been in this room since his mother died. Brushing dust off the bench, he sits. He lifts up the organ cover, and starts pumping. The pedals are stiff. He pumps as best as he can. He decides to play a note. The sound that comes from the organ is not the smooth sound his mother's even pressure on the pedals made. Rather, the organ releases a low moan, like the cry of a ghost. Harold feels the hair on his neck stand up.

Suddenly, he is aware of a presence.

Father! Harold hadn't heard him come in. Harold expects anger. Instead, his father offers a pained smile.

"Lunch?" his father asks.

Harold nods, relieved.

In my mind's eye, Harold pulls the lid shut tightly on that ghostly sound.

In time, Harold and his father would use the parlor again, but for the past 75 years, no one has played the organ.

It is time for a new player to make the organ sing again.

LESSON IN LITERATURE

1. Harold's grandson is telling the story. He is the "I" of the story.

2. The first and last sentences take place in the present. The speaker sounds like an adult.

3. The middle of the story takes place during Harold's childhood. The storyteller tries to project Harold's point of view.

4. Answers will vary. Perhaps he is not permitted to go into the parlor. Perhaps he feels the awful sounds he's making will anger his father. Perhaps his father doesn't want to be reminded of the loss of his wife.

SELECTION VOCABULARY

brood: worry about; think about moodily

chink: crack; narrow opening

clasped: gripped; firmly grasped

concoct: make up; put together many ingredients resulting in something new and different

perch: a high position or resting place

resolved: firmly decided on a course of action

siblings: brothers or sisters

stewed: fretted, worried, fussed

team: two or more horses, oxen or other animals harnessed together to draw a vehicle

undeniable: clearly real and true

brood	clasped	perch	siblings	team
chink	concoct	resolved	stewed	undeniable

1. When the first hen was stolen from the barnyard, Amos was angry. He _____ (fretted) that morning, then forgot all about it.

2. But the next day, when two more hens were gone, he began to _____ (worry, think moodily).

3. Who was stealing their hens? And what would be stolen next? Amos and his three _____ (brothers and sisters) had built the farm from scratch.

4. They had driven a _____ (two or more oxen) of oxen up from Oklahoma City and just stopped in the middle of the wilderness.

5. Before they'd left the city, they had _____ (firmly decided) to build a farm as far from civilization as possible, and they had done just that.

6. They had built a big, solid barn to protect their livestock, and put up fences everywhere to keep out thieves—both human and animal. But there must have been a _____ (crack, narrow opening) in a well somewhere.

7. That things would only get worse if they did nothing was _____ (true).

8. They would have to _____ (put together) a plan to catch the thief.

9. Amos climbed up into the wagon. As he _____ (grasped) the reins, he thought he saw something moving in the distance.

10. From his _____ (high position) on the wagon he could see for miles across the flat Oklahoma landscape. Was that a bushy tail he saw moving among the cornstalks?

Workbook p. 85   Answer Guide p. 8

A Time for Rhyme

Under each vocabulary word, write a two or four line rhyme using that word. To help you out, we've provided you with some rhyming words, though you may use your own rhymes if you prefer. Your poem may be serious, funny, or silly, but it must make sense! If you don't know the meanings of some of the rhyming words, consult your dictionary. Good luck! Below is a sample rhyme:

I asked my Mom—"what's for supper?"
When all she answered was "Food"
I fretted, I worried, I fussed—
As a matter of fact, I stewed.

Brooded: deluded, included, exuded	
Concocted: locked it, mocked it, knocked it, rocked it	
Clasped: grasped, gasped, rasped	
Team: beam, gleam, supreme, extreme	
Perch: lurch, birch, search	
Undeniable: unreliable, viable, flyable, liable, pliable	
Chink: mink, sink, link	
Resolved: involved, evolved, dissolved	
Sibling: nibbling, quibbling	

Workbook p. 86   Answer Guide p. 8

BACKGROUND BYTES

We are indebted to The Women of the West Museum in Los Angeles (Autry National Center, 4700 Western Heritage Way, Los Angeles, CA 90027) for much of the information below.

In our story, Hattie McClintic Burden leaves home for "the distant, promising plains of Nebraska" on a warm May morning in 1873. Do your students know how it was possible that people could go west and claim land? Could a person go to Nebraska these days, find an unoccupied plot of land, and build a house there? The events of the story require a little history lesson.

Maps dating from the middle 1800s called a region that included Nebraska (and Kansas, Montana, North Dakota, South Dakota, Colorado, and Oklahoma) the "Great American Desert." Although some of this land had low annual rainfall, and there were few trees, this was no desert. Large native communities had lived there for centuries.

By the 1860s much of the west was declared public domain. President Abraham Lincoln signed the Homestead Act into law in 1862. Hundreds of thousands of people were given the opportunity to lay claim to parcels of this land. Many of these folks were people whose families had never been able to own land before.

The Homestead Act said that

Any person who is the head of a family, or who has arrived at the age of twenty-one years, and is a citizen of the United States, or who shall have filed his declaration of intention to become such.... Who has never borne arms against the United States Government or given aid and comfort to its enemies, is entitled to 160 free acres of land. For an $18 filing fee, the homesteader could claim property, as long as he resided there for five years. Women who were heads of households and had no husbands were allowed under the law to file claims.

In the 1870s, the climate changed for more than a decade and the U.S. government advertised the land as both free and fertile. By transforming the plains—the so-called Great American Desert—into farmland, the United States expanded its territory significantly. In the last half of the nineteenth century, six new states joined the nation: Kansas in 1861, Nebraska in 1867, Colorado in 1876, North Dakota, South Dakota, and Montana in 1889.

Ask your students what they think it would mean today, if suddenly millions of acres of land were made available, at no cost?

Hattie refers to their house in Nebraska as their "soddy." What was a *soddy*?

Sod is defined as *turf,* as the upper stratum of soil bound by grass and plant roots into a thick mat.

On the great plains, the great American desert, there were no trees and few stones. What were people to build houses from? The soil was the answer.

It was there, all around them, it was cheap, and was good insulation.

Using a tool called a cutting plow, the settlers cut the soil into three to six inch rows, 12" wide. They then cut the rows into bricks. The sod was laid down like bricks, grass side down, in side-by side rows. Three rows of sod made a nice thick wall, strong enough to support the weight of a house. By staggering the seams of the bricks, the walls were made tighter. Every third or fourth layer of sod was laid crosswise to bind the stacks together.

Both men and women worked on the construction of their houses. After the walls were completed, both the inner and outer walls needed to be shaved for smoothness. This was done with a sharp shovel and gave the house a nice finished look. (It also closed the rat and insect holes!) Once the walls were shaved inside, they could be plastered, for those families that could afford it.

Whereas many people living in sod houses were extremely poor, there were also those that lived with comparative ease. In fact, there were even two-story sod houses that had glass windows and were stylishly decorated.

Housekeeping was very difficult in a sod house. Snakes, insects, mice, and dirt fell from the ceilings and walls. People tried covering their walls with cloth to keep things from falling in the food and to keep the house clean. But cleanliness was complicated, as well, by the way the plains-people heated their houses.

There was no wood or coal. In order to heat their houses, Hattie and Otto would have used buffalo or cow droppings, called chips. Chips were a good source of heat and the plains were very cold. People learned to tolerate the smell. A woman named Orval Lookhart of Holyoke, Colorado, wrote about her life in a sod house for *Nebraska Farmer.*

Each picker would tie a rope to the handle of an old washtub and pull it around over the grass and pick up all the chips they could find. They would fill the tubs, then empty them into the wagon until it was full. Then it was unloaded in a pile. This operation was repeated till a pile of chips were built up to 10-12 feet long and as high as they could be piled....But oh the ashes that those chips left and that dust that settled over everything when they were taken up from the ash box.

We always said, 'it took one person to bring in the chips, one to keep the fire going, and another to carry the ashes out. Then mother with her broom and dust pan to brush up the dust.' Some job, but if we could find plenty of chips we were warm and comfortable.

INTO "HATTIE'S BIRTHDAY BOX"

Hattie's Birthday Box has two themes. The first theme is Grandaddy's lie: why he told it, how it affected Hattie, his profound regret about having told it, and his forced confrontation of it at his hundredth birthday party. It is essentially a story of human failing. The failing is not great, and it results in no one's suffering but his own, but it is a product of weakness. The second theme is Hattie's strength of character. Spencer's little lie is a catalyst for Hattie's powerful will to survive and prevail. The reader is meant to walk away from the story uplifted by Hattie's unsinkable spirit and touched by the enduring love the two siblings have for one another.

In this story, Hattie's birthday box is much more than a container. It has been handmade by her brother, and given to her as a birthday gift on the day she leaves for the frontier. Because of what Spencer says to her, the box is never opened (until she returns home to Spencer). She doesn't know what is in the box, but she has been told that it holds something that can help her, if ever she needs help. The box comes to represent shelter in a storm, a last resort. In reality, the box is empty, but what counts is what Hattie imagines to be true.

Although many tales and legends have been written in a similar vein, *Hattie's Birthday Box* is essentially different from them. In those tales, the hero is given a cloak, a hat, a coin—something that the hero (naively) believes imparts special powers to him. The hero's belief frees him of his former inhibitions and he actually behaves in a heroic fashion, all the while thinking that his newfound powers are due to the magical item or blessing he has been given. The best known examples of this type of hero are the Lion, the Woodsman and the Tin Man of *The Wizard of Oz,* all of whom blossom when they are led to believe that they have been given magical powers by the wizard.

The birthday box cherished by Hattie does not free her of any cowardliness or weakness. Nor does she look to it for a miraculous salvation. The box serves only to optimize Hattie's already strong, optimistic nature by helping her to eternally postpone despair. Putting off using her "last resort," becomes a challenge to her, and stiffens her resolve to work through each crisis as it arises.

In sum, the real hero of this piece is Hattie. The birthday box has served only to highlight her heroic nature. Had she not had the birthday box, it is likely she would have devised some other prop to help her fight the temptation to give up in the face of tragedy.

EYES ON...CHANGING POINT OF VIEW

Most often when we read literature, we accept the writing, the author's work, uncritically, without giving it much thought. After all, there it is in print. Someone has published it. Moreover, the author must be right in his or her representation of reality. We tend not to think analytically about what we read. We are reading primarily for pleasure or to gain knowledge, after all.

Hattie's Birthday Box is a nice opportunity for students to first, enjoy the piece, and second, consider two techniques the author, Pam Conrad, has employed. This is a beginning look at how a writer writes, how a writer achieves this or that effect.

Conrad has done two interesting things in the story, for the purpose of telling a story within a story. On page **273,** when the story of Spencer and Hattie's early days is related, which includes the giving of the birthday box, the author begins to write in the past tense and she drops the voice of the narrator. It is as if velvet curtains on a stage rose on a tableau and a short play were performed. There is one foray the narrator makes into the telling of the story, when she writes, *My grandaddy, who was then a young man...* (p. **273**)

Both the use of the past tense and the emergence of third person (no *I*, just *he, she,* and *it*), give us the distance that makes this journey into the past magical and credible.

You will need to base your discussion of person and tense on the level of your students.

For homeschoolers who need additional help, here is a basic table of personal pronouns. This is why we refer to the voice in which stories are told as being in the first person or being in the third person.

	Singular	**Plural**
First Person	I, my, mine, me	we, our, ours, us
Second Person	you, your, yours	you, your, yours
Third Person	he, his, him, she, hers, her, it, its	they, their, theirs, them

Blueprint for Reading

INTO . . . *Hattie's Birthday Box*

Have you ever made a promise you couldn't keep? How did you feel? Did your conscience bother you? Did you imagine the other person feeling disappointed? Did you tell yourself no one would really care? How careful are you to keep your word?

A young man gave his sister a box to take on her journey out West. He told her not to open it until things were their very worst. He said that there was something precious in the box that would help her through the worst times. As the years passed, he never asked if she'd opened the box, and never told her it was really empty. Now his sister is coming to visit. What will she say? What does she think of him? He is afraid.

EYES ON . . . *Changing Point of View*

You have read many stories in which one of the characters is also the narrator. You have seen events through the eyes of Samuel in *Samuel's Choice*, Craig in *The Silent Lobby,* Larry in *The Disappearing Man,* Laura in *By the Shores of Silver Lake,* Yurik in *After School,* and Harry Franklin in *One Throw.* Because each one of these characters is so different from the other, the narration of each is different, too.

The beginning and end of *Hattie's Birthday Box* is told to us by a character in the story who speaks in the first person. The middle of the story, however, goes back into the past. The first-person voice is not used, because that part of the story is being told by the author, not by a character.

- A sign stretches across the ceiling of the recreation room of the nursing home: HAPPY ONE HUNDREDTH BIRTHDAY, SPENCER McCLINTIC.

- Spencer McClintic is my great-great grand-father, and the whole family is coming to celebrate.

Hattie's Birthday Box

The sign stretching across the ceiling of the nursing home's rec room says HAPPY ONE HUNDREDTH BIRTHDAY, SPENCER McCLINTIC, and on the wall in bright numbers and letters it says JULY 5, 1847 to 1947. Spencer McClintic is my great-great-grandfather, and our whole family is coming to celebrate.

Pam Conrad

Hattie's Birthday Box ~ 271

LITERARY COMPONENTS

▶ **1. Exposition; Setting; Characters:** It's a 100th birthday celebration at a nursing home for her great-great grandfather and the whole family is coming.

GUIDING THE READING

LITERAL

Q: Where is the birthday party being held?
A: The birthday party is being held in the recreation room of a nursing home.

Q: What year is it?
A: The year is 1947.

- Grandaddy is nervous. He asks Momma over and over who is coming to the party.

- Then he asks, "But is Hattie coming? My baby sister? Are you sure she's coming?"

- I hear him mumble, "Oh, no, oh, no, not Hattie. She's gonna skin me alive."

- I ask, "Don't you like Aunt Hattie, Grandaddy?"

- Grandaddy says he loves her to pieces, but the last time he saw her, when she was a bride of sixteen, heading out in a wagon with her husband to homestead in Nebraska, he did a terrible thing.

- I ask what he did that was so bad.

LITERARY COMPONENTS

▶ **2. Characterization:** Grandaddy is nervous.

▶ **3. Rising Action:** Grandaddy asks if Hattie his baby sister is coming. "Are you sure she's coming?"

▶ **4. Basic Conflict Introduced; Idioms:** Grandaddy loves Hattie and wants to see her, but the last time he saw her 74 years ago, he did something terrible, so he's also afraid to see her. He uses two idioms. *Skin me alive* means punish severely and *have my hide* means about the same thing. The first comes from early punishment practices that hopefully occur nowhere in the world today. The second comes from killing and skinning animals for their skins.

▶ **5. Characterization:** It is so clear from the great-great granddaughter's words how much she loves him.

Momma and I got here early because Momma wanted me to help her blow up balloons and tack up the decorations before everyone arrived. She says now that the war[1] is over and most everyone is back home and rations are a thing of the past, we're going to *really* celebrate.

② But Grandaddy's nervous. He sits in his chair by the window, rubbing his hands together and asking my mother over and over, "Now who-all is coming, Anna?"

And she keeps reciting the list of everyone who's coming, and he ticks them off on his fingers, but before she's even through, he **③** asks impatiently, "But is Hattie coming? My baby sister? Are you sure she's coming?"

"Hattie's coming, Grandaddy. Don't you worry. Hattie will be here."

④ Momma doesn't hear, but I hear him. He mumbles, "Oh, no, oh, no, not Hattie. She's gonna skin me alive."[2]

I pull up a stool near Grandaddy. "Don't you like Aunt Hattie, Grandaddy?"

"Oh, I love her to pieces," he answers. "But she's gonna have my hide.[3] Last time I saw Hattie, she was a bride of sixteen, heading out in a wagon with her new husband to homestead[4] in Nebraska. And I did a terrible thing, a terrible thing."

All the decorations are up, and now that Momma's sure everything is all set, she tells me to stay with Grandaddy and keep him calm while she runs home to get the cake and soda.

⑤ But there is no way to keep Grandaddy calm. "What'd you do that was so bad, Grandaddy? What was it?"

---

1. *The war* refers to World War II, which ended in 1945.
2. *She's gonna skin me alive* is a humorous slang expression meaning "she is so angry at me that she would like to hurt me in some way." The listener is supposed to understand that this is an exaggeration and that she would not really want to hurt him.
3. *Have my hide* is similar in meaning to "she's gonna skin me alive." Again, Grandaddy is saying that his sister is very angry at him.
4. In 1862, a law was passed whereby anyone who lived and worked on a piece of government-owned land for five years would be given that land. The land given to the person was called a *homestead*. The name of the law was the Homestead Act. Here, Grandaddy is using the word as a verb. Hattie and her husband went *to homestead*, meaning to settle a piece of land, in Nebraska.

GUIDING THE READING

LITERAL

Q: What does the narrator hear Grandaddy say that Momma doesn't hear?

A: She hears him say, "Oh, no, oh, no, not Hattie. She's gonna skin me alive."

Q: When did Grandaddy do something terrible to Hattie?

A: He did something terrible to her the last time he saw her, when she was a bride of sixteen, heading out in a wagon with her new husband to homestead in Nebraska.

Q: Identify the verbs in the first, second, and third sentences of the story. What is their tense?

A: The verbs are *had been, was, hadn't risen, were loading, was, were heading, was, knew, would see.* These verbs are all in the past tense.

ANALYTICAL

Q: Grandaddy loves Hattie but he wants her to come and he is afraid of her coming. This is called feeling ambivalent. That means, feeling two ways about something. Why is Grandaddy ambivalent?

A: Grandaddy loves Hattie and hasn't seen her for nearly three quarters of a century. He wants to see her, yet he did something awful to her and he is afraid to face her.

- This is the story I finally got out of him. It was a May morning in 1873.
- Grandaddy's sister, Hattie McClintic Burden, was a new bride setting out for the Nebraska plains with her husband, Otto.

- It was a happy occasion in that Hattie and her husband were going to build a new life, but it was also sad, because no one knew when they'd see them again.
- There were no telephones, no airplanes, just the U.S. mail, slow but reliable.

- The night before they left, there was a combination going-away and birthday party for Hattie, who was just sixteen.
- Everyone brought special gifts.
- My grandaddy, who was then twenty-six, had stewed and brooded.
- He was ten when Hattie was born, and she had always been his favorite.

I watch Grandaddy wringing his hands and tapping his slippered feet nervously. He keeps glancing out the window to the road outside, like he's waiting for some old lynch mob to come riding over the hill. <u>This is the story I finally got out of him.</u> **6**

<u>It had been a warm May morning in 1873, and Grandaddy's **7** sister Hattie McClintic Burden was a new bride ready to set out for a life on the distant, promising plains of Nebraska.</u> The sun hadn't quite risen yet, and she and her new husband, Otto, were loading the final things into the wagon. While it was a happy occasion in that Hattie and her husband were heading out for a new life, it was also a sad day, <u>because no one knew when they'd **8** ever see them again.</u> <u>Grandaddy, who was a young man at the **9** time, didn't know it would be seventy-four years before he would finally see her.</u> But no one ever knew that back then. No one knew how long it would be before they saw each other or if they would ever see each other at all. There were no telephones, no airplanes, just the U.S. mail, slow but reliable, carrying recipes for pumpkin bread and clippings of hair from new babies, and sad messages of deaths.

The night before Hattie and Otto left, everyone had tried to smile and be happy for them. <u>There was a combination going- **10** away party and birthday party for Hattie, who was just sixteen. Everyone brought special gifts</u>—blankets and lanterns and bolts of cotton,[5] a pair of small sewing scissors, a bottle of ink, and even a canary in a shiny cage.

<u>My grandaddy</u>, who was then a young man of twenty-six, had **11** stewed and brooded. <u>He had been ten years old when Hattie was **12** born, and she had always been his favorite.</u> More than once he had carried her out into the barn on crystal-clear nights to

---

5. A *bolt of cotton* is a roll of many yards of cotton.

WORD BANK	**stewed**(STOOD) *v.*: fretted, worried, fussed
	brooded(BROO did) *v.*: worried about; thought about moodily

LITERARY COMPONENTS

▶ **6. Transition:** This announces that the curtains are going up on the subplot (which is really the main plot).

▶ **7. Switch to Past Tense and Third-Person Tone; Exposition; Setting:** It was 1873, a warm morning in May, and Hattie was a new bride setting out for the plains of Nebraska.

▶ **8. Element of Conflict:** Hattie is leaving and no one knows when they will see her again.

▶ **9. Reference Back to the Future:** Grandaddy didn't know it would be 74 years, until he became the person he is at the beginning of the story.

▶ **10. Rising Action; Motivation:** There was a party the night before and everyone brought presents.

▶ **11. Third Person in Remission for One Sentence:** The speaker breaks through and says, *My grandaddy.* Although, note that grandaddy here is a little different than previously, since it is not capitalized.

▶ **12. Characterization of Relationship Between Grandaddy and Hattie; Motivation:** He was ten when she was born and she was always his favorite.

GUIDING THE READING

LITERAL

Q: What year is it as the story opens?
A: It is 1873.

Q: How many years will it be before Grandaddy sees Hattie again?
A: Seventy-four years will have passed before he sees her again.

Q: What occurred the night before Hattie and Otto left?
A: They were given a combination going-away and birthday party (for Hattie). People brought special gifts.

Q: How old was grandaddy at that time?
A: He was twenty-six years old.

ANALYTICAL

Q: You have learned that ambivalent means feeling two ways about something. As the story opens, people in the family are ambivalent about something else. Why is it both a happy occasion and a sad day?
A: It is a happy occasion because Hattie is a new bride and she and her husband Otto are heading off to a new life, but it is also a sad day because no one knows when the members of the family will be reunited.

Q: Think about the gifts Hattie and her husband were given. Why would they need each one of these items?
A: They would need blankets to keep warm in their beds; lanterns because there was no electricity and they needed to be able to see when it got dark; bolts of cotton, for making clothing and curtains; sewing scissors for sewing clothes and mending; ink for their pens, to be able to write letters and make lists; and a canary for music, comfort, companionship, and bright color.

SUMMING UP THE PLOT

- Grandaddy's heart was breaking that she was going away and he wanted to give her the most special gift.

- But he had no money, nothing to trade, and no real gift to give her.

- Not knowing what the gift would be, he made a wooden box for it.

- At the party that night, Spencer had lied boldly to Hattie.

- He said he had something special for her, something so special she had better not open it right away.

- He told her not to open the box unless times got hard, got to be their very worst, and then it would see her through.

- Hattie had looked at him with love and trust.

LITERARY COMPONENTS

▶ **13. Rising Action; Characterization:** His little sister was going away and he wanted to give her the best gift.

▶ **14. Characterization; Theme:** Grandaddy had no money, no gift to give her, as he saw it. So he made a wooden box to hold the gift he could not give. Apparently, it never occurred to him that a handmade box to hold things could be a gift, which is kind of sad. This is a very important point that can be missed—that he never conceived of the box as the gift.

▶ **15. Motivation; Theme:** Desperation, even born of the finest feelings, may bend morals.

▶ **16. Characterization; Conflict; Creating a Symbol:** He throws caution to the winds and tells Hattie that when she is really in trouble, what is in the box will see her through. It's deplorable, but in doing so, he transforms the box into a symbol of shelter and rescue.

▶ **17. Imagery:** This picture of Hattie with her tongue stuck out to catch the snow is lovely.

show her a calf being born. He had taught her to swim in the cool spring. And he had chased away anyone who came around to ⑬ bother her. His heart was breaking that his little sister was going away, and he had wanted to give her the most special gift. The best gift of all. So she would always remember him and know how much he had loved her.

He would have given her a gold necklace, or a bracelet with diamonds, or earrings with opal jewels, but it had been a rough year, with a few of the cattle dying in a storm and a few others ⑭ lost to a brief sickness. He had no money, nothing to trade, no real gift to give her. Not knowing what the gift would be, he had lovingly hammered together a small wooden box and carved her initials in it, thinking that whatever it would be, it would be about this size.

⑮ It was at the party that night that he realized there was nothing to give her and he concocted his tale. Finding her alone at the punch bowl, Spencer had clasped Hattie's small shoulders in his rough hands, looked straight in her face, and lied boldly.

"I got you something special, Hattie, something so special I ⑯ think you'd better not open it right away. I want you to just hold on to the box, and don't open it unless times get hard, not unless things get to be their very worst, you hear me? And it will see you through."

Hattie had looked at him with such love and trust. He memorized her face, the same small face she had turned to him ⑰ when a birth-wet calf had finally struggled to its feet, or when he had carried her out on snowy nights to turn her tongue to the swirling night sky.[6] Her face was soft with love, and he knew she

---

6. As children, Spencer and Hattie had played outside at night as the snow fell. Spencer had told Hattie to catch snowflakes on her *tongue* as they *swirled* down from the *night sky*.

WORD BANK	**concocted** (kun KAHK ted) *v.*: made up; put together many ingredients resulting in something new and different **clasped** *v.*: gripped; firmly grasped

274 ~ Unit 3

GUIDING THE READING

LITERAL
Q: What did Spencer carve on the box?
A: He carved Hattie's initials.

Q: How did Hattie look at Spencer?
A: She looked at him with love and trust.

ANALYTICAL
Q: Why is young Spencer's heart breaking?
A: Hattie has been his favorite sibling, she is going away, and he wants to give her the most special gift.

Q: Why doesn't Spencer have any money? Give the reason in the book, and see if you can think of another, broader reason.
A: The book tells us that it had been a rough year, with cattle dying in a storm and from sickness. But the bigger reason is that most people did not have money and things the

way we do now in middle-class America. People also did not go shopping at stores all the time.

Q: Why does Spencer make the box?
A: He makes it to hold the present he cannot give.

SUMMING UP THE PLOT

- Grandaddy knew Hattie must have thought his gift was something precious that she could sell if there were a disaster.
- But he lied, he lied.

- That morning before the sun rose, he helped Otto hook up the team of horses to the wagon.
- My young grandaddy slipped the sealed and empty box into Hattie's lap.

- He waved goodbye and never saw her again.
- Until today. Aunt Hattie's flying in from Nebraska.
- "I meant to finally buy her something to put in the box," Grandaddy keeps saying.
- "But then I don't know." He'd gotten married, had his own children, and Hattie'd never mentioned it in any of her letters.

---

⑱ must have thought his gift was something precious that she could sell if crops failed or some other disaster happened. But he lied, he lied.

So that morning before the sun rose, he helped Otto hook up the team to the wagon, and once Hattie was high on her perch beside her husband—looking for all the world like a little child ⑲ playing farmhouse—my young grandaddy had slipped the sealed and empty wooden box into her lap and backed away. He waved goodbye and never saw her again.

⑳ Until today. Aunt Hattie's flying in from Nebraska with cousin Harold and his wife, Mary. Since she was sixteen, Hattie has never set foot off Nebraska soil.

"I meant to finally buy her something to put in the box, I really did," ㉑ Grandaddy keeps saying. "I thought that as soon as things got a little better, as soon as I had a little money, I'd buy those earrings or that necklace and send it right off to her, explaining everything. But then I don't know. Soon I got married myself, and then there were my own children, and Hattie just

WORD BANK	**team** (TEEM) *n.:* two or more horses, oxen, or other animals harnessed together to draw a vehicle
	perch *n.:* a high position or resting place

LITERARY COMPONENTS

▶ **18. Motivation; Characterization; Theme; Repetition; Technique:** The writer is bringing the reader back to the present here. The word *lied*, said twice, gives us Spencer's inner voice.

▶ **19. Bringing Us Up for Air—Back to the Future:** This is done, first, by use of the first person with *My*. We are reminded that this is a story being told by one of the participants. Second, the harsh termination in the terminal sentence: *He waved goodbye and never saw her again.* This final sentence implies the unstated, *until today.*

▶ **20. Return to the Present Tense and the First-Person Narrator:** Now the author says, "Until today."

▶ **21. Motivation; Continuing the Story from the Present Looking Back at the Past:** Grandaddy explains why he never got to send Hattie something to put in the box. He adds that Hattie never mentioned it.

GUIDING THE READING

LITERAL

Q: Has Hattie ever returned before or gone anyplace?
A: Hattie has never set foot off Nebraska soil since she was sixteen.

Q: According to Grandaddy, why didn't he ever do something about the empty box over 74 years?
A: He got married himself, then he had children, and Hattie never mentioned it.

ANALYTICAL

Q: What do you think of Spencer's lie—which seems to get bigger as he keeps talking?
A: Without his necessarily thinking about it, the lie does grow, as if it takes on a life of its own. It is a moving lie, because it tells you how much he wishes he could protect his little sister, and it's a sad lie, because he will have to live with it for 74 years.

Q: When the author repeats the word *lied*, it sounds like the character's internal dialogue—his inner voice. Why?
A: Because that is the way we think and speak in our minds. If we are angry with ourselves, we may say things over and over.

- Grandaddy groans. "Oh mercy, Hattie's coming."
- People are starting to arrive and the room is filling up with children, laughter, and presents.
- And Grandaddy won't even look up at them.

- He gets up and walks slowly to another seat far from the window.
- Out the window, I can see an airport taxi pull up.
- I post myself by Grandaddy and watch.

- Suddenly a hush falls over the whole room.
- The name *Hattie* is whispered across the room, like prairie wind over the flute of a stovepipe.

LITERARY COMPONENTS

▶ **22. Rising Action:** From her perspective, the narrator can see that Hattie has arrived.

▶ **23. Characterization of Relationship:** The narrator is protective of Grandaddy. She *posts* herself behind him. This is a use of the verb that is associated with guards stationed at a post.

▶ **24. The Moment Arrives (What We've Been Building up to); Onomatopoeia; Simile:** Apparently she has come. The author uses onomatopoeia with *hush* and *whispered*. Her name is whispered across the room *like prairie wind over the flute of a stovepipe*.

▶ **25. Interesting Literary Technique; Growing Suspense:** We cannot see Hattie (she has not been described to us as being seen), although clearly the other people in the room can see her—that's why they are uttering her name. But **we are inside Grandaddy's head at this moment.** And the author is building suspense by not letting us see her. The tension cannot be relieved until Grandaddy, who wants to see her and doesn't want to see her, and Hattie establish eye contact.

▶ **26. Building Suspense:** We can only hear, we cannot see.

▶ **27. Characterization:** For Hattie, too, this is the great moment of a lifetime.

▶ **28. Irony:** She's not packing a shotgun.

never mentioned it in any of her letters." Grandaddy groans and lowers his head into his upturned hands. "Oh, mercy, Hattie's coming."

People are starting to arrive now, and the room is filling with children, laughter, and presents. Many of the people are my relatives who live right nearby, and a few came up from Jersey and Washington, people I'd normally see on holidays and such but never all together like this in one place.

And Grandaddy won't even look at them. He just gets up and **(22)** walks slowly to another seat far from the window. <u>Out the window I see an airport taxi pull up.</u>

(23) <u>I post myself behind Grandaddy and watch.</u> His hands are trembling more than usual, and I can tell he's not paying attention as little babies are brought to him to kiss and my father keeps taking flash pictures of him with everybody.

(24) <u>Suddenly a hush falls over everyone. Even the littlest children grow wide-eyed and still. The name "Hattie" is whispered across the room, like prairie wind over the flute of a stovepipe.</u>[7]

(25) "It's Hattie."

"Hattie's here."

"Hattie!"

I put my hand on Grandaddy's shoulder. "Don't worry, Grandaddy. She'll have to get through me first."

Grandaddy takes a deep breath, and his shoulders slump. He doesn't turn toward the door. He just waits in the silence that **(26)** falls over the room. <u>We can hear footsteps, Harold's and Mary's, and Hattie's.</u> They stand in the doorway with Hattie in the middle, **(27)** as though they support her, but <u>when she sees Grandaddy sitting with his back to her, she gently withdraws her arms from them and comes toward us.</u>

(28) She doesn't look like she could swat a fly, and <u>she's not packing a shotgun.</u> The tiny thin net on her hat trembles as she takes tiny steps toward us. "Spencer?" she says softly.

---

7. A *stovepipe* is a pipe that conducts heat away from the stove to the chimney. A *flute* refers to a groove in a pipe. When the prairie wind blows over the groove in the stovepipe, it makes a soft, whispering sound.

GUIDING THE READING

LITERAL

Q: The name, Hattie, is whispered across the room like what?

A: Like prairie wind over the flute of a stovepipe.

Q: According to the narrator, what does Hattie not have with her?

A: Hattie is not packing a shotgun.

ANALYTICAL

Q: Do you think that Grandaddy's reasons for not doing anything about the empty box were good ones or understandable ones?

A: Students will have different opinions about this. That he never had the money to buy anything more and that he was distracted, seem reasonable justification for not buying anything. That Hattie never mentioned it might be persuasive that it wasn't that

important to her. Perhaps talking about something that was so shameful to him was something he avoided at all costs. We all know, too, the snowball effect of putting off an apology—the longer you wait, the harder it gets.

Q: Why is Grandaddy not looking at all the other guests?

A: One possibility is that he is so concerned about how things will be with Hattie that he can't think about anything else.

Q: Why do you think we cannot see Hattie, when other people in the room can see her?

A: This may be a difficult question for fifth

graders. But you can help them with the answer, by guiding them to the knowledge that (1) we are with Spencer, whose back is turned; and (2) the author builds suspense in this fashion.

Q: Why does Grandaddy have his back turned to Hattie?

A: He is afraid of two things: (1) facing his own lie and her possible disappointment in him, after all these years; and (2) this is quite simply an overwhelming moment, difficult to grasp, emotionally so charged.

SUMMING UP THE PLOT

- Hattie says, "Why, Spencer, they told me you were an old man."
- She holds out her hands to him and he takes them.
- The tears stream down his checks.

- All of a sudden one of the cousins starts to clap, and everyone, one at a time, joins in.
- I'm not about to leave Grandaddy's side. If she's ever going to give him the business about the empty box, I want to hear it.

- Someone brings Hattie a chair. I sit down between them right at their feet.
- Then I notice it. On her lap is a small wooden box, and the lid is off.
- Grandaddy sees it, too, and groans, "Oh, Hattie, do you hate me? Can you ever forgive me?"

"Grandaddy," I say more sharply, poking him in the arm. 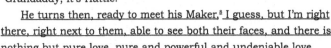 **29**
"Grandaddy, it's Hattie."

He turns then, ready to meet his Maker,[8] I guess, but I'm right **30**
there, right next to them, able to see both their faces, and there is
nothing but pure love, pure and powerful and undeniable love.

"Why, Spencer, they told me you were an old man." She holds
out her hands to him, and he takes them.

Tears stream down his cheeks and drip from his chin. "But **31**
no one told me you were still such a fine young lady," he says.
Still lying, my grandaddy.

"Oh, Spencer, Spencer," she says, "there's been too much time
and space." And I watch her as she steps towards her brother, as
they gaze at each other, sharing their special connection. No one
in the room is breathing. Then all of a sudden, one of the cousins
starts to clap, and everyone, one at a time, joins in, until everyone
is laughing and wiping tears, patting Grandaddy on the shoulder,
and hugging Hattie.

I'm not about to leave Grandaddy's side. If she's ever going to **32**
give him the business[9] about the empty box, I want to hear it.
Someone brings her a chair and sits her down right next to him,
and no one stops me so I sit down between them right at their **33**
feet. And then I notice it. On her lap is a small wooden box, and **34**
the lid is off. Delicately carved into its varnished top are the
initials HMcB. She holds the box in her hands, and I can see the
varnish worn dull in spots where her fingers touch and must have
touched for years.

Grandaddy sees it, too, and groans. "Oh, Hattie, do you hate **35**
me? Can you ever forgive me?"

"Forgive you for what?"

8. When a person is about to die, we say he is *going to meet his Maker* meaning
he is going to meet G-d, Who *made* him.
9. *Give him the business* is an old-fashioned expression for "scold him."

> WORD
> BANK
> **undeniable** (un dee NY uh bul) *adj.:* clearly real and true

LITERARY COMPONENTS

▶ **29. Irony; Nearly the Climax:** The narrator pokes her great-great grandfather to get him to respond.

▶ **30. Climax; Idiom:** When Grandaddy turns ready *to meet his Maker*, he turns to have an experience that will be like being judged for one's sins. Of course, this is said tongue in cheek, and is not meant literally. But when they face each other, the narrator observes nothing but *pure and powerful and undeniable love*.

▶ **31. Characterizations:** When the narrator hears Grandaddy flatter Hattie, her comment is, Still lying, my grandaddy. She has a good sense of him.

▶ **32. Characterization; Idiom:** This girl is protective of her great-great grandfather. The idiom, *the business*, means a scolding or teasing.

▶ **33. Tableau; Rearranged Relationships:** This is a lovely image, her sitting at their feet, as though now the two of them together form a tent of family for her to sit within. She is back to being the child—he doesn't need her protection from his sister—and Hattie is now her great-great grandaunt, instead of a stranger who threatens her beloved Grandaddy.

▶ **34. Moment of Reckoning:** Although the emotional climax has already occurred, when the narrator sees the open birthday box, we know the moment of reckoning is at hand. The box is on Hattie's lap and it is open.

▶ **35. The Conflict Resolved; Theme:** He sees the box on her lap and asks if she can ever forgive him. She sounds surprised and says it is the best present she ever received.

GUIDING THE READING

LITERAL

Q: What does it mean to give someone the business?
A: It means to give them a scolding.

Q: What does Grandaddy say, when he sees the open box?
A: He asks Hattie if she hates him and whether she can ever forgive him.

ANALYTICAL

Q: How does Grandaddy feel when he sees the open box on Hattie's lap?
A: Students may have different answers to this question—and certainly there is not a single answer. They may say he feels awful, guilty, relieved, or ascribe some other emotion to him. Students will need to explain why they have drawn the conclusions they have drawn.

SUMMING UP THE PLOT

- Hattie tells him that the box was the best present she ever received.

- "It wasn't an empty box. It was a box full of good things."

- Grandaddy asks Hattie how she figured that the box was not empty.

- She tells him how she put it in a safe place until they got their soddy built.

- Then Otto made a special chink in the wall where it stayed for years.

- Their first winter they ran out of food, she tells him. She thought to open the box, but neighbors were generous with them. That taught her to let people be neighborly.

- Then one summer they lost their whole crop to a prairie fire, and again she thought of the box.

- But Otto was sure they could make it on their own. This taught her to let him have his pride.

- When their son drowned, she almost opened it just out of despair, but she reminded herself that Spencer had said to open it only if things got their worst. They still had their daughter and she was expecting another child.

- No matter how bad things got they never got their worst. Even when Otto died.

- "Your box taught me that," she said.

- Grandaddy says, "But you did open it."

- He points to the box, open and empty on her lap.

- Hattie says that she opened the box when she knew she was going to be seeing Spencer.

- She thought there might be a piece of jewelry that she could wear when she saw him.

LITERARY COMPONENTS

▶ **36. Theme; Symbol:** It wasn't an empty box. It was full of good things.

▶ **37. Theme; Symbol; The Box As Teacher:** The box teaches Hattie to allow people to be neighborly.

▶ **38. Theme; Symbol; The Box As Teacher; Idiom:** The box teaches Hattie to let her husband *have his pride*, which means to be able to retain his self-respect.

▶ **39. Theme; Symbol; The Box As Teacher:** The box teaches Hattie to appreciate what she still has.

"For the empty box."

"Forgive you? Why, Spencer, it was the best present I've ever gotten."

"An empty box?" Grandaddy is stunned.

36 "It wasn't an empty box. It was a box full of good things."

"How d'you figure that?" Grandaddy asks.

"Well, I put it in a safe place, you know. First I hid it under the seat in the wagon, and when we finally got our soddy[10] built, I had Otto make a special chink in the wall where I hid it and where it stayed for years. And I always knew it was there if things got really bad.

37 "Our first winter, we ran out of food, and I thought to open the box then and see if it would help us, but there were kind neighbors who were generous with us, and I learned to let people be neighborly.

38 "And then one summer we lost our whole crop in a prairie fire, and I thought of the box, but Otto was sure we could make it on our own, and I learned to let him have his pride. Then when our **39** son drowned, just out of despair I almost opened it, but you had said to open it only if things got their worst, and I knew I still had my daughter, and there was another baby already stirring in me.

"No matter how bad things got, Spencer, they never got their worst. Even when Otto finally died a few years ago. Your box taught me that."

"But you did open it." He points to the box, open and empty in her lap.

"I opened it when I knew I'd be seeing you. I always thought maybe there'd be a brooch or a gold stickpin or something." Hattie smiles. I can almost imagine her with her open face turned up to a snowy sky. She laughs. "I was going to wear it for you!"

---

10. A *soddy* is a house made of tightly packed earth.

WORD BANK	**chink** (CHEENK) *n.:* crack; narrow opening

278 ~ Unit 3

GUIDING THE READING

LITERAL
Q: What does Hattie say about the box?
A: She says it was the best present she ever received.

ANALYTICAL
Q: Hattie says that box wasn't empty. What was it filled with for her?
A: She says it was full of good things.

Q: How does the box teach Hattie to be neighborly?
A: Because Spencer told her not to open the box until things were at their worst, Hattie accepted the generosity of her neighbors.

Q: How does the box teach Hattie to let her husband have his pride?
A: Again, if her husband Otto said they would make it, then the stipulations for opening the box had not been met.

Q: How does the box teach Hattie to appreciate what she has?
A: She is forced to the realization that if she still has a child and is expecting, than things are not their worst.

SUMMING UP THE PLOT

- Grandaddy says, "I always meant to fill it, Hattie—"
- Hattie says, "Hush, now, they're bringing your cake."
- Grandaddy and Hattie hold hands while everyone sings Happy Birthday.
- Their hands are like old wisteria vines woven into each other.
- I hold the empty box.
- I bring it to my face.
- I smell it.
- I smell a young farmer's stubbornness, a pioneer mother's sorrow, and a wondrous wild and lasting hope.

"I always meant to fill it, Hattie—"

"Hush now," she says. "They're bringing your cake."

And sure enough, Momma's wheeling over a metal table that has a big iced sheet cake on it. Hattie slips the cover back on her empty box and places it on the floor beside her feet, beside me. I stand to get out of the way of the rolling table and take the box.

Grandaddy and Aunt Hattie hold hands while everyone sings "Happy Birthday." Their hands are like old wisteria vines[11] woven **40** into each other. I hold the empty box. I bring it to my face. I look inside. Nothing. It is empty. And then I smell it. At first I think it smells like wood, and then I smell all the rest—a young farmer's stubbornness, a pioneer mother's sorrow, and a wondrous wild and lasting hope.

---

11. *Wisteria vines* have beautiful bluish purple flowers and are often grown to cover walls.

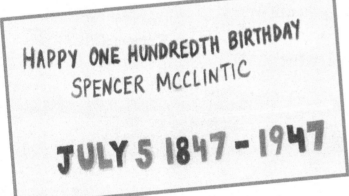

HAPPY ONE HUNDREDTH BIRTHDAY
SPENCER MCCLINTIC

JULY 5 1847 - 1947

LITERARY COMPONENTS

▶ **40. Resolution; Similes; Transferring Values to the Next Generation:** This is a wonderful conclusion with falling action. Their hands together are *like old wisteria vines woven into each other.* The great-great granddaughter smells the empty box. What a nice touch! And it smells like three of the most important markers of the human condition.

About The Author

Pam Conrad was born in Brooklyn in 1947. She grew up in an apartment near her grandparents' home and, throughout her life, felt very close to them. Although Conrad wrote poetry and stories even as a girl, she didn't start her career as a writer until she was the mother of two children. Her first book was entitled *I Don t Live Here;* it was followed by more than twenty others. Conrad's appreciation for older people can be seen in *Hatties Birthday Box.* Sadly, her own life was cut short by illness. She died in 1996.

FIRST IMPRESSIONS

On the one hand, the fact that he has regretted his lie for 76 years tells you he is an ethical person who believes strongly that "a promise is a promise." A less honest person would have long ago put the incident out of his mind, or laughed about it, or excused his younger self, or denied he'd ever really said there was something in the box. On the other hand, there is some childish part of Grandaddy that seems more fearful of his sister's reaction than regretful of having lied. Surely, Grandaddy does not have the robust, upright nature of his sister. The more one considers Grandaddy, the more complex a character Grandaddy appears to be.

Studying the Selection

FIRST IMPRESSIONS

Do you think Grandaddy is basically an honest or a dishonest person?

QUICK REVIEW

1. When the story opens, who is having a birthday party?
2. Who is telling the story?
3. What year is it, when the story opens?
4. When the story goes back in time, to what year does it return?

FOCUS

5. For many years Hattie believed that there was something in the box. What does the box represent to Hattie? Does it matter that the box is really empty?
6. Why do you think the author uses the past tense for pages 273-275? Why does she stop using the first-person voice on those pages?

CREATING & WRITING

7. Find a box to hold slips of paper. Whenever you feel that things are not going your way, do the following. On one side of the paper, write down what you wished had happened. On the other side, write down how things could have been worse!
8. You can learn something about how it felt to live 150 years ago. For one day, you will not use the telephone (unless you have an emergency or your parents request that you do). Every time you want to make a phone call, write a letter to the person you want to call. Have paper, envelopes, stamps, a pen, and addresses ready. Keep a record of your letters for your teacher.
9. Now is your chance to make a beautiful box. You will need a box with a lid, that you can use for your project. If you prefer, you may make a box yourself, using cardboard, oak tag, or another suitable material (and lots of tape!). Have fun. Do something wonderful!

Hattie's Birthday Box ~ 281

QUICK REVIEW

1. Spencer McClintic is about to have a party to celebrate his 100th birthday.
2. The story is being told by Spencer McClintic's great-great-granddaughter.
3. The year is 1947.
4. The story goes back in time to 1873.

FOCUS

5. The box represents many things. It represents a safety net, a last resort if things got too bad, a secret knowledge that there is always help available. It also represents her brother's love; it is a material link to the loving family she left behind. Does it matter that the box is really empty? We think that the point of the story is that it does not matter; that the real treasure is Hattie herself; that the secret safety net is Hattie's own unplumbed depths. Children, however, are very concrete, and they may say, "yes, of course it matters! What if she'd opened it and found nothing?! She'd have been angry and disappointed." If your students say this, ask them, "then what? What do you think Hattie would have done after she got over her disappointment?" The answer is, of course, she'd have done just what she did *without* opening the box—found the strength to go on.
6. Again students will have various things to say, but using the past tense gives the story separation, depth, like a shadow box. The past tense makes the past seem *more* like the past. Changing from first person gives us distance from the young great-great-grandaughter, who certainly was not there at the time.

CREATING & WRITING

7. Ask the students to read some of their slips aloud. You may find yourself inspired or amused.
8. How will you know that your students have completed this assignment? First, you will want to send home a note to parents the week previous, so parents will be prepared for the time it will take for their child to write letters. Second, to make the exercise not too much of a burden, caution your students to write (at least two, but) no more than four letters on their two phone-free nights. Finally, have students bring their unsealed letters to class (but with envelopes addressed and stamped). It may be very entertaining for the class to hear some of the letters read aloud by their writers. This should be a voluntary activity. Then you can have students seal their letters and mail them from the mailboxes closest to school.

9. Please make certain that each student has access to a box and materials to decorate if they do not have these at home.

PULLING IT ALL TOGETHER

- The plot is acted out by the story's **characters**.
- The characters must have **internal conflict, external conflict,** or both, if the story is to be exciting.
- One way we learn about the characters and their conflicts is through the story's **dialogue**.
- The story's **point of view** depends on who is telling the story. The story may be told by a narrator outside the story or by a character in the story.

THINK ABOUT IT!

1. What are two actions of Androcles that tell us about his character?

2. What internal conflict did Androcles have before he decided to escape?

3. What are two examples of how a character's inner thoughts are revealed to us through the dialogue?

4. In response to Androcles' words, the lion does something. If you put the lion's actions into words, what would the lion be saying?

Androcles and the Lion: A Fable Retold

Long ago, during the time of the Roman Empire, a young slave named Androcles had a very harsh master. No matter how hard Androcles worked, his master would whip him and push him harder. One day Androcles decided to escape.

"Though I may be executed if I am caught," Androcles reasoned, "it would be better to die than to live like this." That night, taking only the clothes on his back, he walked all night by the light of the moon, and by sunrise he was exhausted and very hungry. Stepping into a thicket of trees to find a place to hide, Androcles found himself face to face with a lion.

Androcles couldn't believe his bad luck, to have finally escaped slavery only to fall prey to a wild lion. But the lion did not pounce. Rather, the animal held up a front paw as if to shake hands. Androcles realized that the paw was soaked in blood.

"You poor creature," the young man said soothingly. "You're hurt."

As Androcles stepped carefully toward the lion, he saw the source of the problem: a very large thorn stuck in the lion's paw.

Androcles spoke in a low voice. "It's alright. All will be well." He gently took the lion's paw in one hand, and with the other quickly pulled out the thorn. The lion licked its paw, then, in thanks, licked Androcles' hand. From that moment on they were friends.

One day, however, when Androcles was out gathering food for his supper, he was captured by Roman soldiers and—as punishment—taken to the city to be thrown into the arena with hungry lions.

When the day arrived for his execution, Androcles was sent into the arena to face his death. A hush fell over the gathered masses as the Emperor gave the order to release the hungry lion. The fierce creature raced toward the helpless man. Androcles closed his eyes and prepared to be torn limb from limb by a beast certainly gripped with hunger and angry at having been caged. He waited. The attack never came.

Androcles opened his eyes to find the lion laying at his feet. Could it be? It was! Androcles knelt down and patted his friend.

"Poor thing," he said. "They must have captured you the same day they caught me."

Stunned by this escaped slave who could tame a lion, the Emperor ordered both Androcles and the lion to be freed. As Androcles and his friend left the arena together, the crowds roared their approval.

You never know when a kindness shown to another might be repaid.

LESSON IN LITERATURE

1. Androcles runs away from his master, which tells you he hates slavery and loves freedom. Androcles helps the lion, which tells you first, that he is courageous and, second, that he is kindhearted.

2. Androcles, knowing that he would be risking his life in trying to escape, had to decide whether freedom was worth the risk.

3. "it would be better to die than to live like this"; "You poor creature"; "Poor thing"

4. The lion is saying "Thank you."

SELECTION VOCABULARY

beachcomber: one who wanders about looking for food, provisions, or some unexpected find

burrowing: digging down

dunes, dune: sand hills

marshes: areas of waterlogged soil, having no trees and covered with rushes, cattails and other grasses

mottled: marked with spots or blotches of different colors or shades

pottering: (puttering) doing "odds and ends" of small jobs

puckered: drew together tightly, forming wrinkles

quizically: questioningly

shrewdly: sharply and cleverly

vise: a tool with two jaws that can be adjusted to hold an object firmly

---

beachcomber	dunes, dune	mottled	puckered	shrewdly
burrowing	marshes	pottering	quizically	vise

1. Scientists like to study the large variety of plants, insects, fish, and waterfowl that live in or near _____ (areas of waterlogged soil).

2. The basket was gone. We had left it near some sand _____ (hills) on the beach, but now, in the shadows of the evening, we could not tell one _____ (sand hill) from another.

3. It had rained all night, but now the sun shone brightly through the _____ (marked with blotches of different colors) leaves.

4. The baby grabbed the bright yellow lemon and took a big bite. Her lips _____ (drew together tightly) as the sour juice ran into her mouth, and she let out a yelp.

5. Some people like to spend their free time going shopping or attending sports events, but I like to spend mine just _____ (doing odd jobs) around the house.

6. "So what do you really want?" he asked _____ (cleverly).

7. The carpenter put strong glue on each board and stuck the two boards together. He then put them in a _____ (tool with two jaws) to hold them tight until the glue set.

8. The fellow walking on the sand looked like a typical _____ (one who looks along the beach for objects); he sported cut-off jeans, uncombed hair and eyes glued to the ground.

9. The little rabbit was so busy _____ (digging down) into the ground, that it did not notice the cat creeping up behind it.

10. The little boy stood waiting patiently as his father worked at his desk. Finally, his father looked up. "Yes?" he said _____ (questioningly).

Workbook p. 91   Answer Guide p. 9

Unscramble

What insults did the ornithologists hurl at one another?*

SHRAMES

TROPETING

PREEDUCK

FROGARE

"You are __ __ __ __ __ __," said one.

CHAMBBERCOME

DWERSHLY

SNUDE

TELDMOT

SIEV

GROWNIRUB

"Well, you are a __ __ __ __ __ __ __ __ __ __," retorted the other.

*ornithologist: a scientist who specializes in the study of birds

Workbook p. 92   Answer Guide p. 9

BACKGROUND BYTES

John James Audubon (1785-1851) was the best known American wildlife artist for more than fifty years. His seminal work, *Birds of America*, is a compilation of 435 life-size drawings. Even today, it is the work against which bird artists are measured.

He played no part in the Audubon Society, the organization that bears his name. However, his name was used, because it was then—and is still—synonymous with bird conservation across the globe.

The mission of the Audubon Society is to maintain or to restore natural ecosystems. (An ecosystem is a community of organisms and its environment—the whole and all the interrelated parts, which function as an ecological unit.) The Audubon Society focuses on birds and other wildlife, and the places where they need to live. The Audubon Society does this for the benefit of humanity and for global biological diversity.

On January 5, 2005, the Audubon Society celebrated the 100th anniversary of its founding. What was happening on January 5, 1905? What was the world like in those days? A history lesson from the Audubon Society tells us that "Theodore Roosevelt was president, milk cost about 10 cents a gallon, and Albert Einstein published his Theory of Relativity. In the world of high fashion, ladies donned hats adorned with heron and egret plumes, and many even wore elaborate millinery creations containing entire bird bodies."

In fact, it was in response to the wholesale slaughter of plume bird colonies, that several smaller, local Audubon groups came together to take action. Since that time, the Audubon Society has worked steadily to educate people regarding the relationship between the decline of bird populations and the deteriorating human environment. When bird populations begin to die off, this is a signal of threats to all other species.

There are hundreds of Audubon societies across North America. Find out whether there is one close enough to you to be a resource for your students. Many Audubon societies run nature centers.

Since 1997, the National Audubon Society (New York City) and the Cornell Lab of Ornithology (in Ithaca, NY) have conducted an annual Great Backyard Bird Count. People across North America are urged to look at the birds in their backyards and report back to Audubon with their numbers. This is one of the world's largest volunteer efforts. The count gives ordinary citizens the opportunity to celebrate birds. No matter if those who participate are bird experts or newcomers, their efforts are an essential part of helping the birds of North America. The annual count takes place over a period of several days.

Contact the main office of the National Audubon Society for information.

National Audubon Society
700 Broadway
New York, NY 10003
Phone: (212) 979-3000
Fax: (212) 979-3188

According to the Audubon Society, the whimbrel is one of the world's widest ranging birds. Whimbrels nest in the arctic and spend winter on the coasts of southern North America through South America, southern Asia to Australia, and Africa. The whimbrel is a large shorebird, brownish in color. Its down-curved bill is its most distinctive feature. Its cousin, the Eskimo curlew, is now extinct. The number of whimbrels has recently declined. Avian experts assume that this is because the coastal wetlands where they winter are being destroyed across the globe. A whimbrel cannot winter in wetlands that are dry or polluted by toxic waste from factories.

Identification

If you are looking for a whimbrel, look for a large, short-legged bird on the shore that has the famous down-curved bill, a striped head, and brown speckled upperparts. On its neck and upper breast are light underparts with streaking. If you are listening for a whimbrel, its call is described as "*bibibibibibibi*" when it is not the breeding season, and a "*cur-lew*" note during migration. You will need a tape recording if you want to get a better idea of how this sounds.

Population Numbers

The U.S. Shorebird Conservation Plan lists whimbrels among shorebirds that have been shown to be in serious decline. The population of whimbrels in the Hudson Bay area has dropped from an estimated 42,500 in 1973 to only 17,000 in 2004.

What Can You Do?

Audubon is part of the **BirdLife International** alliance. BirdLife member organizations in Canada, the Caribbean, Central America, and South America are working to develop **Important Bird Areas (IBA) Programs** to identify, save, and restore critical habitats that support whimbrels and other species. For more information on their efforts contact the National Audubon Society.

TAKE YOUR STUDENTS BIRDING

Plan an outing with your students to a nearby park, wildlife refuge, Audubon nature center, or other natural area. If you are in the city, don't be discouraged. Take your class "urban birding." City species include doves, gulls, sparrows, pigeons, hawks, and even falcons. If you can brief your students using bird photos and drawings and audio or video tapes before your excursion, all the better.

Help your students to become people who are interested in birds. Lay volunteers are absolutely critical to the success of programs that monitor the long-term status of wintering populations of whimbrels and other bird species. Citizen-science monitoring programs enable anyone to participate in a process that will hopefully help restore the natural balance of our world.

Resources:

Brown, S., C. Hickey, B. Harrington, and R. Gill, eds. 2001. *The U.S. Shorebird Conservation Plan*. Manomet Center for Conservation Sciences, Manomet, MA.

Skeel, Margaret A. and Elizabeth P. Mallory. 1996. Whimbrel (Numenius phaeopus) In *The Birds of North America*, No. 219 (A. Poole and F. Gill, eds.). The Academy of Natural Sciences, Philadelphia, PA, and the American Ornithologists' Union, Washington, D. C. The National Audubon Society, diverse materials.

INTO "THE WHIMBREL"

Briefly put, the idiom and maxim *never say die* and the adage *if at first you don't succeed, try try again!* describe Axel's efforts and Tessa's attitude in this nice little story. (For those who may not know, *Never say die* means "Don't ever give up, do not despair!")

These are thematic elements that you can discuss with your class.

Why would someone bother helping an injured animal?

Why is it wrong to ignore an animal that is suffering?

Confronted with unfamiliar or frightening and difficult events, many of us freeze and feel helpless. We don't even *try* to find help. What practical steps can a person take to get help or to provide assistance?

Another thematic issue in *The Whimbrel* is why a healthy wild animal should be set free rather than kept in a cage. (Of course, when an animal is too injured to manage in the wild, it either must be put down by a veterinarian or be taken care of at a nature center—or by individual families who are able to do so.)

EYES ON...PULLING IT ALL TOGETHER

Once again, we are using the unit's final story to bring together and talk about the literary components that were showcased in the stories that preceded it.

On the board or on paper, review the literary components of the first five stories. Then, with your class, you can look for the ways in which each of these appears in *The Whimbrel.*

Story and Literary Component Showcased
Gramp
    (1) How We Get to Know the Characters
After School
    (2) Internal and External Conflict
One Throw
    (3) Dialogue
The Birds' Peace
    (4) A Character Speaks to One Who Cannot Answer & Internal Dialogue
Hattie's Birthday Box
    (5) Point of View

(1) Do we **get to know the characters** in *The Whimbrel* through
    • **Adjectives** the author uses in the narrative
    • **Dialogue**
    • the **Character's Thoughts** (also called **Internal Dialogue**)
    • the **Character's Actions**
    • what **Other Characters** think, say, and do in response to that character

(2) In *The Whimbrel,* what is the **conflict** for the main characters?

Is the conflict with another person or with a set of circumstances? Remind students that conflicts that occur with events or people *outside* oneself are called **external conflicts.** Is the basic problem one that they have within themselves (as in

Blueprint for Reading

a personal struggle over what is the right thing to do)? A conflict within is called an **internal conflict.**

(3) What do we learn about the main characters in *The Whimbrel* from their **dialogue**?

(4) In *The Whimbrel,* do the characters speak to the bird (who cannot answer)? Do we read their inner thoughts and feelings (**internal dialogue**)?

(5) Is there a narrator that refers to him- or herself as **I**? Is the story written in the present tense or the past tense? Are there any obvious symbols in the story?

The Whimbrel

Colin Thiele

The Whimbrel ~ 285

- About a hundred people live in the little town of Snapper Bay in southern Australia.

- Axel Jorgensen is seventy-two and has a mop of white hair and a cotton-wool beard.

- Tessa Noble is twelve. She lives in a white house in the main street—the only street—in Snapper Bay.

- Axel lives by himself in a wood hut around the curve of the bay, away from town.

- Axel was a fisherman, a forager, a boatman, a talker and a teacher.

LITERARY COMPONENTS

▶ **1. Setting:** We are introduced to the little town and population of Snapper Bay.

▶ **2. Characters; Characterization; Compare/ Contrast:** The two protagonists are introduced, described. Because the descriptions parallel each other, the author presents a contrast. Both characters are equally important in the story.

❶ About a hundred people lived in the little town of Snapper Bay in southern Australia. Some of them were young, and some of them were old, and some of them were in-between.

❷ Axel Jorgensen was seventy-two, with a mop of white hair and a cotton-wool beard, and legs that bowed outward like bananas. He looked something like Father Time.

Tessa Noble was twelve, with a mop of brown hair and tapioca-freckled cheeks, and legs that bowed inward at the knees like bent sticks. She lived in a white house in the main street of Snapper Bay. There was only one street in the whole town, so it had to be the main one anyway. She lived with her father and mother and her grown-up brother, Jody, and Jody's wife, Bridget.

Axel Jorgensen lived by himself in a wooden hut far around the curve of the bay, away from the town. It was the place where the sandy beach ended and the first rocks reared up near the start of the Hammerhead Handle. He was a fisherman, and a forager, a boatman and a beachcomber, a talker and a teacher. He taught Tessa many

> **WORD BANK**
> **forager** (FOR uh jer) *n.*: one who wanders about looking for food, provisions, or some unexpected find
> **beachcomber** (BEECH kohm er) *n.*: one who looks carefully (combs) along the beach for objects of interest

286 ~ Unit 3

GUIDING THE READING

LITERAL

Q: When the story opens, where are we?
A: We are in the little town of Snapper Bay in southern Australia.

Q: Describe Axel Jorgensen.
A: Axel is seventy-two, white hair and white bearded, and his legs bow outward.

Q: Describe Tessa Noble.
A: Tessa is twelve, has brown hair and tapioca-freckled cheeks, and her legs bow inward.

Q: Where does Axel live?
A: He lives in a wooden hut around the curve of the bay, away from the town.

Q: Where, and with whom, does Tessa live?
A: Tessa lives with her parents, her grown-up brother, Jody, and Jody's wife, Bridget, in a white house on the main street of Snapper Bay.

SUMMING UP THE PLOT

- When Axel and Tessa walk along the coast, he tells her about seashells and albatrosses.

- When they walk inland, he teaches her about summer sedges, snails, and spoonbills.

- Axel comes to eat at Tessa's house and goes fishing with Tessa's father.

- Tessa spends as much time near Axel's shack as she does on her own street.

things. When they walked along the coast together he taught her about seashells and albatrosses, and when they walked inland by the lakes and marshes he taught her about summer sedges, snails, and spoonbills in the wildlife sanctuary.[1] She thought he was one of the Wise People of the World.

She had called him Uncle Axel for as long as she could remember, even though they were not related. He often came to have a meal in Tessa's house, and Tessa's father went fishing with him whenever he could. She spent as much time pottering about near his shack as she did in her own little street in Snapper Bay.

1. A *wildlife sanctuary* is an area of land that is preserved in its natural state. There, the plants, birds, fish, and animals native to the area live and grow undisturbed. People may come to observe the wildlife, but may not interfere with it in any way.

WORD BANK

marshes (MAR shiz) *n.:* areas of waterlogged soil, having no trees and covered with rushes, cattails, and other grasses

pottering (usually puttering, PUTT er ing) *v.:* doing "odds and ends" of small jobs

The Whimbrel ~ 287

LITERARY COMPONENTS

▶ **3. Characterization; Background; Exposition:** Axel is characterized and the author describes the relationship between the older man and the young girl. They are both characterized in the sentence, "She thought he was one of the Wise People of the World."

GUIDING THE READING

ANALYTICAL

Q: How can Axel be learned enough to teach, if he has never studied in school?
A: He has learned from the things he has done in his long life. He must also be a person who pays attention to what he sees.

Q: Why do you think Tessa considers Axel one of the Wise People of the World?
A: Likely she thinks this because he knows so much and shares his knowledge so well with her.

SUMMING UP THE PLOT

- Axel's shack is filled with things Tessa's mother calls junk: oars, rusty oarlocks, bits of rope, rudder pins and grappling hooks, boxes, chains, and old craypots.

- Axel has known Tessa since the day she was born.

LITERARY COMPONENTS

▶ **4. Characterization; Humor/Irony:** We get a good picture of Tessa's mother and of Axel, from the author's telling us in such a backhanded way that Tessa's mom would consider Axel's collection of stuff *junk.*

4 The shack was filled with things that Tessa's mother called junk. There were oars and rusty oarlocks, bits of rope, rudder pins and grappling hooks, boxes, chains, and old craypots that seemed ancient enough to have come out of Noah's Ark. For Axel had been a sailor as well as a fisherman. He had known Tessa since the day she was born.

2. A *rudder* is a blade that turns in the water at the stern (rear) of a boat. The rudder is used for steering the boat.
3. A *grappling hook* is an iron-clawed instrument attached to a rope. It is thrown from a boat onto an object such as a wall or an enemy ship. When the object is "hooked," it cannot move away from the boat.

GUIDING THE READING

LITERAL
Q: Name some of the things that are in Axel's shack.
A: The items include oars, rusty oarlocks, bits of rope, rudder pins, grappling hooks, boxes, chains, and old craypots.

ANALYTICAL
Q: Why would Tessa's mother consider the things in Axel's hut to be junk?
A: Answers will vary. Axel has accumulated parts of things, and parts of old things, that might be of use to him sometime. Probably, a mother on main street would not want chains and oarlocks in her living room.

SUMMING UP THE PLOT

- Axel loves all living things, even Rump, a young wombat.
- When the driver of a car hits Rump, he took the injured wombat to Axel, and left him as he would leave a patient in a hospital.

- Rump recovered and stayed on with Axel.
- Axel never calls him a pet. He is a mate, a friend, and a companion.
- One morning Tessa walks to Axel's and finds him busy and excited.

- He is working at the vise on his bench near the door of his shack.
- Tessa asks him what he is doing. "What's up?"
- "You'll never guess, Tessa girl," Axel says.
- Tessa knows something has happened, because Axel never calls her Tessa girl unless he is excited.
- Axel tells Tessa to look inside, but to move slowly.
- She asks if it is a snake.

Axel loved all living things—even Rump, the young wombat, who caused him a lot of trouble. Rump had been run over by a car near the Murray River, and the driver had picked him up and left him with Axel, just like a patient in a hospital. When Rump had recovered he had stayed on, burrowing in the bank behind the hut or wandering down to the town to thin out someone's vegetable garden.

"It's that potbellied wombat again," people used to say when they found out. "Take him back to Axel."

And so Rump would soon be back digging in his bank again or snuffling in a corner of the hut or scrabbling under the floor. Once Axel had disappeared completely into a new wombat hole while he had been stirring the porridge at the stove. But he was never angry with Rump. He wouldn't even call him a pet. He was a mate, he said, a friend and a companion.

One morning when Tessa walked around the long curve of the beach to Axel's hut she found him busy and excited. He was working at the vise on his bench near the door of his shack.

"What are you doing?" she asked. "What's up?"

"You'll never guess, Tessa girl," he said. She knew that something had happened, because he never called her Tessa girl unless he was excited.

"What is it, then?"

"Look inside." He nodded his head at the shack. "But move slowly."

She was suspicious and walked very carefully. "Is it a snake?"

> WORD BANK
> **burrowing** (BURR oh ing) *v.*: digging down
> **vise** (VYZ) *n.*: a tool with two jaws that can be adjusted to hold an object firmly

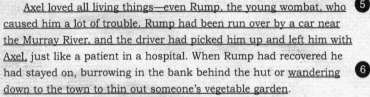

The Whimbrel ~ 289

LITERARY COMPONENTS

▶ **5. Characterization; Subplot:** The story of Rump is a mini-subplot that tells us a lot about Axel and the people in the town.

▶ **6. Humor, Irony:** The author, too, indulges the wombat by describing his activities as "thin[ning] out someone's vegetable garden."

▶ **7. Characterization; Dialect:** Axel doesn't consider Rump a pet. He's his *mate.*

▶ **8. Rising Action:** Tessa visits Axel who is working at the vise and who is excited about something.

▶ **9. Sustaining Suspense:** Notice how the author sustains suspense here. Tessa can't see what Axel has until seven short paragraphs later. If she can't see it, neither can we.

GUIDING THE READING

LITERAL

Q: Who is Rump?
A: Rump is a wombat who was brought to Axel injured. After he healed, he just stayed on with Axel.

Q: What is Axel doing, when Tessa arrives at his hut?
A: He is working at the vise on his bench.

Q: What does Tessa think Axel has got, at first?
A: She asks if it is a snake.

ANALYTICAL

Q: What does it tell us about Axel, that he does not call the wombat his pet?
A: Axel does see himself as owning animals. Rather, they are his fellow creatures that he helps and respects.

Q: Why do you think people in the town are so good-natured about the wombat's thinning out their gardens?
A: It will be interesting to see what students have to say about this. Snapper Bay is a small town and everyone knows everyone else.

Perhaps the slower pace of life and being closer to nature (living near the sea in an area that is not "developed") make people more patient, more tolerant, and less angry.

Q: When Axel greets Tessa, how does she know that he is excited about something?
A: He calls her Tessa girl, which is what he says when he is excited about something.

SUMMING UP THE PLOT

- Tessa can't see anything at all in the shadow. "I can't see a thing."
- Axel chuckles and says that he wouldn't take her out to see things in the marshes.
- Suddenly she sees it.

LITERARY COMPONENTS

▶ **10. Rising Action; Suspense:** In fact, we don't get to see the bird until one paragraph after Tessa sees it.

"Not a snake. Come and see."

At first she couldn't see anything at all in the shadow. She opened her eyes wide and then puckered them quickly to get a clearer view.

"I can't see anything."

"Not very smart, are you?" He chuckled. "Wouldn't take you out to see things in the marshes."

10 "Is it a . . . Oh!" Suddenly she saw it. There was a little silence while she took a breath and looked at it. Axel went on working busily at the vise on his bench.

> WORD BANK — **puckered** *v.:* drew together tightly, forming wrinkles

290 ~ Unit 3

GUIDING THE READING

ANALYTICAL

Q: Why does Axel say he wouldn't take Tessa out to see things in the marshes?

A: He thinks she is not being very observant and doesn't know how to look properly.

- Tessa sees a bird with a long curved beak, lying on its side in a large wire cage, panting.
- It is streaked brown and buff over the wings and body, but its breast is white and its crown has long white stripes above the eyes.

It is beautiful.
- "What is it?" she asks.
- Axel straightens up and stops his filing at the vise. "A whimbrel," he says.
- Tessa tastes the name on her tongue. "I like

that. It's a name with meanings in the sounds."
- Axel says, "Speed and distance, and lonely faraway cries in the night."
- Tessa asks, "Is it hurt?"
- Axel answers, "Pretty bad."

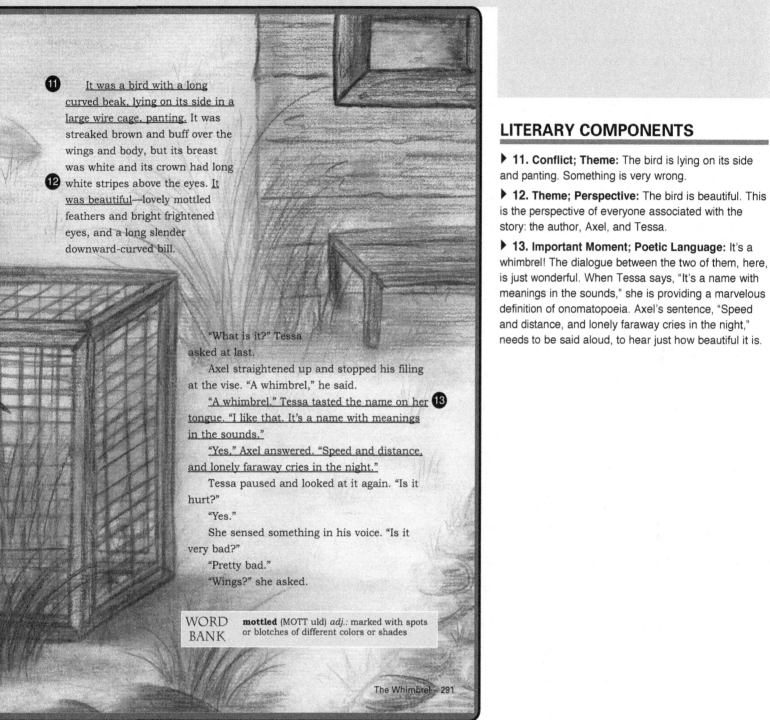

(11) It was a bird with a long curved beak, lying on its side in a large wire cage, panting. It was streaked brown and buff over the wings and body, but its breast was white and its crown had long (12) white stripes above the eyes. It was beautiful—lovely mottled feathers and bright frightened eyes, and a long slender downward-curved bill.

"What is it?" Tessa asked at last.

Axel straightened up and stopped his filing at the vise. "A whimbrel," he said.

"A whimbrel." Tessa tasted the name on her (13) tongue. "I like that. It's a name with meanings in the sounds."

"Yes," Axel answered. "Speed and distance, and lonely faraway cries in the night."

Tessa paused and looked at it again. "Is it hurt?"

"Yes."

She sensed something in his voice. "Is it very bad?"

"Pretty bad."

"Wings?" she asked.

> WORD BANK **mottled** (MOTT uld) *adj.*: marked with spots or blotches of different colors or shades

The Whimbrel ~ 291

LITERARY COMPONENTS

▶ **11. Conflict; Theme:** The bird is lying on its side and panting. Something is very wrong.

▶ **12. Theme; Perspective:** The bird is beautiful. This is the perspective of everyone associated with the story: the author, Axel, and Tessa.

▶ **13. Important Moment; Poetic Language:** It's a whimbrel! The dialogue between the two of them, here, is just wonderful. When Tessa says, "It's a name with meanings in the sounds," she is providing a marvelous definition of onomatopoeia. Axel's sentence, "Speed and distance, and lonely faraway cries in the night," needs to be said aloud, to hear just how beautiful it is.

GUIDING THE READING

LITERAL

Q: When Tessa first sees the bird, where is it and what is it doing?
A: The bird is lying on its side in a large wire cage, panting.

Q: What does Tessa say about the word, whimbrel?
A: She says "It's a name with meanings in the sounds."

Q: What does Axel say about it?
A: He says that it sounds like "Speed and distance, and lonely faraway cries in the night."

ANALYTICAL

Q: What does Tessa mean, when she says that the word whimbrel has meanings in its sounds?
A: This is like onomatopoeia, words that sound like what they do.

Q: Have you ever heard lonely, faraway cries in the night?
A: It will be interesting to see if any students answer yes. If so, ask them if they knew what made the sound, and how the sound made them feel.

SUMMING UP THE PLOT

- Axel takes the thing he is making out of the vise, examines it, and puts it back.

- He says, "He's lost a foot, Tessa. He can't stand up properly."

- Tessa is horrified. "A foot? How on earth could he have lost a foot?"

- Axel says that a bullet probably injured the bird.

- Tessa can't believe that anyone would shoot a whimbrel.

- Tessa asks what is going to happen to the whimbrel.

- Axel tells Tessa that because of its lost foot the whimbrel can't stand properly.

- Tessa tries to imagine how the bird lost its foot.

- Axel thinks that a bullet did the damage.

- Tessa is horrified by the idea that someone would shoot at a whimbrel.

LITERARY COMPONENTS

▶ **14. Conflict; Theme; Characterization; Revelation:** Axel is working on something. Could it be connected with the whimbrel situation? We won't know for another twenty-four short paragraphs! He tells Tessa the bird has lost a foot.

▶ **15. Characterization; Theme:** Tessa expresses her shock that people would try to shoot a whimbrel.

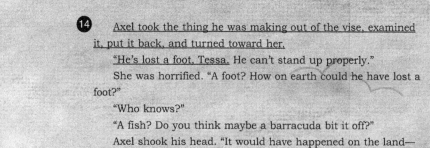

14 Axel took the thing he was making out of the vise, examined it, put it back, and turned toward her.

"He's lost a foot, Tessa. He can't stand up properly."

She was horrified. "A foot? How on earth could he have lost a foot?"

"Who knows?"

"A fish? Do you think maybe a barracuda bit it off?"

Axel shook his head. "It would have happened on the land— or in the air. He likes the inlets and the mud flats."

"A sharp piece of iron, then? Or a piece of wire—a power line he didn't see when he was flying fast?"

Axel's big mop of white hair trembled as he shook his head again. "No. A bullet, more likely."

Tessa was appalled. "Not a bullet!" she said quickly. "Nobody would shoot at a whimbrel!"

"No?" Axel rubbed angrily with a file. "Have you seen the way Tiny Hilbert or Joe Zucci handle a rifle around here? Like maniacs!"

15 "But not at a whimbrel. Surely they wouldn't shoot at a whimbrel."

292 ~ Unit 3

GUIDING THE READING

LITERAL

Q: What is wrong with the whimbrel?

A: The whimbrel has lost a foot.

Q: How does Axel think the whimbrel could have lost a foot?

A: He thinks he was hit in the foot with a bullet.

SUMMING UP THE PLOT

- Axel says, "What do you think? He can't live as he is, can he? He has to fly all the way to Siberia or Canada in a few weeks' time."

- Tessa sits on an old box near the door and asks Axel if the whimbrel can land on one foot and take off again.

- Axel says that most birds can stand on one foot, if it's not too windy. "But his other foot is hurt too—the claw."

- "Can't he stand at all, then?"

- Axel answers that he can tumble about and hop and flap and flop. But how could he live like that? "It would be better to put him away than to let him starve to death."

"They'd shoot at anything. At a stilt or a curlew or an ibis or a pelican, at a spoonbill or a snipe or a swallow or a swan, at a post or a tin or a light bulb or a tank. They ought to be locked up."

"That's awful." She was silent for a while. "What's going to happen to him?"

Old Axel looked up sharply. "What do you think? He can't live as he is, can he? He has to fly all the way to Siberia or Canada in a few weeks time."

"But that's on the other side of the world!"

"Yes. Big enough trip to tackle with two legs."

She sat on an old box near the door and glanced back and forth from Axel to the whimbrel. "Can he land on one foot and take off again?"

"Most birds can stand on one foot—if it's not too windy. But his other foot is hurt too—the claw."

"Can't he stand at all, then?"

"He can tumble about and hop and flap and flop. But how could he live like that? How could he get enough food? It would be better to put him away than to let him starve to death."

The Whimbrel ~ 293

LITERARY COMPONENTS

▶ **16. Information about Whimbrels; Theme:** For readers who may not know, the author tells us that whimbrels migrate long distances. Axel expresses the view that an animal cannot live if it cannot function well enough to be what it is.

▶ **17. Theme; Conflict:** Axel says that it would be better to put the bird away than to let it starve. Tessa doesn't believe that Axel would do that.

GUIDING THE READING

LITERAL

Q: Where will all the whimbrels in Australia be going in a few weeks' time?
A: They will be flying to Canada or to Siberia.

SUMMING UP THE PLOT

- Tessa doesn't believe that Axel would do that—kill the whimbrel kindly.

- Axel says that sometimes we have to do things even when we don't want to.

- Tessa says that she knows he wouldn't do that. She stands up and says, "What are you making?"

- Axel unfastens something very small from the vise: It's a foot. A tiny wooden foot for a whimbrel.

- Tessa holds the whimbrel while Axel tries to

fit the artificial foot. It has a hollow stem to fit over the stump of his leg.

- Although the whimbrel is frightened, it seems to know that they are trying to help.

LITERARY COMPONENTS

▶ **17. Theme; Conflict:** Axel says that it would be better to put the bird away than to let it starve. Tessa doesn't believe that Axel would do that.

▶ **18. Rising Action; Strong Visual Image; Theme; Characterization:** Axel has made a little foot! Ask the class if everyone sees that foot in their mind's eye. Axel is a person who never says die.

---

17 Her eyes opened wide. "Put him away?"

"Yes. Kill him kindly."

"No," she said quickly. "Oh no, you wouldn't do that." She paused for a second and looked at the old man shrewdly. "You couldn't do that, could you?"

He seemed to be so busy at his vise that at first she thought he hadn't heard her. But after a while he went on without looking up. "Sometimes things have to be done even when you don't want to do them. Even when it's very hard."

"I know you wouldn't do it," she said confidently, "even if you could." She stood up and went over to him. "What are you making?"

18 He unfastened something very small from the vise and held it up. It was a foot. A tiny wooden foot—for a whimbrel.

Tessa held the whimbrel while Axel tried to fit the artificial foot. It was not an easy thing to do, even though the little piece of wood was carefully made, with three carved toes, and a hollow stem to fit over the stump of the leg.

Fortunately the whimbrel didn't struggle. Axel showed Tessa how to hold it firmly and gently with the wings wrapped against its body. Although it was frightened it seemed to know that they were trying to help. Its dark eyes blinked and flashed, and when its head moved jerkily its long bill darted about like a probe. Tessa was spellbound.

"It must be four inches long," she said.

Axel didn't even look up. "Four!" he said. "More like sixteen; nice streamlined bird, the whimbrel."

"Not the bird. The bill."

"What about the bill?"

"It must be four inches long."

"The bill is, yes. Not the bird."

"No, the bill, the bill."

"Well, why didn't you say so in the first place?"

Tessa snorted. "Really, Uncle Axel!" She was about to say much more, but decided to hold her peace. She looked down at the whimbrel again, at the great curving beak, as black as ebony, at the white breast, the mottled back, and the light stripe running above the eyebrows and over the curve of his head.

> WORD BANK **shrewdly** (SHROOD lee) *adv.:* sharply and cleverly

294 ~ Unit 3

GUIDING THE READING

LITERAL

Q: What has Axel been working on all this time at the vise on his workbench?

A: He has been creating a wooden foot for the whimbrel.

ANALYTICAL

Q: Do you think that Axel would put the bird down, if the alternative is that it would starve?

A: Yes. He certainly would not just watch the bird struggle.

Q: What do you think it feels like, to hold a whimbrel as Tessa does in this scene?

A: Answers will vary. We think it would be just wonderful. Warm, feathery, big.

- Tessa says to the whimbrel, "Oh, you're a beautiful fellow."
- Old Axel says gently, "Hold still, Willie." We've nearly finished.
- Tessa says, "Is that his name—Willie?"
- Axel says he's finished. "Put him down in his pen."
- The whimbrel flutters for a minute, but settles down quickly. He begins to pace up and down in the cage.
- Tessa says excitedly, "It actually works, Uncle Axel. It actually works."
- Tessa asks whether he thinks the whimbrel will be able to fly now, and land without somersaulting.
- Axel says to give him a day or two to get used to it. "It's not every day that a bird has to learn to fly with a wooden leg."
- It was wise to wait, because two days later the leg has gotten soggy and starts to break up. Willie had walked in his tray of water.

"Oh, you're a beautiful fellow," she said. But the bird suddenly struggled and she had to tighten her grip.

"Hold still, Willie," said old Axel gently. "We've nearly finished." **19**

"Is that his name—Willie?"

"Suits him, I reckon. Will-he walk? Or won't he?"

"Will-he walk! That's a dreadful joke, Uncle Axel."

"Well, we'll soon know."

"Finished?"

"Finished."

Axel put his pliers and other tools aside and straightened up. "Put him down in his pen."

The whimbrel fluttered for a minute, but he settled down quickly and began to pace up and down in the cage. At first he lifted his leg with a high awkward step like a man learning to walk on skis, but before long he grew used to it and stomped about happily. Tessa had her nose pressed against the wire. "It works, Uncle Axel," she said excitedly. "It actually works." **20**

"Of course it works," he answered haughtily.

"D'you think he'll be able to fly now, and land without somersaulting?"

"Give him a day or two to get used to it," Axel said. "It's not every day that a bird has to learn to fly with a wooden leg."

It was wise to wait. Two days later the wooden leg was useless. After Willie had walked in his tray of water a few times the light wood grew soggy and began to break up. **21**

The Whimbrel ~ 295

LITERARY COMPONENTS

▶ **19. Character:** The bird now has a name.

▶ **20. Success, Nearly:** The leg seems to work!

▶ **21. Rising Action; Conflict; Suspense:** The leg has fallen apart. What will they do?

GUIDING THE READING

LITERAL

Q: Does the leg work?
  A: Yes.

Q: What happens to the wooden leg?
  A: It becomes wet when Willie walks in his tray of water, then it deteriorates.

- Axel works at his bench for another whole day and makes a metal foot, of aluminum. But it is too hard to fit to Willie's leg.

- Axel admits at last that it doesn't work. That the

LITERARY COMPONENTS

▶ **22. Theme; Characterization:** *If at first you don't succeed...*

leg would probably do him more harm than good.

- Tessa is downhearted. "Whatever are we going to do, then?"

- Axel assures her that they will win yet. "I've

still got bags of ideas."

- He makes a plastic foot and cuts the shape carefully to match the real foot. He melts out a hollow stem with a red-hot skewer.

"Fat lot of use that was, Willie," said Axel. "Wouldn't have lasted you to Mount Gambier, let alone to the other side of the world. We'll have to do better than that."

So he worked at his bench for another whole day and made a metal foot—of aluminum. It was beautifully shaped, but it was too hard to fit to Willie's leg.

"Won't work," Axel admitted at last. "Might hurt him, probably do more harm than good."

Tessa was downhearted. "Whatever are we going to do, then? He looks so helpless when you take his foot away from him."

㉒ "We'll win yet. I've still got bags of ideas."

This time he made a plastic foot, cutting the shape carefully to match the real one, and melting out a hollow stem with a red-hot skewer. It fitted beautifully. But Axel was still

GUIDING THE READING

LITERAL

Q: What does Axel try next?
A: His next leg is made of aluminum.

Q: What is the problem with the aluminum leg?
A: It is too hard to fit to Willie's leg.

Q: What does Axel try next?
A: Plastic.

ANALYTICAL

Q: Why would aluminum be a good metal to work with?
A: It is lightweight and it does not rust.

- Axel keeps Willie for another week, checking his foot every day.
- By now Willie is quite tame. He eats out of Axel and Tessa's hands.

- Tessa thinks that Axel is becoming so fond of Willie that soon he won't be able to part with him.
- She asks Axel if he is going to keep Willie or set him free.

- Tessa realizes that she has been rude, questioning Axel about his intentions.
- The new leg fits beautifully, but Axel is still not satisfied.
- He experiments for another two days, and makes more and more little feet.
- He varies the length and diameter of the hollow stem until he has one that is perfect.
- It fits snugly over the whole of the stump of Willie's leg, and extends a half inch beyond it so that his two legs—the real one and the artificial one—are exactly the same length.
- Axel fastens a tiny clamp around the stump to be doubly sure.
- Willie walks as if he is marching in a brass band. He looks so pleased.
- Axel lifts Willie out of his cage. "It's time you tested your new foot out in the wide world."

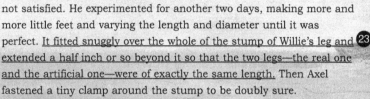

not satisfied. He experimented for another two days, making more and more little feet and varying the length and diameter until it was perfect. It fitted snugly over the whole of the stump of Willie's leg and **23** extended a half inch or so beyond it so that the two legs—the real one and the artificial one—were of exactly the same length. Then Axel fastened a tiny clamp around the stump to be doubly sure.

"Now, Willie," he said, "you ought to be able to dance to music."

Willie walked as if he was marching in a brass band. He looked so pleased that Tessa thought his big bill would break out into a long down-curving smile.

"He's all right this time," she said. "Now he really can look after himself."

Axel kept him for another week, checking the foot carefully every day. By now Willie was quite tame, standing quietly when they came near him and even eating out of their hands. Tessa could see that **24** Axel was becoming so fond of him that soon he wouldn't be able to part with him.

"Are you going to keep Willie?" she asked slyly one day. "Or are you going to set him free?"

Axel looked at her quizzically.

Tessa was very uncomfortable. She knew she had been rude and she was certain that he knew it too.

"Come on then," he said suddenly, lifting Willie out of his cage. **25** "It's time you tested your new foot out in the wide world."

> WORD BANK **quizzically** (KWIZ ik lee) *adv.*: questioningly

The Whimbrel ~ 297

LITERARY COMPONENTS

▶ **23. Turning Point:** Axel has come up with a solution; the plastic leg works!

▶ **24. Rising Action; Characterization; Conflict; Theme:** The bird is doing well and eats from their hands. Will Axel release him? It seems to be the case here that Tessa asks Axel a question that is inappropriate given their relative ages. It is hard to tell if the behavior is considered rude because she is baiting him slightly (note the word, *slyly*) or because she is prying.

▶ **25. Rising to the Challenge:** Axel is brave, too.

GUIDING THE READING

ANALYTICAL

Q: Why would it be hard for Axel to let the bird go?

A: It is hard to separate from something for which you feel love and responsibility. He has gotten used to the whimbrel's company, as well.

Q: Why is it rude for Tessa to ask Axel about this?

A: Tessa is young, Axel is her mentor. It sounds as though she is teasing him or prying.

SUMMING UP THE PLOT

- Tessa and Axel carry Willie to the dunes behind the shack.
- They stop and look at Willie for the last time.
- "Good-bye, Willie," Tessa whispers.

LITERARY COMPONENTS

▶ **26. Poignant:** This is sad.

▶ **27. Climax; Theme:** He sets Willie down. The image of his rising in the air is a strong one.

- "Off you go," says Axel.
- He puts Willie down. Willie stands as if amazed at the sight of everything around him. Then he runs forward and rises easily into the air.

- "Just look at him fly," Tessa says, "so fast and free."

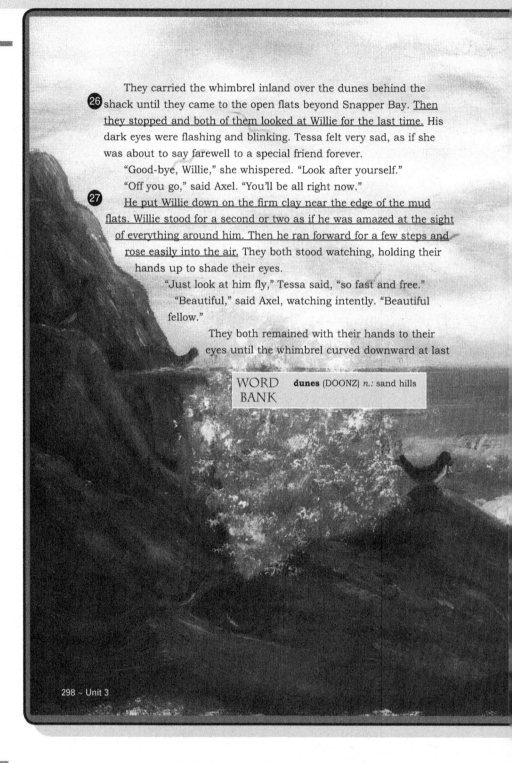

㉖ They carried the whimbrel inland over the dunes behind the shack until they came to the open flats beyond Snapper Bay. Then they stopped and both of them looked at Willie for the last time. His dark eyes were flashing and blinking. Tessa felt very sad, as if she was about to say farewell to a special friend forever.

"Good-bye, Willie," she whispered. "Look after yourself."

"Off you go," said Axel. "You'll be all right now."

㉗ He put Willie down on the firm clay near the edge of the mud flats. Willie stood for a second or two as if he was amazed at the sight of everything around him. Then he ran forward for a few steps and rose easily into the air. They both stood watching, holding their hands up to shade their eyes.

"Just look at him fly," Tessa said, "so fast and free."

"Beautiful," said Axel, watching intently. "Beautiful fellow."

They both remained with their hands to their eyes until the whimbrel curved downward at last

WORD BANK	**dunes** (DOONZ) *n.:* sand hills

298 ~ Unit 3

GUIDING THE READING

LITERAL

Q: What do Tessa and Axel say about Willie as he flies away?

A: Tessa says, "Just look at him fly, so fast and free." Axel says, "Beautiful, beautiful fellow."

ANALYTICAL

Q: Why do you think Axel releases Willie at just that moment?

A: Answers will vary. He may have already planned to do so. He may have been provoked by what Tessa said. He himself may fear that he has gotten too attached to the bird. If he waits any longer it will only get harder.

SUMMING UP THE PLOT

- Though the world is full of birds, it suddenly feels empty to them.
- Axel says that it is time for them to go home.
- Tessa's eyes mist over and her lip trembles.
- Axel tells her not to be sad. It wouldn't have been right for them to keep Willie in a cage, especially when the whimbrels fly to the other side of the world. "Think how lonely he would be then."
- Axel says, "And think what a hero he'll be."
- Axel says that Willie will be super special. "There won't be another whimbrel like him in the whole world."

toward the skyline by the marshes and they lost sight of him. <u>Though</u> **28** <u>the world was full of birds it was suddenly empty.</u>

"Back home, Tessa," said Axel gently. He saw her eyes misting over and her lip trembling. "No need to be sad for Willie," he said quietly. "He's happy back with the other whimbrels—with all his friends. It wouldn't be right to keep him in a cage, especially when they all fly to the other side of the world. Think how lonely he would be then. You wouldn't like that."

She shook her head. "No, I wouldn't like that."

"And think what a hero he'll be. He'll be able to talk about his wooden leg for the rest of his life."

<u>"His plastic leg."</u>　　　　　　　　　　　　　　　　　　　**29**

<u>"Just like old Mrs. Elliot with her operations."</u>

<u>Tessa smiled. "He will be sort of special, won't he?"</u>

<u>"Super special," said Axel. "There won't be another whimbrel like</u> <u>him in the whole world."</u>

The Whimbrel ~ 299

LITERARY COMPONENTS

▶ **28. Falling Action:** This is just how it feels, when someone goes for good.

▶ **29. Conclusion; Theme:** Willie may be handicapped, but that just makes him unique.

GUIDING THE READING

ANALYTICAL

Q: Why does Tessa cry when Willie is released?

A: Students may have varying ideas about this. Certainly she has become attached to the bird. The bird is a part of what she and Axel have been doing together every day for a while. It is hard to say goodbye forever. Also, his beauty and freedom and flight probably move her.

Q: Why will Willie be a hero?

A: Because of his prosthesis he will be unusual, special. Also, he had an unusual experience and survived.

CREATING & WRITING (P. 301)

7. Students will write different pieces. Points that can be made include the following (and likely some things we have not even thought of):

It is important to be humane; it does not matter who the recipient is.

Animals suffer, too.

All living creatures "count," and it is not for us to decide that a bird or a dog or a rabbit doesn't matter.

Animals are kind to us and help us and we should return the favor.

8. Students may legitimately make different choices. Here are examples. You may want to consult the list at **Eyes on**, and to refer your students to that list.

(1) *The Whimbrel* is a good piece for **getting to know the characters** through their dialogue and their actions. The piece is filled with passages that demonstrate this. We also learn about the characters in this piece from the author's description, but not through adjectives. The fourth paragraph is a very good example. We learn what kind of person Axel is, we learn about how he teaches Tessa, and we also learn about both of them when the author writes, "She thought he was one of the Wise People of the World." (*Gramp* was the story used for this literary component.)

(2) The **conflict** in *The Whimbrel* is an **external** one. Axel and Tessa want to help an injured whimbrel. The conflict is sustained because the first and second artificial limbs, made from wood and metal, don't work. Axel has to start over again on another leg made from a different material. Even when he has solved the problem with plastic, he continues to experiment with different measurements.

There are two other auxiliary conflicts regarding (1) whether the most humane thing to do is to put the bird down, if Axel cannot make it an artificial limb (**internal conflict**); and (2) whether it is better for Axel to keep the bird, given the injury that it has sustained, and given his growing attachment to it, or whether the whimbrel should be freed to join other members of its species and live like a bird (both **internal** and **external conflict**). (*After School* was the story used for this literary component.)

(3) This overlaps with number (1). In *The Whimbrel,* we learn a great deal about both Axel and Tessa from their talking with each other. Again, the piece is replete with examples. (*One Throw* was used to showcase dialogue.)

(4) In *The Whimbrel,* the characters speak to the whimbrel briefly at times. There is no internal dialogue. (*The Birds' Peace* was used.)

(5) *The Whimbrel* is written in the third person (omniscient narrator) and the past tense. There are no changes in person or tense. Although the whimbrel himself may seem a symbol of flight and freedom, this is not emphasized in the story. (*Hattie's Birthday Box* was used to discuss these elements.)

Animal Glossary

An *albatross* is a large, white bird with a broad wingspread and the ability to remain aloft for long periods of time.

A *sedge* is a grasslike plant that grows in wet places.

A *barracuda* is a long, slender fish with sharp teeth. It is known for its habit of biting any moving object within reach.

A *snipe* is a plump, long-billed shorebird.

A *cray* is a spiny lobster found in Australian waters. A *craypot* is used for trapping crays.

A *spoonbill* is a large wading bird with a long, flat bill that has a spoonlike tip.

A *curlew* is a large shorebird with a long bill that curves down.

A *stilt* is a black and white wading bird with long, pink legs and a long black bill.

An *ibis* is a large wading bird with a long, thin bill that curves down.

A *wombat* is an Australian marsupial (animals who carry their young in a pouch). The wombat has a thick, bearlike body and short legs.

About the Author

Colin M. Thiele was born in 1920 in a small, South Australian town called Eudunda. As a child, he loved to roam the countryside. His early love of nature is seen in most of his writings. Thiele fought for Australia in WWII. After the war, he worked as a teacher, principal, and college director. All the while, he was writing poetry, novels, storybooks, biographies, and plays. His hometown of Eudunda is so proud of him that, in their civic gardens, they have erected a sculpture of him, seated with a notebook and pencil, a pelican at his side.

300 ~ Unit 3

9. Most libraries have tapes of bird calls available, as well as picture books of bird species. Try to bring some in for your class, before they do this assignment.

For us, it is hard to imagine that the foot will stay attached for good.

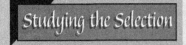

FIRST IMPRESSIONS
Do you think Willie will do well with his plastic foot?

QUICK REVIEW
1. What is the setting of the story?

2. Who are the three main characters?

3. What does the author think Tessa's mother would call the things in Axel's shack?

4. Who is Rump?

FOCUS
5. Why does Axel make an artificial foot for the whimbrel?

6. Imagine that Tessa is telling the story. She will speak in the first person. Rewrite at least five sentences from the story. Here is an example from page 287:

   I had called him Uncle Axel for as long as I could remember, even though we were not related. He often came to have a meal in **my** house, and **my** father went fishing with him whenever he could. I spent as much time pottering about near his shack as I did in **my** own little street in Snapper Bay.

CREATING & WRITING
7. Write several paragraphs in which you explain why helping animals is so important.

8. Choose one of the following elements of a story: character, conflict, dialogue, or first-person narration. Write a paragraph explaining the element you have chosen. Then, use one or two paragraphs to bring examples from the story of how the element is used in *The Whimbrel*.

9. Your assignment is to do an **Outside Bird Count**. You will need a pad and a pencil, and a quiet place outside. Spend half an hour counting the birds you see. Note the different types. If you don't know their names, describe them in brief notes. Count the different bird calls you hear. If you can, make some rough, quick sketches of the birds you see.

The Whimbrel ~ 301

1. The story is set in Snapper Bay, a little town in southern Australia.

2. Axel Jorgensen, a seventy-two-year-old man, Tessa Noble, a twelve-year-old girl, and Willie is a whimbrel of indeterminate age.

3. The author writes that, "The shack was filled with things that Tessa's mother called junk."

4. Rump is a young wombat that Axel brought back to good health after the wombat had been hit by a car.

FOCUS

5. Students may talk about this in different ways. Axel clearly has a history of caring for (and about) injured animals. The bird cannot manage without a foot. Axel makes the foot because it is the only way he knows to restore the bird to something like his natural condition. Clearly, in addition to being compassionate, Axel is extremely clever and good with his hands.

6. You should remind students that more words will need changing than just **she** to **I**. For example, **her** or **hers** will become **my, mine,** and **me,** of course depending upon how the words are used in a sentence.

EYES ON...CONCRETE OR FORM POEMS

Concrete poems are poetry's visual answer to onomatopoeia. Onomatopoeia *sounds* like what it is. Concrete poetry *looks* like what it is. In a concrete or form poem, the words and lines are arranged on the page to look like the topic of the poem.

For your convenience we present the poem without visual distortion. We have interpreted the line breaks. It turns out that *I Am Winding Through a Maze* has—surprise!—a regular pattern of rhyme and rhythm. The author has done this quite cleverly, in fact.

Rhythmic I Am Winding Through a Maze	Rhyme Scheme	Pattern
I am winding through a maze,	a	7
I've been trapped in here for days,	a	7
And I wonder if I ever will get out.	b	11 beats
I am feeling some dismay,	c	7
for I've truly lost my way,	c	7
and my future seems to be		
a bit in doubt.	b	11
As I journey forth and back,	d	7
I'm completely losing track	d	7
of direction, where I've been,		
and where to go.	e	11
Is the exit far or near?	f	7
It is totally unclear,	f	7
and I woefully acknowledge		
I don't know.	e	11
As I take each turn and twist,	g	7
I am certain I have missed	g	7
where I ought to have been		
going all along.	h	11
Now I'm in a cul-de-sac,	d	7
and I have to double back,	d	7
every step I take is obviously wrong.	h	11
It's apparent that I am,	i	7
in a pickle, in a jam,	i	7
in a quandary, in a scrape,		
a squeeze, a spot	j	11
But at last I think I see	k	7
where the exit just might be,	k	7
so I think I'll soon be out...		
whoops! no I'm not.	j	11

This is an example of doing a little extra work with a poem, and making a discovery as a consequence! Who would guess that the poem had such regularity of form? *I Am Winding Through a Maze* is a good subject for student exercises that should be fun for your class. (See the poetry post-curriculum, page **306**.)

Make sure students know the words *cul-de-sac* and *quandary*. A cul-de-sac is a street or passage closed at one end. (The word comes directly from French and literally means, the bottom of the bag.) A quandary is a state of perplexity or doubt. It will be important to remind them that **for the purposes of the poem, *quandary* is only two syllables**.

Make sure, as well, that they know the idioms, *in a pickle, in a jam, in a scrape, in a squeeze,* and *in a spot.* All of these idioms similarly mean *in a difficult, threatening, or embarrassing situation or unable to solve a dilemma.*

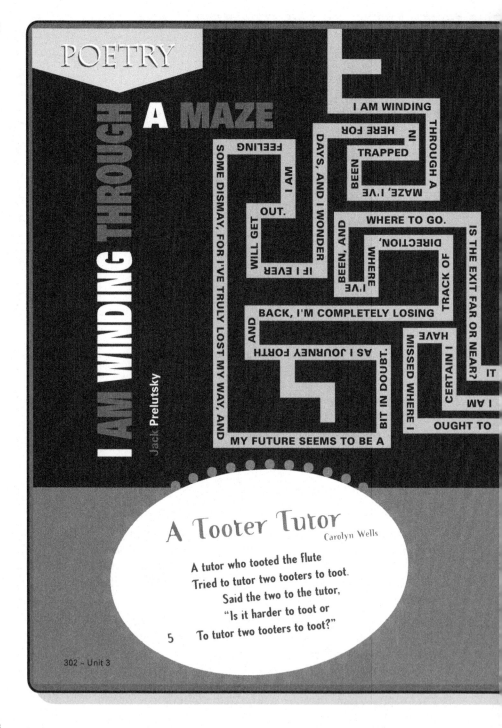

POETRY

I AM WINDING THROUGH A MAZE
Jack Prelutsky

A Tooter Tutor
Carolyn Wells

A tutor who tooted the flute
Tried to tutor two tooters to toot.
Said the two to the tutor,
"Is it harder to toot or
5   To tutor two tooters to toot?"

SOON BE OUT...

I'LL THINK I

WHOOPS!

SO

NO, I'M NOT.

JUST MIGHT BE,

THE EXIT

I THINK I SEE WHERE

IN A JAM, IN A

QUANDARY,

ACKNOWLEDGE

BUT AT LAST

IN A SCRAPE,

A

WOEFULLY

I DON'T KNOW. AS I TAKE

SQUEEZE, A SPOT.

WRONG. IT'S APPARENT THAT I AM IN A PICKLE,

AND I

UNCLEAR,

AND I HAVE

TO

DOUBLE BACK,

IS TOTALLY

EVERY STEP I

EACH TURN AND TWIST,

NOW I'M IN A CUL-DE-SAC,

TAKE

HAVE BEEN GOING

IS

ALL

OBVIOUSLY

ALONG.

A Bear in Reverse

Anonymous

A cheerful old bear at the zoo
Could always find something to do.
When it bored him to go
On a walk to and fro,
5   He reversed it, and walked fro and to.

EYES ON...LIMERICKS

The two limericks that follow are basically like all other limericks in their construction and intent. Limericks are funny, five-line poems with a regular pattern of rhythm and rhyme.

Regarding the pattern of rhyme, Lines 1, 2, and 5 rhyme, and Lines 2 and 3 rhyme. So the rhyme scheme is written:

    aabba

Traditionally, the fifth (and last) line ends with the final word of the first line.

Regarding the rhythmic pattern, Lines 1, 2, and 5 usually have 8 beats. Lines 2 and 3 usually have 5 or 6 beats.

So the basic mode is 8-8-5-5-8 or 8-8-6-6-8.

A Tooter Tutor differs from the basic model. It's 8-9-7-7-8.

A Bear in Reverse is 8-8-6-6-9.

If you are looking for other examples of limericks, check out the extraordinary body of work of Edward Lear (1812-1888), who also produced such brilliant, well-known longer poems as *The Quangle Wangle's Hat* (see pp. 639-641 in the textbook), *The Owl and the Pussycat*, and *The Jumblies* (see *Pearl*, Mosdos Press, 6th Grade Literature Anthology).

Historically, limericks use **hyperbole** to entertain. Hyperbole (hi PURR boh lee) is the use of extravagant exaggeration. Hyperbole is funny, because a reality is conveyed that is impossible.

Neither of these limericks, however, uses hyperbole. *A Tooter Tutor* is funny

(1) because it is a tongue twister; (2) because of the repetition of consonant and vowel sounds; and (3) because it uses homophones. *Homophones* are one of two or more words that are pronounced alike but are spelled differently and are different in meaning. Sometimes people mistakenly use the word *homonym* for *homophone*. A homonym is one of two or more words that are pronounced *and* spelled alike but are different in meaning (as the noun *quail* and the verb *quail*).

These limericks (and most other limericks) do not require any analyzing. They simply entertain and provide students an easy model to imitate so that they can write their own. *A Tooter Tutor* is clever with its homophones. *A Bear in Reverse* has a rather nice reversal of its own with *fro and to*.

INTO "74TH STREET"

74th Street is free verse, and has no regular rhythm or rhyme. The poem relies on informal language (*Hey, kid, you know what?*) to convey tone. The poem uses lots of one-syllable verbs—about fourteen, if you count the repetitions: *gets, puts, stands, flops, sticks, falls, smacks, grabs, sticks, slides, falls, skins, puts, sticks.*

In fact, the poem has a total of 88 words. Only ten have two syllables. That's a little more than ten percent. The poet does this intentionally. Perhaps this is to suggest this kid's driving intensity as she learns how to skate—in the way of most children. This child, as in the way of children, is daring, relentless, and unafraid of injuring herself. The minds and bodies of children can handle flopping over backwards, falling down, smacking their hands, and falling down again. Of course, when the author places the word *again,* alone in vertical and horizontal space, as the last line of the poem, she is expressing her adult amazement.

ANALYZING "THIS IS THE DAY"

This Is the Day is a poem about a longing—the longing to preserve one special day, the *today* of the speaker. The poem has a fairly consistent rhythm and no rhyme.

Repetition is important in this poem. The first line of each of the five stanzas (the *only* line in the fifth) begins with the words *This is....* In fact, the first line of the first stanza is repeated in its entirety in the second and third stanzas: *This is the sort of day....* Also, the second line of each of the first four stanzas begins, *I should like to ....* The specific action verb that follows (describing what the speaker *should like to* do) varies in its specificity, but in each of the stanzas, an action verb does follow. That, in itself, is a form of repetition.

There is an interesting juxtaposition of images. In the first three stanzas, the speaker tells us the ways in which she would like to put away and save—perhaps conceal—the wonderful day, to be brought out at another moment. That other moment is described in the fourth line of each of the first three stanzas. (Although, granted, the fourth line of the second stanza just indicates the *possibility* of bringing out the day once more.) However, the first line of the fourth stanza is like an introduction of this special day to the reader, to the audience. The second line of the fourth stanza tells us exactly what the speaker has been getting at in the first three stanzas. The fifth stanza reveals that day in all of its glory. Thus the first three stanzas hide the day away, and the last two expose it to view.

The poem has a quality of tenderness. All of us have had moments we cherished, then put away in the back closets of our minds, to take out on occasion to warm ourselves. We need to remember that we can do this, hold experiences in our hearts and minds, and move through them again, when we need to retreat to a safe or happy place and nourish ourselves.

74th Street

Myra Cohn Livingston

Hey, this little kid gets roller skates.
She puts them on.
She stands up and almost
flops over backwards.
5   She sticks out a foot like
she's going somewhere and
falls down and
smacks her hand. She
grabs hold of a step to get up and
10   sticks out the other foot and
slides about six inches and
falls and
skins her knee.

   And then, you know what?

15   She brushes off the dirt and the
blood and puts some
spit on it and then
sticks out the other foot

   again.

304 ~ Unit 3

The speaker of the poem tells us about a day she wants to keep, so that even when it is over, it can make her feel as she does today all over again.

The poem speaks to the transitory human experience of joy, and man's eternal quest to somehow preserve it. How to make happiness, joy, pleasure last? We are reminded that, in our memories, the light of good times can continue to shine within us. If we mentally retain rich experiences, the images, with their associated feelings, can be taken out repeatedly in private, quiet times. The ability to do exactly this is an important emotional tool which many, or most, children come by naturally. Who hasn't spent some delightful hours engaged in a "remember when?" conversation with friends? Reliving the good times is a way we can make ourselves feel stronger when the going gets tough.

The poem also shows the silly good feelings many of us have on our birthdays—the somewhat absurd sense of importance and delight we derive, when we are feted (not for a particular accomplishment, but just) because it is the anniversary of our birth. Presumably, then, the speaker is a young person, since few adults would confess to such unabashed pleasure simply from the attention we may get on our birthdays.

EYES ON...METAPHOR

This Is the Day is a good example of how poets use metaphor. You may want to remind students that a metaphor is a comparison between two things—two things that presumably are not alike. After the students have read the poem, you can talk with them about these comparisons. How is a special day the same as a wrapped present? How is it the same as something valuable that is locked away? How is it the same as clothing that keeps us warm in winter? Could a day be wrapped, put in a drawer, or hung? Decidedly not. But the poet's equation suggests that maybe it could be. The comparison evokes in us the sense that these unlike things *are* alike, after all. Through the comparison, we understand far better the feeling the poet is expressing.

These metaphors are fun, because they convey images of concrete but impossible ways to preserve the moment. Because they are concrete actions, the metaphors are interesting. The metaphors are not expressed as nouns with which the day is to be compared. What makes this poem unusual is that the metaphors are *actions* that imply the day is like an object that can be wrapped, hidden, or hung up. Wrapping the day in paper like a gift, hiding it in a secret drawer, and hanging it in the back of the wardrobe are wishful and instructive constructions. The lesson is that we *can* wrap, hide, hang the wonderful moments in our minds.

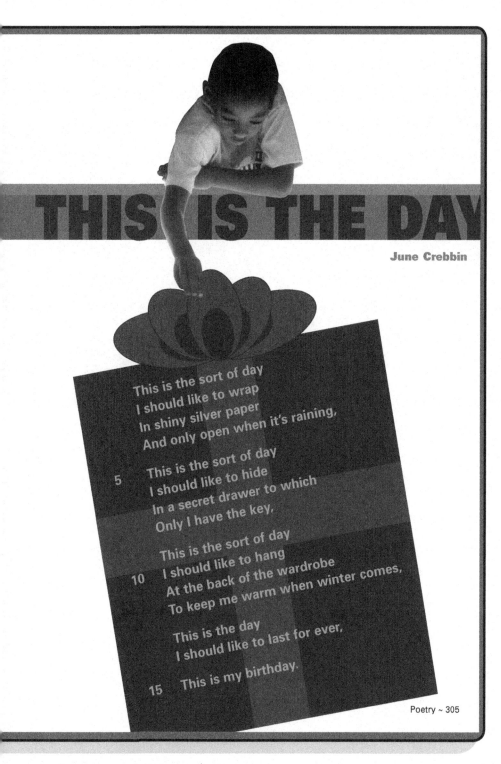

THIS IS THE DAY

June Crebbin

This is the sort of day
I should like to wrap
In shiny silver paper
And only open when it's raining,

5   This is the sort of day
I should like to hide
In a secret drawer to which
Only I have the key,

This is the sort of day
10 I should like to hang
At the back of the wardrobe
To keep me warm when winter comes,

This is the day
I should like to last for ever,

15 This is my birthday.

Poetry ~ 305

LITERARY COMPONENTS

▶ 1. Repetition of Inner Vowel Sound (Assonance): *day, paper, raining*

▶ 2. Repetition of Initial Consonant Sound: *sort, should, shiny, silver*

▶ 3. Repetition of Initial Vowel Sound: *only open*

▶ 4. Repetition of Initial Consonant Sound and Internal Vowel/Consonant Combination: *wardrobe, warm when winter*

EYES ON...RHYTHM

This Is the Day does not have a pattern of rhyme, but it does have a fairly consistent rhythm. It certainly *looks* like it has a regular rhythm or form, which in poetry works on our expectations. Because of our *visual* impressions, we expect this poem to be traditional. And it is, almost. Although the poem has no regular pattern of end rhymes, it is not purely free verse.

Notice the regularity of the rhythm across the first three stanzas:

Stanza I: Beats

This is the sort of *day*,	6	monosyllables
I should like to *wrap*,	5	monosyllables
In *shiny silver paper*	7	2-syllable words
And *only open when*		
it's *raining*.	9	mixed syllables

Stanza II:

This is the sort of *day*,	6	monosyllables
I should like to *hide*,	5	monosyllables
In a *secret drawer* to *which*	7	mixed syllables
Only I have the *key*.	6	mostly monosyllables

Stanza III:

This is the sort of *day*,	6	monosyllables
I should like to *hang*,	5	monosyllables
At the *back* of the *wardrobe*	7	mostly monosyllables
To keep me *warm* when		
winter *comes*.	8	mostly monosyllables

It is precisely this regularity that makes the fourth stanza so strong. The first line, *This is the day,* absent the words *sort of,* consequently is very powerful. The two-line fourth stanza is spoken like a presentation, as if the speaker were saying, "And now, introducing...," with each word a long beat (although, again, *This* and *day* are heavier).

The one-line fifth stanza unrolls to reveal exactly what is so special.

Remember this technique for looking at poems. It is easy to do, to count out the beats. It is easy to display, to write out, or to type. It will not be helpful with every poem, but it may be very instructive with some. It does not take much time to do this.

Finally, the poem is written in one sentence, but it is not really one sentence—it is five.

STUDYING THE SELECTION

I Am Winding Through a Maze

1. A maze is a confusing combination of paths from which it seems there is no exit.
2. See above at **Eyes On...Concrete or Form Poems.**

ABOUT THE AUTHORS

Jack Prelutsky was born in Brooklyn, New York in 1910. Upon reaching adulthood, he could not decide upon a career. He tried carpentry, furniture moving, cab driving, bookselling, and even folk singing. Finally, he tried drawing. To accompany his drawings, he wrote some verses. When he took them to a publisher, she said "You are the worst artist I've ever seen"—but she loved his poems. Prelutsky became a children's poet, writing more than sixty books of poems for children. He lives in Olympia, Washington.

Carolyn Wells was born in New Jersey in 1869. At the age of six, she lost her hearing. As a young woman, she worked as a librarian, but for most of her life she was an author who wrote and wrote and wrote! She completed 180 volumes, most of which were either humorous verse or mystery novels. In 1918 she married Hadwin Houghton and moved to New York. Although her husband died the following year, she remained in New York until her death in 1942.

Myra Cohn Livingston was born in Omaha, Nebraska in 1926. Many of the poems she wrote later were based on her happy childhood in Omaha. As a girl, her main interests were writing and music. Livingston's first published poems were written while she attended Sarah Lawrence College in New York. While working at a bookstore, she decided to submit a manuscript of a children's book she had written to a publishing house. The book was published. It was the first of almost fifty books of poetry and nonfiction that Livingston wrote. She, her husband, and their three children lived in Los Angeles until her death in 1996.

Studying the Selection   POETRY

I Am Winding Through a Maze

1. What is a maze?

2. Write out the first four stanzas of the poem *I Am Winding Through a Maze.* Here are some clues:
   - The poem has 8 stanzas.
   - Each stanza has 3 lines.
   - The first two lines of each stanza rhyme.

To help you, here are the last two stanzas:

It's apparent that I am,
in a pickle, in a jam,
in a quandary, in a scrape, a squeeze, a spot.

But at last I think I see
where the exit just might be,
so I think I'll soon be out . . . whoops! No, I'm not.

3. Write a concrete poem. Remember, it doesn't have to rhyme or have a regular beat. There are lots of ways you can do this. A poem about a house could be in the shape of a house. A poem about a cat could be in the shape of a cat. Try to keep your "drawing" very simple. You will be drawing with lines of words. Here are other possibilities: the sun, the moon, a star, a tree, a box, a circle, a triangle, and so forth.

A Tooter Tutor • A Bear in Reverse

1. What does the tutor try to do in the limerick?

2. What question do the students ask the tutor—in your own words?

3. Write your own limerick. Just remember a limerick is five lines. Lines 1, 2, and 5 rhyme and have 8 beats. Lines 3 and 4 rhyme, and have 5 or 6 beats. Have fun with this.

74th Street

1. Why do you think the poet uses mostly one-syllable words?

2. Write down eight of the verbs in the poem.

3. What is the girl in the poem trying to do?

4. How do you think the poet feels about her?

This Is the Day

1. What is this poem about? Just give a short, simple answer in one or two sentences.

2. What are two phrases in the poem that are repeated?

3. Give an example from the poem of words that begin with the same letter.

4. What is the strongest picture you have in your mind from the poem? (There is no single correct answer to this question.)

A Tooter Tutor / A Bear in Reverse

1. The tutor is trying to teach two students to play the flute.

2. The students ask their tutor whether it is harder to play the flute or to teach two students to play the flute.

3. If you will write your own limerick for the students, perhaps that will amuse and encourage them.

    I had a good student named Nick,
    He scribbled a good limerick.
        He made his friends smile.
        He wrote with great style.
    He shocked us 'cause he was so quick!

74th Street

1. (The poem has 88 words. Ten words have two syllables.) Answers will vary. One-syllable words give the poem a brittle quality that is like the girl's standing and falling, standing and falling. They also give the poem a hard, driving quality—what it takes to learn how to skate.

2. The verbs in the poem include *gets, puts, stands, flops, falls, smacks, grabs, slides, skins, puts,* and *sticks.*

3. The girl in the poem is trying to learn how to roller skate.

4. The poet is amazed by her—that she keeps trying, no matter how many times she falls or is injured. She admires her.

This Is the Day

1. *This Is the Day* is about a person whose birthday is so special, he wants to save it so he can have it again at future times.

2. The poet repeats the first line in the first three stanzas. See other examples above in **ANALYZING THE POEM.**

3. Many words begin with **s**: **s**ort, **s**hould, **s**hiny, **s**ilver, etc. Again, see other examples in the discussion above.

4. Answers will vary.

UNIT THREE WRAP-UP

Gramp • After School • One Throw • The Birds' Peace
Hattie's Birthday Box • The Whimbrel

WHAT MONTH IS IT? WHAT DAY?
HEY, WHAT KIND OF BIRD IS THAT?

Create a Calendar of Birds • Song Sparrow, Canary, Whimbrel

1. You have read three selections in this unit in which birds are
   mentioned. In *The Birds' Peace* and *The Whimbrel,* a song sparrow and
   a whimbrel are main characters. *In Hattie's Birthday Box,* a canary is
   briefly mentioned. Make a table like the one below. Using books from
   the library, or provided by your teacher, fill in all of the columns in the
   table. Make sure your third and fourth columns are big enough for your
   notes.

Selection	Bird	Color & Markings	Habits and Ways
The Birds' Peace			

2. Have you ever seen a calendar that hangs on the wall and has one particular subject? For each month, there is a picture related to the subject of the calendar. Below the picture, there is information about it. Underneath, is the calendar for that month. It looks like this: ———→

Name of Bird

Information about the bird.

Name of Month

Sun	Mon	Tues	Wed	Thurs	Fri	Sat

Complete each of the steps below on a separate sheet of paper, so that if you make a mistake on one part, you can correct it before it is attached to the other parts.

a. Pick one bird for your calendar, and draw a picture of that bird. **Do this on its own sheet of paper.**

b. Write a paragraph of information about your bird. Take the information from the research you did for your table in #1. **Do this on a separate piece of paper.**

c. Choose one month of the year, and copy the page for that month from a calendar. Your teacher may wish to assign different months to different students so that, when the project is completed, the class will have a calendar of the entire school year to hang on the wall. **Again, do this on a separate piece of paper.**

d. Now, put all of the pieces together on one very large piece of paper or oak tag. When the month you have chosen comes, hang your bird calendar on the wall!

WHO ARE THESE TWO PEOPLE?

You and a Classmate Have Come From One of the Stories—Which One?

1. In each of the stories in this unit, two characters have a friendship or important connection. Your teacher will match people to be partners. Together, the two of you will pick one of the selections. Now, you and your partner are going to be one of the character pairs in the story you have selected. Bring some props and costumes. You may even wish to put on some makeup for your presentation.

2. Write down about five sentences each, describing "yourself."

3. Prepare a very short skit in which the two of you talk *to each other.* It must "feel" like part of the story from which your character is taken.

4. For the presentation, first tell the class about "yourself," from the sentences you have prepared. If you can do this without looking at your notes, all the better. Second, act out your skit together.

5. Conclude your presentation by asking your class together, "Who are we?" Don't be afraid to be funny.

6. Remember. It takes practice and rehearsing to do a good job on this.

DRAMATIC PERFORMANCE

The Curtain's Going Up: What Will It Be, Prose or Poetry?

1. Quickly review the six stories and the poems. What is your favorite passage of all?

2. Copy the passage down. (Your passage must be at least fifty words long.) Now, write a paragraph's worth of notes about why you like it. These do not need to be complete sentences, but should express your feelings.

3. Practice reading your passage aloud. Read it clearly and with proper expression.

4. Recite the passage of prose or poetry before your class. Then, with the help of your notes, tell them why this passage is your favorite.

AIMING HIGH

1. What does it mean to aim high?

2. Think about the main characters in each of the prose selections. All of them aim high, one way or the other. Who did you like the most?

3. Now it is time to write several paragraphs. In your first paragraph, explain what it means to aim high. For the final sentence of your first paragraph, write something like, "These words remind me of in *selection name,* and I am going to write about (him or her)." Use your second paragraph to give examples of ways in which your character aimed high. Use your third paragraph to conclude. Here is an example of a conclusion: "These are the reasons (character's name) was the person I liked most in these stories."

- GLOSSARY
- INDEX OF AUTHORS
  AND TITLES

glossary

A

abound (uh BOWND) *v.:* are filled or supplied with

accommodation (uh KOM uh DAY shun) *n.:* place for housing and feeding

accurate (AK yuh rut) *adj.:* perfectly correct

achievement (uh CHEEV ment) *n.:* something accomplished through great effort or skill

activist (AK tih vist) *n.:* one who is very involved in groups and organizations, whose goals are to change existing policies

adamantly (ADD uh munt LEE) *adv.:* firmly and insistently; strongly and definitely

adapted (uh DAPP ted) *v.:* suited by nature or design to a particular use or situation

affidavit (AH fih DAY vit) *n.:* a written statement made with the promise to tell the truth

aide (AYD) *n.:* an assistant or helper

alarmed (uh LARMD) *adj.:* suddenly frightened or worried

altered (ALT urd) *v.:* changed

amateur (AM uh CHOOR) *n.:* not professional or expert; a person who is unskilled or inexperienced in a particular activity

ambition (am BIH shun) *n.:* a strong desire for success, fame, wealth, or the like, and the willingness to work for it

ambled (AM buld) *v.:* walked slowly and casually

analyze (AN uh LYZE) *v.:* to examine each part of something in a careful, logical way

apathy (A puh THEE) *n.:* a complete lack of interest; indifference

aristocratic (uh RISS tuh KRATT ik) *adj.:* belonging to a class of people who are educated, wealthy, and "well-born"

array (uh RAY) *n.:* an orderly grouping or arrangement, especially for troops

B

bandit *n.:* an outlaw, a robber

bank *n.:* the slope or high ground next to a river

banner *n.:* a large sign painted on cloth

barges (BAR juz) *n.:* flat-bottomed vessels, usually pushed or towed through the water, for carrying freight or passengers

barrage (buh RAZH) *n.:* a heavy, prolonged attack

bayonets (BAY uh NETS) *n.:* a long-pointed steel weapon attached to the open end of a gun

glossary

beachcomber (BEECH kohm er) *n.:* one who looks carefully (combs) along the beach for objects of interest

beckoning (BEK uh ning) *v.:* motioning to someone to come closer

belligerent (buh LIJ urr int) *adj.:* argumentative; displaying an eagerness to fight

bellows (BELL oze) *n.:* a device for producing a strong current of air

bias (BY us) *n.:* prejudice; a positive or negative feeling towards something that is not based on logic or sense of fairness

billowing (BIL oh ing) *v.:* swelling and puffing out

blazed (BLAYZD) *v.:* gleamed or glowed brightly

bluffs *n.:* cliffs

bolted (BOLT ed) *v.:* suddenly tried to break free

bombarded (bahm BAR ded) *v.:* pelted; threw objects at a target repeatedly

bounding (BOWND ing) *v.:* leaping in great steps and jumps

boycott (BOY kot) *v.:* refuse to buy, sell, or use a product

brigade (brih GAYD) *n.:* a unit of an army having two or more regiments; several brigades make up a division

broad (BRAWD) *adj.:* wide

broadside (BROAD side) *n.:* the whole side of a ship above the water line

brocades (broe KAYDZ) *n.:* expensive fabrics with raised designs, often woven with gold or silver threads

brooded (BROO did) *v.:* worried about; thought about moodily

buckled (BUK uld) *v.:* collapsed

buffeting (BUFF ih ting) *n.:* repeated hitting and pushing

buoys (BOYS) *n.:* a floating object, fastened or anchored so that it remains in one place, used as a marker for sailors

burrowing (BURR oh ing) *v.:* digging down

burrows (BURR ohz) *n.:* holes or tunnels in the ground made by an animal

C

cajole (kuh JOLE) *v.:* persuade; coax

camaraderie (KAHM uh RAD uh ree) *n.:* a feeling of close and comfortable friendship

canopy (KAN uh pee) *n.:* the cover formed by the leafy upper branches of the trees in a forest

canter (KAN ter) *n.:* an easy gallop

glossary

captivity (kap TIV ih TEE) *n.:* being held as a prisoner

cargo (KAR go) *n.:* freight carried by a ship or airplane

cavorting (kuh VORT ing) *v.:* jumping and prancing merrily about

celebrity (suh LEB rih tee) *n.:* a famous person

chap *n.:* fellow, guy

chink (CHEENK) *n.:* crack; narrow opening

churning (CHURR ning) *v.:* stirring and shaking

clasped *v.:* gripped; firmly grasped

commemoration (kuh MEM uh RAY shun) *n.:* in memory of some person or event

commuters (kum YOO ters) *n.:* people who travel to and from work

complex (kuhm PLEX) *adj.:* complicated and difficult to understand or deal with

concocted (kun KAHK ted) *v.:* made up; put together many ingredients resulting in something new and different

conflagration (KAHN fluh GRAY shun) *n.:* a huge, destructive fire

confront (kun FRONT) *v.:* meet face to face, often with a demand or accusation

congenial (kuhn JEE nee uhl) *adj.:* agreeable; pleasant

congregating (KAHNG ruh gay ting) *v.:* meeting; assembling

conscience (KAHN shuntz) *n.:* the inner sense that directs a person to choose right over wrong

conspicuous (kun SPIK yoo us) *adj.:* noticeable; standing out

constructive (kun STRUK tiv) *adj.:* helping to improve and build (the opposite of destructive)

countered (KOWN terd) *v.:* answered a question with a question

credentials (kruh DENN shulz) *n.:* documents showing that a person has privileges

crevices (KREH viss iz) *n.:* long, deep cracks

cross *adj.:* angry

curtly (KURT lee) *adv.:* briefly and a bit rudely

customary (KUSS tuh MAIR ee) *adj.:* usual

D

dart *v.:* move swiftly and suddenly

debris (duh BREE) *n.:* the remains of anything destroyed; bits of old waste matter lying about

deliberately (de LIB uh rut LEE) *adv.:* carefully and knowingly

delirious (dih LEER ee us) *adj.:* a state of illness in which a person is unconscious but has strange, dreamlike visions

deluges (DELL yooj iz) *n.:* huge rainstorms

depresses (de PRESS iz) *v.:* presses down

descended (dee SEND ed) *v.:* came down

desolate (DEH suh lut) *adj.:* empty, deserted, and lonely

desperation (DESS puh RAY shun) *n.:* a feeling of hopelessness

despondent (dih SPOND ent) *adj.:* extremely discouraged; feeling hopeless

deteriorating (dee TEER ee uh RAYT ing) *v.:* becoming worse in some or many ways

dictate (DIK tayt) *v.:* say or read aloud words so that they can be written down, typed, or recorded

diminished (dih MIN ished) *v.:* lessened

diplomat (DIP luh MAT) *n.:* a person who has been appointed by the government of their country to deal with the governments of other countries on matters concerning both

discriminated (dis KRIM ih NAY ted) *v.:* were treated unfairly because of prejudice

distinctive (diss TINK tiv) *adj.:* unusual; having a special quality or style

distract (diss TRAKT) *v.:* draw someone's attention away

divert (dy VURT) *v.:* turn aside from its intended goal

dominates (DAHM ih nayts) *v.:* rules over; controls

drifted (DRIFF ted) *v.:* slowly moved away

driftwood (DRIFT wood) *n.:* wood floating or cast ashore by a body of water

dunes (DOONZ) *n.:* sand hills

E

earnestly (UR nust lee) *adv.:* seriously, sincerely

edging (EDJ ing) *v.:* moving slowly and cautiously

eerie (EER ee) *adj.:* strange, mysterious, and somewhat frightening

elated (ee LAY ted) *adj.:* immensely happy

elation (ee LAY shun) *n.:* extreme happiness

glossary

embankment (em BANK ment) *n.:* a long mound of raised earth next to a stream or river

embraced (em BRAYST) *v.:* hugged

emerged (ee MURJD) *v.:* came out from

emetic (ee MET ik) *n.:* a medicine to make a person vomit

enduring (in DYOOR ing) *v.:* undergoing suffering with patience and determination

enigma (uh NIG muh) *n.:* a puzzling occurrence; a mystery that seems unsolvable

evacuate (ee VAK yoo AYT) *v.:* leave

excesses (EX sess iz) *n.:* extremes; unusually large amounts or degrees of something

exclusively (ex KLOO siv lee) *adv.:* only; excluding all others

excruciating (ex KROO shee AYT ing) *adj.:* intensely painful

exemplary (egg ZEMP luh ree) *adj.:* perfect; worthy of imitation

exhilaration (egg ZILL uh RAY shun) *n.:* immense and thrilling joy

exploit (ex PLOIT) *v.:* use selfishly for one's own ends

extinguished (ex TING wishd) *v.:* put out (a light or a fire)

exuberant (ex OO ber ent) *adj.:* full of high spirits and enthusiasm

F

facade (fuh SOD) *n.:* the front of a building, especially a decorative one

feeble (FEE bul) *adj.:* weak

filet knife (fih LAY NYF) *n.:* a knife used to remove the bones of meat or fish

fitful (FIT full) *adj.:* stopping and starting

flitted (FLITT ed) *v.:* flew swiftly from one place to another, settling only for a moment

forager (FOR uh jer) *n.:* one who wanders about looking for food, provisions, or some unexpected find

foreman (FOR mun) *n.:* a person in charge of a department or group of workers, as in a factory

forlorn (for LORN) *adj.:* lonely and sad

fragments (FRAG ments) *n.:* bits and pieces of something

frantically (FRAN tik lee) *adv.:* wildly and desperately

fruitlessly (FROOT luss lee) *adv.:* unsuccessfully; with no useful outcome

fund *v.:* pay for

furrow (FUR oh) *n.:* a narrow groove made in the ground by a plow

Glossary ~ 673

futile (FEW tuhl) *adj.:* useless, ineffective

G

gale (GAYL) *n.:* a strong wind

galley (GAL ee) *n.:* the kitchen area of a ship, plane, or camper

gap *n.:* a break or opening in a row of objects or in a wall

gaped (GAYPT) *v.:* to open or part widely

gazed (GAYZD) *v.:* looked intently

genteel (jen TEEL) *adj.:* well-bred; polite (today, used to mean overly polite)

gig (GIG) *n.:* a light boat rowed with four, six, or eight long oars

glass *n.:* mirror

glimpsed (GLIMPST) *v.:* saw for a brief moment

graffiti (gruh FEE tee) *n.:* words or pictures painted illegally on public property

grampus (GRAMP us) *n.:* a large dolphin

grizzled (GRIZ uhld) *adj.:* having gray hair

gurney (GUR nee) *n.:* a narrow, padded table on wheels used for moving patients

gutted *v.:* removed the inner parts, such as the stomach and intestines

H

hastens (HAYS ens) *v.:* hurries

hauled (HAWLD) *v.:* pulled or tugged with force

hazards (HAZZ erds) *n.:* dangers

hectic (HEK tik) *adj.:* rushed and confused

heirloom (AIR loom) *n.:* a family possession handed down from one generation to another

heist *n.:* a robbery or holdup

heralded (HAIR ul dud) *v.:* publicly welcomed

hitched *v.:* fastened, tied

hoarded (HOHRD ed) *v.:* something hidden and guarded–often, money or food

hoist (HOYST) *v.:* raise; lift

horizon (huh RI zun) *n.:* the place in the distance where the sky and earth appear to meet

hutch *n.:* a pen or enclosed coop for animals

I

idealist (i DEEL ist) *n.:* a person who is guided more by spiritual goals than practical ones

glossary

illuminated (ill LOO mih NAY ted) *v.:* lit up

imminent (IM ih nent) *adj.:* about to occur

incident (IN sih dent) *n.:* event, happening

incubating (IN kyew BAY ting) *v.:* sitting on (eggs) for the purpose of hatching

indignation (IN dig NAY shun) *n.:* anger at something because it is unfair or insulting

inert (in URT) *adj.:* still; unmoving

ingenious (in JEEN yuss) *adj.:* clever and original

ingenuity (IN juh NOO ih TEE) *n.:* creativity in solving problems or overcoming obstacles

inhabitants (in HAB ih tunts) *n.:* people or animals who live in a place

injustice (in JUST iss) *n.:* an unfair act

innovation (IN oh VAY shun) *n.:* the introduction of something new or different

inscription (in SKRIP shun) *n.:* a word or words carved on stone or other hard surface; a brief dedication or note written by hand in a book, on a photograph, or on a similar item

inspire (in SPY uhr) *v.:* fill one with a certain feeling, usually, the desire to do good

intercede (IN ter SEED) *v.:* help or defend someone by pleading or arguing on his behalf with another person

intercepted (IN ter SEP ted) *v.:* stopped someone or something on the way to its destination

issue (ISH oo) *v.:* put forth; write out an official document

L

laboriously (luh BORR ee us LEE) *adv.:* with much difficulty and effort

labyrinth (LAB uh rinth) *n.:* a complicated and confusing set of paths, through which it is difficult to find one's way

laden (LAY dun) *adj.:* very full of something

legislators (LEH jiss LAY torz) *n.:* lawmakers

level (LEH vul) *adj.:* sensible; spoken in a calm, even voice

lever (LEH ver or LEE ver) *n.:* a bar or rod

linger (LING er) *v.:* stay longer than usual

litany (LITT uh nee) *n.:* a long prayer in which many of the lines are repeated

lobby (LAH bee) *v.:* to work at influencing lawmakers to vote a certain way

glossary

loner (LO ner) *n.:* a person who has little to do with other people

lull *n.:* a temporary calm or quiet

lurched *v.:* swayed or tipped suddenly

luxurious (lug ZHUR ee us) *adj.:* rich, comfortable, and pleasurable

lyrics (LIHR iks) *n.:* the words of a song

M

makeshift (MAYK shift) *adj.:* temporary

manifest (MAN ih fest) *n.:* a list of the cargo or passengers carried by a ship, plane, truck, or train

marshes (MAR shiz) *n.:* areas of waterlogged soil, having no trees and covered with rushes, cattails, and other grasses

meditative (MEH dih TAY tiv) *adj.:* thoughtful

melodically (muh LODD ih klee) *adv.:* tunefully; with a beautiful melody

melodious (muh LOE dee us) *adj.:* tuneful; sweet-sounding

memorable (MEM uh ruh bl) *adj.:* worth remembering; easily remembered

mercilessly (MURR suh luss lee) *adv.:* without pity

methodical (meth AH dih kul) *adj.:* systematic; slow and careful

milling (MILL ing) *v.:* moving aimlessly

miserly (MY zer lee) *adv.:* stingy

momentum (mo MENT um) *n.:* a feeling or energy that increases once the action is underway

monarch (MAHN ark) *n.:* king; ruler

monotonously (muh NOT uh nuss lee) *adv.:* dully and boringly

monument (MAHN yoo ment) *n.:* any lasting evidence or outstanding example of something

motionless (MO shun luss) *adj.:* not moving, still

mottled (MOTT uld) *adj.:* marked with spots or blotches of different colors or shades

mourned (MORND) *v.:* said in a sad, sorrowful tone

mufflers *n.:* scarves

musket (MUSS kit) *n.:* an old-fashioned gun used by foot soldiers (later replaced by the rifle)

N

naive (NAH eve) *adj.:* lacking in experience, judgment, or information

glossary

naturalist (NACH ruh list) *n.:* a person who is an expert in natural history, especially a zoologist or botanist

negotiate (nuh GO she ATE) *v.:* work towards an agreement through discussion and bargaining

novelty (NAH vul tee) *n.:* new experience

O

occasional (uh KAY zhun ul) *adj.:* occurring or appearing only once in a while

omen (OH mun) *n.:* a sign that something will happen; an omen can be "good" or "evil"

optimist (AHP tuh mist) *n.:* one who generally expects things to turn out well; a person with a positive, upbeat attitude

optimistic (OPP tuh MISS tik) *adj.:* hopeful; positive; having a feeling that all will turn out well

ordeal (or DEEL) *n.:* any extremely trying or severe test or experience

P

panic (PAN ik) *n.:* a sudden, overwhelming fear

peaked (PEEKD) *adj.:* having a pointed top

peddle (PED dl) *v.:* sell

peering (PEER ing) *v.:* looking intensely, in the attempt to see something clearly

perch *n.:* a high position or resting place

periodically (PIH ree AH dik lee) *adv.:* every so often

perish (PAIR ish) *v.:* die

persisted (pur SIS ted) *v.:* continued to make a point in spite of opposition

persistence (pur SISS tuntz) *n.:* firmly keeping to a particular course of action in spite of opposition

perturbed (pur TURBD) *v.:* disturbed; troubled

pesticides (PEST ih SYDS) *n.:* chemicals used for killing insects

petition (puh TISH un) *n.:* a document, signed by many people, that makes a request or demand

piercingly (PEER sing lee) *adv.:* sharply and knowingly

plaque (PLACK) *n.:* a metal plate engraved with the name of a person being honored

plunged (PLUNJD) *v.:* threw himself about

poacher (POE cher) *n.:* one who hunts illegally on property belonging to someone else

Glossary ~ 677

glossary

pottering (usually puttering, PUTT er ing) *v.:* doing "odds and ends" of small jobs

pouted (POW ted) *v.:* showed discontent or ill humor in a gloomy and silent way

preened *v.:* trimmed or smoothed feathers with the beak or tongue

prejudice (PREH juh diss) *n.:* an already formed opinion not based on actual experience; an unreasoning like or dislike

premises (PREH mi suz) *n.:* a building and its grounds

proclamation (PRAHK luh MAY shun) *n.:* an official announcement

prominent (PRAHM ih nent) *adj.:* leading, important, or well-known

puckered *v.:* drew together tightly, forming wrinkles

purling (PURR ling) *adj.:* flowing with a curling or rippling motion, as a shallow stream over stones

purposefully (PUR puss full lee) *adv.:* seriously, with a goal in mind; determinedly

Q

quivering (KWIV er ing) *v.:* trembling; shaking

quizzically (KWIZ ik lee) *adv.:* questioningly

R

radiance (RAY dee unts) *n.:* shining brightness

rallied (RA leed) *v.:* brought together for a common purpose

rarely (RAIR lee) *adv.:* hardly ever

raspy (RASP ee) *adj.:* not smooth; rough and grating

raucous (RAW kus) *adj.:* loud and harsh

receding (ree SEE ding) *adj.:* returning to a lower level; moving back and further away

recruits (rih KROOTS) *n.:* new members of the army

reel *v.:* to pull out of the water by winding a fishing line around a small wheel or spool

regiments (REJ ih ments) *n.:* a unit of soldiers in an army; several regiments make up a brigade

relish (RELL ish) *n.:* great enjoyment

renovated (REN uh VAY tuhd) *v.:* restored to good condition as by repairing or remodeling

representatives (REP ree ZEN tuh TIVZ) *n.:* individuals who speak for and act on behalf of a group

reservoir (REZ urv WAHR) *n.:* a place where water is stored

glossary

resign (ree ZYN) *v.:* give up a position or job

resolved (re ZAHLVD) *v.:* firmly decided on a course of action

resounded (ree ZOWND ed) *v.:* echoed

resounding (ree ZOWN ding) *adj.:* loud and echoing

resourceful (rih SORSS ful) *adj.:* able to deal skillfully and promptly with new situations

responded (ree SPOND ed) *v.:* answered

restraint (ree STRAINT) *n.:* control, holding back

retreat (rih TREET) *v.:* move back, away from the enemy

ridicule (RID ih KYOOL) *v.:* make fun of

rigmarole (RIG muh rohl) *n.:* confused or meaningless talk

riot (RY itt) *n.:* a noisy, violent public disorder caused by a crowd of people

ruckus (RUCK iss) *n.:* uproar; a noisy commotion

rugged (RUG ged) *adj.:* rough; rocky and hilly

rural (RUH rul) *adj.:* characteristic of or having to do with the country (compare to urban: characteristic of or having to do with the city)

ruthless (ROOTH luss) *adj.:* without pity; cruel

S

salvage (SAL vuj) *v.:* to save from being destroyed or thrown out

sapling (SAPP ling) *n.:* a young tree

savage (SA vudg) *adj.:* wild; fierce

scarlet (SKAHR lut) *adj.:* of a deep red color

scorched (SKORCHD) *adj.:* slightly burned

serenely (suh REEN lee) *adv.:* calmly; peacefully

shaft *n.:* a passageway leading deep into the ground

sheath (SHEETH) *n.:* a close-fitting case for the blade of a knife or sword

shimmered *v.:* glowed and softly shone with a flickering light

shrewdly (SHROOD lee) *adv.:* sharply and cleverly

shrubs *n.:* woody plants with many separate stems, smaller than a tree

sibling (SIBB ling) *n.:* a brother or sister

sinister (SIN iss ter) *adj.:* looking a bit frightening or threatening

Glossary ~ 679

glossary

site (SYT) *n.:* area or exact place where something is to be located or built

sleuth (SLOOTH) *n.:* detective

spar (SPAHR) *n.:* a strong pole to which a boat's sail is attached

staggering (STAG er ing) *v.:* walking unsteadily; tottering

steadying (STED ee ing) *adj.:* calming

stealthily (STELL thuh lee) *adv.:* quietly, carefully, and secretly so as not to be discovered

stewed (STOOD) *v.:* fretted; worried; fussed

struggle (STRUH gul) *n.:* a fight

superiors (suh PIH ree urz) *n.:* higher in position; those who have greater power

surpassing (sur PASS ing) *v.:* going beyond; exceeding

surveyed (sur VAYD) *v.:* looked at; inspected

sympathetic (SIM puh THEH tik) *adj.:* to have a positive or favorable feeling about something

T

tackle (TAH kuhl) *n.:* equipment for fishing, such as lines and hooks

team (TEEM) *n.:* two or more horses, oxen, or other animals harnessed together to draw a vehicle

tersely (TURSS lee) *adv.:* briefly

thicket (THIK et) *n.:* a dense growth of bushes or small trees

thrashed *v.:* beat soundly; hit repeatedly

threaded (THRED ed) *v.:* made its way past or around obstacles

thriving (THRY ving) *adj.:* doing very well; prospering

timber (TIM ber) *n.:* trees; an area of woodland or forest

torrent (TAW rent) *n.:* a huge, rushing stream of water

toxic (TOX ik) *adj.:* poisonous

traipsing (TRAYPS ing) *v.:* tramping through

trespassing (TRESS pass ing) *v.:* entering someone's property without the owner's permission

trifle (TRY fl) *adj.:* a bit

triumphant (try UMF unt) *adj.:* expressing joy over a success or victory

triumphed (TRY umft) *v.:* rejoiced over a victory

glossary

truce (TROOSS) *n.:* a temporary peace agreement

U

undeniable (un dee NY uh bul) *adj.:* clearly real and true

union (YOON yun) *n.:* an association of workers formed to protect the rights of its members

urban (URR bun) *adj.:* having to do with a city

V

vandalized (VAN duh LYZD) *v.:* deliberately destroyed or damaged

verify (VAIR ih fy) *v.:* prove the truth of

vigorously (VIG uh russ LEE) *adv.:* energetically; forcefully

virtuous (VUR choo us) *adj.:* good; one who has good character and performs good deeds

visas (VEE zuhz) *n.:* official papers indicating that the bearer has permission to enter a particular country

vise (VYZ) *n.:* a tool with two jaws that can be adjusted to hold an object firmly

void (VOYD) *n.:* emptiness

vulnerable (VUHL nuh ruh buhl) *adj.:* easily hurt physically or emotionally

W

washout (WASH out) *n.:* (informal) a complete failure or disappointment

weaned (WEEND) *v.:* ended the period of time when a baby was fed only milk; introduced the baby to solid food

wharf (HWARF) *n.:* a pier; a wooden walkway built next to or jutting into the water so that boats can come alongside it to load or unload

wizened (WEE zund) *adj.:* withered; shriveled

wounded (WOON ded) *adj.:* injured

wrath (RATH) *n.:* fierce anger

writhed (RYTHD) *v.:* twisted and turned in pain

index of authors and titles

WORKBOOK ANSWER GUIDE
Table of Contents

SAMUEL'S CHOICE (Textbook p. 16)
VOCABULARY—Activity I (p. 1)

1. muskets
2. bayonets
3. recruits
4. wounded
5. wharf
6. gale
7. buoys
8. glimpse
9. retreat
10. barges

VOCABULARY—Activity II (p. 2)

Flag: bayonets, recruits, muskets, wounded, retreat
Sail: barges, buoys, gale, wharf
Eye: glimpsed

Comprehension Questions—In-depth Thinking (p. 3)

1. According to the story, Brooklyn was a town—a small one at that—in those days. There is a flour mill that stands on Gowanus Creek. Gowanus Creek winds out of New York Harbor into green fields and loses itself in ponds and marshes. Brooklyn today, like other big cities, probably has few flour mills, creeks, green fields, ponds, or marshes. These days, to get from one city to another when the cities are separated by bodies of water, one drives across a bridge over the water or through a tunnel under the water.

2. *Freedom* means the quality or state of being free, as in (a) the absence of necessity, coercion, or constraint in choice or in action, and (b) liberation from slavery or restraint or from the power of another.
   Liberty is also defined as the quality or state of being free, as in (a) the power to do as one pleases; (b) freedom from physical restraint; (c) having freedom from arbitrary or despotic control; (d) the positive enjoyment of various social, political, or economic rights and privileges; (e) having the power of choice.
   Obviously, these definitions overlap. We may associate *freedom* with individuals and *liberty* with nations and their populations. Some opposites might be: slavery, imprisonment, colony, jailed, bondage, servitude, tyranny, and so forth.
   Self-governing is clearly a political term and is defined as having control or rule over oneself; specifically, having self-government.
   For your use, we add to the list the word *independence*—the quality of being independent. *Independent* is defined as not subject to control by others; self-governing; not affiliated with a larger controlling unit.

3. Students may have a variety of legitimate answers to the question.

Comprehension Questions—Drawing Conclusions (pp. 3-4)

1. Remind students that the sentences are to be written as if they really are Samuel. This may help them think about why they, themselves, might not want to get involved in the rescue operation. Certainly, Samuel is used to being punished for not doing as he is told or for acting independently. It is not his boat. He can easily be injured or killed. He is frightened by the ongoing battle.

2. Student answers will vary. There is no right answer.

3. Again, student answers will vary. The question should not suggest to students that slavery is appropriate under *any* circumstances. To keep slaves in a nation that has itself fought for freedom is not rational or consistent. But there is an even greater irony and injustice to take people who have fought for national liberty and deprive them of personal freedom and self-governance.

Graphic Organizer (pp. 5-6)

1. "never to row or sail except when he sent me."
2. "Liberty ain't for Africans…And it got nothin' to do with us."
3. "No business for us black slaves, I'm tellin' you."
4. "The sun glinted on rows of brass cannon and bayonets."
5. "Tired, frightened people. Most were sopping wet."
6. "lots of soldiers were being shot like ducks in the marshes."

SLOWER THAN THE REST (Textbook p. 34)
VOCABULARY—Activity I (p. 7)

1. congenial
2. rarely
3. sympathetic
4. ambition
5. achievement
6. drifting
7. frantically
8. occasional
9. beckoning
10. plaque

VOCABULARY—Activity II (p. 8)

Any reasonable answer is acceptable.

Comprehension Questions—In-Depth Thinking (p. 9)

1. In the second paragraph on page 36 of the textbook, we read, "Both his little sisters squealed when the animal stuck its ugly head to look at them, and they thought its claws horrifying, but Leo loved it from the start." The sisters are afraid and repelled. Their feelings are negative ones. Leo is delighted and filled with good feelings.

2. Leo means that it isn't fair that animals die in forest fires just because they move slowly. Leo also is saying that some things are more difficult for the "slow ones." He is cautioning his classmates that a careless attitude towards those who are struggling to keep up is far more damaging than it is to the "fast ones." He wants the students to be aware that not everyone is equally gifted and that care should be taken, whether in class, in sports, or in social situations, not to leave anyone behind.

3. Answers may vary. It is certainly wrong to tell someone in an absolute way that they are slower than the rest. It is also—and stress this—untrue. No one is "slower" in every area. Consider the turtle. He is a slow runner, but quick to be friendly, quick to adjust, and quick to be enthusiastic.

Comprehension Questions—Drawing Conclusions (pp. 9-10)

1. Answers will vary.
2. The story certainly shows us that beauty is in the eye of the beholder. Answers will vary. Certainly species are prejudiced towards their own kind.
3. Leo wins the prize, because he cares about his subject and because what he has learned is based on his own experience. His heart is in his discussion. Students may include additional ideas.

Graphic Organizer (pp. 11-12)

In the turtle's shell:

1. Leo had few friends and stuck to himself. *Charlie was the friendliest turtle anyone had ever seen.*

2. Leo was uninterested in most of what went on around him in school. *The turtle's head was always stretched out, moving left and right, trying to see what was in the world.*
3. Leo was always thinking about how he was slower than the rest. *Put Charlie down and he would sniff at the air a moment, then take off as if no one had ever told him how slow he was supposed to be.*
4. When a skit was presented in school, Leo didn't want to laugh with the other children. *Charlie took care of Leo's happiness, and he did it by being congenial.*

In the chart:
1. beginning of story
2. end of story
3. beginning of story
4. beginning of story
5. end of story
6. beginning of story
7. end of story
8. end of story
9. beginning of story
10. end of story

KATE SHELLEY (Textbook p. 44)
VOCABULARY — Activity I (p. 13)

1. rugged
2. foreman
3. hazards
4. timber
5. lull

6. lingered
7. extinguish
8. recede
9. fragment
10. buffeting

VOCABULARY — Activity II (p. 14)

Answers will vary.

Comprehension Questions — In-depth Thinking (p. 15)

1. The story has many vivid passages, including the following:
   "Kate…discovered his riderless horse beside the Des Moines River…" (p. 46)
   "She loved to ride bareback through the forests in autumn or row a skiff along the broad, smooth surface of the river in high summer." (p. 47)
   "Sometimes she would hear urgent tapping from behind the ticket window…" (p. 47)
   "…and now black clouds were heaping up on the horizon…" (p. 48)
   "…the sky went dark as if a black curtain had been flung across the sun." (p. 48)
   "Thunder rattled loose glass in the window frame, while fierce wind hurled sheets of rain against the house." (p. 49)
   Of course the most powerful images describe the storm. **Sensory images** are listed for each page of the text in the **Literary Components.** If you have reviewed these with students, that will help them with this exercise.
2. Answers will probably vary. Students may talk about how she must have looked after running through a raging storm and crawling over a 700-foot bridge, how disoriented she may have sounded, how no one could have believed she had actually come through the night, and so forth.
3. Students may have a variety of legitimate answers to the question.

Comprehension Questions — Drawing Conclusions (pp. 15-16)

1. Students may give various answers. Their responses may include Mrs. Shelley's poor health, the younger children needing her, and the possibility that she could not have moved as quickly as Kate, which would have slowed Kate down.
2. It is not clear from the story whether the midnight express was halted as a result of Kate's warning, or whether it had already been stopped because of the bad storm. Students may make differing assumptions. It seems that the information she provided regarding the crew of the pusher engine was very important.
3. Again, student answers will vary. Students may talk about her rigorous life, her being unspoiled, her love of the trains, her father's death, her respect for human life, and so forth.

Graphic Organizer (pp. 17-18)

1. "black clouds are heaping up—threatening another storm."
2. fierce lightning, torrents of rain, loud thunder, trees uprooted
3. Honey Creek Bridge collapses with a train on it.
4. First decision: she will go help the men. Second decision: she will stop the midnight train from the west.
5. She must fight the rain and the angry river.
6. The rain extinguishes her lamp.
7. She must cross on her hands and knees.
8. Her clothes catch on the nails and spikes.
9. She almost loses her hold.
10. The angry flood is sweeping a great tree along the river.

NEW PROVIDENCE (Textbook p. 64)
VOCABULARY — Activity I (p. 19)

1. deteriorating
2. facades
3. thriving
4. graffiti; debris
5. vandalized

6. inscription
7. commemorated
8. renovate
9. rural

VOCABULARY — Activity II (p. 20)

Answers will vary.

Comprehension Questions — In-depth Thinking (p. 21)

1. Give examples from 1910 that show New Providence is thriving. The word *thriving* means "to grow vigorously; to flourish; to gain wealth or possessions; to prosper; to progress toward or realize a goal." In 1910, the streets are bustling with activities that suggest people are selling and buying goods. The city has the money to build a commemorative fountain and statue. Business is good, people have money to purchase necessities, the city is in good repair, and children go to school. There is housing for workers.
2. Encourage students to both read the text *and* look at the pictures to find differences.
3. **1910:** a flock of birds fly peacefully
   1935: a biplane and a blimp
   1970: power lines are strong across the horizon and a jet Answers will vary. Technology brings busyness, noise, tension, a move away from the natural world; it brings convenience, ease of travel and communication, better health care and medicines, improved sanitation and living conditions, etc.

Comprehension Questions—Drawing Conclusions
(pp. 21-22)
1. It will help if you can provide students with materials that have photographs of Victorian settings. Otherwise, they can just use their imaginations.
2. Answers will vary.
3. Answers will vary.

Graphic Organizer (pp. 23-24)	19 10	19 35	19 55	19 70	19 80	19 92
The streets are cobblestone.	✓	✗	✗	✗	✗	✗
The streets are paved.	✗	✓	✗	✓	✓	✓
There is a bandstand at the center of town.	✓	✗	✗	✗	✗	✓
Women wear long skirts.	✓	✗	✗	✗	✗	✗
Getz and McClure is open for business.	✓	✓	✓	✓	✓	✓
Victorian homes dot the hillside.	✓	✓	✓	✗	✗	✗
Modern apartment buildings are on the hillside.	✗	✓	✓	✓	✓	✗
Colonel Fleming House is used to house business.	✗	✓	✗	✗	✗	✓
The cars are Model-Ts.	✓	✓	✗	✗	✗	✗
The cars are Fords, A.M., G.M., etc.	✗	✗	✓	✓	✓	✓
A flock of birds flies overhead.	✓	✗	✗	✗	✗	✓
A jet plane is in the sky.	✗	✗	✗	✓	✗	✗

THE SILENT LOBBY (Textbook p. 82)
VOCABULARY—Activity I (p. 25)
1. struggle
2. petition
3. credentials
4. optimist
5. lobby
6. persistence
7. alarmed
8. legislators
9. prejudice
10. affidavit

VOCABULARY—Activity II (p. 26)
1. a
2. a
3. b
4. b
5. a
6. a
7. a
8. b
9. b
10. b

Comprehension Questions—In-depth Thinking (p. 27)
1. Craig's mother feels it is dangerous for the people to travel to Washington by bus—the bus could be bombed. She wants her husband to forget about agitating for the vote, and just let them live in peace. She had not wanted her husband to register two years earlier—in the past, people had been arrested and beaten for trying to register.

   Craig's father says that if people wanted to, they could bomb the house—the bus does not provide a special danger. He feels he cannot have peace—that no one can—if he does not have freedom, rights, equality. Two years earlier, he had insisted on

going to register to vote. He went even though it meant losing his job, even though he risked being arrested or beaten.
2. Answers will vary. Students may say that Craig's dad cannot feel peaceful inside, or at peace with himself, if he doesn't fight for his rights or if he doesn't have rights. Possibly he means that there cannot be peace among the populace in a society, if a group of people are discriminated against and oppressed. That is a situation that is volatile, that can always explode, because one group of people is always angry, deep down.
3. Student answers will vary. There are several reasonable answers: When Craig's father decides to go on the bus to Washington; when he tries to register to vote; when the Freedom Party registers people; when the group gets to Washington; when they stand in the tunnel; when they sit as spectators in the Congress; when the vote is taken— and so forth.

Comprehension Questions—Drawing Conclusions (pp. 27-28)
1. Answers will vary. Students may mention, in their own words, such ideas as:
Without struggle, there can be no change;
Without freedom, there is no peace of mind;
The government must provide equal opportunities to all its citizens;
Every citizen has the right to vote;
If at first you don't succeed, try, try again;
If you show your face to those in government, it is harder for them to be unjust to you.
And so forth.
2. Remind students, if necessary, of the material you presented from **Background Bytes.** Blacks in the South were victimized by the Ku Klux Klan and the general citizenry for centuries, beginning with their enslavement. There were good reasons for Craig's mother's fear of reprisals. She doesn't want anything to happen to her husband or her son. It is reasonable for her to expect that things will not change, and that whatever sacrifice they make may well be for nothing. Craig's father approaches the situation differently, and wants to bring about change. He believes it can be done. He feels driven to go to Washington and to bring his son with him. Both parents are "right."
3. Answers will vary. Encourage students to reread *Samuel's Choice,* so that they will recapture a sense of how Samuel changes in the story. Likely, Samuel would not have had enough sense of himself at the outset of the story to have gone to Washington. Once he has made his choice and experienced self-determination and self-respect, it is likely he would have gotten on that bus.

Graphic Organizer (pp. 29-30)
1. *Papa:* Papa tries to register to vote even though it cost him his job. He went to Washington, helped repair the bus, and, most importantly, refused to turn back.
2. *Craig:* Craig is the boy who tells the story. He participates by being a part of the group and not complaining or expressing fear.

3. *Mrs. Hamer:* Mrs. Hamer helped register black people to vote and ran for Congress.
4. *Sister Phyllis:* Sister Phyllis rode on the bus, insisted that the group be treated humanely, and prayed for everyone's safety.
5. *Congressman Ryan:* Congressman Ryan actively lobbied his fellow congressmen to give blacks equal voting rights.
6. *148 congressmen:* 148 members of Congress voted to seat Mrs. Hamer and members of the Freedom Democratic Party.

GOLD-MOUNTED GUNS (Textbook p. 110)
VOCABULARY—Activity I (p. 31)
1. meditative
2. sinister
3. restraint
4. stealthily
5. piercingly
6. level
7. amble
8. counter
9. novelty
10. desperation

VOCABULARY—Activity II (p. 32)
1. stealthily
2. sinister
3. ambled
4. firm
5. fitful
6. restraint
7. desperation
8. level
9. meditative

Comprehension Questions—In-depth Thinking (p. 33)
1. The author describes him as "hard-faced" four times in the first seven paragraphs. (In paragraph seven, he begins to call him the "lean man.") His gray mustache has a "sinister droop" and his eyes are "steel-blue." The author also makes us think he is bad, because he describes the young man as being so afraid of him—the author makes it seem as though he is going to shoot the young man.
2. His hands are upraised, because in the third paragraph the "hard-faced man made a slight movement—a bare flick of the hand at the gun belt." The hard-faced man has drawn his gun when the stranger steps out of the shadows.
3. At night, darkness and danger seemed to rule. People would lock themselves in against the dark, against the animals, against the criminals. Anything that ventured into this darkness had to be brave. Even the light, "daring" to pierce the darkness, seemed to have a bravery to it.

Comprehension Questions—Drawing Conclusions (pp. 33-34)
1. Ms. Sanderson has worked very hard to earn money to go to college ("Two years you've been away from me. Two years you've slaved in a store."), but all she can think about is comforting her father, when they find the money missing. She must be brave and kind.
2. Answers will vary.
3. Answers will vary. He might very well have continued to rob.

Graphic Organizer (pp. 35-36)
1. Will thinks that Tommy Pecos, being an outlaw, automatically reaches for his gun when he hears his name called.
   The true meaning: The sheriff is on the lookout for Tommy's friends or other outlaws.
2. Will thinks Tommy Pecos is a tough, suspicious outlaw, who wants to know who's been talking about him.

The true meaning: The sheriff is trying to figure out just who Will is and which side of the law he's on, without revealing to Will who he himself is.
3. Will thinks people backed away from the man because he is the ruthless outlaw, Tommy Pecos.
   The true meaning: People actually backed away from this man because he is the sheriff, and no one wants him to question or arrest them for any reason. They don't want to get too near anyone tough enough to kill Tommy Pecos.
4. Will thinks Tommy Pecos will make him a member of his gang.
   The true meaning: The sheriff means he will "take him along" to jail.
5. Will thinks Tommy is just a tough outlaw who wants to be in charge.
   The true meaning: The sheriff wants the money so that he can restore it to its owners.

THE DISAPPEARING MAN (Textbook p. 128)
VOCABULARY—Activity I (p. 37)
1. sleuth
2. amateur
3. loner
4. analyze
5. heists
6. enigma
7. milling
8. peddling
9. edging
10. evacuate

VOCABULARY—Activity II (p. 38)
1. heist
2. peddle
3. edging
4. analyze
5. sleuth
6. loner
7. evacuate
8. enigma
9. milling
10. amateur

Answer to Riddle: They had a mon-key.

Comprehension Questions—In-depth Thinking (p. 39)
1. Larry says to his father, "He's got to have a fence—someone to peddle the jewels." This observation helps Larry to put two and two together when he sees that (a) the building houses a jeweler and (b) someone seems to have given Stockton a key to the building.
2. He knew about Stockton because "Dad is a detective on the force, and he was on the case."
3. He recognizes Stockton from having deduced that if he acquired his police uniform at the costumer's, it would not fit well. The pants of the man he points to end above his ankles.

Comprehension Questions—Drawing Conclusions (pp. 39-40)
1. Answers will vary. Students may talk about his job as a detective, which requires bravery, which makes people hard, and which may make him impatient. He seems a bit brusque. Fearing for his son, or wanting to separate job from home, he may seem unyielding when it comes to his son's interest in detective work.
2. Answers will vary. Students may point to Stockton's having committed many robberies and therefore being "a hardened criminal." Stockton may be older (he is described as a man, whereas Arblaster is described repeatedly as a boy). In point of fact, we know almost nothing about Stockton because, in typi-

cal detective story fashion, the author focuses on the detective far more than on the criminal. *Gold-Mounted Guns*, on the other hand, is very much about the criminal himself.

3. Answers will vary. Bear in mind that this story is not a serious detective story, so the reader is expected to suspend reality while he reads it. In defense of the author, we may invoke Agatha Christie's dictum: people in uniform are not recognized as individuals. The *uniform* and hence, the person's position in life, will be recalled, but not the face or personality of the wearer.

Graphic Organizer (pp. 41-42)

In *The Disappearing Man*, there are two possibilities to consider: Circle the one that **cannot** be true.

Letter D of the first group, *Stockton is not in the building*, cannot be true.

Second Floor

Stockton would have no interest in this business. (Some students may comment that Stockton should have used the tailors to lengthen his pants, but, clearly, he did not.)

Third Floor

1. Stockton could use a costume to disguise himself.
2. Stockton could choose a policeman's uniform.
3. The costume might not fit him.

Top Floor

1. Stockton needs someone to sell his stolen goods for him.
2. Stockton might have entered this store to fence the jewels he stole.

THE SPECKLED HEN'S EGG (Textbook p. 140)
VOCABULARY—Activity I (p. 43)

1. aristocratic
2. brocades
3. prominent
4. heirlooms
5. miserly
6. hoarded
7. omens
8. litany
9. genteel
10. laboriously

VOCABULARY—Activity II (p. 44)

1. Someone who hoards bread would be saving it, not throwing it to the birds.
2. An heirloom is something old, handed down through generations, not something new, bought at a store. Also, an heirloom usually has some intrinsic value.
3. A weatherman, who is a scientist, does not use omens to predict weather. He uses scientific measurements.
4. If the picture were in a prominent place, it would be noticed.
5. A genteel lady has good—or overly good—manners.
6. An aristocratic person is a member of the upper social and economic classes. A baker's son wearing second-hand clothes does not look aristocratic in the least.
7. Brocades are worn for formal, dressy affairs, not play. Moreover, they would be ruined by a washing machine.
8. The description of the skater's "flying over the ice" is just the opposite of laborious. It could be described as appearing "effortless."

Comprehension Questions—In-depth Thinking (p. 45)

1. Even at the beginning of the story, when Madame is described as being stingy, she works taking care of chickens and selling eggs. Moreover, she has no household help and does all of her own cleaning and cooking.
2. The villagers (except for the storekeeper) and the clerk all take the examination of the egg seriously, as well as the interpretation of the picture.
3. The cause of Madame's sparing the hen is her belief that the hen has laid a very special egg.

Comprehension Questions—Drawing Conclusions (pp. 45-46)

1. Answers will vary. Having pride can simply be a matter of proper self-respect. Pride does not necessarily mean excessive self-esteem.
2. Answers will vary. To feel a sense of responsibility for the errors of one's people, of one's nation, or of one's family is showing sensitivity and courage. If one can help alleviate the problems resulting from such errors, that is all to the good. But one should not behave unwisely as a consequence.
3. Answers will vary. Possibilities include (1) hide the cookbook; (2) trade for some of the other hen's eggs; (3) take off for parts unknown.

Graphic Organizer (pp. 47-48)

Original Madame Roberge: a
Proud Madame Roberge: b
Humbled Madame Roberge: c

1. a	7. b
2. b	8. b
3. c	9. a
4. a	10. c
5. b	11. a
6. c	12. c

THE BLACK STALLION (Textbook p. 156)
VOCABULARY—Activity I (p. 49)

1. descended
2. eerie
3. diminish
4. monotonously
5. hectic
6. elated
7. savage
8. ruthless
9. altered
10. quota

VOCABULARY—Activity II (p. 50)

1. ruthless
2. hectic
3. diminished
4. monotonous
5. quota
6. savage
7. altered
8. descended
9. ruthless
10. both! But probably elated

Comprehension Questions—In-depth Thinking (p. 51)

1. There are many instances of Alec's courage in the story. Even his going to India without his family—which is not described in the story—is an example of behaving with courage.
2. Answers will vary. Presumably students will talk about the stallion's being frightened, being in a new situation, being hurt from the whip, and being angry.
3. Answers will vary.

Comprehension Questions—Drawing Conclusions
(p. 51-52)

1. Answers will vary. Captain Watson seems nice enough. He talks with Alec and tries to make him feel comfortable. He behaves well during the crisis with the ship. He is a practical person: The horse is destroying the stall, so when the horse's companion gives him money and he can replace whatever is destroyed, he just shrugs and walks away.

2. Answers may vary. The passage in which Alec recalls his uncle's saying that a pocketknife comes in handy, and those connected with his love of horses are good predictors of what will save Alec in the end.

3. Answers will vary.

Graphic Organizer (pp. 53-54)

SECTION 1—Introduction: 2, 5, 9, 14
SECTION 2—Conflict: 1, 6, 8, 10
SECTION 3—Turning Point: 4, 12
SECTION 4—Conclusion: 3, 7, 11, 13

BY THE SHORES OF SILVER LAKE
(Textbook p. 180)
VOCABULARY—Activity I (p. 55)

1. mufflers
2. steadying
3. glass
4. motionless
5. desolate
6. mourned
7. bank
8. radiance
9. shimmered
10. earnestly

VOCABULARY—Activity II (p. 56)

1. They prefer to wear turtleneck sweaters.
2. "That feller's really taken a shine to me."
3. When she's asleep.
4. Sand dollars.
5. Because it is a light desert.
6. A looking glass.
7. She longed for days gone by.
8. Because he'd had a milkshake for breakfast.

Comprehension Questions—In-depth Thinking (p. 57)

1. Laura says that they mustn't go near the water hole and she leads Carrie along the lakeshore until they are well away from it. When Laura sees the wolf, she doesn't mention it to Carrie—obviously she does not want to frighten her—and simply says she will race her home. This second decision is really quite impressive.

2. Webster's Unabridged says that a *moonpath* is "a lengthened reflection of the moon from slightly agitated water." The usage in the story would allow a broader definition. In *By the Shores of Silver Lake,* the water is frozen, not agitated. We no longer follow the path of the moon, since there are streetlights nearly everywhere we go. Also, children resort to other indoor, perhaps electronic, entertainments more often than they go out on cold nights to slide across frozen ice. Finally, parents today would be far more worried about allowing their children out alone at night (or at any other time).

3. The following passages are good:
"It was so beautiful that they hardly breathed." (p. 183) Students may also point to the description that follows in the remainder of the paragraph, since it really is their perspective.

"'How still it is,' Carrie whispered. 'Listen how still it is.' Laura's heart swelled. She felt herself a part of the wide land, of the far deep sky and the brilliant moonlight." (p. 183)
"He was looking toward her. The wind stirred his fur and the moonlight seemed to run in and out of it." (p. 184)

Comprehension Questions—Drawing Conclusions
(pp. 57-58)

1. Student answers will vary. Laura may be concerned about her father's being hurt. Laura may worry for the wolves. The student Laura may not worry for the wolves. And so forth.

2. Student answers will vary—and their speculation about the return to the den will be interesting to read. Of course one wolf may say that the other insisted they return (for whatever reason). Encourage students to look at every part of the situation that needs explaining. Why did they return to the old den/region? Why did they stay so briefly? Where do they come from that they had to travel so far? Why did they travel home at such a quick pace? Remind students to look for a description of the wolves, to give their answers authenticity: The wolves are life mates, they are old, they are big, they once hunted buffalo before all the buffalo were killed.

3. Student answers will vary. Some possible answers will be that she will see other farms in the distance, that the children of new homesteaders will be playing at the lake too, that there's a herd of cattle grazing in a nearby pasture, that there is another brother or sister toddling around, and so on.

Graphic Organizer (pp. 59-60)
Answers will vary.

GRAMP (Textbook p. 208)
VOCABULARY—Activity I (p. 61)

1. feeble
2. site
3. premises; scarlet
4. chaps
5. rigamarole
6. persisted
7. raucous
8. cross
9. curtly

VOCABULARY—Activity II (p. 62)

1. *Nouns:* site, rigamarole, chap, premises
2. *Verb:* persisted
3. *Adverb:* curtly
4. *Adjective:* cross, raucous, feeble, scarlet

Comprehension Questions—In-depth Thinking (p. 63)

1. Answers will vary. Students ought to mention that he is a person who wants something to love and take care of, and that he behaves responsibly towards his obligations.

2. Answers will vary. Gramp never really says anything about his problem until Simon questions him. After that he is silent. He doesn't complain. He simply withdraws.

3. Answers will vary. Mum's first response to Simon is that Gramp is getting old and that people get "like that" when they are old. When Simon says that Gramp was not like that before they moved to the apartment building, she insists that Gramp is better off at the apartment where it is lighter and cleaner and warmer and dryer than the house where they had lived. She does not acknowledge the problem, let alone how serious it is.

She asks Simon irritably why he is standing there and staring. When he responds that Gramp would be all right if he had a bench, she becomes exasperated. She asks where they could find a workbench in a place like the apartment building. The tenor of the entire discussion is that she is tense and upset and cannot stand to keep talking about this problem, which she feels helpless to solve.

Comprehension Questions—Drawing Conclusions
(pp. 63-64)
1. Answers will vary.
2. Answers will vary. The most likely scenario, however, is that Gramp will be without a place to work—unless he can convince the management to hire him.
3. Answers will vary. They should include the following:
    a. The first step to solving a problem is recognizing that it exists.
    b. The problem should be studied and analyzed.
    c. Someone has to really care about solving the problem.
    d. Ingenuity is a basic ingredient of problem solving, as is—
    e. Persistence.
    f. Belief in yourself, in others, and in the idea that problems can be solved is paramount.

Graphic Organizer (pp. 65-66)
Bottom row of pyramid:
  ["Gramp—come down and look at my guinea pigs."]
  "Too far down there."
  ["Why don't you put a bench up here?"]
  "There's not room."
  ["We could keep it clean."]
  "You don't know what you're talking about."
Middle row of pyramid:
  Simon asks the builders if Grandpa could put a bench in one of the sheds.
  ["This is a building site and no one is allowed on it."]
  Simon asks the men at the gatehouse if there is somewhere Gramp could put his bench.
  ["Get off the premises!"]
Third row of pyramid:
  Simon asks Mr. Gideon if Gramp can use the bench in the basement.
  ["I don't see why not."]

AFTER SCHOOL (Textbook p. 236)
VOCABULARY—Activity I (p. 67)
1. naive
2. cajoling
3. relish
4. dictated
5. triumphant
6. despondent
7. interceded
8. forlorn
9. distracted
10. ridiculed

VOCABULARY—Activity II (p. 68)
  Answers will vary.

Comprehension Questions—In-depth Thinking (p. 69)
1. The chart at **Eyes On...Internal and External Conflict** lists the

conflicts.
2. The chart at **Eyes On...Internal and External Conflict** lists the conflicts.
3. When the neighbor bully asks Seryozha if his sister learned the whole alphabet that day, Seryozha defends her by saying that it takes a whole year to learn the entire alphabet.

Comprehension Questions—Drawing Conclusions
(pp. 69-70)
1. He had reassured the little girl and taken her out of the classroom; he had explained the situation to her brother, so that the brother would not be angry at her and would understand; he had knocked the wind out of a bully's sails; he is going to help the sister and brother write to their parents that night. That's a lot of good to spread in the world in a single day, a lot of pain to have eased.
2. He tells us that he went into the first grade classroom, because he was looking after a neighbor's child. He also understands that this is important to do, because it is the first day of school. Certainly, the neighbor would not have asked him if he were not a reliable sort of person.
3. The narrator always tries to help. The neighbor boy takes pleasure in teasing and hurting. Instead of sympathizing with the children who have lost their mother and father, he delights in saying that now the children will not be able to write to their parents for a whole year. His relationship to the other children is established through cruel barbs. The narrator establishes a relationship by helping out.

Graphic Organizer (pp. 71-72)
1. He draws a funny picture of a girl eating supper with her family.
2. Yurik explains that letters are made from sticks.
3. Yurik explains that it takes a year to learn the alphabet and that the sister didn't know this.
4. Yurik offers to write it for him.
5. Yurik shows the boy that Seryozha is telling the truth.

ONE THROW (Textbook p. 248)
VOCABULARY—Activity I (p. 73)
1. rooming house
2. on my neck
3. needle me
4. egging him on
5. steam a kid up
6. a kick out of anything
7. bawls me out
8. blow the whistle
9. the brass
10. I've got no kick coming

VOCABULARY—Activity II (p. 74)
  Answers will vary.

Comprehension Questions—In-depth Thinking (p. 75)
1. Pete says that he doesn't get along with Al, because he is "on his neck" all the time. Pete also says that if he does something good, Al says nothing about it, but if he does something wrong, he gets bawled out in front of others.
2. Eddie wants to see if Pete is worthy of being a Yankee. In the old days, that meant being fair and square, honest, and a good sportsman.

Comprehension Questions—Drawing Conclusions
(pp. 75-76)

1. Answers will vary.
2. This question can be argued both ways and both arguments have validity. On the one hand, Eddie is testing Pete, knowing that if Pete fails, the Yankees will not be interested in him. As representative of the Yankees, he is obligated to make sure Pete is the man he seems to be. We may view Eddie as being unfair and dishonest. Is every ballplayer put to the test for honesty? Why pick on Pete? Would Eddie himself stop at a bit of dishonesty under the right circumstances? He's lying right here! And so on.
3. The story's Pete Maneri probably felt happy, grateful, and a bit awed. Projecting their own feelings, students may say he was angry at Eddie for trying to trick him, he was glad he could finally show Al Dall a thing or two, he was thrilled to be leaving the two-bit minor league he's been stuck in. But none of these reactions would be true to the spirit of the story.

Graphic Organizer (pp. 77-78)

1. F. Mr. Franklin is really Eddie Brown, a scout for the Yankees.
2. F. Al Dall must be trying to get Pete ready for the majors.
3. F. Al Dall has sent a good report to Eddie Brown, which is why Eddie Brown has come.
4. T.
5. Probably F. Eddie (hopefully) made up this story to test Pete.
6. T.

THE BIRDS' PEACE (Textbook p. 262)
VOCABULARY—Activity I (p. 79)

1. thicket
2. flitted, sapling
3. melodically
4. purling
5. belligerent, serenely
6. incubating
7. conspicuous
8. preened

VOCABULARY—Activity II (p. 80)

1. I don't like that guy. He's always looking for a fight, really belligerent.
2. She's a good teacher; she always speaks serenely.
3. That butterfly! I've been watching it flit from flower to flower.
4. Meet me under that sapling.
5. That is a purling stream.
6. I found this wallet in a thicket.
7. I like watching those birds in the zoo preen.
8. I saw that boy! With his funny hair, he was conspicuous.
9. On the farm, we watched those hens incubating their eggs.
10. She's a good singer. Her voice is sweet and her songs are melodious.

Comprehension Questions—In-depth Thinking (p. 81)

1. At the beginning of the story, Kristy feels *undone* by the loss of her father. She sobs from the deepest well of her being. At the end of the story, she is writing a letter to her father about something she has observed. This is growing.
2. Kristy has an existing relationship with the birds—they are her longtime friends. She has names for them, can identify them, and knows their individual songs and habits.
3. Kristy is comparing the birds with humankind.

Comprehension Questions—Drawing Conclusions
(pp. 81-82)

1. It is Fluter's job to protect the territory and his family from strangers. It is his job to warn strangers to stay away and to warn his wife to get on home to the nest.
2. It doesn't appear to be Dulce's job to worry about intruders. She waits for her husband's signal of warning to fly back to the nest and protect the eggs.
3. No. She will weep and suffer for a long time, but she will become more accustomed to the situation and learn to manage her feelings.

Graphic Organizer (pp. 83-84)

Pictures will vary.

HATTIE'S BIRTHDAY BOX (Textbook p. 270)
VOCABULARY—Activity I (p. 85)

1. stewed
2. brood
3. siblings
4. team
5. resolved
6. chink
7. undeniable
8. concoct
9. clasped
10. perch

VOCABULARY—Activity II (p. 86)

Answers will vary.

Comprehension Questions—In-depth Thinking (p. 87)

1. The narrator shows her feelings for her great-great grandfather in the following actions:
* She thinks the story is important enough to be told.
* She helps her mother prepare for Grandaddy's party.
* She's concerned when she sees that Grandaddy is anxious.
* She asks Grandaddy what happened with Hattie.
* She posts herself behind Grandaddy when Hattie's cab pulls up.
* She puts her hand on Grandaddy's shoulder when Hattie arrives and says, "Don't worry, Grandaddy. She'll have to get through me first."
* She says that she's not about to leave Grandaddy's side. If Hattie's ever going to "give him the business about the empty box," she wants to be there.
2. Students will have different ideas about this, but a canary is bright, yellow (which is the color of hope), and has a wonderful song. A canary is also company.
3. The misfortunes include the following:
* Hattie and her husband ran out of food their first winter.
* One summer they lost their whole crop in a prairie fire.
* Their son drowned.
* Hattie's husband, Otto, died.

Comprehension Questions—Drawing Conclusions
(pp. 87-88)

1. Students may have different ideas about this. First, she brought it back because the author, Pam Conrad, needed to bring things full circle. She brought it back because it was the tangible evidence of her brother's love for her that she had cherished for all those years of separation. She wanted to thank him for it, perhaps to show him how often she had handled it

and how much she had cherished it.

2. It seems that Spencer and Hattie have viewed the box differently throughout the years. Spencer sees only the emptiness of the box, his inability to buy a gift for his beloved sister, his procrastination in explaining to her why the box was empty. His small lie has grown in his imagination into a huge violation of trust. To Hattie, the box is a symbol of her brother's love, to be cherished and handled often. With the passing of years, Hattie must have expected less and less from the supposed gift inside. "I always thought maybe there'd be a brooch or a gold stickpin or something." Hattie, the realist, must have understood that whatever an impoverished twenty-year-old farm boy could have bought was not going to rescue her from financial disaster. As she got older, she loved the box for its good intentions, not for any possible treasure it might have held. So, would Spencer have felt better if she hadn't brought the box? No, because he would never have been able to see how much the box had meant to her and how little she cared about the gift that it was supposed to contain.

3. Students should have all kinds of ideas. Maybe she made him a box of cookies.

Graphic Organizer (pp. 89-90)

1. Samuel could have still been a slave, or he could have been injured or a prisoner of the British. The positive: He is fighting for a just cause and will be free.

2. Leo could have been left to fail in a regular class, and never learn the material. The positive: He can make friends with his classmates and learn at his own pace.

3. The sign could have been a warning of death or disaster. The positive: Madame Roberge is no worse off than she was before, and has learned an important lesson.

4. Answers will vary.

THE WHIMBREL (Textbook p. 284)
VOCABULARY—Activity I (p. 91)

1. marshes
2. dunes, dune
3. mottled
4. puckered
5. pottering
6. shrewdly
7. vise
8. beachcomber
9. burrowing
10. quizzically

VOCABULARY—Activity II (p. 92)

Show the children how these puzzles work if they are not familiar with them. Unscramble each word and write the word on the blank boxes. Then, unscramble the word formed by the letters in the circles and write the word in the quote below each section. The two quotes are the answer to the question at the top.

marshes
pottering
puckered
quizzically
"you are *cheep*" said one.

beachcomber
shrewdly
dunes
mottled
vise
burrowing
"Well, you are a *birdbrain*," retorted the other.

Comprehension Questions—In-depth Thinking (p. 93)

1. Students may give various answers. Axel knows a lot about the sea and about living creatures. He teaches Tessa many things, about seashells and albatrosses, about summer sedges, snails, and spoonbills. He is a doctor to injured animals. He is wise enough to be kind to people and animals. He figures out how to make an artificial foot for the whimbrel. He knows that a whimbrel needs to live like a whimbrel.

2. Of course student answers will vary. You may want to guide students by suggesting they think about what it is like to live out in the open, without being confined, close to nature—the water, the waves, the open sky, the wind—and to living creatures. A person who fishes also probably eats some of what they catch, instead of buying all of their food at a store. They see the relationship between killing and eating. A person who works on a boat is not as protected as someone who is always inside.

3. Likely, Axel treats her like a person, not as just a child. He spends time with her. He also provides companionship. Also, she may find his "junk" interesting— stuff she wouldn't have at home. Students may have other points to make.

Comprehension Questions—Drawing Conclusions (pp. 93-94)

1. Students may say that he would find some other way to enable the bird to live reasonably, but not well enough to free him. Students may also say that he would put the animal down to be humane.

2. Hopefully students will approach the question with a bit of humor. Perhaps someone will suggest that the other whimbrels will be clamoring for a fancy-looking new foot.

3. Answers will vary.

Graphic Organizer (pp. 95-96)

Answers will vary.

THE DAY OF THE TURTLE (Textbook p. 316)
VOCABULARY—Activity I (p. 97)

1. bombarded
2. wizened
3. spar
4. salvage
5. cargo
6. gig
7. purposefully
8. cavorting
9. fruitlessly
10. driftwood

VOCABULARY—Activity II (p. 98)

1. Driftwood is wood floating on a body of water.
2. Wizened means shriveled or withered.
3. Bombarded means pelted.
4. A spar is a strong pole to which a boat's sail is attached.
5. Fruitlessly means unsuccessfully.
6. A gig is a light boat rowed with four, six, or eight oars.
7. Cargo is freight carried on a ship or plane.
8. Salvage is a verb meaning to save from being thrown out.
9. Cavorting is jumping and prancing about.
10. Purposefully means seriously, with a goal in mind.

Comprehension Questions—In-depth Thinking (p. 99)

1. Both Laura Perryman and Laura Ingalls have respect for a wild creature and they want it to continue to live. Both girls have intense feelings about this. Each wishes to save a creature

that can in no way ever pay her back or show her gratitude or even recognition. Each girl also has a father who is a threat to the life, respectively, of a giant turtle and a giant wolf.

2. In *The Whimbrel*, Tessa is not the one who finds the injured animal. Tessa is not alone with the situation for the better part of two days, as Laura is. Tessa is introduced to the animal by a reliable adult who cares that the bird survive. Up until the moment that Granny May says, "Let's try shrimps," Laura believes that any adult will represent an additional threat to the turtle's survival. Their experience is the same at the end, when neither girl wants the wild creature to go.

3. Laura is lucky to have a grandmother who understands how she feels, and who respects and supports her feelings. She is also fortunate that they are able to help the turtle to get back into the ocean.

Comprehension Questions—Drawing Conclusions
(pp. 99-100)

1. Laura should tell her father about the turtle because (1) people shouldn't lie; (2) it feels terrible to lie to our parents; and (3) the turtle represents a lot of meat and everyone is very hungry. Laura shouldn't tell her father, because he will kill the turtle. She believes it should be saved. She needs to see something good happen. Her spirit may need more nourishing than her body.

2. Students' answers will vary. But Granny means that when something concrete, something in the material world, is broken, it is possible to fix it, with time, proper supplies, and (sometimes) money. However, when the human spirit breaks, when people see terrible things happen that they are helpless to change, it is not always possible for them to recover their joy in life and their faith in others. Her granddaughter, Laura, is hoping to save the giant turtle.

3. Hopefully, your students will have an enthusiastic reaction.

Graphic Organizer (pp. 101-102)

Answers will vary.

PRAIRIE FIRE (Textbook p. 332)
VOCABULARY—Activity I (p. 103)

1. conflagration
2. bounding
3. billowed
4. staggering
5. congregating
6. quivering
7. thrashed
8. scorched
9. bluffs
10. furrow

VOCABULARY—Activity II (p. 104)

Movement: *bounding, staggering, quivering, congregating*
Fire: *thrashed, scorched, conflagration*
Earth: *furrow, bluffs*
Wind: *billowing*

Comprehension Questions—In-depth Thinking (p. 105)

1. Ma and Pa Ingalls are creating a fire line. A fire line is a barrier of cleared or plowed land that checks the spread of a fire. In order to burn, fire needs fuel. Here, the fuel is the prairie grass. If there is a space with no prairie grass (because it has already been burned), there is a border with no fuel. Moreover, if there is a furrow (a trench, a narrow depression) in the ground, the fire has to jump from one side of the border to the other. The furrow also separates burning grass from unburned grass. So,

Pa first plows a furrow to encircle the advancing fire. Pa then sets fire to the grass. Then Ma puts that fire out by beating it with wet sacks. It is difficult for the advancing fire to cross that line. Also, Pa's little fire creates a backfire: *The little fire went backing slowly away against the wind. It went slowly crawling to meet the racing furious big fire. And suddenly the big fire swallowed the little one.*

2. There is repetition of sounds: *bound, plow, shout, house; thousands; hurry* and *furrow.*
There is repetition of words: *bound, plow, shout, house; hurry* and *furrow; run, rabbit(s), scream, thousands, tub.*
There is repetition of images regarding the absence of the sun, darkness, and black. Fleeing leaping and bounding rabbits are mentioned five times in seven short paragraphs. Pa Ingalls also *bounds*, at least twice. Everyone runs—the horses from the field, Ma to the well, Laura to tug the tub, and even the fire is moving *faster than a horse can run.* There is also a lot of roaring.

3. *...black clouds billowing up in the south, across the sun...*
The sky was black now, the air was as dark as if the sun had set.
...the red fire coming under the billows of smoke...
...the red undersides of the rolling smoke...
...the flames that tried to cross the furrow...
The fire blew wildly, snatching at the dry grass inside the furrow.
The prairie fire was roaring now, roaring louder and louder...
Great flames came roaring, flaring and twisting high.
Twists of flame broke loose and came down on the wind to blaze up in the grasses far ahead of the roaring wall of fire.
A red light came from the rolling black clouds of smoke overhead.
The orange, yellow, terrible flames were coming faster than horses can run, and their quivering light danced over everything.
And so forth.

Comprehension Questions—Drawing Conclusions
(pp. 105-106)

1. This adage means that although at first everything went wrong, the final outcome was good, and that's all that counts.

2. One person would not have had time to dig the furrow, fill the tub with water, drag the tub over, set the fire, and put out flames.

3. The Indians had always burned the prairie to make green grass grow more quickly and to make traveling by horse over the prairie easier. Their ponies couldn't gallop through thick, tall, dead grass.

Graphic Organizer (pp. 107-108)
First chart:
- *Ma:* pulls up buckets of water
- *Pa:* plows and furrows around the house
- *Rabbits:* bound past Pa
- *Jack:* shivers and whines, then howls
- *Birds:* fly from the fire
- *Snakes:* ripple across the yard
- *Prairie hens:* run silently

Second chart:

- *Gophers:* come up from their holes
- *Birds:* come flying back
- *Snakes:* crawl out of the creek bottoms
- *Prairie hens:* come walking
- *Ma and Pa:* are cheerful

HOW TO BRING UP A LION (Textbook p. 346)
VOCABULARY—Activity I (p. 109)
1. monarch
2. captivity
3. raspy
4. trifle
5. triumphed
6. perished
7. wean
8. broad
9. canter
10. hoisted

VOCABULARY—Activity II (p. 110)
1. b
2. b
3. b
4. a
5. a
6. a
7. a
8. b
9. a (hoist indicates "up")
10. b (a rider in a hurry would make the horse gallop)

Comprehension Questions—In-depth Thinking (p. 111)
1. (1) That Daniel and Una's mother goes into the house "to give orders," suggests that she is in charge. (2) When the keeper comes with the baby lion, she comes out of the house with a bottle and she fills it with milk and warm water for the baby lion. (3) She says that she is going to bring up the baby lion, and that "he is *not* going to die." (4) She immediately starts feeding him with the bottle as soon as he arrives. (5) She directs the narrator to weigh the baby on the meat scales, and gives orders that he be weighed once a week, so that they can keep track of his weight. (6) She instructs people regarding what he is to be fed and how often. (7) She also says that his bottle must be cleaned with boiling water after each meal. (8) She instructs the narrator to go find out how the lion is to be brought up, because, as she says once again, "this lion is not going to die."
2. The parents of the baby lion were Matabele lions. The Matabele word for lion is *umlibaan.* This sounds like the familiar Celtic name Sullivan, and so, he was called Sullivan "for short" (although this hardly sounds shorter!).
3. The family fed the baby lion mutton broth in a baby bottle and brushed him every day with a dandy brush (to make up for his mother's not being able to lick him with her tongue).

Comprehension Questions—Drawing Conclusions
(pp. 111-112)
1. Answers will vary, presumably from pessimistic (the lion lives in a cage or the lion is released and is shot and killed) to optimistic (the lion is able to walk around outside in a large fenced-in area or is released and lives happily ever after).
2. At the outset of the story, people thought the baby lion would die, and in fact the family knew nothing about raising a baby lion when they agreed to take it. But as Kipling writes, the lion grew to weigh more than fifteen pounds when they had to leave him, and they were very proud of this. They had "triumphed over the keeper and the other people who had said we could

never bring him up by hand."
3. Answers will vary. Students may talk about the scenery he envisions, the animals he would like to stalk, the good meals he would eat as a consequence, and the other lion friends he would have.

Graphic Organizer (pp. 113-114)
1. Moms do not bite their babies or hurt them in any way.
2. Babies are kept in cradles and cribs.
3. Babies are kept in the house.
4. Same
5. Same
6. Similar; babies are weighed on baby scales.
7. We would do this if the baby was underweight.
8. Same
9. Same
10. We make a bed of soft cotton sheets.
11. Same
12. Absolutely not
13. What is cuter or funnier than a baby? And yes, most babies are big show-offs!

THE STREETS ARE FREE (Textbook p. 364)
VOCABULARY—Activity I (p. 115)
1. banner
2. aide
3. urban
4. confront
5. riot
6. constructive
7. site
8. shrubs
9. ruckus
10. saplings

VOCABULARY—Activity II (p. 116)
Answers will vary.

Comprehension Questions—In-depth Thinking (p. 117)
1. The Librarian (1) asks why the three children are sad; (2) explains how the city grew up without a playground; (3) asks them what *they* would do to fix up an "empty" lot with garbage and broken glass, in order to turn it into a playground; (4) gets a pencil and pad of paper for writing down their ideas; (5) appoints the negative Camila the official list-maker; and so forth. Her presence is very important, as advisor, guide, helper, *and* provider of emotional support.
2. Answers will vary. Some students may say that Camila is only being realistic. Perhaps she has grown up in such a way as to make her negative. Maybe she has seen sad things happen. Maybe she has seen her parents struggle. And so forth.
3. The media helps a cause by bringing attention to it. From the news and the newspapers, many people learn of a problem that needs to be solved. Ideally, the public will become concerned about the problem. Public officials need to respond to their concern, or presumably they will not be re-elected. However, media attention can also be misleading. If there are photos in the newspaper of the Mayor dedicating the plot of land, as in this story, people will mistakenly assume that the problem has been taken care of. We know how important the media can be at election time.

Comprehension Questions—Drawing Conclusions
(pp. 117-118)
1. Answers will vary. The Mayor is not an ethical person. He

doesn't keep his word. He says things so that he will appear to be a caring and responsive public official. But his concern is superficial. He likes the sound of his words. He likes to have his picture taken. But he does not follow through. He may be lazy. He may be forgetful. But he could be worse! At least he doesn't allow the police to take the children away, and he *does* dedicate the land, which means it is there for the citizens to fix up.

2. Answers will vary. The town is a poor one, and playgrounds cost money to build. Perhaps the Mayor doesn't care much about children. The government is less organized or caring than ours; in most American cities there are ordinances that require a certain amount of land be made into parks.

3. Answers will vary. It seems likely that the children would have made another fuss. Certainly their parents and the librarian could have contacted the media once more and forced the Mayor's hand. Likely, other citizens would also have joined the fight. Students may legitimately answer that the whole project would have fallen on its face and the citizenry would have tired of fighting for it. Certainly, a subsequent issue will be maintenance of the park, since people litter unmercifully.

Graphic Organizer (pp. 119-120)

Answers will vary.

ONE DAY IN THE DESERT (Textbook p. 384)
VOCABULARY—Activity I (p. 121)

1. torrents
2. distinctive
3. deluges
4. retreat
5. labyrinth
6. dominates
7. reservoir
8. wrath
9. adapt
10. ruthless

VOCABULARY—Activity II (p. 122)

Answers will vary.

Comprehension Questions—In-depth Thinking (p. 123)

1. Here is the material that students can gather from the story, from which they can write their answer:

The scent of lion reached the nose of a coyote who was cooling off under the dark embankment of the dry river not far from the Papago Indian hut. He lifted his head, flicked his ears nervously, and got to his feet. He ran swiftly into his burrow beneath the roots of the ancient saguaro cactus that grew beside the hut. (p. 391)

The crash of the saguaro terrified the coyote. He darted out of his den under the tree and back to the dry riverbed. (p. 400)

A drumroll sounded up Scorpion Pass…The coyote rushed out of the dry riverbed. (p. 401)

The coyote was washed out from under the embankment. He tumbled head over heels, swam to the surface, and climbed onto an uprooted mass of prickly pears. On this he sailed into the valley and was dropped safely onto the outwash plain when the water went into the ground. Stunned, he shook himself and looked around. Before him the half-drowned pack rat struggled. Recovering his wits, the coyote pounced upon him. (p. 401)

2. (1) The first mention of the lion tells us how much he is suffering. The intensity of his suffering, his desperation, make him the central character of the piece. His suffering, and the hope on the part of the reader that it will be alleviated, are the focus

of the piece. (2) We learn more about him, even, than we do about Bird Wing and her mother. (3) The lion's feelings are expressed not in the omniscient third person, but in a voice that is very nearly internal dialogue. For example, the author writes *He must eat and drink.* (p. 386); *He was afraid of people, but this morning he was desperate.* (p. 387) The voice, the perspective, is very close to the lion's internal voice (if he had one). (4) The mountain lion's journey down the mountain is the thread that unites all of the creatures and the events of the story, except when the author moves into the *really* omniscient third person of the "science" passages. (5) The suspense in the story is generated by the mountain lion: (a) Is he going to attack the people? (b) Is he going to get something to relieve his hunger and thirst? (c) Is there anything that will relieve the pain of his wound? This is why his disappearance into the water near the end of the story is so painful to us—not just because he was trying so hard, but because he is the core of the piece.

3. The saguaro cactus is enormous and very old. It is like the matriarch or patriarch of a family. With the aged, we associate wisdom. Also, the saguaro provides so much for so many: It is shelter, shade, protection, and nourishment. Such a venerable institution would seem to have been around—and would last—forever.

Comprehension Questions—Drawing Conclusions (pp. 123-124)

1. (a) Microclimates are small shelters out of the terrible heat. The microclimates are burrows in the ground where it is cool, crevices and caves in rocks, or the shade. Because of the dryness, the thin desert air does not hold heat. Shady spots can be 20° F cooler than out in the sun.

(b) The mountain lion seeks the shade of a giant saguaro cactus and lies down to rest. (p. 391, paragraph 2)

The coyote cools off under the dark embankment of the dry river. (p. 391, paragraph 3)

The coyote has a burrow beneath the roots of the ancient saguaro cactus. (p. 391, paragraph 3)

Humans boil the fruit from the saguaro cactus to make a sweet, nourishing syrup. (p. 391, paragraph 4)

The roadrunner uses the tall grass for shade, and hides from the lion under the embankment of the dry riverbed. (p. 392, paragraph 3)

The peccaries stay alive in the dry desert by eating the water-storing prickly pear cactus. They lie in the cool of the paloverde trees that grow in thickets. (p. 392, paragraph 4)

A headstand beetle hides under the grass plant by a tarantula's doorway. (p. 394, paragraph 1)

A tortoise eats the fruit of a prickly pear cactus. Because of the moisture of the plant and her huge bladder that stores the moisture, she is never thirsty. (p. 394, paragraph 2)

The tortoise has a burrow under the paloverde bushes. (p. 395, paragraph 1)

A cactus wren has a nest in a teddy-bear cactus. (p. 395, paragraph 3)

Hundreds of lizards seek shelter from the heat under sticks and stones. (p. 395, paragraph 4)

A kangaroo rat has a labyrinth under the ocotillo plants. She has dug a tunnel that leads deeper to a room under the giant saguaro cactus. The kangaroo rat eats seeds of the mesquite tree. (p. 396, paragraph 1)

The roadrunner seeks sanctuary in the saguaro forest. **(p. 396, paragraph 2)**

The Gila woodpecker has a hole for a home in the giant saguaro. **(p. 397, paragraph 1)**

Honeypot ants gets sweets from plants. **(p. 398, paragraph 1)**

The peccaries find safety from the flood in the saguaro forest. **(p. 398, paragraph 2)**

The coyote uses an uprooted mass of prickly pears as a raft. **(p. 401, paragraph 6)**

The peccaries eat billions of seeds that have been dumped on the land by the flood. **(p. 402, paragraph 6)**

(c) The tarantula eats moist crickets and other insects to quench her thirst. **(p. 393, paragraph 4)**

A headstand beetle uses a tarantula's hole to escape the heat of the day. **(p. 394, paragraph 1)**

A cottontail rabbit takes refuge in a tortoise's burrow to get out of the hot sun. **(p. 395, paragraph 2)**

A spiny-tailed lizard and a Texas banded gecko take refuge from the heat in the tortoise's burrow. **(p. 395, paragraph 2)**

The lion drinks water that the humans have brought back to their hut in a bucket. **(p. 396, paragraph 3)**

The sparrow-sized elf owl uses for a nest one of the old nests of the Gila woodpecker. **(p. 397, paragraph 1)**

Honeypot ants store the sweets from plants in the bellies of hanging ants. **(p. 398, paragraph 1)**

A rattlesnake takes refuge from the heat in the pack rat's nest. **(p. 398, paragraph 8)**

The coyote eats the pack rat. **(p. 401, paragraph 6)**

The humans feel they owe their surviving the flood to the presence of the lion, because they fled him. **(p. 402, paragraph 3)**

The roadrunner eats a snake. **(p. 403, paragraph 1)**

2. Answers will vary. Students need to consider whether the question is just about how the story would have turned out, or about whether there would have been a story at all. If the lion had gone up, likely he would not have died. Although with his wound infected (which we can deduce from his being feverish), his not being drowned in the flood may simply have meant that his suffering was prolonged. Finally, as the story is constructed —the story that the author thinks needs to be told, of the lion's journey downward, with the reactions of the animals that he passes and his ultimate death—it would not have been, without his descent to the Papago hut.

3. Students should have learned about the importance of predators from the discussion of wolves in the **Background Bytes** of *By the Shores of Silver Lake* **(p. 179)**. Without wolves, bears, and mountain lions, the number of smaller predators increases and the animals that these smaller predators feed on decreases. The disappearance of large predators means that the balance of nature is upset. The population of animals they feed on grows so large that there is not enough food for all of them. Those prey animals begin to starve.

Graphic Organizer (pp. 125-126)

Answers according to temperature, from bottom up.

- 80 Lion
- 81 Coyote
- 112 Bird Wing and her mother
- 112 roadrunner
- 112 peccaries
- 112 spider
- 117 tortoise
- 118 cactus wren
- 119 kangaroo rat
- 120 lion
- 121 Bird Wing

THE MEMORY BOX (Textbook p. 422)
VOCABULARY—Activity I (p. 127)

1. tackle	6. filet knife
2. reel	7. horizon
3. haul	8. darted
4. sheath	9. bandit
5. gutted	10. bolted

VOCABULARY—Activity II (p. 128)

1. reel	6. sheath
2. dart	7. bolted
3. tackle	8. tackle
4. gutted	9. dart
5. reel	10. bolted

1. bandit
2. filet
3. horizon

Comprehension Questions—In-depth Thinking (p. 129)

1. Gramps means that their experience fishing together on that day is so fine that it is worthy of preserving in the memory box.

2. The Cook's Rule is, "Nothing but good smells at the cook's dinner table." To comply with the Cook's Rule, Gramps and Zach clean the fish and wash themselves in the shed before coming into the house.

3. In *Gramp*, Gramp has lost his independence because of the family's move to an apartment building that is completely inappropriate for his life experience and his time of life. He feels useless and angry, because there is nothing for him to do. He may have some trouble getting up and down long flights of stairs, but his health of body and mind otherwise seem good. However, he is no longer head of the family and his wife is gone. On the other hand, Gramps lives in a wonderful place and has been happy. He still is the head of the family and he and his wife are good partners. But he has Alzheimer's and he knows it.

Comprehension Questions—Drawing Conclusions (pp. 129-130)

1. Answers will vary. Gramps feels love, devotion, respect, gratitude and, now, dependence upon, Gram. Gram feels love, devotion, respect, concern for and protective of Gramps. Zach feels love, respect, concern for, anxiety about and sadness towards Gramps.

2. Gramps is sufficiently aware to know that he got lost on or near his own property. It is humiliating for an adult to feel like a baby or a small child. What can be more frightening than to lose one's mind?

3. We vote for Yes, since by next summer Gramps' condition may be considerably worse.

Graphic Organizer (pp. 131-132)

Answers will vary.

THE GREATEST SNOWBALL FIGHT IN HISTORY (Textbook p. 436)

VOCABULARY—Activity I (p. 133)

1. brigades
2. array
3. regiments
4. truce
5. barrage
6. momentum
7. rally
8. vigorously
9. grizzled
10. imminent

VOCABULARY—Activity II (p. 134)

1. array
2. vigorously
3. rallied
4. imminent
5. truce
6. barrage
7. grizzled
8. battalion

Comprehension Questions—In-depth Thinking (p. 135)

1. The Yankees, who were used to cold, snowy winters, just groaned and clutched their heavy blankets more tightly about them. The Confederate soldiers had never seen snow before and were delighted with the cold white stuff. They left their huts and tents to throw snowballs.
2. Both are fights, and so both involve aggression. But a snowball fight is fun because it is just a good-natured copy of the real thing. Even if we want to hit people in a snowball fight, we don't usually want to injure or kill them.
3. Given the lack of supplies, it is hard to believe that the soldiers would have had extra clothing. They may have wrapped themselves in their blankets and hung their (very dirty) clothes on sticks or branches near fires, so that they could dry out.

Comprehension Questions—Drawing Conclusions (pp. 135-136)

1. After the Battle of Fredericksburg, both sides were waiting until spring to fight again. In war, soldiers are often waiting for the weather and for the officers to make decisions. Fighting is not continuous.
2. Probably not. It would have been dangerous for the men on either side to let down their guard that much. Also, in order to kill people, you can't allow yourself to just see them as people—they are the enemy.

Graphic Organizer (pp. 137-138)

Snowflake A: First Regiment of Texas Brigade
Snowflake B: Fourth Regiment of Texas Brigade
Snowflake C: Fifth Regiment of Texas Brigade
Snowflake D: Third Arkansas Regiment of Texas Brigade
Triangle: Texas Brigade
Square: Georgia Brigade
Snowball A: Generals Hood and Anderson's Division
Snowball B: General Lafayette McLaw's Division

FOUNDERS OF THE CHILDREN'S RAIN FOREST (Textbook p. 446)

VOCABULARY—Activity I (p. 139)

1. threaded
2. canopy
3. optimistic
4. naturalist
5. resourceful
6. ingenuity
7. prominent
8. inspire
9. monument

VOCABULARY—Activity II (p. 140)

Answers will vary.

Comprehension Questions—In-depth Thinking (p. 141)

1. (1) They held a "rain forest evening" for which they charged admission. At the evening, they performed a play about death in the rain forest, after which they collected donations. They had made rain forest books and written rain forest poems which they sold. They raised $240 from the evening's activities.
   (2) Their teacher brought in a list of prominent and wealthy people. They wrote a letter to at least one person on the list.
   (3) They wrote to the king of Sweden.
   (4) They made a recording of their own rain forest songs and created a tape. They sold five hundred tapes for ten dollars apiece.
   (5) They had a fair with a magician, a pony riding contest, a market, a bearded lady, the strongest lady in the world, and a rabbit-jumping contest.
   (6) They formed an organization called Barnens Regnskog and opened a bank account. And so forth.
2. In both situations, the children are very persistent. The obstacles faced by the children in *The Streets are Free* were of a more local nature. They had to get the attention of an indifferent mayor and of the local press. The problem they were trying to solve was of a local nature, although it certainly can inspire others to do the same in their own cities. The children in *Founders of the Children's Rain Forest* wanted to buy as much rain forest acreage as they could afford. They needed to raise a *lot* of money. For this they needed to do a great deal of fundraising and outreach. The problem they were trying to solve was (and is) of a global nature. In both situations, the children needed to be relentless and fearless.
3. The children were helped by Eha Kern, their teacher, who showed them slides, described the problem, and really shepherded them through the entire project. Sharon Kinsman showed the children a map and slides of the Monte Verde forest and told them how they could preserve it. The citizens of the children's town helped by coming to their fundraisers and generously contributing money to the cause. The king of Sweden contributed some funds and, presumably some publicity, to their cause. A music teacher helped them write songs and make tapes to sell. Mr. Kern helped them form Barnens Regnskog.

Comprehension Questions—Drawing Conclusions (pp. 141-142)

1. Answers will vary. Most people making a presentation would want a mature and thoughtful response to their slide show. They would like the students to show interest, ask questions, and offer to help.

2. If the rain forest is not preserved, virtually all of the rain forest life, both plants and animals, will become extinct. Global warming will increase and weather patterns may change. The 50 million people who live in the rain forest, who do not have the skills for living in urban society, will likely become impoverished.

Graphic Organizer (pp. 143-144)

1. *The class learns about the rain forests. They learn:*
   a. half the types of plants and animals in the whole world are there.
   b. rain forests are being destroyed at 100 acres a minute.
   c. nearly half have been cut down.
2. *Some of the animals, birds, reptiles and plants of the rain forest are:*
   a. monkeys
   b. leopards
   c. sloths
   d. jaguars
   e. ocelots
   f. tapirs
   g. butterflies
   h. golden toad
3. *Some of the ideas for raising money:*
   a. performed a play about the rain forest
   b. sold rain forest books and poems
   c. wrote letters asking for donations
   d. made a tape of rain forest songs and sold it
   e. had a fair
   f. charged for chores they did all day
4. *The happy ending:*
   a. children donate $25,000 to Monte Verde Conservation League.
   b. children from all over the world have raised more than two million dollars.
   c. 33,000 acres have been preserved.

JESSICA GOVEA (Textbook p. 464)
VOCABULARY—Activity I (p. 145)

1. injustice
2. activist
3. pesticide
4. exploited
5. unions
6. negotiate
7. boycott
8. bias
9. apathy
10. discriminated

VOCABULARY—Activity II (p. 146)

Answers will vary.

Comprehension Questions—In-depth Thinking (p. 147)

1. When Jessica Govea was in eighth grade, her best friend, Virginia, was hit by a truck and killed, as she tried to cross a dangerous road. She had been taking her younger siblings to the nearest park to play—a park that was three miles away. As a consequence, the members of the Junior CSO drew up a petition that they took door-to-door, in order to convince county officials to create another park closer to their neighborhood. The focus of the children's protests in *The Streets are Free* was also the need for a local park.

2. When Jessica and her father were working for CSO, he talked with Mexican-Americans who "told him stories of how they had been discriminated against in jobs, hospitals, schools, public office." (**p. 468**) Jessica's father encouraged Mexican-Americans to "protest. To register to vote. To become strong by acting together." (**p. 470**) When Cesar Chavez tried to organize a new labor union for farmworkers in order to change poor working conditions, they feared "they would be 'blacklisted,' which meant that no grower would hire them." (**p. 470**)

   In *The Silent Lobby*, courageous southern blacks register to vote, in spite of great social pressure not to do so. Craig's father is threatened with the loss of his job if he does so. The story makes clear that people become strong by acting together. When the Governor does not send their elected representatives to the Congress, the blacks are being discriminated against in public office.

3. A boycott occurs when a group of people join together and agree not to have anything to do with the services or products of a business or a nation (or some other entity). The group of people agree to withhold themselves (and their money), in order to express disapproval of that business's or that nation's policies. When people refuse to buy products or services, they are conducting an economic boycott. This is what blacks in the south did when they refused to ride the buses. The bus companies could not afford to operate without the fares paid by the blacks. In this way, the blacks forced the bus companies to allow them to sit anywhere on the bus. A boycott is like a strike. People who want conditions changed, but who are powerless when working individually, can bring about change by working together. [Of course, like any other tool, the boycott is only as just as the cause it is promoting. The boycott in the hands of those who wish to isolate innocent or good people, can be an effective weapon of prejudice and unfounded hate.]

Comprehension Questions—Drawing Conclusions (pp. 147-148)

1. The people in the story are citizens of the United States. They are called Mexican-Americans, because their parents and grandparents and great-grandparents came from Mexico, and they look Hispanic.
2. Student answers will vary.
3. When people can vote, it means that they have a say in what is done by government officials—because through voting, we choose our public officials. Registered voters can contact their elected officials in the county, the state, or the federal government, and express a view or report a problem.

Graphic Organizer (pp. 149-150)

Answers will vary.

THE STREET BOY (Textbook p. 478)
VOCABULARY—Activity I (p. 151)

1. adamant
2. responded
3. intercepted
4. commuters
5. panic
6. emerged
7. deliberately
8. inhabitants
9. delirious
10. pouted

VOCABULARY—Activity II (p. 152)

The sentence endings will, of course, vary from student to student. The answers for the words to be replaced are:

1. luxurious
2. adamantly
3. emerged from
4. commuters
5. intercepted
6. delirious
7. deliberately
8. panic
9. responded

Comprehension Questions—In-depth Thinking (p. 153)

1. The answers will be determined by how the student feels about dogs and bikes. Clearly, a bike is hard and made of metal; a dog is soft and warm. A bike does not have to be fed, but a dog doesn't get a flat tire. You can ride a bike, but a dog can be a friend. And so forth.

2. *The city…sprawled out in all directions, had a huge number of inhabitants, and had streets that were always busy.* **(p. 479)**

Their comfortable house overlooked a subway station. **(p. 479)**

At night, the street boy slept in the doorway of a store that was boarded up and empty. He lay on a few sheets of cardboard and slept in a dark green sleeping bag. **(p. 480)**

But before his birthday came along, the weather turned freezing cold. There was a shimmering of frost on the grass in the morning, and puddles turned into sheets of ice that cracked if you stepped on them. Flurries of snow fell from time to time. **(p. 482)**

Students may find additional passages on which to base their descriptions.

3. It seems that the main point of the story is that the boy does *not* want to live on the street but has no alternative. Blaming the victim is a ruse typically used by people who do not wish to help the victim.

Comprehension Questions—Drawing Conclusions
(pp. 153-154)

1. Answers will vary. The best guess is that he is subjected to the street boy's life in order to learn the importance of taking personal responsibility and intervening when someone needs help. The street boy may also be a kind of double for Hedley.

2. Hedley is turned back into Hedley, when he tries to save the street boy's life. For Hedley, this may be the ultimate good act, given that the boy has taken his place. Hedley might understandably wish him ill. When Hedley tries to keep the boy from being killed, and risks his own life doing so, perhaps he earns the right to be himself.

3. One would expect the street boy's experience to mirror Hedley's, but the street boy seems convinced that he *is* Hedley during their first encounter. After the switch back, the street boy doesn't seem to recall his Hedley existence.

Graphic Organizer (pp. 155-156)

Hedley's bedroom—a comfortable bedroom vs. ground next to the subway

Hedley's clothes—new, good quality clothing vs. secondhand sweater

Hedley's meals—wholesome, filling meals vs. little food from the food kitchen

Hedley's spending money—we guess that he had some vs. what-

ever coins people put in his cap

Hedley's hygiene—we assume he was clean and well groomed vs. smelling and unwashed in a shelter for the homeless

Hedley's friends—we assume he had other boys and girls like himself as friends vs. no one but other street people

SMALL STEPS—PART I (Textbook p. 514)
VOCABULARY—Activity I (p. 157)

1. periodically
2. fund
3. accurate
4. verify
5. ordeal
6. lyrics
7. bellows
8. buckle
9. gurney
10. vulnerable

VOCABULARY—Activity II (p. 158)

Answers will vary. Although we do list below the word that, to us, is the most obvious choice, students may give you a different word to good effect.

Example: accurate

1. verify
2. ordeal
3. lyrics
4. buckled
5. fund
6. vulnerable
7. gurney
8. periodically
9. bellows

Comprehension Questions—In-depth Thinking (p. 159)

1. *Paralysis* means the complete or partial loss of function, especially motion or sensation in a part of the body; the loss of the ability to move; a state of powerlessness or incapacity to act. Peg can only move her head, swallow, speak, breathe, blink, and cry.

2. Based on the story, the doctor may be checking to see if the lower leg can move or bounce upward.

3. Answers may vary. Writing about her illness may have helped her resolve some old feelings she had about that difficult time in her life. She probably wanted to leave a written record for her children and others to read and gain inspiration from. By writing her story, Peg helped others in many ways. She gave healthy people insight into what a polio survivor needs in the way of understanding and physical help, and she surely provided hope and strength for those who found themselves in similar circumstances to hers.

Comprehension Questions—Drawing Conclusions
(pp. 159-160)

1. Answers will vary. The point of the question is to have children think about one avenue of work that enables us to serve others.

2. Answers will vary. She had no choice. She slept a lot. She had—and even developed more so—inner strength.

3. The climax of Chapter 1 is the last sentence: *When I woke up, I was paralyzed.* The climax of Chapter 2 is either the doctor's telling Peg that she has bulbar polio, the worst kind of polio, or the moment of absurdity when he tells her to call the nurse if she starts to choke. The climax of Chapter 3 is Peg's drinking the chocolate milkshake (and at that point, we are so relieved, we can even taste it ourselves).

Graphic Organizer (pp. 161-162)

102 fever: When Peg came home from school, she had a temperature of 102. When the fever did not go down, the doctor recommended she be put in the hospital.

Sheltering Arms: This was the name of the hospital that specialized in children with polio.

Isolation ward: Because polio is so contagious, Peg had to be kept from any contact with anyone, including her own parents. This was very difficult for Peg.

Spinal polio and respiratory polio are two different types of polio with which Peg was afflicted.

Oxygen tent: In an oxygen tent, the air has a higher percentage of oxygen, making breathing easier for someone whose lungs are not strong enough to take in sufficient air.

Iron lung: This was a large metal tube, big enough for someone to lie in. Many polio patients were put into iron lungs, which mechanically helped them breathe. Peg dreaded this happening to her, and, fortunately, it never became necessary.

SMALL STEPS—PART II (Textbook p. 538)
VOCABULARY—Activity I (p. 163)

1. exhilaration
2. virtuous
3. herald
4. exclusively
5. camaraderie
6. endure
7. excruciating
8. surpassed
9. impeccable

VOCABULARY—Activity II (p. 164)

1. excruciating
2. a celebrity
3. exhilaration
4. indignation
5. elation
6. virtuous
7. exemplary
8. surpassing
9. camaraderie
10. exclusively

Comprehension Questions—In-depth Thinking (p. 165)

1. *...I felt sorry for Tommy who was still stuck in the iron lung, unable to hold a book. I was clearly getting better; he was not.* (p. 540)

   Disappointment filled me, and I could tell the others were disappointed, too. (p. 541)

   ...I wondered why I got better and some of the other patients did not. Tommy might spend the rest of his life in the iron lung. It didn't seem fair. (p. 542)

   But it wasn't all luck, I thought; it was quick action by my parents. They helped create my good luck. (p. 542)

   It had to be hard for her to watch new patients arrive, get better, and leave... (p. 545)

   We had the kind of camaraderie that I imagine exists between soldiers who have fought... (p. 549)

   As I thought about them, I realized that even if I had never grown strong enough to leave Silver, I still would have been able to lead a happy life. (p. 550)

Of course, students may find additional passages.

2. See Dr. Bevis's words on p. 543: *Many people have polio and never know it. They are highly contagious, but because their symptoms are so slight, they don't see a doctor.*

3. Her mother took her initial symptoms seriously. Her parents called the doctor the first night. Her doctor came right away. In less than 24 hours, he did a spinal tap. He told her parents to take her to the hospital. Her parents took her without waiting.

Comprehension Questions—Drawing Conclusions (pp. 165-166)

1. Peg no longer thinks that the ordinary concerns of kids her age—clothing, haircuts, tests, homework, ballgames—are any big deal. Peg has faced death, experienced loneliness, and lived through excruciating pain. She still doesn't know if she will ever walk again. See pages 543-544.

2. See page 544: *I felt closer now to Tommy, whose head was the only part of him I had ever seen, than I did to the kids who used to be my dearest friends. Tommy understood what it was like to have polio; my school friends could never know.* It is also true that Tommy and Peg have had a relationship with no props. They have been with each other through the hardest times, and have seen each other at their most vulnerable.

3. She misses her home, her room, the special things she does with her mother, her father, and her grandfather. She misses her dog. Students may also think of what *they* would miss and add those things to Peg's list.

Graphic Organizer (pp. 167-168)

Students should write a sentence or two linking the picture to the story.

Walking sticks: Peg used walking sticks to help her walk as she was on the road to recovery. By the end of the story, she is able to walk on her own.

Books: When Peg is sick in the hospital, she reads many books to entertain her. All of her reading keeps her from falling behind her classmates.

Letters: Peg's classmates write letters to her. She finds their concerns petty and unimportant.

Radio: Peg listens to the radio with Tommy. This distracts and entertains both of them. Their hero is the Lone Ranger. A strong bond of friendship is forged by the two radio fans. When Peg leaves the hospital, she gives her radio to Tommy.

Doctor: The doctors are professional, caring, and straight talking. Dr. Bevis will stand out in the students' mind as the doctor who helped cure Peg.

Music: Peg and her friends in the hospital raise their spirits by singing.

SMALL STEPS—PART III (Textbook p. 552)
VOCABULARY—Activity I (p. 169)

1. nostalgia
2. celebrity
3. mimic
4. gait
5. commentary
6. mutual
7. discard
8. frigid
9. elation
10. epilogue

VOCABULARY—Activity II (p. 170)

1. elation
2. celebrity
3. epilogue
4. frigid
5. mutual
6. discard
7. gait

Comprehension Questions—In-depth Thinking (p. 171)

1. Dr. Bevis's role is a critical hospital role. He is responsible for earlier stage life-and-death decisions, as well as appropriate treatment decisions for a patient who is paralyzed from the neck down. Miss Ballard's role is the role of physical therapist at a rehabilitation center. She teaches Peg how to learn to use her muscles, once more, so that she will be able to walk, or to get about with the least difficulty. Their roles are similar, because both are devoted to their patients. Both use encouragement and humor as healing tools.

2. As Peg is learning to walk without walking sticks, Dorothy is trying hard to walk using new braces and walking sticks. If she is not able to do this, she will always be in a wheelchair. Renée is doing better than Dorothy. She needs assistance to put her leg braces on, but once she is standing, she can move about with her walking sticks.

3. Peg wonders whether everyone will stare at her, and whether even kids she doesn't know will want to hear about her time in the hospital. Will she feel like a freak in a sideshow? Will her friendship be valued only because she is different?

Comprehension Questions—Drawing Conclusions
(pp. 171-172)

1. Peg mentions that she had become a celebrity, because she was the only person in Austin to get polio that year and the whole town followed her progress. The people of Austin had been pulling for her. Perhaps they had a sense of the difficulty of her struggle. She may also have been a person that people liked a lot—because she is a person of integrity and compassion.

2. What didn't she learn (that matters in life)? She was trained to withstand pain, fear, and loneliness. She learned that there are people who will do whatever they can to help. If she had any doubt before, she learned just how much her family cared. She saw other people suffer and cared about them. She learned the value of things.

3. The singing makes a very nice frame to the story. She tells us at the outset how much she likes to sing. What greater sign of joy than that she can sing at the end, after such struggle?! She also tells us how much she likes *Give Me Your Tired, Your Poor*. This is a song about the bringing of solace and freedom to those who suffer. Peg understands suffering.

WHAT A WILD IDEA (Textbook p. 566)
VOCABULARY—Activity I (p. 173)

1. complex
2. futile
3. memorable
4. ingenious
5. lever
6. resounding
7. resourceful
8. churning
9. innovation
10. washout

VOCABULARY—Activity II (p. 174)

Answers will vary, but here are some possibilities:

1. Food processor, smoothie maker, blender
2. Ice cream maker
3. Some electric lawn mowers, some electric tools
4. The portable phone, cell phone, etc.
5. Dryer, oven
6. Answers will vary.
7. Computer, etc.
8. Answers will vary.
9. Possibly—rotary telephone, brownie camera, black and white television, transistor radio

Comprehension Questions—In-depth Thinking (p. 175)

1. Every hardworking chicken deserves a pair of sun-goggles.
2. Every fat chicken needs to combine eating and exercising, such as the spinning platform designed by William J. Manly. Guaranteed to produce scrambled eggs.
3. Alfred Clark's Rocking Chair Butter Churn is what every butter-loving, rocker-addicted, churn hater needs.

Comprehension Questions—Drawing Conclusions
(pp. 175-176)

1. Wild ideas, as exemplified by the inventions in the story, are impractical, too complex, and a lot more trouble than they are worth. Students may also define the word.
2. Answers will vary. If any students say they would *like* it, make sure they tell you why.
3. Answers will vary. Surely some people would rather find themselves on the floor, rather than being hit in the head (even by corks), especially if they have a carpet.

Graphic Organizer (pp. 177-178)

Answers and pictures will vary.

FLIGHT INTO DANGER (Textbook p. 580)
VOCABULARY—Activity I (p. 179)

1. perturbed
2. hastens
3. manifest
4. galley
5. methodical
6. divert
7. depresses
8. toxic
9. emetic
10. exuberant

VOCABULARY—Activity II (p. 180)

airplane: galley, divert, manifest
masks: perturbed, methodical, exuberant
pill bottles: toxic, emetic
elevator: hasten, depress

Comprehension Questions—In-depth Thinking (p. 181)

1. One-dimensional characters are those who lack complexity. They are portrayed as having one "dimension," or side, to their personality. Most people are a complicated mix of sometimes conflicting personality traits; a one-dimensional character does not display that mix. To help the students round out the character each has chosen, you may have the class make up a list of possible personality or character traits. The list might include such characteristics as sense of humor, lazy, sly, forthright,

vain, neat, and so on.

2. Answers will vary. Our choice is the moment that the captain appears to be too sick to fly the plane.

3. Answers will vary.

Comprehension Questions—Drawing Conclusions
(pp. 181-182)

1. There would have been chaos on board. Spencer might have been too frightened to fly the plane; Baird could not have helped the passengers; the stewardess could not have comforted anyone; and so on.

2. Humor is an outlet for tension. The passenger who makes some humorous remarks to Baird helps himself and others remain calm. Spencer's humor keeps his fear under control and helps him master the situation.

3. Answers will vary.

Graphic Organizer (pp. 183-184)

1. filled in.
2. "This woman has to be gotten to a hospital immediately."
3. very sick
4. fog
5. takes sick
6. fish
7. ate fish
8. fog
9. to be very sick
10. he didn't fly big planes
11. 125
12. panics
13. "He can't fly the bloody thing!"
14. "Watch the air speed! Your nose is too high!"
15. "I ground looped!"
16. filled in

THE QUANGLE WANGLE'S HAT (Textbook p. 638)
Comprehension Questions—In-depth Thinking (p. 185)

1. How students say this will differ, but the basic idea is that nonsense literature uses language and names, describes conduct, events, places, and creatures, and presents ideas—and combinations of circumstances—that are absurd or contrary to what we know is possible.

2. **Stanza I:**

   There is no such tree as *the Crumpetty Tree.*

   The Quangle Wangle's hat is a hundred and two feet wide.

   What or *who* is the Quangle Wangle?

   A hat could not be that large.

   Bibbons is not a real word.

   Has anyone's face ever been forever hidden by their hat?

   Stanza II:

   The Quangle Wangle's diet is not a healthy one. No one lives just on jam, jelly, and bread.

   Stanza III:

   Well, it is unlikely that a canary couple would come and ask to build a nest in the Quangle Wangle's hat.

   Stanza IV:

Suddenly, many creatures arrive, when previously, few people ever came that way. How can it be? The Stork, the Duck, the Owl, the Snail, the Bumble-Bee, the Frog, and the Fimble Fowl.

The use of the word *the* makes it sound as though these are the only ones of their kind. Would all of these animals come together? And, there is no such thing as a Fimble Fowl—especially one with a Corkscrew leg! (If students don't know, a corkscrew is a device for drawing corks from bottles that has a pointed spiral piece of metal turned by a handle.) *And,* all of these creatures humble beg as one to live in the Quangle Wangle's hat! A snail lives on the ground! A bee in a hive!

Stanza V:

What is a *pobble?* Why does he have no toes? What is a small Olympian bear? The Dong with a luminous nose? *Luminous* means emitting or reflecting usually steady, suffused, or glowing light. But who is the Dong? And why is his nose glowing? A Blue Baboon who plays the flute? The Orient Calf? The Land of Tute? *Attery* is not in the dictionary. *Squash* refers to a vegetable or a crushed mass. And what is a Bisky Bat? Whatever or whoever these creatures are, they all come to live in the Quangle Wangle's hat. All of this is wonderful, believable nonsense with lots of nonsense language.

Stanza VI:

Have you ever heard of a Mulberry moon? More silliness, except for the Quangle Wangle Quee's happiness that all of these creatures have come to live with him, in the Crumpetty Tree.

3. Answers will vary. Make sure students know that in the poem, not much is said about the Crumpetty Tree, except that it has broad green leaves. Students may infer things from its name. Do your students know to look in the dictionary for similar words? Do they know that a *crumpet* is a small round unsweetened bread cooked on a griddle and usually split and toasted before serving? Students may also infer characteristics of the tree from the number of creatures it is able to accommodate.

Comprehension Questions—Drawing Conclusions
(pp. 185-186)

1. A list of the characters:

   The Quangle Wangle Quee

   Mr. and Mrs. Canary

   The Stork

   The Duck

   The Owl

   The Snail

   The Bumble-Bee

   The Frog

   The Fimble Fowl (with the Corkscrew leg)

   The Golden Grouse

   The Pobble (who has no toes)

   The small Olympian bear

   The Dong (with a luminous nose)

   The Blue Baboon (who plays the flute)

   The Orient Calf (from the Land of Tute)

The Attery Squash
The Bisky Bat
2. Again, try to make certain that each creature has student representation. Answers, of course, will vary.
3. This is an exercise of the imagination.

PASSAGE TO FREEDOM (Textbook p. 646)
VOCABULARY—Activity I (p. 187)
1. visa
2. diplomats
3. superior
4. conscience
5. incident
6. gazing
7. issued
8. inspired
9. peered
10. embraced

VOCABULARY—Activity II (p. 188)
Answers will vary.

Comprehension Questions—In-depth Thinking (p. 189)
1. The Sugiharas are not being discriminated against. The racial and religious group to which they belong is not being victimized. They are saving thousands of people from a totally different culture, people with whom they might easily not identify.
2. Altruism means unselfish regard for or devotion to the welfare of others. Altruism also refers to behavior by an animal that is not beneficial to, or that may be harmful to, itself, but that benefits others of its species. The word comes from the French altruisme, and from autrui, which means "other people." The French words come from the Latin alter, which means "the one …the other."
3. Yukiko and Aunt Setsuko encourage Mr. Sugihara to issue the visas. They risk their own lives and futures by helping him.

Yukiko offers to help write the visas and, although Mr. Sugihara insists on writing them all himself, she assists him in other ways. The three adults act as a unit throughout.

Comprehension Questions—Drawing Conclusions (pp. 189-190)
1. Chiune Sugihara saw that each person had the right to participate in a decision that would affect them. He was not the sort of person who acts like the boss of the family or like a tyrant. He was also wise enough to seek counsel. The Sugihara family was a moral unit, in which each family member had a say. Mr. Sugihara does not accept Mrs. Sugihara's offer of help because if anyone is to be punished for this, it will only be he. He is a brave person and a wonderful husband.
2. This was a good idea because it calmed the people in the crowd, and enabled Mr. Sugihara to find out what their needs were—without his being overwhelmed by their numbers.
3. We learn that there may come a time, when our obligation to obey the law of the state is superseded by our obligation to do what is right.

Graphic Organizer (pp. 191-192)
The following are sample answers, although many other answers would be correct, too.
Mrs. Sugihara: caring (compassionate), self-sacrificing. She encourages her husband to disobey the Japanese government in order to save the Jews.
The Japanese government: uncaring (at best—in this story only. In reality, they were cruel, ruthless, etc.). They do not give permission to Mr. Sugihara to write more visas.
The Germans: cruel, evil. There are no words to describe the depth of their depravity. They seek to murder innocent Jews.
The Sugihara survivors: grateful, caring. They do not forget Mr. Sugihara and honor him long after the war is over.